A TREATISE ON THE
CONSTITUTIONAL LIMITATIONS

Da Capo Press Reprints in

AMERICAN CONSTITUTIONAL AND LEGAL HISTORY

GENERAL EDITOR: LEONARD W. LEVY

Claremont Graduate School

A TREATISE ON THE CONSTITUTIONAL LIMITATIONS

Which Rest Upon the Legislative Power
of the States of the American Union

By Thomas M. Cooley

DA CAPO PRESS • NEW YORK • 1972

Library of Congress Cataloging in Publication Data

Cooley, Thomas McIntyre, 1824-1898.
    A treatise on the constitutional limitations which
rest upon the legislative power of the States of the
American Union.
    (Da Capo Press reprints in American constitutional
and legal history)
    Reprint of the 1st ed. published in 1868.
    1. Legislative power—U. S. —States. 2. State
rights. 3. U. S.—Constitutional law. I. Title.
KF4600.C6   1972   342'.73'05   78-87510
ISBN 0-306-71403-5

This Da Capo Press edition of *A Treatise on the Constitutional
Limitations* is an unabridged republication of the first edition published in Boston in 1868. It is reprinted by permission from a copy of the original edition in the Library
of the University of Michigan Law School.

Published by Da Capo Press, Inc.
A Subsidiary of Plenum Publishing Corporation
227 West 17th Street, New York, N.Y. 10011

Manufactured in the United States of America

A TREATISE ON THE
CONSTITUTIONAL LIMITATIONS

A

TREATISE

ON THE

CONSTITUTIONAL LIMITATIONS

WHICH REST UPON

THE LEGISLATIVE POWER OF THE STATES
OF THE AMERICAN UNION.

BY

THOMAS M. COOLEY,

ONE OF THE JUSTICES OF THE SUPREME COURT OF MICHIGAN, AND JAY PROFESSOR
OF LAW IN THE UNIVERSITY OF MICHIGAN.

———

BOSTON:
LITTLE, BROWN, AND COMPANY.
1868.

UNIVERSITY PRESS: WELCH, BIGELOW, & Co.,
CAMBRIDGE.

PREFACE.

IF the following work shall furnish to the practitioner and the student in the law such a presentation of elementary constitutional principles as shall serve, with the aid of its references to judicial decisions, legal treatises, and historical events, as a convenient guide in the examination of questions respecting the constitutional limitations which rest upon the power of the several State legislatures, the purpose of its preparation will be fully accomplished. The need of some work bringing together those principles in a manner that would enable them to be examined as a comprehensive system, and their relative bearing and influence considered, has, it is believed, been quite generally felt; and, in view of the rapid multiplication of judicial decisions upon points of constitutional law, was daily becoming more urgent. The valuable treatises of Mr. Smith and Mr. Sedgwick were very complete and satisfactory on the points which they undertook to cover by their discussions; but the plan which each of them marked out for his labors excluded from examination many of the topics here presented, while others were but incidentally alluded to by them, and still others have acquired their importance in a considerable degree from subsequent events or decisions. Valuable as those treatises are, therefore, they do not so completely cover the ground of State constitutional law as to make a work specially devoted to that subject unimportant, and the present work is submitted to the profession, rather as supplementary to their labors than as a substitute for them.

In these pages the author has faithfully endeavored to state the law as it has been settled by the authorities, rather than to present his own views. At the same time he will not attempt to deny — what will probably be sufficiently apparent — that he has written in full sympathy with all those restraints which the caution of the fathers has imposed upon the exercise of the powers of government, and with greater faith in the checks and balances of our republican system, and in correct conclusions by the general public sentiment, than in a judicious, prudent, and just exercise of unbridled authority by any one man or body of men, whether sitting as a legislature or as a court. In this sympathy and faith he has written of jury trial and the other safeguards to personal liberty, of liberty of the press, and of vested rights ; and he has also endeavored to point out that there are on all sides definite limitations which circumscribe the legislative authority, aside from the specific restrictions which the people impose by their constitutions. But while he has not been predisposed to discover in any part of our system the rightful existence of any power created by the Constitution, and by that instrument made unlimited save in its own discretion, neither, on the other hand, has he designed to advance new doctrines, or to do more than to state clearly and with reasonable conciseness the principles to be deduced from the judicial decisions. Those decisions he has made reference to and in many cases quoted from ; not, however, deeming it important to cumber his pages with many references to the English reports on those points on which the American authorities were sufficiently numerous and uniform to be fairly regarded as having settled the law for this country. And trusting that fair criticism may discover in his work sufficient of practical utility to justify its publication, he submits it to the judgment of an enlightened and generous profession.

ANN ARBOR, MICHIGAN,
September, 1868.

In quoting from the constitutions of such of the Southern States as came under the operation of the Congressional Reconstruction Acts, the author has referred to the instruments in force before the Rebellion, as modified by conventions held in 1864, 1865, and 1866. While this work has been passing through the press, several of these States have adopted constitutions under the Reconstruction Acts, and have been admitted to representation in Congress. Maryland has also adopted a new constitution. The changes, however, which have been made by these constitutions, in particulars important to the present work, are not numerous, nor often important.

The new constitutions of Arkansas and Florida forbid special legislative acts authorizing the sale of lands of infants and other persons under disability.

In the clauses from the constitutions of Florida and North Carolina quoted in the note on page 352, the word *freeman* is changed to *person* by the new instruments.

Regarding liberty of speech and of the press, no changes are made by the new constitutions of Alabama, Florida, Georgia, and Louisiana, and only a change of the word *liberty* to *privilege* in that of Maryland. The following are the clauses on this subject in the other new constitutions : —

" The liberty of the press shall forever remain inviolate. The free communication of thoughts and opinions is one of the invaluable rights of man, and all persons may freely speak, write, and publish their sentiments on all subjects, being responsible for the abuse of such right. In all criminal prosecutions for libel the truth may be given in evidence to the jury, and if it shall appear to the jury that the matter charged as libellous is true, and was published with good motives, and for justifiable ends, the party shall be acquitted." — *Const. of Arkansas*, Art. 1, § 2.

" The freedom of the press is one of the great bulwarks of liberty, and therefore ought never to be restrained ; but every individual shall be held responsible for the abuse of the same." — *Const. of North Carolina*, Art. 1, § 20.

"All persons may freely speak, write, and publish their sentiments on any subject, being responsible for the abuse of that right, and no laws shall be enacted to restrain or abridge the liberty of speech or of the press. In prosecutions for the publication of papers investigating the official conduct of officers or men in public capacity, or when the matter published is proper for public information, the truth thereof may be given in evidence ; and in all indictments for libel, the jury shall be the judges of the law and the facts." — *Const. of South Carolina*, Art. 1, §§ 7, 8.

The new constitution of Maryland forbids any religious test as a qualification for any office of profit or trust " other than a declaration of belief in the existence of God."

The new constitution of North Carolina disqualifies for office " all persons who shall deny the being of Almighty God." The clause in the original constitution of 1776 was as follows : " That no person who shall deny the being of God, or the truth of the Protestant religion, or the divine authority of either the Old or New Testaments, or who shall hold religious principles incompatible with the freedom and safety of the State, shall be capable of holding any office or place of trust or profit in the civil department within this State." This was amended in 1835 by substituting the word *Christian* for *Protestant*, and in that form it remained until the present year, when the disqualification was narrowed as above shown.

Voting by ballot, instead of *viva voce*, is established by the new constitutions of Arkansas and Georgia.

TABLE OF CONTENTS.

CHAPTER I.

DEFINITIONS.

CHAPTER II.

THE CONSTITUTION OF THE UNITED STATES.

CHAPTER III.

THE FORMATION AND AMENDMENT OF STATE CONSTITUTIONS.

CHAPTER IV.

CONSTRUCTION OF STATE CONSTITUTIONS.

CHAPTER V.

THE POWERS WHICH THE LEGISLATIVE DEPARTMENT MAY EXERCISE.

CHAPTER VI.

THE ENACTMENT OF LAWS.

CHAPTER VII.

THE CIRCUMSTANCES UNDER WHICH A LEGISLATIVE ACT MAY BE DECLARED UNCONSTITUTIONAL.

CHAPTER VIII.

THE SEVERAL GRADES OF MUNICIPAL GOVERNMENT.

CHAPTER IX.

PROTECTION TO PERSON AND PROPERTY UNDER THE CONSTITUTION OF THE UNITED STATES.

CHAPTER X.

THE CONSTITUTIONAL PROTECTIONS TO PERSONAL LIBERTY.

CHAPTER XI.

OF THE PROTECTION OF PROPERTY BY THE "LAW OF THE LAND."

CHAPTER XII.

LIBERTY OF SPEECH AND OF THE PRESS.

CHAPTER XIII.

RELIGIOUS LIBERTY.

CHAPTER XIV.

THE POWER OF TAXATION.

CHAPTER XV.

THE EMINENT DOMAIN.

CHAPTER XVI.

THE POLICE POWER OF THE STATES.

CHAPTER XVII.

THE EXPRESSION OF THE POPULAR WILL.

TABLE OF CASES CITED.

CONSTITUTIONAL LIMITATIONS

STATE LEGISLATIVE POWER.

CHAPTER I.

DEFINITIONS.

A STATE is a body politic, or society of men, united together for the purpose of promoting their mutual safety and advantage by the joint efforts of their combined strength.[1] The terms *nation* and *state* are frequently employed, both in the law of nations and in common parlance, as importing the same thing;[2] but the term *nation* is more strictly synonymous with *people*, and while a single state may embrace different nations or peoples, a single nation will be sometimes so divided as to constitute several states.

In American constitutional law, the word *state* is applied to the several members of the American Union, while the word *nation* is applied to the whole body of the people embraced within the jurisdiction of the Federal government.

Sovereignty, as applied to states, imports the supreme, absolute, uncontrollable power by which any state is governed.[3] A state is called a *sovereign state* when this supreme power resides within itself, whether resting in a single individual, or in a number of individuals, or in the whole body of the people.[4] In the view of international law, all sovereign states are equal in rights,

---

[1] Vattel, b. 1, c. 1, § 1; Story on Const. § 207; Wheat. Int. Law, pt. 1, c. 2, § 2; Halleck, Int. Law, 63; Bouv. Law Dict. "State."

[2] Thompson, J. in Cherokee Nation v. Georgia, 5 Pet. 52; Vattel, supra.

[3] Story on Const. § 207; 1 Blackstone, Com. 49; Wheat. Int. Law, pt. 1, c. 2, § 5; Halleck, Int. Law, 63, 64; Chipman on Government, 137.

[4] Vattel, b. 1, c. 1, § 2; Story on Const. § 207; Halleck, Int. Law, 65. In other words, when it is an *independent* state. Chipman on Government, 137.

1

since, from the very definition of a sovereign state, it is impossible that there can be in respect to it any political superior.

The sovereignty of a state commonly extends to all the subjects of government within the territorial limits occupied by the associated society, and, except upon the high seas which belong equally to all men, like the air, and no part of which can rightfully be appropriated by any nation,[1] the dividing line between sovereignties is usually a territorial line. In American constitutional law, however, there is a division of the powers of sovereignty between the national and state governments by subjects; the former being possessed of supreme, absolute, and uncontrollable power over certain subjects throughout all the States and Territories while the latter have the like complete power, within their respective territorial limits, over other subjects.[2] In regard to certain other subjects, the States possess powers of regulation which are not sovereign powers, inasmuch as they are liable to be controlled, or for the time being to become altogether dormant, by the exercise of a power vested in the general government in respect to the same subjects.

A *constitution* is sometimes defined as the fundamental law of a state, containing the principles upon which the government is founded, regulating the division of the sovereign powers, and directing to what persons each of these powers is to be confided, and the manner in which it is to be exercised.[3] Perhaps an equally complete definition would be, that body of rules and maxims in accordance with which the powers of sovereignty are habitually exercised.

In a very qualified and imperfect sense, every state may be said to possess a constitution; that is to say, some leading principle has prevailed in the administration of its government, until it has become an understood part of its system, to which obedi-

---

[1] Vattel, b. 1, c. 23, § 281; Wheat. Int. Law, pt. 2, c. 4, § 10.

[2] McLean, J. in License Cases, 5 How. 588. " The powers of the general government, and of the State, although both exist and are exercised within the same territorial limits, are yet separate and distinct sovereignties, acting separately and independently of each other within their respective spheres. And the sphere of action appropriated to the United States is as far beyond the reach of the judicial process issued by a State judge or a State court, as if the line of division was traced by landmarks and monuments visible to the eye." Taney, J. in Ableman v. Booth, 21 How. 516.

[3] 1 Bouv. Inst. 9; Duer, Const. Juris. 26.

ence is expected and habitually yielded ; like the hereditary principle in most monarchies, and the principle of choosing the chieftain by the body of the people, which prevails among some barbarous tribes. But the term *constitutional government* is applied only to those whose fundamental rules or maxims not only locate the sovereign power in individuals or bodies designated or chosen in some prescribed manner, but also define the limits of its exercise so as to protect individual rights and shield them against the exercise of arbitrary power. The number of these is not great, and the protection they afford to individual rights is far from being uniform.

In American constitutional law the word *constitution* is used in a restricted sense, as implying the written instrument agreed upon by the people of the Union, or of any one of the States, as the absolute rule of action and decision for all departments and officers of the government, in respect to all the points covered by it, until it shall be changed by the authority which established it, and in opposition to which any act or rule of any department or officer of the government, or even of the people themselves, will be altogether void.

The term *unconstitutional law* must vary in its meaning in different states, according as the powers of sovereignty are or are not possessed by the individual or body which exercises the powers of ordinary legislation. Where the law-making department of a state is restricted in its powers by a written fundamental law, as in the American States, we understand by unconstitutional law one which, being opposed to the fundamental law, is therefore in excess of legislative power, and void. Indeed, the term *unconstitutional law*, in American jurisprudence, is a misnomer and implies a contradiction ; that enactment which is opposed to the Constitution being in fact no law at all. But where, by the theory of the government, the complete sovereignty is vested in the same individual or body which enacts the ordinary laws, any law, being an exercise of power by the sovereign authority, could not be void, but, if it conflicted with any existing constitutional principle, must have the effect to change or abrogate such principle, instead of being nullified by it. This must be so in Great Britain with every law not in harmony with pre-existing constitutional principles ; since, by the theory of its government, Parliament is sovereign, and may change the constitution at any time, as in many instances it has done, by declaring its will to that effect.[1] And when thus the power to control and modify the constitution resides in the ordinary lawmaking power of the state, the term *unconstitutional law* can mean no more than this: a law which, being opposed to the settled maxims upon which the government has been habitually conducted, *ought not* to be, or to have been, adopted. It follows, therefore, that in Great Britain constitutional questions are for the most part to be discussed before the people or the Parliament, since the declared will of the Parliament is the final law; but in America, after a constitutional question has been passed upon by the legislature, there is generally a right of appeal to the courts, when it is attempted to put the will of the legislature in force. For the will of the people, as declared in the Constitution, is the final law; and the will of the legislature is only law when it is in harmony with, or at least is not opposed to, that controlling instrument which governs the legislative body equally with the private citizen.

[1] 1 Blackstone, Com. 160 ; De Tocqueville, Democracy in America, c. 6.

CHAPTER II.

THE CONSTITUTION OF THE UNITED STATES.

THE government of the United States is the existing representative of the national government which has always, in some form, existed over the American States. Before the Revolution the powers of government which were exercised over all the Colonies in common were so exercised either by the crown of Great Britain or by the Parliament ; but the extent of those powers, and how far vested in the crown and how far in the Parliament, were questions never definitely settled, and which constituted subjects of dispute between the mother country and the people of the Colonies, finally resulting in hostilities.[1] That the power over peace and war, the general direction of commercial intercourse, and the control of such subjects generally as fall within the province of international law, were vested in the home government, and that the Colonies were not, therefore, sovereign states, except in a very qualified sense, were not seriously disputed in America, and indeed were often formally conceded ; and the disputes related to questions as to what were or were not matters of internal regulation, the control of which the colonists insisted should be left exclusively to themselves.

Besides the tie uniting the several Colonies through the crown of Great Britain, there had always been a strong tendency to a more intimate and voluntary union, whenever circumstances of danger threatened them, and which had led to the New England Confederacy of 1643, to the temporary Congress of 1690, to the plan of union agreed upon in convention in 1754, but rejected by the Colonies as well as by the crown, to the Stamp Act Congress of 1765, and finally to the Continental Congress of 1774. When the difficulties with Great Britain culminated in actual war, the Congress of 1775 assumed to itself those powers of external control which before had been conceded to the crown or to the Par-

---

[1] Story on Const. § 183 et seq. ; 1 Pitkin's Hist. U. S. c. 6 ; 5 Bancroft's U. S. c. 18 ; 2 Marshall's Washington, c. 2 ; Declaration of Rights by Colonial Congress of 1765 ; Ramsay's Revolution in South Carolina, pp. 6 – 11.

liament, together with such other powers of sovereignty as it seemed essential a general government should exercise, and became the national government of the United Colonies.   By this body war was conducted, independence declared, treaties formed, and admiralty jurisdiction exercised.   It is evident, therefore, that the States, though declared to be " sovereign and independent," were never strictly so in their individual character, but that they were always, in respect to the higher powers of sovereignty, subject to the control of a central power, and were never separately known as members of the family of nations.[1]   The Declaration of Independence made them sovereign and independent States by altogether abolishing the foreign jurisdiction, and substituting a national government of their own creation.

But while national powers were assumed by and conceded to

---

[1] " All the country now possessed by the United States was [prior to the Revolution] a part of the dominions appertaining to the crown of Great Britain. Every acre of land in this country was then held, mediately or immediately, by grants from that crown.   All the people of this country were then subjects of the king of Great Britain, and owed allegiance to him ; and all the civil authority then existing or exercised here flowed from the head of the British empire. They were in a strict sense fellow-subjects, and in a variety of respects one people.   When the Revolution commenced, the patriots did not assert that only the same affinity and social connection subsisted between the people of the Colonies which subsisted between the people of Gaul, Britain, and Spain, while Roman provinces, namely, only that affinity and social connection which result from the mere circumstance of being governed by one prince ; different ideas prevailed, and gave occasion to the Congress of 1774 and 1775.

" The Revolution, or rather the Declaration of Independence, found the people already united for general purposes, and at the same time providing for their more domestic concerns by State conventions and other temporary arrangements. From the crown of Great Britain the sovereignty of their country passed to the people of it ; and it was not then an uncommon opinion that the unappropriated lands which belonged to the crown passed, not to the people of the Colony or State within whose limits they were situated, but to the whole people.   On whatever principles this opinion rested, it did not give way to the other, and thirteen sovereignties were considered as emerged from the principles of the Revolution, combined with local convenience and considerations ; the people nevertheless continued to consider themselves, in a national point of view, as one people ; and they continued without interruption to manage their national concerns accordingly.   Afterwards, in the hurry of the war, and in the warmth of mutual confidence, they made a confederation of the States the basis of a general government. Experience disappointed the expectations they had formed from it ; and then the people, in their collective capacity, established the present Constitution."   Per Jay, Ch. J. in Chisholm v. Georgia, 2 Dall. 470.

the Congress of 1775 – 76, that body was nevertheless strictly revolutionary in its character, and, like all revolutionary bodies, its authority was undefined, and could be limited only, *first*, by instructions to individual delegates by the States choosing them; *second*, by the will of the Congress; and *third*, by the power to enforce that will.[1] As in the latter particular it was essentially feeble, the necessity for a clear specification of powers which should be exercised by the national government became speedily apparent, and led to the adoption of the Articles of Confederation. But these articles did not concede the full measure of power essential to the efficiency of a national government at home, the enforcement of respect abroad, or the preservation of the public faith or public credit; and the difficulties experienced induced the election of delegates to the Constitutional Convention held in 1787, by which a Constitution was formed which was put into operation in 1789. As much larger powers were vested by this instrument in the general government than had ever been exercised in this country, by either the crown, the Parliament, or the Revolutionary Congress, and larger than those conceded to the Congress under the Articles of Confederation, the assent of the people of the several States was essential to its acceptance, and a provision was inserted in the Constitution that the ratification

---

[1] See remarks of Iredell, J. in Penhallow *v.* Doane's Adm'r, 3 Dall. 91, and of Blair, J. in same case, p. 111. " It has been inquired what powers Congress possessed from the first meeting, in September, 1774, until the ratification of the Articles of Confederation on the 1st of March, 1781. It appears to me that the powers of Congress during that whole period were derived from the people they represented, expressly given, through the medium of their State conventions or State legislatures; or that after they were exercised they were impliedly ratified by the acquiescence and obedience of the people. After the confederacy was completed, the powers of Congress rested on the authority of the State legislatures and the implied ratification of the people, and was a government over governments. The powers of Congress originated from necessity, and arose out of and were only limited by events, or, in other words, they were revolutionary in their very nature. Their extent depended on the exigencies and necessities of public affairs. It was absolutely and indispensably necessary that Congress should possess the power of conducting the war against Great Britain, and therefore, if not expressly given by all, as it was by some of the States, I do not hesitate to say that Congress did rightfully possess such power. The authority to make war of necessity implied the power to make peace, or the war must be perpetual. I entertain this general idea, that the several States retained all internal sovereignty, and that Congress properly possessed the great rights of external sovereignty." Per Chase, J. in Ware *v.* Hylton, 3 Dall. 231.

of the conventions of nine States should be sufficient for the establishment of the Constitution between the States so ratifying the same. In fact, the Constitution was ratified by conventions of delegates chosen by the people in eleven of the States before the new government was organized under it ; and the remaining two, North Carolina and Rhode Island, by their refusal to accept, and by the action of the others in proceeding separately, were excluded altogether from that national jurisdiction which before had embraced them. This exclusion was not warranted by anything contained in the Articles of Confederation, which purported to be articles of " perpetual union," and the action of the eleven States in making radical revision of the Constitution, and excluding their associates for refusal to assent, was really revolutionary in its character, and only to be justified by that absolute necessity for a stronger government which had been fully demonstrated.[1]

[1] " Two questions of a very delicate nature present themselves on this occasion : 1. On what principle the Confederation, which stands in the form of a solemn compact among the States, can be superseded without the unanimous consent of the parties to it; 2. What relation is to subsist between the nine or more States ratifying the Constitution and the remaining few who do not become parties to it. The first question is answered at once by recurring to the absolute necessity of the case ; to the great principle of self-preservation; to the transcendent law of nature and of nature's God, which declares that the safety and happiness of society are the objects at which all political institutions aim, and to which all such institutions must be sacrificed. *Perhaps*, also, an answer may be found without searching beyond the principles of the compact itself. It has been heretofore noted, among the defects of the Confederation, that in many of the States it had received no higher sanction than a mere legislative ratification. The principle of reciprocality seems to require that its obligation on the other States should be reduced to the same standard. A compact between independent sovereigns, founded on acts of legislative authority, can pretend to no higher validity than a league or treaty between the parties. It is an established doctrine on the subject of treaties, that all of the articles are mutually conditions of each other ; that a breach of any one article is a breach of the whole treaty ; and that a breach committed by either of the parties absolves the others, and authorizes them, if they please, to pronounce the compact violated and void. Should it unhappily be necessary to appeal to these delicate truths for a justification for dispensing with the consent of particular States to a dissolution of the Federal pact, will not the complaining parties find it a difficult task to answer the multiplied and important infractions with which they may be confronted ? The time has been when it was incumbent on us all to veil the ideas which this paragraph exhibits. The scene is now changed, and with it the part which the same motives dictate. The second question is not less delicate, and the flattering prospect of its being merely hypothetical forbids an over-curious discussion of it. It is one

Left at liberty now to assume complete powers of sovereignty, as independent governments, these two States saw fit soon to resume their place in the American family, under a permission contained in the Constitution; and new States have since been added from time to time, all of them, with the exception of one, organized by the consent of the general government with territory before under its control. The exception was Texas, which had previously been an independent sovereign state, but which, by the conjoint action of its government and that of the United States, was received into the Union on an equal footing with the other States.

Without therefore discussing, or even designing to allude to, any abstract theories as to the precise position and actual power of the several States at the time of forming the present Constitution, it may be said of them generally that they have at all times been subject to some common national government, which has exercised control over the subjects of war and peace, and other matters pertaining to external sovereignty; and that when the only three States which ever exercised complete sovereignty accepted the Constitution and came into the Union on an equal footing with all the other States, they thereby accepted the same relative position to the general government, and divested themselves permanently of those national powers which the others had never exercised.

The government of the United States is one of *enumerated powers;* the national Constitution being the instrument which specifies them, and in which authority should be found for the exercise of any power which the national government assumes to possess.[1]   In this respect it differs from the constitutions of the

of those cases which must be left to provide for itself. In general, it may be observed, that although no political relation can subsist between the assenting and dissenting States, yet the moral relations will remain uncancelled. The claims of justice, both on one side and on the other, will be in force, and must be fulfilled; the rights of humanity must in all cases be duly and mutually respected; whilst considerations of a common interest, and above all the remembrance of the endearing scenes which are past, and the anticipation of a speedy triumph over the obstacles to reunion, will, it is hoped, not urge in vain *moderation* on one side and *prudence* on the other." Federalist, No. 43 (by Madison).

[1] "The government of the United States can claim no powers which are not granted to it by the Constitution; and the powers actually granted must be such as are expressly given, or given by necessary implication." Per Marshall, Ch. J. in Martin v. Hunter's Lessee, 1 Wheat 326. "This instrument contains an enumeration of the powers expressly granted by the people to their government.

several States, which are not grants of power to the States, but which apportion and impose restrictions upon powers which the States inherently possess. The general purpose of the Constitution of the United States is declared by its founders to be, " to form a more perfect union, establish justice, insure domestic tranquillity, provide for the common defence, promote the general welfare, and secure the blessings of liberty to ourselves and our posterity." To accomplish these purposes the Congress is empowered by the eighth section of article one : —

1. To lay and collect taxes, duties, imposts, and excises ; to pay the debts and provide for the common defence and general welfare of the United States ; but all duties, imposts, and excises shall be uniform throughout the United States.

2. To borrow money on the credit of the United States.

3. To regulate commerce with foreign nations, and among the several States, and with the Indian tribes.

4. To establish a uniform rule of naturalization, and uniform laws on the subject of bankruptcy, throughout the United States.

5. To coin money, regulate the value thereof, and of foreign coin, and fix the standard of weights and measures.

6. To provide for the punishment of counterfeiting the securities and current coin of the United States.

7. To establish post-offices and post-roads.

8. To promote the progress of science and useful arts, by securing for limited terms to authors and inventors the exclusive right to their respective writings and discoveries.

9. To constitute tribunals inferior to the Supreme Court. To define and punish piracies and felonies committed upon the high seas, and offences against the law of nations.

10. To declare war, grant letters of marque· and reprisal, and make rules concerning captures on land and water.

11. To raise and support armies ; but no appropriation of money to that use shall be for a longer term than two years.

12. To provide and maintain a navy.

13. To make rules for the government and regulation of the land and naval forces.

Marshall, Ch. J. in Gibbons v. Ogden, 9 Wheat. 187. See Weister v. Hall, 52 Penn. St. 477. The tenth amendment to the Constitution provides that " The powers not delegated to the United States by the Constitution, nor prohibited by it to the States, are reserved to the States respectively, or to the people."

14. To provide for calling forth the militia to execute the laws of the Union, suppress insurrections, and repel invasions.

15. To provide for organizing, arming, and disciplining the militia, and for governing such part of them as may be employed in the service of the United States, reserving to the States respectively the appointment of the officers, and the authority of training the militia according to the discipline prescribed by Congress.

16. To exercise exclusive legislation in all cases whatsoever over such district not exceeding ten miles square, as may by cession of particular States, and the acceptance of Congress, become the seat of government of the United States, and to exercise like authority over all places purchased, by the consent of the legislature of the State in which the same shall be, for the erection of forts, magazines, arsenals, dock-yards, and other needful buildings.

17. To make all laws which shall be necessary and proper for carrying into execution the foregoing powers, and all other powers vested by the Constitution in the government of the United States, or in any department or officer thereof.

The executive power is vested in a President, who is made commander-in-chief of the army and navy, and of the militia of the several States when called into the service of the United States; and who has power, by and with the consent of the Senate, to make treaties, provided two thirds of the Senate concur, and with the same advice and consent to appoint ambassadors, and other public ministers, and consuls, judges of the Supreme Court, and other officers of the United States whose appointments are not otherwise provided for.[1]

The judicial power of the United States extends to all cases in law and equity arising under the national Constitution, the laws of the United States, and treaties made, or which shall be made, under their authority; to all cases affecting ambassadors, other public ministers, and consuls; to all cases of admiralty and maritime jurisdiction; to controversies to which the United States shall be a party; to controversies between two or more States; between a State and citizens of another State; between citizens of different States; between citizens of the same State claiming lands under grants of different States; and between a

[1] U. S. Const. art. 2.

State or citizens thereof and foreign states, citizens, or subjects.[1] But a State is not subject to be sued in the courts of the United States by the citizens of another State, or by citizens or subjects of any foreign state.[2]

The Constitution, and the laws of the United States made in pursuance thereof, and all treaties made under the authority of the United States, are declared to be the supreme law of the land; and the judges of every State are to be bound thereby, anything in the Constitution or laws of any State to the contrary notwithstanding.[3]

It is essential to the protection of the national jurisdiction, and to prevent collision between State and national authority, that the final decision upon all questions arising in regard thereto should rest with the courts of the Union;[4] and as such questions must often arise first in the State courts, provision is made by the Judiciary Act of 1789 for removing to the Supreme Court of the United States the final judgment or decree in any suit, rendered in the highest court of law or equity of a State, in which a decision could be had, in which was drawn in question the validity of a treaty, or statute of or authority exercised under the United States, and the decision was against their validity; or where was drawn in question the validity of a statute of, or an authority exercised under, any State, on the ground of their being repugnant to the Constitution, treaties, or laws of the United States, and the decision was in favor of such their validity; or where was drawn in question the construction of any clause of the Constitution, or of a treaty, or statute of, or commission held under, the United States, and the decision was against the right,

---

[1] U. S. Const. art. 3, § 2.

[2] U. S. Const. 11th Amendment.

[3] U. S. Const. art. 6; Owings v. Norwood's Lessee, 5 Cranch, 348; Foster v. Neilson, 2 Pet. 253, 314. When a treaty has been ratified by the proper formalities, it is, by the Constitution, the supreme law of the land, and the courts have no power to examine into the authority of the persons by whom it was entered into on behalf of the foreign nation; Doe v. Braden, 16 How. 635, 657; or the powers or rights recognized by it in the nation with whom it was made; Maiden v. Ingersoll, 6 Mich. 373. A State law in conflict with it must give way to its superior authority. Yeaker v. Yeaker, 4 Met. Ky. 33.

[4] Martin v. Hunter's Lessee, 1 Wheat. 304, 334; Cohens v. Virginia, 6 Wheat. 264; Bank of United States v. Norton, 3 Marsh. 423; Braynard v. Marshall, 8 Pick. 196, per Parker, Ch. J.; Spangler's Case, 11 Mich. 298.

title, privilege, or exemption specially set up or claimed by either party under such clause of the said Constitution, treaty, statute, or commission.[1]

But to authorize the removal, it must appear from the record, either expressly or by clear and necessary intendment, that some one of the enumerated questions did arise in the State court, and was there passed upon. It is not sufficient that it might have arisen or been applicable.[2] And if the decision of the State court is in favor of the right, title, privilege, or exemption so claimed, the Judiciary Act does not authorize such removal.[3] Neither does it where the validity of a State law is drawn in question, as opposed to the Constitution, laws, or treaties of the United States, and the decision of the State court is against its validity.[4]

But the same reasons which require that the final decision upon all questions of national jurisdiction should be left to the national courts, will also hold the national courts bound to respect the decisions of the State courts, upon all questions arising under the State constitutions and laws, where no question of national authority is involved, and to accept those decisions as correct, and to follow them whenever the same questions arise in the national courts.[5] With the power to revise the decisions of the State

[1] 1 Statutes at Large, 83 ; Brightly's Digest, 259.

[2] Owings v. Norwood's Lessee, 5 Cranch, 344 ; Martin v. Hunter's Lessee, 1 Wheat. 304 ; Inglee v. Coolidge, 2 Wheat. 363 ; Miller v. Nicholls, 4 Wheat. 311 ; Williams v. Norris, 12 Wheat. 117 ; Hickie v. Starke, 1 Pet. 98 ; Harris v. Dennie, 3 Pet. 292 ; Fisher's Lessee v. Cockerell, 5 Pet. 256 ; New Orleans v. De Armas, 9 Pet. 223, 234 ; Keene v. Clark, 10 Pet. 291 ; Crowell v. Randell, 10 Pet. 368 ; McKinney v. Carroll, 12 Pet. 66 ; Holmes v. Jennison, 14 Pet. 540 ; Scott v. Jones, 5 How. 343 ; Smith v. Hunter, 7 How. 738 ; Williams v. Oliver, 12 How. 111 ; Calcote v. Stanton, 18 How. 243 ; Maxwell v. Newbold, 18 How. 511 ; Hoyt v. Shelden, 1 Black, 518 ; Farney v. Towle, 1 Black, 350 ; Day v. Gallup, 2 Wal. 97. It is not sufficient that the presiding judge of the State court certifies that a right claimed under the national authority was brought into question. Railroad Co. v. Rock, 4 Wal. 177.

[3] Gordon v. Caldcleugh, 3 Cranch, 268 ; McDonogh v. Millaudon, 3 How. 693 ; Fulton v. McAffee, 16 Pet. 149 ; Linton v. Stanton, 12 How. 423 ; Burke v. Gaines, 19 How. 388 ; Reddall v. Bryan, 24 How. 420 ; Ryan v. Thomas, 4 Wal. 603.

[4] Commonwealth Bank v. Griffith, 14 Pet. 56 ; Walker v. Taylor, 5 How. 64.

[5] McKeen v. De Lancy's Lessee, 5 Cranch, 22 ; Polk's Lessee v. Wendal, 9 Cranch, 87 ; Jackson v. Chew, 12 Wheat. 153, 167 ; Henderson v. Griffin, 5 Pet. 151 ; Green v. Neal's Lessee, 6 Pet. 291 ; Massingill v. Downs, 7 How. 767 ;

courts, in the cases already pointed out, the due observance of
this rule will prevent those collisions of judicial authority which
would otherwise be inevitable, and which, besides being unseemly,

Nesmith v. Sheldon, 7 How. 812; Van Rensselaer v. Kearney, 11 How. 297; Webster v. Cooper, 14 How. 503; Luther v. Borden, 7 How. 1; Leffingwell v. Warren,
2 Black, 599; Greene v. James, 2 Curt. 189; Dubois v. McLean, 4 McLean, 488;
Woolsey v. Dodge, 6 McLean, 150; Thompson v. Phillips, Baldw. 246; Jefferson
Branch Bank v. Skelly, 1 Black, 436; Sumner v. Hicks, 2 Black, 532. The Judiciary Act of 1789 recognizes this principle in providing that " the laws of the several States, except where the Constitution, treaties, or statutes of the United States
shall otherwise require or provide, shall be regarded as rules of decision in trials
at common law in the courts of the United States, where they apply." Sec. 34.
In Suydam v. Williamson, 24 How. 427, the Supreme Court of the United States
overruled several of its former decisions, in order to make its rulings conform to
a more recent decision in the State of New York, — the question involved being
as to the law of that State. And in Leffingwell v. Warren, 2 Black, 599, the
court reiterate the doctrine of former cases, that if the highest tribunal of a
State adopt new views on a matter of State law, reversing its former decisions,
the Supreme Court of the United States will follow the latest settled adjudica-
tions. In the Sixth American Edition of Smith's Leading Cases, vol. i. p. 747,
is a note bearing upon this point. Speaking of the case of Diamond v. Lawrence
County, 37 Penn. St. 358, where certain county bonds were held not to be negotiable, it is said : " It may be added that, since the decisions of the Supreme Court
of the United States, as reported in 1 Wallace, 83, 206, and 384, the decision in
Diamond v. Lawrence County, or any decision like it in any State court, may be
regarded as unimportant. A Pennsylvanian, indeed, suing a Pennsylvania city
or county, and who must accordingly sue in a State court, could not recover
more than the amount which the county actually received ; but a citizen of any
other State, or any foreigner, to both of whom the courts of the United States are
open, would recover the whole amount. Of course, as the bonds are payable to
bearer, no Pennsylvanian, if he can help it, will sue on them. By selling them
— if sold in good faith — to a citizen of New York or New Jersey, or any other
State than his own, since the bonds are declared to have ' all the qualities of commercial paper,' suit could be brought by the new purchaser in the Federal courts,
and the whole amount be recovered." This note does not appear to us to be warranted by the Federal decisions. Before the national courts can disregard the
rulings of the State courts on questions respecting the validity and operation of
contracts deriving their vitality and force from State statutes, and made and payable within the State, and where the State decisions are not at variance, they must
disregard many of their own well-considered opinions, besides establishing for themselves a correctional power in regard to the decisions of the State courts, neither
given by the Constitution nor consistent with the general division of powers in
the American system. However desirable it may be that the rules in the various
States should be uniform, especially on questions of commercial law, it is certain
that no power is conferred on the Supreme Court of the United States to make
them so, where no question of national authority is involved.

would be dangerous to the peace, harmony, and stability of the Union under our peculiar system.

Besides conferring specified powers upon the national government, the Constitution contains also certain prohibitions upon the action of the States, a portion of them designed to prevent encroachments upon the national authority, and another portion to protect individual rights against possible abuse of State power. Of the first class are the following : No State shall enter into any treaty, alliance, or confederation ; grant letters of marque or reprisal ; coin money ; emit bills of credit ; [1] or make anything but gold and silver coin a tender in payment of debts. No State shall, without the consent of Congress, lay any imposts or duties upon imports or exports, except what may be absolutely necessary for executing its inspection laws ; and the net produce of all duties and imposts laid by any State on imports or exports shall be for the use of the treasury of the United States, and all such laws shall be subject to the revision and control of Congress. No State shall, without the consent of Congress, lay any duty of tonnage, keep troops or ships of war in time of peace, enter into any agreement or compact with another State or with a foreign power, or engage in war, unless actually invaded, or in such imminent danger as will not admit of delay. Of the second class are the following : No State shall pass any bill of attainder, *ex post facto* law, or law impairing the obligation of contracts.[2]

Other provisions have for their object to prevent discrimination by the several States against the citizens and public proceedings of other States. Of this class are the provisions that the citizens of each State shall be entitled to all the privileges and immunities of citizens in the several States ; [3] that fugitives from justice shall

---

[1] To constitute a bill of credit within the meaning of the Constitution, it must be issued by a State, involve the faith of the State, and be designed to circulate as money on the credit of the State in the ordinary uses of business. Briscoe *v.* Bank of Kentucky, 11 Pet. 257 ; Woodruff *v.* Trapnall, 10 How. 205. And see Craig *v.* Missouri, 4 Pet. 410 ; Darrington *v.* State Bank of Alabama, 13 How. 12 ; Curran *v.* Arkansas, 15 How. 317.

[2] Const. of U. S. art. 1, § 10.

[3] Const. of U. S. art. 4. " What are the privileges and immunities of citizens in the several States ? We feel no hesitation in confining these expressions to those privileges and immunities which are in their nature *fundamental;* which belong of right to the citizens of all free governments; and which have, at all times, been enjoyed by the citizens of the several States which compose this Union, from the time of their becoming free, independent, and sovereign. What

be delivered up;[1] and that full faith and credit shall be given in

those fundamental principles are, it would perhaps be more tedious than difficult to enumerate. They may, however, be all comprehended under the following general heads: protection by the government; the enjoyment of life and liberty, with the right to acquire and possess property of every kind, and to pursue and obtain happiness and safety; subject, nevertheless, to such restraints as the government may justly prescribe for the general good of the whole. The right of a citizen of one State to pass through or to reside in any other State, for purposes of trade, agriculture, professional pursuits, or otherwise; to claim the benefit of the writ of habeas corpus; to institute and maintain actions of every kind in the courts of the State; to take, hold, and dispose of property, either real or personal; and an exemption from higher taxes or impositions than are paid by the other citizens of the State, may be mentioned as some of the particular privileges and immunities of citizens, which are clearly embraced by the general description of privileges deemed to be fundamental; to which may be added the elective franchise, as regulated and established by the laws or constitution of the State in which it is to be exercised. These, and many others which might be mentioned, are, strictly speaking, *privileges and immunities*, and the enjoyment of them by the citizens of each State, in every other State, was manifestly calculated (to use the expressions of the preamble of the corresponding provision in the old Articles of Confederation) 'the better to secure and perpetuate mutual friendship and intercourse among the people of the different States of the Union.'" Washington, J. in Corfield v. Coryell, 4 Wash. C. C. 380. The Supreme Court will not describe and define these privileges and immunities in a general classification, preferring to decide each case as it may come up. Conner v. Elliott, 18 How. 591. For discussions upon this subject, see Murray v. McCarty, 2 Munf. 393; Lemmon v. People, 26 Barb. 270, and 20 N. Y. 562; Campbell v. Morris, 3 Har. & McH. 554; Amy v. Smith, 1 Lit. 326; Crandall v. State, 10 Conn. 340; Butler v. Farnsworth, 4 Wash. C. C. 101; Commonwealth v. Towles, 5 Leigh, 743; Haney v. Marshall, 9 Md. 194; Slaughter v. Commonwealth, 13 Grat. 767; State v. Medbury, 3 R. I. 138; People v. Imlay, 20 Barb. 68; People v. Coleman, 4 Cal. 46: Fire Department v. Noble, 3 E. D. Smith, 441; Same v. Wright, Ibid. 453.

[1] For decisions under this clause, see Ex parte Joseph Smith, 3 McLean, 133; Dow's Case, 18 Penn. St. 39; Matter of Clark, 9 Wend. 221; Johnson v. Riley, 13 Geo. 97; Matter of Fetter, 3 Zab. 311. The alleged offence need not be an offence at the common law; it is sufficient that it be a crime against the State from which the accused has fled. Johnson v. Riley; Matter of Clark and Matter of Fetter, supra. But the crime must have been actually committed within the State reclaiming the alleged offender, and he must have been an actual fugitive therefrom. Ex parte Smith, supra. The whole subject was considered in Commonwealth of Kentucky v. Dennison, 24 How. 66. One Lago was indicted in Kentucky for enticing and assisting a slave to escape from his master, and a requisition was made upon the Governor of Ohio for his surrender to the Kentucky authorities as a fugitive from justice. The Governor of Ohio refused to surrender him, on the ground that the act with which he was charged was an offence not known to the laws of Ohio, and not affecting the public safety, nor regarded as *malum in se* by the general judgment and conscience of civilized na-

each State to the public acts, records, and judicial proceedings of every other State.[1]

The last provisions which we shall here notice are, that the United States shall guarantee to every State in the Union a republican form of government,[2] and that no State shall grant any title of nobility.[3] The purpose of these is to protect a Union founded on republican principles, and composed entirely of re-

tions. Application was then made to the Supreme Court of the United States for a mandamus to compel the Governor of Ohio to perform this duty. The application was denied on the ground that, although the governor erred in this refusal, no power was delegated to the general government, either through the judicial department or any other department, to use any coercive means to compel him.

[1] Const. of U. S. art. 4. This clause of the Constitution has been the subject of a good deal of discussion in the courts. It is well settled that if the record of a judgment shows that it was rendered without service of process or appearance of the defendant, or if that fact can be shown without contradicting the recitals of the record, it will be treated as void in any other State, notwithstanding this constitutional provision. Benton v. Bergot, 10 S. & R. 242 ; Thurber v. Blackbourne, 1 N. H. 242 ; Hall v. Williams, 6 Pick. 232 ; Aldrich v. Kinney, 4 Conn. 380 ; Bradshaw v. Heath, 13 Wend. 407 ; Robinson v. Ward's Ex'rs, 8 Johns. 86 ; Fenton v. Garlick, Ibid. 194 ; Kilburn v. Woodworth, 5 Johns. 37 ; Pawling v. Bird's Ex'rs, 13 Johns. 192 ; Starbuck v. Murray, 5 Wend. 161 ; Woodworth v. Tremere, 6 Pick. 354 ; Lincoln v. Tower, 2 McLean, 473 ; Westervelt v. Lewis, Ibid. 511 ; Bimelar v. Dawson, 4 Scam. 536 ; Gleason v. Dodd, 4 Met. 333 ; Noyes v. Butler, 6 Barb. 613 ; Warren v. McCarthy, 25 Ill. 95 ; Rape v. Heaton, 9 Wis. 328 ; Wood v. Watkinson, 17 Conn. 500 ; Norwood v. Cobb, 24 Texas, 551 ; McLawrine v. Monroe, 30 Mo. 462. But whether it would be competent to show, in opposition to the recitals in the record, that a judgment of another State was rendered without jurisdiction having been obtained of the person of the defendant, is not clear on the authorities. Many cases hold not. Field v. Gibbs, 1 Pet. C. C. 156 ; Green v. Sarmiento, Ibid. 76 ; Lincoln v. Tower, 2 McLean, 473 ; Westervelt v. Lewis, Ibid. 511 ; Pearce v. Olney, 20 Conn. 544 ; Hoxie v. Wright, 2 Vt. 263 ; Newcomb v. Peck, 17 Vt. 302 ; Wilcox v. Kassick, 2 Mich. 165 ; Bimelar v. Dawson, 4 Scam. 536 ; Welch v. Sykes, 3 Gil. 197 ; Roberts v. Caldwell, 5 Dana, 512. Other cases admit such evidence. Starbuck v. Murray, 5 Wend. 148 ; Holbrook v. Murray, Ibid. 161 ; Shumway v. Stillman, 6 Wend. 447 ; Borden v. Fitch, 15 Johns. 121 ; Hall v. Williams, 6 Pick. 232 ; Aldrich v. Kinney, 4 Conn. 380 ; Bradshaw v. Heath, 13 Wend. 407 ; Gleason v. Dodd, 4 Met. 333 ; Noyes v. Butler, 6 Barb. 613 ; Norwood v. Cobb, 24 Texas, 551. The same defences may be made to a judgment, when sued in another State, which could have been made to it in the State where rendered. Hampton v. McConnel, 3 Wheat. 234 ; Mills v. Duryea, 7 Cranch, 484 ; Steel v. Smith, 7 W. & S. 447 ; Bank of the State v. Dalton, 9 How. 528.

[2] Const. of U. S. art. 4, § 4.

[3] Const. of U. S. art. 1, § 10.

2

publican members against aristocratic and monarchical innovations.[1]

So far as a particular consideration of the foregoing prohibitions falls within the design of our present work, it will be more convenient to treat of them hereafter, especially as such of them as are designed for the protection of rights of persons or property are usually repeated in the bills of rights contained in the State constitutions.

Where powers are conferred upon the general government, the exercise of the same powers by the States is impliedly prohibited, wherever the intent of the grant to the national government might be defeated by such exercise. On this ground it is held that the States cannot tax the agencies or loans of the general government; since the power to tax, if possessed by the States in regard to these objects, might be so exercised as to altogether destroy such agencies or destroy the national credit.[2] And where, by the national Constitution, jurisdiction is given to the national courts with a view to the more efficient and harmonious working of the system organized under it, it is competent for Congress in its wisdom to make that jurisdiction exclusive of the State courts.[3] On some other subjects State laws may be valid until the power of Congress is exercised, when they become superseded, either wholly, or so far as they conflict. The States may legislate on the subject of bankruptcy, if there be no law of Congress conflicting therewith.[4] State laws for organizing and disciplining the militia are valid except as they may conflict with national legislation;[5] and the States may constitutionally provide for punishing the counterfeiting of coin[6] and the passing of counterfeit money,[7] since these acts are offences against the State, notwithstanding they may be offences against the nation also.

[1] Federalist, Nos. 43 and 84.

[2] M'Culloch v. Maryland, 4 Wheat. 316, 427; Weston v. Charleston, 2 Pet. 449. And see chapter on taxation, post.

[3] Martin v. Hunter's Lessee, 1 Wheat. 334; The Moses Taylor v. Hammons, 4 Wal. 411. The Ad. Hine v. Trevor, Ibid. 555. And see note to these cases in Western Jurist, vol. 1, 241.

[4] Sturgis v. Crowninshield, 4 Wheat. 122; McMillan v. McNiell, Ibid. 209. See Chapter IX.

[5] Houston v. Moore, 5 Wheat. 1, 51.

[6] Harlan v. People, 1 Doug. Mich. 207.

[7] Fox v. Ohio, 5 How. 410; United States v. Marigold, 9 How. 560. And see Hendrick's case, 5 Leigh, 707; Moore v. People, 14 How. 13.

The tenth amendment to the Constitution provides that the powers not delegated to the United States by the Constitution, nor prohibited by it to the States, are reserved to the States respectively, or to the people. And it is to be observed as a settled rule of construction of the national Constitution, that the limitations it imposes upon the powers of government are in all cases to be understood as limitations upon the government of the Union only, except where the States are expressly mentioned.[1]

With other rules for the construction of the national Constitution we shall have little occasion to deal. They have been the subject of very elaborate treatises, judicial opinions, and legislative debates, which are familiar not only to the legal profession, but to the public at large. So far as that instrument apportions powers to the national judiciary, it must be understood, for the most part, as simply authorizing Congress to confer jurisdiction to exercise those powers, and not as directly conferring them upon the courts. The Constitution does not, of its own force, give to the national courts jurisdiction of the several cases which it enumerates, but an act of Congress is essential to create courts, and to apportion the jurisdiction among them. The exceptions are of those few cases of which the Constitution confers jurisdiction upon the Supreme Court by name. And although the courts of the United States administer the common law in many cases, they do not derive from the common law authority to take cognizance of and punish offences against the government.[2]

[1] Barron v. Mayor of Baltimore, 7 Pet. 243 ; Livingston's Lessee v. Moore, 7 Pet. 551 ; Fox v. Ohio, 5 How. 432, 434 ; Smith v. Maryland, 18 How. 71 ; Purvear v. Commonwealth, 5 Wal. 475 ; Bonaparte v. Camden & Amboy Railroad Co., Baldw. 220 ; James v. Commonwealth, 12 S. & R. 221 ; Barker v. People, 3 Cow. 686 ; Colt v. Eves, 12 Conn. 243 ; Jane v. Commonwealth, 3 Met. (Ky.) 18 ; Lincoln v. Smith, 27 Vt. 336 ; Matter of Smith, 10 Wend. 449 ; State v. Barnett, 3 Kansas, 250 ; Reed v. Rice, 2 J. J. Marsh. 45.

[2] Demurrer to an indictment for a libel upon the President and Congress. By the Court : " The only question which this case presents is, whether the Circuit Courts can exercise a common law jurisdiction in criminal cases. . . . . The general acquiescence of legal men shows the prevalence of opinion in favor of the negative of· the proposition. The course of reasoning which leads to this conclusion is simple, obvious, and admits of but little illustration. The powers of the general government are made up of concessions from the several States : whatever is not expressly given to the former, the latter expressly reserve. The judicial power of the United States is a constitutional part of these concessions : that power is to be exercised by courts organized for the purpose, and brought

into existence by an effort of the legislative power of the Union. Of all the courts which the United States may, under their general powers, constitute, one only, the Supreme Court, possesses jurisdiction derived immediately from the Constitution, and of which the legislative power cannot deprive it. All other courts created by the general government possess no jurisdiction but what is given them by the power that created them, and can be vested with none but what the power ceded to the general government will authorize them to confer. It is not necessary to inquire whether the general government, in any and what extent, possesses the power of conferring on its courts a jurisdiction in cases similar to the present; it is enough that such jurisdiction has not been conferred by any legislative act, if it does not result to those courts as a consequence of their creation." U. S. v. Hudson, 7 Cranch, 32. See U. S. v. Coolidge, 1 Wheat. 415. "It is clear there can be no common law of the United States. The Federal government is composed of twenty-four sovereign and independent States, each of which may have its local usages, customs, and common law. There is no principle which pervades the Union, and has the authority of law, that is not embodied in the Constitution or laws of the Union. The common law could be made a part of our Federal system only by legislative adoption." Per McLean, J., Wheaton v. Peters, 8 Pet. 658. As to the adoption of the common law by the States, see Van Nest v. Pacard, 2 Pet. 144, per Story, J.

CHAPTER III.

THE FORMATION AND AMENDMENT OF STATE CONSTITUTIONS.

THE Constitution of the United States assumes the existence of thirteen distinct State governments, over whose people its authority was to be extended if ratified by conventions chosen for the purpose. Each of these States was exercising the powers of government under some form of written constitution, and that instrument would remain unaffected by the adoption of the national Constitution, except in those particulars in which the two would come in conflict, and then the latter would modify and control the former. But besides this fundamental law, every State had also a body of laws, prescribing the rights, duties, and obligations of persons within its jurisdiction, and establishing those minute rules for all the relations of life which are deemed out of place in the Constitution, andmust be left to the regulation of the ordinary law-making power.

By far the larger and more valuable portion of that body of laws consisted of the *common law of England*, which had been transplanted in the American wilderness, and which the Colonists, now become an independent nation, had found a shelter of protection during all the long contest with the mother country at length brought to so fortunate a conclusion.

The common law of England consisted of those maxims of freedom, order, enterprise, and thrift which had prevailed in the conduct of public affairs, the management of private business, the regulation of domestic relations, and the acquisition, control, and transfer of property from time immemorial. It was the outgrowth of the habits of thought and action of the people, and was modified from time to time as those habits became modified, and as civilization advanced, and new inventions changed the modes of business. Springing from the very nature of the people themselves, it was obviously the best body of laws to which they were suited, and as they took with them their nature, so they would take with them these laws, whenever they should transfer their domicile from one country to another.

To eulogize the common law is no part of our present purpose. Many of its features were exceedingly harsh and repulsive, and gave unmistakable indications that they had their origin in times of profound ignorance, superstition and barbarism. The feudal system, which was essentially a system of violence, disorder, and rapine,[1] fastened many of its maxims upon the common law system, and these maxims are still to be traced, especially in the rules which govern the acquisition, control, and enjoyment of real estate. The criminal code was also marked by cruel and absurd features, some of which have clung with wonderful tenacity, long after even the most stupid could perceive their inconsistency with justice and civilization. But on the whole the system was the best foundation on which to erect an enduring structure of civil liberty which the world has ever known. It was the peculiar excellence of the common law that it recognized the worth, and sought specially to protect the rights and the privileges of the individual man. Its maxims were those of a sturdy and independent race, accustomed in an unusual degree to freedom of thought and action, and to a share in the administration of public affairs : arbitrary power and uncontrolled authority were not recognized in its principles. Awe surrounded and majesty clothed the king, but the humblest subject might shut the door of his cottage against him, and defend from intrusion that privacy which was as sacred as the kingly prerogatives. The system was the opposite of servile ; its features implied boldness and independent self-reliance on the part of the people ; and if the criminal code was harsh, it at least escaped the inquisitorial system which fastened itself upon criminal procedure in other civilized countries, and has ever been fruitful of injustice, oppression, and terror.

For several hundred years, however, changes had from time to time been made in the common law by means of statutes. The purpose of general statutes originally was mainly declaratory of common-law principles, which, by reason of usurpations and abuses, had come to be of doubtful force, and which therefore

---

[1] " A feudal kingdom was a confederacy of a numerous body, who lived in a state of war against each other, and of rapine towards all mankind, in which the king, according to his ability and vigor, was either a cipher or a tyrant, and a great portion of the people were reduced to personal slavery." Mackintosh, History of England, Chap. III.

needed to be authoritatively pronounced, that king and subject alike might understand and observe them. Such was the purpose of the first great statute, promulgated at a time when the legislative power was exercised by the king alone, and which is still known as the Magna Charta of King John. Such also was the purpose of the several confirmations of that charter, as well as of the Petition of Right[1] and the Bill of Rights,[2] each of which became necessary by reason of usurpations. But statutes also became important because old customs and modes of business were unsuited to new conditions of things, when property had become more valuable, wealth greater, commerce more extended, and all these changes had brought with them new dangers against which society as well as the individual subject was to be guarded. For this purpose the Statute of Wills[3] and the Statute of Frauds and Perjuries[4] became important; and the Habeas Corpus Act[5] was also necessary, not so much to change the law as to secure existing principles of the common law against being habitually set aside and violated by those in power.

From the first the Colonists in America claimed the benefit and protection of the common law. In some particulars, however, the common law was not suited to their condition and circumstances in this country, and those particulars they omitted as it was put in practice by them.[6] They also claimed the benefit of

[1] 1 Charles I. c. 1.

[2] 1 William & Mary, sess. 2, c. 2.

[3] 32 Hen. VIII. c. 7, and 34 & 35 Hen. VIII. c. 5.

[4] 29 Charles II. c. 3.

[5] 31 Charles II. c. 2.

[6] " The common law of England is not to be taken, in all respects, to be that of America. Our ancestors brought with them its general principles, and claimed it as their birthright; but they brought with them and adopted only that portion which was applicable to their situation." Story, J. in Van Nest v. Pacard, 2 Pet. 144. " The settlers of Colonies in America did not carry with them the laws of the land as being bound by them wherever they should settle. They left the realm to avoid the inconveniences and hardships they were under, where some of these laws were in force : particularly ecclesiastical laws, those for payment of tithes, and others. Had it been understood that they were to carry these laws with them, they had better have stayed at home among their friends, unexposed to the risks and toils of a new settlement. They carried with them a right to such parts of laws of the land as they should judge advantageous or useful to them ; a right to be free from those they thought hurtful ; and a right to make such others as they should think necessary, not infringing the general rights of Englishmen ; and such new laws they were to form as agreeable as might be to the

such statutes as from time to time had been enacted in modification of this body of rules. And when the difficulties sprung
up with the home government, it was a source of immense moral
power to the Colonists that they were able to show that the
rights they claimed were conferred by the common law, and
that the king or the Parliament was seeking to deprive them of
the common birthright of Englishmen. Did Parliament attempt
to levy taxes in America; its people demanded the benefit of
that maxim with which for many generations every English child
had been familiar, that those must vote the tax who are to pay
it.[1] Did Parliament order offenders against the laws in America
to be sent to England for trial; every American was roused to
indignation, and protested against the trampling under foot of
that time-honored principle that trials for crime must be by a
jury of the vicinage. Contending thus behind the bulwarks of
the common law, Englishmen would appreciate and sympathize
with their position; and Americans would feel doubly strong in a
cause that was right not only, but the justice of which must be
confirmed by an appeal to the consciousness of their enemies
themselves.

The evidence of the common law consisted in part of the declaratory statutes we have mentioned,[2] in part of the commenta-
ries of such men learned in the law as had been accepted as authority, but mainly of the decisions of the courts applying the

laws of England." Franklin, Works by Sparks, vol. 4, p. 275. See Morgan v.
King, 30 Barb. 9; Mayo v. Wilson, 1 N. H. 58; Houghton v. Page, 2 N. H. 44
State v. Rollins, 8 N. H. 550.

[1] "The blessing of Judah and Issachar will never meet; that the same people
or nation should be both the lion's whelp and the ass between burdens; neither
will it be that a people overlaid with taxes should ever become valiant and mar-
tial. It is true that taxes levied by consent of the estate do abate men's courage
less, as it hath been seen notably in the exercises of the Low Countries, and in
some degree in the subsidies of England, for you must note that we speak now of
the heart, and not of the purse; so that although the same tribute or tax laid by
consent or by imposing be all one to the purse, yet it works diversely upon the
courage. So that you may conclude that no people overcharged with tribute is
fit for empire." Lord Bacon on The True Greatness of Kingdoms.

[2] These statutes upon the points which are covered by them are the best evidence possible. They are the living charters of English liberty to the present
day; and as the forerunners of the American constitutions and the source of their
bills of rights, they are constantly appealed to where personal liberty or private
rights are placed in apparent antagonism to the government.

law to actual controversies. While Colonization continued, —
that is to say, until the war of the Revolution actually commenced, — these decisions were authority in the Colonies, and
the changes made in the common law up to the same period were
operative in America also, if suited to the condition of things
here. The opening of the war of the Revolution is the point of
time at which the continuous stream of the common law became
divided, and that portion which had been adopted in America
flowed on by itself, no longer subject to changes from across the
ocean, but liable to be still gradually modified through changes
in the modes of thought and of business among the people, as
well as through statutory enactments.

The Colonies also had legislatures of their own, by which laws
had been passed which were in force at the time of the separation,
and which remained unaffected thereby. When therefore they
emerged from the colonial condition into that of independence,
the laws which governed them consisted, *first*, of the common law
of England so far as they had tacitly adopted it as suited to their
condition ; *second*, of the statutes of England or of Great Britain
amendatory of the common law which they had in like manner
adopted ; and *third*, of the colonial statutes. The first and second
constituted the American common law, and by this in great part
are rights adjudged and wrongs redressed in the American States
to this day.[1]

---

[1] A few of the States, to get rid of confusion in the law, deemed it desirable to
repeal the acts of Parliament, and to re-enact such portions of them as were regarded important here. See the Michigan repealing statute, copied from that of
Virginia, in Code of 1820, p. 459. In some of the new States there were also other
laws in force than these to which we have above alluded. Although it has been
said in La Plaisance Bay Harbor Co. *v.* The City of Monroe, Wal. Ch. 155, and
Depew *v.* The Trustees of the Wabash and Erie Canal, 5 Ind. 8, that the Ordinance of 1787 was superseded in each of the States formed out of the Northwest
Territory by the adoption of a State constitution and admission to the Union, yet
the weight of judicial authority is probably the other way. In Hogg *v.* The
Zanesville Canal Manufacturing Co. 5 Ohio, 410, it was held that the provision
of the ordinance that the navigable waters of the Territory and the carrying places
between should be common highways and forever free, was permanent in its
character, and could not be altered without the assent, both of the people of the
State and of the United States, given through their representatives. " It is an
article of compact ; and until we assume the principle that the sovereign power
of a State is not bound by compact, this clause must be considered obligatory."
Justices McLean and Leavitt, in Spooner *v.* McConnell, 1 McLean, 337, exam-

Every Colony had also its charter emanating from the crown
and constituting its Colonial constitution. All but two of these
were swept away by the whirlwind of revolution, and others substituted by the people themselves, through the agency of conventions which they had chosen. The exceptions were of the States
of Connecticut and Rhode Island, each of which had continued
its government as a State under the Colonial charter, finding it
sufficient and satisfactory for the time being, and accepting it as
the constitution for the State.[1] New States have since from time

ine this subject at considerable length, and both arrive at the same conclusion
with the Ohio court. The view taken of the ordinance in that case was, that
such parts of it as were designed temporarily to regulate the government of the
Territory were abolished by the change from a Territorial to a State government,
while the other parts, which were designed to be permanent, are unalterable
except by common consent. Some of these, however, being guaranteed by the
Federal Constitution, afterwards adopted, may be considered as practically annulled, while any others which are opposed to the constitution of any State
formed out of the Territory must also be considered as annulled by common consent : the people of the State assenting in forming their constitution, and Congress in admitting the State into the Union under it.   The article in regard to
navigable waters is therefore still in force. The same was also said in regard to
the article prohibiting slavery, so that the prohibition of involuntary servitude
does not rest merely upon State constitutions, inasmuch as the subject is taken
beyond their control by the compact, except with the assent of Congress. The
same opinion was subsequently expressed in Palmer v. Commissioners of Cuyahoga Co. 3 McLean, 226, and in Jolly v. Terre Haute Drawbridge Co. 6 McLean,
237. See also Doe v. Douglass, 8 Blackf. 12 ; Connecticut Mutual Life Insurance Co. v. Cross, 18 Wis. 109. In the cases in 1st and 3d McLean, however,
the opinion was expressed that the States might lawfully improve the navigable
waters and the carrying places between, and charge tolls upon the use of the improvement to obtain reimbursement of their expenditures.

In some of the States formed out of territory acquired by the United States
from foreign countries, traces will be found of the laws existing before the change
of government. Louisiana has a code peculiar to itself, based upon the civil law.
Much of Mexican law, and especially in regard to lands and land titles, is retained in the systems of Texas and California. In Michigan, when the acts of
Parliament were repealed, it was also deemed important to repeal all laws derived from France, through connection with the Canadian provinces, including
the contumé de Paris, or ancient French common law. In the mining States and
Territories a peculiar species of common law, relating to mining rights and titles,
has sprung up, having its origin among the miners, but recognized and enforced
by the courts.

[1] It is worthy of note that the first case in which a legislative enactment was
declared unconstitutional and void by the courts of a State, on the ground of incompatibility with the State constitution, was that of Trevett v. Weeden, decided

to time formed constitutions, either regularly in pursuance of enabling acts passed by Congress, or irregularly by the spontaneous action of the people, or under the direction of the legislative or executive authority of the Territory to which the State succeeded. Where irregularities existed, they must be regarded as having been cured by the subsequent admission of the State into the Union by Congress ; and there were not wanting in the case of some States plausible reasons for insisting that such admission

by the Superior Court of Rhode Island in 1786. In the spring of that year a paper-money bank of £100,000 was created by the State legislature, whose bills were to be loaned to the people of the State according to the apportionment of the last tax, upon a pledge of real estate of double their value, and to be paid into the treasury at the end of fourteen years. As the bills immediately began to depreciate, a forcing act was passed, which subjected any person who should refuse to receive them on the same terms as specie, or in any way discourage their circulation, to a penalty of £100 on the first conviction, and the loss of the rights of a freeman on the second. A subsequent act moderated the penalty, but provided for a summary trial without jury, and prohibited any appeal. Under these acts Trevett entered complaint before the chief justice against Weedon, a butcher of Newport, for refusing to receive paper money at par in payment for meat. The case was heard before a full bench, and was argued by the ablest counsel of the State, amidst intense excitement. The court unanimously held the forcing acts void, because depriving the accused of the right to trial by jury, which was secured by the Colonial charter. A great outcry followed. The Assembly was immediately convened in special session, and by resolution reciting that whereas the said court had "declared and adjudged an act of the Supreme legislature of this State to be unconstitutional and so absolutely void ; and whereas it is suggested that the aforesaid judgment is unprecedented in this State, and may tend to abolish the legislative authority thereof," it was ordered that the judges be cited to give their immediate attendance on the Assembly to assign the reasons and grounds of their judgment. The judges obeyed the summons, and one of the number defended the opinion of the bench in an able argument upon the unconstitutionality of the bill, and asserted the independence of the court ; contending that the supreme judiciary of the State were not accountable to the General Assembly, or to any other power on earth for their judgments. The Assembly resolved that no satisfactory reasons had been rendered by the judges for their judgment, and when their terms expired at the end of the year, supplanted four of the five members of the court with more pliant instruments, with whose aid the public and private debts of the State were extinguished on the pretence of payment, or tender of payment in the paper money, which had fallen to one sixth of its nominal value, while debtors out of the State to creditors within it were not allowed the same privilege. See Arnold's History of Rhode Island, vol. 2, ch. 24. The printed argument for the defence in the case is now before us, and is able and conclusive. A citizen of the State can now look back with satisfaction to the upright, fearless, and dignified deportment of the prosecuted judges, even if no other feature of the case is calculated to excite emotions of pleasure.

had become a matter of right, and that the necessity for an enabling act by Congress was dispensed with by the previous stipulations of the national government in acquiring the territory from which such States were formed.[1]   Some of these constitutions pointed out the mode for their own modification ; others were silent on that subject ; but it has been assumed that in such cases the power to originate proceedings for that purpose rests with the legislature of the State, as the department most nearly representing its general sovereignty.   And this is doubtless the correct view to take of this subject.[2]

The theory of our political system is that the ultimate sovereignty is in the people, from whom springs all legitimate authority.[3]   They have created a national Constitution, and conferred upon it powers of sovereignty over certain subjects, and they create State governments upon which they confer the remaining powers of sovereignty, so far as they are disposed to allow them to be exercised at all.   By the constitutions which they form, they tie up alike their own hands and the hands of their agencies ; and neither the officers of the State, nor the whole people as an aggregate body, are at liberty to take action in opposition to these fundamental laws.   But in every State, although all persons are under the protection of the government, and obliged to conform their action to its laws, there are some who are altogether excluded from participation in the government, and are compelled to submit to be ruled by an authority in the creation of which they have no choice.   This patent fact suggests the inquiry, Who are the *people* in whom is vested the sovereignty of the State ? — since it is evident that they cannot include the whole population, and that the maxim that government rests upon the consent of the governed is in practice subject to exceptions.

---

[1] This was the claim made on behalf of Michigan ; it being insisted that whenever the Territory acquired the requisite population, its citizens had an absolute right to form a constitution and be admitted to the Union under the provisions of the Ordinance of 1787.   See Scott v. Detroit Young Men's Society's Lessee, 1 Doug. Mich. 119, and the contrary opinion in Myers v. Manhattan Bank, 20 Ohio, 283.   See also the opinions of the Attorney-General, vol. 2, p. 726.   The debates in the Senate of the United States on the admission of Michigan to the Union, go fully into this question.   See Benton's Abridgment of Congressional Debates, vol. 13, p. 69 to 72.

[2] See Jameson on Constitutional Conventions, ch. 8.

[3] McLean, J. in Spooner v. McConnell, 1 McLean, 347.

What *should be* the correct rule on this subject, it does not fall within our province to consider. That is a question which lies back of the formation of the Constitution, and is addressed to the people themselves. As a practical fact, the sovereignty is vested in those persons who by the constitution of the State are allowed to exercise the elective franchise. Such persons may have been designated by description in the enabling act of Congress permitting the formation of the Constitution, if such an act there was, or the convention which framed the constitution may have determined upon the qualifications of electors without external dictation. In either case, however, it was essential to subsequent good order and satisfaction with the government, that those persons generally should be admitted to a voice in the government whose exclusion on the ground of want of capacity or of moral fitness could not reasonably and to the general satisfaction be defended.

Certain classes have been almost universally excluded, — the slave, because he is wanting alike in the intelligence and the freedom of will essential to the proper exercise of the right; the woman from mixed motives, but mainly, perhaps, because, in the natural relation of marriage, she was supposed to be, and under the common law actually was, in a condition of dependence upon and subjection to the husband; the infant, for reasons similar to those which exclude the slave; the idiot, the lunatic, and the felon, on obvious grounds; and sometimes other classes for whose exclusion it is difficult to assign reasons so generally satisfactory.

The theory in these cases we take to be that classes are excluded because they lack either the intelligence, the virtue, or the freedom of action essential to the proper exercise of the elective franchise. But the rule by which the presence of these qualities is to be determined, it is not easy to establish on grounds the reason and propriety of which shall be accepted by all. It must be one that is definite and easy of application, and it must be made permanent, or an accidental majority may at any time change it, so as to usurp all power to themselves. But to be definite and easy of application, it must also be arbitrary. The infant of tender years is wanting in competency, but he is daily acquiring it, and a period is fixed at which he shall conclusively be presumed to possess what is requisite. The alien may know nothing of our political system and laws, and he is excluded until he has been domiciled in the country for a period judged to be sufficiently long to make him familiar with its institutions; races are sometimes excluded arbitrarily; and there have been times when in some of the States the possession of a certain amount of property, or the capacity to read, were regarded the only satisfactory proof of sufficient freedom of action and intelligence.[1]

Whatever the rule that is once established, it must remain fixed until those who by means of it have the power of the State put into their hands see fit to invite others to participate with them in its exercise. Any attempt of the excluded classes to assert their right to a share in the government, otherwise than by operating upon the public opinion of those who possess the right of suffrage, would be regarded as an attempt at revolution, to be put down by the strong arm of the government of the State, assisted, if need be, by the military power of the Union.[2]

In regard to the formation and amendment of State constitutions, the following appear to be settled principles of American constitutional law: —

I. The people of the several Territories may form for themselves State constitutions whenever enabling acts for that purpose are passed by Congress, but only in the manner allowed by such enabling acts, and through the action of such persons as the enabling acts shall clothe with the elective franchise to that end. If the people of a Territory shall, of their own motion, without such enabling act, meet in convention, frame and adopt a constitution, and demand admission to the Union under it, such action does not entitle them, as matter of right, to be recognized as States; but the power that can admit can also refuse, and the Territorial status must be continued until Congress shall be satisfied to suffer the Territory to become a State. There are always in these cases questions of policy as well as of constitutional law

---

[1] State v. Woodruff, 2 Day, 504; Catlin v. Smith, 2 S. & R. 267; Opinions of Judges, 18 Pick. 575. For some local elections it is quite common still to require property qualification or the payment of taxes in the voter; but statutes of this description are generally construed liberally. See Crawford v. Wilson, 4 Barb. 504. Many special statutes, referring to the people of a municipality the question of voting aid to internal improvements, have confined the right of voting on the question to tax-payers.

[2] The case of Rhode Island and the "Dorr Rebellion," so popularly known, will be fresh in the minds of all. For a discussion of the legal aspects of the case, see Luther v. Borden, 7 How. 1.

to be determined by the Congress before admission becomes a matter of right: whether the constitution formed is republican; whether the proper State boundaries have been fixed upon; whether the population is sufficient; whether the proper qualifications for the exercise of the elective franchise have been agreed to; whether any inveterate evil exists in the Territory which is now subject to control, but which might be perpetrated under a State government, — these and the like questions, in which the whole country is interested, cannot be finally solved by the people of the Territory for themselves, but the final decision must rest with Congress, and the judgment must be favorable before admission can be claimed or expected.

II. In the original States, and all others subsequently admitted to the Union, the power to amend or revise their constitutions resides in the great body of the people as an organized body politic, who, being vested with ultimate sovereignty, and the source of all State authority, have power to control and alter the law which they have made at their will. But the people, in the legal sense, must be understood to be those who, by the existing constitution, are clothed with political rights, and who, while that instrument remains, will be the sole organs through which the will of the body politic can be expressed.

III. But the will of the people to this end can only be expressed in the legitimate modes by which such a body politic can act, and which must either be prescribed by the constitution whose revision or amendment is sought, or by an act of the legislative department of the State, which alone would be authorized to speak for the people upon this subject, and to point out a mode for the expression of their will in the absence of any provision for amendment or revision contained in the constitution itself.[1]

[1] Opinions of the judges, 6 Cush. 573; Collier v. Frierson, 24 Ala. 100. The first constitution of New York contained no provision for its own amendment, and Mr. Hammond, in his political history of New York, vol. 1, ch. 26, gives a very interesting account of the controversy before the legislature and in the council of revision as to the power of the legislature to call a convention for revision, and as to the mode of submitting its work to the people. In Collier v. Frierson, 24 Ala. 108, it appeared that the legislature had proposed eight different amendments to be submitted to the people at the same time; the people had approved them, and all the requisite proceedings to make them a part of the constitution had been had, except that in the subsequent legislature the resolution for their ratification had by mistake omitted to recite one of them. On the question

IV. In accordance with universal practice, and from the very necessity of the case, amendments to an existing constitution, or entire revisions of it, must be prepared and matured by some body of representatives chosen for the purpose. It is obviously impossible for the whole people to meet, prepare, and discuss the proposed alterations, and there seems no feasible mode by which an expression of their will can be obtained, except by asking it upon the single point of assent or disapproval. But no body of representatives, unless specially clothed with power for that purpose by the people when choosing them, can rightfully take definitive action upon amendments or revisions ; but they must submit the result of their deliberations to the people — who alone are competent to exercise the powers of sovereignty in framing the fundamental law — for ratification or rejection. The constitutional convention is the representative of sovereignty only in a very qualified sense, and for the specific purpose, and with the restricted authority, to put in proper form the questions of amendment upon which the people are to pass ; but the changes in the

whether this one had been adopted, we quote from the opinion of the court : " The constitution can be amended in but two ways, either by the people who originally framed it, or in the mode prescribed by the instrument itself. If the last mode is pursued, the amendments must be proposed by two thirds of each house of the General Assembly ; they must be published in print, at least three months before the next general election for representatives ; it must appear from the returns made to the Secretary for State that a majority of those voting for representatives have voted in favor of the proposed amendments, and they must be ratified by two thirds of each house of the next General Assembly after such election, voting by yeas and nays, the proposed amendments having been read at each session three times on three several days in each house. We entertain no doubt that to change the constitution in any other mode than by a convention, every requisition which is demanded by the instrument itself must be observed, and the omission of any one is fatal to the amendment. We scarcely deem any argument necessary to enforce this proposition. The constitution is the supreme and paramount law. The mode by which amendments are to be made under it is clearly defined. It has been said that certain acts are to be done, certain requisitions are to be observed, before a change can be effected. But to what purpose are those acts required or those requisitions enjoined, if the legislature or any department of the government can dispense with them ? To do so would be to violate the instrument which they are sworn to support, and every principle of public law and sound constitutional policy requires the courts to pronounce against any amendment which is not shown to have been made in accordance with the rules prescribed by the fundamental law.   See also State v. McBride, 4 Mo. 303.

fundamental law of the State must be enacted by the people themselves.[1]

V. The power of the people to amend or revise their constitutions is limited by the Constitution of the United States in the following particulars: —

1. It must not abolish the republican form of government, since such act would be revolutionary in its character, and would call for and demand direct intervention on the part of the government of the United States.[2]

2. It must not provide for titles of nobility, or assume to violate the obligation of any contract, or attaint persons of crime, or provide *ex post facto* for the punishment of acts by the courts which were innocent when committed, or contain any other provision which would, in effect, amount to the exercise of any power expressly or impliedly prohibited to the States by the Constitution of the Union. For while such provisions would not call for the direct and forcible intervention of the government of the Union, it would be the duty of the courts, both State and national, to refuse to enforce them, and to declare them altogether void, as much when enacted by the people in their primary capacity as makers of the fundamental law, as when enacted in the form of statutes through the delegated power of their legislatures.[3]

VI. Subject to the foregoing principles and limitations, each State must judge for itself what provisions shall be inserted in its constitution; how the powers of government shall be apportioned in order to their proper exercise; what protection shall be thrown around the person or property of the citizen; and to what extent private rights shall be required to yield to the general good.[4]

[1] See upon this subject Jameson on the Constitutional Convention, §§ 415 – 418 and 479 – 520. This work is so complete and satisfactory in its treatment of the general subject, as to leave little to be said by one who shall afterwards attempt to cover the same ground.

[2] Const. of U. S. art. 4, § 4; Federalist, No. 43.

[3] Cummings *v.* Missouri, 4 Wal. 277; Jefferson Branch Bank *v.* Skelly, 1 Black, 436.

[4] Matter of the Reciprocity Bank, 22 N. Y. 9; McMullen *v.* Hodge, 5 Texas, 34; Matter of Oliver Lee and Co.'s Bank, 21 N. Y. 9. In the case last cited, Denio, J. says: "The [constitutional] convention was not obliged, like the legislative bodies, to look carefully to the preservation of vested rights. It was competent to deal, subject to ratification by the people, and to the Constitution of the Federal government, with all private and social rights, and with all the existing laws and institutions of the State. If the convention had so willed, and the

And the courts of the State, still more the courts of the Union, would be precluded from inquiring into the justice of their action, or questioning its validity, because of any supposed conflict with fundamental rules of right or of government, unless they should be able to show collision at some point between the instrument thus formed and that paramount law which constitutes, in regard to the subjects it covers, the fundamental rule of action throughout the whole United States.[1]

How far the constitution of a State shall descend into the particulars of government is a question of policy addressed to ·the convention which forms it. Certain things are to be looked for in all these instruments; though even as to these there is great variety, not only of substance, but also in the minuteness of their provisions to meet particular cases.

I. We are to expect a general framework of government to be designed, under which the sovereignty of the people is to be exercised by representatives chosen for the purpose, in such manner as the instrument provides, and with such ·reservations as it makes.

II. Generally the qualifications for the right of suffrage will be declared, as well as the conditions under which it shall be exercised.

III. Separate departments will be created for the exercise of legislative, executive, and judicial power, and care taken to keep the three as separate and distinct as possible, except so far as each is made a check upon the other to keep it within proper bounds, or to prevent hasty and improvident action. The exec-

people had concurred, all former charters and grants might have been annihilated. When therefore we are seeking for the true construction of a constitutional provision, we are constantly to bear in mind that its authors were not executing a delegated authority, limited by other constitutional restraints, but are to look upon them as the founders of a State, intent only upon establishing such principles as seemed best calculated to produce good government and promote the public happiness, at the expense of any and all existing institutions which might stand in their way."

[1] All the State constitutions now contain within themselves provisions for their amendment. Some require the question of calling a convention to revise the constitution to be submitted to the people at stated periods; others leave it to the legislature to call a convention or to submit to the people the question of calling one; while the major part allow the legislature to mature specific amendments to be submitted to the people separately, and these become a part of the constitution if adopted by the requisite vote.

utive is a check upon the legislature in the veto power, which most States allow; the legislature is a check upon both the other departments through its power to prescribe rules for the exercise of their authority, and through its power to impeach their officers; and the judiciary is a check upon the legislature by means of its authority to annul unconstitutional laws.

IV. Local self-government having always been a part of the English and American system, we shall look for its recognition in any such instrument. And even if not expressly recognized, it is still to be understood that all these instruments are framed with its present existence and anticipated continuance in view.

V. We shall also expect a declaration of rights for the protection of. individuals and minorities. This declaration usually contains the following classes of provisions: —

1. Those declaratory of the general principles of republican government; such as, that all freemen, when they form a social compact, are equal, and no man, or set of men, is entitled to exclusive, separate public emoluments or privileges from the community, but in consideration of public services; that absolute, arbitrary power over the lives, liberty, and property of freemen exists nowhere in a republic, not even in the largest majority; that all power is inherent in the people, and all free governments are founded on their authority, and instituted for their peace, safety, happiness, security, and the protection of property; that for the advancement of these ends they have at all times an inalienable and indefeasible right to alter, reform, or abolish their government in such manner as they may think proper; that all elections shall be free and equal; that no power of suspending the laws shall be exercised except by the legislature or its authority; that standing armies are not to be maintained in time of peace; that representation shall be in proportion to population; that the people shall have the right freely to assemble to consult of the common good, to instruct their representatives, and petition for redress of grievances; and the like.

2. Those declaratory of the fundamental rights of the citizen; as that all men are by nature free and independent, and have certain inalienable rights, among which are those of enjoying and defending life and liberty, acquiring, possessing, and protecting property, and pursuing and obtaining safety and happiness; that the right to property is before and higher than any constitutional

sanction; that the free exercise and enjoyment of religious profession and worship, without discrimination or preference, shall
forever be allowed; that every man may freely speak, write, and
publish his sentiments on all subjects, being responsible for the
abuse of that right; that every man may bear arms for the defence of himself and of the State; that the right of the people
to be secure in their persons, houses, papers, and effects against
unreasonable searches and seizures shall not be violated, nor shall
soldiers be quartered upon citizens in time of peace; and the like.

3. Those declaratory of the principles which insure to the
citizen an impartial trial, and protect him in his life, liberty,
and property against the arbitrary action of those in authority;
as that no bill of attainder or *ex post facto* law shall be passed;
that the right to trial by jury shall be preserved; that excessive
bail shall not be required, or excessive punishments inflicted;
that no person shall be subject to be twice put in jeopardy for
the same offence, or be compelled in any criminal case to be a
witness against himself, nor be deprived of life, liberty, or property without due process of law; that private property shall not
be taken for public use without compensation; and the like.

Other clauses are sometimes added declaratory of the principles of morality and virtue; and it is also sometimes expressly
declared, — what indeed is implied without the declaration, —
that everything in the declaration of rights contained is excepted
out of the general powers of government, and all laws contrary
thereto shall be void.

Many other things are commonly found in these charters of
government; but since, while they continue in force, they are to
remain absolute and unchangeable rules of action and decision, it
is obvious that they should not be made to embrace within their
iron grasp those subjects in regard to which the policy or interest
of the State or of its people may vary from time to time, and
which are therefore more properly left to the control of the legislature, which can more easily and speedily make the required
changes.

In considering State constitutions we must not commit the mistake of supposing that, because individual rights are guarded
and protected by them, they must also be considered as owing
their origin to them. These instruments measure the powers of
the rulers, but they do not measure the rights of the governed.

" What is a constitution, and what are its objects ?   It is easier to
tell what it is not than what it is.   It is not the beginning of a
community, nor the origin of private rights ; it is not the fountain
of law, nor the incipient state of government ; it is not the cause,
but consequence, of personal and political freedom ; it grants no
rights to the people, but is the creature of their power, the instrument of their convenience.   Designed for their protection in the
enjoyment of the rights and powers which they possessed before
the constitution was made, it is but the framework of the political government, and necessarily based upon the pre-existing
condition of laws, rights, habits, and modes of thought.   There
is nothing primitive in it : it is all derived from a known source.
It presupposes an organized society, law, order, property, personal
freedom, a love of political liberty, and enough of cultivated intelligence to know how to guard it against the encroachments of
tyranny.   A written constitution is in every instance a limitation
upon the powers of government in the hands of agents ; for there
never was a written republican constitution which delegated to
functionaries all the latent powers which lie dormant in every
nation, and are boundless in extent, and incapable of definition."[1]

[1] Hamilton *v.* St. Louis County Court, 15 Mo. 13, per Bates, *arguendo.*   And
see Matter of Oliver Lee & Co.'s Bank, 21 N. Y. 9.

CHAPTER IV.

OF THE CONSTRUCTION OF STATE CONSTITUTIONS.

THE deficiencies of human language are such that if written instruments were always carefully drawn, and by persons skilled in the use of words, we should not be surprised to find their meaning often drawn in question, or at least to meet with difficulties in their practical application. But these difficulties are greatly increased when draughtsmen are careless or incompetent, and they multiply rapidly when the instruments are to be applied, not only to the subjects directly within the contemplation of those who framed them, but also to a great variety of new circumstances which could not have been anticipated, but which must nevertheless be governed by the general rules which the instruments establish. So, also, the different stand-points which diverse interests occupy incline men to take different views of the instruments which affect those interests; and from all these considerations the subject of construction is always prominent in the practical administration of the law.[1] From the earliest periods in the his-

[1] In what we shall say in this chapter, the word *construction* will be employed in a sense embracing all that is covered by the two words *interpretation* and *construction* when used in their strictly accurate and technical sense. Their meaning is not the same, though they are frequently used as expressing the same idea. Lieber distinguishes thus: "Interpretation is the act of finding out the true sense of any form of words, that is, the sense which their author intended to convey, and of enabling others to derive from them the same idea which the author intended to convey. Construction is the drawing of conclusions respecting subjects that lie beyond the direct expressions of the text, from elements known from and given in the text; conclusions which are in the spirit, though not in the letter of the text. Interpretation only takes place if the text conveys some meaning or other. But construction is resorted to when, in comparing two different writings of the same individual, or two different enactments by the same legislative body, there is found contradiction where there was evidently no intention of such contradiction one of another, or where it happens that part of a writing or declaration contradicts the rest. When this is the case, and the nature of the document or declaration, or whatever else it may be, is such as not to allow us to consider the whole as being invalidated by a partial or other contradiction, then resort must be had to construction; so, too, if found to act in cases which have not been foreseen by the framers of those rules, by which we are

tory of written law, rules of construction, sometimes based upon sound reason, and seeking the real intent of the instrument, and at other times altogether arbitrary or fanciful, have been laid down by those who have assumed to instruct in the law, or who have been called upon to administer it, by the aid of which the meaning of the instrument was to be resolved. Some of these rules have been applied to particular classes of instruments only ; others are more general in their application, and so far as they are sound, may be made use of in any case where the meaning of a writing is in dispute. To such of these as seem important in constitutional law we shall refer, and illustrate them by reference to reported cases, where they have been applied.

A few preliminary words may not be out of place, upon the questions, who are to apply these rules ; what person, body, or department is to enforce the construction ; and how far a determination, when once made, is to be binding upon other persons, bodies, or departments.

We have already seen that we are to expect in every constitution an apportionment of the powers of government. We shall also find certain duties imposed upon the several departments, as well as upon specified officers in each, and we shall likewise discover that the constitution has sought to hedge about their action in various ways, with a view to the protection of individual rights, and the proper separation of duties. And wherever any one is called upon to perform any constitutional duty, or to do any act in respect to which it can be supposed that the constitution has spoken, it is obvious that a question of construction may at once arise, upon which some one must decide before the duty is performed or the act done. From the very nature of the case, this decision must commonly be made by the person, body, or department upon whom the duty is devolved, or from whom the act is required.

Let us suppose that the constitution requires of the legislature,

nevertheless obliged, for some binding reason, faithfully to regulate as well as we can our action respecting the unforeseen case." Legal and Political Hermeneutics. See Smith on Stat. and Const. Construction, 600. Bouvier defines the two terms succinctly as follows : "*Interpretation*, the discovery and representation of the true meaning of any signs used to convey ideas." "*Construction*, in practice, determining the meaning and application as to the case in question of the provisions of a constitution, statute, will, or other instrument, or of an oral agreement." Law Dic.

that, in establishing municipal corporations, it shall restrict their powers of taxation ; and a city charter is proposed which confines the right of taxation to the raising of money for certain specified purposes, but in regard to those purposes leaves it unlimited ; or which allows to the municipality unlimited choice of purposes, but restricts the rate ; or which permits persons to be taxed indefinitely, but limits the taxation of property : in either of these cases the question at once arises, whether the limitation in the charter is such a restriction as the constitution intends. Let us suppose, again, that a board of supervisors is, by the constitution, authorized to borrow money upon the credit of the county for any county purpose, and they are asked to issue bonds in order to purchase stock in some railway company which proposes to construct a road across the county ; the proposition is met with the query, Is this a county purpose, and can the issue of bonds be regarded as a borrowing of money, within the meaning of the people as expressed in the constitution ? And once again, let us suppose that the governor is empowered to convene the legislature on extraordinary occasions, and he is requested to do so in order to provide for a class of private claims whose holders are urgent ; can this with any propriety be deemed an extraordinary occasion ?

In these and the like cases our constitutions have provided no tribunal for the specific duty of solving in advance the questions which arise. In a few of the States, indeed, the legislative department has been empowered by the constitution to call upon the courts for their opinion upon the constitutional validity of a proposed law, in order that, if it be adjudged without warrant, the legislature may abstain from enacting it.[1] But these provisions are not often to be met with, and judicial decisions, especially upon delicate and difficult questions of constitutional law, can seldom be entirely satisfactory when made, as they commonly will be under such calls, without the benefit of argument at the bar, and of that light upon the points involved which might

---

[1] By the constitutions of Maine, New Hampshire, and Massachusetts, the judges of the Supreme Court are required when called upon by the Governor, Council, or either house of the legislature, to give their opinions " upon important questions of law, and upon solemn occasions." In Missouri they are to give their opinions " upon important questions of constitutional law, and upon solemn occasions."

be afforded by counsel learned in the law, and interested in giving them a thorough investigation.

It follows, therefore, that every department of the government and every official of every department may at any time, when a duty is to be performed, be required to pass upon a question of constitutional construction.[1] Sometimes the case will be such that the decision when made must, from the nature of things, be conclusive and subject to no appeal or review, however erroneous it may be in the opinion of other departments or other officers ; but in other cases the same question may be required to be passed upon again before the duty is completely performed. The first of these classes is where, by the constitution, a particular question is plainly addressed to the discretion or judgment of some one department or officer, so that the interference of any other department or officer, with a view to the substitution of its own discretion or judgment in the place of that to which the constitution has confided the decision, would be impertinent and intrusive.   Under every constitution cases of this description are to be met with ; and though it will sometimes be found difficult to classify them, there can be no doubt, when the case is properly determined to be one of this character, that the rule must prevail which makes the decision final.

We will suppose, again, that the constitution empowers the executive to convene the legislature on extraordinary occasions, and does not in terms authorize the intervention of any one else in determining what is and what is not such an occasion in the constitutional sense ; it is obvious that the question is addressed exclusively to the executive judgment, and neither the legislature nor the judicial department can intervene to compel action if he decide against it, or to enjoin action if, in his opinion, the proper occasion has arisen.[2] And again, if, by the constitution,

---

[1] " It is argued that the legislature cannot give a construction to the constitution relative to private rights secured by it. It is true that the legislature, in consequence of their construction of the constitution, cannot make laws repugnant to it. But every department of government, invested with certain constitutional powers, must, in the first instance, but not exclusively, be the judge of its powers, or it could not act." Parsons, Ch. J., in Kendall v. Inhabitants of Kingston, 5 Mass. 524.

[2] In exercising his power to call out the militia in certain exigencies, the President is the exclusive and final judge when the exigency has arisen. Martin v. Mott, 12 Wheat. 29.

laws are to take effect at a specified time after their passage, unless the legislature, for urgent reasons, shall otherwise order, we must perceive at once that the legislature alone is competent to pass upon the urgency of the alleged reasons.[1] And to take a judicial instance : if a court is required to give an accused person a trial at the first term after indictment, unless good cause be shown for continuance, it is obvious that the question of good cause is one for the court alone to pass upon, and that its judgment when exercised is, and must be from the nature of the case, final. And when in any of these and similar cases the decision is once made, other departments or other officers, whatever may have been their own opinions, must assume the decision to be correct, and are not at liberty to raise any question concerning it, unless some duty is devolved upon them which raises the same question anew.

But there are cases where the question of construction is equally addressed to two or more departments of the government, and it then becomes important to know whether the decision by one is binding upon the others, or whether each is to act upon its own judgment. Let us suppose once more that the governor, being empowered by the constitution to convene the

---

[1] In Gillinwater v. Mississippi & Atlantic Railroad Co. 13 Ill. 1, it was urged that a certain restriction imposed upon railroad corporations by the general railroad law was a violation of the provision of the constitution which enjoins it upon the legislature " to encourage internal improvements by passing liberal general laws of incorporation for that purpose." The court say of this provision : " This is a constitutional command to the legislature, as obligatory on it as any other of the provisions of that instrument; but it is one which cannot be enforced by the courts of justice. It addresses itself to the legislature alone, and it is not for us to say whether it has obeyed the behest in its true spirit. Whether the provisions of this law are liberal, and tend to encourage internal improvements, is matter of opinion, about which men may differ ; and as we have no authority to revise legislative action on the subject, it would not become us to express our views in relation to it. The law makes no provision for the construction of canals and turnpike roads, and yet they are as much internal improvements as railroads, and we might as well be asked to extend what we might consider the liberal provisions of this law to them, because they are embraced in the constitutional provision, as to ask us to disregard such provisions of it as we might regard as illiberal. The argument proceeds upon the idea that we should consider that as done which ought to be done ; but that principle has no application here. Like laws upon other subjects within legislative jurisdiction, it is for the courts to say what the law is, not what it should be." It is clear that courts cannot interfere with matters of legislative discretion. Maloy v. Marietta, 11 Ohio, N. S. 639.

legislature upon extraordinary occasions, has regarded a particular event to be such an occasion, and has issued his proclamation calling them together with a view to the enactment of some particular legislation which the event seems to call for, and which he specifies in his proclamation. Now the legislature are to enact laws upon their own view of necessity and expediency; and they will refuse to pass the desired statute if they regard it as unwise or unimportant. But in so doing they indirectly review the governor's decision, as in refusing to pass the law they also decide that the specific event was not one calling for action on their part. In such a case it is clear that, while the decision of the governor is final so far as to require the legislature to meet, it is not final in any sense that would bind the legislative department to accept and act upon it when they are called to enter upon the performance of their duty in the making of laws.

So also there are cases where, after the two houses of the legislature have passed upon the question, their decision is in a certain sense subject to review by the governor. If a bill is introduced the constitutionality of which is disputed, the passage of the bill by the two houses must be regarded as the expression of their judgment that, if approved, it will be a valid law. But if the constitution confers upon the governor a veto power, the same question of constitutional power will be brought by the bill before him, since it is manifestly his duty to withhold approval from any bill which, in his opinion, the legislature ought not for any reason to pass. And what reason so valid as that the constitution confers upon them no authority to that end? In all these and the like cases, each department must act upon its own judgment, and cannot be required to do that which it regards as a violation of the constitution, on the ground solely that another department which, in the course of the discharge of its own duty, was called upon first to act, has reached the conclusion that it will not be violated by the proposed action.

But setting aside now those cases to which we have referred where from the nature of things, and perhaps from explicit terms of the constitution, the judgment of the department or officer acting must be final, we shall find the general rule to be, that whenever an act is done which may become the subject of a proceeding in court, any question of constitutional authority that was open for consideration when the act was done will also be open in such proceeding, and that as the courts must finally settle the controversy, so also will they finally determine the question of constitutional law.

For the constitution of the State is higher in authority than any law, direction, or decree made by any body or any officer assuming to act under it, since such body or officer must exercise a delegated authority, and that must necessarily be subservient to the instrument by which the delegation is made. In any case of conflict the fundamental law must govern, and the act in conflict with it must be treated as of no legal validity. But no mode has yet been devised by which these questions of conflict are to be discussed and settled as abstract questions, and their determination is necessary or practicable only when public or private rights would be affected thereby. They then become the subject of legal controversy, and legal controversies must be settled by the courts. The courts have thus devolved upon them the duty to pass upon the constitutional validity, sometimes of legislative, and sometimes of executive acts. And as judicial tribunals have authority, not only to judge, but also to enforce their judgments, the result of a decision against the constitutionality of a legislative or executive act will be to render it invalid through the enforcement of the paramount law in the controversy which has raised the question.[1]

[1] " When laws conflict in actual cases, they [the courts] must decide which is the superior law, and which must yield ; and as we have seen that, according to our principles, every officer remains answerable for what he officially does, a citizen, believing that the law he enforces is incompatible with the superior law, the constitution, simply sues the officer before the proper court as having unlawfully aggrieved him in the particular case. The court, bound to do justice to every one, is bound also to decide this case as a simple case of conflicting laws. The court does not decide directly upon the doings of the legislature. It simply decides for the case in hand, whether there actually are conflicting laws, and if so which is the higher law that demands obedience, when both may not be obeyed at the same time. As, however, this decision becomes the leading decision for all future cases of the same import, until, indeed, proper and legitimate authority should reverse it, the question of constitutionality is virtually decided, and it is decided in a natural, easy, legitimate, and safe manner, according to the principle of the supremacy of the law, and the dependence of justice. It is one of the most interesting and important evolutions of the government of law, and one of the greatest protections of the citizen. It may well be called a very jewel of Anglican liberty, and one of the best fruits of our political civilization." Lieber, Civil Liberty and Self-Government.

" Whenever a law which the judge holds to be unconstitutional is argued in a

The same conclusion is reached by stating in consecutive order a few familiar maxims of the law. The administration of public justice is referred to the courts. To perform this duty, the first requisite is to ascertain the facts, and the next to determine the law that is applicable. The constitution is the fundamental law of the State, in opposition to which any other law, or any direction or decree, must be inoperative and void. If, therefore, such other law, direction, or decree seems to be applicable to the facts, but on comparison with the fundamental law it is found to be in conflict, the court, in declaring what the law of the case is, must necessarily determine its invalidity, and thereby in effect annul it.[1] The right and the power of the courts to do this are so plain,

tribunal of the United States, he may refuse to admit it as a rule; this power is the only one which is peculiar to the American magistrate, but it gives rise to immense political influence. Few laws can escape the searching analysis; for there are few which are not prejudicial to some private interest or other, and none which may not be brought before a court of justice by the choice of parties, or by the necessity of the case. But from the time that a judge has refused to apply any given law in a case, that law loses a portion of its moral sanction. The persons to whose interest it is prejudicial learn that means exist for evading its authority; and similar suits are multiplied until it becomes powerless. One of two alternatives must then be resorted to, — the people must alter the constitution, or the legislature must repeal the law." De Tocqueville, Democracy in America, c. 6.

[1] " It is idle to say that the authority of each branch of the government is defined and limited by the constitution, if there be not an independent power able and willing to enforce the limitations. Experience proves that the constitution is thoughtlessly but habitually violated; and the sacrifice of individual rights is too remotely connected with the objects and contests of the masses to attract their attention. From its very position it is apparent that the conservative power is lodged in the judiciary, which, in the exercise of its undoubted rights, is bound to meet any emergency; else causes would be decided, not only by the legislature, but sometimes without hearing or evidence." Per Gibson, Ch. J. in De Chastellux v. Fairchild, 15 Penn. St. 18.

" Nor will this conclusion, to use the language of one of our most eminent jurists and statesmen, by any means suppose a superiority of the judicial to the legislative power. It will only be supposing that the power of the people is superior to both; and that where the will of the legislature, declared in its statutes, stands in opposition to that declared by the people in the constitution, the judges ought to be governed by the latter rather than the former. They ought to regulate their decisions by the fundamental laws rather than by those which are not fundamental. Neither would we, in doing this, be understood as impugning the honest intentions, or sacred regard to justice, which we most cheerfully accord to the legislature. But to be above error is to possess an entire attribute of the De-

and the duty is so generally — we may now say universally — conceded, that we should not be justified in wearying the patience of the reader in quoting from the very numerous authorities upon the subject.[1]

ity;" and to spurn its correction, is to reduce to the same degraded level the most noble and the meanest of his works." Bates v. Kimball, 2 Chip. 77.

" Without the limitations and restraints usually found in written constitutions, the government could have no elements of permanence and durability ; and the distribution of its powers and the vesting their exercise in separate departments would be an idle ceremony." Brown, J. in People v. Draper, 15 N. Y. 558.

[1] 1 Kent, 500 – 507 ; Marbury v. Madison, 1 Cranch, 137 ; Webster on the Independence of the Judiciary, Works, vol. 3, p. 29. In this speech Mr. Webster has forcibly set forth the necessity of leaving with the courts the power to enforce constitutional restrictions. " It cannot be denied," says he, " that one great object of written constitutions is, to keep the departments of government as distinct as possible ; and for this purpose to impose restraints designed to have that effect. And it is equally true that there is no department on which it is more necessary to impose restraints than upon the legislature. The tendency of things is almost always to augment the power of that department in its relation to the judiciary. The judiciary is composed of few persons, and those not such as mix habitually in the pursuits and objects which most engage public men. They are not, or never should be, political men. They have often unpleasant duties to perform, and their conduct is often liable to be canvassed and censured where their reasons for it are not known or cannot be understood. The legislature holds the public purse. It fixes the compensation of all other departments ; it applies as well as raises all revenue. It is a numerous body, and necessarily carries along with it a great force of public opinion. Its members are public men, in constant contact with one another and with their constituents. It would seem to be plain enough that, without constitutional provisions which should be fixed and certain, such a department, in case of excitement, would be able to encroach on the judiciary." " The constitution being the supreme law, it follows, of course, that every act of the legislature contrary to that law must be void. But who shall decide this question ? Shall the legislature itself decide it ? If so, then the constitution ceases to be a legal, and becomes only a moral restraint upon the legislature. If they, and they only, are to judge whether their acts be conformable to the constitution, then the constitution is admonitory or advisory only, not legally binding ; because if the construction of it rests wholly with them, their discretion, in particular cases, may be in favor of very erroneous and dangerous constructions. Hence the courts of law, necessarily, when the case arises, must decide on the validity of particular acts." " Without this check, no certain limitation could exist on the exercise of legislative power." See also, as to the dangers of legislative encroachments, De Tocqueville, Democracy in America, c. 6. The legislature, though possessing a larger share of power, no more represents the sovereignty of the people than either of the other departments ; it derives its authority from the same high source. Bailey v. Philadelphia, &c. Railroad Co. 4 Harr. 402 ; Whittington v. Polk, 1 H. & J. 244.

The Doctrine of res adjudicata and stare decisis.

But a question which has arisen and been passed upon in one case may arise again in another, or it may present itself under different circumstances before some other department of the government. Will the principle once declared be held conclusive upon other courts and other departments, or does it settle only the particular controversy, and may a different decision be looked upon as possible in any new controversy that may arise? These questions resolve themselves into two others : when can a matter be said to be *res adjudicata?* and what is the extent of the doctrine known in the books as *stare decisis?*

And as to the first, we understand the rule to be, that a decision once made in a case, by the highest court empowered to pass upon it, is conclusive upon the parties to the controversy and their privies, who are not allowed afterwards to revive it in a new proceeding for the purpose of raising the same or any other questions. The matter in controversy has become *res judicata,* a thing definitely settled by judicial decision ; and the judgment of the court imports absolute verity. Whatever the question involved, — whether the interpretation of a private contract, the legality of an individual act, or the validity of a legislative enactment, — the rule of finality is the same. The controversy has been adjudged, and once finally passed upon is never to be renewed.[1] It must frequently happen, therefore, that a question of constitutional law will be decided in a private litigation, and the parties to the controversy, and all others subsequently acquiring rights under them, in the subject-matter of the suit, will thereby become absolutely and forever precluded from renewing the question in respect to the matter then involved. The rule of conclusiveness to this extent is one of the most inflexible prin-

---

[1] Duchess of Kingston's case, 2 Smith's Lead. Cas. 424 ; Etheridge *v.* Osborn, 12 Wend. 399 ; Hayes *v.* Reese, 34 Barb. 151 ; Hyatt *v.* Bates, 35 Barb. 308 ; Harris *v.* Harris, 36 Barb. 88 ; Young *v.* Black, 7 Cranch, 567 ; Chapman *v.* Smith, 16 How. 114 ; Wales *v.* Lyon, 2 Mich. 276 ; Prentiss *v.* Holbrook, 2 Mich. 372 ; Van Kleek *v.* Eggleston, 7 Mich. 511 ; Newberry *v.* Trowbridge, 13 Mich. 278 ; Crandall *v.* James, 6 R. I. 144 ; Babcock *v.* Camp, 12 Ohio, N. S. 11 ; Warner *v.* Scott, 39 Penn. St. 274 ; Kerr *v.* Union Bank, 18 Md. 396 ; Eimer *v.* Richards, 25 Ill. 289 ; Wright *v.* Leclaire, 3 Iowa, 241 ; Whittaker *v.* Johnson County, 12 Iowa, 595 ; Peay *v.* Duncan, 20 Ark. 85 ; Madox *v.* Graham, 2 Met. (Ky.) 56 ; George *v.* Gillespie, 1 Greene (Iowa), 421 ; Clark *v.* Sammons, 12 Iowa, 368 ; Taylor *v.* Chambers, 1 Iowa, 124 ; Skelding *v.* Whitney, 3 Wend. 154.

ciples of the law ; insomuch that even if it were subsequently held by the courts that the decision in the particular case was erroneous, such holding would not authorize the reopening of the old controversy in order that the final conclusion might be applied thereto.[1]

But if important principles of constitutional law can thus be disposed of in suits involving only private rights, and when private individuals and their counsel alone are heard, it becomes of interest to know how far, if at all, other individuals and the public at large are affected by the decision. And here it will be discovered that quite a different rule prevails, and that a judicial decision has no such force of absolute conclusiveness as to other parties as it is allowed to possess between the parties to the litigation in which the decision has been made, and those who have succeeded to their rights.

A party is estopped by a judgment against him from disputing its correctness, so far as the point directly involved in the case was concerned, whether the reasons upon which it was based were sound or not, and even if no reasons were given therefor. And if the parties themselves are estopped, so also should be all those who, since the decision, claim to have acquired interests in the subject-matter of the judgment from or under the parties, as personal representatives, heirs at law, donees, or purchasers, and who are therefore considered in the law as privies. But if strangers who have no interest in that subject-matter are to be in like manner concluded, because their controversies are supposed to involve the same question of law, we shall not only be forced into a series of endless inquiries, often resulting in little satisfaction, in order to ascertain whether the question is the same, but we shall also be met by the query, whether we are not concluding parties by decisions which others have obtained in fictitious controversies and by collusion, or suffered to pass without sufficient consideration and discussion, and which might have been given otherwise had these parties had an opportunity of being heard.

---

[1] McLean v. Hugarin, 13 Johns. 184 ; Morgan v. Plumb, 9 Wend. 287 ; Wilder v. Case, 16 Wend. 583 ; Baker v. Rand, 13 Barb. 152 ; Kelley v. Pike, 5 Cush. 484 ; Hart v. Jewett, 11 Iowa, 276 ; Colburn v. Woodworth, 31 Barb. 381 ; Newberry v. Trowbridge, 13 Mich. 278 ; Skildin v. Herrick, 3 Wend. 154 ; Brockway v. Kinney, 2 Johns. 210 ; Platner v. Best, 11 Johns. 530 ; Phillips v. Berick, 16 Johns. 136.

We have already seen that the force of a judgment does not depend upon the reasons given therefor, or upon the circumstance that any were or were not given. If there were, they may have covered portions of the controversy only, or they may have had such reference to facts peculiar to that case, that in any other controversy, though somewhat similar in its facts, and apparently resembling it in its legal bearings, grave doubts might arise whether it ought to fall within the same general principle. If one judgment was absolutely to conclude the parties to any similar controversy, we ought at least to be able to look into the judicial mind, in order that we might ascertain of a surety that all those facts which influence the questions of law were substantially the same in each, and we ought also to be able to see that the first litigation was conducted in entire good faith, and that all those considerations were presented to the court which could properly have weight in the construction and application of the law. All these things, however, are manifestly impossible; and the law therefore wisely excludes judgments from being used to the prejudice of strangers to the controversy, and restricts their conclusiveness to parties thereto and their privies.[1] Even parties and privies are bound only so far as regards the subject-matter then involved, and would be at liberty to raise the same questions anew in a distinct controversy affecting some distinct subject-matter.[2]

All judgments, however, are supposed to apply the existing law to the facts of the case; and the reasons which are sufficient to influence the court to a particular conclusion in one case ought to be sufficient to bring it or any other court to the same conclusion in all other like cases where no modification of the law has intervened. There would thus be uniform rules for the administration of justice, and the same measure that is meted out

---

[1] Burrill v. West, 2 N. H. 190; Davis v. Wood, 1 Wheat. 6; Jackson v. Vedder, 3 Johns. 8; Case v. Reeve, 14 Johns. 79; Alexander v. Taylor, 4 Denio, 302; Van Bokkelin v. Ingersoll, 5 Wend. 315; Smith v. Ballantyne, 10 Paige, 101; Orphan House v. Lawrence, 11 Paige, 80; Thomas v. Hubbell, 15 N. Y. 405; Wood v. Stephen, 1 Serg. & R. 175; Peterson v. Lothrop, 34 Penn. St. 223; Twambly v. Henley, 4 Mass. 441; Este v. Strong, 2 Ohio, 401; Cowles v. Harts, 3 Conn. 516; Floyd v. Mintsey, 5 Rich. 361; Riggins's Ex'rs v. Brown, 12 Geo. 271; Persons v. Jones, Ibid. 371.

[2] Van Alstine v. Railroad Co., 34 Barb. 28; Taylor v. McCracken, 2 Blackf. 260; Cook v. Vimont, 6 T. B. Monr. 284.

4

to one would be received by all others. And even if the same or any other court, in a subsequent case, should be in doubt concerning the correctness of the decision which has been made, there are consequences of a very grave character to be contemplated and weighed before the experiment of disregarding it should be ventured upon. That state of things, when judicial decisions conflict, so that a citizen is always at a loss in regard to his rights and his duties, is a very serious evil; and the alternative of accepting adjudged cases as precedents in future controversies resting upon analogous facts, and brought within the same reasons, is obviously preferable. Precedents, therefore, become important, and counsel are allowed and expected to call the attention of the court to them, not as concluding controversies, but as guides to the judicial mind. Chancellor Kent says: " A solemn decision upon a point of law arising in any given case becomes an authority in a like case, because it is the highest evidence which we can have of the law applicable to the subject, and the judges are bound to follow that decision so long as it stands unreversed, unless it can be shown that the law was misunderstood or misapplied in that particular case. If a decision has been made upon solemn argument and mature deliberation, the presumption is in favor of its correctness, and the community have a right to regard it as a just declaration or exposition of the law, and to regulate their actions and contracts by it. It would therefore be extremely inconvenient to the public if precedents were not duly regarded, and implicitly followed. It is by the notoriety and stability of such rules that professional men can give safe advice to those who consult them, and people in general can venture to buy and trust, and to deal with each other. If judicial decisions were to be lightly disregarded, we should disturb and unsettle the great landmarks of property. When a rule has once been deliberately adopted and declared, it ought not to be disturbed unless by a court of appeal or review, and never by the same court, except for very urgent reasons, and upon a clear manifestation of error; and if the practice were otherwise, it would be leaving us in a perplexing uncertainty as to the law." [1]

[1] 1 Kent, 475. And see Cro. Jac. 527; Goodtitle v. Otway, 7 T. R. 416; Selby v. Bardons, 3 B. & Ad. 17; Fletcher v. Lord Somers, 3 Bing. 588; Anderson v. Jackson, 16 Johns. 402; Goodell v. Jackson, 20 Johns. 722; Bates v. Releyea, 23 Wend. 340; Emerson v. Atwater, 7 Mich. 12; Nelson v. Allen, 1

The doctrine of *stare decisis*, however, is only applicable, in its
full force, within the territorial jurisdiction of the courts making

Yerg. 376; Palmer *v.* Lawrence, 5 N. Y. 389; Kneeland *v.* Milwaukee, 15 Wis.
458; Boon *v.* Bowers, 30 Miss. 246; Rex *v.* Cox, 2 Burr. 787; King *v.* Younger,
5 T. R. 450; Hammond *v.* Anderson, 4 B. & P. 69; Broom's Maxims, 109. Dr.
Lieber thinks the doctrine of the precedent especially valuable in a free country.
"Liberty and steady progression require the principle of the precedent in all
spheres. It is one of the roots with which the tree of liberty fastens in the soil of
real life, and through which it receives the sap of fresh existence. It is the
weapon by which interference is warded off. The principle of the precedent is
eminently philosophical. The English Constitution would not have developed
itself without it. What is called the English Constitution consists of the fundamentals of the British polity, laid down in custom, precedent, decisions, and statutes; and the common law in it is a far greater portion than the statute law.
The English Constitution is chiefly a common-law constitution; and this reflex of
a continuous society in a continuous law is more truly philosophical, than the the-
oretic and systematic, but lifeless constitutions of recent France." Civ. Lib. and
Self-Gov. See also his chapter on precedents in the Hermeneutics. In Nelson
v. Allen, 1 Yerg. 376, where the constitutionality of the "Betterment Law" came
under consideration, the court (White, J.) say: "Whatever might be my own
opinion upon this question, not to assent to its settlement now, after two solemn
decisions of this court, the last made upwards of fourteen years ago, and not
only no opposing decision, but no attempt even by any case, during all this time,
to call the point again in controversy, forming a complete acquiescence, would
be, at the least, inconsistent, perhaps mischievous, and uncalled for by a correct
discharge of official duty. Much respect has always been paid to the contemporaneous construction of statutes, and a forbidding caution hath always accompanied any approach towards unsettling it, dictated no doubt by easily foreseen
consequences attending a sudden change of a rule of property, necessarily introductory at least of confusion, increased litigation, and the disturbance of the
peace of society. The most able judges and the greatest names on the bench
have held this view of the subject, and occasionally expressed themselves to that
effect, either tacitly or openly, intimating that if they had held a part in the first
construction they would have been of a different opinion; but the construction
having been made, they give their assent thereto. Thus Lord Ellenborough, in
2 East, 302, remarks: 'I think it is better to abide by that determination, than
to introduce uncertainty into this branch of the law, it being often more important to have the rule settled, than to determine what it shall be. I am not, however, convinced by the reasoning in this case, and if the point were new I should
think otherwise.' Lord Mansfield, in 1 Burr. 419, says: 'Where solemn determinations acquiesced under had settled precise cases, and a rule of property, they
ought, for the sake of certainty, to be observed, as if they had originally formed
a part of the text of the statute.' And Sir James Mansfield, in 4 B. & P. 69,
says: 'I do not know how to distinguish this from the case before decided in the
court. It is of greater consequence that the law should be as uniform as possible,
than that the equitable claim of an individual should be attended to.'" And see
People *v.* Cicotte, 16 Mich.

the decisions, since there alone can such decisions be regarded as having established any rules. Rulings made under a similar legal system elsewhere may be cited and respected for their reasons, but are not to be necessarily accepted as guides except in so far as those reasons commend themselves to the judicial mind.[1] Great Britain and the thirteen original States had each substantially the same system of common law originally, and a decision now by one of the higher courts of Great Britain as to what the common law is upon any point is certainly entitled to great respect in any of the States, though not necessarily to be accepted as binding authority any more than the decisions in any one of the other States upon the same point. It gives us the opinions of able judges as to what the law is, but its force as an authoritative declaration must be confined to the country for which the court sits and judges. But an English decision before the Revolution is in the direct line of authority ; and where a particular statute or clause of the constitution has been adopted in one State from the statutes or constitution of another, after a judicial construction had been put upon it in such last-mentioned State, it is but just to regard the construction to have been adopted, as well as the words, and all the mischiefs of disregarding precedents would follow as legitimately here as in any other case.[2]

It will of course sometimes happen that a court will find a former decision so unfounded in law, so unreasonable in its deductions, or so mischievous in its consequences, as to feel compelled to disregard it. Before doing so, however, it will be well to consider whether the point involved is such as to have become a rule of property, so that titles have been acquired in reliance upon it, and vested rights will be disturbed by any change ; for in such a case it may be better that the correction of the error be left to the legislature, which can control its action so

---

[1] Caldwell v. Gale, 11 Mich. 77.

[2] Commonwealth v. Hartnett, 3 Gray, 450 ; Bond v. Appleton, 8 Mass. 472 ; Rutland v. Mendon, 1 Pick. 154 ; Campbell v. Quinlin, 3 Scam. 288 ; Little v. Smith, 4 Scam. 402 ; Tyler v. Tyler, 19 Ill. 151 ; Pennock v. Dialogue, 2 Pet. 18 ; Adams v. Field, 21 Vt. 266 ; Turnpike Co. v. People, 9 Barb. 167 ; Drennan v. People, 10 Mich. 169 ; Myrick v. Hasey, 27 Me. 9 ; People v. Coleman, 4 Cal. 46 ; Attorney-General v. Brunst, 3 Wis. 787 ; Langdon v. Applegate, 5 Ind. 327. But it does not necessarily follow that the prior decision construing the law must be inflexibly followed, since the circumstances in the State adopting it may be so different as to require a different construction. Little v. Smith, 4 Scam. 402.

as to make it prospective only, and thus prevent unjust consequences.[1]

Whenever the case is such that judicial decisions which have been made are to be accepted as law, and followed by the courts in future cases, it is equally to be expected that they will be followed by other departments of the government also. Indeed in the great majority of cases the officers of other departments have no option; for the courts possess the power to enforce their construction of the law as well as to declare it; and a failure to accept and follow it in one case would only create necessity for new litigation with similar result. Nevertheless, there are exceptions to this rule which embrace all those cases where new action is asked of another department, which that department is at liberty to grant or refuse for any reasons which it may regard as sufficient. We cannot conceive that, because the courts have declared an expiring corporation to have been constitutionally created, the legislature would be bound to renew its charter, or the executive to sign an act for that purpose, if doubtful of the constitutional authority, even though no other adverse reasons existed. In the enactment of laws the legislature must act upon its own reasons; mixed motives of power, justice, and policy influence its action; and it is always justifiable and laudable to lean against a violation of the constitution. Indeed cases must sometimes occur when a court should refrain from declaring a statute

---

[1] Emerson v. Atwater, 7 Mich. 12. "It is true that when a principle of law, doubtful in its character or uncertain in the subject-matter of its application, has been settled by a series of judicial decisions, and acquiesced in for a considerable time, and important rights and interests have become established under such decisions, courts will hesitate long before they will attempt to overturn the result so long established. But when it is apparently indifferent which of two or more rules is adopted, the one which shall have been adopted by judicial sanction will be adhered to, though it may not, at the moment, appear to be the preferable rule. But when a question arises involving important public or private rights, extending through all coming time, has been passed upon on a single occasion, and which decision can in no just sense be said to have been acquiesced in, it is not only the right, but the duty of the court, when properly called upon, to re-examine the questions involved, and again subject them to judicial scrutiny. We are by no means unmindful of the salutary tendency of the rule *stare decisis*, but at the same time we cannot be unmindful of the lessons furnished by our own consciousness, as well as by judicial history, of the liability to error and the advantages of review." Per Smith, J. Pratt v. Brown, 3 Wis. 609. And see Kneeland v. Milwaukee, 15 Wis. 458.

unconstitutional, because not clearly satisfied that it is so, when if the judges were to act as legislators upon the question of its enactment, they ought with the same views to withhold their assent, from grave doubts upon that subject. The duty is different in the two cases, and presumptions may control in one which do not exist in the other. But those cases where new legislation is sought stand by themselves, and are not precedents for those which involve only considerations concerning the constitutional validity of existing enactments. The general acceptance of judicial decisions as authoritative, by each and all, can alone prevent confusion, doubt, and uncertainty, and any other course is incompatible with a true government of law.

Construction to be Uniform.

A cardinal rule in dealing with written instruments is that they shall receive an unvarying interpretation, and that their practical construction is to be uniform. A constitution is not to be made to mean one thing at one time, and another at some subsequent time when the circumstances may have so changed as perhaps to make a different rule in the case seem desirable. A principal share of the benefit expected from written constitutions would be lost if the rules they established were so flexible as to bend to circumstances or be modified by public opinion. It is with special reference to the varying moods of public opinion, and with a view to putting the fundamentals of government beyond their control, that these instruments are framed; and there can be no such steady and imperceptible change in their rules as inheres in the principles of the common law. Those beneficent maxims of the common law which guard person and property have grown and expanded until they mean vastly more to us than than they did to our ancestors, and are more minute, particular, and pervading in their protections; and we may confidently look forward in the future to still further modifications in the direction of improvement. Public sentiment and action effect such changes, and the courts recognize them; but a court or legislature which should allow a change in public sentiment to influence it in giving construction to a written constitution not warranted by the intention of its founders, would be justly chargeable with reckless disregard of official oath and public duty; and if its course could become a precedent, these instruments would be of little avail. The violence of public passion is quite as likely to be in the direction of oppression as in any other; and the necessity for bills of rights in our fundamental laws lies mainly in the danger that the legislature will be influenced by temporary excitements and passions among the people to adopt oppressive enactments. What a court is to do, therefore, is *to declare the law as written,* leaving it to the people themselves to make such changes as new circumstances may require.[1] The meaning of the constitution is fixed when it is adopted, and it is not different at any subsequent time when a court has occasion to pass upon it.[2]

The Intent to govern.

The object of construction, as applied to a written constitution, is *to give effect to the intent of the people in adopting it.* In the case of all written laws, it is the intent of the lawgiver that is to be enforced. But this intent is to be found in the instrument itself. It is to be presumed that language has been employed with sufficient precision to convey it, and unless examination demonstrates that the presumption does not hold good in the particular case, nothing will remain except to enforce it. "Where a law is plain and unambiguous, whether it be expressed in general or limited terms, the legislature should be intended to mean what they have plainly expressed, and consequently no room is left for construction."[3] Possible or even probable meanings, when one is

[1] People *v.* Morrell, 21 Wend. 584; Newell *v.* People, 7 N. Y. 109; McKoan *v.* Devries, 3 Barb. 196.

[2] Campbell, J. in People *v.* Blodgett, 13 Mich. 138.

[3] United States *v.* Fisher, 2 Cranch, 399; Bosley *v.* Mattingley, 14 B. Monr. 89; Sturgis *v.* Crowninshield, 4 Wheat. 202; Schooner Paulina's Cargo *v.* United States, 7 Cranch, 60; Ogden *v.* Strong, 2 Paine, C. C. 584; United States *v.* Ragsdale, 1 Hemp. 497; Southwark Bank *v.* Commonwealth, 26 Penn. St. 446; Ingalls *v.* Cole, 47 Me. 530; McCluskey *v.* Cromwell, 11 N. Y. 593; Furman *v.* New York, 5 Sandf. 16; Newell *v.* People, 7 N. Y. 83; People *v.* N. Y. Central R. R. Co., 24 N. Y. 492; Bidwell *v.* Whittaker, 1 Mich. 479; Alexander *v.* Worthington, 5 Md. 471; Cantwell *v.* Owens, 14 Md. 215; Case *v.* Wildridge, 4 Ind. 51; Spencer *v.* State, 5 Ind. 49; Putnam *v.* Flint, 10 Pick. 504; Heirs of Ludlow *v.* Johnson, 3 Ohio, 553; District Township *v.* Dubuque, 7 Iowa, 262; Pattison *v.* Yuba, 13 Cal. 175. The remarks of Mr. Justice Bronson in People *v.* Prudy, 2 Hill, 35, are very forcible in showing the impolicy and danger of looking beyond the instrument itself to ascertain its meaning, when the terms employed are positive and free from all ambiguity. "It is said that the Constitution does not extend to *public* corporations, and therefore a majority vote was sufficient. I do not so read the Constitution. The language of the clause is:

plainly declared in the instrument itself, the courts are not at liberty to search for elsewhere.

'The assent of two thirds of the members elected to each branch of the legislature shall be requisite to *every* bill creating, continuing, altering, or renewing *any* body politic or corporate.' These words are as broad in their signification as any which could have been selected for the occasion from our vocabulary, and there is not a syllable in the whole instrument tending in the slightest degree to limit or qualify the universality of the language. If the clause can be so construed that it shall not extend alike to *all* corporations, whether public or private, it may then, I think, be set down as an established fact that the English language is too poor for the framing of fundamental laws which shall limit the powers of the legislative branch of the government. No one has, I believe, pretended that the Constitution, looking at that alone, can be restricted to any particular class or description of corporations. But it is said that we may look beyond the instrument for the purpose of ascertaining the mischief against which the clause was directed, and thus restrict its operation. But who shall tell us what that mischief was? Although most men in public life are old enough to remember the time when the Constitution was framed and adopted, they are not agreed concerning the particular evils against which this clause was directed. Some suppose the clause was intended to guard against legislative corruption, and others that it was aimed at monopolies. Some are of opinion that it only extends to private without touching public corporations, while others suppose that it only restricts the power of the legislature when creating a single corporation, and not when they are made by the hundred. In this way a solemn instrument — for so I think the Constitution should be considered — is made to mean one thing by one man and something else by another, until, in the end, it is in danger of being rendered a mere dead letter; and that, too, where the language is so plain and explicit that it is impossible to mean more than one thing, unless we first lose sight of the instrument itself, and allow ourselves to roam at large in the boundless fields of speculation. For one, I dare not venture upon such a course. Written constitutions of government will soon come to be regarded as of little value if their injunctions may be thus lightly overlooked; and the experiment of setting a boundary to power will prove a failure. We are not at liberty to presume that the framers of the Constitution, or the people who adopted it, did not understand the force of language." See also same case, 4 Hill, 384. In the language of the Supreme Court of Indiana, we add : " This power of construction in courts is a mighty one, and, unrestrained by settled rules, would tend to throw a painful uncertainty over the effect that might be given to the most plainly worded statutes, and render courts, in reality, the legislative power of the State. Instances are not wanting to confirm this. Judge-made law has overrode the legislative department. It was the boast of Chief Justice Pemberton, one of the judges of the despot Charles II., and not the worst even of those times, that he had entirely outdone the Parliament in making law. We think that system of jurisprudence best and safest which controls most by fixed rules, and leaves least to the discretion of the judge; a doctrine constituting one of the points of superiority in the common law over that system which has been administered in France, where authorities had no force, and the law of each case was what the judge of the case

" Whether we are considering an agreement between parties, a statute, or a constitution, with a view to its interpretation, the thing which we are to seek is *the thought which it expresses.* To ascertain this, the first resort in all cases is to the natural signification of the words employed, in the order of grammatical arrangement in which the framers of the instrument have placed them. If thus regarded the words embody a definite meaning, which involves no absurdity and no contradiction between different parts of the same writing, then that meaning, apparent on the face of the instrument, is the one which alone we are at liberty to say was intended to be conveyed. In such a case there is no room for construction. That which the words declare is the meaning of the instrument, and neither courts nor legislatures have a right to add to or take away from that meaning." [1]

The whole Instrument to be examined.

Nor is it lightly to be inferred that any portion of a written law is so ambiguous as to require extrinsic aid in its construction. Every such instrument is adopted as a whole, and a clause which, standing by itself, might seem of doubtful import, may yet be made plain by comparison with other clauses or portions of the same law. It is therefore a rule of construction, that *the whole is to be examined with a view to arriving at the true intention of each part;* and this Sir Edward Coke regards the most natural and genuine method of expounding a statute.[2] " If any section [of a law] be intricate, obscure, or doubtful, the proper mode of discovering its true meaning is by comparing it with the other sections, and finding out the sense of one clause by the words or obvious intent of another." [3] And in making this comparison it is not to be supposed that any words have been employed without occasion, or without intent that they should have effect as part of

saw fit to make it. We admit that the exercise of an unlimited discretion may, in a particular instance, be attended with a salutary result; still history informs us that it has often been the case that the arbitrary discretion of a judge was the law of a tyrant, and warns us that it may be so again." Spencer *v.* State, 5 Ind. 76.

[1] Newell *v.* People, 7 N. Y. 97. And see Den *v.* Reid, 10 Pet. 524; Greencastle Township *v.* Black, 5 Ind. 569; Broom's Maxims (5th Am. edit.), 551, marg.

[2] Co. Lit. 381, *a.*

[3] Stowell *v.* Lord Zouch, Plowd. 365 ; Broom's Maxims, 521.

the law. The rule applicable here is, that *effect is to be given, if possible, to the whole instrument,* and to every section and clause. If different portions seem to conflict, the courts must harmonize them, if practicable, and lean in favor of a construction which will render every word operative, rather than one which may make some idle and nugatory.[1]

This rule is especially applicable to written constitutions, in which the people will be presumed to have expressed themselves in careful and measured terms, corresponding with the immense importance of the powers delegated, leaving as little as possible to implication.[2] It is scarcely conceivable that a case can arise where a court would be justifiable in declaring any portion of a written constitution nugatory because of ambiguity. One part may qualify another so as to restrict its operation, or apply it otherwise than the natural construction would require if it stood by itself; but one part is not to be allowed to defeat another, if by any reasonable construction the two can be made to stand together.[3]

In interpreting clauses we must presume that *words have been employed in their natural and ordinary meaning.* Says Marshall, Ch. J.: " The framers of the Constitution, and the people who adopted it, must be understood to have employed words in their natural sense, and to have understood what they meant." [4] This is but saying that no forced or unnatural construction is to be put upon their language; and it seems so obvious a truism that one

---

[1] Attorney-General v. Detroit and Erin Plank Road Co., 2 Mich. 138 ; People v. Burns, 5 Mich. 114 ; District Township v. Dubuque, 7 Iowa, 262 ; Manly v. State, 7 Md. 135 ; Parkinson v. State, 14 Md. 184 ; Belleville Railroad Co. v. Gregory, 15 Ill. 20 ; Ogden v. Strong, 2 Paine, C. C. 584 ; Ryegate v. Wardsboro, 30 Vt. 746 ; Brooks v. Mobile School Commissioners, 31 Ala. 227 ; Den v. Dubois, 1 Harrison, 285 ; Den v. Schenck, 3 Halst. 34.

[2] Wolcott v. Wigton, 7 Ind. 49 ; People v. Purdy, 2 Hill, 36, per Bronson, J. ; Greencastle Township v. Black, 5 Ind. 570 ; Green v. Weller, 32 Miss. 650.

[3] It is a general rule, in the construction of writings, that, a general intent appearing, it shall control the particular intent ; but this rule must sometimes give way, and effect must be given to a particular intent plainly expressed in one part of a constitution, though apparently opposed to a general intent deduced from other parts. Warren v. Sherman, 5 Texas, 441. In Quick v. Whitewater Township, 7 Ind. 570, it was said that if two provisions of a written constitution are irreconcilably repugnant, that which is last in order of time and in local position is to be preferred.

[4] Gibbons v. Ogden, 9 Wheat. 188.

expects to see it universally accepted without question ; but the attempt is so often made by interested subtlety and ingenious refinement to induce the courts to force from these instruments a meaning which their framers never held, that it frequently becomes necessary to re-declare this fundamental maxim.[1] Narrow and technical reasoning is misplaced when it is brought to bear upon an instrument framed by the people themselves, for themselves, and designed as a chart upon which every man, learned and unlearned, may be able to trace the leading principles of government.

But it must not be forgotten, in construing our constitutions, that in many particulars they are but the legitimate successors of the great charters of English liberty, whose provisions declaratory of the rights of the subject have acquired a well-understood meaning, which the people must be supposed to have had in view in adopting them. We cannot understand these provisions unless we understand their history ; and when we find them expressed in

[1] State v. Mace, 5 Md. 337 ; Manly v. State, 7 Md. 135 ; Green v. Weller, 32 Miss. 650 ; Greencastle Township v. Black, 5 Ind. 570 ; People v. N. Y. Central Railroad Co., 34 Barb. 137, and 24 N. Y. 488 ; Story on Const. § 453. " The true sense in which words are used in a statute is to be ascertained generally by taking them in their ordinary and popular signification, or if they be terms of art, in their technical signification. But it is also a cardinal rule of exposition, that the intention is to be deduced from the whole and every part of the statute, taken and compared together, from the words of the context, and such a construction adopted as will best effectuate the intention of the lawgiver. One part is referred to in order to help the construction of another, and the intent of the legislature is not to be collected from any particular expression, but from a general view of the whole act. Dwarris, 658, 698, 702, 703. And when it appears that the framers have used a word in a particular sense generally in the act, it will be presumed that it was intended to be used in the same sense throughout the act, unless an intention to give it a different signification plainly appears in the particular part of the act alleged to be an exception to the general meaning indicated. Ibid. 704, et seq. When words are used to which the legislature has given a plain and definite import in the act, it would be dangerous to put upon them a construction which would amount to holding that the legislature did not mean what it has expressed. It follows from these principles that the statute itself furnishes the best means of its own exposition ; and if the sense in which words were intended to be used can be clearly ascertained from all its parts and provisions, the intention thus indicated shall prevail, without resorting to other means of aiding in the construction. And these familiar rules of construction apply with at least as much force to the construction of written constitutions as to statutes ; the former being presumed to be framed with much greater care and consideration than the latter." Green v. Weller, 32 Miss. 678.

technical words, and words of art, we must suppose these words to be employed in their technical sense. When the constitution speaks of an *ex post facto* law, it means a law technically known by that designation ; the meaning of the phrase having become defined in the history of constitutional law, and being so familiar to the people that it is not necessary to employ language of a more popular character to designate it. The technical sense in these cases is the sense popularly understood, because that is the sense fixed upon the words in legal and constitutional history where they have been employed for the protection of popular rights.[1]

The Common Law to be kept in View.

In the same connection it may be remarked that the constitutions are be construed in the light of the common law, and of the fact that its rules are still left in force. By this we do not mean that the common law is to control the constitution, or that the latter is to be warped and perverted in its meaning in order that no inroads, or as few as possible, may be made in the system of common-law rules, but only that for its definitions we are to draw from that great fountain, and that, in judging what it means, we

---

[1] It is quite possible, however, in applying constitutional maxims, to overlook entirely the reason upon which they rest, and " considering merely the letter, go but skin deep into the meaning." On the great debate on the motion for withdrawing the confidence of Parliament from the ministers, after the surrender of Cornwallis, — a debate which called out the best abilities of Fox and Pitt as well as of the ministry, and necessarily led to the discussion of the primary principle in free government, that taxation and representation shall go together, — Sir James Mariott rose, and with great gravity proceeded to say, that if taxation and representation were to go hand in hand, then Britain had an undoubted right to tax America, because she was represented in the British Parliament. She was represented by the members for the county of Kent, of which the thirteen Provinces were a part and parcel ; for in their charters they were to hold of the manor of Greenwich in Kent, of which manor they were by charter to be parcel ! The opinion, it is said, " raised a very loud laugh," but Sir James continued to support it, and concluded by declaring that he would give the motion a hearty negative. Thus would he have settled a great principle of constitutional right, for which a seven years' bloody war had been waged, by putting it in the form of a meaningless legal fiction. Hansard's Debates, vol. 22, p. 1184. Lord Mahon, following Lord Campbell, refers the origin of this wonderful argument to Mr. Hardinge, a Welsh judge, and nephew of Lord Camden. 7 Mahon's Hist. 139. He was said to have been a good lawyer, but must have read the history of his country to little purpose.

are to keep in mind that it is not the beginning of law for the State, but that it assumes the existence of a well-understood system, which is still to be administered, but under such limitations and restrictions as that instrument imposes. It is a maxim with the courts that statutes in derogation of the common law shall be construed strictly ;[1] a maxim which we fear is sometimes perverted to the overthrow of the legislative intent; but the same maxim could seldom be properly applied to constitutions. When these instruments assume to make any change in the common law, the change designed is generally a radical one ; but as they do not go minutely into particulars, like the statutes, it will sometimes be easy to defeat a provision, if courts are at liberty to say that they will presume against any intention to alter the common law further than is expressly declared. A reasonable construction is what such an instrument demands and should receive ; and the real question is, what the people meant, and not how meaningless their words can be made by the application of arbitrary rules.[2]

---

[1] Broom's Maxims, 33 ; Sedg. on Stat. & Const. Law, 313.

[2] Under a clause of the Constitution of Michigan which provided that " the real and personal estate of every female acquired before marriage, and all property to which she may afterwards become entitled, by gift, grant, inheritance, or devise, shall be and remain the estate and property of such female, and shall not be liable for the debts, obligations, or engagements of her husband, and may be devised or bequeathed by her as if she were unmarried," it was held that a married woman could not sell her personal property without the consent of her husband, inasmuch as the power to do so was not expressly conferred, and the clause, being in derogation of the common law, was not to be extended by construction. Brown v. Fifield, 4 Mich. 322. The danger of applying arbitrary rules in the construction of constitutional principles might well, as it seems to us, be illustrated by this case. For while on the one hand it might be contended that, as a provision in derogation of the common law, the one quoted should receive a strict construction, on the other hand it might be insisted with perhaps equal reason that, as a remedial provision, in furtherance of natural right and justice, it should be liberally construed, to effect the beneficial purpose had in view. Thus arbitrary rules, of directly opposite tendency and force, would be contending for the mastery in the same case. The subsequent decisions under the same provision do not appear to have followed this lead. See White v. Zane, 10 Mich. 333 ; McKee v. Wilcox, 11 Mich. 358 ; Farr v. Sherman, 11 Mich. 33 ; Watson v. Thurber, 11 Mich. 457 ; Bardeno v. Amperse, 14 Mich. 91 ; Tong v. Marvin, 15 Mich. 60 ; Tillman v. Shackleton, 15 Mich. 447. The common law is certainly to be kept in view in the interpretation of such a clause, since otherwise we do not ascertain the evil designed to be remedied, and perhaps are not able to fully understand and explain the terms employed ; but it is to be looked at with a view to the real intent, rather than for the purpose of arbitrarily restraining it.

As a general thing, it is to be supposed that the same word is used in the same sense wherever it occurs in a constitution. Here again, however, great caution must be observed in applying an arbitrary rule; for, as Mr. Story has well observed, " It does not follow, either logically or grammatically, that because a word is found in one connection in the Constitution with a definite sense, therefore the same sense is to be adopted in every other connection in which it occurs. This would be to suppose that the framers weighed only the force of single words, as philologists or critics, and not whole clauses and objects, as statesmen and practical reasoners. And yet nothing has been more common than to subject the Constitution to this narrow and mischievous criticism.[1] Men of ingenious and subtle minds, who seek for symmetry and harmony in language, having found in the Constitution a word used in some sense, which falls in with their favorite theory of interpreting it, have made that the standard by which to measure its use in every other part of the instrument. They have thus stretched it, as it were, on the bed of Procrustes, lopping off its meaning when it seemed too large for their purposes, and extending it when it seemed too short. They have thus distorted it to the most unnatural shapes, and crippled where they have sought only to adjust its proportions according to their own opinions." [2] And he gives many instances where, in the national Constitution, the same word is very plainly used with different meanings. So that, while the rule may be sound as one of presumption merely, its force is but slight, and it must readily give way to a different intent appearing in the instrument.

Operation to be Prospective.

We shall venture also to express the opinion that *a constitution is to be construed to operate prospectively only*, unless its terms clearly imply that it should have a retrospective effect. This is the rule in regard to statutes, and it is " one of such obvious convenience and justice, that it must always be adhered to in the construction of statutes, unless there is something on the face of the enactment putting it beyond doubt that the legislature meant it to operate retrospectively.[3] Retrospective legislation, except

---

[1] See remarks of Johnson, J. in Ogden v. Sanders, 12 Wheat. 290.

[2] Story on Const. § 454. And see Cherokee Nation v. Georgia, 5 Pet. 19.

[3] Moon v. Durden, 2 Exch. 22. See Dash v. Van Kleek, 7 Johns. 477; Sayre

when designed to cure formal defects, or otherwise operate reme-
dially, is commonly objectionable in principle, and apt to result in
injustice; and it is a sound rule of construction which refuses
lightly to imply an intent to enact it. And we are aware of no
reasons applicable to ordinary legislation which do not, upon this
point, apply equally well to constitutions.[1]

Implications.

The implications from the provisions of a constitution are sometimes exceedingly important, and have large influence upon its
construction. In regard to the Constitution of the United States
the rule has been laid down, that where a general power is conferred or duty enjoined, every particular power necessary for the
exercise of the one, or the performance of the other, is also conferred.[2] The same rule has been applied to the State constitution,
with an important modification, by the Supreme Court of Illinois.
"That other powers than those expressly granted may be, and
often are, conferred by implication, is too well settled to be

v. Wisner, 8 Wend. 661; State v. Atwood, 11 Wis. 422; Hastings v. Lane, 3
Shep. 134; Brown v. Wilcox, 14 S. & M. 127; Price v. Mott, 52 Penn. St. 315;
Broom's Maxims, 28.

[1] In Allbyer v. State, 10 Ohio, N. S. 588, a question arose under the provision
of the constitution that "all laws of a general nature shall have a uniform operation throughout the State." Another clause provided that all laws then in force,
not inconsistent with the constitution, should continue in force until amended or
repealed. Allbyer was convicted and sentenced to imprisonment under a crimes
act previously in force, applicable to Hamilton County only, and the question was,
whether that act was not inconsistent with the provision above quoted, and therefore repealed by it. The court held that the provision quoted evidently had regard
to future and not to past legislation, and therefore was not repealed. A similar
decision was made in State v. Barbee, 3 Ind. 258. In Matter of Oliver Lee & Co.'s
Bank, 21 N. Y. 12, Denio, J. says: "The rule laid down in Dash v. Van Kleek,
7 Johns. 477, and other cases of that class, by which the courts are admonished to
avoid, if possible, such an interpretation as would give a statute a retrospective
operation, has but a limited application, if any, to the construction of a constitution. When, therefore, we read in the provision under consideration, that the
stockholders of every banking corporation shall be subject to a certain liability,
we are to attribute to the language its natural meaning, without inquiring whether
private interests may not be prejudiced by such a sweeping mandate." The remark was *obiter*, as it was found that enough appeared in the constitution to show
clearly that it was intended to apply to existing, as well as to subsequently created banking institutions.

[2] Story on Const. § 430. See also United States v. Fisher, 2 Cranch, 358;
McCulloch v. Maryland, 4 Wheat. 428.

doubted. Under every constitution implication must be resorted to, in order to carry out the general grants of power. A constitution cannot from its very nature enter into a minute specification of all the minor powers naturally and obviously included in and flowing from the great and important ones which are expressly granted. It is therefore established as a general rule, that when a constitution gives a general power, or enjoins a duty, it also gives, by implication, every particular power necessary for the exercise of the one or the enjoyment of the other. The implication under this rule, however, must be a necessary, not a conjectural or argumentative one. And it is further modified by another rule, that where the means for the exercise of a granted power are given, no other or different means can be implied, as being more effective or convenient."[1] The rule applies to the exercise of power by all departments and all officers, and will be touched upon incidentally hereafter.

Akin to this is the rule that " where a power is granted in general terms, the power is to be construed as coextensive with the terms, unless some clear restriction upon it is deducible [expressly or by implication] from the context."[2] This rule has been so frequently applied in restraining the legislature from encroaching upon the grant of power to the judiciary, that we shall content ourselves in this place with a reference to the cases collected upon this subject and given in another chapter.

Another rule of construction is, that when the constitution defines the circumstances under which a right may be exercised or a penalty imposed, the specification is an implied prohibition against legislative interference, to add to the condition, or to extend the penalty to other cases. On this ground it has been held by the Supreme Court of Maryland, that where the constitution defined the qualifications of an officer, it was not in the power of the legislature to change or superadd to them, unless the power to do so was expressly or by necessary implication conferred by the constitution itself.[3]

---

[1] Field v. People, 2 Scam. 83.

[2] Story on Const. §§ 424 – 426.

[3] Thomas v. Owens, 4 Md. 189. To the same effect see Matter of Dorsey, 7 Port. 293. So the legislature cannot add to the constitutional qualifications of voters. Rison v. Farr, 24 Ark. 161.

The Light which the Purpose to be accomplished may afford in Construction.

The considerations thus far suggested are such as have no regard to extrinsic circumstances, but are those by the aid of which we seek to arrive at the meaning of the constitution from an examination of the words employed. It is possible, however, that after we shall have made use of all the lights which the instrument itself affords, there may still be doubts to clear up and ambiguities to explain. Then, and only then, are we warranted in seeking elsewhere for aid. We are not to import difficulties into a constitution, by a consideration of extrinsic facts, when none appear upon its face. If, however, a difficulty really exists, which an examination of every part of the instrument does not enable us to remove, there are certain extrinsic aids which may be resorted to, and which are more or less satisfactory in the light they afford. Among these aids is, a contemplation of *the object to be accomplished or the mischief designed to be remedied or guarded against* by the clause in which the ambiguity is met with.[1] "When we once know the reason which alone determined the will of the law-makers, we ought to interpret and apply the words used in a manner suitable and consonant to that reason, and as will be best calculated to effectuate the intent. Great caution should always be observed in the application of this rule to particular given cases; that is, we ought always to be certain that we do know, and have actually ascertained, the true and only reason which induced the act. It is never allowable to indulge in vague and uncertain conjecture, or in supposed reasons and views of the framers of an act, where there are none known with any degree of certainty."[2] The prior state of the law will sometimes furnish the clew to the real meaning of the ambiguous provision,[3] and it is especially important to look into it if the constitution is the successor to another, and in the particular in question essential changes have apparently been made.[4]

[1] Alexander *v.* Worthington, 5 Md. 471; District Township *v.* Dubuque, 7 Iowa, 262.

[2] Smith on Stat. and Const. Construction, 634. See also remarks of Bronson, J. in Purdy *v.* People, 2 Hill, 35 – 37.

[3] Baltimore *v.* State, 15 Md. 376; Henry *v.* Tilson, 21 Vt. 485; Hamilton *v.* St. Louis County Court, 15 Mo. 30; Story on Const. § 428.

[4] People *v.* Blodgett, 13 Mich. 147.

5

Proceedings of the Constitutional Convention.

When the inquiry is directed to ascertaining the mischief designed to be remedied, or the purpose sought to be accomplished by a particular provision, it may be proper to examine the proceedings of the convention which framed the instrument.[1] Where the proceedings clearly point out the purpose of the provision, the aid will be valuable and satisfactory ; but where the question is one of abstract meaning, it will be difficult to derive from this source much reliable assistance in interpretation. Every member of such a convention acts upon such motives and reasons as influence him personally, and the motions and debates do not necessarily indicate the purpose of a majority of a convention in adopting a particular clause. It is quite possible for a clause to appear so clear and unambiguous to the members of a convention as to require neither discussion nor illustration ; and the few remarks made concerning it in the convention might have a plain tendency to lead directly away from the meaning in the minds of the majority. It is equally possible for a part of the members to accept a clause in one sense and a part in another. And even if we were certain we had attained to the meaning of the convention, it is by no means to be allowed a controlling force, especially if that meaning appears not to be the one which the words would most naturally and obviously convey.[2] For as the constitution does not derive its force from the convention which framed, but from the people who ratified it, the intent to be arrived at is that of the people, and it is not to be supposed that they have looked for any dark or abstruse meaning in the words employed, but rather that they have accepted them in the sense most obvious to the common understanding, and ratified the instrument in the belief that that was the sense designed to be conveyed.[3] These proceedings therefore are less conclusive of the proper construction of the instrument than are legislative proceedings of the proper construction of a statute ; since in the latter case it is the intent of the legisla-

[1] Per Walworth, Chancellor, Coutant v. People, 11 Wend. 518, and Clark v. People, 26 Wend. 602 ; Per Bronson, J., Purdy v. People, 2 Hill, 37 ; People v. N. Y. Central Railroad Co., 24 N. Y. 496. See State v. Kennon, 7 Ohio, N. S. 563.

[2] Taylor v. Taylor, 10 Minn. 126. And see Eakin v. Racob, 12 S. & R. 352 ; Aldridge v. Williams, 3 How. 1.

[3] State v. Mace, 5 Md. 348; Manly v. State, 7 Md. 147.

ture we seek, while in the former we are endeavoring to arrive at the intent of the people through the discussions and deliberations of their representatives. The history of the calling of the convention, the causes which led to it, and the discussions and issues before the people at the time of the election of the delegates, will sometimes be quite as instructive and satisfactory as anything to be gathered from the proceedings of the convention.

Contemporaneous and Practical Construction.

An important question which now suggests itself is this: How far the contemporaneous construction, or the subsequent practical construction of any particular provision of the constitution, is to have weight with the courts when the time arrives at which a judicial decision becomes necessary. Contemporaneous construction may consist simply in the understanding with which the people received it at the time, or in the acts done in putting it in operation, and which necessarily assume that it is to be construed in a particular way. In the first case it can have very little force, because the evidences of the public understanding, when nothing has been done under the provision in question, must always necessarily be vague and indecisive. But where there has been a practical construction, which has been acquiesced in for a considerable period, considerations in favor of adhering to this construction sometimes present themselves to the courts with a plausibility and force which it is not easy to resist. Indeed, where a particular construction has been generally accepted as correct, and especially when this has occurred contemporaneously with the adoption of the constitution, and by those who had opportunity to understand the intention of the instrument, it is not to be denied that a strong presumption exists that the construction rightly interprets the intention. Especially where this has been given by officers in the discharge of their duty, and rights have accrued in reliance upon it, which would be divested by a decision that the construction was erroneous, the argument *ab inconvenienti* is sometimes allowed to have very great weight.

The Supreme Court of the United States has had frequent occasion to consider this question. In Stewart *v.* Laird,[1] decided in 1803, that court sustained the authority of its members to sit as Circuit judges on the ground of a practical construction, com-

---

[1] 1 Cranch, 299.

mencing with the organization of the government. In Martin *v.* Hunter's Lessee,[1] Justice Story, after holding that the appellate power of the United States extends to cases pending in the State courts, and that the 25th section of the Judiciary Act, which authorized its exercise, was supported by the letter and spirit of the Constitution, proceeds to say : " Strong as this conclusion stands upon the general language of the Constitution, it may still derive support from other sources. It is an historical fact, that this exposition of the Constitution, extending its appellate power to State courts; was, previous to its adoption, uniformly and publicly avowed by its friends, and admitted by its enemies, as the basis of their respective reasonings both in and out of the State conventions. It is an historical fact, that at the time when the Judiciary Act was submitted to the deliberations of the First Congress, composed, as it was, not only of men of great learning and ability, but of men who had acted a principal part in framing, supporting, or opposing that Constitution, the same exposition was explicitly declared and admitted by the friends and by the opponents of that system. It is an historical fact, that the Supreme Court of the United States have from time to time sustained this appellate jurisdiction in a great variety of cases, brought from the tribunals of many of the most important States in the Union, and that no State tribunal has ever breathed a judicial doubt on the subject, or declined to obey the mandate of the Supreme Court until the present occasion. This weight of contemporaneous exposition by all parties, this acquiescence by enlightened State courts, and these judicial decisions by the Supreme Court through so long a period, do, as we think, place the doctrine upon a foundation of authority which cannot be shaken without delivering over the subject to perpetual and irremediable doubts." The same doctrine was subsequently supported by Chief Justice Marshall in a case involving the same point, and in which he says that " great weight has always been attached, and very rightly attached, to contemporaneous exposition." [2]

In Bank of United States *v.* Halstead [3] the question was made, whether the laws of the United States authorizing the courts of the Union so to alter the form of process of execution used in the Supreme Courts of the States in September, 1789, as to subject to

[1] 1 Wheat. 351.

[2] Cohens *v.* Virginia, 6 Wheat. 418.   [3] 10 Wheat. 63.

execution lands and other property not thus subject by the State laws in force at that time, were constitutional ; and Mr. Justice Thompson, in language similar to that of Chief Justice Marshall in the preceding case, says : " If any doubt existed whether the act of 1792 vests such power in the courts, or with respect to its constitutionality, the practical construction given to it ought to have great weight in determining both questions." And Mr. Justice Johnson assigns a reason for this in a subsequent case : " Every candid mind will admit that this is a very different thing from contending that the frequent repetition of wrong will create a right. It proceeds upon the presumption that the contemporaries of the Constitution have claims to our deference on the question of right, because they had the best opportunities of informing themselves of the understanding of the framers of the Constitution, and of the sense put upon it by the people when it was adopted by them." [1]

Great deference has been paid in all cases to the action of the executive departments, where its officers have been called upon, under the responsibilities of their official oaths, to inaugurate a new system, and when, it is to be presumed, they have carefully and conscientiously weighed all considerations, and endeavored to keep within the letter and the spirit of the Constitution. If the question involved is really one of doubt, the force of their judgment, especially in view of the injurious consequences that may result from disregarding it, is fairly entitled to turn the scale in the judicial mind. [2]

Where, however, no ambiguity or doubt appears in the law, we think the same rule obtains here as in other cases, that the court should confine its attention to the law, and not allow extrinsic circumstances to introduce a difficulty where the language is plain. To allow force to practical construction in such a case would be to suffer manifest perversions to defeat the evident purpose of the

---

[1] Ogden v. Saunders, 12 Wheat. 290.

[2] Union Insurance Co. v. Hoge, 21 How. 66 ; Edward's Lessee v. Darby, 12 Wheat. 210 ; Hughes v. Hughes, 4 T. B. Monr. 42 ; Chambers v. Fisk, 22 Texas, 504 ; Britton v. Ferry, 14 Mich. 66 ; Plummer v. Plummer, 37 Miss. 185 ; Burgess v. Pue, 2 Gill, 11 ; State v. Mayhew, Ibid. 487 ; Coutant v. People, 11 Wend. 511 ; Baltimore v. State, 15 Md. 376 ; Farmers and Mechanics' Bank v. Smith, 3 S. & R. 63 ; Norris v. Clymer, 2 Penn. St. 277 ; Moers v. City of Reading, 21 Penn. St. 188 ; Washington v. Murray, 4 Cal. 388 ; Surgett v. Lapice, 8 How. 68 ; Bissell v. Penrose, Ibid. 336 ; Troup v. Haight, Hopk. 267.

law-makers. " Contemporary construction . . . . can never abrogate
the text; it can never fritter away its obvious sense ; it can never
narrow down its true limitations; it can never enlarge its natural
boundaries." [1] While we conceive this to be the true and only
safe rule, we shall be obliged to confess that some of the cases
appear, on first reading, not to have observed these limitations.
In the case first cited of Stewart v. Laird,[2] the practical construction was regarded as conclusive.   To the objection that the
judges of the Supreme Court had no right to sit as Circuit judges,
the court say : " It is sufficient to observe that practice and acquiescence under it for a period of several years, commencing with
the organization of the judicial system, affords an irresistible answer, and has indeed fixed the construction. It is a contemporary
interpretation of the most forcible nature. This practical exposition is too strong and obstinate to be shaken or controlled.   Of
course the question is at rest, and ought not now to be disturbed."
This is certainly very strong language ; but that of a very similar
character was used by the Supreme Court of Massachusetts in one
case where large and valuable estates depended upon a particular
construction of a statute, and very great mischief would follow
from changing it.   The court said that, " although if it were now
res integra, it might be very difficult to maintain such a construction, yet at this day the argument *ab inconvenienti* applies with
great weight.   We cannot shake a principle which in practice has
so long and so extensively prevailed.   If the practice originated
in error, yet the error is now so common that it must have the
force of law.   The legal ground on which this provision is now
supported is, that long and continued usage furnishes a contemporaneous construction which must prevail over the mere technical
import of the words." [3] Language nearly as strong was also used
by the Supreme Court of Maryland, where the point involved was
the possession of a certain power by the legislature, which it had
constantly exercised for nearly seventy years.[4]

It is believed, however, that in each of these cases an examination of the Constitution left in the minds of the judges sufficient

---

[1] Story on Constitution, § 407.   And see Evans v. Myers, 25 Penn. St. 116;
Sadler v. Langham, 34 Ala. 311; Barnes v. First Parish in Falmouth, 6 Mass.
417.

[2] 1 Cranch, 299.

[3] Rogers v. Goodwin, 2 Mass. 478.

[4] State v. Mayhew, 2 Gill, 487.

doubt upon the question of its violation to warrant their looking elsewhere for aids in interpretation, and that the cases are not in conflict with the general rule as above laid down. Acquiescence for no length of time can legalize a clear usurpation of power, where the people have plainly expressed their will in the constitution, and appointed judicial tribunals to enforce it. A power is frequently yielded to merely because it is claimed, and it may be exercised for a long period, in violation of the constitutional prohibition, without the mischief which the Constitution was designed to guard against appearing, or without any one being sufficiently interested in the subject to raise the question ; but these circumstances cannot be allowed to sanction a clear infraction of the Constitution.[1] We think we allow to contemporary and practical construction its full legitimate force when we suffer it, where it is clear and uniform, to solve in its own favor the doubts which arise on reading the instrument to be construed.[2]

[1] See further, on this subject, the case of Sadler v. Langham, 34 Ala. 311.

[2] There are cases which clearly go further than any we have quoted, and which sustain legislative action which they hold to be usurpation, on the sole ground of long acquiescence. Thus in Brigham v. Miller, 17 Ohio, 446, the question was, Has the legislature power to grant divorces ? The court say : " Our legislature have assumed and exercised this power for a period of more than forty years, although a clear and palpable assumption of power, and an encroachment upon the judicial department, in violation of the Constitution. To deny this long-exercised power, and declare all the consequences resulting from it void, is pregnant with fearful consequences. If it affected only the rights of property, we should not hesitate ; but second marriages have been contracted and children born, and it would bastardize all these, although born under the sanction of an apparent wedlock, authorized by an act of the legislature before they were born, and in consequence of which the relation was formed which gave them birth. On account of these children, and for them only, we hesitate. And in view of this, we are constrained to content ourselves with simply declaring that the exercise of the power of granting divorces, on the part of the legislature, is unwarranted and unconstitutional, an encroachment upon the duties of the judiciary, and a striking down of the dearest rights of individuals, without authority of law. We trust we have said enough to vindicate the Constitution, and feel confident that no department of state has any disposition to violate it, and that the evil will cease." So in Johnson v. Joliet and Chicago Railroad Co., 23 Ill. 207, the question was whether railroad corporations could be created by special law, without a special declaration by way of preamble that the object to be accomplished could not be attained by general law. The court say : " It is now too late to make this objection, since by the action of the General Assembly under this clause, special acts have been so long the order of the day and the ruling passion with every legislature which has convened under the Constitution, until their acts of this de-

Unjust Provisions.

We have elsewhere expressed the opinion that a statute cannot
be declared void because opposed to a supposed general intent or

scription fill a huge and misshapen volume, and important and valuable rights
are claimed under them. The clause has been wholly disregarded, and it would
now produce far-spread ruin to declare such acts unconstitutional and void. It
is now safer and more just to all parties, to declare that it must be understood,
that in the opinion of the General Assembly, at the time of passing the special
act, its object could not be attained under the general law, and this without any
recital by way of preamble, as in the act to incorporate the Central Railroad
Company. That preamble was placed there by the writer of this opinion, and a
strict compliance with this clause of the Constitution would have rendered it
necessary in every subsequent act. But the legislature, in their wisdom, have
thought differently, and have acted differently, until now our special legislation
and its mischiefs are beyond recovery or remedy." These cases certainly presented very strong motives for declaring the law to be what it was not; but it
would have been interesting and useful if either of these learned courts had enumerated the evils that must be placed in the opposite scale when the question is
whether a constitutional rule shall be disregarded; not the least of which is, the
encouragement of a disposition on the part of legislative bodies to set aside constitutional restrictions, in the belief that, if the unconstitutional law can once be
put in force, and large interests enlisted under it, the courts will not venture to
declare it void, but will submit to the usurpation, no matter how gross and dar-
ing. We agree with the Supreme Court of Indiana, that in construing constitutions, courts have nothing to do with the argument *ab inconvenienti*, and should
not " bend the Constitution to suit the law of the hour." Greencastle Township
v. Black, 5 Ind. 565. And with Bronson, Ch. J., in what he says in Oakley *v.*
Aspinwall, 3 N. Y. 568 : " It is highly probable that inconveniences will result
from following the Constitution as it is written. But that consideration can have
no force with me. It is not for us, but for those who made the instrument, to
supply its defects. If the legislature or the courts may take that office upon
themselves, or if, under color of construction, or upon any other specious ground,
they may depart from that which is plainly declared, the people may well despair
of ever being able to set any boundary to the powers of the government. Written constitutions will be more than useless. Believing as I do that the success of
free institutions depends upon a rigid adherence to the fundamental law, I have
never yielded to considerations of expediency in expounding it. There is always
some plausible reason for latitudinarian constructions which are resorted to for
the purpose of acquiring power; some evil to be avoided or some good to be attained by pushing the powers of the government beyond their legitimate boundary. It is by yielding to such influences that constitutions are gradually under-
mined and finally overthrown. My rule has ever been to follow the fundamental
law as it is written, regardless of consequences. If the law does not work well,
the people can amend it; and inconveniences can be borne long enough to await
that process. But if the legislature or the courts undertake to cure defects by
forced and unnatural constructions, they inflict a wound upon the Constitution

spirit which it is thought pervades or lies concealed in the Constitution, but wholly unexpressed, or because, in the opinion of the court, it violates fundamental rights or principles, if it was passed in the exercise of a power which the Constitution confers. Still less will the injustice of a constitutional provision authorize the courts to disregard it, or indirectly to annul it by construing it away. It is quite possible that the people may, under the influence of temporary prejudice, or mistaken view of public policy, incorporate provisions in their charter of government, infringing upon the right of the individual man, or upon principles which ought to be regarded as sacred and fundamental in republican government; and quite probable that obnoxious classes will be unjustly disfranchised. The remedy for such injustice must rest with the people themselves, through an amendment of their work when better counsels prevail. Such provisions, when free from doubt, must receive the same construction as any other. We do not say, however, that if a clause should be found in a constitution which should appear at first blush to demand a construction leading to monstrous and absurd consequences, it might not be the duty of the court to question and cross-question such clause closely, with a view to discover in it, if possible, some other meaning more consistent with the general purpose and aims of these instruments. When such a case arises, it will be time to consider it.[1]

Duty in Case of Doubt.

But when all the legitimate lights for ascertaining the meaning of the Constitution have been made use of, it may still happen that the construction remains a matter of doubt. In such a case it seems clear that every one called upon to act where, in his

which nothing can heal. One step taken by the legislature or the judiciary, in enlarging the powers of the government, opens the door for another which will be sure to follow; and so the process goes on until all respect for the fundamental law is lost, and the powers of the government are just what those in authority please to call them." Whether there may not be circumstances under which the State can be held justly estopped from alleging the invalidity of its own action in apportioning the political divisions of the State, and imposing burdens on citizens, where such action has been acquiesced in for a considerable period, and rights have been acquired through bearing the burdens under it, see Ramsey *v.* People, 19 N. Y. 41; People *v.* Maynard, 15 Mich. 470; Kneeland *v.* Milwaukee, 15 Wis. 454.

[1] McMullen *v.* Hodge, 5 Texas, 34.

opinion, the proposed action would be of doubtful constitutionality, is bound upon the doubt alone to abstain from acting. Whoever derives power from the Constitution to perform any public function, is disloyal to that instrument, and grossly derelict in duty, if he does that which he is not reasonably satisfied the Constitution permits. Whether the power be legislative, executive, or judicial, there is manifest disregard of constitutional and moral obligation by one who, having taken an oath to observe that instrument, takes part in an action which he cannot say he believes to be no violation of its provisions. A doubt of the constitutionality of any proposed legislative enactment should in any case be reason sufficient for refusing to adopt it; and, if legislators do not act upon this principle, the reasons upon which are based the judicial decisions sustaining legislation in very many cases will cease to be of force.

Directory and Mandatory Provisions.

An important question sometimes presents itself, whether we are authorized in any case, when the meaning of a clause of the Constitution is arrived at, to give it such practical construction as will leave it optional with the department or officer to which it is addressed to obey it or not as he shall see fit. In respect to statutes it has long been settled that particular provisions may be regarded as *directory* merely; by which is meant that they are to be considered as giving directions which *ought* to be followed, but not as so limiting the power in respect to which the directions are given that it cannot be effectually exercised without observing them. The force of many of the decisions on this subject will be readily assented to by all; while others are sometimes thought to go to the extent of nullifying the intent of the legislature in essential particulars. It is not our purpose to examine the several cases critically, or to attempt — what we deem impossible — to reconcile them all; but we shall content ourselves with quoting from a few, with a view, if practicable, to ascertaining some line of principle upon which they can be classified.

There are cases where, whether a statute was to be regarded as merely directory or not, was made to depend upon the employment or failing to employ negative words which imported that the act should be done in a particular manner or time, *and not otherwise*.[1] The use of such words is often very conclusive of an intent to impose a limitation ; but their absence is by no means equally conclusive that the statute was not destined to be mandatory.[2] Lord Mansfield would have the question whether mandatory or not depend upon whether that which was directed to be done was or was not of the essence of the thing required.[3] The Supreme Court of New York, in an opinion afterwards approved by the Court of Appeals, laid down the rule as one settled by authority, that " statutes directing the mode of proceeding by public officers are directory, and are not regarded as essential to the validity of the proceedings themselves, unless it be so declared in the statute." [4] This rule strikes us as very general, and as likely to include within its scope, in many cases, things which are of the very essence of the proceeding. The questions in that case were questions of irregularity under election laws, not in any way hindering the complete expression of the will of the electors ; and the court was doubtless right in holding that the election was not to be avoided for a failure in the officers appointed for its conduct to comply in all respects with the directions of the statute there in question. The same court in another case say : " Statutory requisitions are deemed directory only when they relate to some immaterial matter, where a compliance is a matter of convenience rather than of substance." [5] The Supreme Court of Michigan, in a case involving the validity of proceedings in the sale of lands for taxes, laid down the rule that " what the law requires to be done for the protection of the tax-payer is mandatory, and cannot be regarded as directory merely." [6] A similar rule was recognized in a recent case in Illinois. Commissioners had been appointed to ascertain and assess the damage and recompense due to the owners of land which might be taken, on the real estate of the persons benefited by a certain local improvement, in proportion as nearly as might be to the benefits resulting to each. By the statute, when the assessment was completed, the commissioners were to sign and return the same to the

---

[1] Slayton *v.* Hulings, 7 Ind. 144 ; King *v.* Inhabitants of St. Gregory, 2 Ad. & El. 99 ; King *v.* Inhabitants of Hipswell, 8 B. & C. 466.

[2] District Township *v.* Dubuque, 7 Iowa, 284.

[3] Rex *v.* Locksdale, 1 Burr. 447.

[4] People *v.* Cook, 14 Barb. 290 ; Same case, 8 N. Y. 67.

[5] People *v.* Schermerhorn, 19 Barb. 558.

[6] Clark *v.* Crane, 5 Mich. 154.

city council within forty days of their appointment. This provision was not complied with, but return was made afterwards, and the question was raised as to its validity when thus made. In the opinion of the court, this question was to be decided by ascertaining whether any advantage would be lost, or right destroyed, or benefit sacrificed, either to the public or to any individual, by holding the provision directory. After remarking that they had held an assessment under the general revenue law, returned after the time appointed by law, as void, because the person assessed would lose the benefit of an appeal from the assessment,[1] they say of the statute before the court : " There are no negative words used declaring that the functions of the commissioners shall cease after the expiration of the forty days, or that they shall not make their return after that time ; nor have we been able to discover the least right, benefit, or advantage which the property owner could derive from having the return made within that time, and not after. No time is limited and made dependent on that time, within which the owner of the property may apply to have the assessment reviewed or corrected. The next section requires the clerk to give ten days' notice that the assessment has been returned, specifying the day when objections may be made to the assessment before the common council by parties interested, which hearing may be adjourned from day to day ; and the common council is empowered in its discretion to confirm or annul the assessment altogether, or to refer it back to the same commissioners, or to others to be by them appointed. As the property owner has the same time and opportunity to prepare himself to object to the assessment and have it corrected, whether the return be made before or after the expiration of the forty days, the case differs from that of Chestnut v. Marsh,[2] at the very point on which that case turned. Nor is there any other portion of the chapter which we have discovered, bringing it within the principle of that case, which is the well-recognized rule in all the books." [3]

The rule is nowhere more clearly stated than by Chief Justice Shaw, in Torrey v. Milbury,[4] which was also a tax case. " In

---

[1] Marsh v. Chestnut, 14 Ill. 223.

[2] Ibid.

[3] Wheeler v. Chicago, 24 Ill. 108.

[4] 21 Pick. 67.

considering the various statutes regulating the assessment of taxes, and the measures preliminary thereto, it is not always easy to distinguish which are conditions precedent to the legality and validity of the tax, and which are directory merely, and do not constitute conditions. One rule is very plain and well settled, that all those measures that are intended for the security of the citizen, for insuring equality of taxation, and to enable every one to know with reasonable certainty for what polls and for what real estate he is taxed, and for what all those who are liable with him are taxed, are conditions precedent; and if they are not observed, he is not legally taxed; and he may resist it in any of the modes authorized by law for contesting the validity of the tax. But many regulations are made by statutes designed for the information of assessors and officers, and intended to promote method, system, and uniformity in the modes of proceeding, a compliance or non-compliance with which does in no respect affect the rights of tax-paying citizens. These may be considered directory. Officers may be liable to legal animadversion, perhaps to punishment, for not observing them; but yet their observance is not a condition precedent to the validity of the tax."

We shall quote further only from a single other case upon this point. The Supreme Court of Wisconsin, in considering the validity of a statute not published within the time required by law, " understand the doctrine concerning directory statutes to be this: that where there is no substantial reason why the thing to be done might not as well be done after the time prescribed as before, no presumption that by allowing it to be so done it may work an injury or wrong, nothing in the act itself, or in other acts relating to the same subject-matter, indicating that the legislature did not intend that it should rather be done after the time prescribed than not to be done at all, there the courts assume that the intent was, that if not done within the time prescribed it might be done afterwards. But when any of these reasons intervene, then the limit is established." [1]

These cases perhaps sufficiently indicate the rules, so far as any of general application can be declared, which are to be made use of in determining whether the provisions of a statute are mandatory or directory. Those directions which are not of the essence of the thing to be done, but which are given with a view merely

[1] State v. Lean, 9 Wis. 292.

to the proper, orderly, and prompt conduct of the business, and by a failure to obey which the rights of those interested will not be prejudiced, are not commonly to be regarded as mandatory; and if the act is performed, but not in the time or in the precise mode indicated, it may still be sufficient, if that which is done accomplishes the substantial purpose of the statute.[1] But this rule presupposes that no negative words are employed in the statute which expressly or by necessary implication forbid the doing of the act at any other time or in any other manner than as directed. Even as thus laid down and restricted, the doctrine is one to be applied with much circumspection; for it is not to be denied that the courts have sometimes, in their anxiety to sustain the proceedings of careless or incompetent officers, gone very far in substituting a judicial view of what was essential for that declared by the legislature.[2]

But courts tread upon very dangerous ground when they venture to apply the rules which distinguish directory and mandatory statutes to the provisions of a constitution. Constitutions do not usually undertake to prescribe mere rules of proceeding, except when such rules are looked upon as essential to the thing to be done; and they must then be regarded in the light of limitations upon the power to be exercised. It is the province of an instrument of this solemn and permanent character to establish those fundamental maxims, and fix those unvarying rules, by which all

---

[1] The following, in addition to those cited, are some of the cases in this country in which statutes have been declared directory only: Pond v. Negus, 3 Mass. 230; Williams v. School District, 21 Pick. 75; City of Lowell v. Hadley, 8 Met. 180; Holland v. Osgood, 8 Vt. 280; Corliss v. Corliss, Ibid. 390; People v. Allen, 6 Wend. 486; Marchant v. Langworthy, 6 Hill, 646; Ex parte Heath, 3 Hill, 43; People v. Holley, 12 Wend. 481; Jackson v. Young, 5 Cow. 269; Striker v. Kelley, 7 Hill, 9; People v. Peck, 11 Wend. 604; Matter of Mohawk and Hudson Railroad Co. 19 Wend. 143; People v. Runkel, 9 Johns. 147; Gale v. Mead, 2 Denio, 160; Doughty v. Hope, 3 Denio, 252; Elmendorf v. Mayor, &c. of New York, 25 Wend. 696; Thames Manufacturing Co. v. Lathrop, 7 Conn. 550; Colt v. Eves, 12 Conn. 243; People v. Doe, 1 Mich. 451; Parks v. Goodwin, 1 Doug. (Mich.) 56; Hickey v. Hinsdale, 8 Mich. 267; People v. Hartwell, 12 Mich. 508; State v. McGinley, 4 Ind. 7; Stayton v. Hulings, 7 Ind. 144; New Orleans v. St. Rowes, 9 La. An. 573; Edwards v. James, 13 Texas, 52; State v. Click, 2 Ala. 26; Savage v. Walshe, 26 Ala. 620; Webster v. French, 12 Ill. 302; McKim v. Weller, 11 Cal. 47. The list might easily be largely increased.

[2] See upon this subject the remarks of Mr. Sedgwick in his work on Statutory and Constitutional Law, p. 375, and those of Hubbard, J. in Briggs v. Georgia, 15 Vt. 72.

departments of the government must at all times shape their conduct; and if it descends to prescribing mere rules of order in unessential matters, it is lowering the proper dignity of such an instrument, and usurping the proper province of ordinary legislation. We are not therefore to expect to find in a constitution provisions which the people, in adopting it, have not regarded as of high importance, and worthy to be embraced in an instrument which, for a time at least, is to control alike the government and the governed, and to form a standard by which is to be measured the power which can be exercised as well by the delegate as by the sovereign people themselves. If directions are given respecting the times or modes of proceeding in which a power should be exercised, there is at least a strong presumption that the people designed it should be exercised in that time and mode only; and we impute to the people a want of due appreciation of the purpose and proper province of such an instrument, when we infer that such directions are given to any other end. Especially when, as has been already said, it is but fair to presume that the people in their constitution have expressed themselves in careful and measured terms, corresponding with the immense importance of the powers delegated, and with a view to leave as little as possible to implication.[1]

There are some cases, however, where the doctrine of directory statutes has been applied to constitutional provisions; but they are at variance with the weight of authority upon the precise points considered, and we do not think, therefore, we should be warranted in saying that the judicial decisions as they now stand sanction the application. In delivering the opinion of the New York Court of Appeals in one case, Mr. Justice Willard had occasion to consider the constitutional provision, that on the final passage of a bill the question shall be taken by ayes and noes, which shall be duly entered upon the journals; and he expressed the opinion that it was only directory to the legislature.[2] The remark was *obiter dictum*, as the court had already decided that the provision had been fully complied with; and those familiar with the reasons which have induced the insertion of this clause in our

[1] Wolcott *v.* Wigdon, 7 Ind. 49; Per Bronson, J. in People *v.* Purdy, 2 Hill, 36; Greencastle Township *v.* Black, 5 Ind. 566; Opinions of Judges, 6 Shep. 458. See People *v.* Lawrence, 36 Barb. 177.

[2] People *v.* Supervisors of Chenango, 8 N. Y. 328.

constitutions will not readily concede that its sole design was to establish a mere rule of order for legislative proceedings, which might be followed or not at discretion. Mr. Chief Justice Thurman, of Ohio, in a case not calling for a discussion of the subject, has considered a statute whose validity was assailed on the ground that it was not passed in the mode prescribed by the Constitution. " By the term *mode*," he says, " I do not mean to include the *authority* in which the law-making power resides, or the number of votes a bill must receive to become a law. That the power to make laws is vested in the Assembly alone, and that no act has any force that was not passed by the number of votes required by the Constitution, are nearly, or quite, self-evident propositions. These essentials relate to the authority by which, rather than the mode in which, laws are to be made. Now to secure the careful exercise of this power, and for other good reasons, the Constitution prescribes or recognizes certain things to be done in the enactment of laws, which things form a course or mode of legislative procedure. Thus we find, *inter alia*, the provision that every bill shall be fully and distinctly read on three different days, unless, in case of urgency, three fourths of the house in which it shall be pending shall dispense with this rule. This is an important provision without doubt, but, nevertheless, there is much reason for saying that it is merely directory in its character, and that its observance by the Assembly is secured by their sense of duty and official oaths, and not by any supervisory power of the courts. Any other construction, we incline to think, would lead to very absurd and alarming consequences. If it is in the power of every court (and if one has the power, every one has it) to inquire whether a bill that passed the Assembly was " fully " and " distinctly " read three times in each house, and to hold it invalid if, upon any reading, a word was accidentally omitted, or the reading was indistinct, it would obviously be impossible to know what is the statute law of the State. Now the requisition that bills shall be fully and distinctly read is just as imperative as that requiring them to be read three times ; and as both relate to the mode of procedure merely, it would be difficult to find any sufficient reason why a violation of one of them would be less fatal to an act than a violation of the other." [1]

A requirement that a law shall be read *distinctly*, whether man-

---

[1] Miller *v.* State, 3 Ohio, N. S. 483.

datory or directory, is, from the very nature of the case, addressed to the judgment of the legislative body, whose decision as to what is or what is not a compliance cannot be subject to review. But in the absence of authority to the contrary, we should not have supposed that the requirement of three successive readings on different days stood upon the same footing.[1] To this extent a definite and certain rule is capable of being, and has been, laid down, which can be literally obeyed; and the legislative body cannot suppose or adjudge it to have been done if the fact is otherwise. The requirement has an important purpose, in making legislators proceed in their action with caution and deliberation; and there cannot often be difficulty in ascertaining from the legislative records themselves if the constitution has been violated in this particular. There is, therefore, no inherent difficulty in the question being reached and passed upon by the courts in the ordinary mode, if it is decided that the constitution intends legislation shall be reached through the three readings, and not otherwise.

The opinion above quoted was recognized as law by the Supreme Court of Ohio in a case soon after decided. In that case the court proceed to say : " The . . . . provision . . . . that no bill shall contain more than one subject, which shall be clearly expressed in its title, is also made a permanent rule in the introduction and passage of bills through the houses. The subject of the bill is required to be clearly expressed in the title for the purpose of advising members of its subject, when voting in cases in which the reading has been dispensed with by a two-thirds vote. The provision that a bill shall contain but one subject was to prevent combinations by which various and distinct matters of legislation should gain a support which they could not if presented separately. As a rule of proceeding in the General Assembly, it is manifestly an important one. But if it was intended to effect any practical object for the benefit of the people in the examination, construction, or operation of acts passed and published, we are unable to perceive it. The title of an act may indicate to the reader its subject, and under the rule each act would contain one subject. To suppose that for such a purpose the Constitutional Convention adopted the rule under consideration, would impute to them a most minute provision for a very imperfect heading of the chapters of laws and their subdivision. This pro-

---

[1] See People v. Campbell, 3 Gilm. 466 ; McCulloch v. State, 11 Ind. 432.

6

vision being intended to operate upon bills in their progress
through the General Assembly, it must be held to be directory
only. It relates to bills, and not to acts. It would be most mischievous in practice to make the validity of every law depend
upon the judgment of every judicial tribunal of the State, as to
whether an act or a bill contained more than one subject, or
whether this one subject was clearly expressed in the title of the
act or bill. Such a question would be decided according to the
mental precision and mental discipline of each justice of the peace
and judge. No practical benefit could arise from such inquiries.
We are therefore of opinion that in general the only safeguard
against the violation of these rules of the houses is their regard
for, and their oath to support, the constitution of the State. We
say, *in general*, the only safeguard ; for whether a manifestly gross
and fraudulent violation of these rules might authorize the court
to pronounce a law unconstitutional, it is unnecessary to determine. It is to be presumed no such case will ever occur." [1]

If the prevailing doctrine of the courts were in accord with
this decision, it might become important to consider whether
the object of the clause in question, as here disclosed, was not
of such a character as to make the provision mandatory even in a
statute. But we shall not enter upon that subject here, as elsewhere we shall have occasion to refer to decisions in New York,
Iowa, Indiana, New Jersey, Louisiana, Georgia, Kentucky, Minnesota, Michigan, Texas, and Maryland, which have recognized
similar provisions as mandatory, and to be enforced by the courts.
And we concur fully in what was said by Mr. Justice Emmot, in
speaking of this very provision, that " it will be found upon full
consideration to be difficult to treat any constitutional provision
as merely directory and not imperative." [2] And with what is said
by Mr. Justice Lumpkin, as to the duty of the courts : " It has
been suggested that the prohibition in the seventeenth section of
the first article of the constitution, ' Nor shall any law or ordinance pass containing any matter different from what is expressed
in the title thereof,' is directory only to the legislative and executive or law-making departments of the government. But we do
not so understand it. On the contrary, we consider it as much a

---

[1] Pim *v.* Nicholson, 6 Ohio, N. S. 179. See also the case of Washington *v.*
Murray, 4 Cal. 388, for similar views.

[2] People *v.* Lawrence, 36 Barb. 186.

matter of judicial cognizance as any other provision in that instrument. If the courts would refuse to execute a law suspending the writ of habeas corpus when the public safety did not require it, a law violatory of the freedom of the press, or trial by jury, neither would they enforce a statute which contained matter different from what was expressed in the title thereof." [1]

We have thus indicated some of the rules which we think are to be observed in the construction of constitutions. It will be perceived that we have not thought it important to quote and to dwell upon those arbitrary rules to which so much attention is sometimes given, and which savor rather of the closet than of actual life. Our observation would lead us to the conclusion that they are more often resorted to as aids in ingenious attempts to make the constitution seem to say what it does not, than with a view to make that instrument express its real intent. All external aids, and especially all arbitrary rules, applied to instruments of this popular character, are of very uncertain value ; and we do not regard it as out of place to repeat here, what we have had occasion already to say in the course of this chapter, that they are to be made use of with hesitation, and only with much circumspection. [2]

[1] Protho v. Orr, 12 Geo. 36.   See also Opinions of Judges, 6 Shep. 458 ; Indiana Central Railroad Co. v. Potts, 7 Ind. 683.

[2] See People v. Cowles, 13 N. Y. 360, per Johnson, J. ; Temple v. Mead, 4 Vt. 540, per Williams, J.   " In construing so important an instrument as a constitution, especially those parts which affect the vital principle of republican government, the elective franchise, or the manner of exercising it, we are not, on the one hand, to indulge ingenious speculations which may lead us wide from the true sense and spirit of the instrument, nor, on the other, to apply to it such narrow and constrained views as may exclude the real object and intent of those who framed it. We are to suppose that the authors of such an instrument had a thorough knowledge of the force and extent of the words they employ ; that they had a beneficial end and purpose in view ; and that, more especially in any apparent restriction upon the mode of exercising the right of suffrage, there was some existing or anticipated evil which it was their purpose to avoid. If an enlarged sense of any particular form of expression should be necessary to accomplish so great an object as a convenient exercise of the fundamental privilege or right, — that of election, — such sense must be attributed. We are to suppose that those who were delegated to the great business of distributing the powers which emanated from the sovereignty of the people, and to the establishment of the rules for the perpetual security of the rights of person and property, had the wisdom to adapt their language to future as well as existing emergencies, so that words competent to the then existing state of the community, and at the same time ca-

pable of being expanded to embrace more extensive relations, should not be restrained to their more obvious and immediate sense, if, consistently with the general object of the authors and the true principles of the compact, they can be extended to other relations and circumstances which an improved state of society may produce. *Qui hæret in litera hæret in cortice* is a familiar maxim of the law. The letter killeth, but the spirit maketh alive, is the more forcible expression of Scripture." Parker, Ch. J. in Henshaw v. Foster, 9 Pick. 316.

CHAPTER V.

OF THE POWERS WHICH THE LEGISLATIVE DEPARTMENT MAY EXERCISE.

IN considering the powers which may be exercised by the legislative department of a State, it is natural that we should recur to those possessed by the Parliament of Great Britain, upon which, in a measure, the American legislatures have been modelled, and from which we derive our legislative usages and customs, or parliamentary common law, as well as the precedents upon which the exercise of legislative power in this country has been based. It is natural, also, that we should incline to measure the power of the legislative department in America by the power of the like department in Britain; and to concede without reflection that whatever the legislature of the country from which we derive our laws could do, might also be done by the department created for the exercise of legislative authority in this country. But to guard against being misled by a comparison between the two, we must bear in mind the important distinction already pointed out, that with the Parliament rests the sovereignty of the country, and it may therefore exercise all the powers of the government if it wills so to do; while the legislatures of the American States are not the sovereign authority, and, though vested with the exercise of one branch of the sovereignty, they are nevertheless, in wielding it, hedged in on all sides by important limitations, some of which are imposed in express terms, and others by implications which are equally imperative.

" The power and jurisdiction of Parliament," says Sir Edward Coke,[1] " is so transcendent and absolute, that it cannot be confined, either for persons or causes, within any bounds. And of this high court it may truly be said: ' Si antiquitatem spectes, est vetustissima; si dignitatem est honoratissima; si jurisdictionem, est capacissima.' It hath sovereign and uncontrolled authority in the making, confirming, enlarging, restraining, abrogating, repealing, reviving, and expounding of laws, concerning matters of all possible denominations, ecclesiastical or temporal,

---

[1] 4 Inst. 36.

civil, military, maritime, or criminal: this being the place where that absolute despotic power, which must in all governments reside somewhere, is entrusted by the constitution of these kingdoms. All mischiefs and grievances, operations and remedies, that transcend the ordinary course of the laws, are within the reach of this extraordinary tribunal. It can regulate or new-model the succession to the crown, as was done in the reign of Henry VIII. and William III. It can alter the established religion of the land ; as was done in a variety of instances, in the reign of King Henry VIII. and his three children. It can change and create afresh even the constitution of the kingdom and of Parliaments themselves, as was done by the Act of Union, and the several statutes for triennial and septennial elections. It can, in short, do everything that is not naturally impossible ; and therefore some have not scrupled to call its power, by a figure rather too bold, the omnipotence of Parliament. True it is, that what the Parliament doth, no authority upon earth can undo ; so that it is a matter most essential to the liberties of this kingdom that such members be delegated to this important trust as are most eminent for their probity, their fortitude, and their knowledge ; for it was a known apothegm of the great Lord Treasurer Burleigh, ' that England could never be ruined but by a Parliament '; and as Sir Matthew Hale observes : ' This being the highest and greatest court, over which none other can have jurisdiction in the kingdom, if by any means a misgovernment should fall upon it, the subjects of this kingdom are left without all manner of remedy.' " [1]

The strong language in which the complete jurisdiction of Parliament is here described is certainly inapplicable to any authority in the American States, unless it be to the people of the States when met in their primary capacity for the formation of their fundamental law ; and even then there rest upon them the restraints of the Constitution of the United States, which bind them as absolutely as they do the governments which they create. It becomes important, therefore, to ascertain in what respect the State legislatures resemble the Parliament in the powers they exercise, and how far we may extend the comparison without losing sight of the fundamental ideas and principles of the American system.

[1] 1 Bl. Com. 160.

The first and most notable difference is that to which we have already alluded, and which springs from the different theory on which the British Constitution rests.   When Parliament is recognized as possessing the sovereign power of the country, it is evident that the resemblance between it and American legislatures in regard to their ultimate powers cannot be carried very far. The American legislatures only exercise a certain portion of the sovereign power.   The sovereignty is in the people ; and the legislatures which they have created are only to discharge a trust of which they have been made a depository, but with well-defined restrictions.

Upon this difference it is to be observed, that while Parliament, to any extent it may choose, may exercise judicial authority, one of the most noticeable features in American constitutional law is, the care taken to separate legislative, executive, and judicial functions.   It has evidently been the intention of the people in every State that the exercise of each should rest with a separate department.   The different classes of power have been apportioned to different departments ; and this being all done by the same instrument, there is an implied exclusion of each department from exercising the functions conferred upon the others.

There are two fundamental rules by which we may measure the extent of legislative authority in the States : —

1. In creating a legislative department and conferring upon it the legislative power, the people must be understood to have conferred the full and complete power as it rests in, and may be exercised by, the sovereign power of any country, subject only to such restrictions as they may have seen fit to impose, and to the limitations which are contained in the Constitution of the United States.   The legislative department is not made a special agency, for the exercise of specifically defined legislative powers, but is entrusted with the general authority to make laws at discretion.

2. But the apportionment to this department of legislative power does not sanction the exercise of executive or judicial functions, except in those cases, warranted by parliamentary usage, where they are incidental, necessary, or proper to the exercise of legislative authority, or where the constitution itself, in specified cases, may expressly permit it.   Executive power is so intimately connected with legislative, that it is not easy to draw a line of separation ; but the grant of the judicial power to the department

created for the purpose of exercising it must be regarded as an exclusive grant, covering the whole power, subject only to the limitations which the constitutions impose, and to the incidental exceptions before referred to. While, therefore, the American legislatures may exercise the legislative powers which the Parliament of Great Britain wields, except as restrictions are imposed, they are at the same time excluded from other functions which may be, and sometimes habitually are, exercised by the Parliament.

"The people in framing the constitution," says Denio, Ch. J., "committed to the legislature the whole law-making power of the State, which they did not expressly or impliedly withhold. Plenary power in the legislature, for all purposes of civil government, is the rule. A prohibition to exercise a particular power is an exception. In inquiring, therefore, whether a given statute is constitutional, it is for those who question its validity to show that it is forbidden. I do not mean that the power must be expressly inhibited, for there are but few positive restraints upon the legislative power contained in the instrument. The first article lays down the ancient limitations which have always been considered essential in a constitutional government, whether monarchical or popular; and there are scattered through the instrument a few other provisions in restraint of legislative authority. But the affirmative prescriptions and the general arrangements of the constitution are far more fruitful of restraints upon the legislature. Every positive direction contains an implication against everything contrary to it, or which would frustrate or disappoint the purpose of that provision. The frame of the government, the grant of legislative power itself, the organization of the executive authority, the erection of the principal courts of justice, create implied limitations upon the law-making authority as strong as though a negative was expressed in each instance; but independently of these restraints, express or implied, every subject within the scope of civil government is liable to be dealt with by the legislature."[1]

"It has never been questioned, so far as I know," says Redfield, Ch. J., "that the American legislatures have the same unlimited power in regard to legislation which resides in the British Parliament, except where they are restrained by written constitutions.

[1] People v. Draper, 15 N. Y. 543.

That must be conceded, I think, to be a fundamental principle in the political organization of the American States. We cannot well comprehend how, upon principle, it should be otherwise. The people must, of course, possess all legislative power originally. They have committed this in the most general and unlimited manner to the several State legislatures, saving only such restrictions as are imposed by the Constitution of the United States, or of the particular State in question." [1]

" I entertain no doubt," says Comstock, J., " that aside from the special limitations of the Constitution, the legislature cannot exercise powers which are in their nature essentially judicial or executive. These are, by the Constitution, distributed to other departments of the government. It is only the 'legislative power' which is vested in the senate and assembly. But where the constitution is silent, and there is no clear usurpation of the powers distributed to other departments, I think there would be great difficulty and great danger in attempting to define the limits of this power. Chief Justice Marshall said : ' How far the power of giving the law may involve every other power, in cases where the constitution is silent, never has been, and perhaps never can be, definitely stated.' [2] That very eminent judge felt the difficulty ; but the danger was less apparent then than it is now, when theories, alleged to be founded in natural reason or inalienable rights, but subversive of the just and necessary powers of government, attract the belief of considerable classes of men, and when too much reverence for government and law is certainly among the least of the perils to which our institutions are exposed. I am reluctant to enter upon this field of inquiry, satisfied, as I am, that no rule can be laid down in terms which may not contain the germ of great mischief to society, by giving to private opinion and speculation a license to oppose themselves to the just and legitimate powers of government." [3]

Numerous other opinions might be cited to the same effect with

[1] Thorpe v. Rutland & Burlington Railroad Co. 27 Vt. 142. See also Leggett v. Hunter, 19 N. Y. 445 ; Cochran v. Van Surlay, 20 Wend. 365 ; People v. Morrell, 21 Wend. 563 ; Sears v. Cottrell, 5 Mich. 251 ; Mason v. Wait, 4 Scam. 134 ; People v. Supervisors of Orange, 27 Barb. 593 ; Taylor v. Porter, 4 Hill, 144, per Bronson, J.

[2] Fletcher v. Peck, 6 Cranch, 136.

[3] Wynehamer v. People, 13 N. Y. 391.

those from which we have here quoted ; but as we shall have occasion to refer to them elsewhere, in considering the circumstances under which a statute may be declared unconstitutional, we shall refrain from further references in this place. Nor shall we enter upon a discussion of the question suggested by Chief Justice Marshall as above quoted ;[1] since, however interesting it may be as an abstract question, it is made practically unimportant by the careful separation of duties between the several departments of the government which has been made by each of the State constitutions. Had no such separation been made, the disposal of executive and judicial duties must have devolved upon the department vested with the general authority to make laws ;[2] but assuming them to be apportioned already, we are only at liberty to liken the power of the State legislature to that of the Parliament, when it assumes to exercise legislative functions ; and such authority as is in its nature either executive or judicial is beyond its constitutional powers, with the few exceptions to which we have already referred.

It will be important therefore to consider those cases where legislation has been questioned as encroaching upon judicial authority ; and to this end it may be useful, at the outset, to endeavor to define legislative and judicial power respectively, that we may the better be enabled to point out the proper line of distinction when questions arise in their practical application to actual cases.

The legislative power is the authority, under the Constitution, to make laws, and to alter and repeal them. Laws, in the sense in which the word is here employed, are rules of civil conduct, or statutes, which the legislative will has prescribed. " The laws of a State," observes Mr. Justice Story, " are more usually understood to mean the rules and enactments promulgated by the legislative authority thereof, or long-established local customs having

---

[1] The power to distribute the judicial power, except so far as that has been done by the constitution, rests with the legislature ; but when the constitution has conferred it upon certain specified courts, this must be understood to embrace the whole judicial power, and the legislature cannot vest any portion of it elsewhere. State v. Maynard, 14 Ill. 420 ; Gibson v. Emerson, 2 Eng. 173 ; Chandler v. Nash, 5 Mich. 409.

[2] Calder v. Bull, 2 Root, 350, and 3 Dall. 386 ; Ross v. Whitman, 6 Cal. 361 ; Smith v. Judge, 17 Cal. 547 ; per Patterson, J. in Cooper v. Telfair, 4 Dall. 19 ; Martin v. Hunter's Lessee, 1 Wheat. 304.

the force of laws." [1] " The difference between the departments undoubtedly is, that the legislature makes, the executive executes, and the judiciary construes, the law." [2] And it is said that that which distinguishes a judicial from a legislative act is, that the one is a determination of what the existing law is in relation to some existing thing already done or happened, while the other is a predetermination of what the law shall be for the regulation of all future cases falling under its provisions.[3] And in another case it is said : " The legislative power extends only to the making of laws, and in its exercise it is limited and restrained by the paramount authority of the Federal and State constitutions. It cannot directly reach the property or vested rights of the citizen by providing for their forfeiture or transfer to another, without trial and judgment in the courts ; for to do so would be the exercise of a power which belongs to another branch of the government, and is forbidden to the legislative." [4] " That is not legislation which adjudicates in a particular case, prescribes the rule contrary to the general law, and orders it to be enforced. Such power assimilates itself more closely to despotic rule than any other attribute of government.[5]"

On the other hand, to adjudicate upon, and protect, the rights and interests of individual citizens, and to that end to construe and apply the laws, is the peculiar province of the judicial department.[6] " No particular definition of judicial power," says Woodbury, J., " is given in the constitution [of New Hampshire], and, considering the general nature of the instrument, none was to be expected. Critical statements of the meanings in which all important words were employed would have swollen into volumes ; and when those words possessed a customary signification, a definition of them would have been useless. But ' powers judicial,'

---

[1] Swift v. Tyson, 16 Pet. 18.

[2] Per Marshall, Ch. J. in Wayman v. Southard, 10 Wheat. 46 ; Per Gibson, Ch. J. in Greenough v. Greenough, 11 Penn. St. 494.

[3] Bates v. Kimball, 2 Chip. 77.

[4] Newland v. Marsh, 19 Ill. 382.

[5] Ervine's Appeal, 16 Penn. St. 266. See also Greenough v. Greenough, 11 Penn. St. 494 ; Dechastellux v. Fairchild, 15 Penn. St. 18.

[6] Cincinnati &c. Railroad Co. v. Commissioners of Clinton Co. 1 Ohio N. S. 81. See also King v. Dedham Bank, 15 Mass. 454 ; Gordon v. Inghram, 1 Grant's Cases, 152 ; People v. Supervisors of New York, 16 N. Y. 432 ; Beebe v. State, 6 Ind. 515 ; Greenough v. Greenough, 11 Penn. St. 494 ; Taylor v. Place, 4 R. I. 324.

'judiciary powers,' and 'judicatures' are all phrases used in the constitution; and though not particularly defined, are still so used to designate with clearness that department of government which it was intended should interpret and administer the laws. On general principles, therefore, those inquiries, deliberations, orders, and decrees, which are peculiar to such a department, must in their nature be judicial acts. Nor can they be both judicial and legislative ; because a marked difference exists between the employment of judicial and legislative tribunals. The former decide upon the legality of claims and conduct, and the latter make rules upon which, in connection with the constitution, those decisions should be founded. It is the province of judges to determine what is the law upon existing cases. In fine, the law is *applied* by the one, and *made* by the other. To do the first, therefore, — to compare the claims of parties with the law of the land before established, — is in its nature a judicial act. But to do the last — to pass new rules for the regulation of new controversies — is in its nature a legislative act; and if these rules interfere with the past, or the present, and do not look wholly to the future, they violate the definition of a law as ' a rule of civil conduct ' ; [1] because no rule of conduct can with consistency operate upon what occurred before the rule itself was promulgated.

" It is the province of judicial power, also, to decide private disputes between or concerning persons ; but of legislative power to regulate public concerns, and to make laws for the benefit and welfare of the State. Nor does the passage of private statutes conflict with these principles; because such statutes, when lawful, are enacted on petition, or by the consent of all concerned ; or else they forbear to interfere with past transactions and vested rights." [2]

With these definitions and explanations, we shall now proceed to consider some of the cases in which the courts have attempted to draw the line of distinction between the proper functions of the legislative and judicial departments, in cases where it has been claimed that the legislature have exceeded their power by invading the domain of judicial authority.

---

[1] 1 Bl. Com. 44.

[2] Merrill *v.* Sherburne, 1 N. H. 204. See Jones *v.* Perry, 10 Yerg. 69 ; Taylor *v.* Porter, 4 Hill, 144 ; Ogden *v.* Blackledge, 2 Cranch, 272 ; Dash *v.* Van Kleek, 7 Johns. 498 ; Wilkinson *v.* Leland, 2 Pet. 657 ; Leland *v.* Wilkinson, 10 Pet. 297.

Declaratory Statutes.

Legislation is either introductory of new rules, or it is declaratory of existing rules. " A declaratory statute is one which is passed in order to put an end to a doubt as to what is the common law, or the meaning of another statute, and which declares what it is and ever has been.[1] Such a statute, therefore, is always in a certain sense retrospective ; because it assumes to determine what the law was before it was passed ; and as a declaratory statute is important only in those cases where doubts have already arisen, the statute, when passed, may be found to declare the law to be different from what it has already been adjudged to be by the courts. Thus Mr. Fox's Libel Act declared that, by the law of England, juries were judges of the law in prosecutions for libel ; it did not purport to introduce a new rule, but to declare a rule already and always in force. Yet previous to the passage of this act the courts had repeatedly held that the jury in these cases were only to pass upon the fact of publication and the truth of the innuendoes ; and whether the publication was libellous or not was a question of law addressed exclusively to the court. Thus the legislature declared the law to be what the courts had declared it was not. So in the State of New York, after the courts had held that insurance companies were taxable to a certain extent under an existing statute, the legislature passed another act, declaring that such companies were only taxable at a certain other rate ; and it was thereby declared that such was the intention and true construction of the original statute.[2] In these cases it will be perceived that the courts, in the due exercise of their authority as interpreters of the laws, have declared what the rule established by the common law or by statute is, and that the legislature has then interposed, put its own construction upon the existing law, and in effect declared the judicial interpretation to be unfounded and unwarrantable. The courts in these cases have clearly kept within the proper limits of their jurisdiction, and if they have erred, the error has been one of judgment only, and has not extended to usurpation of power. Was the legislature also within the limits of its authority when it passed the declaratory statute ?

[1] Bouv. Law Dic. " Statute."

[2] People *v.* Supervisors of New York, 16 N. Y. 424.

The decision of this question must depend upon the practical application which is sought to be made of the declaratory statute, and whether it is designed to have practically a retrospective operation, or only to establish a construction of the doubtful law for the determination of cases that may arise in the future. It is always competent to change an existing law by a declaratory statute ; and where it is only to operate upon future cases, it is no objection to its validity that it assumes the law to have been in the past what it is now declared that it shall be in the future. But the legislative action cannot be made to retroact upon past controversies, and to reverse decisions which the courts, in the exercise of their undoubted authority, have made ; for this would not only be the exercise of judicial power, but it would be its exercise in the most objectionable and offensive form, since the legislature would in effect sit as a court of review to which parties might appeal when dissatisfied with the rulings of the courts.[1]

As the legislature cannot set aside a construction of the law already applied by the courts to actual cases, neither can it compel the courts for the future to adopt a particular construction of a law which the legislature permits to remain in force. " To declare what the law *is, or has been*, is a judicial power ; to declare what the law *shall be*, is legislative. One of the fundamental principles of all our governments is, that the legislative power

[1] In several different cases the courts of Pennsylvania had decided that a testator's mark to his name, at the foot of a testamentary paper, but without proof that the name was written by his express direction, was not the signature required by the statute, and the legislature, to use the language of Chief Justice Gibson, " declared, in order to overrule it, that every last will and testament heretofore made, or hereafter to be made, except such as may have been fully adjudicated prior to the passage of this act, to which the testator's name is subscribed by his direction, or to which the testator has made his mark or cross, shall be deemed and taken to be valid. How this mandate to the courts to establish a particular interpretation of a particular statute, can be taken for anything else than an exercise of judicial power in settling a question of interpretation, I know not. The judiciary had certainly recognized a legislative interpretation of a statute before it had itself acted, and consequently before a purchaser had been misled by its udgment ; but he might have paid for a title on the unmistakable meaning of plain words ; and for the legislature subsequently to distort or pervert it, and to enact that white meant black, or that black meant white, would in the same degree be an exercise of arbitrary and unconstitutional power." Greenough *v.* Greenough, 11 Penn. St. 494. The act in this case was held void so far as its operation was retrospective, but valid as to future cases. And see Reiser *v.* Tell Association, 39 Penn. St. 137.

shall be separate from the judicial."[1] If the legislature would prescribe a different rule for the future from that which the courts enforce, it must be done by statute, and cannot be done by a mandate to the courts, which leaves the law unchanged, but seeks to compel the courts to construe and apply it, not according to the judicial, but according to the legislative judgment.[2] But in any case the substance of the legislative action should be regarded rather than the form; and if it appears to be the intention to establish by declaratory statute a rule of conduct for the future, the courts should accept and act upon it, without too nicely inquiring whether the mode by which the new rule is established is the best, most decorous and suitable that could have been adopted or not.

If the legislature cannot thus indirectly control the action of the courts, by requiring of them a construction of the law according to its own views, it is very plain it cannot do so directly, by setting aside their judgments, compelling them to grant new trials, ordering the discharge of offenders,[3] or directing what particular steps shall be taken in the progress of a judicial inquiry.[4]

[1] Dash v. Van Kleek, 7 Johns. 498, per Thompson, J.; Ogden v. Blackledge, 2 Cranch, 272.

[2] Govenor v. Porter, 5 Humph. 165; People v. Supervisors, &c. 16 N. Y. 424; Reiser v. Tell Association, 39 Penn. St. 137; O'Conner v. Waner, 4 W. & S. 227; Lamberton v. Hogan, 2 Penn. St. 25.

[3] In State v. Fleming, 7 Humph. 152, a legislative resolve that "no fine, forfeiture, or imprisonment should be imposed or recovered under the act of 1837 [then in force], and that all causes pending in any of the courts for such offence should be dismissed," was held void as an invasion of judicial authority.

[4] Opinions of judge^ on the Dorr case, 3 R. I. 299. In the case of Picquet, appellant, 5 Pick. 64, the Judge of Probate had ordered letters of administration to issue to an applicant therefor, on his giving bond in the penal sum of $50,000, with sureties within the commonwealth, for the faithful performance of his duties. He was unable to give the bond, and applied to the legislature for relief. Thereupon a resolve was passed "empowering" the Judge of Probate to grant the letters of administration, provided the petitioner should give bond with his brother, a resident of Paris, France, as surety, and "that such bond should be in lieu of any and all bond or bonds by any law or statute in this commonwealth now in force required," &c. The Judge of Probate refused to grant the letters on the terms specified in this resolve, and the Supreme Court, while holding that it was not compulsory upon him, also declared their opinion that, if it were so, it would be inoperative and void. In Bradford v. Brooks, 2 Aik. 284, it was decided that the legislature had no power to revive a commission for proving claims against an estate after it had once expired. See also Bagg's Appeal, 43 Penn. St. 512. In Hill

And as a court must act as an organized body of judges, and, where differences of opinion arise, they can only decide by majorities, it has been held that it would not be in the power of the legislature to provide that, in certain contingencies, the opinion of the minority of a court, vested with power by the constitution, should prevail, and so that the decision of the court in such cases should be rendered against the judgment of its members.[1]

Nor is it in the power of the legislature to bind parties by a recital of facts in a statute, thereby making them evidence against parties interested. A recital of facts in the preamble of a statute may perhaps be evidence, where they relate to matters of a public nature, as that riots or disorders exist in a certain part of the country;[2] but where the facts concern the rights of individuals, the legislature cannot adjudicate upon them. As private statutes are generally obtained on the application of some party interested, and are put in form to suit his wishes, perhaps their exclusion from being made evidence against any other party would result from other general principles; but it is clear that the recital could have no force, except as a judicial finding of facts; and that such finding is not a legislative act.[3]

v. Sunderland, 3 Vt. 507; and Burch v. Newberry, 10 N. Y. 374, it was held that the legislature had no power to grant to parties a right to appeal after it was gone under the general law. Besides the authorities referred to, to show that the legislature cannot grant a new trial, see Lewis v. Webb, 3 Greenl. 326; Durham v. Lewiston, 4 Greenl. 140; Bates v. Kimball, 2 Chip. 77; Staniford v. Barry, 1 Aik. 314; Merrill v. Sherburne, 1 N. H. 199; Dechastellux v. Fairchild, 15 Penn. St. 18; Taylor v. Place, 4 R. I. 324; Young v. State Bank, 4 Ind. 301; Lanier v. Gallatas, 13 La. An. R. 175; Miller v. State, 8 Gill, 145; Beebe v. State, 6 Ind. 515; Atkinson v. Dunlap, 50 Me. 111. In Burt v. Williams, 24 Ark. 91, it was held that the granting of continuances of pending cases was the exercise of judicial authority, and a legislative act assuming to do this was void.

[1] In Clapp v. Ely, 3 Dutch. 622, it was held that a statute which provided that no judgment of the Supreme Court should be reversed by the Court of Errors and Appeals, unless a majority of those members of the court who were competent to sit on the hearing and decision should concur in the reversal, was unconstitutional. Its effect would be, if the court were not full, to make the opinion of the minority in favor of affirmance, control that of the majority in favor of reversal, unless the latter were a majority of the whole court. Such a provision in the constitution might be proper and unexceptionable; but if the constitution has created a Court of Appeals, without any restriction of this character, the ruling of this case is that the legislature cannot impose it. The court was nearly equally divided, standing 7 to 6.

[2] Rex v. Sutton, 4 M. & S. 532.

[3] Elmendorf v. Carmichael, 3 Litt. 478; Parmelee v. Thompson, 7 Hill, 80.

We come now to a class of cases in regard to which there has been serious contrariety of opinion; springing from the fact, perhaps, that the purpose sought to be accomplished by the statutes is generally effected by judicial proceedings, so that if the statutes are not a direct invasion of judicial authority, they at least cover ground which the courts usually occupy under general laws which confer the jurisdiction upon them. We refer to

Statutes conferring Power upon Guardians and other Trustees to sell Lands.

Whenever it becomes necessary or proper to sell the estate of a decedent for the payment of debts, or of a lunatic or other incompetent person for the same purpose, or for future support, or of a minor to provide the means for his education and nurture, or for the more profitable investment of the proceeds, or of tenants in common to effectuate a partition between them, it will probably be found in every State that some court is vested with jurisdiction to make the necessary order, if the facts seem to render it important after a hearing of the parties in interest. The case is eminently one for judicial investigation. There are facts to be inquired into, in regard to which it is always possible that disputes may arise; the party in interest is often incompetent to act on his own behalf, and his interest is carefully to be inquired into and guarded ; and as the proceeding will usually be *ex parte*, there is more than the ordinary opportunity for fraud upon the party interested, as well as upon the authority which grants permission. It is highly and peculiarly proper, therefore, that by general laws judicial inquiry should be provided for these cases, and that these laws should provide for notice to all proper parties, and an opportunity for the presentation of any facts which might bear upon the propriety of granting the applications.

But it will sometimes be found that the general laws provided for these cases are not applicable to some which arise ; or if applicable, that they do not always accomplish fully all that seems desirable ; and in these cases, and perhaps also in some others without similar excuse, it has not been unusual for legislative authority to intervene, and by special statute to grant the power which, under the general law, is granted by the courts. The

7

power to pass such statutes has often been disputed, and it may be well to see upon what basis of authority as well as of reason it rests.

If in fact judicial inquiry is essential in these cases, it would seem clear that such statutes must be ineffectual and void. But if judicial inquiry is not essential, and the legislature may confer the power of sale in such a case upon an *ex parte* presentation of evidence, or upon the representations of the parties without any proof whatever, then we must consider the general laws to be passed, not because the cases fall within the province of judicial action, but because the courts can more conveniently consider, and properly, safely, and inexpensively pass upon such cases, than the legislative body, where the power primarily rests.[1]

The rule upon this subject, as we deduce it from the authorities, seems to be this: If the party standing in position of trustee applies for permission to make the sale, for a purpose apparently for the interest of the *cestuis que trust*, and there are no adverse interests to be considered and adjudicated, the case is not one which requires judicial action, but it is optional with the legislature to grant the relief by statute, or to refer the case to the courts for consideration, according as the one course or the other, on considerations of policy, may seem desirable.

In the case of Rice *v.* Parkman,[2] it appeared that, certain minors having become entitled to real estate by descent from their mother, the legislature passed a special statute empowering their father as guardian for them, and, after giving bond to the judge of probate, to sell and convey the lands, and put the proceeds at interest on good security for the benefit of the minor owners. A sale was made accordingly; but the children, after coming of age, brought suit against the party claiming under the sale, insisting that the special statute was void. There was in force at the time this special statute was passed a general statute, under which license might have been granted by the courts; but it was held that this general law did not deprive the legislature of that full

---

[1] There are constitutional provisions in Kentucky, Virginia, Missouri, Oregon, Nevada, Indiana, Maryland, New Jersey, and Michigan, forbidding special laws licensing the sale of the lands of minors and other persons under legal disability. Perhaps the general provision in some other constitutions, forbidding special laws in cases where a general law could be made applicable, might also be held to exclude such special authorization.

[2] 16 Mass. 326.

and complete control over such cases which it would have possessed had no such statute existed. " If," say the court, " the power by which the resolve authorizing the sale in this case was passed were of a judicial nature, it would be very clear that it could not have been exercised by the legislature without violating an express provision of the constitution. But it does not seem to us to be of this description of power; for it was not a case of controversy between party and party, nor is there any decree or judgment affecting the title to property. The only object of the authority granted by the legislature was to transmute real into personal estate, for purposes beneficial to all who were interested therein. This is a power frequently exercised by the legislature of this State, since the adoption of the constitution, and by the legislature of the Province and of the Colony, while under the sovereignty of Great Britain, analogous to the power exercised by the British Parliament on similar subjects, time out of mind. Indeed, it seems absolutely necessary for the interest of those who, by the general rules of law, are incapacitated from disposing of their property, that a power should exist somewhere of converting lands into money. For otherwise many minors might suffer, although having property, it not being in a condition to yield an income. This power must rest in the legislature, in this Commonwealth ; that body being alone competent to act as the general guardian and protector of those who are disabled to act for themselves.

" It was undoubtedly wise to delegate this authority to other bodies, whose sessions are regular and constant, and whose structure may enable them more easily to understand the merits of the particular application brought before them. But it does not follow that, because the power has been delegated by the legislature to courts of law, it is judicial in its character. For aught we see, the same authority might have been given to the selectmen of each town, or to the clerks or registers of the counties, it being a mere ministerial act, certainly requiring discretion, and sometimes knowledge of law, for its due exercise, but still partaking in no degree of the characteristics of judicial power. It is doubtless included in the general authority granted by the people to the legislature by the constitution. For full power and authority is given from time to time to make, ordain, and establish all manner of wholesome and reasonable orders, laws, statutes, and ordinances, directions and restrictions (so as the same be not repugnant or contrary to the constitution), as they shall judge to be for the good and welfare of the Commonwealth, and of the subjects thereof. No one imagines that, under this general authority, the legislature could deprive a citizen of his estate, or impair any valuable contract in which he might be interested. But there seems to be no reason to doubt that, upon his application, or the application of those who properly represent him if disabled from acting himself, a beneficial change of his estate, or a sale of it for purposes necessary and convenient for the lawful owner, is a just and proper subject for the exercise of that authority. It is, in fact, protecting him in his property, which the legislature is bound to do, and enabling him to derive subsistence, comfort, and education from property which might otherwise be wholly useless during that period of life when it might be most beneficially employed.

" If this be not true, then the general laws, under which so many estates of minors, persons *non compos mentis*, and others, have been sold and converted into money, are unauthorized by the constitution, and void. For the courts derive their authority from the legislature, and, it not being of a judicial nature, if the legislature had it not, they could not communicate it to any other body. Thus, if there were no power to relieve those from actual distress who had unproductive property, and were disabled from conveying it themselves, it would seem that one of the most essential objects of government — that of providing for the welfare of the citizens — would be lost. But the argument which has most weight on the part of the defendants is, that the legislature has exercised its power over this subject in the only constitutional way, by establishing a general provision ; and that, having done this, their authority has ceased, they having no right to interfere in particular cases. And if the question were one of expediency only, we should perhaps be convinced by the argument, that it would be better for all such applications to be made to the courts empowered to sustain them. But as a question of right, we think the argument fails. The constituent, when he has delegated an authority without an interest, may do the act himself which he has authorized another to do ; and especially when that constituent is the legislature, and is not prohibited by the constitution from exercising the authority. Indeed, the whole authority might be revoked, and the legislature resume the burden of this business to itself, if in its wisdom it should determine that the common welfare required it. It is not legislation which must be by general acts and rules, but the use of a parental or tutorial power, for purposes of kindness, without interfering with or prejudice to the rights of any but those who apply for specific relief. The title of strangers is not in any degree affected by such an interposition."

A similar statute was sustained by the Court for the Correction of Errors in New York. "It is clearly," says the Chancellor, "within the powers of the legislature, as *parens patria*, to prescribe such rules and regulations as it may deem proper for the superintendence, disposition, and management of the property and effects of infants, lunatics, and other persons who are incapable of managing their own affairs. But even that power cannot constitutionally be so far extended as to transfer the beneficial use of the property to another person, except in those cases where it can legally be presumed the owner of the property would himself have given the use of his property to the other, if he had been in a situation to act for himself, as in the case of a provision out of the estate of an infant or lunatic for the support of an indigent parent or other near relative." [1]

[1] Cochran *v.* Van Surlay, 20 Wend. 373. See the same case in the Supreme Court, *sub nom.* Clarke *v.* Van Surlay, 15 Wend. 436. See also Suydam *v.* Williamson, 24 How. 427 ; Heirs of Holman *v.* Bank of Norfolk, 12 Ala. 369 ; Florentine *v.* Barton, 2 Wal. 210. In Opinions of the Judges, 4 N. H. 572, the validity of such a special statute, under the constitution of New Hampshire, was denied. The judges say : "The objection to the exercise of such a power by the legislature is, that it is in its nature both legislative and judicial. It is the province of the legislature to prescribe the rule of law, but to apply it to particular cases is the business of the courts of law. And the thirty-eighth article in the Bill of Rights declares that 'in the government of the State the three essential powers thereof, to wit, the legislative, executive, and judicial, ought to be kept as separate from, and independent of, each other as the nature of a free government will admit, or as consistent with that chain of connection that binds the whole fabric of the Constitution in one indissoluble bond of union and amity.' The exercise of such a power by the legislature can never be necessary. By the existing laws, judges of probate have very extensive jurisdiction to license the sale of real estate of minors by their guardians. If the jurisdiction of the judges of probate be not sufficiently extensive to reach all proper cases, it may be a good reason why that jurisdiction should be extended, but can hardly be deemed a sufficient reason for the particular interposition of the legislature in an individual case. If there be a defect in the laws, they should be amended. Under our

The same ruling has been made in analogous cases. In Ohio, a special act of the legislature authorizing commissioners to make sale of lands held in fee tail, by devisees under a will, in order to cut off the entailment and effect a partition between them, — the statute being applied for by the mother of the devisees and the executor of the will, and on behalf of the devisees, — was held not obnoxious to constitutional objection, and as sustainable on immemorial legislative usage, and on the same ground which would support general laws for the same purpose.[1] In a case in the Supreme Court of the United States, where an executrix who had proved a will in New Hampshire made sale of lands without authority in Rhode Island, for the purpose of satisfying debts against the estate, a subsequent act of the Rhode Island legisla-

institutions all men are viewed as equal, entitled to enjoy equal privileges, and to be governed by equal laws. If it be fit and proper that license should be given to one guardian, under particular circumstances, to sell the estate of his ward, it is fit and proper that all other guardians should, under similar circumstances, have the same license. This is the very genius and spirit of our institutions. And we are of opinion that an act of the legislature to authorize the sale of the land of a particular minor by his guardian cannot be easily reconciled with the spirit of the article in the Bill of Rights which we have just cited. It is true that the grant of such a license by the legislature to the guardian is intended as a privilege and a benefit to the ward. But by the law of the land no minor is capable of assenting to a sale of his real estate in such a manner as to bind himself. And no guardian is permitted by the same law to determine when the estate of his ward ought and when it ought not to be sold. In the contemplation of the law, the one has not sufficient discretion to judge of the propriety and expediency of a sale of his estate, and the other is not to be intrusted with the power of judging. Such being the general law of the land, it is presumable that the legislature would be unwilling to rest the justification of an act authorizing the sale of a minor's estate upon any assent which the guardian or the minor could give in the proceeding. The question then is, as it seems to us, Can a ward be deprived of his inheritance without his consent by an act of the legislature which is intended to apply to no other individual? The fifteenth article of the Bill of Rights declares that no subject shall be deprived of his property but by the judgment of his peers or the law of the land. Can an act of the legislature, intended to authorize one man to sell the land of another without his consent, be 'the law of the land' in a free country? If the question proposed to us can be resolved into these questions, as it appears to us it may, we feel entirely confident that the representatives of the people of this State will agree with us in the opinion we feel ourselves bound to express on the question submitted to us, that the legislature cannot authorize a guardian of minors, by a special act or resolve, to make a valid conveyance of the real estate of his wards."

[1] Carroll v. Lessee of Olmsted, 16 Ohio, 251.

ture, confirming the sale, was held not an encroachment upon the judicial power. The land, it was said, descended to the heirs subject to a lien for the payment of debts, and there is nothing in the nature of the act of authorizing a sale to satisfy the lien, which requires that it should be performed by a judicial tribunal, or that it should be performed by a delegate rather than by the legislature itself. It is remedial in its nature, to give effect to existing rights.[1] The case showed the actual existence of debts, and indeed a judicial license for the sale of lands to satisfy them had been granted in New Hampshire before the sale was made. The decision was afterwards followed in a carefully considered case in the same côurt.[2] In each of these cases it is assumed that the legislature does not by the special statute determine the existence or amount of the debts, and disputes concerning them would be determinable in the usual modes. Many other decisions have been made to the same effect.[3]

This species of legislation may perhaps be properly called prerogative remedial legislation. It hears ahd determines no rights ; it deprives no one of his property. It simply authorizes one's real estate to be turned into personal, on the application of the person representing his interest, and under such circumstances that the consent of the owner, if capable of giving it, would be presumed. It is in the nature of the grant of a privilege to one person, which at the same time effects injuriously the rights of no other.[4]

But a different case is presented when the legislaturé assumes to authorize a person who does not occupy a fiduciary relation to

---

[1] Wilkinson v. Leland, 2 Pet. 660.

[2] Watkins v. Holman's Lessee, 16 Pet. 25 – 60. See also Florentine v. Barton, 2 Wal. 210 ; Doe v. Douglass, 8 Blackf. 10.

[3] Thurston v. Thurston, 6 R. I. 296 ; Williamson v. Williamson, 3 S. & M. 715 ; McComb v. Gilkey, 29 Miss. 146 ; Boon v. Bowers, 30 Miss. 246 ; Stewart v. Griffith, 33 Mo. 13 ; Estep v. Hutchman, 14 S. & R. 435 ; Snowhill v. Snowhill, 2 Green, Ch. 20 ; Dorsey v. Gilbert, 11 G. & J. 87 ; Norris v. Clymer, 2 Penn. St. 277 ; Coleman v. Carr, Walker, 258 ; Davison v. Johonnot, 7 Met. 388 ; Towle v. Forney, 14 N. Y. 423 ; Leggett v. Hunter, 19 N. Y. 445 ; Kibby v. Chetwood's Adm'rs, 4 T. B. Monr. 94 ; Shehan's Heirs v. Barnett's Heirs, 6 T. B. Monr. 594 ; Davis v. State Bank, 7 Ind. 316. In Moore v. Maxwell, 18 Ark. 469, a special statute authorizing the administrator of one who held the mere naked legal title to convey to the owner of the equitable title was held valid.

[4] It would be equally competent for the legislature to authorize a person under legal disability — e. g. an infant — to convey his estate, as to authorize it to be conveyed by guardian. McComb v. Gilkey, 29 Miss. 146.

the owner, to make sale of real estate, to satisfy demands which he asserts, but which are not judicially determined, or for any other purpose not connected with the convenience or necessity of the owner himself. An act of the legislature of Illinois undertook to empower a party who had applied for it to make sale of the lands pertaining to the estate of a deceased person, in order to raise a certain specified sum of money which the legislature assumed to be due to him and another person, for moneys by them advanced and liabilities incurred on behalf of the estate, and to apply the same to the extinguishment of their claims. Now it is evident that this act was in the nature of a judicial decree, passed on the application of parties adverse in interest to the estate, and in effect adjudging a certain amount to be due them, and ordering lands to be sold for its satisfaction. As was well said by the Supreme Court of Illinois, in adjudging the act void : " If this is not the exercise of a power of inquiry into, and a determination of facts, between debtor and creditor, and that, too, ex parte and summary in its character, we are at a loss to understand the meaning of terms ; nay, that it is adjudging and directing the application of one person's property to another, on a claim of indebtedness, without notice to, or hearing of, the parties whose estate is divested by the act. That the exercise of such power is in its nature clearly judicial we think too apparent to need argument to illustrate its truth. It is so self-evident from the facts disclosed that it proves itself." [1]

[1] Lane v. Dorman, 3 Scam. 242. In Dubois v. McLean, 4 McLean, 486, Judge Pope assumes that the case of Lane v. Dorman decides a special act, authorizing an executor to sell lands of the testator to pay debts against his estate, would be unconstitutional. We do not so understand that decision. On the contrary, another case in the same volume, Edwards v. Pope, p. 465, fully sustains the cases before decided, distinguishing them from Lane v. Dorman. But that indeed is also done in the principal case, where the court, after referring to similar cases in Kentucky, say : " These cases are clearly distinguished from the case at bar. The acts were for the benefit of all the creditors of the estates, without distinction ; and in one case, in addition, for the purpose of perfecting titles contracted to be made by the intestate. The claims of the creditors of the intestate were to be established by judicial or other satisfactory legal proceedings, and, in truth, in the case last cited, the commissioners were nothing more than special commissioners. The legislative department, in passing these acts, investigated nothing, nor did an act which could be deemed a judicial inquiry. It neither examined proof, nor determined the nature or extent of claims ; it merely authorized the application of the real estate to the payment of debts generally, discriminating in favor

A case in harmony with the one last referred to was decided by the Supreme Court of Michigan. Under the act of Congress " for the relief of citizens of towns upon the lands of the United States, under certain circumstances," approved May 23, 1844, and which provided that the trust under said act should be conducted under such rules and regulations as may be prescribed by the legislative authority of the State," &c., the legislature passed an act authorizing the trustee to give deeds to a person named therein, and those claiming under him; thus undertaking to dispose of the whole trust to the person thus named and his grantees, and authorizing no one else to be considered or to receive any relief. This was very plainly an attempted adjudication upon the rights of the parties concerned; it did not establish regulations for the administration of the trust, but it adjudged the trust property to certain claimants exclusively, in disregard of any rights which might exist in others; and it was therefore declared to be void.[1] And it has also been held that, whether a

of no one creditor, and giving no one a preference over another. Not so in the case before us; the amount is investigated and ascertained, and the sale is directed for the benefit of two persons exclusively. The proceeds are to be applied to the payment of such claims and none other, for liabilities said to be incurred but not liquidated or satisfied; and those, too, created after the death of the intestate." See also Mason v. Wait, 4 Scam. 127 – 134. The case of Estep v. Hutchman, 14 S. & R. 435, would seem to be more open to question on this point than any of the others before cited. It was the case of a special statute, authorizing the guardian of infant heirs to convey their lands in satisfaction of a contract made by their ancestor; and which was sustained. Compare this with Jones v. Perry, 10 Yerg. 59, where an act authorizing a guardian to sell lands to pay the ancestor's debts was held void.

[1] Cash, Appellant, 6 Mich. 193. The case of Powers v. Bergen, 6 N. Y. 358, is perhaps to be referred to another principle than that of encroachment upon judicial authority. That was a case where the legislature, by special act, had undertaken to authorize the sale of property, not for the purpose of satisfying liens upon it, or of meeting or in any way providing for the necessities or wants of the owners, but solely, after paying expenses, for the investment of the proceeds. It appears from that case that the executors under the will of the former owner held the lands in trust for a daughter of the testator during her natural life, with a vested remainder in fee in her two children. The special act assumed to empower them to sell and convey the complete fee, and apply the proceeds, *first*, to the payment of their commissions, costs, and expenses; *second*, to the discharge of assessments, liens, charges, and encumbrances on the land, of which, however, none were shown to exist; and, *third*, to invest the proceeds and pay over the income, after deducting taxes and charges, to the daughter during her life, and after her decease to convey, assign, or pay over the same to the per-

corporation has been guilty of abuse of authority under its charter, so as justly to subject it to forfeiture,[1] and whether a widow
is entitled to dower in a specified parcel of land,[2] are judicial questions which cannot be decided by the legislature. In these cases
there are necessarily adverse parties; the questions that would
arise are essentially judicial, and over which the courts possess
jurisdiction at the common law; and it is presumable that legislative acts of this character must have been adopted carelessly, and
without a due consideration of the proper boundaries which mark
the separation of legislative from judicial duties.[3]

sons who would be entitled under the will. The court regarded this as an unauthorized interference with private property upon no necessity, and altogether
void, as depriving the owners of their property contrary to the "law of the land."
At the same time the authority of those cases, where it has been held that the
legislature, acting as the guardian and protector of those who are disabled to act
for themselves by reason of infancy, lunacy, or other like cause, may constitutionally pass either general or private laws, under which an effectual disposition of
their property might be made, was not questioned. The court cite, with apparent approval, the cases, among others, of Rice v. Parkman, 16 Mass. 326; Cochran v. Van Surlay, 20 Wend. 365; and Wilkinson v. Leland, 2 Pet. 657. The
case of Ervine's Appeal, 16 Penn. St. 256, was similar, in the principles involved,
to Powers v. Bergen, and was decided in the same way. See also Kneass's Appeal, 31 Penn. St. 87, and compare with Kerr v. Kitchell, 17 Penn. St. 438, and
Martin's Appeal, 23 Penn. St. 437.

  [1] State v. Noyes, 47 Me. 189; Campbell v. Union Bank, 6 How. (Miss.) 661;
Canal Co. v. Railroad Co., 4 G. & J. 122; Regents of University v. Williams, 9
G. & J. 365. In Miner's Bank of Dubuque v. United States, 1 Morris, 482, a
clause in a charter authorizing the legislature to repeal it for any abuse or mis-
user of corporate privileges was held to refer the question of abuse to the legislative judgment. The appointment of a receiver by the legislature for an insolvent bank was sustained in Carey v. Giles, 9 Geo. 253.

  [2] Edwards v. Pope, 3 Scam. 465.

  [3] The injustice and dangerous character of legislation of this description are
well stated by the Supreme Court of Pennsylvania: "When, in the exercise of
proper legislative powers, general laws are enacted which bear, or may bear, on
the whole community, if they are unjust and against the spirit of the constitution, the whole community will be interested to procure their repeal by a voice
potential. And that is the great security for just and fair legislation. But
when individuals are selected from the mass, and laws are enacted affecting
their property, without summons or notice, at the instigation of an interested
party, who is to stand up for them, thus isolated from the mass, in injury and injustice, or where are they to seek relief from such acts of despotic power? They
have no refuge but in the courts, the only secure place for determining conflicting rights by due course of law. But if the judiciary give way, and, in the language
of the Chief Justice in Greenough v. Greenough, in 11 Penn. St. 494, 'confesses
itself too weak to stand against the antagonism of the legislature and the bar,' one

We have elsewhere referred to a number of cases where statutes have been held unobjectionable which validated legal proceedings, notwithstanding irregularities apparent in them.[1] These statutes may as properly be made applicable to judicial as to ministerial proceedings; and although, when they refer to such proceedings, they may at first seem like an interference with judicial authority, yet if they are only in aid of judicial proceedings, and tend to their support by precluding parties from taking advantage of errors which do not affect their substantial rights, they cannot be obnoxious to the charge of usurping judicial power. The legislature does, or may, prescribe the rules under which the judicial power is exercised by the courts; and in doing so, it may dispense with any of those formalities which are not essential to the jurisdiction of the court; and whatever it may dispense with by statute anterior to the proceedings, we believe it may also dispense with by statute after the proceedings have been taken, if the court has failed to observe any of those formalities. But it would not be competent for the legislature to authorize a court to proceed and adjudicate upon the rights of parties, without giving them an opportunity to be heard before it; and, for the same reason, it would be incompetent for it, by retrospective legislation, to make valid proceedings which had been had in the courts, but which were void for want of jurisdiction over the parties. Such a legislative enactment would be doubly objectionable: *first*, as an exercise of judicial power, since, the proceedings in court being void, it would be the statute alone which would constitute an adjudication upon the rights of the parties; and, *second*, because, in all judicial proceedings, notice to parties and an opportunity to defend are essential, — both of which they would be deprived of in such a case.[2] And for like reasons a statute validating pro-

---

independent co-ordinate branch of the government will become the subservient handmaid of the other, and a quiet, insidious revolution will be effected in the administration of the government, whilst its form on paper remains the same." Ervine's Appeal, 16 Penn. St. 268.

[1] See Chapter XI.

[2] In McDaniel *v.* Correll, 19 Ill. 226, it appeared that a statute had been passed to make valid certain legal proceedings by which an alleged will was adjudged void, and which were had against non-resident defendants, over whom the courts had obtained no jurisdiction. The court say: " If it was competent for the legislature to make a void proceeding valid, then it has been done in this case. Upon this question we cannot for a moment doubt or hesitate. They can no more impart a binding efficacy to a void proceeding, than they can take one man's

ceedings had before an intruder into a judicial office, before whom
no one is authorized or required to appear, and who could have
jurisdiction neither of the parties nor of the subject-matter, would
also be void.[1]

property from him and give it to another. Indeed, to do the one is to accomplish
the other. By the decree in this case the will in question was declared void,
and, consequently, if effect be given to the decree, the legacies given to those
absent defendants by the will are taken from them and given to others, according
to our statute of descents. Until the passage of the act in question, they were
not bound by the verdict of the jury in this case, and it could not form the basis
of a valid decree. Had the decree been rendered before the passage of the act, it
would have been as competent to make that valid as it was to validate the antecedent proceedings upon which alone the decree could rest. The want of jurisdiction over the defendants was as fatal to the one as it could be to the other. If
we assume the act to be valid, then the legacies which before belonged to the
legatees have now ceased to be theirs, and this result has been brought about
by the legislative act alone. The effect of the act upon them is precisely the
same as if it had declared in direct terms that the legacies bequeathed by this will
to these defendants should not go to them, but should descend to the heirs at law
of the testator, according to our law of descents. This it will not be pretended
that they could do directly, and they had no more authority to do it indirectly,
by making proceedings binding upon them which were void in law."

 [1] In Denny v. Mattoon, 2 Allen, 361, a judge in insolvency had made certain
orders in a case pending in another jurisdiction, and which the courts subsequently declared to be void. The legislature then passed an act declaring that
they " are hereby confirmed, and the same shall be taken and deemed good and
valid in law, to all intents and purposes whatsoever." On the question of the
validity of this act the court say : " The precise question is, whether it can be
held to operate so as to confer a jurisdiction over parties and proceedings which
it has been judicially determined do not exist, and give validity to acts and processes which have been adjudged void. The statement of this question seems to
us to suggest the obvious and decisive objection to any construction of the statute
which would lead to such a conclusion. It would be a direct exercise by the
legislature of a power in its nature clearly judicial, from the use of which it is
expressly prohibited by the thirtieth article of the Declaration of Rights. The
line which marks and separates judicial from legislative duties and functions is
often indistinct and uncertain, and it is sometimes difficult to decide within which
of the two classes a particular subject falls. All statutes of a declaratory nature,
which are designed to interpret or give a meaning to previous enactments, or to
confirm the rights of parties either under their own contracts or growing out of
the proceedings of courts or public bodies, which lack legal validity, involve in
a certain sense the exercise of a judicial power. They operate upon subjects
which might properly come within the cognizance of the courts and form the basis of judicial consideration and judgment. But they may, nevertheless, be supported as being within the legitimate sphere of legislative action, on the ground
that they do not declare or determine, but only confirm rights ; that they give

Legislative Divorces.

There is another class of cases where it would seem that action ought to be referred exclusively to the judicial tribunals, but in respect to which the prevailing doctrine seems to be, that the legis-

effect to the acts of parties according to their intent ; that they furnish new and more efficacious remedies, or create a more beneficial interest or tenure, or, by supplying defects and curing informalities in the proceedings of courts, or of public officers acting within the scope of their authority, they give effect to acts to which there was the express or implied assent of the parties interested. Statutes which are intended to accomplish such purposes do not necessarily invade the province, or directly interfere with the action of judicial tribunals. But if we adopt the broadest and most comprehensive view of the power of the legislature, we must place some limit beyond which the authority of the legislature cannot go without trenching on the clear and well-defined boundaries of judicial power." " Although it may be difficult, if not impossible, to lay down any general rule which may serve to determine, in all cases, whether the limits of constitutional restraint are overstepped by the exercise by one branch of the government of powers exclusively delegated to another, it certainly is practicable to apply to each case as it arises some test by which to ascertain whether this fundamental principle is violated. If, for example, the practical operation of a statute is to determine adversary suits pending between party and party, by substituting in place of the well-settled rules of law the arbitrary will of the legislature, and thereby controlling the action of the tribunal before which the suits are pending, no one can doubt that it would be an unauthorized act of legislation, because it directly infringes on the peculiar and appropriate functions of the judiciary. It is the exclusive province of the courts of justice to apply established principles to cases within their jurisdiction, and to enforce their jurisdiction by rendering judgments and executing them by suitable process. The legislature have no power to interfere with this jurisdiction in such manner as to change the decision of cases pending before courts, or to impair or set aside their judgments, or to take cases out of the settled course of judicial proceeding. It is on this principle that it has been held, that the legislature have no power to grant a new trial or direct a rehearing of a cause which has been once judicially settled. The right to a review, or to try anew facts which have been determined by a verdict or decree, depends on fixed and well-settled principles, which it is the duty of the court to apply in the exercise of a sound judgment and discretion. These cannot be regulated or governed by legislative action. Taylor v. Place, 4 R. I. 324, 337 ; Lewis v. Webb, 3 Me. 326 ; Dechastellux v. Fairchild, 15 Penn. St. 18. A fortiori, an act of the legislature cannot set aside or amend final judgments or decrees." The court further consider the general subject at length, and adjudge the particular enactment under consideration void, both as an exercise of judicial authority, and also because, in declaring valid the void proceedings in insolvency against the debtor, under which assignees had been appointed, it took away from the debtor his property, " not by due process of law or the law of the land, but by an arbitrary exercise of legislative will."

lature has complete control unless, specially restrained by the State constitution. The granting of divorces from the bonds of matrimony was not confided to the courts in England, and from the earliest days the Colonial and State legislatures in this country have assumed to possess the same power over the subject which was possessed by the Parliament, and from time to time have passed special laws declaring a dissolution of the bonds of matrimony in special cases. Now it is clear that " the question of divorce involves investigations which are properly of a judicial nature, and the jurisdiction over divorces ought to be confined exclusively to the judicial tribunals, under the limitations to be prescribed by law " ; [1] and so strong is the general conviction of this fact, that the people in framing their constitutions, in a majority of the States, have positively forbidden any such special laws.[2]

[1] 2 Kent, 106. See Levins v. Sleaton, 2 Greene (Iowa), 607.

[2] The following are constitutional provisions : — *Alabama :* Divorces from the bonds of matrimony shall not be granted but in the cases by law provided for, and by suit in chancery ; but decrees in chancery for divorce shall be final, unless appealed from in the manner prescribed by law, within three months from the date of the enrolment thereof. *Arkansas :* The General Assembly shall not have power to pass any bill of divorce, but may prescribe by law the manner in which such cases may be investigated in the courts of justice, and divorces granted. *California :* No divorce shall be granted by the legislature. The provision is the same or similar in Iowa, Indiana, Maryland, Michigan, Minnesota, Nevada, Nebraska, Oregon, New Jersey, Texas, and Wisconsin. *Florida :* Divorces from the bonds of matrimony shall not be allowed but by the judgment of a court, as shall be prescribed by law. *Georgia :* The Superior Court shall have exclusive jurisdiction in all cases of divorce, both total and partial. *Illinois :* The General Assembly shall have no power to grant divorces, but may authorize the courts of justice to grant them for such causes as may be specified by law ; provided that such laws be general and uniform in their operation. *Kansas :* And power to grant divorces is vested in the District Courts, subject to regulations by law. *Kentucky :* The General Assembly shall have no power to grant divorces, ... but by general laws shall confer such powers on the courts of justice. *Louisiana :* The legislature may enact general laws regulating the . . . . granting of divorce ; but no special laws shall be enacted relating to particular or individual cases. *Massachusetts :* All causes of marriage, divorce, and alimony . . . . shall be heard and determined by the Governor and Council, until the legislature shall by law make other provision. *Mississippi :* Divorces from the bonds of matrimony shall not be granted but in cases provided for by law, and by suit in chancery. *New Hampshire :* All causes of marriage, divorce, and alimony . . . . shall be heard and tried by the Superior Court, until the legislature shall by law make other provision. *New York :* No law shall be passed abridging the right of the people peaceably to assemble and petition the government, or any

Of the judicial decisions on·the subject of legislative power over divorces there seem to be three classes of cases. The doctrine of the first class seems to be this: The granting of a divorce may be either a legislative or a judicial act, according as the legislature shall refer its consideration to the courts, or reserve it to itself. The legislature has the same full control over the *status* of husband and wife which it possesses over the other domestic relations, and may permit or prohibit it according to its own views of what is for the interest of the parties or the good of the public. In dissolving the relation, it proceeds upon such reasons as to it seem sufficient; and if inquiry is made into the facts of the past, it is no more than is needful when any change of the law is contemplated, with a view to the establishment of more salutary rules for the future. The inquiry, therefore, is not judicial in its nature, and it is not essential that there be any particular finding of misconduct or unfitness in the parties. As in other cases of legislative action, the reasons or the motives of the legislature cannot be inquired into; the relation which the law permitted before is now forbidden, and the parties are absolved from the obligations growing out of that relation which continued so long as the relation existed, but which necessarily cease with its termination. Marriage is not a contract, but a *status;* the parties cannot have vested rights of property in a domestic relation; therefore the legislative act does not come under condemnation as depriving parties of

department thereof, nor shall any divorce be granted otherwise than by due judicial proceedings. *North Carolina:* The General Assembly shall have power to pass general laws regulating divorce and alimony, but shall not have power to grant a divorce or secure alimony in any particular case. *Ohio:* The General Assembly shall grant no divorce, nor exercise any judicial power, not herein expressly conferred. *Pennsylvania:* The legislature shall not have power to enact laws annulling the contract of marriage in any case where by law the courts of this Commonwealth are, or hereafter may be, empowered to decree a divorce. *Tennessee:* The legislature shall have no power to grant divorces, but may authorize the courts of justice to grant them for such causes as may be specified by law; provided that such laws be general and uniform throughout the State. *Virginia:* The legislature shall confer on the courts the power to grant divorces, ... but shall not, by special legislation, grant relief in such cases, or in any other case of which the courts or other tribunals may have jurisdiction. *Missouri:* The legislature shall not pass special laws divorcing any named parties. Under the Constitution of Michigan it was held that, as the legislature was prohibited from granting divorces, they could pass no special act authorizing the courts to divorce for a cause which was not a legal cause for divorce under the general laws. Teft *v.* Teft, 3 Mich. 67. See also Clark *v.* Clark, 10 N. H. 387.

rights contrary to the law of the land, but, as in other cases within the scope of the legislative authority, the legislative will must be regarded as sufficient reason for the rule which it promulgates.[1]

---

[1] The leading case on this subject is Starr v. Pease, 8 Conn. 541. On the question whether a divorce is necessarily a judicial act, the court say : " A further objection is urged against this act, viz. that, by the new constitution of 1818, there is an entire separation of the legislative and judicial departments, and that the legislature can now pass no act or resolution not clearly warranted by that constitution; that the constitution is a grant of power, and not a limitation of powers already possessed; and, in short, that there is no reserved power in the legislature since the adoption of this constitution. Precisely the opposite of this is true. From the settlement of the State there have been certain fundamental rules by which power has been exercised. These rules were embodied in an instrument called by some a constitution, by others a charter. All agree that it was the first constitution ever made in Connecticut, and made, too, by the people themselves. It gave very extensive powers to the legislature, and left too much (for it left everything almost) to their will. The constitution of 1818 proposed to, and in fact did, limit that will. It adopted certain general principles by a preamble called a Declaration of Rights; provided for the election and appointment of certain organs of the government, such as the legislative, executive, and judicial departments; and imposed upon them certain restraints. It found the State sovereign and independent, with a legislative power capable of making all laws necessary for the good of the people, not forbidden by the Constitution of the United States, nor opposed to the sound maxims of legislation; and it left them in the same condition, except so far as limitations were provided. There is now and has been a law in force on the subject of divorces. The law was passed a hundred and thirty years ago. It provides for divorces *a vinculo matrimonii* in four cases, viz. adultery, fraudulent contract, wilful desertion, and seven years' absence unheard of. The law has remained in substance the same as it was when enacted in 1667. During all this period the legislature has interfered like the Parliament of Great Britain, and passed special acts of divorce *a vinculo matrimonii;* and at almost every session since the Constitution of the United States went into operation, now forty-two years, and for the thirteen years of the existence of the Constitution of Connecticut, such acts have been, in multiplied cases, passed and sanctioned by the constituted authorities of our State. We are not at liberty to inquire into the wisdom of our existing law upon this subject ; nor into the expediency of such frequent interference of the legislature. We can only inquire into the constitutionality of the act under consideration. The power is not prohibited either by the Constitution of the United States or by that of this State. In view of the appalling consequences of declaring the general law of the State, or the repeated acts of our legislature, unconstitutional and void, consequences easily perceived, but not easily expressed, — such as bastardizing the issue and subjecting the parties to punishment for adultery, — the court should come to the result only on a solemn conviction that their oaths of office and these constitutions imperiously demand it. Feeling myself no such conviction, I cannot pronounce the act void." Per Daggett, J., Hosmer, Ch. J., and Bissell, J., concurring. Peters, J., dissented. Upon the same subject, see Crane v.

The second class of cases to which we have alluded hold that divorce is a judicial act in those cases upon which the general laws confer on the courts power to adjudicate ; and that consequently in those cases the legislature cannot pass special laws, but its full control over the relation of marriage will leave it at liberty to grant divorces in other cases, for such causes as shall appear to its wisdom to justify them.[1]

A third class of cases deny altogether the authority of these special legislative enactments, and declare the act of divorce to be in its nature judicial, and not properly within the province of the legislative power.[2] The most of these decisions, however, lay more or less stress upon clauses in the constitutions other than those which in general terms separate the legislative and judicial functions, and some of them would perhaps have been differently decided but for those other clauses. But it is safe to say, that the general sentiment in the legal profession is against the rightfulness of special legislative divorces ; and it is believed that, if the question could originally have been considered by the courts, unembarrassed by any considerations of long acquiescence, and of the serious consequences which must result from affirming their unlawfulness, after so many had been granted and new relations formed, it is highly probable that these enactments would have been held to be usurpations of judicial authority, and we should have been spared the necessity for the special constitutional provisions which have since been introduced. Fortunately, these provisions render the question now discussed of little practical importance ; at the same time that they refer the decision

Meginnis, 1 G. & J. 463 ; Wright v. Wright, 2 Md. 429 ; Gaines v. Gaines, 9 B. Monr. 295 ; Cabell v. Cabell, 1 Met. (Ky.) 319 ; Dickson v. Dickson, 1 Yerg. 110 ; Melizet's Appeal, 17 Penn. St. 449 ; Townsend v. Griffin, 4 Harr. 440 ; Noel v. Ewing, 9 Ind. 37 ; and the examination of the whole subject by Mr. Bishop, in his work on Marriage and Divorce.

[1] Levins v. Sleator, 2 Greene (Iowa), 604 ; Opinions of Judges, 16 Me. 479 ; Adams v. Palmer, 51 Me. 480. See also Townsend v. Griffin, 4 Harr. 440. It is a well-reasoned case in Kentucky, it was held that a legislative divorce, obtained on the application of one of the parties while suit for divorce was pending in a court of competent jurisdiction, would not affect the rights to property of the other, growing out of the relation. Gaines v. Gaines, 9 B. Monr. 295.

[2] Bingham v. Miller, 17 Ohio, 445 ; Clark v. Clark, 10 N. H. 380 ; Ponder v. Graham, 4 Flor. 23 ; State v. Fry, 4 Mo. 120 ; Bryson v. Campbell, 12 Mo. 498 ; Bryson v. Bryson, 17 Mo. 590. See also Jones v. Jones, 12 Penn. St. 353, 354.

upon applications for divorce to those tribunals which must proceed upon inquiry, and cannot condemn unheard.[1]

The force of a legislative divorce must in any case be confined to a dissolution of the relation; it can only be justified on the ground that it merely lays down a rule of conduct for the parties to observe towards each other for the future. It cannot inquire into the past, with a view to punish the parties for their offences against the marriage relation, except so far as the divorce itself is a punishment. It cannot order the payment of alimony, for that would be a judgment;[2] it cannot adjudge upon conflicting claims to property between the parties, but it must leave all questions of this character to the courts. Those rights of property which depend upon the continued existence of the relation will be terminated by the dissolution, but only as in any other case rights in the future may be incidentally affected by a change in the law.[3]

Legislative Encroachments upon Executive Power.

If it is difficult to point out the precise boundary which separates legislative from judicial duties, it is still more difficult to discriminate, in particular cases, between what is properly legislative and what is properly executive duty. The authority that makes the laws has large discretion in determining the means through which they shall be executed; and the performance of

---

[1] If marriage is a natural right, then it would seem that any particular marriage that parties might lawfully form they must have a lawful right to continue in, unless by misbehavior they subject themselves to a forfeiture of the right. And if the legislature can annul the relation in one case, without any finding that a breach of the marriage contract has been committed, then it would seem that they might annul it in every case, and even prohibit all parties from entering into the same relation in the future. The recognition of a full and complete control of the relation in the legislature, to be exercised at its will, leads inevitably to this conclusion; so that, under the "rightful powers of legislation" which our constitutions confer upon the legislative department, a relation essential to organized civil society might be abrogated entirely. Single legislative divorces are but single steps towards this barbarism which the application of the same principle to every individual case, by a general law, would necessarily bring upon us. See what is said by the Supreme Court of Missouri in Bryson v. Bryson, 17 Mo. 593, 594.

[2] Crane v. Meginnis, 1 G. & J. 463.

[3] Star v. Pease, 8 Conn. 545.

many duties which they may provide for by law, they may refer
either to the chief executive of the State, or, at their option, to
any other executive or ministerial officer, or even to a person
specially named for the duty. What can be definitely said on
this subject is this: that such powers as are specially conferred
by the constitution upon the governor, or any specified officer,
the legislature cannot confer upon any other officer or authority;
and from those duties which the constitution requires of him he
cannot be excused by law.[1]   But other powers or duties the executive cannot exercise or assume except by legislative authority,
and the power which in its discretion it confers it may also withhold or confer in other directions.[2]   Whether in those cases where
power is conferred by the constitution upon the governor, the
legislature have the same authority to make rules for the exercise
of the power, that they have to make rules to govern the proceedings in the courts, may perhaps be a question.[3]   It would seem

[1] Attorney-General *v.* Brown, 1 Wis. 522. "Whatever power or duty is expressly given to, or imposed upon, the executive department, is altogether free
from the interference of the other branches of the government. Especially is
this the case where the subject is committed to the *discretion* of the chief executive officer, either by the constitution or by the laws. So long as the power
is vested in him, it is to be by him exercised, and no other branch of the government can control its exercise." Under the constitution of Ohio, which forbids
the exercise of any appointing power by the legislature, except as therein authorized, it was held that the legislature could not, by law, constitute certain designated persons a State board, with power to appoint commissioners of the State
House, and directors of the penitentiary, and to remove such directors for cause.
State *v.* Kennon, 7 Ohio St. 546. And see Davis *v.* State, 7 Md. 161.

[2] "In deciding this question [as to the authority of the governor], recurrence
must be had to the constitution. That furnishes the only rule by which the court
can be governed. That is the charter of the governor's authority. All the
powers delegated to him by, or in accordance with that instrument, he is entitled
to exercise, and no others. The constitution is a limitation upon the powers of
the legislative department of the government, but it is to be regarded as a grant
of powers to the other departments. Neither the executive nor the judiciary,
therefore, can exercise any authority or power except such as is clearly granted
by the constitution." Field *v.* People, 2 Scam. 80.

[3] Whether the legislature can constitutionally remit a fine, when the pardoning
power is vested in the governor by the constitution, has been made a question; and
the cases of Haley *v.* Clarke, 26 Ala. 439, and People *v.* Bircham, 12 Cal. 50, are opposed to each other upon the point. If the fine is payable to the State, perhaps the
legislature should be considered as having the same right to discharge it that they
would have to release any other debtor to the State from his obligation. In Morgan *v.* Buffington, 21 Mo. 549, it was held that the State Auditor was not obliged

that this must depend generally upon the nature of the power, and upon the question whether the constitution, in conferring it, has furnished a sufficient rule for its exercise. If complete power to pardon is conferred upon the executive, it may be doubted if the legislature can impose restrictions under the name of rules or regulations; but when the governor is made commander-in-chief of the military forces of the State, his authority must be exercised under such proper rules as the legislature may prescribe, because the military forces are themselves under the control of the legislature, and military law is prescribed by that department. There would be this clear limitation upon the power of the legislature to prescribe rules for the executive department, that they must not be such as, under pretence of regulation, divest the executive of, or preclude his exercising, any of his constitutional prerogatives or powers. Those matters which the constitution specifically confides to him the legislature cannot take from his control.

Delegating Legislative Power.

One of the settled maxims in constitutional law is, that the power conferred upon the legislature to make laws cannot be delegated by that department to any other body or authority. Where the sovereign power of the State has located the authority, there it must remain; and by the constitutional agency alone

to accept as conclusive the certificate from the Speaker of the House as to the sum due a member of the House for attendance upon it, but that he might lawfully inquire whether the amount had been actually earned by attendance or not. The legislative rule, therefore, cannot go to the extent of compelling an executive officer to do something else than his duty, under any pretence of regulation. The power to pardon offenders is vested by the several State constitutions in the governor. It is not, however, a power which necessarily inheres in the executive. State v. Dunning, 9 Ind. 22. And several of the State constitutions have provided that it shall be exercised under such regulations as shall be prescribed by law. There are provisions more or less broad to this purport in those of Kansas, Florida, Alabama, Arkansas, Texas, Mississippi, Oregon, Indiana, Iowa, and Virginia. In State v. Dunning, 9 Ind. 20, an act of the legislature requiring the applicant for the remission of a fine or forfeiture to forward to the governor, with his application, the opinion of certain county officers as to the propriety of the remission, was sustained as an act within the power conferred by the constitution upon the legislature to prescribe regulations in these cases. And see Branham v. Lange, 16 Ind. 500. The power to reprieve is not included in the power to pardon. Ex parte Howard, 17 N. H. 545.

the laws must be made until the constitution itself is changed. The power to whose judgment, wisdom, and patriotism this high prerogative has been intrusted cannot relieve itself of the responsibility by choosing other agencies upon which the power shall be devolved, nor can it substitute the judgment, wisdom, and patriotism of any other body for those to which alone the people have seen fit to confide this sovereign trust.[1]

But it is not always essential that a legislative act should be a completed statute which must in any event take effect as law, at the time it leaves the hands of the legislative department. A statute may be *conditional*, and its taking effect may be made to depend upon some subsequent event.[2] Affirmative legislation may in some cases be adopted, of which the parties interested are at liberty to avail themselves or not at their option. A private act of incorporation cannot be forced upon the corporators ; they may refuse the franchise if they so choose.[3] In these cases the legislative

---

[1] "These are the bounds which the trust that is put in them by the society, and the law of God and nature, have set to the legislative power of every commonwealth, in all forms of government : —

" *First.* They are to govern by promulgated established laws, not to be varied in particular cases, but to have one rule for rich and poor, for the favorite at court and the countryman at plough.

" *Secondly.* These laws also ought to be designed for no other end ultimately but the good of the people.

" *Thirdly.* They must not raise taxes on the property of the people without the consent of the people, given by themselves or their deputies. And this properly concerns only such governments where the legislative is always in being, or at least where the people have not reserved any part of the legislative to deputies, to be from time to time chosen by themselves.

" *Fourthly.* The legislative neither must nor can transfer the power of making laws to anybody else, or place it anywhere but where the people have." Locke on Civil Government, § 142.

That legislative power cannot be delegated, see Thorne *v.* Cramer, 15 Barb. 112 ; Bradley *v.* Baxter, Ib. 122 ; Barto *v.* Himrod, 8 N. Y. 483 ; People *v.* Stout, 23 Barb. 349 ; Rice *v.* Foster, 4 Harr. 479 ; Santo *v.* State, 2 Iowa, 165 ; Geebrick *v.* State, 5 Iowa, 491 ; State *v.* Beneke, 9 Iowa, 203 ; People *v.* Collins, 3 Mich. 243 ; Railroad Co. *v.* Commissioners of Clinton County, 1 Ohio, N. S. 77 ; Parker *v.* Commonwealth, 6 Penn. St. 507 ; Commonwealth *v.* McWilliams, 11 Penn. St. 61 ; Maize *v.* State, 4 Ind. 342 ; Meshmeier *v.* State, 11 Ind. 482 ; State *v.* Parker, 26 Vt. 362 ; State *v.* Swisher, 17 Texas, 441 ; State *v.* Copeland, 3 R. I. 33.

[2] Brig Aurora *v.* United States, 7 Cranch, 382 ; Bull *v.* Read, 13 Grat. 78 ; State *v.* Parker, 26 Vt. 357.

[3] Ang. & Ames on Corp. § 81.

act is regarded as complete when it has passed through the constitutional formalities necessary to perfected legislation, notwithstanding its actually going into operation as law may depend upon its subsequent acceptance. We have elsewhere spoken of municipal corporations, and of the powers of legislation which may be and commonly are bestowed upon them, and the bestowal of which is not to be considered as trenching upon the maxim that legislative power is not to be delegated, since that maxim is to be understood in the light of the immemorial practice of this country and of England, which has always recognized the propriety of vesting in the municipal organizations certain powers of local regulation, in respect to which the parties immediately interested may fairly be supposed more competent to judge of their needs than any central authority. As municipal organizations are mere auxiliaries of the State government in the important business of municipal rule, the legislature may create them at will from its own views of propriety or necessity, and without consulting the parties interested; and it also possesses the like power to abolish them, without stopping to inquire what may be the desire of the corporators on that subject.[1]

Nevertheless, as the corporators have a special and peculiar interest in the terms and conditions of the charter, in the powers conferred and liabilities imposed, as well as in the general question whether they shall originally be or afterwards remain incorporated at all or not, and as the burdens of municipal government must rest upon their shoulders, and especially as by becoming incorporated they are held, in law, to contract to discharge the duties the charter imposes, it seems eminently proper that their voice should be heard on the question of their incorporation, and that their decision should be conclusive, unless, for strong reasons of state policy or local necessity, it should seem important to overrule the opinion of the local majority. The right to refer any legislation of this character to the people peculiarly interested does not seem to be questioned, and the reference is by no means unusual.[2]

---

[1] City of Patterson v. Society, &c., 4 Zab. 385 ; Cheany v. Hooser, 9 B. Monr. 330; Berlin v. Gorham, 34 N. H. 266. See Ang. & Ames on Corp. § 31 and note. See also *post*, Chap. VIII.

[2] Bull v. Read, 13 Grat. 78 ; Corning v. Greene, 23 Barb. 33 ; Morford v. Unger, 8 Iowa, 82 ; City of Patterson v. Society, &c., 4 Zab. 385 ; Commonwealth

For the like reasons the question whether a county or township shall be divided and a new one formed,[1] or two townships or school districts formerly one be reunited,[2] or a county seat located at a particular place, or after its location removed elsewhere,[3] or the municipality contract particular debts, or engage in works of local improvement,[4] is always a question which may with propriety be referred to the voters of the municipality for decision.

The question then arises, whether that which may be done in

v. Judges of Quarter Sessions, 8 Penn. St. 391; Commonwealth v. Painter, 10 Penn. St. 214; Call v. Chadbourne, 46 Me. 206; State v. Scott, 17 Mo. 521; Hobart v. Supervisors, &c., 17 Cal. 23; Bank of Chenango v. Brown, 26 N. Y. 467; Steward v. Jefferson, 3 Harr. 335; Burgess v. Pue, 2 Gill, 11.

[1] State v. Reynolds, 5 Gilm. 1.

[2] Commonwealth v. Judges, &c., 8 Penn. St. 391; Call v. Chadbourne, 46 Me. 206.

[3] Commonwealth v. Painter, 10 Penn. St. 214.

[4] Goddin v. Crump, 8 Leigh, 120; Bridgeport v. Housatonic Railroad Co., 15 Conn. 475; Thomas v. Leland, 24 Wend. 65; Clark v. Rochester, 24 Barb. 446; Benson v. Mayor, &c. of Albany, 24 Barb. 248; Corning v. Greene, 23 Barb. 33; Grant v. Courter, 24 Barb. 232; Starin v. Genoa, 29 Barb. 442, and 23 N. Y. 439; Bank of Rome v. Village of Rome, 18 N. Y. 38; Prettyman v. Supervisors, &c., 19 Ill. 406; Robertson v. Rochford, 21 Ill. 451; Johnson v. Stack, 24 Ill. 75; Perkins v. Perkins, Ibid. 208; Bushnell v. Beloit, 10 Wis. 195; Clark v. Janesville, Ibid. 136; Mayor of Wetumpka v. Winter, 29 Ala. 651; Patterson v. Yuba, 13 Cal. 175; Blanding v. Burr, Ibid. 343; Hobart v. Supervisors, &c., 17 Cal. 23; Dubuque County v. Railroad Co., 4 Greene (Iowa), 1; State v. Bissell, Ibid. 328; Clapp v. Cedar County, 5 Iowa, 15; Gaines v. Robb, 8 Iowa, 193; McMillen v. Boyles, 6 Iowa, 304; Taylor v. Newberne, 2 Jones, Eq. 141; Caldwell v. Justices of Burke, 4 Jones, Eq. 323; Louisville, &c. Railroad Co. v. Davidson, 1 Sneed, 637; Nichol v. Mayor of Nashville, 9 Humph. 252; Railroad Co. v. Commissioners of Clinton Co., 1 Ohio, N. S. 77; Trustees of Paris v. Cherry, 8 Ohio, N. S. 564; Cass v. Dillon, 2 Ohio, N. S. 607; State v. Commissioners of Clinton Co., 6 Ohio, N. S. 280; State v. Van Horne, 7 Ohio, N. S. 327; State v. Trustees of Union, 8 Ohio, N. S. 394; Trustees, &c. v. Shoemaker, 12 Ohio, N. S. 624; State v. Commissioners of Hancock, 12 Ohio, N. S. 596; Commonwealth v. McWilliams, 11 Penn. St. 61; Sharpless v. Mayor, &c., 21 Penn. St. 147; Moers v. Reading, Ibid. 188; Talbot v. Dent, 9 B. Monr. 526; Slack v. Railroad Co., 13 B. Monr. 1; City of St. Louis v. Alexander, 23 Mo. 483; City of Aurora v. West, 9 Ind. 74; Cotton v. Commissioners of Leon, 6 Flor. 610; Copes v. Charleston, 10 Rich. 491; Commissioners of Knox County v. Aspinwall, 21 How. 539, and 24 How. 326; Same v. Wallace, 21 How. 547; Zabriske v. Railroad Co., 23 How. 381; Amey v. Mayor, &c., 24 How. 365; Gelpecke v. Dubuque, 1 Wal. 175; Thompson v. Lee County, 3 Wal. 327; Rogers v. Burlington, Ibid. 654; Butler v. Dunham, 27 Ill. 474; Gibbons v. Mobile & Great Northern Railroad Co., 36 Ala. 410.

reference to any municipal organization within the State may not also be done in reference to the State at large ? May not any law framed for the State at large be made conditional on its acceptance by the people at large, declared through the ballot-box ? If it is not unconstitutional to delegate to a single locality the power to decide whether it will be governed by a particular charter, must it not quite as clearly be within the power of the legislature to refer to the people at large, from whom all power is derived, the decision upon any proposed statute affecting the whole State ? And can that be called a delegation of power which consists only in the agent or trustee referring back to the principal the final decision in a case where the principal is the party concerned, and where perhaps there are questions of policy and propriety involved which no authority can decide so satisfactorily and so conclusively as the principal to whom they are referred.

If the decision of these questions is to depend upon the weight of judicial authority up to the present time, it must be held that there is no power to refer the adoption or rejection of a general law to the people of the State, any more than there is to refer it to any other authority. The prevailing doctrine in the courts appears to be, that, except in those cases where, by the constitution, the people have expressly reserved to themselves a power of decision, the function of legislation cannot be exercised by them, even to the extent of accepting or rejecting a law which has been framed for their consideration. " The exercise of this power by the people in other cases is not expressly and in terms prohibited by the constitution, but it is forbidden by necessary and unavoidable implication. The Senate and Assembly are the only bodies of men clothed with the power of general legislation. They possess the entire power, with the exception above stated. The people reserved no part of it to themselves [with that exception], and can therefore exercise it in no other case." It is therefore held that the legislature have no power to submit a proposed law to the people, nor have the people power to bind each other by acting upon it. They voluntarily surrendered that power when they adopted the constitution. The government of the State is democratic, but it is a representative democracy, and in passing general laws the people act only through their representatives in the legislature.[1]

[1] Per Ruggles, Ch. J. in Barto v. Himrod, 8 N. Y. 489. It is worthy of con-

Nor, it seems, can such legislation be sustained as legislation of a conditional character, whose force is to depend upon the happening of some future event, or upon some future change of circumstances. " The event or change of circumstances on which a law may be made to take effect must be such as, in the judgment of the legislature, affects the question of the expediency of the law ; an event on which the expediency of the law in the opinion of the law-makers depends. On this question of expediency, the legislature must exercise its own judgment definitively and finally. When a law is made to take effect upon the happening of such an event, the legislature in effect declare the law inexpedient if the event should not happen, but expedient if it should happen. They appeal to no other man or men to judge for them in relation to its present or future expediency. They exercise that power themselves, and then perform the duty which the constitution imposes upon them." But it was held that in the case of the submission of a proposed free-school law to the people, no such event or change of circumstances affecting the expediency of the law was expected to happen. The wisdom or expediency of the School Act, abstractly considered, did not depend on the vote of the people. If it was unwise or inexpedient before that vote was taken, it was equally so afterwards. The event on which the act was to take effect was nothing else than the vote of the people on the identical question which the constitution makes it the duty of the legislature itself to decide. The legislature has no power to make a statute dependent on such a

---

sideration, however, whether there is anything in the reference of a statute to the people for acceptance or rejection which is inconsistent with the representative system of government. To refer it to the people to frame and agree upon a statute for themselves would be equally impracticable and inconsistent with the representative system ; but to take the opinion of the people upon a bill already framed by representatives and submitted to them, is not only practicable, but is in precise accordance with the mode in which the constitution of the State is adopted, and with the action which is taken in many other cases. The representative in these cases has fulfilled precisely those functions which the people as a democracy could not fulfil ; and where the case has reached a stage when the body of the people can act without confusion, the representative has stepped aside to allow their opinion to be expressed. The legislature is not attempting in such a case to delegate its authority to a new agency, but the trustee, vested with a large discretionary authority, is taking the opinion of the principal upon the necessity, policy, or propriety of an act which is to govern the principal himself.

contingency, because it would be confiding to others that legislative discretion which they are bound to exercise themselves, and
which they cannot delegate or commit to any other man or men
to· be exercised.[1]

---

[1] Per Ruggles, Ch. J. in Barto v. Himrod, 8 N. Y. 490. And see Santo v.
State, 2 Iowa, 165 ; State v. Beneke, 9 Iowa, 203 ; State v. Swisher, 17 Texas,
441 ; State v. Field, 17 Mo. 529 ; Bank of Chenango v. Brown, 26 N. Y. 470 ;
People v. Stout, 23 Barb. 349. But upon this point there is great force in what
is said by Redfield, Ch. J. in State v. Parker, 26 Vt. 357 : "If the operation of
a law may fairly be made to depend upon a future contingency, then, in my apprehension, it makes no essential difference what is the nature of the contingency,
so it be an equal and fair one, a moral and legal one, not opposed to sound policy, and so far connected with the object and purpose of the statute as not to be
a mere idle and arbitrary one. And to us the contingency, upon which the present statute was to be suspended until another legislature should meet and have
opportunity of reconsidering it, was not only proper and legal, and just and
moral, but highly commendable and creditable to the legislature who passed the
statute ; for at the very threshold of inquiry into the expediency of such a law
lies the other and more important inquiry, Are the people prepared for such a
law ? Can it be successfully enforced ? These questions being answered in the
affirmative, he must be a bold man who would even vote against the law ; and
something more must he be who would, after it had been passed with that assur-
ance, be willing to embarrass its operation or rejoice at its defeat.

"After a full examination of the arguments by which it is attempted to be
sustained that statutes made dependent upon such contingencies are not valid
laws, and a good deal of study and reflection, and I must declare that I am fully
convinced — although at first, without much examination, somewhat inclined to
the same opinion — that the opinion is the result of false analogies, and so founded
upon a latent fallacy. It seems to me that the distinction attempted between
the contingency of a popular vote and other future contingencies is without all
just foundation in sound policy or sound reasoning, and that it has too often been
made more from necessity than choice, — rather to escape from an overwhelming
analogy than from any obvious difference in principle in the two classes of cases ;
for . . . . one may find any number of cases in the legislation of Congress, where
statutes have been made dependent upon the shifting character of the revenue
laws, or the navigation laws, or commercial rules, edicts, or restrictions of other
countries. In some, perhaps, these laws are made by representative bodies, or,
it may be, by the people of these states, and in others by the lords of the treasury, or the boards of trade, or by the proclamation of the sovereign ; and in all
these cases no question can be made of the perfect legality of our acts of Congress
being made dependent upon such contingencies. It is, in fact, the only possible
mode of meeting them, unless Congress is kept constantly in session. The same
is true of acts of Congress by which power is vested in the President to levy
troops or draw money from the public treasury, upon the contingency of a declaration or an act of war committed by some foreign state, empire, kingdom, prince,
or potentate. If these illustrations are not sufficient to show the fallacy of the

The same reasons which preclude the original enactment of a law from being referred to the people would render it equally incompetent to refer to their decision the question, whether an existing law should be repealed. If the one is " a plain surrender to the people of the law-making power," so also is the other.[1] It would seem, however, that if a legislative act is, by its terms, to take effect in any contingency, it is not unconstitutional to make the *time* when it shall take effect depend upon the event of a popular vote being for or against it, — the time of its going into operation being postponed to a later day in the latter contingency.[2] It would also seem that if the question of the acceptance or rejection of a municipal charter can be referred to the voters of the locality specially interested, it would be equally competent to refer to them the question whether a State law establishing a particular police regulation should be of force in such locality or not. Municipal charters refer most questions of local government, including police regulations, to the local authorities; on the supposition that they are better able to decide for themselves upon the needs, as well as the sentiments, of their constituents, than the legislature possibly can be, and are therefore more competent to judge what local regulations are important, and also how far the local sentiment will assist in their enforcement. The same reasons would apply in favor of allowing the people of the locality to accept or reject for themselves a particular police regulation, since this is only allowing them less extensive powers of local government than a municipal charter would confer; and the fact that the rule of law on that subject might be different in different

argument, more would not avail." See also State *v.* Noyes, 10 Fost. 292 ; Bull *v.* Read, 13 Grat. 78 ; Johnson *v.* Rich, 9 Barb. 680 ; State *v.* Reynolds, 5 Gilm. 1 ; Robinson *v.* Bidwell, 22 Cal. 349.

[1] Geebrick *v.* State, 5 Iowa, 491 ; Rice *v.* Foster, 4 Harr. 492 ; Parker *v.* Commonwealth, 6 Penn. St. 507.

[2] State *v.* Parker, 26 Vt. 357. The act under consideration in that case was, by its terms, to take effect on the second Tuesday of March after its passage, unless the people, to whose votes it was submitted, should declare against it, in which case it should take effect in the following December. The case was distinguished from Barto *v.* Himrod, 8 N. Y. 483, and the act sustained. At the same time the court express their dissent from the reasoning upon which the New York case rests. In People *v.* Collins, 3 Mich. 343, the court was equally divided in a case similar to that in Vermont, except that in the Michigan case the law, which was passed and submitted to the people in 1853, was not to go into effect until 1870, if the vote of the people was against it.

localities, according as the people accepted or rejected the regulation, would not seem to affect the principle, when the same result is brought about by the different regulations which municipal corporations establish for themselves in the exercise of an undisputed authority.[1] The current of authority, however, is perhaps against the constitutionality of any such reference.

The legislature of Delaware, in 1847, passed an act to authorize the citizens of the several counties of the State to decide by ballot whether the license to retail intoxicating liquors should be permitted. By this act a general election was to be held: and if a majority of votes in any county should be cast against license, it should not thereafter be lawful for any person to retail intoxicating liquors within such county ; but if the majority should be cast in favor of license, then licenses might be granted in the county so voting, in the manner and under the regulations in said act prescribed. The Court of Errors and Appeals of that State held this act void, as an attempted delegation of the trust to make laws, and upon the same reasons which support the cases before cited, where acts have been held void which referred to the people of the State for approval a law of general application.[2] The same decision was made near the same time by the Supreme

---

[1] In New Hampshire a statute was passed making bowling-alleys, situate within twenty-five rods of a dwelling-house, nuisances ; but the statute was to be in force only in those towns in which it should be adopted in town meeting. In State v. Noyes, 10 Fost. 293, this act was held to be constitutional. " Assuming," say the court, " that the legislature has the right to confer the power of local regulation upon cities and towns, that is, the power to pass ordinances and by-laws, in such terms and with such provisions, in the classes of cases to which the power extends, as they may think proper, it seems to us hardly possible seriously to contend that the legislature may not confer the power to adopt within such municipality a law drawn up and framed by themselves. If they may pass a law authorizing towns to make ordinances to punish the keeping of billiard-rooms, bowling-alleys, and other places of gambling, they may surely pass laws to punish the same acts, subject to be adopted by the town before they can be of force in it." And it seems to us difficult to answer this reasoning, if it be confined to such laws as fall within the proper province of local government, and which are therefore usually referred to the judgment of the municipal authorities or their constituency. A similar question arose in Smith v. Village of Adrian, 1 Mich. 495, but was not decided. In Bank of Chenango v. Brown, 26 N. Y. 467, it was held competent to authorize the electors of an incorporated village to determine for themselves what sections of the general act for the incorporation of villages should apply to their village.

[2] Rice v. Foster, 4 Harr. 479.

Court of Pennsylvania,[1] followed afterwards in an elaborate opinion by the Supreme Court of Iowa.[2]

By statute in Indiana it was enacted that no person should retail spirituous liquors, except for sacramental, mechanical, chemical, medicinal, or culinary purposes, without the consent of the majority of the legal voters of the proper township who might cast their votes for license at the April election, nor without filing with the county auditor a bond as therein provided; upon the filing of which the auditor was to issue to the person filing the same a license to retail spirituous liquors, which was to be good for one year from the day of the election. This act was held void upon similar reasons to those above quoted.[3] This case follows the decisions in Pennsylvania and Delaware,[4] and it has since been followed by another decision of the Supreme Court of that State, except that while in the first case only that portion of the statute which provided for submission to the people was held void, in the later case that unconstitutional provision was held to affect the whole statute with infirmity, and render the whole invalid.[5]

Irrepealable Laws.

Similar reasons to those which forbid the legislative department of the State from delegating its authority will also forbid its passing any irrepealable law. The constitution, in conferring the legislative authority, has prescribed to its exercise any limitations which the people saw fit to impose; and no other power than the people can superadd other limitations. To say that the legislature may pass irrepealable laws, is to say that it may alter the very constitution from which it derives its authority; since in so far as one legislature could bind a subsequent one by its enactments, it could in the same degree reduce the legislative power of its successors, and the process might be repeated until, one by one, the subjects of legislation would be excluded altogether from their control, and the constitutional provision, that the

---

[1] Parker v. Commonwealth, 6 Penn. St. 507.

[2] Geebrick v. State, 5 Iowa, 495.

[3] Maize v. State, 4 Ind. 342.

[4] Parker v. Commonwealth, 6 Penn. St. 507; Rice v. Foster, 4 Harr. 479. See also State v. Field, 17 Mo. 529; Commonwealth v. McWilliams, 11 Penn. St. 61; State v. Copeland, 3 R. I. 33.

[5] Meshmeier v. State, 11 Ind. 484.

legislative power shall be vested in two houses, would be to a greater or less degree rendered ineffectual.[1]

" Acts of Parliament," says Blackstone, " derogatory to the power of subsequent Parliaments, bind not ; so the statute 11 Henry VII. ch. 1, which directs that no person for assisting a king *de facto* shall be attainted of treason by act of Parliament or otherwise, is held to be good only as to common prosecutions for high treason, but it will not restrain or clog any parliamentary attainder. Because the legislature, being in truth the sovereign power, is always of equal, and always of absolute authority ; it acknowledges no superior upon earth, which the prior legislature must have been if its ordinances could bind a subsequent Parliament. And upon the same principle, Cicero, in his letters to Atticus, treats with a proper contempt those restraining clauses which endeavor to tie up the hands of succeeding legislatures. ' When you repeal the law itself,' says he, ' you at the same time repeal the prohibitory clause which guards against such repeal.' " [2]

Although this reasoning does not in all its particulars apply to the American legislatures, the principle applicable in each case is the same. There is a modification of the principle, however, by an important provision of the Constitution of the United States, forbidding the State from passing any laws impairing the obligation of contracts. Legislative acts are sometimes in substance contracts between the State and the party who is to derive some right under them, and they are not the less under the protection of the clause quoted because of having assumed this form. Charters of incorporation, except those of a municipal character, — and which as we have already seen are mere agencies of govern-

---

[1] " Unlike the decision of a court, a legislative act does not bind a subsequent legislature. Each body possesses the same power, and has a right to exercise the same discretion. Measures, though often rejected, may receive legislative sanction. There is no mode by which a legislative act can be made irrepealable, except it assume the form and substance of a contract. If in any line of legislation, a permanent character could be given to acts, the most injurious consequences would result to the country. Its policy would become fixed and unchangeable on great national interests, which might retard, if not destroy, the public prosperity. Every legislative body, unless restricted by the constitution, may modify or abolish the acts of its predecessors ; whether it would be wise to do so is a matter for legislative discretion." Bloomer v. Stolley, 5 McLean, 161. In Kellogg v. Oshkosh, 14 Wis. 623, it was held that one legislature could not bind a future one to a particular mode of repeal.

[2] 1 Bl. Com. 90.

ment, — are held to be contracts between the State and the corporators, and not subject to modification or change by the act of the State alone, except as may be authorized by the terms of the charters themselves.[1]   And it now seems to be settled, by the decisions of the Supreme Court of the United States, that a State, by contract to that effect, based upon a consideration, may exempt the property of an individual or corporation from taxation for any specified period or permanently.   And it is also settled, by the same decisions, that where a charter containing an exemption from taxes, or an agreement that the taxes shall be to a specified amount only, is accepted by the corporators, the exemption is presumed to be upon sufficient consideration, and consequently binding upon the State.[2]

Territorial Limitation to State Legislative Authority.

'The legislative authority of every State must spend its force

[1] Dartmouth College v. Woodward, 4 Wheat. 518 ; Planters' Bank v. Sharp, 6 How. 301.

[2] Gordon v. Appeal Tax Court, 3 How. 133 ; New Jersey v. Wilson, 7 Cranch, 164 ; Piqua Branch Bank v. Knoop, 16 How. 369 ; Ohio Life Ins. and Trust Co. v. Debolt, 16 How. 416, 432 ; Dodge v. Woolsey, 18 How. 331 ; Mechanics and Traders' Bank v. Debolt, 18 How. 381 ; Jefferson Branch Bank v. Skelly, 1 Black, 436.   See also Hunsaker v. Wright, 30 Ill. 146 ; Spooner v. McConnell, 1 McLean, 347.   The right of a State legislature to grant away the right of taxation, which is one of the essential attributes of sovereignty, has been strenuously denied. Debolt v. Ohio Life Ins. and Trust Co., 1 Ohio, N. S. 563 ; Mechanics and Traders' Bank v. Debolt, Ibid. 591 ; Brewster v. Hough, 10 N. H. 143 ; Mott v. Pennsylvania Railroad Co., 30 Penn. St. 9.   And see Thorpe v. Rutland and B. Railroad Co., 27 Vt. 146.   In Brick Presbyterian Church v. Mayor, &c. of New York, 5 Cow. 538, it was held that a municipal corporation had no power as a party to make a contract which should control or embarrass its discharge of legislative duties.   In Coats v. Mayor, &c. of New York, 7 Cow. 585, it was decided that though a municipal corporation grant lands for cemetery purposes, and covenant for their quiet enjoyment, it will not thereby be estopped afterwards to forbid the use of the land, by by-law, for that purpose, when such use becomes or is likely to become a nuisance.   See also, on the same subject, Morgan v. Smith, 4 Minn. 104 ; Hamrick v. Rouse, 17 Geo. 56, where it was held that the legislature could not bind its successors not to remove a county seat ; Bass v. Fontleroy, 11 Texas, 698 ; Shaw v. Macon, 21 Geo. 280 ; Regents of University v. Williams, 9 G. & J. 390 ; Mott v. Pennsylvania Railroad Co., 30 Penn. St. 9.   In Bank of Republic v. Hamilton, 21 Ill. 53, it was held that, in construing a statute, it will not be intended that the legislature designed to abandon its right as to taxation.   This subject will be referred to again in the chapter on the Eminent Domain.

within the territorial limits of the State. The legislature of one
State cannot make laws by which people outside the State must
govern their actions, except as they may have occasion to resort
to the remedies which the State provides, or to deal with property
situated within the State. It can have no authority upon the
high seas beyond State lines, because there is the point of contact with other nations, and all international questions belong to
the national government.[1] It cannot provide for the punishment
as crimes of acts committed beyond the State boundary, because
such acts, if offences at all, must be offences against the sovereignty within whose limits they have been done.[2] But if the
consequences of an unlawful act committed outside the State
have reached their ultimate and injurious result within it, it
seems that the perpetrator may be punished as an offender against
such State.[3]

Other Limitations of Legislative Authority.

Besides the limitations of legislative authority to which we
have referred, others exist which do not seem to call for special
remark. Some of these are prescribed by constitutions,[4] but

---

[1] 1 Bish. Cr. Law, § 120.

[2] State v. Knight, 2 Hayw. 109 ; People v. Merrill, 2 Park. Cr. R. 590 ; Adams
v. People, 1 N. Y. 173 ; Tyler v. People, 8 Mich. 320 ; Morrissey v. People, 11
Mich. 327 ; Bromley v. People, 7 Mich. 472 ; State v. Main, 16 Wis. 398.

[3] In Tyler v. People, 8 Mich. 320, it was held constitutional to punish in Michigan a homicide committed by a mortal blow in Canadian waters, from which death
resulted in the State. In Morrissey v. People, 11 Mich. 327, the court was divided on the question whether the State could lawfully provide for the punishment of persons who, having committed larceny abroad, brought the stolen
property within the State. And see Bromley v. People, 7 Mich. 472 ; State v.
Main, 16 Wis. 398.

[4] The restrictions upon State legislative authority are much more extensive
in some constitutions than in others. The constitution of Missouri has the following provision : " The General Assembly shall not pass special laws divorcing any
named parties, or declaring any named person of age, or authorizing any named
minor to sell, lease, or encumber his or her property, or providing for the sale of
the real estate of any named minor or other person laboring under legal disability, by any executor, administrator, guardian, trustee, or other person, or
establishing, locating, altering the course, or effecting the construction of roads,
or the building or repairing of bridges, or establishing, altering, or vacating any
street, avenue, or alley in any city or town, or extending the time for the assessment or collection of taxes, or otherwise relieving any assessor or collector of

others spring from the very nature of free government. The latter must depend for their enforcement upon legislative wisdom, discretion, and conscience. The legislature is to make laws for the public good, and not for the benefit of individuals. It has control of the public moneys, and should provide for disbursing them only for public purposes. Taxes should only be levied for those purposes which properly constitute a public burden. But what is for the public good, and what are public purposes, and what does properly constitute a public burden, are questions which the legislature must decide upon its own judgment, and in respect to which it is vested with a large discretion which cannot be controlled by the courts, except perhaps where its action is clearly evasive, and where, under pretence of a lawful authority, it has assumed to exercise one that is unlawful. Where the power which is exercised is legislative in its character, the courts can enforce only those limitations which the constitution imposes, and not those implied restrictions which, resting in theory only, the people have been satisfied to leave to the judgment, patriotism, and sense of justice of their representatives.

taxes from the due performance of his official duties, or giving effect to informal or invalid wills or deeds, or legalizing, except as against the State, the unauthorized or invalid acts of any officer, or granting to any individual or company the right to lay down railroad tracks in the streets of any city or town, or exempting any property of any named person or corporation from taxation. The General Assembly shall pass no special law for any case for which provision can be made by a general law, but shall pass general laws providing, so far as it may deem necessary, for the cases enumerated in this section, and for all other cases where a general law can be made applicable." Constitution of Missouri, art. 4, § 27. See Thomas v. Board of Commissioners, 5 Ind. 4, for a decision under a similar clause. We should suppose that so stringent a provision would, in some of these cases, lead to the passage of general laws of doubtful utility in order to remedy the hardships of particular cases. As to when a general law can be made applicable, see Thomas v. Board of Commissioners, 5 Ind. 4 ; Johnson v. Railroad Co. 23 Ill. 202. In State v. Hitchcock, 1 Kansas, 178, it was held that the constitutional provision, that " in all cases where a general law can be made applicable, no special law shall be enacted," left a discretion with the legislature to determine the cases in which special laws should be passed.

CHAPTER VI.

OF THE ENACTMENT OF LAWS.

WHEN the supreme power of a country is wielded by a single man, or by a single body of men, few questions can arise in the courts concerning the manner of its exercise, and any discussion of rules by which it is to be governed, in the enactment of laws, can be of very little practical value. For whenever the sovereign power expresses its will that a certain rule shall be established, that expression must be conclusive, whether such forms have been observed in making the declaration as are customary and proper or not. We may query whether the will has been declared; we may question and cross-question the words employed, to ascertain the real sense that they express; we may doubt and hesitate as to the intent; but when discovered, it must govern, and it is idle to talk of forms that should have surrounded the expression, but do not. But when the legislative power of a State is to be exercised by a department composed of two branches, or as, in most of the American States, of three branches, and these branches have their several duties marked out and prescribed by the law to which they owe their origin, and which provides for the exercise of their powers in certain modes and under certain forms, there are other questions to arise than those of the mere intent of the law-makers, and sometimes forms become of the last importance. For not only is it essential that the will of the law-makers be expressed, but it is also essential that it be expressed in due form of law; since nothing is law simply and solely because the legislators will that it shall be, unless they have expressed their determination to that effect, in the mode pointed out by the instrument which invests them with the power, and under all the forms which that instrument has rendered essential. And if, when the constitution was adopted, there were known and settled rules and usages, forming a part of the law of the country, in reference to which the constitution has evidently been framed, and these rules and usages required the observance of particular forms, the constitution itself must also be understood as requiring them, because, in assuming the existence of such laws and usages, and being framed with reference to them, it has in effect adopted them as a part of itself, as much as if they were expressly incorporated in its provisions. Where, for an instance, the legislative power is to be exercised by two houses, and by settled and well-understood parliamentary law, these two houses are to hold separate sessions for their deliberations, and the determination of the one upon a proposed law is to be submitted to the separate determination of the other, the constitution, in providing for two houses, has evidently spoken in reference to this settled custom, incorporating it as a rule of constitutional interpretation ; so that it would require no prohibitory clause to forbid the two houses from combining in one, and jointly enacting laws by the vote of a majority of all. All those rules which are of the essentials of law-making must be observed and followed ; and it is only the customary rules of order and routine, such as in every deliberative body are always understood to be under its control, and subject to constant change at its will, that the constitution can be understood to have left as matters of discretion, to be established, modified, or abolished by the bodies for whose government in non-essential matters they exist.

Of the two Houses of the Legislature.[1]

In the enactment of laws the two houses of the legislature are of equal importance, dignity, and power, and the steps which result in laws may originate indifferently in either. This is the general rule ; but as one body is more numerous than the other and more directly represents the people, and in many of the States, is renewed more often by elections, the power to originate all money bills, or bills for the raising of revenue, is left exclusively, by the constitutions of some of the States, with this body, in accordance with the custom in England which does not permit bills of this character to originate with the House of Lords.[2] To these

---

[1] The wisdom of a division of the legislative department has been demonstrated by the leading writers on constitutional law, as well as by general experience. See De Lolme, Const. of England, b. 2, ch. 3 ; Federalist, No. 22 ; 1 Kent, 208 ; Story on Const. §§ 545 – 570. The early experiments in Pennsylvania and Georgia, based on Franklin's views, for which see his Works, vol. 5, p. 165, are the only ones made by any of the American States with a single house.

[2] There are provisions in the constitutions of Alabama, Massachusetts, Delaware, Minnesota, Mississippi, New Hampshire, New Jersey, Pennsylvania, South Carolina, Vermont, Indiana, Oregon, Kentucky, Louisiana, and Maine, requiring

bills, however, the other house may propose alterations, and they require the assent of that house to their passage, the same as other bills. The time for the meeting of the legislature will be such time as is fixed by the constitution or by statute ; but it may be called together by the executive in special session as the constitution may prescribe, and the two houses may also adjourn any general session to a time fixed by them for the holding of a special session, if an agreement to that effect can be arrived at; and if not, power is conferred by a majority of the constitutions upon the executive to prorogue and adjourn them. And if the executive in any case undertake to exercise this power to prorogue and adjourn, on the assumption that a disagreement exists between the two houses which warrants his interference, and his action is acquiesced in by those bodies, who thereupon cease to hold their regular sessions, the legislature must be held in law to have adjourned, and no inquiry can be entered upon as to the rightfulness of the governor's assumption that such a disagreement existed.[1]

revenue bills to originate in the more popular branch of the legislature, but allowing the Senate the power of amendment usual in other cases. In England the Lords are not allowed to amend money bills, and by resolutions of 5th and 6th July, 1860, the Commons deny their right even to reject them.

[1] This question became important and was passed upon in People v. Hatch, 33 Ill. 9. The Senate had passed a resolution for an adjournment of the session *sine die* on a day named, which was amended by the house by fixing a different day. The Senate refused to concur, and the House then passed a resolution expressing a desire to recede from its action in amending the resolution, and requesting a return of the resolution by the Senate. While matters stood thus, the governor, assuming that such a disagreement existed as empowered him to interfere, sent in his proclamation, declaring the legislature adjourned to a day named, and which was at the very end of the official term of the members. The message created excitement; it does not seem to have been at once acquiesced in, and a protest against the governor's authority was entered upon the journal; but for eleven days in one house and twelve in the other no entries were made upon their journals, and it was unquestionable that practically they had acquiesced in the action of the governor, and adjourned. At the expiration of the twelve days, a portion of the members came together again, and it was claimed by them that the message of the governor was without authority, and the two houses must be considered as having been, in point of law, in session during the intervening period, and that consequently any bills which had before been passed by them and sent to the governor for his approval, and which he had not returned within ten days, Sundays excepted, had become laws under the constitution. The Supreme Court held that, as the two houses had practically asquiesced in the action of the governor, the session had come to an end, and that the mem-

There are certain matters which each house determines for itself, and in respect to which its decision is conclusive. It chooses its own officers, except where, by constitution or statute, it is otherwise provided ; it determines its own rules of proceeding, it decides upon the election and qualification of its own members.[1] These powers it is obviously proper should rest with the body immediately interested, as essential to enable it to enter upon and proceed with its legislative functions, without liability to interruption and confusion. In determining questions concerning contested seats, the house will exercise judicial power, but generally in accordance with a course of practice which has sprung from precedents in similar cases, and no other authority is at liberty to interfere.

Each house has also the power to punish members for disorderly behavior, and other contempts of its authority, and also to expel a member for any cause which seems to the body to render it unfit that he continue to occupy one of its seats. This power is sometimes conferred by the constitution, but it exists whether expressly conferred or not. It is " a necessary and incidental power, to enable the house to perform its high functions, and is necessary to the safety of the State. It is a power of protection. A member may be physically, mentally, or morally wholly unfit ; he may be affected with a contagious disease, or insane, or noisy, violent, and disorderly, or in the habit of using profane, obscene, and abusive language." And, " independently of parliamentary customs and usages, our legislative houses have the power to protect themselves by the punishment and expulsion of a member " ; and the courts cannot inquire into the justice of the decision, or look into the proceedings to see whether opportunity for defence was furnished or not.[2]

bers had no power to re-convene on their own motion, as had been attempted. The case is a very full and valuable one on several points pertaining to legislative proceedings and authority.

[1] In People v. Mahaney, 13 Mich. 481, it was held that the correctness of a decision by one of the houses, that certain persons had been chosen members, could not be inquired into by the courts. In that case a law was assailed as void, on the ground that a portion of the members who voted for it, and without whose votes it would not have had the requisite majority, had been given their seats in the House in defiance of law, and to the exclusion of others who had a majority of legal votes. See the same principle in State v. Jarrett, 17 Md. 309. See also Lamb v. Lynd, 44 Penn. St. 336.

[2] Hiss v. Bartlett, 3 Gray, 468. And see Anderson v. Dunn, 6 Wheat. 204.

Each house may also punish contempts of its authority by other persons, whether express authority is conferred by the constitution or not;[1] but where imprisonment is imposed as a punishment, it must terminate with the final adjournment of the house, and if the prisoner be not then discharged by its order, he may be released on habeas corpus.[2]

By common parliamentary law, the members of the legislature are privileged from arrest on civil process during the session of that body, and for a reasonable time before and after to enable them to go to and return from the same. By the constitutions of some of the States this privilege has been enlarged, so as to exempt the persons of legislators from any service of civil process,[3] and in others their estates are exempt from attachment for some prescribed period.[4] For any arrest contrary to the parliamentary law or to these provisions, the house of which the person arrested is a member may give summary relief by ordering his discharge, and if the order is not complied with, by punishing the persons concerned in the arrest as for a contempt of its authority. The remedy of the party, however, is not confined to this mode of relief. His privilege is not the privilege of the house merely, but of the people, and to enable him to discharge the trust confided to him by his constituents;[5] and if the house neglected to interfere, the court from which the process issued· should set it aside on the facts being represented, and any court or officer having authority to issue writs of habeas corpus might also in-

---

[1] Anderson v. Dunn, 6 Wheat. 204; Burdett v. Abbott, 14 East, 1; Stockdale v. Hansard, 9 Ad. & El. 231; Burnham v. Morrissey, 14 Gray, 226; State v. Matthews, 37 N. H. 450.

[2] Jefferson's Manual, § 18; Prichard's case, 1 Lev. 165.

[3] " Senators and representatives shall, in all cases except treason, felony, or breach of the peace, be privileged from arrest. They shall not be subject to any civil process during the session of the legislature, or for fifteen days next before the commencement and after the termination of each session." Const. of Mich. art. 4, § 7. The same exemption from civil process is found in the constitution of Kansas, art. 2, § 22, and in that of Nebraska, art. 2, § 15.

[4] The constitution of Rhode Island provides that " the person of every member of the General Assembly shall be exempt from arrest, and his estate from attachment, in any civil action, during the session of the General Assembly, and two days before the commencement and two days after the termination thereof, and all process served contrary hereto shall be void." Art. 4, § 5.

[5] Coffin v. Coffin, 4 Mass. 27.

quire into the case, and release the party from the unlawful imprisonment.[1]

Each house must also be allowed to proceed in its own way in the collection of such information as may seem important to a proper discharge of its functions; and whenever it is deemed desirable that witnesses should be examined, the power and authority to do so is very properly referred to a committee, with any such powers short of final legislative or judicial action as may seem necessary or expedient in the particular case. Such a committee has no authority to sit during a recess of the house which has appointed it, without its permission to that effect; but the house is at liberty to confer such authority if it see fit.[2] A refusal to appear or to testify before such committee, or to produce books or papers, would be a contempt of the house;[3] but the committee cannot punish for contempts; it can only report the conduct of the offending party to the house for its action. The power of the committee will terminate with the final dissolution of the house appointing it.

Each house keeps a journal of its proceedings, which is a public record, and of which the courts are at liberty to take judicial notice.[4] If it should appear from these journals that any act did not receive the requisite majority, or that in respect to it the legislature did not follow any requirement of the constitution, or that in any other respect the act was not constitutionally adopted, the courts may act upon this evidence, and adjudge the statute void.[5] But whenever it is acting in the apparent performance of legal functions, every reasonable presumption is to be made in favor of the action of a legislative body; it will not be presumed in any case, from the mere silence of the journals, that either house has exceeded its authority, or disregarded a consti-

---

[1] On this subject, Cushing on Law and Practice of Parliamentary Assemblies, §§ 546 – 597, will be consulted with profit.

[2] Branham v. Lange, 16 Ind. 497; Marshall v. Harwood, 7 Md. 466. See also parliamentary cases, 5 Grey, 374; 9 Grey, 350; 1 Chandler, 50.

[3] Burnham v. Morrissey, 14 Grey, 226.

[4] Spangler v. Jacoby, 14 Ill. 297; Miller v. State, 3 Ohio, N. S. 475; People v. Mahaney, 13 Mich. 481; Southwark Bank v. Commonwealth, 2 Penn. St. 446; McCulloch v. State, 11 Ind. 430; State v. Moffitt, 5 Ohio, 358; Turley v. Logan Co., 17 Ill. 151; People v. Supervisors of Chenango, 8 N. Y. 317.

[5] See cases cited in preceding note. Also Prescott v. Trustees of Ill. & Mich. Canal, 19 Ill. 324.

tutional requirement in the passage of legislative acts, unless where the constitution has expressly required the journals to show the action taken, as, for instance, where it requires the yeas and nays to be entered.[1]

The law also seeks to cast its protection around legislative sessions, and to shield them against corrupt and improper influences, by making void all contracts which have for their object to influence legislation in any other manner than by such open and public presentation of facts and arguments and appeals to reason as are recognized as proper and legitimate with all public bodies. While counsel may be properly employed to present the reasons in favor of any public measure to the body authorized to pass upon it, or to any of its committees empowered to collect facts and hear arguments, and parties interested may lawfully contract to pay for this service, yet the secret approach of members of such a body with a view to influence their action, at a time and in a manner that do not allow the presentation of opposite views, is improper and unfair to the opposing interest; and a contract to pay for this irregular and improper service would not be enforced by the law.[2]

---

[1] Miller *v.* State, 3 Ohio, N. S. 475; McCulloch *v.* State, 11 Ind. 424; Supervisors *v.* People, 25 Ill. 181.

[2] This whole subject was very fully considered in the case of Frost *v.* Inhabitants of Belmont, 6 Allen, 152, which was a bill filed to restrain the payment by the town of demands to the amount of nearly $ 9,000, which the town had voted to pay as expenses in obtaining their act of incorporation. By the court, Chapman, J.: " It is to be regretted that any persons should have attempted to procure an act of legislation in this commonwealth by such means as some of these items indicate. By the regular course of legislation, organs are provided through which any parties may fairly and openly approach the legislature, and be heard with proofs and arguments respecting any legislative acts which they may be interested in, whether public or private. These organs are the various committees appointed to consider and report upon the matters to be acted upon by the whole body. When private interests are to be affected, notice is given of the hearings before these committees; and thus opportunity is given to adverse parties to meet face to face and obtain a fair and open hearing. And though these committees properly dispense with many of the rules which regulate hearings before judicial tribunals, yet common fairness requires that neither party shall be permitted to have secret consultations, and exercise secret influences that are kept from the knowledge of the other party. The business of ' lobby members ' is not to go fairly and openly before the committees, and present statements, proofs, and arguments that the other side has an opportunity to meet and refute, if they are wrong, but to go secretly to the members and ply them with statements and argu-

The Introduction and Passage of Bills.

Any member may introduce a bill in the house to which he belongs, in accordance with its rules; and this he may do at any

ments that the other side cannot openly meet, however erroneous they may be, and to bring illegitimate influences to bear upon them. If the 'lobby member' is selected because of his political or personal influence, it aggravates the wrong. If his business is to unite various interests by means of projects that are called ' log rolling,' it is still worse. The practice of procuring members of the legislature to act under the influence of what they have eaten and drank at houses of entertainment tends to render those who yield to such influences wholly unfit to act in such cases. They are disqualified from acting fairly towards interested parties or towards the public. The tendency and object of these influences are to obtain by corruption what it is supposed cannot be obtained fairly.

" It is a well-established principle, that all contracts which are opposed to public policy, and to open, upright, and fair dealing, are illegal and void. The principle was fully discussed in Fuller v. Dame, 18 Pick. 472. In several other States it has been applied to cases quite analogous to the present case.

" In Pingrey v. Washburn, 1 Aiken, 264, it was held in Vermont that an agreement, on the part of a corporation, to grant to individuals certain privileges in consideration that they would withdraw their opposition to the passage of a legislative act touching the interests of the corporation, is against sound policy, prejudicial to just and correct legislation, and void. In Gulick v. Ward, 5 Halst. 87, it was decided in New Jersey that a contract which contravenes an act of Congress, and tends to defraud the United States, is void. A had agreed to give B $100, on condition that B would forbear to propose or offer himself to the Postmaster-General to carry the mail on a certain mail route, and it was held that the contract was against public policy and void. The general principle as to contracts contravening public policy was discussed in that case at much length. In Wood v. McCann, 6 Dana, 366, the defendant had employed the plaintiff to assist him in obtaining a legislative act in Kentucky legalizing his divorce from a former wife, and his marriage with his present wife. The court say : ' A lawyer may be entitled to compensation for writing a petition, or even for making a public argument before the legislature or a committee thereof; but the law should not hold him or any other person to a recompense for exercising any personal influence in any way, in any act of legislation. It is certainly important to just and wise legislation, and therefore to the most essential interest of the public, that the legislature should be perfectly free from any extraneous influence which may either corrupt or deceive the members, or any of them.'

" In Clippinger v. Hepbaugh, 5 Watts & S. 315, it was decided in Pennsylvania that a contract to procure or endeavor to procure the passage of an act of the legislature, by using personal influence with the members, or by any sinister means, was void, as being inconsistent with public policy and the integrity of our political institutions. And an agreement for a contingent fee to be paid on the passage of a legislative act was held to be illegal and void, because it would be

time when the house is in session, unless the constitution, the law, or the rules of the house forbid.   The constitution of Michigan

a strong incentive to the exercise of personal and sinister influences to effect the object.

" The subject has been twice adjudicated upon in New York. In Harris *v.* Roof, 10 Barb. 489, the Supreme Court held that one could not recover for services performed in going to see individual members of the house, to get them to aid in voting for a private claim, the services not being performed before the house as a body, nor before its authorized committees. In Sedgwick *v.* Stanton, 4 Kernan, 289, the Court of Appeals held the same doctrine, and stated its proper limits. Selden, J., makes the following comments on the case of Harris *v.* Roof : ' Now the court did not mean by this decision to hold that one who has a claim against the State may not employ competent persons to aid him in properly presenting such claim to the legislature, and in supporting it with the necessary proofs and arguments. Mr. Justice Hand, who delivered the opinion of the court, very justly distinguishes between services of the nature of those rendered in that case, and the procuring and preparing the necessary documents in support of a claim, or acting as counsel before the legislature or some committee appointed by that body. Persons may, no doubt, be employed to conduct an application to the legislature, as well as to conduct a suit at law ; and may contract for and receive pay for their services in preparing documents, collecting evidence, making statements of facts, or preparing and making oral or written arguments, provided all these are used or designed to be used before the legislature or some committee thereof as a body; but they cannot, with propriety, be employed to exert their personal influence with individual members, or to labor in any form privately with such members out of the legislative halls. Whatever is laid before the legislature in writing, or spoken openly or publicly in its presence or that of a committee, if false in fact, may be disproved, or if wrong in argument may be refuted; but that which is whispered into the private ear of individual members is frequently beyond the reach of correction. The point of objection in this class of cases then is, the personal and private nature of the services to be rendered.'

" In Fuller *v.* Dame, cited above, Shaw, Ch. J., recognizes the well-established right to contract and pay for professional services when the promissee is to act as attorney and counsel, but remarks that ' the fact appearing that persons do so act prevents any injurious effects from such proceeding. Such counsel is considered as standing in the place of his principal, and his arguments and representations are weighed and considered accordingly.' He also admits the right of disinterested persons to volunteer advice ; as when a person is about to make a will, one may represent to him the propriety and expediency of making a bequest to a particular person ; and so may one volunteer advice to another to marry another person ; but a promise to pay for such service is void.

" Applying the principles stated in these cases to the bills which the town voted to pay, it is manifest that some of the money was expended for objects that are contrary to public policy, and of a most reprehensible character, and which could not, therefore, form a legal consideration for a contract."

See further a full discussion of the same subject, and reaching the same conclusion, by Mr. Justice Grier, in Marshall *v.* Baltimore & Ohio R. R. Co., 16 How. 314.   See also Hatzfield *v.* Gulden, 7 Watts, 152.

provides that no new bill shall be introduced into either house of the legislature after the first fifty days of the session shall have expired;[1] and the constitution of Maryland provides that no bill shall originate in either house within the last ten days of the session.[2] The purpose of these clauses is to prevent hasty and improvident legislation, and to compel, so far as any previous law can accomplish that result, the careful examination of proposed laws, or at least the affording of opportunity for that purpose; which will not always be done when bills may be introduced up to the very hour of adjournment, and, with the concurrence of the proper majority, put immediately upon their passage.[3]

For the same reason it is required by the constitutions of several of the States, that no bill shall have the force of law until on three several days it be read in each house, and free discussion allowed thereon; unless, in case of urgency, four fifths or some other specified majority of the house shall deem it expedient to dispense with this rule. The journals which each house keeps of its proceedings ought to show whether this rule is complied with or not; but in case they do not, the passage in the manner provided by the constitution must be presumed, in accordance with the general rule which presumes the proper discharge of official duty.[4]

---

[1] Art. 4, § 28.

[2] Art. 3, § 26.

[3] A practice has sprung up of evading these constitutional provisions by introducing a new bill after the time has expired when it may constitutionally be done, as an amendment to some pending bill, the whole of which, except the enacting clause, is struck out to make way for it. Thus, the member who thinks he may possibly have occasion for the introduction of a new bill after the constitutional period has expired, takes care to introduce sham bills in due season which he can use as stocks to graft upon, and which he uses irrespective of their character or contents. The sham bill is perhaps a bill to incorporate the city of Siam. One of the member's constituents applies to him for legislative permission to construct a dam across the Wild Cat River. Forthwith, by *amendment*, the bill entitled a bill to incorporate the city of Siam has all after the enacting clause stricken out, and it is made to provide, as its sole object, that John Doe may construct a dam across the Wild Cat. With this title and in this form it is passed; but the house then considerately amends the title to correspond with the purpose of the bill, and the law is passed, and the constitution at the same time saved! This dodge is so transparent, and so clearly in violation of the constitution, and the evidence at the same time so fully spread upon the record, that it is a matter of surprise to find it so often resorted to.

[4] Supervisors of Schuyler Co. *v.* People, 25 Ill. 181; Miller *v.* State, 3 Ohio, N. S. 480. The clause in the constitution of Ohio is: "Every bill shall be fully

As to what shall constitute a reading of a bill, it seems to be held sufficient to read the written instrument that is adopted by the two houses ; and if anything else becomes law in consequence of its passage, and by reason of being referred to in it, it is nevertheless not essential that it be read with the reading of the bill.[1] Thus, a statute which incorporated a military company by reference to its constitution and by-laws, was held valid, notwithstanding the constitution and by-laws, which would acquire the force of law by its passage, were not read in the two houses as a part of it.[2]

It is also provided in the constitutions of some of the States, that on the final passage of every bill the yeas and nays shall be entered on the journal. Such a provision is designed to serve an important purpose in compelling each member present to assume as well as to feel his due share of responsibility in legislation ; and also in furnishing definite and conclusive evidence whether the bill has been passed by the requisite majority or not. " The constitution prescribes this as the test by which to determine whether the requisite number of members vote in the affirmative. The office of the journal is to record the proceedings of the house, and authenticate and preserve the same. It must appear on the face of the journal that the bill passed by a constitutional majority. These directions are all clearly imperative. They are

and distinctly read on three different days, unless, in case of urgency, three fourths of the house in which it shall be pending shall dispense with this rule "; and in Miller v. State, 3 Ohio, N. S. 481, and Pim v. Nicholson, 6 Ohio, N. S. 178, this provision was held to be merely directory. The *distinctness* with which any bill must be read cannot possibly be defined by any law ; and it must always, from the necessity of the case, rest with the house to determine finally whether in this particular the constitution has been complied with or not ; but the rule respecting three several readings on different days is specific, and capable of being precisely complied with, and we do not see how, even under the rules applied to statutes, it can be regarded as directory merely, provided it has a purpose beyond the mere regular and orderly transaction of business. That it has such a purpose, that it is designed to prevent hasty and improvident legislation, and is therefore not a mere rule of order, but one of protection to the public interests and to the citizens at large, is very clear, and independent of the question whether definite constitutional principles can be dispensed with in any case on the ground of their being merely directory, we cannot see how this can be treated as anything but mandatory. See People v. Campbell, 3 Gilm. 466 ; McCulloch v. State, 11 Ind. 424.

[1] Dew v. Cunningham, 28 Ala. 466.

[2] Bibb County Loan Association v. Richards, 21 Geo. 592.

expressly enjoined by the fundamental law, and cannot be dispensed with by the legislature." [1]

For the vote required in the passage of any particular law, the reader is referred to the constitution of his State. A simple majority of a quorum is sufficient, unless the constitution establishes some other rule; and where, by the constitution, a two-thirds or three-fourths vote is made essential to the passage of any particular class of bills, two thirds or three fourths of a quorum will be understood, unless it is expressly declared that this proportion of all the members, or of all those elected, shall be requisite. [2]

The Title of a Statute.

The title of an act was formerly considered no part of it; and although it might be looked to as a guide to the intent of the law-makers when the body of the statute appeared to be in any respect ambiguous or doubtful, [3] yet it was not supposed to control, and the law might be good when that and the title were in conflict. The reason for this was that anciently titles were not prefixed at all, and when afterwards they came to be introduced, they were usually prepared by the clerk of the house in which the bill first passed, and attracted but little attention from the members. They indicated the clerk's idea of the contents or purpose of the bills, rather than that of the house; and they therefore were justly regarded as furnishing very little insight into the legislative intention. Titles to legislative acts, however, have recently, in some States, come to possess very great importance, by reason of constitutional provisions, which not only require that they should correctly indicate the purpose of the law, but which absolutely make the title to control, and exclude everything from effect and operation as law which is incorporated in the body of the act but is not within the purpose indicated by the title. These provisions are given in the note, and it will readily be perceived that they make a very great change in the law. [4]

---

[1] Spangler v. Jacoby, 14 Ill. 297 ; Supervisors of Schuyler Co. v. People, 25 Ill. 183.

[2] Southworth v. Palmyra & Jacksonburg Railroad Co. 2 Mich. 287; State v. McBride, 4 Mo. 303.

[3] United States v. Palmer, 3 Wheat. 610 ; Burgett v. Burgett, 1 Ohio, 480 ; Eastman v. McAlpin, 1 Kelley, 157 ; Cohen v. Barrett, 5 Cal. 195. See Dwarris on Statutes, 502.

[4] The constitutions of Minnesota, Kansas, Maryland, Kentucky, Nebraska,

In considering these provisions it is important to regard, —

1. *The evils designed to be remedied.* The constitution of
New Jersey refers to these as " the improper influences which
may result from intermixing in one and the same act such
things as have no proper relation to each other." In the
language of the Supreme Court of Louisiana, speaking of the
former practice : " The title of an act often afforded no clew to its
contents. Important general principles were found placed in acts
private or local in their operation ; provisions concerning matters,
of practice or judicial proceedings were sometimes included in
the same statute with matters entirely foreign to them, the result
of which was that on many important subjects the statute law
had become almost unintelligible, as they whose duty it has been
to examine or act under it can well testify. To prevent any further accumulation to this chaotic mass was the object of the
constitutional provision under consideration." [1] The Supreme
Court of Michigan say : " The history and purpose of this constitutional provision are too well understood to require any elu-

Ohio, and Pennsylvania provide that " no law shall embrace more than one subject, which shall be expressed in its title." Those of Michigan, Louisiana, and
Texas are the same, substituting the word *object* for *subject.* The constitutions
of South Carolina, Alabama, and California contain similar provisions. The constitution of New Jersey provides that, " to avoid improper influences which may
result from intermixing in one and the same act such things as have no proper
relation to each other, every law shall embrace but one object, and that shall be
expressed in the title." The constitution of Missouri contains a similar provision, with the addition, that, " if any subject embraced in an act be not expressed
in the title, such act shall be void only as to so much thereof as is not so expressed." The constitutions of Indiana and Iowa provide that " every act shall
embrace but one subject, and matters properly connected therewith, which subject shall be expressed in the title. But if any subject shall be embraced in an
act which shall not be expressed in the title, such act shall be void only as to so
much thereof as shall not be expressed in the title." The constitution of Nevada provides that " every law enacted by the legislature shall embrace but one
subject, and matters properly connected therewith, which subject shall be briefly
expressed in the title." The constitutions of New York, Wisconsin, and Illinois
provide that " no private or local bill which may be passed by the legislature
shall embrace more than one subject, and that shall be expressed in the title."
Whether the word *object* is to have any different construction from the word *subject,* as used in these provisions, is a question which may some time require discussion ; but as it is evidently employed for precisely the same purpose, it would seem
that it ought not to have. Compare Hingle *v.* State, 24 Ind. 28, and People *v.*
Lawrence, 36 Barb. 192.

[1] Walker *v.* Caldwell, 4 La. An. 298.

cidation at our hands. The practice of bringing together into one bill subjects diverse in their nature and having no necessary connection, with a view to combine in their favor the advocates of all, and thus secure the passage of several measures, no one of which could succeed upon its own merits, was one both corruptive of the legislator and dangerous to the State. It was scarcely more so, however, than another practice, also intended to be remedied by this provision, by which, through dexterous management, clauses were inserted in bills of which the titles gave no intimation, and their passage secured through legislative bodies whose members were not generally aware of their intention and effect. There was no design by this clause to embarrass legislation, by making laws unnecessarily restrictive in their scope and operation, and thus multiplying their number ; but the framers of the constitution meant to put an end to legislation of the vicious character referred to, which was little less than a fraud upon the public, and to require that in every case the proposed measure should stand upon its own merits, and that the legislature should be fairly satisfied of its design when required to pass upon it."[1] The Court of Appeals of New York declare the object of this provision to be " that neither the members of the legislature nor the people should be misled by the title."[2] The Supreme Court of Iowa say : " The intent of this provision of the constitution was, to prevent the union, in the same act, of incongruous matters, and of objects having no connection, no relation. And with this it was designed to prevent surprise in legislation, by having matter of one nature embraced in a bill whose title expressed another."[3] And similar expressions will be found in many other reported cases.[4] It may therefore be assumed as settled that the purpose of these provisions was: *first*, to prevent *hodge-podge*, or " log-rolling " legislation ; *second*, to prevent surprise or fraud upon the legislature, by means of provisions in bills of which the titles

---

[1] People *v.* Mahaney, 13 Mich. 494. And see Board of Supervisors *v.* Heenan, 2 Minn. 336.

[2] Sun Mutual Insurance Co. *v.* Mayor, &c. of New York, 8 N. Y. 253.

[3] State *v.* County Judge of Davis Co., 2 Iowa, 282.

[4] See Conner *v.* Mayor, &c. of New York, 5 N. Y. 293 ; Davis *v.* State, 7 Md. 151. The Supreme Court of Indiana also understand the provision in the constitution of that State to be designed, among other things, to assist in the codification of the laws. Indiana Central Railroad Co. *v.* Potts, 7 Ind. 685 ; Hingle *v.* State, 24 Ind. 28.

gave no intimation, and which might therefore be overlooked and carelessly and unintentionally adopted; and, *third*, to fairly apprise the people, through such publication of legislative proceedings as is usually made, of the subjects of legislation that are being considered, in order that they may have opportunity of being heard thereon, by petition or otherwise, if they shall so desire.

2. *The particularity required in stating the object.* The general purpose of these provisions is accomplished when a law has but one general object, which is fairly indicated by its title. To require every end and means necessary or convenient for the accomplishment of this general object to be provided for by a separate act relating to that alone, would not only be unreasonable, but would actually render legislation impossible. It has accordingly been held that the title of " an act to establish a police government for the city of Detroit," was not objectionable for its generality, and that all matters properly connected with the establishment and efficiency of such a government, including taxation for its support, and courts for the examination and trial of offenders, might constitutionally be included in the bill under this general title. Under any different ruling, it was said, " the police government of a city could not be organized without a distinct act for each specific duty to be devolved upon it, and these could not be passed until a multitude of other statutes had taken the same duties from other officers before performing them. And these several statutes, fragmentary as they must necessarily be, would often fail of the intended object, from the inherent difficulty in expressing the legislative will when restricted to such narrow bounds." [1] The generality of a title is therefore no objection to it, so long as it is not made a cover to legislation incongruous in itself, and which by no fair intendment can be considered as having a necessary or proper connection.[2] The legislature must determine for itself how broad and comprehensive shall be the object of a statute, and how much particularity shall be employed in the title in defining it.[3] One thing, however, is very

---

[1] People *v.* Mahaney, 13 Mich. 495. See also Morford *v.* Unger, 8 Iowa, 82, and Whiting *v.* Mount Pleasant, 11 Iowa, 482.

[2] Indiana Central Railroad Co. *v.* Potts, 7 Ind. 681.

[3] In State *v.* Powers, 14 Ind. 195, an act came under consideration the title to which was " An act to amend the first section of an act entitled ' An act concern-

plain; that the use of the words " other purposes," which has heretofore been so common in the title to acts, with a view to cover any and every thing, whether connected with the main purpose indicated by the title or not, can no longer be of any avail where these provisions exist. As was said by the Supreme Court of New York, in a case where these words had been made use of in the title to a local bill : " The words ' for other purposes ' must be laid out of consideration. They express nothing, and amount to nothing as a compliance with this constitutional requirement. Nothing which the act could not embrace without them can be brought in by their aid." [1]

3. *What is embraced by the title.* The repeal of a statute on a given subject, it is held, is properly connected with the subject-matter of a new statute on the same subject ; and therefore a repealing section in the new statute is valid, notwithstanding the title is silent on that subject.[2] So an act to incorporate a railroad

ing licenses to vend foreign merchandise, to exhibit any caravan, menagerie, circus, rope and wire dancing puppet-shows, and legerdemain,' approved June 15, 1852, and for the encouragement of agriculture, and concerning the licensing of stock and exchange brokers." It was held that the subject of the act was licenses, and that it was not unconstitutional as containing more than one subject. But it was held also that, as the licenses which it authorized and required were specified in the title, the act could embrace no others, and consequently a provision in the act requiring concerts to be licensed was void. In State *v.* County Judge of Davis County, 2 Iowa, 280, the act in question was entitled " An act in relation to certain State roads therein named." It contained sixty-six sections, in which it established some forty-six roads, vacated some, and provided for the re-location of others. The court sustained the act. " The object of an act may be broader or narrower, more or less extensive ; and the broader it is, the more particulars will it embrace. . . . . There is undoubtedly great objection to uniting so many particulars in one act, but so long as they are of the same nature, and come legitimately under one general determination or object, we cannot say that the act is unconstitutional." P. 284.   Upon this subject see Indiana Central Railroad Co. *v.* Potts, 7 Ind. 684, where it is considered at length. Also Brewster *v.* Syracuse, 19 N. Y. 116 ; Hall *v.* Bunte, 20 Ind. 304. An act entitled " An act fixing the time and mode of electing State printer, defining his duties, fixing compensation, and repealing all laws coming in conflict with this act,' was sustained in Walker *v.* Dunham, 17 Ind. 483.

[1] Town of Fishkill *v.* Fishkill and Beekman Plank Road Co., 22 Barb. 642. See, to the same effect, Ryerson *v.* Utley, 16 Mich. 269. But see Martin *v.* Broach, 6 Geo. 21.

[2] Gabbert *v.* Railroad Co., 11 Ind. 365. The constitution under which this decision was made required the law to contain but one subject, *and matters properly connected therewith ;* but the same decision was made under the New York con-

company may authorize counties to subscribe to its stock, or otherwise aid the construction of the road.[1] So an act to incorporate the Firemen's Benevolent Association may lawfully include under this title provisions for levying a tax upon the income of foreign insurance companies, at the place of its location, for the benefit of the corporation.[2] So an act to provide a homestead for widows and children was held valid, though what it provided for was the pecuniary means sufficient to purchase a homestead.[3] So an act " to regulate proceedings in the county court " was held to properly embrace a provision giving an appeal to the District Court, and regulating the proceedings therein on the appeal.[4] So an act entitled " an act for the more uniform doing of township business " may properly provide for the organization of townships.[5] So it is held that the changing of the boundaries of existing counties is a matter properly connected with the subject of forming new counties out of those existing.[6] So a provision for the organization and sitting of courts in new counties is properly connected with the subject of the formation of such counties, and may be included in " an act to authorize the formation of new counties, and to change county boundaries." [7] Many other cases are referred to in the note which will further illustrate the views of the courts upon this subject. There has been a general disposition to construe the constitutional provision liberally, rather than to embarrass legislation by a construction whose strictness is unnecessary to the accomplishment of the beneficial purposes for which it has been adopted.[8]

stitution, which omits the words here italicized ; and it may well be doubted whether the legal effect of the provision is varied by the addition of those words. See Guilford v. Cornell, 18 Barb. 640.

[1] Supervisors, &c. v. People, 25 Ill. 181.

[2] Firemen's Association v. Lounsbury, 21 Ill. 511.

[3] Succession of Lanzetti, 9 La. An. 329.

[4] Murphey v. Menard, 11 Texas, 673.

[5] Clinton v. Draper, 14 Ind. 295.

[6] Haggard v. Hawkins, 14 Ind. 299. And see Duncombe v. Prindle, 12 Iowa, 1.

[7] Brandon v. State, 16 Ind. 197. In this case, and also in State v. Bowers, 14 Ind. 198, it was held that if the title to an original act is sufficient to embrace the matters covered by the provisions of an act amendatory thereof, it is unnecessary to inquire whether the title of an amendatory act would, of itself, be sufficient. And see Morford v. Unger, 8 Iowa, 82.

[8] Green v. Mayor, &c., R. M. Charlt. 368 ; Martin v. Broach, 6 Geo. 21 ; Protho

4. *The effect if the title embrace more than one object.* Perhaps in those States where this constitutional provision is limited

v. Orr, 12 Geo. 36 ; Wheeler *v.* State, 23 Geo. 9 ; Hill *v.* Commissioners, 22 Geo.
203 ; Jones *v.* Columbus, 25 Geo. 610 ; Denham *v.* Holeman, 26 Geo. 182 ; Can-
non *v.* Hemphill, 7 Texas, 184 ; Battle *v.* Howard, 13 Texas, 345 ; Robinson *v.*
State, 15 Texas, 311 ; Conner *v.* Mayor, &c. of New York, 2 Sandf. 355, and 5
N. Y. 285 ; Fishkill *v.* Plank Road Co., 22 Barb. 634 ; Brewster *v.* Syracuse, 19
N. Y. 116 ; People *v.* McCann, 16 N. Y. 58 ; Williams *v.* People, 24 N. Y. 405 ;
People *v.* Lawrence, 36 Barb. 177 ; Sharp *v.* Mayor, &c. of New York, 31 Barb.
572 ; Davis *v.* State, 7 Md. 51 ; Keller *v.* State, 11 Md. 525 ; Parkinson *v.* State,
14 Md. 184 ; Bossier *v.* Steele, 13 La. An. 433 ; Læfon *v.* Dufoe, 9 La. An. 329 ;
State *v.* Harrison, 11 La. An. 722 ; Williams *v.* Payson, 14 La. An. 7 ; Mewherter *v.* Price, 11 Ind. 199 ; Gabbert *v.* Railroad Co., Ibid. 365 ; Railroad Co. *v.*
Whiteneck, 8 Ind. 217 ; Wilkins *v.* Miller, 9 Ind. 100 ; Foley *v.* State, 9 Ind.
363 ; Gillespie *v.* State, Ibid. 380 ; Henry *v.* Henry, 13 Ind. 250 ; Igoe *v.* State,
14 Ind. 239 ; Haggard *v.* Hawkins, Ibid. 299 ; Reed *v.* State, 12 Ind. 641 ; Stur-
geon *v.* Hitchens, 22 Ind. 107 ; Lauer *v.* State, Ibid. 461 ; Central Plank Road
Co. *v.* Hannaman, Ibid. 484 ; Gifford *v.* Railroad Co., 2 Stockt. 171 ; Johnson *v.*
Higgins, 3 Met. (Ky.) 566 ; Chiles *v.* Drake, 2 Met. (Ky.) 146 ; Louisville, &c.
Co. *v.* Ballard, Ibid. 165 ; Phillips *v.* Covington, &c. Co., Ibid. 219 ; Chiles *v.*
Monroe, 4 Met. (Ky.) 72 ; Commonwealth *v.* Dewey, 15 Grat. 1 ; Whiting *v.*
Mount Pleasant, 11 Iowa, 482 ; Tuttle *v.* Strout, 7 Minn. 465 ; Supervisors, &c. *v.*
Heenan, 2 Minn. 330 ; Railroad Co. *v.* Gregory, 15 Ill. 20 ; People *v.* Mellen, 32
Ill. 181.   In Davis *v.* Woolnough, 9 Iowa, 104, an act entitled " An act for revising and consolidating the laws incorporating the city of Dubuque, and to establish a city court therein," was held to express by its title but one object, which
was, the revising and consolidating the laws incorporating the city ; and the city
court, not being an unusual tribunal in such a municipality, might be provided
for by the act, whether mentioned in the title or not.   " An act to enable the
supervisors of the city and county of New York to raise money by tax," provided for raising money to pay judgments then existing and also any thereafter to be recovered ; and it also contained the further provision, that whenever
the controller of the city should have reason to believe that any judgment then
of record or thereafter obtained had been obtained by collusion, or was founded
in fraud, he should take the proper and necessary means to open and reverse the
same, &c.   This provision was held constitutional, as properly connected with
the subject indicated by the title, and necessary to confine the payments of the
tax to the objects for which the moneys were intended to be raised.   Sharp *v.*
Mayor, &c. of New York, 31 Barb. 572.   In O'Leary *v.* Cook Co., 28 Ill. 534, it
was held that a clause in an act incorporating a college, prohibiting the sale of
ardent spirits within a distance of four miles, was so germane to the primary object of the charter as to be properly included within it.   By the first section
of " an act for the relief of the creditors of the Lockport and Niagara Falls
Railroad Company," it was made the duty of the president of the corporation, or
one of the directors to be appointed by the president, to advertise and sell the
real and personal estate, including the franchise of the company, at public auc-

in its operation to private and local bills, it might be held that an act was not void for embracing two or more objects which were indicated by its title, provided one of them only was of a private and local nature. It has been held in New York that a local bill was not void because embracing general provisions also ; [1] and if they may constitutionally be embraced in the act, it is presumed they may also be constitutionally embraced in the title. But if the title to the act actually indicates, and the act itself actually embraces, two distinct objects, when the constitution says it shall embrace but one, the whole act must be treated as void, from the manifest impossibility in the court choosing between the two, and holding the act valid as to the one and void as to the other.

5. *The effect where the act is broader than the title.* But if the act is broader than the title, it may happen that one part of it can stand because indicated by the title, while as to the object not indicated by the title it must fail. Some of the State constitutions, it will be perceived, have declared that this shall be the rule ; but the declaration was unnecessary ; as the general rule, that so much of the act as is not in conflict with the constitution must be sustained, would have required the same declaration from the courts. If by striking from the act all that relates to the object not indicated by the title, that which is left is complete in itself, sensible, capable of being executed, and wholly independent of that which is rejected, it must be sustained as constitutional.

tion to the highest bidder. It was then declared that the sale should be absolute, and that it should vest in the purchaser or purchasers of the property, real or personal, of the company, all the franchise, rights, and privileges of the corporation, as fully and as absolutely as the same were then possessed by the company. The money arising from the sale, after paying costs, was to be applied, first, to the payment of a certain judgment, and then to other liens according to priority ; and the surplus, if any, was to be divided ratably among the other creditors, and then if there should be an overplus, it was to be divided ratably among the then stockholders. By the second section of the act, it was declared that the purchaser or purchasers should have the right to sell and distribute stock to the full amount which was authorized by the act of incorporation, and the several amendments thereto ; and to appoint an election, choose directors, and organize a corporation anew, with the same powers as the existing company. There was then a proviso, that nothing in the act should impair or affect the subscriptions for new stock, or the obligations or liabilities of the company which had been made or incurred in the extension of the road from Lockport to Rochester, &c. The whole act was held to be constitutional. Mosier *v.* Hilton, 15 Barb. 657.

[1] People *v.* McCann, 16 N. Y. 58.

The principal questions in each case will therefore be, whether the act is in truth broader than the title; and if so, then whether the other objects in the act are so intimately connected with the one indicated by the title that the portion of the act relating to them cannot be rejected, and leave a complete and sensible enactment which is capable of being executed.

As the legislature may make the title to an act as restrictive as they please, it is obvious that they may sometimes so frame it as to preclude many matters being included in the act which might with entire propriety have been embraced in one enactment with the matters indicated by the title, but which must now be excluded, because the title has been made unnecessarily restrictive. The courts cannot enlarge the scope of the title; they are vested with no dispensing power; the constitution has made the title the conclusive index to the legislative intent as to what shall have operation; it is no answer to say that the title might have been made more comprehensive, if in fact the legislature have not seen fit to make it so. Thus, " An act concerning promissory notes and bills of exchange " provided that all promissory notes, bills of exchange, *or other instruments in writing*, for the payment of money, or for the delivery of specific articles, or to convey property, or to perform any other stipulation therein mentioned, should be negotiable, and assignees of the same might sue thereon in their own names. It was held that this act was void, as to all the instruments mentioned therein except promissory notes and bills of exchange;[1] though it is obvious that it would have been easy to frame a title to the act which would have embraced them all, and which would have been unobjectionable. It has also been held that an act for the preservation of the Muskegon River Improvement could not lawfully provide for the levy and collection of tolls for the payment of the expense of *constructing* the improvement, as the operation of the act was carefully limited by its title to the future.[2] So also it has been held that " an act to limit the number of grand jurors, and to point out the mode of their selection, defining their jurisdiction, and repealing all laws inconsistent therewith," could not constitutionally contain provisions which should authorize a defendant in a criminal case, on a trial for any offence, to be found guilty of any lesser offence necessarily in-

---

[1] Mewherter *v.* Price, 11 Ind. 199.
[2] Ryerson *v.* Utley, 16 Mich. 269.

cluded therein.[1] These cases must suffice upon this point;
though the cases before referred to will furnish many similar
illustrations.

In all we have said upon this subject we have assumed the constitutional provision to be mandatory. Such has been the view
of the courts almost without exception. In California, however,
a different view has been taken, the court saying: " We regard
this section of the constitution as merely directory; and, if we
were inclined to a different opinion, would be careful how we
lent ourselves to a construction which must in effect obliterate
almost every law from the statute-book, unhinge the business and
destroy the labor of the last three years. The first legislature
that met under the constitution seems to have considered this
section as directory ; and almost every act of that and the subsequent sessions would be obnoxious to this objection. The contemporaneous exposition of the first legislature, adopted or acquiesced in by every subsequent legislature, and tacitly assented to
by the courts, taken in connection with the fact that rights have
grown up under it, so that it has become a rule of property, must
govern our decision." [2] Similar views have also been expressed
in the State of Ohio.[3] These cases, and especially what is said by
the California court, bring forcibly before our minds a fact, which
cannot be kept out of view in considering this subject, and which
has a very important bearing upon the precise point which these
decisions cover. The fact is this: that whatever constitutional
provision can be looked upon as directory merely is very likely to
be treated by the legislature as if it was devoid even of moral
obligation, and to be therefore habitually disregarded. To say
that a provision is directory seems, with many persons, to be
equivalent to saying that it is not law at all. That this ought not
to be so must be conceded ; that it is so we have abundant reason
and good authority for saying. If, therefore, a constitutional provision is to be enforced at all, it must be treated as mandatory.
And if the legislature habitually disregard it, it seems to us that
there is all the more urgent necessity that the courts should enforce it. And it also seems to us that there are few evils which

---

[1] Foley v. State, 9 Ind. 363 ; Gillespie v. State, Ibid. 380. See also Indiana
Cent. Railroad Co. v. Potts, 7 Ind. 681 ; Kuhns v. Krammis, 20 Ind. 490.

[2] Washington v. Murray, 4 Cal. 388.

[3] Miller v. State, 3 Ohio, N. S. 475 ; Pim v. Nicholson, 6 Ohio, N. S. 177.

can be inflicted by a strict adherence to the law, so great as that which is done by the habitual disregard, by any department of the government, of a plain requirement of that instrument from which it derives its authority, and which ought, therefore, to be scrupulously observed and obeyed. Upon this subject we need only refer here to what we have said concerning it in another place.[1]

Amendatory Statutes.

It has also been deemed important, in some of the States, to provide by their constitutions, that "no act shall ever be revised or amended by mere reference to its title; but the act revised or section amended shall be set forth and published at full length."[2] Upon this provision an important query arises. Does it mean that the act or section revised or amended shall be set forth and published at full length as it stood before, or does it mean only that it shall be set forth and published at full length as amended or revised? Upon this question perhaps a consideration of the purpose of the provision may throw some light. "The mischief designed to be remedied was the enactment of amendatory statutes in terms so blind that legislators themselves were sometimes deceived in regard to their effects, and the public, from the difficulty in making the necessary examination and comparison, failed to become apprised of the changes made in the laws. An amendatory act which purported only to insert certain words, or to substitute one phrase for another in an act or section which was only referred to, but not published, was well calculated to mislead the careless as to its effect, and was, perhaps, sometimes drawn in that form for the express purpose. Endless confusion was thus introduced into the law, and the constitution wisely prohibited such legislation."[3] If this is a correct view of the purpose of the provision, it does not seem to be at all important to its accomplishment that the old law should be republished, if the law as amended is given in full, with such reference to the old law as will show for what the new law is substituted. Neverthe-

---

[1] Ante, p. 74.

[2] This is the provision as it is found in the constitutions of Indiana, Louisiana, Nevada, Oregon, Texas, and Virginia. In Kansas, Ohio, Nebraska, Michigan, Missouri, and Maryland there are provisions of similar import.

[3] People v. Mahaney, 13 Mich. 497.

less, it has been decided in Louisiana that the constitution requires the old law to be set forth and published;[1] and the courts of Indiana, assuming the provision in their own constitution to be taken from that of Louisiana after the decisions referred to had been made, adopt and follow them as precedents.[2] It is believed, however, that the general understanding of the provision in question is different, and that it is fully complied with, in letter and spirit, if the act or section revised or amended is set forth and published as revised or amended, and that anything more only tends to render the statute unnecessarily cumbrous. Statutes which amend others by implication, however, are not within this provision; and it is not essential that they even refer to the acts or sections which by implication they amend.[3]

It was a parliamentary rule that a statute should not be repealed at the same session of its enactment, unless a clause permitting it was inserted in the statute itself;[4] but this rule did not apply to repeals by implication,[5] and it is possibly not recognized in this country at all, except where it is incorporated in the State constitution.[6]

Signing of Bills.

When a bill has passed the two houses, it is engrossed for the signatures of the presiding officers. This is a constitutional requirement in most of the States, and therefore cannot be dispensed with; though, in the absence of any such requirement, it would seem not to be essential.[7] And if, by the constitution of

---

[1] Walker v. Caldwell, 4 La. An. 297; Heirs of Duverge v. Salter, 5 La. An. 94.

[2] Langdon v. Applegate, 5 Ind. 327; Rogers v. State, 6 Ind. 31.

[3] People v. Mahaney, 13 Mich. 496; Spencer v. State, 5 Ind. 41; Branham v. Lange, 16 Ind. 497. Repeals by implication, however, are not favored. Ibid. And see Naylor v. Field, 5 Dutch. 287; State v. Berry, 12 Iowa, 58; Attorney-General v. Brown, 1 Wis. 525; Dodge v. Gridley, 10 Ohio, 177; Hirn v. State, 1 Ohio, N. S. 20; McCool v. Smith, 1 Black, 459; New Orleans v. Southern Bank, 15 La. An. 89.

[4] Dwarris on Statutes, vol. 1, p. 269; Sedgw. on Stat. and Const. Law, 122; Smith on Stat. and Const. Construction, 908.

[5] Ibid. And see Spencer v. State, 5 Ind. 41.

[6] Spencer v. State, 5 Ind. 41; Attorney-General v. Brown, 1 Wis. 513; Smith on Stat. and Const. Construction, 908; Mobile & Ohio Railroad Co. v. State, 29 Ala. 573.

[7] Speer v. Plank Road Co., 22 Penn. St. 376.

the State, the governor is a component part of the legislature, the
bill is then presented to him for his approval.

Approval of Laws.

The qualified veto power of the governor is regulated by the
constitutions of those States which allow it, and little need be
said here beyond referring to the constitutional provisions for
information concerning them.   It has been held that if the governor, by statute, was entitled to one day, previous to the adjournment of the legislature, for the examination and approval of laws,
this is to be understood as a full day of twenty-four hours, before
the hour of the final adjournment.[1]   It has also been held that,
in the approval of laws, the governor is a component part of the
legislature, and that unless the constitution allows further time
for the purpose, he must exercise his power of approval before
the two houses adjourn, or his act will be void.[2]   But under a
provision of the constitution of Minnesota, that the governor may
approve and sign " within three days of the adjournment of the
legislature any act passed during the last three days of the session," it has been held that Sundays were not to be included as
a part of the prescribed time ;[3] and under the constitution of
New York, which provided that, " if any bill shall not be returned
by the governor within ten days, Sundays excepted, after it shall
have been presented to him, the same shall be a law, in like manner as if he had signed it, unless the legislature shall, by their
adjournment, prevent its return, in which case it shall not be a
law," it was held that the governor might sign a bill after the
adjournment, at any time within the ten days.[4]   The governor's
approval is not complete until the bill has passed beyond his con-

---

[1] Hyde v. White, 24 Texas, 137.

[2] Fowler v. Peirce, 2 Cal. 165.   The court also held in this case that, notwithstanding an act purported to have been approved before the actual adjournment,
it was competent to show by parol evidence that the actual approval was not
until the next day.   In support of this ruling, People v. Purdy, 2 Hill, 31, was
cited, where it was held that the court might go behind the statute-book and inquire whether an act to which a two-thirds vote was essential had constitutionally passed.   That, however, would not be in direct contradiction of the record,
but it would be inquiring into a fact concerning which the statute was silent, and
other records supplied the needed information.

[3] Stinson v. Smith, 8 Minn. 366.   [4] People v. Bowen, 30 Barb. 24.

trol by the constitutional and customary mode of legislation ; and at any time prior to that he may reconsider and retract any approval previously made.[1] His disapproval of a bill is communicated to the house in which it originated, with his reasons ; and it is there reconsidered, and may be again passed over the veto by such vote as the constitution prescribes.[2]

[1] People v. Hatch, 19 Ill. 283. An act apportioning the representatives was passed by the legislature and transmitted to the governor, who signed his approval thereon by mistake, supposing at the time that he was subscribing one of several other bills then lying before him, and claiming his official attention ; his private secretary thereupon reported the bill to the legislature as approved, not by the special direction of the governor, nor with his knowledge or special assent, but merely in his usual routine of customary duty, the governor not being conscious that he had placed his signature to the bill until after information was brought to him of its having been reported approved ; whereupon he sent a message to the speaker of the house to which it was reported, stating that it had been inadvertently signed and not approved, and on the same day completed a veto message of the bill which was partially written at the time of signing his approval, and transmitted it to the house where the bill originated, having first erased his signature and approval. It was held that the bill had not become a law. It had never passed out of the governor's possession after it was received by him until after he had erased his signature and approval, and the court was of opinion that it did not pass from his control until it had become a law by the lapse of ten days under the constitution, or by his depositing it with his approval in the office of the secretary of state. It had long been the practice of the governor to report, formerly through the secretary of state, but recently through his private secretary, to the house where bills originated, his approval of them ; but this was only a matter of formal courtesy, and not a proceeding necessary to the making or imparting vitality to the law. By it no act could become a law which without it would not be a law. Had the governor returned the bill itself to the house, with his message of approval, it would have passed beyond his control, and the approval could not have been retracted, unless the bill had been withdrawn by consent of the house ; and the same result would have followed his filing the bill with the secretary of state with his approval subscribed.

The constitution of Indiana provides, art. 5, § 14, that, "if any bill shall not be returned by the governor within three days, Sundays excepted, after it shall have been presented to him, it shall be a law without his signature, unless the general adjournment shall prevent its return ; in which case it shall be a law unless the governor, within five days next after the adjournment, shall file such bill with his objections thereto, in the office of the secretary of state," &c. Under this provision it was held that where the governor, on the day of the final adjournment of the legislature, and after the adjournment, filed a bill received that day, in the office of the secretary of state, without approval or objections thereto, it thereby became a law, and he could not file objections afterwards. Tarlton v. Peggs, 18 Ind. 24.

[2] In practice the veto power, although very great and exceedingly important in

Other Powers of the Governor.

The power of the governor as a branch of the legislative department is almost exclusively confined to the approval of bills. As executive, he communicates to the two houses information concerning the condition of the State, and may recommend measures to their consideration, but he cannot originate or introduce bills. He may convene the legislature in extra session whenever extraordinary occasion seems to have arisen; but their powers when convened are not confined to a consideration of the subjects to which their attention is called by his proclamation or his message, and they may legislate on any subject as at the regular sessions.[1] An exception to this statement exists in those States where, by the express terms of the constitution, it is provided that when convened in extra session the legislature shall consider no subject except that for which they were specially called together, or which may have been submitted to them by special message of the governor.[2]

When Acts are to take Effect.

The old rule was that statutes, unless otherwise ordered, took effect from the first day of the session on which they were passed;

this country, is obsolete in Great Britain, and no king now ventures to resort to it. As the Ministry must at all times be in accord with the House of Commons, — except where the responsibility is taken of dissolving the Parliament and appealing to the people, — it must follow that any bill which the two houses have passed must be approved by the monarch. The approval has become a matter of course, and the governing power in Great Britain is substantially in the House of Commons.

[1] The constitution of Iowa — art. 4, § 11 — provides that the governor "may, on extraordinary occasions, convene the General Assembly by proclamation, and shall state to both houses, when assembled, the purpose for which they have been convened." It was held in Morford v. Unger, 8 Iowa, 82, that the General Assembly, when thus convened, were not confined in their legislation to the purposes specified in the message. "When lawfully convened, whether in virtue of the provision in the constitution or the governor's proclamation, it is the 'General Assembly' of the State, in which the full and exclusive legislative authority of the State is vested. Where its business at such session is not restricted by some constitutional provision, the General Assembly may enact any law at a special or extra session that it might at a regular session. Its powers, not being derived from the governor's proclamation, are not confined to the special purpose for which it may have been convened by him."

[2] Provisions to this effect will be found in the constitutions of Illinois, Michigan, Missouri, and Nevada; perhaps in some others.

but this rule was purely arbitrary, based upon no good reason, and frequently working very serious injustice. The present rule is that an act takes effect from the time when it actually becomes a law under the constitution, unless it is otherwise ordered, or unless there is some constitutional or statutory rule on the subject which prescribes otherwise. By the constitution of Mississippi,[1] " no law of a general nature, unless otherwise provided for, shall be enforced until sixty days after the passage thereof." By the constitution of Illinois,[2] no public act can take effect or be in force until the expiration of sixty days from the end of the session at which the same may be passed, unless in case of emergency the General Assembly shall otherwise direct. By the constitution of Michigan,[3] no public act shall take effect, or be in force, until the expiration of ninety days from the end of the session at which the same is passed, unless the legislature shall otherwise direct by a two-thirds vote of the members elected to each house. These and similar provisions are designed to secure, as far as possible, the public promulgation of the law before parties are bound to take notice of and act under it ; and to obviate the injustice of a rule which should compel parties at their peril to know and obey a law of which, in the nature of things, they could not possibly have heard, they give to all parties the full constitutional period in which to become acquainted with the terms of the statutes which are passed, except when the legislature has otherwise directed ; and no one is bound to govern his conduct by the new law until that period has elapsed.[4] And the fact that, by the terms of the statute, something is to be done under it before the expiration of the constitutional period for it to take effect, will not amount to a legislative direction that the act shall take effect at that time, if the act itself is silent as to the period when it shall go into operation.[5]

[1] Art. 7, § 6.

[2] Art. 3, § 23.

[3] Art. 4, § 20.

[4] Price v. Hopkin, 13 Mich. 318. And where a law has failed to take effect for want of publication, all parties are chargeable with notice of that fact. Clark v. Janesville, 10 Wis. 136.

[5] Supervisors of Iroquois Co. v. Keady, 34 Ill. 293. An act for the removal of a county seat provided for taking the vote of the electors of the county upon it on the 17th of March, 1863, at which time the legislature had not adjourned. It was not expressly declared in the act at what time it should take effect, and it

The constitution of Indiana provides[1] that "no act shall take effect until the same shall have been published and circulated in the several counties of this State, by authority, except in case of emergency; which emergency shall be declared in the preamble, or in the body of the law." Unless the emergency is thus declared, it is plain that the act cannot take earlier effect.[2] But the courts will not inquire too nicely into the mode of publication. If the laws are distributed in bound volumes, in a manner and shape not substantially contrary to the statute on that subject, and by the proper authority, it will be held sufficient, notwithstanding a failure to comply with some of the directory provisions of the statute on the subject of publication.[3]

The constitution of Wisconsin, on the other hand, provides[4] that "no general law shall be in force until published"; thus leaving the time when it should take effect to depend, not alone upon the legislative direction, but upon the further fact of publication. But what shall be the mode of publication seems to be left to the legislative determination. It has been held, however, that a general law was to be regarded as *published* although printed in the volume of private laws, instead of the volume of public laws as the statute of the State would require.[5] But an unauthorized publication — as, for example, of an act for the incorporation of a city in two local papers instead of the State paper — is no publication in the constitutional sense.[6]

was therefore held that it would not take effect until sixty days from the end of the session, and a vote of the electors taken on the 17th of March was void. And it was also held in this case, and in Wheeler v. Chubbuck, 16 Ill. 361, that "the direction must be made in a clear, distinct, and unequivocal provision, and could not be helped out by any sort of intendment or implication," and that the act must all take effect at once, and not by piecemeal.

[1] Art. 4, § 28.

[2] Carpenter v. Montgomery, 7 Blackf. 415; Hendrickson v. Hendrickson, 7 Ind. 13; Mark v. State, 15 Ind. 98.

[3] State v. Bailey, 16 Ind. 46. See further, as to this constitutional provision, Jones v. Cavins, 4 Ind. 305.

[4] Art. 7, § 21.

[5] Matter of Boyle, 9 Wis. 264. Under this provision it has been decided that a law establishing a municipal court in a city is a general law. Matter of Boyle, supra. Also a statute for the removal of a county seat. State v. Lean, 9 Wis. 279. Also a statute incorporating a municipality, or authorizing it to issue bonds in aid of a railroad. Clark v. Janesville, 10 Wis. 136. And see Scott v. Clark, 1 Iowa, 70.

[6] Clark v. Janesville, 10 Wis. 136.

The constitution of Iowa provides that " no law of the General Assembly, passed at a regular session, of a public nature, shall take effect until the fourth day of July next after the passage thereof. Laws passed at a special session shall take effect ninety days after the adjournment of the General Assembly by which they were passed. If the General Assembly shall deem any law of immediate importance, they may provide that the same shall take effect by publication in newspapers in the State." [1] Under this section it is not competent for the legislature to confer upon the governor the discretionary power which the constitution gives to that body, to fix an earlier day for the law to take effect. [2]

[1] Art. 3, § 26.
[2] Scott *v.* Clark, 1 Iowa, 70 ; Pilkey *v.* Gleason, Ibid. 522.

CHAPTER VII.

OF THE CIRCUMSTANCES UNDER WHICH A LEGISLATIVE ENACTMENT MAY BE DECLARED UNCONSTITUTIONAL.

WE have now examined somewhat briefly the legislative power of the State, and the bounds which expressly or by implication are set to it, and also some of the conditions necessary to its proper and valid exercise. We have also seen that, under some circumstances, it may become the duty of the courts to declare that what the legislature has assumed to enact is void, either from want of constitutional power to enact it, or because the constitutional forms or conditions have not been observed. In the further examination of our subject, it will be important to consider what the circumstances are under which the courts will feel impelled to exercise this high prerogative, and what precautions should be observed before assuming to do so.

It must be evident to any one that the power to declare a legislative enactment void is one which the judge, conscious of the fallibility of the human judgment, will shrink from exercising in any case where he can conscientiously and with due regard to duty and official oath decline the responsibility. The legislative and judicial are co-ordinate departments of the government, of equal dignity ; each is alike supreme in the exercise of its proper functions, and cannot directly or indirectly, while acting within the limits of its authority, be subjected to the control or supervision of the other, without an unwarrantable assumption by that other of power which, by the constitution, is not conferred upon it. The constitution apportions the powers of government, but it does not make any one of the three departments subordinate to another, when exercising the trust committed to it. The courts may declare legislative enactments unconstitutional and void in some cases, but not because the judicial power is superior in degree or dignity to the legislative. Being required to declare what the law is in the cases which come before them, they must enforce the constitution as the paramount law, whenever a legislative enactment comes in conflict with it.[1] But the courts sit, not to review or revise the legislative action, but to enforce the legislative will; and it is only where they find that the legislature has failed to keep within its constitutional limits, that they are at liberty to disregard its action; and in doing so, they only do what every private citizen may do in regard to the action of the courts when the judges assume to act and to render judgments or decrees without jurisdiction. " In exercising this high authority, the judges claim no judicial supremacy; they are only the administrators of the public will. If an act of the legislature is held void, it is not because the judges have any control over the legislative power, but because the act is forbidden by the constitution, and because the will of the people, which is therein declared, is paramount to that of their representatives expressèd in any law." [2]

Nevertheless, in declaring a law unconstitutional, a court must necessarily cover the same ground which has already been covered by the legislative judgment, and must indirectly overrule the decision of that co-ordinate department. The task is therefore a delicate one, and only to be entered upon with reluctance and hesitation. It is a solemn act in any case to declare that that body to whom the people have committed the sovereign function of making the laws for the commonwealth, have deliberately disregarded the limitations imposed upon this delegated authority, and usurped power which the people have been careful to withhold; and it is almost equally so when the act which is adjudged to be unconstitutional appears to be chargeable rather to careless and improvident action, or error in judgment, than to intentional disregard of obligation. But it is a duty which the courts, in a proper case, are not at liberty to decline; and whatever doubts may at one time have been suggested regarding it, they have long since been removed, if indeed they were ever seriously entertained.[3]

----

[1] Rice v. State, 7 Ind. 334 ; Bloodgood v. Mohawk & Hudson Railroad Co., 18 Wend. 53.

[2] Lindsay v. Commissioners, &c., 2 Bay, 61.

[3] There are at least two cases in American judicial history where judges have been impeached as criminals for refusing to enforce unconstitutional enactments. One of these we have referred to, ante, p. 26 ; concerning the other, we copy from the Western Law Monthly, " Sketch of Hon. Calvin Pease," vol. 5, p. 3, June, 1863 : " The first session of the Supreme Court [of Ohio] under the con-

I. In view of the considerations which have been suggested, the rule which is adopted by some courts, that they will not

stitution was held at Warren, Trumbull County, on the first Tuesday of June, 1803. The State was divided into three circuits. . . . . The Third Circuit of the State was composed of the counties of Washington, Belmont, Jefferson, Columbiania, and Trumbull. At this session of the legislature Mr. Pease was appointed President Judge of the Third Circuit in April, 1803, and though nearly twenty-seven years old, he was very youthful in his appearance. He held the office until March 4, 1810, when he sent his resignation to Governor Huntingdon. . . . . During his term of service upon the bench many interesting questions were presented for decision, and among them the constitutionality of some portion of the act of 1805, defining the duties of justices of the peace; and he decided that so much of the fifth section as gave justices of the peace jurisdiction exceeding $20, and so much of the twenty-ninth section as prevented plaintiffs from recovering costs in actions commenced by original writs in the Court of Common Pleas, for sums between $20 and $50, were repugnant to the Constitution of the United States and of the State of Ohio, and therefore null and void. . . . . The clamor and abuse to which this decision gave rise was not in the least mitigated or diminished by the circumstance that it was concurred in by a majority of the judges of the Supreme Court, Messrs. Huntingdon, and Tod. . . . . At the session of the legislature of 1807 – 8 steps were taken to impeach him and the judges of the Supreme Court who concurred with him; but the resolutions introduced into the house were not acted upon during the session. But the scheme was not abandoned. At an early day of the next session, and with almost indecent haste, a committee was appointed to inquire into the conduct of the offending judges, and with leave to exhibit articles of impeachment, or report otherwise, as the facts might justify. The committee without delay reported articles of impeachment against Messrs. Pease and Tod but not against Huntingdon, who in the mean time had been elected governor of the State. . . . . The articles of impeachment were preferred by the House of Representatives on the 23d day of December, 1808. He was summoned at once to appear before the Senate as a high court of impeachment, and he promptly obeyed the summons. The managers of the prosecution on the part of the House were Thomas Morris, afterwards Senator in Congress from Ohio, Joseph Sharp, James Pritchard, Samuel Marrett, and Othniel Tooker. . . . . Several days were consumed in the investigation, but the trial resulted in the acquittal of the respondent." Sketch of Hon. George Tod, August number of same volume : " At the session of the legislature of 1808 – 9 he was impeached for concurring in decisions made by Judge Pease, in the counties of Trumbull and Jefferson, that certain provisions of the act of the legislature passed in 1805 defining the duties of justices of the peace were in conflict with the Constitution of the United States and of the State of Ohio, and therefore void. These decisions of the courts of Common Pleas and of the Supreme Court, it was insisted, were not only an assault upon the wisdom and dignity, but also upon the supremacy of the legislature, which passed the act in question. This could not be endured; and the popular fury against the judges rose to a very high pitch, and the senator from the county of Trumbull in the legislature at that time, Cal-

decide a legislative act to be unconstitutional by a majority of
a bare quorum of the judges only, — less than a majority of all,
— but will instead postpone the argument until the bench is full,
seems a very prudent and proper precaution to be observed before
entering upon questions so delicate and so important. The
benefit of the wisdom and deliberation of every judge ought to
be had under circumstances so grave. Something more than
private rights are involved ; the fundamental law of the State is
in question, as well as the correctness of legislative action ; and
considerations of courtesy, as well as of the importance of the
question involved, should lead the court to decline to act at all,
where they cannot sustain the legislative action, until a full
bench has been consulted, and its deliberate opinion is found
against it. But this is a rule of propriety, not of constitutional
obligation ; and though generally adopted and observed, each
court will regulate, in its own discretion, its practice in this
particular.[1]

vin Cone, Esq., took no pains to soothe the offended dignity of the members of
that body, or their sympathizing constituents, but pressed a contrary line of conduct. The judges must be brought to justice, he insisted vehemently, and be
punished, so that others might be terrified by the example and deterred from committing similar offences in the future. The charges against Mr. Tod were substantially the same as those against Mr. Pease. Mr. Tod was first tried, and acquitted. The managers of the impeachment, as well as the result, were the same
in both cases."

[1] Briscoe v. Commonwealth Bank of Kentucky, 8 Pet. 118. It has been intimated that inferior courts should not presume to pass upon constitutional questions, but ought in all cases to treat statutes as valid. Ortman v. Greenman, 4
Mich. 291. But no tribunal can exercise judicial power, unless it is to decide
according to its judgment ; and it is difficult to discover any principle of justice
which can require a magistrate to enter upon the execution of a statute when
he believes it to be invalid, especially when he must thereby subject himself to
prosecution, without any indemnity in the law if it proves to be invalid. Undoubtedly when the highest courts in the land hesitate to declare a law unconstitutional, and allow much weight to the legislative judgment, the inferior courts
should be still more reluctant to exercise this power, and a becoming modesty
would at least be expected of those judicial officers who have not been trained to
the investigation of legal and constitutional questions. But in any case a judge
or justice, being free from doubt in his own mind, and unfettered by any judicial
decision properly binding upon him, must follow his own sense of duty upon constitutional as well as upon any other questions. See Miller v. State, 3 Ohio, N.
S. 483 ; Pim v. Nicholson, 6 Ohio, N. S. 180 ; Mayberry v. Kelly, 1 Kansas,
116. In the case last cited it is said : " It is claimed by counsel for the plaintiff
in error, that the point raised by the instruction is, that inferior courts and minis-

II. Neither will a court, as a general rule, pass upon a constitutional question, and decide a statute to be invalid, unless a decision upon that very point becomes necessary to the determination of the cause. "While the courts cannot shun the discussion of constitutional questions when fairly presented, they will not go out of their way to find such topics. They will not seek to draw in such weighty matters collaterally, nor on trivial occasions. It is both more proper and more respectful to a co-ordinate department to discuss constitutional questions only when that is the very *lis mota*. Thus presented and determined, the decision carries a weight with it to which no extra-judicial disquisition is entitled."[1] In any case, therefore, where a constitutional question is raised, though it may be legitimately presented by the record, yet if the record also presents some other and clear ground upon which the court may rest its judgment, and thereby render the constitutional question immaterial to the case, the court will take that course, and leave the question of constitutional power to be passed upon when a case arises which cannot be otherwise disposed of, and which consequently renders a decision upon such question necessary.[2]

III. Nor will a court listen to an objection made to the constitutionality of an act by a party whose rights it does not affect, and who has consequently no interest in defeating it. On this ground it has been held that the objection that a legislative act was unconstitutional, because divesting the rights of remainder-men against their will, could not be successfully urged by the owner of the particular estate, and could only be made on behalf

terial officers have no right to judge of the constitutionality of a law passed by a legislature. But is this law ? If so, a court created to interpret the law must disregard the constitution in forming its opinions. The constitution is law, — the fundamental law, — and must as much be taken into consideration by a justice of the peace as by any other tribunal. When two laws apparently conflict, it is the duty of all courts to construe them. If the conflict is irreconcilable, they must decide which is to prevail ; and the constitution is not an exception to this rule of construction. If a law were passed in open, flagrant violation of the constitution, should a justice of the peace regard the law and pay no attention to the constitutional provision ? If that is his duty in a plain case, is it less so when the construction becomes more difficult ? "

[1] Hoover *v.* Wood, 9 Ind. 287.

[2] Ex parte Randolph, 2 Brock. 447 ; Frees *v.* Ford, 6 N. Y. 177, 178 ; White *v.* Scott, 4 Barb. 56 ; Mobile and Ohio Railroad Co. *v.* State, 29 Ala. 573.

of the remainder-men themselves.[1] And a party who has assented to his property being taken under a statute cannot afterwards object that the statute is in violation of a provision in the constitution designed for the protection of private property.[2] The statute is assumed to be valid, until some one complains whose rights it invades. "*Prima facie*, and on the face of the act itself, nothing will generally appear to show that the act is not valid ; and it is only when some person attempts to resist its operation, and calls in the aid of the judicial power to pronounce it void, as to him, his property or his rights, that the objection of unconstitutionality can be presented and sustained. Respect for the legislature, therefore, concurs with well-established principles of law in the conclusion that such an act is not void, but voidable only ; and it follows, as a necessary legal inference from this position, that this ground of avoidance can be taken advantage of by those only who have a right to question the validity of the act, and not by strangers. To this extent only is it necessary to go, in order to secure and protect the rights of all persons against the unwarranted exercise of legislative power, and to this extent only, therefore, are courts of justice called on to interpose."[3]

IV. Nor can a court declare a statute unconstitutional and void, solely on the ground of unjust and oppressive provisions, or because it is supposed to violate the natural, social, or political rights of the citizen, unless it can be shown that such injustice is prohibited or such rights guaranteed or protected by the constitution. It is true there are some reported cases in which judges have been understood to intimate a doctrine different from what is here asserted ; but it will generally be found, on an examination of those cases, that what is said is rather by way of argument and illustration, to show the unreasonableness of putting upon constitutions such a construction as would permit legislation of the objectionable character then in question, and to induce a more cautious and patient examination of the statute, with a view to

[1] Sinclair v. Jackson, 8 Cow. 543.

[2] Embury v. Conner, 3 N. Y. 511 ; Baker v. Braman, 6 Hill, 47 ; Mobile and Ohio Railroad Co. v. State, 29 Ala. 586.

[3] Wellington, Petitioner, 16 Pick. 96. And see Hingham, &c. Turnpike Co. v. Norfolk Co., 6 Allen, 353 ; De Jarnette v. Haynes, 23 Miss. 600 ; Sinclair v. Jackson, 8 Cow. 543, 579 ; Heyward v. Mayor, &c. of New York, 8 Barb. 489 ; Matter of Albany St., 11 Wend. 149.

discover in it, if possible, some more just and reasonable legislative intent, than as laying down a rule by which courts would be at liberty to limit, according to their own judgment and sense of justice and propriety, the extent of legislative power in directions in which the constitution had imposed no restraint.   Mr. Justice Story, in one case, in examining the extent of power granted by the charter of Rhode Island, which authorized the General Assembly to make laws in the most ample manner, " so as such laws, &c., be not contrary and repugnant unto, but as near as may be agreeable to, the laws of England, considering the nature and constitution of the place and people there," expresses himself thus : " What is the true extent of the power thus granted must be open to explanation as well by usage as by construction of the terms in which it is given.   In a government professing to regard the great rights of personal liberty and of property, and which is required to legislate in subordination to the general laws of England, it would not lightly be presumed that the great principles of Magna Charta were to be disregarded, or that the estates of its subjects were liable to be taken away without trial, without notice, and without offence.   Even if such authority could be deemed to have been confided by the charter to the General Assembly of Rhode Island, as an exercise of transcendental sovereignty before the Revolution, it can scarcely be imagined that that great event could have left the people of that State subjected to its uncontrolled and arbitrary exercise.   That government can scarcely be deemed to be free, where the rights of property are left solely dependent upon the will of a legislative body, without any restraint.   The fundamental maxims of a free government seem to require that the rights of personal liberty and private property should be held sacred.   At least no court of justice in this country would be warranted in assuming that the power to violate and disregard them — a power so repugnant to the common principles of justice and civil liberty — lurked under any general grant of legislative authority, or ought to be implied from any general expressions of the will of the people.   The people ought not to be presumed to part with rights so vital to their security and well-being, without very strong and direct expressions of such an intention."   " We know of no case in which a legislative act to transfer the property of A to B, without his consent, has ever been held a constitutional exercise of legislative power in any State in the Union. On the contrary, it has been constantly resisted, as inconsistent with just principles, by every judicial tribunal in which it has been attempted to be enforced." [1] The question discussed by the learned judge in this case is perceived to have been, What is the scope of a grant of legislative power to be exercised in conformity with the laws of England? Whatever he says is pertinent to that question; and the considerations he suggests are by way of argument, to show that the power to do certain unjust and oppressive acts was not covered by the grant of legislative power. It is not intimated that if they were within the grant, they would be impliedly prohibited because unjust and oppressive.

In another case arising in the Supreme Court of New York, one of the judges, in considering the rights of the city of New York to certain corporate property, has said: "The inhabitants of the city of New York have a vested right in the City Hall, markets, water-works, ferries, and other public property, which cannot be taken from them any more than their individual dwellings or storehouses. Their rights, in this respect, rest *not merely upon the constitution*, but upon the great principles of eternal justice which lie at the foundation of all free governments." [2] The great principles of eternal justice which affected the particular case had been incorporated in the constitution, and it therefore became unnecessary to consider what would otherwise have been the rule; nor do we understand the court as intimating any opinion upon that subject. It was sufficient for the case, to find

---

[1] Wilkinson v. Leland, 2 Pet. 657. See also what is said by the same judge in Terrett v. Taylor, 9 Cranch, 43. "It is clear that statutes passed against plain and obvious principles of common right and common reason are absolutely null and void, so far as they are calculated to operate against those principles." Ham v. McClaws, 1 Bay, 98. But the question in that case was one of construction; whether the court should give to a statute a construction which should make it operate against common right and common reason. In Bowman v. Middleton, 1 Bay, 282, the court held an act which divested a man of his freehold and passed it over to another, was void "as against common right as well as against Magna Charta." In Regents of University v. Williams, 9 Gill & J. 365, it was said that an act was void as opposed to fundamental principles of right and justice inherent in the nature and spirit of the social compact. But the court had already decided that the act was opposed, not only to the constitution of the State, but to that of the United States also. See Mayor, &c. of Baltimore v. State, 15 Md. 376.

[2] Benson v. Mayor, &c. of New York, 10 Barb. 244.

that the principles of right and justice had been recognized and protected by the constitution, and that the people had not assumed to confer upon the legislature a power to deprive the city of rights which did not come from the constitution, but from principles antecedent to and recognized by it.

So it is said by Hosmer, Ch. J., in a Connecticut case : " With those judges who assert the omnipotence of the legislature in all cases where the constitution has not interposed an explicit restraint, I cannot agree. Should there exist, what I know is not only an incredible supposition, but a most remote improbability, a case of direct infraction of vested rights, too palpable to be questioned and too unjust to admit of vindication, I could not avoid considering it as a violation of the social compact, and within the control of the judiciary. If, for example, a law were made without any cause to deprive a person of his property, or to subject him to imprisonment, who would not question its legality, and who would aid in carrying it into effect? On the other hand, I cannot harmonize with those who deny the power of the legislature, in any case, to pass laws which, with entire justice, operate on antecedent legal rights. A retrospective law may be just and reasonable, and the right of the legislature to enact one of this description I am not speculatist enough to question." [1]   The cases here supposed of unjust and tyrannical enactments would probably be held not to be within the power of any legislative body in the Union. One of them would be clearly a bill of attainder; the other, unless it was in the nature of remedial legislation, and susceptible of being defended on that theory, would be an exercise of judicial power, and therefore in excess of legislative authority, because not included in the apportionment of power made to that department. No question of implied prohibition would arise in either of these cases ; but if the grant of power had covered them, and there had been no express limitation, there would, as it seems to us, be very great probability of unpleasant and dangerous conflict of authority if the courts were to deny validity to legislative action on subjects within their control, on the assumption that the legislature had disregarded justice or sound policy. The moment a court ventures to substitute its own judgment for that of the legislature, in any case where the constitution has vested the legislature with power over the subject, that moment it enters

[1] Goshen v. Stonington, 4 Conn. 225.

upon a field where it is impossible to set limits to its authority, and where its discretion alone will measure the extent of its interference.[1]

The rule of law upon this subject appears to be, that, except where the constitution has imposed limits upon the legislative power, it must be considered as practically absolute, whether it operate according to natural justice or not in any particular case. The courts are not the guardians of the rights of the people of the State, unless those rights are secured by some constitutional provision which comes within the judicial cognizance. The remedy for unwise or oppressive legislation, within constitutional bounds, is by an appeal to the justice and patriotism of the representatives of the people. If this fail, the people in their sovereign capacity can correct the evil; but courts cannot assume their rights.[2] The judiciary can only arrest the execution of a statute when it conflicts with the constitution. It cannot run a race of opinions upon points of right, reason, and expediency with the law-making power.[3] Any legislative act which does not encroach upon the other departments of the government, being *prima facie* valid, must be enforced, unless restrictions upon the legislative power can be pointed out in the constitution, and the case shown to come within them.[4]

---

[1] "If the legislature should pass a law in plain and unequivocal language, within the general scope of their constitutional powers, I know of no authority in this government to pronounce such an act void, merely because, in the opinion of the judicial tribunals, it was contrary to the principles of natural justice; for this would be vesting in the court a latitudinarian authority which might be abused, and would necessarily lead to collisions between the legislative and judicial departments, dangerous to the well-being of society, or at least not in harmony with the structure of our ideas of natural government." Per Rogers, J., in Commonwealth v. McCloskey, 2 Rawle, 374. "All the courts can do with odious statutes is to chasten their hardness by construction. Such is the imperfection of the best human institutions, that, mould them as we may, a large discretion must at last be reposed somewhere. The best and in many cases the only security is in the wisdom and integrity of public servants, and their identity with the people. Governments cannot be administered without committing powers in trust and confidence." Beebe v. State, 6 Ind. 528, per Stuart, J. And see Johnston v. Commonwealth, 1 Bibb, 603; Flint River Steamboat Co. v. Foster, 5 Geo. 194.

[2] Bennett v. Bull, Baldw. 74.

[3] Perkins, J., in Madison & Indianapolis Railroad Co. v. Whiteneck, 8 Ind. 222.

[4] Sill v. Village of Corning, 15 N. Y. 303; Varick v. Smith, 5 Paige, 137;

V. If the courts are not at liberty to declare statutes void because of their apparent injustice or impolicy, neither can they do so because they appear to the minds of the judges to violate fundamental principles of republican government, unless it shall be found that those principles are placed beyond legislative encroachment by the constitution. The principles of republican government are not a set of inflexible rules, vital and active in the constitution, though unexpressed, but they are subject to variation and modification from motives of policy and public necessity ; and it is only in those particulars in which experience has demonstrated any departure from the settled practice to work injustice or confusion, that we shall discover an incorporation of them in the constitution in such form as to make them definite rules of action under all circumstances. It is undoubtedly a maxim of republican government, as we understand it, that taxation and representation should be inseparable ; but where the legislature interferes, as in many cases it may do, to compel taxation by a .municipal corporation for local purposes, it is evident that this maxim is allowed very little force in the case, since the

Cochran *v.* Van Surlay, 20 Wend. 365; Morris *v.* People, 3 Denio, 381 ; Wyne-hamer *v.* People, 13 N. Y. 430 ; People *v.* Supervisors of Orange, 17 N. Y. 235 ; People *v.* New York Central Railroad Co., 34 Barb. 138; People *v.* Toynbee, 2 Park. Cr. R. 490 ; Dow *v.* Norris, 4 N. H. 16 ; Derby Turnpike Co. *v.* Parks, 10 Conn. 522, 543; Hartford Bridge Co. *v.* Union Ferry Co., 29 Conn. 210; Holden *v.* James, 11 Mass. 396; Norwich *v.* County Commissioners, 13 Pick. 60; Dawson *v.* Shaver, 1 Blackf. 206; Beauchamp *v.* State, 6 Blackf. 305 ; Doe *v.* Douglass, 8 Blackf. 10; Maize *v.* State, 4 Ind. 342; Stocking *v.* State, 7 Ind. 327; Beebe *v.* State, 6 Ind. 528 ; Newland *v.* Marsh, 19 Ill. 376, 384 ; Bliss *v.* Commonwealth, 2 Litt. 90; State *v.* Ashley, 1 Ark. 513; Campbell *v.* Union Bank, 6 How. Miss. 672 ; Tate's Ex'r *v.* Bell, 4 Yerg. 206 ; Whittington *v.* Polk, 1 Harr. & J. 236 ; Norris *v.* Abingdon Academy, 7 Gill & J. 7 ; State *v.* Lyles, 1 McCord, 238 ; Myers *v.* English, 9 Cal. 341 ; Ex parte Newman, Ibid. 502; Hobart *v.* Supervisors, 17 Cal. 23 ; Crenshaw *v.* Slate River Co., 6 Rand. 245; Lewis *v.* Webb, 3 Greenl. 326 ; Durham *v.* Lewiston, 4 Greenl. 140 ; Lunt's case, 6 Greenl. 412 ; Scott *v.* Smart's Ex'rs, 1 Mich. 306 ; Williams *v.* Detroit, 2 Mich. 560; Tyler *v.* People, 8 Mich. 320 ; Colton *v.* Commissioners of Leon County, 6 Flor. 610 ; State *v.* Robinson, 1 Kansas, 27 ; Santo *v.* State, 2 Iowa, 165; Morrison *v.* Springer, 15 Iowa, 304 ; Stoddart *v.* Smith, 5 Binn. 355 ; Moore *v.* Houston, 3 S. & R. 169 ; Braddee *v.* Brownfield, 2 W. & S. 271 ; Harvey *v.* Thomas, 10 Watts, 63 ; Commonwealth *v.* Maxwell, 27 Penn. St. 456 ; Carey *v.* Giles, 9 Geo. 253 ; Macon and Western Railroad Co. *v.* Davis, 13 Geo. 68 ; Franklin Bridge Co. *v.* Wood, 14 Geo. 80 ; Boston *v.* Cummins, 16 Geo. 102 ; Van Horn *v.* Dorrance, 2 Dall. 309 ; Calder *v.* Bull, 3 Dall. 386 ; Cooper *v.* Telfair, 4 Dall. 18 ; Fletcher *v.* Peck, 6 Cranch, 128.

representation of the locality taxed is but slight in the body imposing the tax, and the burden may be imposed, not only against the protest of the local representative, but against the general opposition of the municipality. The property of married women is taxable, notwithstanding they are not allowed a voice in choosing representatives.[1] The maxim is not entirely lost sight of in such cases, but its application in the particular case, and the determination how far it can properly and justly be made to yield to considerations of policy and expediency, must rest exclusively with the law-making power, in the absence of any definite constitutional provisions so embodying the maxim as to make it a limitation upon legislative authority. It is also a maxim of republican government that local concerns shall be managed in the local districts, which shall choose their own administrative and police officers, and establish for themselves police regulations ; but this maxim is subject to such exceptions as the legislative power of the State shall see fit to make ; and when made, it must be presumed that the public interest, convenience, and protection are subserved thereby.[2] The State may interfere to establish new regulations against the will of the local constituency ; and if it shall think proper in any case to assume to itself those powers of local police which should be executed by the people immediately concerned, we must suppose it has been done because the local administration has proved imperfect and inefficient, and a regard to the general well-being has demanded the change. In these cases the maxims which have prevailed in the government address themselves to the wisdom of the legislature ; and to adhere to them as far as possible is doubtless to keep in the path of wisdom ; but they do not constitute restrictions so as to warrant the other departments in treating the exceptions which are made as unconstitutional.[3]

---

[1] Wheeler v. Wall, 6 Allen, 558.

[2] People v. Draper, 15 N. Y. 547.

[3] In People v. Mahaney, 13 Mich. 500, where the Metropolitan Police Act of Detroit was claimed to be unconstitutional on various grounds, the court say : " Besides the specific objections made to the act as opposed to the provisions of the constitution, the counsel for respondent attacks it on ' general principles,' and especially because violating fundamental principles in our system, that governments exist by consent of the governed, and that taxation and representation go together. The taxation under the act, it is said, is really in the hands of a police board, a body in the choice of which the people of Detroit have no voice. This argument

VI. Nor are the courts at liberty to declare an act void, because in their opinion it is opposed to a *spirit* supposed to pervade the constitution, but not expressed in words. " When the fundamental law has not limited, either in terms or by necessary implication, the general powers conferred upon the legislature, we cannot declare a limitation under the notion of having discovered something in the *spirit* of the constitution which is not even mentioned in the instrument." [1] " It is difficult," says Mr. Senator Verplanck, " upon any general principles, to limit the omnipotence of the sovereign legislative power by judicial interposition, except so far as the express words of a written constitution give that authority. There are indeed many *dicta* and some great authorities holding that acts contrary to the first principles of right are void. The principle is unquestionably

is one which might be pressed upon the legislative department with great force, if it were true in point of fact. But as the people of Detroit are really represented throughout, the difficulty suggested can hardly be regarded as fundamental. They were represented in the legislature which passed the act, and had the same proportionate voice there with the other municipalities in the State, all of which receive from that body their powers of local government, and such only as its wisdom shall prescribe within the constitutional limit. They were represented in that body when the present police board were appointed by it, and the governor, who is hereafter to fill vacancies, will be chosen by the State at large, including their city. There is nothing in the maxim that taxation and representation go together which requires that the body paying the tax shall alone be consulted in its assessment; and if there were, we should find it violated at every turn in our system. The State legislature not only has a control in this respect over inferior municipalities, which it exercises by general laws, but it sometimes finds it necessary to interpose its power in special cases to prevent unjust or burdensome taxation, as well as to compel the performance of a clear duty. The constitution itself, by one of the clauses referred to, requires the legislature to exercise its control over the taxation of municipal corporations, by restricting it to what that body may regard as proper bounds. And municipal bodies are frequently compelled most unwillingly to levy taxes for the payment of claims, by the judgments or mandates of courts in which their representation is quite as remote as that of the people of Detroit in this police board. It cannot therefore be said that the maxims referred to have been entirely disregarded by the legislature in the passage of this act. But as counsel do not claim that, in so. far as they have been departed from, the constitution has been violated, we cannot, with propriety, be asked to declare an act void on any such general objection." And see Wynehamer *v.* People, 13 N. Y. 429, per Selden, J.; Benson *v.* Mayor, &c. of Albany, 24 Barb. 256 et seq.; Baltimore *v.* State, 15 Md. 376 ; People *v.* Draper, 15 N. Y. 532.

[1] People *v.* Fisher, 24 Wend. 220.

sound as the governing rule of a legislature in relation to its own acts, or even those of a preceding legislature. It also affords a safe rule of construction for courts, in the interpretation of laws admitting of any doubtful construction, to presume that the legislature could not have intended an unequal and unjust operation of its statutes. Such a construction ought never to be given to legislative language if it be susceptible of any other more conformable to justice; but if the words be positive and without ambiguity, I can find no authority for a court to vacate or repeal a statute on that ground alone. But it is only in express constitutional provisions, limiting legislative power and controlling the temporary will of a majority, by a permanent and paramount law, settled by the deliberate wisdom of the nation, that I can find a safe and solid ground for the authority of courts of justice to declare void any legislative enactment. Any assumption of authority beyond this would be to place in the hands of the judiciary powers too great and too undefined either for its own security or the protection of private rights. It is therefore a most gratifying circumstance to the friends of regulated liberty, that in every change in their constitutional polity which has yet taken place here, whilst political power has been more widely diffused among the people, stronger and better-defined guards have been given to the rights of property." And after quoting certain express limitations, he proceeds: "Believing that we are to rely upon these and similar provisions as the best safeguards of our rights, as well as the safest authorities for judicial direction, I cannot bring myself to approve of the power of courts to annul any law solemnly passed, either on an assumed ground of its being contrary to natural equity, or from a broad, loose, and vague interpretation of a constitutional provision beyond its natural and obvious sense." [1]

The accepted theory upon this subject appears to be this: In every sovereign state there resides an absolute and uncontrolled power of legislation. In Great Britain this complete power rests in the Parliament; in the American States it resides in the people themselves as an organized body politic. But the people, by

---

[1] Cochran v. Van Surlay, 20 Wend. 381 – 383. See also People v. Gallagher, 4 Mich. 244; Benson v. Mayor, &c. of Albany, 24 Barb. 252 et seq.; Grant v. Courter, Ibid. 232; Wynehamer v. People, 13 N. Y. 391, per Comstock, J.; Ibid. p. 453, per Selden, J.; Ibid. p. 477, per Johnson, J.

creating the Constitution of the United States, have delegated this power as to certain subjects, and under certain restrictions, to the Congress of the Union ; and that portion they cannot resume, except as it may be done through amendment of the national Constitution. For the exercise of the legislative power, subject to this limitation, they create, by their State constitution, a legislative department upon which they confer it ; and granting it in general terms, they must be understood to grant the whole legislative power which they possessed, except so far as at the same time they saw fit to impose restrictions. While, therefore, the Parliament of Britain possesses completely the absolute and uncontrolled power of legislation, the legislative bodies of the American States possess the same power except, *first*, as it may have been limited by the Constitution of the United States ; and, *second*, as it may have been limited by the constitution of the State. A legislative act cannot, therefore, be declared void, unless its conflict with one of these two instruments can be pointed out.[1]

It is to be borne in mind, however, that there is a broad difference between the Constitution of the United States and the constitutions of the States as regards the power which may be exercised under them. The government of the United States is one of *enumerated* powers ; the governments of the States are possessed of all the general powers of legislation. When a law of Congress is assailed as void, we look in the national Constitution to see if the grant of specified powers is broad enough to embrace it ; but when a State law is attacked on the same ground, it is presumably valid in any case, and this presumption is a conclusive one, unless in the Constitution of the United States or of the State we are able to discover that it is prohibited. We look in the Constitution of the United States for *grants* of legislative power, but in the constitution of the State to ascertain if any *limitations* have been imposed upon the complete power with which the legislative department of the State was vested in its creation. Congress can pass no laws but such as the Constitution authorizes either expressly or by clear implication ; while the State legislature has jurisdiction of all subjects on which its legislation is not prohibited.[2] " The law-making power of the

[1] People *v.* New York Central Railroad Co., 34 Barb. 138. And see the cases cited, ante, p. 168, note 4.

[2] Sill *v.* Village of Corning, 15 N. Y. 303 ; People *v.* Supervisors of Orange,

State," it is said in one case, " recognizes no restraints, and is bound by none, except such as are imposed by the Constitution. That instrument has been aptly termed a legislative act by the people themselves in their sovereign capacity, and is therefore the paramount law. Its object is not to grant legislative power, but to confine and restrain it. Without the constitutional limitations, the power to make laws would be absolute. These limitations are created and imposed by express words, or arise by necessary implication. The leading feature of the constitution is the separation and distribution of the powers of the government. It takes care to separate the executive, legislative, and judicial powers, and to define their limits. The executive can do no legislative act, nor the legislature any executive act, and neither can exercise judicial authority." [1]

It does not follow, however, that in every case the courts, before they can set aside a law as invalid, must be able to find in the constitution some specific inhibition which has been disregarded, or some express command which has been disobeyed. Prohibitions are only important where they are in the nature of exceptions to a general grant of power ; and if the authority to do an act has not been granted by the sovereign to its representative, it cannot be necessary to prohibit its being done. If in one department was vested the whole power of the government, it might be essential for the people, in the instrument delegating this complete authority, to make careful and particular exception of all those cases which it was intended to exclude from its cognizance ; for without such exception the government might do whatever the people themselves, when met in their sovereign capacity, would have power to do. But when only the legislative power is delegated to one department, and the judicial to another, it is not important that the one should be expressly forbidden to try causes, or the other to make laws. The assumption of judicial power by the legislature in such a case is unconstitutional, because, though not expressly forbidden, it is nevertheless incon-

27 Barb. 593; People v. Gallagher, 4 Mich. 244 ; Sears v. Cottrell, 5 Mich. 257 ; People v. New York Central Railroad Co., 24 N. Y. 497, 504 ; People v. Toynbee, 2 Park. Cr. R. 490 ; State v. Gutierrez, 15 La. An. 190 ; Walpole v. Elliott, 18 Ind. 258 ; Smith v. Judge, 17 Cal. 547 ; Commonwealth v. Hartman, 17 Penn. St. 119 ; Kirby v. Shaw, 19 Penn. St. 260 ; Weister v. Hade, 52 Penn. St. 477.

[1] Sill v. Corning, 15 N. Y. 303.

sistent with the provisions which have conferred upon another department the power the legislature is seeking to exercise. And for similar reasons a legislative act which should undertake to make a judge the arbiter in his own controversies would be void, because, though in form a provision for the exercise of judicial power, in substance it would be the creation of an arbitrary and irresponsible power, neither legislative, executive, nor judicial, and wholly unknown to constitutional government. It could not be necessary to forbid the judiciary to render judgment without suffering the party to make defence; because it is implied in judicial authority that there shall be a hearing before condemnation. Taxation cannot be arbitrary, because its very definition includes apportionment. The bills of rights in the American constitutions forbid that parties shall be deprived of property except by the law of the land; but if the prohibition had been omitted, a legislative enactment to pass one man's property over to another would nevertheless be void. If the act proceeded upon the assumption that such other person was justly entitled to the estate, and therefore it was transferred, it would be void, because judicial in its nature; and if it proceeded without reasons, it would be equally void, as neither legislative nor judicial, but a mere arbitrary fiat.[1] There is no difficulty in saying that any such act, which, under pretence of exercising one power is usurping another, is opposed to the constitution and void. It is assuming a power which the people, if they have not granted it at all, have reserved to themselves. The maxims of Magna Charta and the common law are the interpreters of constitutional grants of power, and those acts which by those maxims the several departments of government are forbidden to do cannot be considered within any grant or apportionment of power which the people in general terms have made to those departments. The Parliament of Great Britain, indeed, as possessing the sovereignty

---

[1] Bowman v. Middleton, 1 Bay, 252; Wilkinson v. Leland, 2 Pet. 657; Terrett v. Taylor, 9 Cranch, 43; Ervine's Appeal, 16 Penn. St. 266. "It is now considered an universal and fundamental proposition in every well-regulated and properly administered government, whether embodied in a constitutional form or not, that private property cannot be taken for a strictly private purpose at all, nor for public without a just compensation; and that the obligation of contracts cannot be abrogated or essentially impaired. These and other vested rights of the citizen are held sacred and inviolable, even against the plenitude of power in the legislative department." Nelson, J. in People v. Morris, 13 Wend. 328.

of the country, has the power to disregard fundamental principles, and pass arbitrary and unjust enactments; but it cannot do
this rightfully, and it has the power to do so simply because there
is no written constitution from which its authority springs or on
which it depends, and by which the courts can test the validity of
its declared will. The rules which confine the discretion of Parliament within the ancient landmarks are rules for the construction of the powers of the American legislatures; and however
proper and prudent it may be expressly to prohibit those things
which are not understood to be within the proper attributes of
legislative power, such prohibition can never be regarded as essential, when the extent of the power apportioned to the legislative
department is considered, and appears not to be broad enough to
cover the obnoxious authority. The absence of such prohibition
cannot, by implication, confer power.

Nor, where fundamental rights are declared by the constitution,
is it necessary at the same time to prohibit the legislature, in express terms, from taking them away. The declaration is itself a
prohibition, and is inserted in the constitution for the express
purpose of operating as a restriction upon legislative power.[1]
Many things, indeed, which are contained in the bills of rights
to be found in the American constitutions are not, and from the
very nature of the case cannot be, so certain and definite in character as to form rules for judicial decisions; and they are declared
rather as guides to the legislative judgment than as marking an
absolute limitation of power. The nature of the declaration will
generally enable us to determine without difficulty whether it is
the one thing or the other. If it is declared that all men are free,
and no man can be slave to another, a definite and certain rule of
action is laid down, which the courts can administer; but if it be
said that " the blessings of a free government can only be maintained by a firm adherence to justice, moderation, temperance,
frugality, and virtue," we should not be likely to commit the
mistake of supposing that this declaration would authorize the
courts to substitute their own view of justice for that which may
have impelled the legislature to pass a particular law, or to inquire into the moderation, temperance, frugality, and virtue of
its members, with a view to set aside their action, if it appears to
have been influenced by the opposite qualities. It is plain that

---

[1] Beebe v. State, 6 Ind. 518.

what in the one case is a rule, in the other is an admonition addressed to the judgment and the conscience of all persons in authority, as well as of the people themselves.

So the forms prescribed for legislative action are in the nature of limitations upon its authority. The constitutional provisions which establish them are equivalent to a declaration that the legislative power shall be exercised under these forms, and shall not be exercised under any other. A statute which does not observe them will plainly be ineffectual.

Statutes unconstitutional in Part.

It will sometimes be found that an act of the legislature is opposed in some of its provisions to the constitution, while others, standing by themselves, would be unobjectionable. So the forms observed in passing it may be sufficient for some of the purposes sought to be accomplished by it, but insufficient for others. In any such case the portion which conflicts with the constitution, or in regard to which the necessary conditions have not been observed, must be treated as a nullity. Whether the other parts of the statute must also be adjudged void because of the association must depend upon a consideration of the object of the law, and in what manner and to what extent the unconstitutional portion affects the remainder. A statute, it has been said, is judicially held to be unconstitutional, because it is not within the scope of legislative authority; it may either propose to accomplish something prohibited by the constitution, or to accomplish some lawful, and even laudable object, by means repugnant to the Constitution of the United States or of the State. A statute may contain some such provisions, and yet the same act, having received the sanction of all branches of the legislature, and being in the form of law, may contain other useful and salutary provisions, not obnoxious to any just constitutional exception. It would be inconsistent with all just principles of constitutional law to adjudge these enactments void, because they are associated in the same act, but not connected with or dependent on others which are unconstitutional.[1] Where, therefore, a part of a

---

[1] Commonwealth v. Clapp, 5 Gray, 100. See, to the same effect, Fisher v. McGirr, 1 Gray, 1; Warren v. Mayor, &c. of Charlestown, 2 Gray, 84; Wellington, Petitioner, 16 Pick. 95; Commonwealth v. Hitchings, 5 Gray, 482; Com-

statute is unconstitutional, that fact does not authorize the courts to declare the remainder void also, unless all the provisions are connected in subject-matter, depending on each other, operating together for the same purpose, or otherwise so connected together in meaning, that it cannot be presumed the legislature would have passed the one without the other.[1] The constitutional and unconstitutional provisions may even be contained in the same section, and yet be perfectly distinct and separable, so that the first may stand though the last fall. The point is not whether they are contained in the same section ; for the distribution into sections is purely artificial ; but whether they are essentially and inseparably connected in substance.[2] If, when the unconstitutional portion is stricken out, that which remains is complete in itself, and capable of being executed wholly independent of that which was rejected, it must be sustained. The difficulty is in determining whether the good and bad parts of the statute are capable of being separated within the meaning of this rule. If a statute attempts to accomplish two or more objects, and is void as to one, it may still be in every respect complete and valid as to the other. But if its purpose is to accomplish a single object only, and some of its provisions are void, the whole must fail unless sufficient remains to effect the object without the aid of the invalid portion.[3] And if they are so mutually connected with and depend-

monwealth *v.* Pomeroy, 5 Gray, 486 ; State *v.* Copeland, 3 R. I. 33 ; State *v.* Snow, 3 R. I. 64 ; McCulloch *v.* State, 11 Ind. 432 ; People *v.* Hill, 7 Cal. 97 ; Lathrop *v.* Mills, 19 Cal. 513 ; Thomson *v.* Grand Gulf Railroad Co., 3 How. Miss. 240 ; Campbell *v.* Union Bank, 6 How. Miss. 625 ; Mobile and Ohio Railroad Co. *v.* State, 29 Ala. 573 ; Santo *v.* State, 2 Iowa, 165 ; State *v.* Cox, 3 Eng. 436 ; Mayor, &c. of Savannah *v.* State, 4 Geo. 26 ; Exchange Bank *v.* Hines, 3 Ohio, N. S. 1 ; Robinson *v.* Bank of Darien, 18 Geo. 65 ; State *v.* Wheeler, 25 Conn. 290 ; People *v.* Lawrence, 36 Barb. 190 ; Williams *v.* Payson, 14 La. An. 7 ; Ely *v.* Thompson, 3 A. K. Marsh. 70 ; Davis *v.* State, 7 Md. 151 ; Bank of United States *v.* Dudley's Lessee, 2 Pet. 526. " To the extent of the collision and repugnancy, the law of the State must yield ; and to that extent, and no further, it is rendered by such repugnancy inoperative and void." Commonwealth *v.* Kimball, 24 Pick. 361, per Shaw, Ch. J. ; Norris *v.* Boston, 4 Met. 288.

[1] Commonwealth *v.* Hitchings, 5 Gray, 485.

[2] Commonwealth *v.* Hitchings, 5 Gray, 485 ; Willard *v.* People, 4 Scam. 470 ; Eells *v.* People, 4 Scam. 512 ; Robinson *v.* Bidwell, 22 Cal. 379.

[3] Santo *v.* State, 2 Iowa, 165. But perhaps the doctrine of sustaining one part of a statute when the other is void was carried to an extreme in this case. A

ent on each other, as conditions, considerations, or compensations for each other, as to warrant the belief that the legislature intended them as a whole, and if all could not be carried into effect, the legislature would not pass the residue independently, then if some parts are unconstitutional, all the provisions which are thus dependent, conditional, or connected must fall with them.[1]

It has accordingly been held where a statute submitted to the voters of a county the question of the removal of their county seat, and one section imposed the forfeiture of certain vested rights in case the vote was against the removal, that this portion of the act being void, the whole must fall, inasmuch as the whole was submitted to the electors collectively, and the threatened forfeiture would naturally affect the result of the vote.[2]

And where a statute annexed to the city of Racine certain lands previously in the township of Racine, but contained an express provision that the lands so annexed should be taxed at a different and less rate than other lands in the city; the latter provision being held unconstitutional, it was also held that the whole statute must fail, inasmuch as such provision was clearly intended as a compensation for the annexation.[3]

And where a statute, in order to obtain a jury of six persons,

prohibitory liquor law had been passed which was not objectionable on constitutional grounds, except that the last section provided that " the question of prohibiting the sale and manufacture of intoxicating liquor " should be submitted to the electors of the State, and if it should appear " that a majority of the votes cast as aforesaid, upon said question of prohibition, shall be for the prohibitory liquor law, then this act shall take effect on the first day of July, 1855." The court held this to be an attempt by the legislature to shift the exercise of legislative power from themselves to the people, and therefore void; but they also held that the remainder of the act was complete without this section, and must therefore be sustained on the rule above given. The reasoning of the court by which they are brought to this conclusion is ingenious; but one cannot avoid feeling, especially after reading the dissenting opinion of Chief Justice Wright, that by the decision the court gave effect to an act which the legislature did not design should take effect unless the result of the unconstitutional submission to the people was in its favor. For a similar ruling, see Maize v. State, 4 Ind. 342; overruled in Meshmeier v. State, 11 Ind. 482.

[1] Warren v. Mayor, &c. of Charlestown, 2 Gray, 99 ; State v. Commissioners of Perry County, 5 Ohio, N. S. 507 ; Slauson v. Racine, 13 Wis. 398 ; Allen County Commissioners v. Silvers, 22 Ind. 491.

[2] State v. Commissioners of Perry County, 5 Ohio, N. S. 507.   And see Jones v. Robbins, 8 Gray, 338.

[3] Slauson v. Racine, 13 Wis. 398.

provided for the summoning of twelve jurors, from whom six were to be chosen and sworn, and under the constitution the jury must consist of twelve, it was held that the provision for reducing the number to six could not be rejected and the statute sustained, inasmuch as this would be giving to it a construction and effect different from that the legislature designed.[1]

On the other hand, — to illustrate how intimately the valid and invalid portions of a statute may be associated, — a section of the criminal code of Illinois provided that " if any person shall harbor or secrete any negro, mulatto, or person of color, the same being a slave or servant, owing service or labor to any other persons, whether they reside in this State or in any other State, or Territory, or district, within the limits and under the jurisdiction of the United States, or shall in any wise hinder or prevent the lawful owner or owners of such slaves or servants from retaking them in a lawful manner, every person so offending shall be deemed guilty of a misdemeanor," &c., and it was held that, although the latter portion of the section was void within the decision in Prigg v. Pennsylvania,[2] yet that the first portion, being a police regulation for the preservation of order in the State, and important to its well-being, and capable of being enforced without reference to the rest, was not affected by the invalidity of the rest.[3]

A legislative act may be entirely valid as to some classes of cases, and clearly void as to others. A general law for the punishment of offences, which should endeavor to reach, by its retroactive operation, acts before committed, as well as to prescribe a rule of conduct for the citizen in the future, would be void so far as it was retrospective, but such invalidity would not affect the operation of the law in regard to the cases which were within the legislative control. A law might be void as violating the obligation of existing contracts, but valid as to all contracts which should be entered into subsequent to its passage, and which therefore would have no legal force except such as the law itself would allow.[4] In any such case the unconstitutional law must operate as far as it can,[5] and it will not be held invalid on the objection

---

[1] Campau v. Detroit, 14 Mich. 272.

[2] 16 Pet. 539.

[3] Willard v. People, 4 Scam. 470 ; Eells v. People, Ibid. 512.

[4] Mundy v. Monroe, 1 Mich. 68 ; Cargill v. Power, 1 Mich. 369.

[5] Baker v. Braman, 6 Hill, 47.

of a party whose interests are not affected by it in a manner which the constitution forbids. If there are any exceptions to this rule, they must be of cases only where it is evident, from a contemplation of the statute and of the purpose to be accomplished by it, that it would not have been passed at all, except as an entirety, and that the general purpose of the legislature will be defeated if it shall be held valid as to some cases and void as to others.

Waiving a Constitutional Objection.

There are cases where a law must be sustained, because the party who makes objection has, by prior action, precluded himself from being heard against it. Where a constitutional provision is designed for the protection solely of the property rights of the citizen, it is competent for him to waive the protection, and to consent to such action as would be invalid if taken against his will. On this ground it has been held that an act appropriating the private property of one person for the private purposes of another, on compensation made, was valid if he whose property was taken assented thereto ; and that he did assent and waive the constitutional privilege, if he received the compensation awarded, or brought an action to recover it.[1] So if an act providing for the appropriation of property for a public use shall authorize more to be taken than the use requires, although such act would be void without the owner's assent, yet with it all objection on the ground of unconstitutionality is removed.[2] And where parties were authorized by statute to erect a dam across a river, provided they should first execute a bond to the people conditioned to pay such damages as each and every person might sustain in consequence of the erection of the dam, the damages to be assessed by a'justice of the peace, and the dam was erected and damages assessed as provided by the statute, it was held, in an action on the bond to recover those damages, that the party erecting the dam was precluded by acting under the statute from objecting to its validity, and insisting upon his right to a common-law trial by jury.[3] In these and the like cases the statute must be read with

---

[1] Baker v. Braman, 6 Hill, 47.

[2] Embury v. Conner, 3 N. Y. 511. And see Heyward v. Mayor, &c. of New York, 8 Barb. 489 ; Mobile and Ohio Railroad Co. v. State, 29 Ala. 586.

[3] People v. Murray, 5 Hill, 468. See Lee v. Tillotson, 24 Wend. 339.

an implied proviso that the party to be affected shall assent thereto ; and such consent removes all obstacle, and lets the statute in to operate the same as if it had in terms contained the condition.[1] In criminal cases, however, the doctrine that a constitutional privilege may be waived, must be true to a very limited extent only.

Judicial Doubts on Constitutional Questions.

It has been said by an eminent jurist, that when courts are called upon to pronounce the invalidity of an act of legislation, passed with all the forms and ceremonies requisite to give it the force of law, they will approach the question with great caution, examine it in every possible aspect, and ponder upon it as long as deliberation and patient attention can throw any new light upon the subject, and never declare a statute void, unless the nullity and invalidity of the act are placed, in their judgment, beyond reasonable doubt.[2] A reasonable doubt must be solved in favor of the legislative action, and the act be sustained.[3]

" The question whether a law be void for its repugnancy to the constitution is at all times a question of much delicacy, which ought seldom, if ever, to be decided in the affirmative in a doubtful case. The court when impelled by duty to render such a judgment would be unworthy of its station could it be unmindful

[1] Embury v. Conner, 3 N. Y. 518. And see Matter of Albany St., 11 Wend. 149 ; Chamberlain v. Lyell, 3 Mich. 448 ; Beecher v. Baldy, 7 Mich. 488 ; Mobile and Ohio Railroad Co. v. State, 29 Ala. 586.

[2] Wellington, Petitioner, 16 Pick. 95, per Shaw, Ch. J.

[3] Cooper v. Telfair, 4 Dall. 18 ; Dow v. Norris, 4 N. H. 16 ; Flint River Steamboat Co. v. Foster, 5 Geo. 194 ; Carey v. Giles, 9 Geo. 253 ; Macon and Western Railroad Co. v. Davis, 13 Geo. 68 ; Franklin Bridge Co. v. Wood, 14 Geo. 80 ; Kendall v. Kingston, 5 Mass. 524 ; Foster v. Essex Bank, 16 Mass. 245 ; Nórwich v. County Commissioners of Hampshire, 13 Pick. 61 ; Hartford Bridge Co. v. Union Ferry Co., 29 Conn. 227 ; Rich v. Flanders, 39 N. H. 312 ; Eason v. State, 6 Eng. 481 ; Hedley v. Commissioners of Franklin Co., 4 Blackf. 116 ; Stocking v. State, 7 Ind. 327 ; La Fayette v. Jenners, 10 Ind. 79 ; Ex parte McCollum, 1 Cow. 564 ; Coutant v. People, 11 Wend. 511 ; Clark v. People, 26 Wend. 606 ; Morris v. People, 3 Denio, 381 ; Baltimore v. State, 15 Md. 376 ; Cotton v. Commissioners of Leon Co., 6 Flor. 610 ; Lane v. Dorman, 3 Scam. 238 ; Newland v. Marsh, 19 Ill. 381 ; Farmers and Mechanics' Bank v. Smith, 3 S. & R. 63 ; Weister v. Hade, 52 Penn. St. 477 ; Sears v. Cottrell, 5 Mich. 251 ; People v. Tyler, 8 Mich. 320 ; Allen County Commissioners v. Silvers, 22 Ind. 491 ; State v. Robinson, 1 Kansas, 17.

of the solemn obligation which that station imposes; but it is not on slight implication and vague conjecture that the legislature is to be pronounced to have transcended its powers, and its acts to be considered as void. The opposition between the constitution and the law should be such that the judge feels a clear and strong conviction of their incompatibility with each other." [1] Mr. Justice Washington gives a reason for this rule, which has been repeatedly recognized in other cases which we have cited. After expressing the opinion that the particular question there presented, and which regarded the constitutionality of a State law, was involved in difficulty and doubt, he says: "But if I could rest my opinion in favor of the constitutionality of the law on which the question arises, on no other ground than this doubt so felt and acknowledged, that alone would, in my estimation, be a satisfactory vindication of it. It is but a decent respect due to the wisdom, the integrity, and the patriotism of the legislative body by which any law is passed, to presume in favor of its validity, until its violation of the constitution is proved beyond all reasonable doubt." [2]

The constitutionality of a law, then, is to be presumed, because the legislature, which was first required to pass upon the question, acting, as they must be deemed to have acted, with integrity, and with a just desire to keep within the restrictions laid by the constitution upon their action, have adjudged that it is so. They are a co-ordinate department of the government with the judiciary, invested with very high and responsible duties, as to some of which their acts are not subject to judicial scrutiny, and they legislate under the solemnity of an official oath, which it is not to be supposed they will disregard. It must, therefore, be supposed that their own doubts of the constitutionality of their action have been deliberately solved in its favor, so that the courts may with some confidence repose upon their conclusion as one based upon their best judgment. For although it is plain, upon the authorities, that the courts should sustain legislative action when not clearly satisfied of its invalidity, it is equally plain in reason that the legislature should abstain from adopting such action if not fully assured of their power to do so. Respect for the instrument under which they exercise their power should impel the

---

[1] Fletcher v. Peck, 6 Cranch, 128, per Marshall, Ch. J.

[2] Ogden v. Saunders, 12 Wheat. 270.

legislature in every case to solve their doubts in its favor, and it is only because we are to presume they do so, that courts are warranted in giving weight in any case to their decision. If it were understood that legislators refrained from exercising their judgment, or that, in cases of doubt, they allowed themselves to lean in favor of the action they desired to accomplish, the foundation for the cases we have cited would be altogether taken away.

As to what the doubt shall be upon which the court is to act, we conceive that it can make no difference whether it springs from an endeavor to arrive at the true interpretation of the constitution, or from a consideration of the law after the meaning of the constitution has been judicially determined. It has sometimes been supposed that it was the duty of the court, first, to interpret the constitution, placing upon it a construction that must remain unvarying, and then test the law in question by it; and that any other rule would lead to differing judicial decisions, if the legislature should put one interpretation upon the constitution at one time and a different one at another. But the decided cases do not sanction this rule,[1] and the difficulty suggested is rather imaginary than real, since it is but reasonable to expect that, where a construction has once been placed upon a constitutional provision, it will be followed afterwards, even though its original adoption may have sprung from deference to legislative action rather than from settled convictions in the judicial mind.[2]

The duty of the court to uphold a statute when the conflict between it and the constitution is not clear, and the implication which must always exist that no violation has been intended by the legislature, may require it in some cases, where the meaning of the constitution is not in doubt, to lean in favor of such a construction of the statute as might not at first view seem most obvious and natural. For as a conflict between the statute and constitution is not to be implied, it would seem to follow, where the meaning of the constitution is clear, *that the court, if possible, must give the statute such a construction as will enable it to have effect.* This is only saying, in another form of words, that the court must construe the statute in accordance with the legis-

---

[1] Sun Mutual Insurance Co. *v.* New York, 5 Sandf. 14; Clark *v.* People, 26 Wend. 606; Baltimore *v.* State, 15 Md. 457.

[2] People *v.* Blodgett, 13 Mich. 162.

lative intent ; since it is always to be presumed the legislature designed the statute to take effect, and not to be a nullity.

The rule upon this subject is thus stated by the Supreme Court of Illinois : " Whenever an act of the legislature can be so construed and applied as to avoid conflict with the constitution and give it the force of law, such construction will be adopted by the courts. Therefore, acts of the legislature, in terms retrospective, and which, literally interpreted, would invalidate and destroy vested rights, are upheld by giving them prospective operation only ; for, applied to, and operating upon, future acts and transactions only, they are rules of property under and subject to which the citizen acquires property rights, and are obnoxious to no constitutional limitation ; but as retroactive laws, they reach to and destroy *existing* rights, through force of the legislative will, without a hearing or judgment of law. So will acts of the legislature, having elements of limitation, and capable of being so applied and administered, although the words are broad enough to, and do, literally read, strike at the right itself, be construed to limit and control the remedy ; for as such they are valid, but as weapons destructive of vested rights they are void ; and such force only will be given the acts as the legislature could impart to them." [1]

The Supreme Court of New Hampshire, where a similar question is involved, recognizing their obligation " so to construe every act of the legislature as to make it consistent, if it be possible, with the provisions of the constitution," proceed to the examination of a statute by the same rule, " without stopping to inquire what construction might be warranted by the natural import of the language used." [2]

And Harris, J., delivering the opinion of the majority of the Court of Appeals of New York, says : " A legislative act is not to be declared void upon a mere conflict of interpretation between the legislative and the judicial power. Before proceeding to annul, by judicial sentence, what has been enacted by the law-making power, it should clearly appear that the act cannot be supported by any reasonable intendment or allowable presumption." [3] And the Supreme Court of New York consider this but

---

[1] Newland *v.* Marsh, 19 Ill. 384.
[2] Dow *v.* Norris, 4 N. H. 17.
[3] People *v.* Supervisors of Orange, 17 N. Y. 241.

the application of the familiar rule, that in the exposition of a statute, it is the duty of the court to seek to ascertain and carry out the intention of the legislature in its enactment, and to give full effect to such intention, and they are bound so to construe the statute, if practicable, as to give it force and validity, rather than to avoid it, or render it nugatory.[1]

The rule is not different when the question is whether any portion of a statute is void, than when the whole is assailed. The excess of power, if there is any, is the same in either case, and is not to be implied in any instance.

And on this ground it has been held that where the repealing clause in an unconstitutional statute repeals all inconsistent acts, the repealing clause is to stand and have effect, notwithstanding the invalidity of the rest.[2]   But other cases hold that such repealing clause is to be understood as designed to repeal all conflicting provisions, in order that those of the new statute can have effect; and that if the statute is invalid, nothing can conflict with it, and therefore nothing is repealed.[3]   Great caution is necessary in some cases, or the rule which was designed to ascertain and effectuate the legislative intent will be pressed to the extreme of giving effect to part of a statute exclusively, when the legislative intent was that it should not stand except as a component part of the whole.

Inquiry into Legislative Motives.

From what examination has been given to this subject, it appears that whether a statute is constitutional or not is always a question of power; that is, whether the legislature in the particular case, in respect to the subject-matter of the act, the manner in which its object is to be accomplished, and the mode of enacting it, has kept within the constitutional limits and observed the constitutional conditions. If so, the courts are not at liberty to inquire into the proper exercise of the power in any case. They must assume that legislative discretion has been properly exer-

---

[1] Clarke v. Rochester, 24 Barb. 471.

[2] Meshmeier v. State, 11 Ind. 489; Ely v. Thompson, 3 A. K. Marsh. 70.

[3] Shepardson v. Milwaukee and Beloit Railroad Co., 6 Wis. 605; State v. Judge of County Court, 11 Wis. 50; Tims v. State, 26 Ala. 165; Sullivan v. Adams, 3 Gray, 476; Devoy v. Mayor, &c. of New York, 35 Barb. 264; Campau v. Detroit, 14 Mich. 276; Childs v. Shower, 18 Iowa, 261.

cised.[1] If evidence was required, it must be supposed that it was before the legislature when the act was passed;[2] and if any special finding was required to warrant the passage of the particular act, it would seem that the passage of the act itself might be held equivalent to such finding.[3] And although it has sometimes been urged at the bar, that the courts ought to inquire into the motives of the legislature where fraud and corruption were alleged, and annul their action if the allegation were established, the argument has in no case been acceded to by the judiciary, and they have never allowed the inquiry to be entered upon.[4]

[1] People v. Lawrence, 36 Barb. 193 ; People v. New York Central Railroad Co., 34 Barb. 137 ; Baltimore v. State, 15 Md. 376.

[2] DeCamp v. Eveland, 19 Barb. 81.

[3] Johnson v. Joliet and Chicago Railroad Co., 23 Ill. 207. The constitution of Illinois provided that " corporations not possessing banking powers or privileges may be formed under general laws, but shall not be created by special acts, except for municipal purposes, and in cases where, in the judgment of the General Assembly, the objects of the corporation cannot be attained under general laws." A special charter being passed without any legislative declaration that its object could not be attained under a general law, the Supreme Court sustained it, but placed their decision mainly on the ground, that the clause had been wholly disregarded, " and it would now produce far-spread ruin to declare such acts unconstitutional and void." It is very clearly intimated in the opinion, that the legislative practice, and this decision sustaining it, did violence to the intent of the constitution. A provision in the constitution of Indiana that " no act shall take effect until the same shall have been published and circulated in the several counties of this State, by authority, except in case of emergency," adds the words, " which emergency shall be declared in the preamble, or in the body of the law " ; thus clearly making the legislative declaration necessary. Carpenter v. Montgomery, 7 Blackf. 415 ; Mark v. State, 15 Ind. 98 ; Hendrickson v. Hendrickson, 7 Ind. 13.

[4] Sunbury and Erie Railroad Co. v. Cooper, 33 Penn. St. 278 ; Ex parte Newman, 9 Cal. 502 ; Baltimore v. State, 15 Md. 376 ; Johnson v. Higgins, 3 Met. (Ky.) 566. " The courts cannot impute to the legislature any other but public motives for their acts." People v. Draper, 15 N. Y. 545, per Denio, Ch. J. " We are not made judges of the motives of the legislature, and the court will not usurp the inquisitorial office of inquiry into the bona fides of that body in discharging its duties." Shankland, J. in same case, p. 555. " The powers of the three departments are not merely equal ; they are exclusive in respect to the duties assigned to each. They are absolutely independent of each other. It is now proposed that one of the three powers shall institute an inquiry into the conduct of another department, and form an issue to try by what motives the legislature were governed in the enactment of a law. If this may be done, we may also inquire by what motives the executive is induced to approve a bill or withhold his approval, and in case of withholding it corruptly, by our mandate compel

Consequences if a Statute is Void.

When a statute is adjudged to be unconstitutional, it is as if it had never been. Rights cannot be built up under it ; contracts which depend upon it for their consideration are void ; it constitutes a protection to no one who has acted under it, and no one can be punished for having refused obedience to it before the decision was made.[1] And what is true of an act void *in toto* is true also as to any part of an act which is found to be unconstitutional, and which, consequently, is to be regarded as having never, at any time, been possessed of any legal force.

its approval. To institute the proposed inquiry would be a direct attack upon the independence of the legislature, and a usurpation of power subversive of the constitution." Wright *v.* Defrees, 8 Ind. 302, per Gookins, J. And see McCulloch *v.* State, 11 Ind. 431.

[1] Strong *v.* Daniel, 5 Ind. 348 ; Astrom *v.* Hammond, 3 McLean, 107.

CHAPTER VIII.

THE SEVERAL GRADES OF MUNICIPAL GOVERNMENT.

IN the examination of American constitutional law, we shall not fail to notice the care taken and the means adopted to bring the agencies by which power is to be exercised as near as possible to the subjects upon which the power is to operate.

In contradistinction to those governments where power is concentrated in one man, or one or more bodies of men, whose supervision and active control extends to all the objects of government within the territorial limits of the State, the American system is one of complete *decentralization*, the primary and vital idea of which is, that local affairs shall be managed by local authorities, and general affairs only by the central authority. It was under the control of this idea that a national constitution was formed, under which the States, while yielding to the national government complete and exclusive jurisdiction over external affairs, conferred upon it such powers only, in regard to matters of internal regulation, as seemed to be essential to national union, strength, and harmony, and without which the purpose in organizing the national authority might have been defeated. It is this, also, that impels the several States, as if by common arrangement, to subdivide their territory into counties, towns, road and school districts, and to confer upon each powers of local legislation, and also to incorporate cities, boroughs, and villages wherever a dense population renders different rules important from those which are needful for the rural districts.

The system is one which almost seems a part of the very nature of the race to which we belong. A similar subdivision of the realm for the purposes of municipal government has existed in England from the earliest ages;[1] and in America, the first settlers, as if instinctively, adopted it in their frame of government, and

---

[1] Crabbe's History of English Law, ch. 2; 1 Bl. Com. 114; Hallam's Middle Ages, ch. 8, pt. 1; 2 Kent, 278; Vaughan's Revolutions in English History, b. 2, ch. 8.

no other has ever supplanted it, or even found advocates. In most of the Colonies the central power created and provided for the organization of the towns;[1] in one at least the towns preceded and created the central authority;[2] but in all, the final result was substantially the same, that towns, villages, boroughs, cities, and counties exercised the powers of local government, and the Colony or State the powers of a more general nature.[3]

The several State constitutions have been framed with this system in view, and the delegations of power which they make, and the express and implied restraints which they impose thereupon, can only be correctly understood and construed by keeping in view its present existence and anticipated continuance. There are few of the general rules of constitutional law that are not more or less affected by the fact that the powers of government are not concentrated in any one body of men, but are carefully distributed, with a view to being easily, cheaply, and

[1] For an interesting history of the legislation in Connecticut on this subject, see Webster v. Harwinton, 32 Conn. 131. In New Hampshire, see Bow v. Allenstown, 34 N. H. 351. The learned note to Commonwealth v. Roxbury, 9 Gray, 503, will give similar information concerning the organization and authority of towns in the Massachusetts provinces.

[2] Rhode Island; see Arnold's History, ch. 7.

[3] " The townships," says De Tocqueville, " are only subordinate to the State in those interests which I shall term *social*, as they are common to all of the citizens. They are independent in all that concerns themselves, and among the inhabitants of New England, I believe that not a man is to be found who would acknowledge that the State has any right to interfere in their local interests. The towns of New England buy and sell, prosecute or are indicted; augment or diminish their rates, without the slightest opposition on the part of the administrative authority of the State. They are bound, however, to comply with the demands of the community. If a State is in need of money, a town can neither give nor withhold the supplies. If a State projects a road, the township cannot refuse to let it cross its territory; if a police regulation is made by the State it must be enforced by the town. An uniform system of instruction is organized all over the country, and every town is bound to establish the schools which the law ordains. . . . . Strict as this obligation is, the government of the State imposes it in principle only, and in its performance the township assumes all its independent rights. Thus taxes are voted by the State, but they are assessed and collected by the township; the existence of a school is obligatory, but the township builds, pays, and superintends it. In France, the state collector receives the local imposts; in America, the town collector receives the taxes of the State. Thus the French government lends its agents to the commune; in America, the township is the agent of the government. The fact alone shows the extent of the differences which exist between the two nations." Democracy in America, ch. 5.

intelligently exercised, and as far as possible by the persons more immediately interested.

We have already seen that the legislature cannot delegate its power to make laws ; but fundamental as this maxim is, it is so qualified by the customs of our race, and by other maxims which regard local government, that the right of the legislature, in the entire absence of authorization or prohibition, to create towns and other inferior municipal organizations, and to confer upon them the powers of local government, and especially of local taxation and police regulations usual with such corporations, would always pass unchallenged. The legislature in these cases is not regarded as delegating its authority, because the regulation of such local affairs as are commonly left to local boards and officers is not understood to properly belong to the State ; and when it interferes, as sometimes it must, to restrain and control the local action, there must be reasons of State policy or dangers of local abuse to warrant the interposition.[1]

The people of the municipalities, however, do not define for themselves their own rights, privileges, and powers, nor is there any common law which draws any definite line of distinction between the powers which may be exercised by the State and those which must be left to the local governments.[2] The municipalities must look to the State for such charters of government as the legislature shall see fit to provide ; and they cannot prescribe for themselves the details, though they have a right to expect that those charters will be granted with a recognition of the general

---

[1] " It seems to be generally conceded that powers of local legislation may be granted to cities, towns, and other municipal corporations. And it would require strong reasons to satisfy us that it could have been the design of the framers of our constitution to take from the legislature a power which has been exercised in Europe by governments of all classes from the earliest history, and the exercise of which has probably done more to promote civilization than all other causes combined ; which has been constantly exercised in every part of our country from its earliest settlement, and which has raised up among us many of our most valuable institutions." State v. Noyes, 10 Fost. 292, per Bell, J. See also Tanner v. Trustees of Albion, 5 Hill, 121 ; Dalby v. Wolf, 14 Iowa, 228 ; State v. Simonds, 3 Mo. 414 ; McKee v. McKee, 8 B. Monr. 433 ; Smith v. Levinus, 8 N. Y. 472 ; People v. Draper, 15 N. Y. 532 ; Burgess v. Pue, 2 Gill, 11 ; New Orleans v. Turpin, 13 La. An. 56 ; Gilkeson v. The Frederick Justices, 13 Grat. 577 ; Mayor, &c. of New York v. Ryan, 2 E. D. Smith, 368 ; St. Louis v. Russell, 9 Mo. 503.

[2] As to common law affecting these corporate existencies, and the effect of usage, see 2 Kent, 278, 279.

principles with which we are familiar. The charter, or the general law under which they exercise their powers, is their constitution, in which they must show authority for the acts they assume to perform. They have no inherent jurisdiction to make laws or adopt regulations of government; they are governments of enumerated powers, acting by a delegated authority; so that while the State legislature may exercise such powers of government coming within the designation of legislative power as are not expressly or impliedly prohibited, the local authorities can exercise those only which are expressly or impliedly conferred, and subject to such regulations or restrictions as are annexed to the grant.[1]

The creation of municipal corporations, and the conferring upon them of certain powers and subjecting them to corresponding duties, does not deprive the legislature of the State of that complete control over their citizens which was before possessed. It still has authority to amend their charters, enlarge or diminish their powers, extend or limit their boundaries, consolidate two or more into one, overrule their action whenever it is deemed unwise, impolitic, or unjust, and even abolish them altogether in the legislative discretion.[2] The rights and franchises of such a corporation, being granted for the purposes of the government, can never

---

[1] Stetson v. Kempton, 13 Mass. 272; Willard v. Killingworth, 8 Conn. 254; Abendroth v. Greenwich, 29 Conn. 363; Baldwin v. North Branford, 32 Conn. 47; Webster v. Harwinton, Ibid. 131; Douglass v. Placerville, 18 Cal. 643; Lackland v. Northern Missouri Railroad Co., 31 Mo. 180; Mays v. Cincinnati, 1 Ohio, N. S. 268; Frost v. Belmont, 6 Allen, 152.

[2] St. Louis v. Allen, 13 Mo. 400; Coles v. Madison Co., Breese, 115; Richland County v. Lawrence County, 12 Ill. 1; Trustees of Schools v. Tatman, 13 Ill. 27; Robertson v. Rockford, 21 Ill. 451; People v. Power, 25 Ill. 187; St. Louis v. Russell, 9 Mo. 503; State v. Cowan, 29 Mo. 330; Harrison Justices v. Holland, 3 Grat. 247; Brighton v. Wilkinson, 2 Allen, 27; Sloan v. State, 8 Blackf. 361; Mills v. Williams, 11 Ired. 558; Langworthy v. Dubuque, 16 Iowa, 271; Weeks v. Milwaukee, 10 Wis. 242; State v. Branin, 3 Zab. 484; City of St. Louis v. Cafferata, 24 Mo. 94; People v. Draper, 15 N. Y. 532; Aspinwall v. Commissioners, &c., 22 How. 364. This power is not defeated or affected by the circumstance that the municipal corporation was by its charter made the trustee of a charity; and in such case, if the corporation is abolished, the Court of Chancery may be empowered and directed by the repealing act to appoint a new trustee to take charge of the property and execute the trust. Montpelier v. East Montpelier, 29 Vt. 12. And See Harrison v. Bridgeton, 16 Mass. 16; Montpelier Academy v. George, 14 La. An. 406; Reynolds v. Baldwin, 1 La. An. 162; Police Jury v. Shreveport, 5 La. An. 665.

become such vested rights as against the State that they cannot be taken away; nor does the charter constitute a contract in the sense of the constitutional provision which prohibits the obligation of contracts being violated.[1] Restraints on the legislative power of control must be found in the constitution of the State, or they must rest alone in the legislative discretion.[2] If the legislative action in these cases operates injuriously to individuals, the remedy is not with the courts. They have no power to interfere, and the people must be looked to, to right through the ballot-box all these wrongs.[3] This is the general rule; and the exceptions to it are not numerous, and will be indicated hereafter.

[1] This principle was recognized by the several judges in Dartmouth College v. Woodward, 4 Wheat. 518.   And see People v. Morris, 13 Wend. 331; St. Louis v. Russell, 9 Mo. 507; Montpelier v. East Montpelier, 29 Vt. 12; Trustees of Schools v. Tatman, 13 Ill. 30; Brighton v. Wilkinson, 2 Allen, 27; Reynolds v. Baldwin, 1 La. An. 162; Police Jury v. Shreveport, 5 La. An. 665.

[2] " Where a corporation is the mere creature of legislative will, established for the general good, and endowed by the State alone, the legislature may, at pleasure, modify the law by which it was created.   For in that case there would be but one party affected, — the government itself, — and therefore not a contract within the meaning of the constitution.   The trustees of such a corporation would be the mere mandatories of the State, having no personal interest involved, and could not complain of any law that might abridge or destroy their agency." Montpelier Academy v. George, 14 La. An. 406.   In Trustees of Schools v. Tatman, 13 Ill. 30, the court say : " Public corporations are but parts of the machinery employed in carrying on the affairs of the State; and they are subject to be changed, modified, or destroyed, as the exigencies of the public may demand. The State may exercise a general superintendence and control over them and their rights and effects, so that their property is not diverted from the uses and objects for which it was given or purchased."   It is a lawful exercise of legislative authority upon the division of counties, towns, &c., to confer a part of the corporate property of the old corporation upon the new, and to direct the old body to pay it over to the new.   Harrison v. Bridgeton, 16 Mass. 16; Bristol v. New Chester, 3 N. H. 524.   But it seems that this apportionment of property can only be made at the time of the division.   Windham v. Portland, 4 Mass. 390; Hampshire v. Franklin, 16 Mass. 76.   See Richland v. Lawrence, 12 Ill. 8; Bowdoinham v. Richmond, 6 Greenl. 112.   In the latter case, it was held that the apportionment of debts between an old town and one created from it was in the nature of a contract; and it was not in the power of the legislature afterwards to release the new township from payment of its share as thus determined.   But the case of Layton v. New Orleans, 12 La. An. 515, is contra.   See also Borough of Dunmore's Appeal, 52 Penn. St. 374, which in principle seems to accord with the Louisiana case.

[3] " The correction of these abuses is as readily attained at the ballot-box as it would be by subjecting it to judicial revision.   A citizen or a number of citizens

13

Powers of Public Corporations.

The powers of these corporations are either express or implied. The former are those which the legislative act under which they exist confers in express terms; the latter are such as are necessary in order to carry into effect those expressly granted, and which must, therefore, be presumed to have been within the intention of the legislative grant.[1] Certain powers are also incidental to corporations, and will be possessed unless expressly or by implication prohibited. Of these an English writer has said: " A municipal corporation has at common law few powers beyond those of electing, governing, and removing its members, and regulating its franchises and property. The power of its governing officers can only extend to the administration of the by-laws and other ordinances by which the body is regulated."[2] But without being expressly empowered so to do, they may sue and be sued; may have a common seal; may purchase and hold lands and other

may be subtracted from a county free from debt, having no taxation for county purposes, and added to an adjacent one, whose debts are heavy and whose taxing powers are exercised to the utmost extent allowed by law, and this, too, without consulting their wishes. It is done every day. Perhaps a majority of the people thus annexed to an adjacent or thrown into a new county by the division of an old one may have petitioned the legislature for this change; but this is no relief to the outvoted minority, or the individual who deems himself oppressed and vexed by the change. Must we, then, to prevent such occasional hardships, deny the power entirely?

" It must be borne in mind that these corporations, whether established over cities, counties, or townships (where such incorporated subdivisions exist), are never intrusted and can never be intrusted with any legislative power inconsistent or conflicting with the general laws of the land, or derogatory to those rights either of person or property which the constitution and the general laws guarantee. They are strictly subordinate to the general laws, and merely created to carry out the purposes of those laws with more certainty and efficiency. They may be and sometimes are intrusted with powers which properly appertain to private corporations, and in such matters their power as mere municipal corporations ceases." City of St. Louis v. Allen, 13 Mo. 414.

[1] 2 Kent, 278, note; Halstead v. Mayor, &c. of New York, 3 N. Y. 433; Hodges v. Buffalo, 2 Denio, 112; New London v. Brainerd, 22 Conn. 552; State v. Ferguson, 33 N. H. 424; McMillan v. Lee County, 3 Iowa, 311; La Fayette v. Cox, 5 Ind. 38; Clark v. Des Moines, 19 Iowa, 212; Beaty v. Knowler, 4 Pet. 162; Mills v. Gleason, 11 Wis. 470. In this last case, it was held that these corporations had implied power to borrow money for corporate purposes. And see also Ketcham v. Buffalo, 14 N. Y. 356.

[2] Willcock on Municipal Corporations, tit. 769.

property for corporate purposes, and convey the same ; may make by-laws whenever necessary to accomplish the design of the incorporation, and enforce the same by penalties; and may enter into contracts to effectuate the corporate purposes.[1] Except as to these incidental powers, and which need not be, though they usually are, mentioned in the charter, the charter itself, or the general law under which they exist, is the measure of the authority to be exercised.

And the general disposition of the courts in this country has been to confine municipalities within the limits that a strict construction of the grants of powers in their charters will assign to them ; thus applying substantially the same rule that is applied to charters of private incorporation.[2]

[1] Angell & Ames on Corp. §§ 111, 239 ; 2 Kyd on Corp. 102 ; State v. Ferguson, 33 N. H. 430.

[2] Under a city charter which authorized the common council to appoint assessors for the purpose of awarding damages to those through whose property a street might be opened, and to assess such damages on the property benefited, it was decided that the council were not empowered to levy a tax to pay for the other expenses of opening the street. Reed v. Toledo, 18 Ohio, 161. So a power to enact by-laws and ordinances to abate and remove nuisances will not authorize the passing of an ordinance to *prevent* nuisances, or to impose penalties for creation thereof. Rochester v. Collins, 12 Barb. 559. A power to impose penalties for *obstructions* to streets would not authorize the like penalties for *encroachments* upon streets, where under the general laws of the State the offences are recognized as different and distinct. Grand Rapids v. Hughes, 15 Mich. 54. Authority to levy a tax on real and personal estate would not warrant an income tax, especially when such a tax is unusual in the State. Mayor of Savannah v. Hartridge, 8 Geo. 23. It will appear, therefore, that powers near akin to those expressly conferred are not, for that reason, to be taken by implication. And see Commonwealth v. Erie and N. E. Railroad Co., 27 Penn. St. 339. This rule has often been applied where authority has been asserted on behalf of a municipal corporation to loan its credit to corporations formed to construct works of internal improvement. See La Fayette v. Cox, 5 Ind. 38. A power to pass ordinances to prohibit the sale or giving away of intoxicating liquors in certain special cases is an implied exclusion of the power to prohibit the sale or giving away in other cases. State v. Ferguson, 33 N. H. 424. In Dunham v. Rochester, 5 Cow. 465, it is said : " For all the purposes of jurisdiction corporations are like the inferior courts, and must show the power given them in every case. If this be wanting, their proceedings must be holden void whenever they come in question, even collaterally ; for they are not judicial and subject to direct review on *certiorari*. 2 Kyd on Corp. 104 – 107." See also Milhau v. Sharp, 17 Barb. 435, 28 Barb. 228, and 27 N. Y. 611 ; Douglass v. Placerville, 18 Cal. 643 ; Mount Pleasant v. Breeze, 11 Iowa, 399 ; Hopple v. Brown, 13 Ohio, N. S. 311 ; Lackland v. Northern Missouri Railroad Co., 31 Mo. 180 ; Smith v. Morse, 2 Cal. 524 ; Bennett v. Borough of Birmingham, 31 Penn. St. 15.

It must follow that, if in any case a party assumes to deal with a corporation on the supposition that it possesses powers which it does not, or to contract in any other manner than is permitted by the charter, he will not be permitted, notwithstanding he may have complied with the undertaking on his part, to maintain an action against the corporation based upon its unauthorized action. Even if a party is induced to enter upon work for a corporation by the false representations of corporation officers, that certain preliminary action had been taken on which the power of the corporation to enter upon the work depended, these false representations cannot have the effect to validate a contract otherwise void, and can afford no ground of action against the corporation ; but every party contracting with it must take notice of any want of authority which the public records would show.[1]

---

[1] The common council of Williamsburg had power to open, regulate, grade, and pave streets, but only upon petition signed by one third of the persons owning lands within the assessment limits. A party entered into a contract with the corporation for improving a street upon the false representations of the council that such a petition had been presented. Held, that the provision of the law being public, and all the proceedings leading to a determination by the council to make a particular improvement being matters of record, all persons were chargeable with notice of the law and such proceedings; and that, notwithstanding the false representations, no action would lie against the city for work done under the contract. Swift v. Williamsburg, 24 Barb. 427. "If the plaintiff can recover on the state of facts he has stated in his complaint, the restrictions and limitations which the legislature sought to impose upon the powers of the common council will go for nothing. And yet, these provisions are matters of substance, and were designed to be of some service to the constituents of the common council. They were intended to protect the owners of lands and the tax-payers of the city, as well against the frauds and impositions of the contractors who might be employed to make local improvements, as against the illegal acts of the common council themselves in employing the contractors. But if the plaintiff can recover in this action, of what value or effect are all these safeguards ? If the common council desire to make a local improvement, which the persons to be benefited thereby, and to be assessed therefor, are unwilling to have made, the consent of the owners may be wholly dispensed with, according to the plaintiff's theory. The common council have only to represent that the proper petition has been presented and the proper proceedings have been taken, to warrant the improvement. They then enter into the contract. The improvement is made. Those other safeguards for an assessment of the expenses and for reviewing the proceedings may or may not be taken. But when the work is completed and is to be paid for, it is found that the common council have no authority to lay any assessment or collect a dollar from the property benefited by the improvement. The contractor then brings his action, and recovers from the city the damages he

Many corporations exist in England by prescription, by which is understood that corporate powers have been exercised from time immemorial, of which it is impossible to show the commencement by any particular charter or act of Parliament, and the law presumes that such exercise of powers has been rightful, and that a charter or act of Parliament conferring the corporate powers once existed, but has been lost by such accidents as length of time may produce.[1] The same presumption in support of corporate rights has been judicially declared in this country,[2] with this difference, that in analogy to the statute of limitations, it is held that an uninterrupted and unquestioned user of the corporate franchise for twenty years, with the assent of the government, would furnish a conclusive presumption of a grant from the State of the corporate rights exercised.[3] And in these cases we apprehend the same rule as to construction of powers would apply.

has sustained by the failure of the city to pay him the contract price. The ground of his action is the falsity of the representations made to him. But the truth or falsity of such representations might have been ascertained by the party with the use of the most ordinary care and diligence. The existence of the proper petition, and the taking of the necessary initiatory steps to warrant the improvement, were doubtless referred to and recited in the contract made with the plaintiff. And he thus became again directly chargeable with notice of the contents of all these papers. It is obvious that the restrictions and limitations imposed by the law cannot be thus evaded. The consent of the parties interested in such improvements cannot be dispensed with ; the responsibility, which the conditions precedent created by the statute impose, cannot be thrown off in this manner. For the effect of doing so is to shift entirely the burden of making these local improvements, to relieve those on whom the law sought to impose the expense, and to throw it on others who are not liable either in law or morals."

So where the charter of Detroit provided that no public work should be contracted for or commenced until an assessment had been levied to defray the expense, and that no such work should be paid or contracted to be paid for, except out of the proceeds of the tax thus levied, it was held, that the city corporation had no power to make itself responsible for the price of any public work, and that such work could only be paid for by funds actually in the hands of the city treasurer, provided for the specific purpose. Goodrich v. Detroit, 12 Mich. 279.

[1] 1 Kyd on Corp. 14 ; Angell & Ames on Corp. §§ 69 – 71.

[2] Dillingham v. Snow, 5 Mass. 547 ; Stockbridge v. West Stockbridge, 12 Mass. 400 ; New Boston v. Dunbarton, 12 N. H. 409 ; Same case, 15 N. H. 201 ; Watkins v. Peck, 13 N. H. 360 ; Wallace v. Fletcher, 10 Fost. 434 ; Bow v. Allenstown, 34 N. H. 365 ; Robie v. Sedgwick, 35 Barb. 326.

[3] Watkins v. Peck, 13 N. H. 360 ; Wallace v. Fletcher, 10 Fost. 434 ; Bow v. Allenstown, 34 N. H. 374. The other cases referred to in the preceding note were cases of the proof of corporations by presumptions and reputation.

The presumption as to the powers granted would be limited by the proof of usage, and nothing could be taken by intendment which the usage did not warrant.

Municipal By-Laws.

The power of municipal corporations to make by-laws is limited in various ways.

1. It is controlled by the Constitution of the United States and of the State. The restrictions imposed by those instruments, and which directly limit the legislative power of the State, rest equally upon all the instruments of government created by it. If a State cannot pass an *ex post facto* law, or law impairing the obligation of contracts, neither can any agency do so which acts under the State with delegated authority.[1] By-laws, therefore, which in their operation would be *ex post facto*, or violate contracts, are not within the power of municipal corporations; and whatever the people by the State constitution have forbidden the State government from doing, it cannot do indirectly through the local governments.

2. Municipal by-laws must also be in harmony with the general laws of the State, and with the provisions of the charter. Whenever they come in conflict with either, the by-law must give way.[2] The charter, however, may expressly or by necessary implication exclude the general laws of the State on any particular subject, and allow the corporation to pass local laws, at discretion, which may differ from the rule in force elsewhere. But in these cases the control of the State is not excluded if the legislature afterward see fit to exercise it; nor will conferring a power upon a

---

[1] Angell & Ames on Corporations, § 332; Stuyvesant v. Mayor, &c. of New York, 7 Cow. 588; Brooklyn Central Railroad Co. v. Brooklyn City Railroad Co., 32 Barb. 358; Illinois Conference Female College v. Cooper, 25 Ill. 148. The last was a case where a by-law of an educational corporation was held void, as violating the obligation of a contract previously entered into by the corporation in a certificate of scholarship which it had issued. See also Davenport, &c. Co. v. Davenport, 13 Iowa, 229; Saving Society v. Philadelphia, 31 Penn. St. 175.

[2] Wood v. Brooklyn, 14 Barb. 428; Mayor, &c. of New York v. Nichols, 4 Hill, 209; Petersburg v. Metzker, 21 Ill. 205; Southport v. Ogden, 23 Conn. 128; Carr v. St. Louis, 9 Mo. 191; Commonwealth v. Erie and Northeast Railroad Co., 27 Penn. St. 339; Burlington v. Kellar, 18 Iowa, 59; Conwell v. O'Brien, 11 Ind. 419. See Baldwin v. Green, 10 Mo. 410; Cowen v. West Troy, 43 Barb. 48.

corporation to pass by-laws and impose penalties upon any specified subject necessarily supersede the State law on the same subject, but the State law and the by-law may both stand together if
not inconsistent.[1] Indeed, the same act may constitute an offence
both against the State and the municipal corporation, and both
may punish it without violation of any constitutional principle.[2]

[1] City of St. Louis v. Bentz, 11 Mo. 61; City of St. Louis v. Cafferata, 24 Mo.
97; Rogers v. Jones, 1 Wend. 261; Levy v. State, 6 Ind. 281; Mayor, &c. of
Mobile v. Allaive, 14 Ala. 400.

[2] Such is the clear weight of authority, though the decisions are not uniform.
In Rogers v. Jones, 1 Wend. 261, it is said: "But it is said that the by-law of a
town or corporation is void, if the legislature have regulated the subject by law.
If the legislature have passed a law regulating as to certain things in a city, I
apprehend the corporation are not thereby restricted from making further regulations. Cases of this kind have occurred and never been questioned on that
ground; it is only to notice a case or two out of many. The legislature have
imposed a penalty of one dollar for servile labor on Sunday; the corporation of
New York have passed a by-law imposing the penalty of five dollars for the same
offence. As to storing gunpowder in New York, the legislature and corporation
have each imposed the same penalty. Suits to recover the penalty have been
sustained under the corporation law. It is believed that the ground has never
been taken that there was a conflict with the State law. One of these cases is
reported in 12 Johns. 122. The question was open for discussion, but not noticed."
In Mayor, &c. of Mobile v. Allaire, 14 Ala. 400, the validity of a municipal by-
law imposing a fine of fifty dollars, for an assault and battery committed within
the city, was brought in question. Collier, Ch. J. says, p. 403: "The object of
the power conferred by the charter, and the purpose of the ordinance itself, was,
not to punish for an offence against the criminal justice of the country, but to
provide a mere *police regulation*, for the enforcement of good order and quiet
within the limits of the corporation. So far as an offence has been committed
against the public peace and morals, the corporate authorities have no power to
inflict punishment, and we are not informed that they have attempted to arrogate
it. It is altogether immaterial whether the State tribunal has interfered and
exercised its powers in bringing the defendant before it to answer for the assault
and battery; for whether he has there been punished or acquitted is alike unimportant. The offence against the corporation and the State we have seen are
distinguishable and wholly disconnected, and the prosecution at the suit of each
proceeds upon a different hypothesis; the one contemplates the observance of the
peace and good order of the city; the other has a more enlarged object in view,
the maintainance of the peace and dignity of the State." See also Mayor, &c.
of Mobile v. Rouse, 8 Ala. 515; Intendant, &c. of Greensboro v. Mullins, 13 Ala.
341; Mayor, &c. of New York v. Hyatt, 3 E. D. Smith, 156; People v. Stevens,
13 Wend. 341; Blatchley v. Moser, 15 Wend. 215; Levy v. State, 6 Ind. 281;
Ambrose v. State, Ibid. 351; Lawrenceburg v. Wuest, 16 Ind. 337; St. Louis v.
Bentz, 11 Mo. 61; St. Louis v. Cafferata, 24 Mo. 94. On the other hand, it was
held in State v. Cowan, 29 Mo. 330, that where a municipal corporation was

3. Municipal by-laws must also be reasonable. Whenever they
appear not to be so, the court must, as a matter of law, declare
them void.[1] To render them reasonable, they should tend in some
degree to the accomplishment of the objects for which the cor-

authorized to take cognizance of and punish an act as an offence against its ordinances which was also an offence against the general laws of the State, and this
power was exercised and the party punished, he could not afterwards be proceeded against under the State law. " The constitution," say the court, " forbids
that a person shall be twice punished for the same offence. To hold that a
party can be prosecuted for an act under the State laws, after he has been punished for the same act by the municipal corporation within whose limits the act
was done, would be to overthrow the power of the General Assembly to create
corporations to aid in the management of the affairs of the State. For a power
in the State to punish, after a punishment had been inflicted by the corporate authorities, could only find a support in the assumption that all the proceedings on
the part of the corporation were null and void. The circumstance that the municipal authorities have not exclusive jurisdiction over the acts which constitute
offences within their limits does not affect the question. It is enough that their
jurisdiction is not excluded. If it exists, — although it may be concurrent, — if
it is exercised, it is valid and binding so long as it is a constitutional principle that
no man may be punished twice for the same offence." This case seems to stand
alone, though the case of Slaughter v. People, cited below, goes still further.
Those which hold that the party may be punished under both the State and the
municipal law are within the principle of Fox v. State, 5 How. 410; Moore v.
People, 14 How. 13. In Jefferson City v. Courtmire, 9 Mo. 692, it was held that
authority to a municipal corporation to " regulate the police of the city," gave it
no power to pass an ordinance for the punishment of indictable offences. And
in Slaughter v. People, 2 Doug. (Mich.) 334, it was held not competent to punish, under city by-laws, an indictable offence.

Where an act is expressly or by implication permitted by the State law, it cannot be forbidden by the corporation. Thus, the statutes of New York established
certain regulations for the putting up and marking of pressed hay, and provided
that such hay might be sold without deduction for tare, and by the weight as
marked, or any other standard weight that should be agreed upon. It was held
that the city of New York had no power to prohibit under a penalty the sale of
such hay without inspection; this being obviously inconsistent with the statute
which gave a right to sell if its regulations were complied with. Mayor, &c. of
New York v. Nichols, 4 Hill, 209.

[1] 2 Kyd on Corporations, 107; Davies v. Morgan, 1 Cromp. & J. 587; Cham-
berlain of London v. Compton, 7 D. & R. 597; Clark v. Le Cren, 9 B. & C. 52;
Gosling v. Veley, 12 Q. B. 347; Dunham v. Rochester, 5 Cow. 462; Ex parte
Burnett, 30 Ala. 461; Craig v. Burnett, 32 Ala. 728; Austin v. Murray, 16 Pick.
121; Godard, Petitioner, Ibid. 504; Commonwealth v. Worcester, 3 Pick. 462;
Commonwealth v. Gas Co., 12 Penn. St. 318; State v. Jersey City, 5 Dutch. 170;
Gallatin v. Bradford, 1 Bibb, 209; Carew v. Western Union Telegraph Co., 15
Mich. 525.

poration was created and its powers conferred. A by-law, that persons chosen annually as stewards of the Society of Scriveners shall furnish a dinner on election day to the freemen of the society, — the freemen not being the electors nor required to attend, and the office of steward being for no other purpose but that of giving the dinner, — is not connected with the business of the corporation, and does not tend to promote its objects, and is therefore unreasonable and void.[1] And where a statute permitted a municipal corporation to license the sale of intoxicating drinks and to charge a license fee therefor, a by-law requiring the payment of a license fee of one thousand dollars was held void, as not advancing the purpose of the law, but as being in its nature prohibitory.[2] And if a corporation has power to prohibit the carrying on of dangerous occupations within its limits, a by-law which should permit one person to carry on such an occupation and prohibit another, who had an equal right, from pursuing the same business, or which should allow the business to be carried on in existing buildings, but prohibit the erection of others for it, would be unreasonable.[3] And a right to license an employment does not imply a right to charge a license fee therefor with a view to revenue, unless such seems to be the manifest purpose of the power; but the authority of the corporation will be limited to such a charge for the license as will cover the necessary expenses of issuing it and the additional labor of officers and expenses thereby imposed. A license is issued under the police power; but the exaction of a license fee with a view to revenue would be an exercise of the power of taxation; and the charter must plainly show an intent to confer that power, or the municipal corporation cannot assume it.[4]

[1] Society of Scriveners v. Brooking, 3 Q. B. 95.

[2] Ex parte Burnett, 30 Ala. 461; Craig v. Burnett, 32 Ala. 728.

[3] Mayor, &c. of Hudson v. Thorne, 7 Paige, 261. A power to prevent and regulate the carrying on of manufactures dangerous in causing or promoting fires does not authorize an ordinance prohibiting the erection of wooden buildings within the city, or to limit the size of buildings which individuals shall be permitted to erect on their own premises. Ibid.

[4] State v. Roberts, 11 Gill & J. 506; Mays v. Cincinnati, 1 Ohio, N. S. 268; Cincinnati v. Bryson, 15 Ohio, 625; Freeholders v. Barber, 2 Halst. 64; Kip v. Paterson, 2 Dutch. 298; Bennett v. Borough of Birmingham, 31 Penn. St. 15; Commonwealth v. Stodder, 2 Cush. 562; Chilvers v. People, 11 Mich. 43; Mayor, &c. of Mobile v. Yuille, 3 Ala. 144. Nevertheless, the courts will not inquire

A by-law to be reasonable should be certain. If it affixes a penalty for its violation, it would seem that such penalty should be a fixed and certain sum, and not left to the discretion of the officer or court which is to impose it on conviction; though a by-law imposing a penalty *not exceeding* a certain sum has been held not to be void for uncertainty.[1]

So a by-law to be reasonable should be in harmony with the common law. If it is in general restraint of trade, — as a by-law that no person shall exercise the art of painter in the city of London, not being free of the company of painters, — it will be void on this ground.[2] So a by-law of a bank, that all payments made or received by the bank must be examined at the time, and mistakes corrected before the dealer leaves the town, is unreasonable and invalid, and a recovery may be had against the bank for an overpayment discovered afterwards, notwithstanding the by-law.[3] So a by-law of a town which, under pretence of regulating the fishery of clams and oysters within its limits, prohibits all persons except the inhabitants of the town from taking shell-fish in a navigable river, is void as in contravention of common right.[4]

very closely into the expense of a license with a view to adjudge it a tax, where it does not appear to be unreasonable in amount in view of its purpose as a regulation. Ash *v.* People, 11 Mich. 347. And in some cases it has been held that license fees might be imposed under the police power with a view to operate as a restriction upon the business or thing licensed. Carter *v.* Dow, 16 Wis. 299; Tenney *v.* Lenz, Ibid. 567. But in such cases, where the right to impose such license fees can be fairly deduced from the charter, it would perhaps be safer and less liable to lead to confusion and difficulty to refer the corporate authority to the taxing power, rather than exclusively to the power of regulation. See Dunham *v.* Trustees of Rochester, 5 Cow. 462, upon the extent of the police power.

[1] Mayor, &c. of Huntsville *v.* Phelps, 27 Ala. 55, overruling Mayor, &c. of Mobile *v.* Yuille, 3 Ala. 144. And see Piper *v.* Chappell, 14 M. & W. 624.

[2] Clark *v.* Le Cren, 9 B. & C. 52; Chamberlain of London *v.* Compton, 7 D. & R. 597. But a by-law is not void, as in restraint of trade, which requires loaves of bread baked for sale to be of specified weight and properly stamped, or which requires bakers to be licensed. Mayor, &c. of Mobile *v.* Yuille, 3 Ala. 137.

[3] Mechanics and Farmers' Bank *v.* Smith, 19 Johns. 115; Gallatin *v.* Bradford, 1 Bibb, 209.

[4] Hayden *v.* Noyes, 5 Conn. 391. As it had been previously held that every person has a common-law right to fish in a navigable river or arm of the sea, until by some legal mode of appropriation this common right was extinguished, — Peck *v.* Lockwood, 5 Day, 22, — the by-law in effect deprived every citizen, except residents of the township, of rights which were *vested* so far as from the

And for like reasons a by-law is void which abridges the rights and privileges conferred by the general laws of the State, unless authority therefor can be pointed out in the corporate charter.[1] And if it assumes to be a police regulation, but deprives a party of the use of his property without regard to the public good, under the pretence of the preservation of health, when it is manifest that such is not the object and purpose of the regulation, it will be set aside as a clear and direct infringement of the right of property without any compensating advantages.[2]

nature of the case a right could be vested.   That a right to *regulate* does not include a right to prohibit, see also Ex parte Burnett, 30 Ala. 461 ; Austin *v.* Murray, 16 Pick. 121.   And see Milhau *v.* Sharp, 17 Barb. 435, 28 Barb. 228, and 27 N. Y. 611.

[1] Dunham *v.* Trustees of Rochester, 5 Cow. 462 ; Mayor, &c. of New York *v.* Nichols, 4 Hill, 209.

[2] By a by-law of the town of Charlestown all persons were prohibited, without license from the selectmen, from burying any dead body brought into town on any part of their own premises or elsewhere within the town.   By the court, Wilde, J. : " A by-law to be valid must be reasonable ; it must be *legi, fidei, rationi consona*.   Now if this regulation or prohibition had been limited to the populous part of the town, and were made in good faith for the purpose of preserving the health of the inhabitants, which may be in some degree exposed to danger by the allowance of interments in the midst of a dense population, it would have been a very reasonable regulation.   But it cannot be pretended that this by-law was made for the preservation of the health of the inhabitants.   Its restraints extend many miles into the country, to the utmost limits of the town. Now such an unnecessary restraint upon the right of interring the dead we think essentially unreasonable.   If Charlestown may lawfully make such a by-law as this, all the towns adjoining Boston may impose similar restraints, and consequently all those who die in Boston must of necessity be interred within the precincts of the city.   That this would be prejudicial to the health of the inhabitants, especially in the hot seasons of the year, and when epidemic diseases prevail, seems to be a well-established opinion.   Interments, therefore, in cities and large populous towns, ought to be discountenanced, and no obstacles should be permitted to the establishment of cemeteries at suitable places in the vicinity.   The by-law in question is, therefore, an unreasonable restraint upon many of the citizens of Boston, who are desirous of burying their dead without the city, and for that reason void.   And this by-law would seem to be void for another reason.   A by-law for the total restraint of one's right is void ; as if a man be barred of the use of his land.   Com. Dig. By-Law, c. 4.   The land where the bodies were interred was the land of the Catholic Bishop of Boston, purchased by him in 1830, and then consecrated as a Catholic burying-ground, and has ever since been used as such, for the interment of Catholics dying in Charlestown and Boston.   It is true the by-law does not operate to the total restraint or deprivation of the bishop's right, but it is a total restraint of the

Delegation of Municipal Powers.

Another and very important limitation which rests upon municipal powers is, that they shall be executed by the municipality
itself, or by such agencies or officers as the statute has pointed
out.   So far as its functions are legislative, they rest in the discretion and judgment of the municipal body intrusted with them,
and that body cannot refer the exercise of the power to the discretion and judgment of its subordinates or of any other authority.   So strictly is this rule applied, that when a city charter
authorized the common council of the city to make by-laws and
ordinances ordering and directing any of the streets to be pitched,
levelled, paved, flagged, &c., or for the altering or repairing the

right of the burying the dead in Boston, for which a part of the burying-ground was
appropriated.   The illegality of the by-law is the same, whether it may deprive
one of the use of a part or the whole of his property ; no one can be so deprived,
unless the public good requires it.   And the law will not allow the right of private
property to be invaded under the guise of a police regulation for the preservation of health, when it is manifest that such is not the object and purpose of the
regulation.   Now we think this is manifest from the case stated in regard to the
by-law in question.   It is a clear and direct infringement of the right of property,
without any compensating advantages, and not a police regulation made in good
faith for the preservation of health.   It interdicts, or in its operation necessarily
intercepts, the sacred use to which the Catholic burying-ground was appropriated
and consecrated, according to the forms of the Catholic religion ; and such an interference, we are constrained to say, is wholly unauthorized and most unreasonable." Austin v. Murray, 16 Pick. 125.   So in Wreford v. People, 14 Mich. 41, the
common council of Detroit, under a power granted by statute to compel the owners and occupants of slaughter-houses to cleanse and abate them whenever necessary for the health of the inhabitants, assumed to pass an ordinance altogether
prohibiting the slaughtering of animals within certain limits in the city ; and it
was held void.   See further, State v. Jersey City, 5 Dutch. 170.   Upon the
whole subject of municipal by-laws, see Angell & Ames on Corp. c. 10 ; Grant on
Corp. 76 et seq.   See also Redfield on Railways (3d ed.), vol. 1, p. 88.   The subject of the reasonableness of by-laws was considered at some length in People v.
Medical Society of Erie, 24 Barb. 570, and Same v. Same, 32 N. Y. 187.   In the
first case, it was held that a regulation subjecting a member of the County Medical Society to expulsion, for charging less than the established fees, was unreasonable and void.   In the second, it was decided that where a party had the prescribed qualifications for admission to the society, he could not be refused admission, on the ground of his having previous to that time failed to observe the code
of medical ethics prescribed by the society for its members.   Municipal by-laws
may impose penalties on parties guilty of a violation thereof, but they cannot
impose forfeiture of property or rights, without express legislative authority.
State v. Ferguson, 33 N. H. 430 ; Phillips v. Allen, 41 Penn. St. 481.

same, " within such time and in such manner as they may prescribe under the superintendence and direction of the city superintendent," and the common council passed an ordinance directing
a certain street to be pitched, levelled, and flagged, " in such manner as the city superintendent, under the direction of the committee on roads of the common council, shall direct and require,"
the ordinance was held void, because it left to the city superintendent and the committee of the common council the decision
which, under the law, must be made by the council itself. The
trust was an important and delicate one, as the expenses of the
improvement were, by the statute, to be paid by the owners of
the property in front of which it was made. It was in effect a
power of taxation, which is the exercise of sovereign authority;
and nothing short of the most positive and explicit language
could justify the court in holding that the legislature intended
to confer such a power on a city officer or committee. The statute in question not only contained no such language, but, on
the contrary, clearly expressed the intention of confiding the exercise of this power to the common council, the members of which
were elected by and responsible to those whose property they were
thus allowed to tax.[1]

This restriction, it will be perceived, is the same which rests
upon the legislative power of the State, and it springs from the
same reasons. The people in the one case in creating the legislative department, and the legislature in the other in conferring
the corporate powers, have selected the depository of the power
which they have designed should be exercised, and in confiding it
to such depository have impliedly prohibited its being exercised
by any other agency. A trust created for any public purpose
cannot be assignable at the will of the trustee.[2]

[1] Thompson v. Schermerhorn, 6 N. Y. 92. See also Smith v. Morse, 2 Cal.
524.

[2] The charter of Washington gave the corporation authority " to authorize the
drawing of lotteries, for effecting any important improvement in the city, which
the ordinary funds or revenue thereof will not accomplish; provided that the
amount raised in each year shall not exceed ten thousand dollars. And provided
also that the object for which the money is intended to be raised shall be first
submitted to the President of the United States, and shall be approved by him."
Per Marshall, Ch. J. speaking of this authority: " There is great weight in the
argument that it is a trust, and an important trust, confided to the corporation
itself, for the purpose of effecting important improvements in the city, and ought,

Equally incumbent upon the State legislature and these municipal bodies is the restriction that they shall adopt no irrepealable
legislation. No legislative body can so part with its powers by
any proceeding as not to be able to continue the exercise of them.
It can and should exercise them again and again, as often as the
public interests require.[1] Such a body has no power, even by
contract, to control and embarrass its legislative powers and duties. On this ground it has been held, that a grant of land by a
municipal corporation, for the purposes of a cemetery, with a covenant for quiet enjoyment by the grantee, could not preclude the
corporation, in the exercise of its police powers, from prohibiting
any further use of the land for cemetery purposes, when the advance of population threatened to make such use a public nuisance.[2] So when " a lot is granted as a place of deposit for
gunpowder, or other purpose innocent in itself at the time ; it
is devoted to that purpose till, in the progress of population, it
becomes dangerous to the property, the safety, or the lives of
hundreds ; it cannot be that the mere form of the grant, because
the parties choose to make it particular instead of general and absolute, should prevent the use to which it is limited being regarded and treated as a nuisance, when it becomes so in fact. In
this way the legislative powers essential to the comfort and preservation of populous communities might be frittered away into

therefore, to be executed under the immediate authority and inspection of the
corporation. It is reasonable to suppose that Congress, when granting a power
to authorize gaming, would feel some solicitude respecting the fairness with which
the power should be used, and would take as many precautions against its abuse
as was compatible with its beneficial exercise. Accordingly, we find a limitation
upon the amount to be raised, and on the object for which the lottery may be
authorized. It is to be for any important improvement in the city, which the
ordinary funds or revenue thereof will not accomplish ; and it is subjected to the
judgment of the President of the United States. The power thus cautiously
granted is deposited with the corporation itself, without an indication that it is
assignable. It is to be exercised like other corporate powers, by the agents of
the corporation under its control. While it remains where Congress has placed
it, the character of the corporation affords some security against its abuse, — some
security that no other mischief will result from it than is inseparable from the
thing itself. But if the management, control, and responsibility may be transferred to any adventurer who will purchase, all the security for fairness which is
furnished by character and responsibility is lost." Clark v. Washington, 12
Wheat. 54.

[1] East Hartford v. Hartford Bridge Co., 10 How. 535.

[2] Brick Presbyterian Church v. City of New York, 5 Cow. 540.

perfect insignificance. To allow rights thus to be parcelled out and secured beyond control would fix a principle by which our cities and villages might be broken up. Nuisances might and undoubtedly would be multiplied to an intolerable extent." [1]

And on the same ground it is held, that a municipal corporation, having power to establish, make, grade, and improve streets, does not, by once establishing the grade, preclude itself from changing it as the public needs or interest may seem to require, notwithstanding the incidental injury which must result to those individuals who have erected buildings with reference to the first grade.[2] So a corporation having power under the charter to establish and regulate streets cannot under this authority, without explicit legislative consent, permit individuals to lay down a railway in one of its streets, and confer privileges exclusive in their character and designed to be perpetual in duration. In a case where this was attempted, it has been said by the court: " The corporation has the exclusive right to control and regulate the use of the streets of the city. In this respect, it is endowed with legislative sovereignty. The exercise of that sovereignty has no limit, so long as it is within the objects and trusts for which the power is conferred. An ordinance regulating a street is a legislative act, entirely beyond the control of the judicial power of the State. But the resolution in question is not such an act. Though it relates to a street, and very materially affects the mode in which that street is to be used, yet in its essential features it is a contract. Privileges exclusive in their nature and designed to be perpetual in their duration are conferred. Instead of regulating the use of the street, the use itself to the extent specified in the resolution is granted to the associates. For what has been deemed an adequate consideration, the corporation has assumed to surrender a portion of their municipal authority, and has in legal effect agreed with the defendants that, so far as they may have occasion to use the street for the purpose of constructing and operating their railroad, the right to regulate

---

[1] Coats v. Mayor, &c. of New York, 7 Cow. 605. See also Davis v. Mayor, &c. of New York, 14 N. Y. 506; Attorney-General v. Mayor, &c. of New York, 3 Duer, 119 ; State v. Graves, 19 Md. 51 ; Gozzle v. Georgetown, 6 Wheat, 597.

[2] Callender v. Marsh, 1 Pick. 417; O'Connor v. Pittsburg, 18 Penn. St. 187; Smith v. Washington, 20 How. 135 ; Skinner v. Hartford Bridge Co., 29 Conn. 523 ; Graves v. Otis, 2 Hill, 466 ; La Fayette v. Bush, 19 Ind. 326 ; Creal v. Keokuk, 4 Green (Iowa), 47 ; Roberts v. Chicago, 26 Ill. 249. And see post, ch. 15.

and control the use of that street shall not be exercised. . . . . It cannot be that powers vested in the corporation as an important public trust can thus be frittered away, or parcelled out to individuals or joint-stock associations, and secured to them beyond control." [1]

So it has been held, that the city of Philadelphia exercised a portion of the public right of eminent domain in respect to the streets within its limits, subject only to the higher control of the State and the use of the people; and therefore a written license granted by the city, though upon a valuable consideration, authorizing the holder to connect his property with the city railway by a turnout and track, was not such a contract as would prevent the city from abandoning or removing the railway wherever, in the opinion of the city authorities, such action would tend to the benefit of its police. [2]

Thus hedged in by the limitations which control the legislative power of the State, these corporations are also entitled to the same protection which surrounds the exercise of State legislative power. One of these is that no right of action shall arise in favor of an individual for incidental injury suffered by him in consequence of their adopting or failing to adopt legislative action. [3] Another is that the same presumption that they have proceeded upon sufficient information and with correct motives shall support their legislative action which supports the statutes of the State, and precludes judicial inquiry on these points. [4] These rules, however, must be confined to those cases where the corpo-

[1] Milhau v. Sharp, 17 Barb. 435; Same case, 28 Barb. 228, and 27 N. Y. 611. See also Davis v. Mayor, &c. of New York, 14 N. Y. 506; State v. Mayor, &c., 3 Duer, 119. The consent of the legislature in any such case would relieve it of all difficulty, except so far as questions might arise concerning the right of individuals to compensation, as to which see post, ch. 15. In the case of Milhau v. Sharp, above cited, it was also held that, under authority " from time to time to regulate the rates of fare to be charged for the carriage of persons," the corporation could not pass a resolution that, in respect to the carriages employed on a street-railway therein authorized to be constructed, that power should never be exercised.

[2] Bryson v. Philadelphia, 47 Penn. St. 329.

[3] Larkin v. Saginaw County, 11 Mich. 88; Radcliffe's Ex'rs v. Mayor, &c. of Brooklyn, 4 N. Y. 195; Duke v. Mayor, &c. of Rome, 20 Geo. 655; St. Louis v. Gurno, 12 Mo. 414; Griffin v. Mayor, &c. of New York, 9 N. Y. 456; Weightman v. Washington, 1 Black, 39; Western College v. Cleveland, 12 Ohio, N. S. 375; Barton v. Syracuse, 37 Barb. 292; Commonwealth v. Duckett, 20 Md. 468.

[4] Milhau v. Sharp, 15 Barb. 193; New York and Harlaem Railroad Co. v. Mayor, &c. of New York, 1 Hilton, 562.

ration is exercising a discretionary power, and where the reasons which are to determine whether it shall act or not, and if it does, what the action shall be, are addressed to the municipal body exclusively.

Among the implied powers of such an organization is one to defend and indemnify its officers where they have incurred liability in the *bona fide* discharge of their duty. It has been held that, where irregularities occurred in assessment of taxes, in consequence of which the tax was void, and the assessors refunded to the persons taxed the moneys which had been collected and paid into the town, county, and State treasuries, the town had authority to vote to raise a sum of money to refund to the assessors what had been so paid by them, and that such vote was a legal promise to pay, on which the assessors might maintain action against the town. " The general purpose of this vote was just and wise. The inhabitants, finding that three of their townsmen who had been elected by themselves to an office, which they could not, without incurring a penalty, refuse to accept, had innocently and inadvertently committed an error which in strictness of law annulled their proceedings, and exposed them to a loss perhaps to the whole extent of their property, if all the inhabitants individually should avail themselves of their strict legal rights, — finding also that the treasury of the town had been supplied by the very money which these unfortunate individuals were obliged to refund from their own estates, and that, so far as the town tax went, the very persons who had rigorously exacted it from the assessors, or who were about to do it, had themselves shared in due proportion the benefits and use of the money which had been paid into the treasury, in the shape of schools, highways, and various other objects which the necessities of a municipal institution call for, — concluded to re-assess the tax, and to provide for its assessment in a manner which would have produced perfect justice to every individual of the corporation, and would have protected the assessors from the effects of their inadvertence in the assessment which was found to be invalid. The inhabitants of the town had a perfect right to make this re-assessment, if they had a right to raise the money originally. The necessary supplies to the treasury of a town cannot be intercepted, because of an inequality in the mode of apportioning the sum upon the individuals. Debts must be incurred, duties must be performed, by every town;

14

the safety of each individual depends upon the execution of the corporate duties and trusts. There is and must be an inherent power in every town to bring the money necessary for the purposes of its creation into the treasury; and if its course is obstructed by the ignorance or mistakes of its agents, they may proceed to enforce the end and object by correcting the means; and whether this be done by resorting to their original power of voting to raise money a second time for the same purposes, or by directing to re-assess the sum before raised by vote, is immaterial; perhaps the latter mode is best, at least it is equally good." [1]

It has also been held competent for a town to appropriate money to indemnify the school committee for expenses incurred in defending an action for an alleged libel contained in a report made by them in good faith, and in which action judgment had been rendered in their favor. [2] And although it should appear that the officer had exceeded his legal right and authority, yet if he has acted in good faith in an attempt to perform duty, the town has the right to adopt his act and to bind itself to indemnify him. [3]

---

[1] Per Parker, Ch. J. in Nelson v. Milford, 7 Pick. 23.

[2] Fuller v. Inhabitants of Groton, 11 Gray, 340. See also Hadsell v. Inhabitants of Hancock, 3 Gray, 526.

[3] A surveyor of highways cut a drain for the purpose of raising a legal question as to the bounds of the highway, and the town appointed a committee to defend an action brought against the surveyor therefor, and voted to defray the expenses incurred by the committee. By the court: "It is the duty of a town to repair all highways within its bounds, at the expense of the inhabitants, so that the same may be safe and convenient for travellers; and we think it has the power, as incident to this duty, to indemnify the surveyor or other agent against any charge or liability he may incur in the *bona fide* discharge of this duty, although it may turn out on investigation that he mistook his legal rights and authority. The act by which the surveyor incurred a liability was the digging a ditch, as a drain for the security of the highway; and if it was done for the purpose of raising a legal question as to the bounds of the highway, as the defendants offered to prove at the trial, the town had, nevertheless, a right to adopt the act, for they were interested in the subject, being bound to keep the highway in repair. They had, therefore, a right to determine whether they would defend the surveyor or not; and having determined the question, and appointed the plaintiffs a committee to carry on the defence, they cannot now be allowed to deny their liability, after the committee have paid the charges incurred under the authority of the town. The town had a right to act on the subject-matter which was within their jurisdiction; and their votes are binding and create a legal obligation, although they were under no previous obligation to indemnify the surveyor. That towns have an authority to defend and indemnify their agents who may incur a liability

And perhaps the legislature may even have power to compel the town, in such a case, to reimburse its officers the expenses incurred by them in the honest but mistaken discharge of what they believed to be their duty, notwithstanding the town, by vote, has refused to do so.[1]

Construction of Municipal Powers.

The powers conferred upon municipalities must be construed with reference to the object of their creation, namely, as agencies of the State in local government. The State can create them for no other purpose, and it can confer powers of government to no other end, without at once coming in conflict with the constitutional maxim, that legislative power cannot be delegated, or with other maxims designed to confine all the agencies of government to the exercise of their proper functions. And wherever the municipality shall attempt to exercise powers not within the proper province of local self-government, whether the right to do so be claimed under express legislative grant, or by implication from the charter, the act must be considered as altogether *ultra vires*.

A reference to a few of the adjudged cases will perhaps best illustrate this principle. The common council of the city of Buffalo undertook to provide an entertainment and ball for its citizens and certain expected guests on the 4th of July, and for that purpose entered into contract with a hotel keeper to provide the entertainment at his house, at the expense of the city. The entertainment was furnished and in part paid for, and suit was brought to recover the balance due. The city had authority, under its charter, to raise and expend moneys for various specified purposes, and also " to defray the contingent and other expenses of the city." But providing an entertainment for its citizens is no part of municipal self-government, and it has never been con-

---

by an inadvertent error, or in the performance of their duties imposed on them by law, is fully maintained by the case of Nelson *v.* Milford, 7 Pick. 18." Bancroft *v.* Lynnfield, 18 Pick. 568.

[1] Guilford *v.* Supervisors of Chenango, 13 N. Y. 143. But where officers make themselves liable to penalties for refusal to perform duty, the corporation has no authority to indemnify them. Halstead *v.* Mayor, &c. of New York, 3 N. Y. 430. See Frost *v.* Belmont, 6 Allen, 152.

sidered, where the common law has prevailed, that the power to do so pertained to the government in any of its departments. The contract was therefore held void, as not within the province of the city government.[1]

The supervisors of the city of New York refused to perform a duty imposed upon them by law, and were prosecuted severally for the penalty which the law imposed for such refusal, and judgment recovered. The board of supervisors then assumed, on behalf of the city and county, the payment of these judgments, together with the costs of defending the suits, and caused drafts to be drawn upon the treasurer of the city for these amounts. It was held, that these drafts upon the public treasury to indemnify officers for disregard of duty were altogether unwarranted and void, and that it made no difference that the officers had acted conscientiously in refusing to perform their duty, and in the honest belief that the law imposing the duty was unconstitutional. The city had no interest in the suits against the supervisors, and appropriating the public funds to satisfy the judgments and costs was not within either the express or implied powers conferred upon the board.[2] It was in fact appropriating the public money for private purposes, and a tax levied therefor must consequently be invalid, on general principles controlling the right of taxation, which will be considered in another place. In a recent case in Iowa it is said: " No instance occurs to us in which it would be competent for [a municipal corporation] to loan its credit or make its accommodation paper for the benefit of citizens to enable them to execute private enterprises ";[3] and where it cannot loan its credit to private undertakings, it is equally with-

---

[1] Hodges v. Buffalo, 2 Denio, 110. See also the case of New London v. Brainard, 22 Conn. 552, which follows and approves this case. The cases differ in this only, that in the first suit was brought to enforce the illegal contract, while in the second the city was enjoined from paying over moneys which it had appropriated for the purposes of the celebration. The cases of Tash v. Adams, 10 Cush. 252, and Hood v. Lynn, 1 Allen, 103, are to the same effect. Where a municipal corporation enters into a contract *ultra vires*, no implied contract arises to compensate the contractor for anything he may have done under it, notwithstanding the corporation may have reaped a benefit therefrom. McSpedon v. New York, 7 Bosw. 601; Zottman v. San Francisco, 20 Cal. 96.

[2] Halsted v. Mayor, &c. of New York, 3 N. Y. 430. See a similar case in People v. Lawrence, 6 Hill, 244. See also Carroll v. St. Louis, 12 Mo. 444; Vincent v. Nantucket, 12 Cush. 103; Parsons v. Goshen, 11 Pick. 396.

[3] Clark v. Des Moines, 19 Iowa, 224.

out power to appropriate the moneys in its treasury, or by the conduct of its officers to subject itself to implied obligations.[1]

The powers conferred upon the municipal governments must also be construed as confined in their exercise to the territorial limits embraced within the municipality ; and the fact that these powers are conferred in general terms will not warrant their exercise except within those limits.   A general power " to purchase, hold, and convey estate, real and personal, for the public use " of the corporation, will not authorize a purchase outside the corporate limits for that purpose.[2] Without some special provision they cannot, as of course, possess any control or rights over lands lying outside ;[3] and the taxes they levy of their own authority, and the moneys they expend, must be for local purposes only.[4]

But it is another question, how far the legislature of the State may authorize the corporation to extend its action to objects outside the city limits, and to engage in enterprises of a public nature which may benefit the citizens of the municipality in common with the people of the State at large, and also in some special and peculiar manner, but which nevertheless are not under the control of the corporation, and are so far aside from the ordinary purposes of local governments that assistance by the municipality in such enterprises would not be warranted under any general grant of power.   For a few years past the sessions of the legislative bodies of the several States have been prolific in a

---

[1] " In determining whether the subject-matter is within the legitimate authority of the town, one of the tests is to ascertain whether the expenses were incurred in relation to a subject specially placed by law in other hands. . . . . It is a decisive test against the validity of all grants of money by towns for objects liable to that objection, but it does not settle questions arising upon expenditures for objects not specially provided for.   In such cases the question will still recur, whether the expenditure was within the jurisdiction of the town.   It may be safely assumed that, if the subject of the expenditure be in furtherance of some duty enjoined by statute, or in exoneration of the citizens of the town from a liability to a common burden, a contract made in reference to it will be valid and binding upon the town."   Allen v. Taunton, 19 Pick. 487.

[2] Riley v. Rochester, 9 N. Y. 64.

[3] Per Kent, Chancellor, Denton v. Jackson, 2 Johns. Ch. 336.   And see Bullock v. Curry, 2 Met. (Ky.) 171 ; Weaver v. Cherry, 8 Ohio, N. S. 564 ; North Hempstead v. Hempstead, Hopk. 294 ; Concord v. Boscawen, 17 N. H. 465.

[4] In Parsons v. Goshen, 11 Pick. 396, the action of a town appropriating money in aid of the construction of a county road, was held void and no protection to the officers who had expended it.   See also Concord v. Boscawen, 17 N. H. 465.

species of legislation which has flooded the country with municipal securities issued in aid of works of public improvement, to
be owned, controlled, and operated by private parties, or by corporations created for the purpose ; the works themselves being
designed for the benefit of the State at large, or some particular
portion of it, but supposed to be specially beneficial to certain
localities because running near or through them, and therefore
justifying, it is supposed, the imposition of a special burden by
taxation upon such localities to aid in construction.[1] We have
elsewhere collected the cases in which it has been held that the
legislature may constitutionally authorize cities, townships, and
counties to subscribe to the stock of railroad companies, or to
loan their credit to these enterprises, and to tax their citizens to
pay these subscriptions, or the bonds or other securities issued,
where a peculiar benefit to the municipality was anticipated from
the improvement. The rulings in these cases, if sound, must
rest upon the same right which allows such municipalities to
impose burdens upon their citizens to construct local streets or
roads, and they can only be defended on the ground that " the
object to be accomplished is so obviously connected with the
[municipality] and its interests as to conduce obviously and in
a special manner to their prosperity and advancement." [2]

---

[1] In Merrick v. Inhabitants of Amherst, 12 Allen, 500, it was held competent
for the legislature to authorize a town to raise money by taxation for a State
agricultural college, to be located therein. The case, however, we think, stands
on different reasons from those where aid has been voted by municipalities to public improvements.

[2] Talbot v. Dent, 9 B. Monr. 526. See Hasbrouck v. Milwaukee, 13 Wis. 44.
" I confess it appears to me, notwithstanding the weight of authority on this head,
that a delegation of the power to municipal corporations to tax their citizens for
works of such a large and general utility as railroads cannot be fairly called a
taxation for local purposes, nor justified on that ground. The road may benefit
the locality, but it is not easy to see how it can properly be called a local object."
Sedgwick on Statutory and Const. Law, 464. See also Cass v. Dillon, 2 Ohio, N. S.
624, per Thurman, J. ; dissenting opinion of Ranney, J. in same case ; Griffith
v. Commissioners of Crawford County, 20 Ohio, 609, per Spaulding, J. And see
the following cases in Iowa, where it has been held incompetent under the constitution of that State to confer any such power upon the municipality : Stokes v.
Scott County, 10 Iowa, 166 ; State v. Wapello County, 13 Iowa, 388 ; Myers v.
Johnson County, 14 Iowa, 47 ; Smith v. Henry County, 15 Iowa, 385 ; Ten Eyck
v. Mayor, &c. of Keokuk, Ibid. 486 ; Clark v. Des Moines, 19 Iowa, 212.
" The corporation of St. Louis might be intrusted with power to borrow
money, and with funds thus procured enter upon some great scheme of improve-

The first requisite to the validity of any such subscriptions or securities would seem, then, to be a special legislative authority to make or issue them ; an authority which does not reside in the general words in which the powers of local self-government are usually conferred,[1] and which must be followed by the municipality in all essential particulars, or the subscription or security will be void. And while mere irregularities of action, not going to the essentials of the power, would not prevent parties who had acted in reliance upon the securities enforcing them, yet as the doings of these corporations are matters of public record, and they have no general power to issue negotiable securities, any one who becomes holder of such securities, even though they be negotiable in form, will take them with constructive notice of any want of power in the corporation to issue them, and cannot enforce them when their issue was unauthorized.[2]

---

ment supposed to be beneficial to the city and the State. It must then, to this extent and for this purpose, be like any other incorporated company established for making roads, digging canals, or engaging in manufactures. I should doubt the power of the legislature to compel any man to become a shareholder in such a company without his consent." City of St. Louis v. Allen, 13 Mo. 415.

[1] Bullock v. Curry, 2 Met. (Ky.) 171. A general power to borrow money or incur indebtedness to aid in the construction of " any road or bridge " must be understood to have reference only to the roads or bridges within the municipality. Stokes v. Scott County, 10 Iowa, 173; State v. Wapello County, 13 Iowa, 388; La Fayette v. Cox, 5 Ind. 38. There are decisions in the Supreme Court of the United States which appear to be to the contrary. The city charter of Muscatine conferred in detail the usual powers, and then authorized the city " to borrow money for any object in its discretion," after a vote of the city in favor of the loan. In Meyer v. Muscatine, 1 Wal. 384, the court seem to have construed this clause as authorizing a loan for *any object whatever;* whereas we think such phrases are understood usually to be confined in their scope to the specific objects before enumerated ; or at least to those embraced within the ordinary functions of municipal governments. This case was followed in Rogers v. Burlington, 3 Wal. 654, four justices dissenting. A municipal corporation having power to borrow money, it is held, may make its obligations payable wherever it shall agree. Meyer v. Muscatine, 1 Wal. 384. There are cases, however, which hold that such obligations can only be made payable at the corporation treasury, unless there is express legislative authority to make them payable elsewhere. People v. Tazewell County, 22 Ill. 147; Pekin v. Reynolds, 31 Ill. 529. Such corporations cannot give their obligations all the qualities of negotiable paper, without express legislative permission. Dively v. Cedar Falls, 21 Iowa, 565.

[2] There is considerable confusion in the cases on this subject. If the corporation has no authority to issue negotiable paper, or if the officers who assume to do so have no power under the charter for that purpose, there can be no doubt that

In some of the cases involving the validity of the subscriptions made or bonds issued by municipal corporations in aid of inter-

the defence of want of power may be made by the corporation in any suit brought on the securities. Smith *v.* Cheshire, 13 Gray, 318; Gould *v.* Sterling, 23 N. Y. 458; Andover *v.* Grafton, 7 N. H. 298; Clark *v.* Des Moines, 19 Iowa, 209. And in any case, if the holder has received the securities with notice of any valid defence, he takes them subject thereto. But where the corporation has power to issue negotiable paper in some cases, and it has assumed to do so in cases not within the charter, whether a *bona fide* holder would be chargeable with notice of the want of authority in the particular case, or, on the other hand, would be entitled to rely on the securities themselves as sufficient evidence that they were properly issued when nothing appeared on their face to apprise him of the contrary, is a question still open to some dispute.

In Stoney *v.* American Life Insurance Co., 11 Paige, 635, it was held that a negotiable security of a corporation which upon its face appears to have been duly issued by such corporation, and in conformity with the provisions of its charter, is valid in the hands of a *bona fide* holder thereof without notice, although such security was in fact issued for a purpose and at a place not authorized by the charter of the company, and in violation of the laws of the State where it was actually issued. In Gelpecke *v.* Dubuque, 1 Wal. 203, the law is stated as follows: " Where a corporation has power, under any circumstances, to issue negotiable securities, the *bona fide* holder has a right to presume they were issued under the circumstances which give the requisite authority, and they are no more liable to be impeached for any infirmity in the hands of such holder than any other commercial paper." In Farmers and Mechanics' Bank *v.* The Butchers and Drovers' Bank, 16 N. Y. 125, it is said: " A citizen who deals directly with a corporation, or who takes its negotiable paper, is presumed to know the extent of its corporate powers. But when the paper is, upon its face, in all respects such as the corporation has authority to issue, and its only defect consists in some extrinsic fact, — such as the purpose or object for which it was issued, — to hold that the person taking the paper must inquire as to such extraneous fact, of the existence of which he is in no way apprised, would obviously conflict with the whole policy of the law in regard to negotiable paper." In Madison and Indianapolis Railroad Co. *v.* The Norwich Saving Society, 24 Ind. 461, this doctrine is approved, and a distinction made, in the earlier case of Smead *v.* Indianapolis, &c. Railroad Co., 11 Ind. 104, between paper executed *ultra vires* and that executed within the power of the corporation, but, by an abuse of the power in that particular instance, was repudiated. In Halstead *v.* Mayor, &c. of New York, 5 Barb. 218, action was brought upon warrants drawn by the corporation of New York upon its treasurer, not in the course of its proper and legitimate business. It was held that the corporation under its charter had no general power to issue negotiable paper, though not being prohibited by law it might do so for any debt contracted in the course of its proper legitimate business. We quote from the opinion of Edwards, J.: " It was contended on the argument, that the rule of law-merchant which protects the *bona fide* holder of negotiable paper, without notice, was of universal application; and that, if the defendants had a right to issue negotiable paper, it must *ex necessitate* be subject to the same rules as the

nal improvements, there has been occasion to consider clauses in the State constitutions designed to limit the power of the legisla-

negotiable paper of an individual. This view seems plausible, but will it bear the test of examination? In the first place, the defendants have no general power, either express or implied, to issue negotiable paper. They have only a special or conditional implied power for that purpose; that it is necessary as a condition precedent to the validity of such paper that the debt which forms the consideration should be contracted in the proper legitimate business of the defendant. The act under which they were incorporated is declared to be a public act. Every person who takes their negotiable paper is bound to know the extent of their powers, and is presumed to receive it with a full knowledge that they have only a limited and conditional power to issue it. He is thus put on his inquiry, and takes it at his peril. The circumstances under which a *bona fide* holder, without notice, receives the negotiable paper of a natural person, or of a corporation having the general express power to issue negotiable paper, are very different. In both those instances, the power to issue such paper is general and unconditional; and hence the rules which have been established by commercial policy, for the purpose of giving currency to mercantile paper, are applicable. It results from the views which have been expressed, that the drafts in question, not having been issued by the defendants in their proper and legitimate business, are void in the hands of the plaintiff, although received by him without actual notice of their consideration." This decision was affirmed in 3 N. Y. 430. In Gould *v.* Town of Stirling, 23 N. Y. 458, it was held that where a town had issued negotiable bonds, which could only be issued when the written assent of two thirds the resident persons taxed in the town had been obtained and filed in the county clerk's office, the bonds issued without such assent were invalid, and that the purchaser of them could not rely upon the recital in the bonds that such assent had been obtained, but must ascertain for himself at his peril. Say the court: "One who takes a negotiable promissory note or bill of exchange, purporting to be made by an agent, is bound to inquire as to the power of the agent.. Where the agent is appointed and the power conferred, but the right to exercise the power has been made to depend upon the existence of facts of which the agent may be supposed to be in an especial manner cognizant, the *bona fide* holder is protected; because he is presumed to have taken the paper upon the faith of the representation as to those facts. The mere fact of executing the note or bill amounts in itself, in such a case, to a representation by the agent to every person who may take the paper that the requisite facts exist. But the holder has no such protection in regard to the existence of the power itself. In that respect the subsequent *bona fide* holder is in no better situation than the payee, except in so far as the latter would appear of necessity to have had cognizance of facts which the other cannot [must?] be presumed to have known." And the case is distinguished from that of the Farmers and Mechanics' Bank *v.* Butchers and Drovers' Bank, 16 N. Y. 125, where the extrinsic fact affecting the authority related to the state of accounts between the bank and one of its customers, which could only be known to the teller and other officers of the bank. The subject is reviewed in Clark *v.* City of Des Moines, 19 Iowa, 209. The action was brought upon city warrants, negotiable in form, and of which the plaintiff claimed to be *bona fide*

ture to incur indebtedness on behalf of the State, and which clauses, it has been urged, were equally imperative in restraining indebtedness on behalf of the several political divisions of the State. The constitution of Kentucky prohibited any act of the legislature authorizing any debt to be contracted on behalf of the Commonwealth, except for certain specified purposes, unless provision should be made in such act for an annual tax sufficient to pay such debt within thirty years ; and the act was not to have effect unless approved by the people. It was contended that this provision was not to apply to the Commonwealth as a mere ideal abstraction, unconnected with her citizens and her soil, but to the Commonwealth as composed of her people, and their territorial organizations of towns, cities, and counties, which make up the State, and that it embraced in principle every legislative act which authorized a debt to be contracted by any of the local organizations of which the Commonwealth was composed. The Supreme Court of that State held otherwise. " The clause in question," they say, " applies in terms to a debt contracted on behalf of the Commonwealth as a distinct corporate body ; and the distinction between a debt on behalf of the Commonwealth, and a debt or debts on behalf of one county, or of any number of counties, is too broad and palpable to admit of the supposition that the latter class of

assignee, without notice of any defects. The city offered to show that the warrants were issued without any authority from the city council, and without any vote of the council authorizing the same. It was held that the evidence should have been admitted, and that it would constitute a complete defence. See further, Head v. Providence, &c. Co., 2 Cranch, 169 ; Royal British Bank v. Turquand, 6 El. & Bl. 327 ; Knox County v. Aspinwall, 21 How. 544 ; Bissell v. Jeffersonville, 24 How. 287 ; Sanborn v. Deerfield, 2 N. H. 254 ; Alleghany City v. McClurkan, 14 Penn. St. 83 ; Morris Canal and Banking Co. v. Fisher, 1 Stock. 667 ; Clapp v. Cedar Co., 5 Iowa, 15 ; Commissioners, &c. v. Cox, 6 Ind. 403. It is of course impossible to reconcile these authorities ; but the doctrine in the case of Gould v. Town of Sterling appears to us to be sound, and that, wherever a want of power exists, a purchaser of the securities is chargeable with notice of it, if the defect is disclosed by the corporate records, or, as in that case, by other records where the power is required to be shown. That the powers of the agents of municipal corporations are matters of record, and the corporation not liable for an unauthorized act, see further, Baltimore v. Eschbach, 18 Md. 276 ; Johnson v. Common Council, 16 Ind. 227. Those who deal with a corporation must take notice of the restrictions in its charter, and see to it that the contracts on which they rely are entered into in the manner the charter authorizes. Brady v. Mayor, &c. of New York, 2 Bosw. 173 ; Same case, 20 N. Y. 312 ; Swift v. Williamsburg, 24 Barb. 427.

debts was intended to be embraced by terms specifically designating the former only." [1]   The same view has been taken by the courts of Iowa, Wisconsin, and Illinois of the provisions in the constitutions of those States restricting the power of the legislature to contract debts on behalf of the State in aid of internal improvements; [2] but the decisions of the first-named State have since been doubted. [3]

Another class of legislation has recently demanded the attention of the courts, which has not been less troublesome, from the new, varied, and peculiar questions involved, than that in relation to municipal subscriptions in aid to internal improvements.   As the power to declare war and to conduct warlike operations rests in the national government, which is vested with unlimited control of all the resources of the country to that end, the duty of national defence, and, consequently, to defend all the citizens as well as all the property of all the municipal organizations in the several States, rests upon the national authorities.   This much is conceded, though in a qualified degree, also, and subordinate to the national government, a like duty rests upon the State governments, which may employ the means and services of their citizens for the purpose.   But it is no part of the duty of a township, city, or county, as such, to raise men or money for warlike operations, nor have they any authority, without express legislative sanction, to impose upon their people any burden by way of taxation for any such purpose. [4]   Nevertheless, when a war arises which taxes all the energies of the nation, which makes it necessary to put into the field a large percentage of all the able-bodied men of the country, and which renders imperative a resort to all available means for filling the ranks of the army, recruiting the navy, and replenishing the national treasury, the question be-

---

[1] Slack v. Railroad Co., 13 B. Monr. 16.

[2] Dubuque County v. Railroad Co., 4 Greene (Iowa), 1; Clapp v. Cedar County, 5 Iowa, 15; Clark v. Janesville, 10 Wis. 136; Bushnell v. Beloit, Ibid. 195; Prettyman v. Supervisors, 19 Ill. 406; Robertson v. Rockford, 21 Ill. 451; Johnson v. Stark County, 24 Ill. 75; Perkins v. Lewis, Ibid. 208; Butler v. Dunham, 27 Ill. 474.

[3] State v. Wapello County, 13 Iowa, 388.   And see People v. Supervisor, &c., 16 Mich. 254.

[4] Stetson v. Kempton, 13 Mass. 272; Gove v. Epping, 41 N. H. 545; Crowell v. Hopkinton, 45 N. H. 9; Baldwin v. North Branford, 32 Conn. 47; Webster v. Harwinton, Ibid. 131.   See also Claflin v. Hopkinton, 4 Gray, 502; Cover v. Baytown, 12 Minn. 124.

comes a momentous one, whether the local organizations, those which are managed most immediately by the people themselves, may not be made important auxiliaries to the national and State governments in accomplishing the great object in which all are alike interested ; and if so, whether there is any constitutional principle which would be violated by making use of these organizations in a cause where failure on the part of the central authority would precipitate general dismay and ruin. Indeed, as the general government, with a view to convenience, economy, and promptness of action, will be very likely to adopt, for any purposes of conscription, the existing municipal divisions of the States, so that its demand for recruits for its armies will seem to impose the special duty of meeting it on the people whose municipal organization embraces the territory covered by the demand, the question we have stated would appear to be rather one of form than of substance, and it would hardly seem to be open to doubt, that the duty which rests upon the citizens of the municipality may properly be assumed by the municipality itself, and then be discharged like any other municipal burden, if the legislature shall grant permission for that purpose.

One difficulty that suggests itself in adopting any such doctrine is, that, by the existing law of the land, able-bodied men between certain specified ages are alone liable to be summoned to the performance of military duty ; and if the obligation is assumed by the municipal organizations of the State, and discharged by the payment of money or the procurement of substitutes, the taxation required for this purpose can be claimed, with some show of reason, to be taxation of the whole community for the particular benefit of those upon whom the obligation rests. When the public funds are used for the purpose, it will be insisted that they are appropriated to discharge the liabilities of private individuals. Those who are already past the legal age of service, and who have stood their chance of being called into the field, or perhaps have actually rendered the required service, will be able to urge with considerable force that the State can no longer honorably require them to contribute to the public defence, but ought to insist that those within the legal ages should perform their legal duty ; and if any upon whom that duty rests shall actually have enrolled themselves in the army with a view to discharge it, such persons may claim, with even greater reason, that every consideration of equality and justice demands that the property they leave behind them shall not be taxed to relieve others from a duty equally imperative.

Whatever may be the abstract reasoning on this subject, there can be no question, in the light of the judicial decisions which have been made, that the people of any municipal corporation or political division of a State have such a general interest in relieving that portion of their fellow-citizens who are liable to the performance of military duty, as will support taxation or render valid indebtedness contracted for the purpose of supplying their places, or filling any call of the national authorities for men, with volunteers who shall be willing to enter the ranks for such pecuniary inducements as may be offered them. The duty of national defence rests upon every person under the protection of the government who is able to contribute to it, and not solely upon those who are within the legal ages. The statute which has prescribed those ages has for its basis the presumption that those between the limits fixed are best able to discharge the burden of military service to the public benefit, and it does not absolve any others from being summoned to the duty, if at any time the public exigency should seem to demand it. Exemption from military duty is a privilege rather than a right, and, like other statutory privileges, may be recalled at any time when reasons of public policy or necessity seem to demand the recall. Moreover, there is no valid reason, in the nature of things, why those who are incapable of performing military service, by reason of age, physical infirmity, or other cause, should not contribute, in proportion to their ability, to the public defence by such means as are within their power; and it may well happen that taxation, for the purpose of recruiting the armies of the nation, will distribute the burden more equally and justly among all the citizens than any other mode which could be devised. Whether it will be just and proper to allow it in any instance must rest with the legislature to determine; but it is unquestionably competent, with legislative permission, for towns, cities, and counties to raise money by loans or by taxation to pay bounty moneys to those who shall volunteer to fill any call made upon such towns, cities, or counties to supply men for the national armies.[1]

[1] " The power to create a public debt, and liquidate it by taxation, is too clear for dispute. The question is therefore narrowed to a single point : Is the purpose

Relief of the community from an impending or possible draft is not, however, the sole consideration which will support taxation by the municipal corporations of the State to raise money for the purpose of paying bounties to soldiers. Gratitude to those who have entered the military service, whether as volunteers or drafted men, or as substitute for others who were drafted or were

in this instance a public one? Does it concern the common welfare and interest of the municipality? Let us see. Civil war was raging, and Congress provided in the second section of the act of 24th February, 1864, that the quota of the troops of each ward of a city, town, township, precinct, &c., should be as nearly as possible in proportion to the number of men resident therein liable to render military service. Section three provided that all volunteers who may enlist after a draft shall be ordered shall be deducted from the number ordered to be drafted in such ward, town, &c. Volunteers are therefore by law to be accepted in relief of the municipality from a compulsory service to be determined by lot or chance. Does the relief involve the public welfare or interest? The answer rises spontaneously in the breast of every one in a community liable to the military burden. It is given, not by the voice of him alone who owes the service, but swells into a chorus from his whole family, relatives, and friends. Military service is the highest duty and burden the citizen is called to obey or to bear. It involves life, limb, and health, and is therefore a greater 'burden' than the taxation of property. The loss or the injury is not confined to the individual himself, but extends to all the relations he sustains. It embraces those bound to him in the ties of consanguinity, friendship, and interest; to the community which must furnish support to his family, if he cannot, and which loses in him a member whose labor, industry, and property contribute to its wealth and its resources; who assists to bear its burdens, and whose knowledge, skill, and public spirit contribute to the general good. Clearly the loss of that part of the population upon whom the greatest number depend, and who contribute most to the public welfare, by their industry, skill, and property, and good conduct, is a common loss, and therefore a general injury. These are alike subject to the draft. The blind and relentless lot respects no age, condition, or rank in life. It is therefore clearly the interest of the community that those should serve who are willing, whose loss will sever the fewest ties, and produce the least injury.

"The bounty is not a private transaction in which the individual alone is benefited. It benefits the public by inducing and enabling those to go who feel they can best be spared. It is not voluntary in those who pay it. The community is subject to the draft, and it is paid to relieve it from a burden of war. It is not a mere gift or reward, but a consideration for services. It is therefore not a confiscation of one man's property for another's use, but it is a contribution from the public treasury for a general good. In short, it is simply taxation to relieve the municipality from the stern demands of war, and avert a public injury in the loss of those who contribute most to the public welfare." Speer v. School Directors of Blairsville, 50 Penn. St. 159. See also Waldo v. Portland, 33 Conn. 363; Bartholomew v. Harwinton, Ibid. 408; Fowler v. Danvers, 8 Allen, 80; Lowell v. Oliver, Ibid. 247.

liable to be, is a consideration which the State may well recognize, and compensate either by the payment of bounty moneys directly to them, or by provision for the support of those dependent upon them while they shall be absent from their homes. Whether we regard such persons as public benefactors, who, having taken upon themselves the most severe and dangerous duty a citizen is ever called upon to perform, have thereby entitled themselves to public reward as an incentive to fidelity and courage, or as persons who, having engaged in the public service for a compensation inadequate to the toil, privation, and danger incurred, are deserving of the bounty as a further recognition on the part of the community of the worth of their services, there seems in either case to be no sufficient reason to question the right of the legislature to authorize the municipal divisions of the State to raise moneys in any of the usual modes, for the purpose of paying bounties to them or their families in recognition of such services.[1]

[1] The act under which the Pennsylvania case, cited in the preceding note, was decided, authorized the borough to contract a debt for the payment of three hundred dollars to each non-commissioned officer and private who might thereafter volunteer and enter the service of the United States, and be credited upon the quota of the borough under an impending draft. The whole purpose, therefore, was to relieve the community from the threatened conscription. But in the case of Brodhead v. Milwaukee, 19 Wis. 652, it was held constitutional, not only to provide for the future by such municipal taxation, but also to raise moneys to pay bounties to volunteers previously enlisted, as well as to those who should thereafter procure substitutes for themselves, and have them credited on the municipal quota. Chief Justice Dixon, in delivering the opinion of the court, says : "I think the consideration of gratitude alone to the soldier for his services, be he volunteer, substitute, or drafted man, will sustain a tax for bounty-money to be paid to him or his family. Certainly no stronger consideration of gratitude can possibly exist than that which arises from the hardships, privations, and dangers which attend the citizen in the military service of his country ; and all nations have ever so regarded it. Who will say that the legislature may not, in consideration of such services, either directly or indirectly, or through the agency of the municipality or district to which he is credited, give to the soldier or his family a suitable bounty after his enlistment, or even after his term of service has expired ? I certainly cannot. It is a matter which intimately concerns the public welfare ; and that nation will live longest in fact, as well as in history, and be most prosperous, whose people are most sure and prompt in the reasonable and proper acknowledgment of such obligations.

"But the act provides for paying the same bounties ' to persons who shall procure substitutes for themselves before being drafted, and have them credited to such town, city, or village upon its quota,' under the then pending call of the President, or any call which should thereafter be made ; and it is said that

And if a municipal corporation shall have voted moneys for such purpose without legislative authority, it is competent for the

clearly no debt of gratitude is due to such persons. To my mind it is not quite so clear. Suppose that during the late rebellion citizens enough in the loyal States, liable to military service, had furnished substitutes so as promptly to have answered the calls of the President, and kept the armies of the Union replenished with new soldiers, and so as to have avoided the evils and expenses of the drafts; is it clear that all the communities thus relieved would have been under no obligation of gratitude to such citizens? Suppose still further, that, under the system of apportionment adopted by Congress, a sufficient number of such citizens had been found in any town, city, or election precinct to have filled its quota by substitutes; would there have been no cause for thankfulness on the part of the inhabitants of such town, city, or precinct for their having done so? I must confess that I think there would. War, though often unavoidable, is always a most deplorable public misfortune; and among its calamities, not the least, I may say the greatest, is the forcible separation of husbands, fathers, sons, and brothers from their homes, kindred, and friends, to be made bloody sacrifices on the field of battle, or to die of loathsome diseases contracted in camps or upon campaigns; and those who avert the evils of such forcible separation, I care not from what motive of private or individual interest, so that the duty of furnishing men for the army is performed, cannot but be regarded as in some sense public benefactors.

"But it is not for those who have furnished substitutes in the past that the act provides bounties, but for those who shall do so under a pending call before being drafted, and have them credited to the town, city, or village, so as to avoid or help to avoid an approaching draft. In such case the power to tax may not rest upon the ground of gratitude. It can be sustained upon consideration of the benefit accruing to the town, city, or village from the credit, which is direct and palpable. The procuring of substitutes was lawful and proper in itself. The act of Congress authorizes it, and the credit to the town, city, or village. Substitutes must be persons not liable to the draft, so as not to affect the interests of those who were, otherwise than by directly relieving them from the burden of it. The provision for substitutes was a necessity. Other obligations exist as strong, sometimes almost stronger, than that of carrying arms in the public defence; and they could not be ignored. Some were so situated that personal service seemed impossible. Others might not go without greater loss to the community at home than gain to the public at large. The procuring of substitutes was therefore not only proper, but in many cases commendable. Persons procuring them performed their whole duty under the law. They furnished soldiers for the field, and relieved the communities in which they resided, the same as if they had themselves enlisted. So far as the public interest is concerned in being relieved from the draft, I can see no distinction between paying bounties to them and to those who volunteer. Both contribute precisely in the same degree to such relief. The error of counsel, I think, consists in looking exclusively to the motives of private advantage by which the persons were governed. That such motives existed, and were most frequently the predominant cause of their procuring substitutes, will not be denied. But there is no public good without at the same time some private gain; and in the language of Chief Justice Black, it is enough that we can

legislature afterwards to legalize their action if it shall so choose.[1]

see any possible public interest in the act, or public benefit to be derived from it. All beyond that is a question of expediency for the legislature, not of law, much less of constitutional law to be determined by the courts."

[1] The town of Woodbury, being subject to a call for thirty-two men for service in the national army, passed a resolution appropriating six thousand four hundred dollars from the treasury of the township for the purpose of procuring substitutes to fill such call. There was no legislation at the time which would warrant this resolution, but a special statute was afterwards passed authorizing the town to confirm this action, which it did by vote of a legal meeting called for the purpose. Bill being filed to restrain action under these votes, it was alleged that they were illegal, unjust to the tax-payers, unconstitutional, and disloyal to the government of the United States; that they were intended to defeat the proper effect of the law of the United States and the call of the President; and that the town thereby unlawfully undertook to transfer the individual liability of each person drafted by the United States to widows, orphans, and non-military subjects, as well as to those liable in their own persons to do military duty on behalf of the United States. The court state the question involved in the case to be this: " Whether it is competent for the State legislature to give gratuities to such of its citizens as are called, under the allegiance they owe to the national government, and independent of the allegiance they owe to the State government, by distinctive and independent national enactments, to render to that national government distinct and independent military service, and tax the citizens generally therefor. For if they have the power to do it, they may impose the duty or confer the power of doing it upon the towns." And after saying that the State constitutions do not, in express terms, confer any such power, nor expressly forbid it, and that the question therefore is, whether it is within the grant of legislative power, they proceed to show that the special statute was not such an infringement of natural justice as would warrant the court in holding it inoperative, as in excess of legislative authority, for several reasons.

" In the first place, if it be conceded that it is not competent for the legislative power to make a gift of the common property, or of a sum of money to be raised by taxation, where no possible public benefit, direct or indirect, can be derived therefrom, such exercise of the legislative power must be of an extraordinary character to justify the interference of the judiciary. And this is not that case.

" Second. If there be the least possibility that making the gift will be promotive in any degree of the public welfare, it becomes a question of policy, and not of natural justice; and the determination of the legislature is conclusive. And such is this case. Such gifts to unfortunate classes of society, as the indigent blind, the deaf and dumb, or insane, or grants to particular colleges or schools, or grants of pensions, swords, or other mementoes for past services, involving the general good indirectly and in slight degree, are frequently made and never questioned.

" Third. The government of the United States was constituted by the people of the State, although acting in concert with the people of other States, and the general good of the people of this State is involved in the maintenance of that

The cases to which we have referred in the notes assume that, if the purpose is one for which the State might properly levy a tax upon its citizens at large, the legislature would also have power to apportion and impose the duty, or confer the power of assuming it upon the towns and other municipal or political divisions. And the rule which is thus laid down opens a broad field to legislative discretion, when it allows the raising and

general government. In many conceivable ways the action of the town of Wood-bury might not only mitigate the burdens imposed upon a class, but render the service of that class more efficient to the general government, and therefore it must be presumed that the legislature found that the public good was in fact thereby promoted.

" And fourth, it is obviously possible, and therefore to be intended, that the General Assembly found a clear equity to justify their action.

" Every citizen is bound to take up arms when necessary in defence of his government; not as a matter of strict law, but as an incident of citizenship; and the selection of a class only of a certain age, of whom that service is to be im-mediately demanded in a particular case, although wise, is arbitrary, not based on any peculiar or special obligation resting upon the class, or on their liability alone to render the service, or to render it with less pecuniary or social sacrifice, but on the wants of the government, and the supposed fitness of the class to sub-serve the purposes of the government with more efficiency than others. But if all owe the service, and it is for the common good, and there is the usual provis-ion that it may be rendered by substitute or commutation, it is not easy to see why men above forty-five years of age, if able bodied, may not be called upon as well as those of less age. If not as able to endure the hardships of the field, they may answer equally well for garrison duty, or as details, and presumptively they are better able to procure substitutes, or commute, for they have more generally accu-mulated property or received it by inheritance. Indeed, if substitution and com-mutation are made elements of the conscription, — and they were of the law in question, — the *ability* to procure a substitute or commute may well be an element without regard to age, and therefore when all above a certain age are exempt, they are favored; and it is clearly equitable and just that they equalize the bur-den by bounties to those who are drafted and serve, or by making provision for the support of their families. On this obvious equity rests the general law mak-ing provision for the families of all drafted men and their substitutes."

The court were therefore of opinion that it was competent for the General Assembly to pass votes in reference to all the drafted men of the State like those which this town had passed, and that it was equally competent for them to dele-gate that power to the towns, and of course to authorize the towns to ratify votes of that character which they had before adopted. Booth *v.* Town of Woodbury, 32 Conn. 118. See, to the same effect, Bartholomew *v.* Harwinton, 33 Conn. 408; Crowell *v.* Hopkinton, 45 N. H. 9; Shackford *v.* Newington, 46 N. H. 415; Low-ell *v.* Oliver, 8 Allen, 247; Ahl *v.* Gleim, 52 Penn. St. 432; Weister *v.* Hade, Ibid. 474.

appropriation of moneys whenever, in the words of one of the cases, there is " the least possibility that it will be promotive in any degree of the public welfare." The same rule, substantially, has been recognized by the Court of Appeals of New York. " The legislature is not confined in its appropriation of the public moneys, or of the sums to be raised by taxation in favor of individuals, to cases in which a legal demand exists against the State. It can thus recognize claims founded in equity and justice in the largest sense of these terms, or in gratitude or charity. Independently of express constitutional restrictions, it can make appropriations of money whenever the public well-being requires or will be promoted by it, and it is the judge of what is for the public good. It can, moreover, under the power to levy taxes, apportion the public burdens among all the tax-paying citizens of the State, or among those of a particular section or political division." [1]   And where citizens have voluntarily advanced moneys for the purpose of paying bounties to recruits who fill the quota of a municipal corporation, on an understanding, based upon informal corporate action, that the moneys should be refunded when a law should be passed permitting it, a subsequent act of the legislature authorizing taxation for this purpose is valid.[2]

However broad are the terms employed in describing the legislative power over taxation in these cases, it is believed that no one of them has gone so far as to sanction taxation or the appropriation of public moneys in order to refund to individuals moneys which they may have paid to relieve themselves from an impending draft, or have voluntarily contributed to any public purposes, from any motives purely personal to themselves, and where they could have no reason to rely upon the credit of the State, or of any municipal corporation, for reimbursement, and where the circumstances are not such as fairly to challenge the public gratitude. Taxation in such a case, where no obligation, honorary or otherwise, rests upon the public, would be nothing else than a naked case of appropriating the property of the tax-payer for private purposes, and that without compensation.[3]

---

[1] Guilford v. Supervisors of Chenango, 13 N. Y. 149.

[2] Weister v. Hade, 52 Penn. St. 474.

[3] Tyson v. School Directors, &c., 51 Penn. St. 9. A meeting of persons liable to draft under the law of the United States was called, and an association formed,

But it has been held by the Supreme Court of Massachusetts that towns might be authorized by the legislature to raise moneys by taxation for the purpose of refunding sums contributed by individuals to a common fund, in order to fill the quota of such towns under a call of the President, notwithstanding such moneys might have been contributed without promise or expectation of reimbursement. The court were of opinion that such contribu-

called the Halifax Bounty Association, which levied an assessment of thirty dollars on each person liable to military duty in the township, and solicited contributions from others. Afterwards, an act was passed by the legislature, with a preamble reciting that certain citizens of Halifax township, associated as the Halifax Bounty Association, for freeing the said township from the late drafts, advanced moneys, which were expended in paying bounties to volunteers to. fill the quota of the township. The act then authorized and required the school directors to borrow such sums of money as would fully reimburse the said Halifax Bounty Association for moneys advanced to free said township from the draft, and then further authorized the school directors to levy and collect a tax to repay the sums borrowed. The court say: " We are bound to regard the statute as an authority to reimburse what was intended by the Association as advances made to the township with the intent or understanding to be reimbursed or returned to those contributing. This was the light in which the learned judge below regarded the terms used; and unless this appears in support of the present levy by the school directors, they are acting without authority. But the learned judge, if I properly comprehend his meaning, did not give sufficient importance to these terms, and hence, I apprehend, he fell into error. He does not seem to have considered it essential whether the Association paid its money voluntarily in aid of its own members, or expressly to aid the township in saving its people from a draft, with the understanding that it was advanced in the character of a loan if the legislature chose to direct its repayment, and the school directors chose to act on the authority conferred. This we cannot agree to. Such an enactment would not be legislation at all. It would be in the nature of judicial action, it is true; but wanting the justice of notice to the parties to be affected by the hearing, trial, and all that gives sanction and force to regular judicial proceedings, it would much more resemble an imperial rescript than constitutional legislation: first, in declaring an obligation where none was created or previously existed; and next, in decreeing payment by directing the money or property of the people to be sequestered to make the payment. The legislature can exercise no such despotic functions; and as it is not apparent in the act that they attempted to do so, we are not to presume that they did. They evidently intended the *advancements* to be reimbursed to be only such as were made on the faith that they were to be returned." See also Crowell v. Hopkinton, 45 N. H. 9; Miller v. Grandy, 13 Mich. 540; Pease v. Chicago, 21 Ill. 508. In Freeland v. Hastings, 10 Allen, 570, it was held that the legislature could not empower towns to raise money by taxation for the purpose of refunding what had been paid by individuals for substitutes in military service.

tions might well be considered as advancements to a public purpose, and, being such, the legislature might well recognize the
obligation and provide for its discharge.[1]

[1] Freeland v. Hastings, 10 Allen, 585. The court, after considering the general subject of the power to authorize the towns to raise money by tax for the payment of bounties to volunteers, proceed to say: "It would seem to follow as a
necessary consequence, that not only was the payment of bounties by the commonwealth, and by cities and towns, for the purpose of procuring volunteers, a
proper and legitimate object of expenditure of public money, raised or to be raised
by taxation, but also that money contributed voluntarily by individuals to raise a
fund for the same purpose may well have been considered by the legislature as
an advancement of money for a public object. When in the summer of 1864 it
became necessary to furnish a large additional number of soldiers to the army of
the United States by filling the quotas allotted to the several cities and towns, a
public exigency had arisen for which no adequate provision had been made by
the legislature. The alternative was presented to the people of the Commonwealth of procuring volunteers to enlist by the payment of bounties, or of submitting to the evils and hardships attendant upon an attempt to recruit the army
by a draft. In most if not all of the cities and towns, it was deemed to be wise
and expedient, and most for the interest of the inhabitants, to embrace the former
branch of this alternative; and accordingly, as no authority was then vested in
towns or cities to raise money by taxation or otherwise for the payment of bounties, resort was had to the method of procuring voluntary contributions to raise a
fund in each town for such purpose. But these contributions, though voluntarily
made, and without any legal claim on the town or city for reimbursement, or any
expectation of legislative sanction, were nevertheless given in aid of the performance of a public duty, which devolved on the city or town, and for which it would
have been competent for the legislature, in anticipation of the exigency, to
authorize money to be raised, by taxation or otherwise, on the credit of a town or
city. In this view the question as to the validity of the statute resolves itself
into this: whether it was competent for the legislature to authorize towns and
cities to repay to individuals money which, in the opinion of the legislature, they
had advanced in a pressing public exigency to enable a town or city to discharge
a duty which was legally devolved upon it, and which it could not have performed
without such adventitious aid. Upon the best consideration which we have been
able to give the subject, we can see no legal or constitutional objection to the
action of the legislature. We are not called upon to determine the wisdom or
expediency of the act. Confining ourselves to the question whether the legislature
have transcended their authority in passing it, we are of opinion that no private
right is invaded, and no constitutional barrier overstepped, in giving authority to
cities and towns to raise money by taxation to reimburse individuals for contributions made in aid of an object of a public or municipal nature; or, in other
words, that as it is competent for the legislature to authorize the imposition of
taxes to raise money to be expended for a public purpose, so it is competent for
them to sanction an expenditure already made for a like object, and to give
authority for its repayment by means of taxation. If these views are correct, then

Whether the legislature has power, against the will of a municipal corporation, to compel its citizens to assume an obligation, and
to discharge it by taxation, where the obligation is one which it
would not fall within the ordinary functions of municipal government to enter into, is a question which, if it is to be decided by
authority, is not entirely free from difficulty. There are cases
which deny to the legislature the possession of any such power;
and which claim for the municipal organizations the same exemption from compulsory burdens, outside the circle of their ordinary
and legal duties, that protects the individual citizen. And even
where a moral obligation may fairly be said to rest upon the municipality, it is denied, in some cases, that the legislature can convert
it into a legal demand, and enforce its payment, though it is conceded that it may authorize the citizens of the municipality to
assume the burden and discharge it if they choose to do so.[1]

it follows that the statute under consideration is not obnoxious to the objections
to its validity urged by the petitioners. It cannot in any just sense be said that
the legislature authorized an assessment, by means of which money could be
capriciously taken from one individual or class and given to another, or that it
sanctioned the appropriation of public money to the payment of claims which had
no just or equitable existence. The clear and decisive answer to all such objections is, that the money which the statute authorized towns to repay by means of
taxation was raised and contributed for a public object. This seems to us not only
to constitute a test by which the validity of the statute is proved, but also a safe
limit by which the power of the legislature to authorize taxation for repayments
or reimbursements of money advanced without legislative sanction may be restrained." This case should be compared and contrasted with that of Tyson v.
School Directors, 51 Penn. St. 9, given fully in a preceding note.

[1] In Hasbrouck v. Milwaukee, 13 Wis. 37, it appeared that the city of Milwaukee had been authorized to issue bonds to an amount not exceeding fifty
thousand dollars, to raise money to expend in the construction of a harbor in that
city. The city authorities entered into a contract for that purpose, at a cost
largely exceeding the limit thus fixed. Subsequent acts of the legislature extended the authority to issue bonds to such an amount as should be necessary to
complete the harbor. Whether these acts had the effect to render valid the contract before entered into by the city was made a question in the court. It did
not appear that the city petitioned for such subsequent acts, or had in any way
expressed its assent to them. "Under these circumstances," say the court, "the
question is, Can the legislature, by recognizing the existence of a previously void
contract, and authorizing its discharge by the city, or in any other way, coerce
the city against its will into a performance of it; or does the law require the assent of the city as well as of the legislature, in order to make the obligation binding and efficacious?

"I must say that, in my opinion, the latter act, as well as the former, is necessary

There are other cases, however, which seem to go to the extent of holding that municipal corporations and organizations are so completely under the legislative control, that, whatever the legislature may *permit* them to do, with a view to the general benefit, it may compel them to do, whether their citizens are willing or not. If, for instance, the legislature may constitutionally authorize a town or city to take stock in a railroad enterprise, for the convenience and benefit of its citizens, and on the supposition that the work, though not local in its character, will be productive of local benefits, it may also compel such action by the town or city, or oblige it to refund moneys which individuals may have advanced for the purpose. And where a State or county building is to be erected, the effect of which may be locally beneficial, the legislature, on the principle of equalizing, as far as practicable, the benefits and the burdens, may oblige the town where it is to be built to contribute to that object such sum as it shall deem just, over and above the ratable proportion as assessed upon the State or county at large.[1]

for that purpose, and that without it the obligation cannot be enforced. A contract void for want of capacity in one or both of the contracting parties to enter into it is as no contract; it is as if no attempt at an agreement had ever been made. And to admit that the legislature, of its own choice, and against the wishes of either or both of the contracting parties, can give it life and vigor, is to admit that it is within the scope of legislative authority to divest settled rights of property, and to take the property of one individual or corporation and transfer it to another. It is certainly unnecessary at this day to enter into an argument, or to cite authorities, to show that under a constitutional government like ours the legislature has no such power.

"It is undoubtedly true that, in cases like the present, where there is a strong moral, but no legal obligation to pay, courts have often seized, and may again seize upon very slight circumstances of assent in order to give effect to the contract. And in this case, if it appeared that the city did by some authorized action procure the passage of the act, or had subsequently acquiesced in it by ratifying the contract, there would be little difficulty in the way of holding it bound by its terms. In such cases it is the contemporaneous or subsequent assent of the parties to be bound, coupled with the power or ability on their part to give such assent, which makes the contract obligatory. But the giving of such assent is a matter which depends upon their own free will. It is a voluntary act which they may do or not as they see fit, and in case they think proper to withhold it, the legislature has no power to compel it." See also Hampshire *v.* Franklin, 16 Mass. 83, for somewhat similar views.

[1] Kirby *v.* Shaw, 19 Penn. St. 258. In this case, by an act of April 3, 1848, the commissioners of Bradford county were to add five hundred dollars annually, until 1857, to the usual county rates and levies of the borough of Towanda in

If these cases, which are referred to in the note, are sound, the
limitations which rest upon the power of the legislature to compel

said county, for the purpose of defraying the expenses of erecting the court-
house and jail, then in process of erection in that borough.   The act was held
constitutional, on the principle of assessment of benefits.   In Thomas v. Leland,
24 Wend. 67, it appeared that certain citizens of Utica had given their bond to
the people of the State of New York, conditioned for the payment into the canal
fund of the sum of thirty-eight thousand six hundred and fifteen dollars, the estimated difference between the cost of connecting the Chenango Canal with the
Erie at Utica, instead of at Whitesborough as the canal commissioners had contemplated ; and it was held within the constitutional powers of the legislature to
require this sum to be assessed upon the taxable property of the city of Utica,
supposed to be benefited by the canal connection.   The court treat the case as
" the ordinary one of local taxation to make or improve a public highway.   If
such an act," says Cowen, J., " be otherwise constitutional, we do not see how
the circumstance that a bond had been before given securing the same money
can detract from its validity.   Should an individual volunteer to secure a sum of
money in itself properly leviable by way of tax on a town or county, thefe would
be nothing in the nature of such an arrangement which would preclude the legislature from resorting, by way of tax, to those who are primarily and more justly
liable.   Even should he pay the money, what is there in the constitution to preclude his being reimbursed by a tax ? "   The same general views have been
acted upon in other cases, which assert the complete power of the legislature over
the subject of taxation, and that it must determine what sums shall be raised,
either in the State at large, or in any particular portion of the State, and also to
what objects the sums so raised shall be applied.   See particularly Guilford v. Supervisors of Chenango, 18 Barb. 615 ; Same case, 13 N. Y. 143 ; People v.
Mitchell, 45 Barb. 208 ; Same case, 35 N. Y. 551 ;. People v. Power, 25 Ill. 187 ;
People v. Mayor, &c. of Brooklyn, 4 N. Y. 419 ; Slack v. Maysville and Lexington Railroad Co., 13 B. Monr. 26 ; Cheaney v. Hooser, 9 B. Monr. 330.   See also
Borough of Dunmore's Appeal, 52 Penn. St. 374.   In that case it appeared that
a township which was considerably indebted, had had four boroughs carved out of
it.   Afterwards an act was passed by which the Court of Common Pleas was
directed to appoint three commissioners, for the purpose of ascertaining the indebtedness of the township, and what amount, if any, was due and owing from
the boroughs, and make an equitable adjustment thereof between them all, and
allowing no appeal by the boroughs from their decision.   It was held that the
act was valid.   Per Woodworth, Ch. J.: " This legislation is unprecedented, and
perhaps severe ; but it denies trial by jury only to municipal corporations, who,
being creatures of the legislative power, are subject to the legislative will in a
manner and to an extent to which citizens are not.   The constitutional guaranties
of the citizen were respected in giving him a right of appeal ; the municipal
corporations, having no such guaranties, the right of appeal was not given to
them.   The theory of the act was therefore unexceptionable, and we have no
reason to doubt that its operation in the peculiar circumstances of the case will
be beneficent and just."   Similar views were expressed by the Supreme Court of

municipal corporations to assume and discharge obligations, can only be such as spring from the general principles governing taxation, namely, that the demand or purpose for which the tax is levied shall be such as to constitute a proper charge or burden upon the State or portion of the State taxed to pay or to accomplish it. But upon this question the legislature is vested with discretionary and compulsory power, and its decisions are not subject to review in the courts. They must be final, unless in clear cases, where, there being no ground to adjudge the purpose to be a proper one for taxation, the legislature may be held to have proceeded unwarrantably. And perhaps there is still a further limitation, that if the claim is unadjusted and in dispute, the legislature have no authority to adjudicate upon it, but must leave the exercise of the judicial function to the ordinary tribunals.[1]

Louisiana in Layton v. New Orleans, 12 La. An. 515. In consolidating three distinct municipalities into one, the statute had provided that the territory which had been embraced in each should pay the pre-existing debts. Afterwards a statute was passed that no tax should be levied, " except the same be equal and uniform within the entire limits of the city." This was held to be constitutional. By the court: " As respects municipal corporations, it has always been held that the law of the State creating them, and conferring upon their officers a part of the sovereign authority as mandataries of the government, is not a contract, and as a consequence that the legislature may modify such acts of incorporation at its pleasure. If it has the power to create, modify, or abolish, it has the power to provide in what manner the taxes shall be levied for their support, and how their debts shall be paid upon their dissolution. This is a discretion vested in the legislature (with whom is vested the power of judging of the necessity of taxation), and nothing prevents it from changing its policy if it shall deem the necessities of the public so require. The courts can only interfere when it has overstepped the limits prescribed by the constitution." The Pennsylvania and Louisiana cases above quoted are directly opposed to the case of Hampshire v. Franklin, 16 Mass. 83, cited in the preceding note.

[1] The courts of New York have perhaps gone further than any others in holding that the legislature has complete control over the subject of municipal taxation. Nevertheless it was held, in People v. Hawes, 37 Barb. 440, that the legislature had no right to direct a municipal corporation to satisfy a claim made against it for damages for breach of contract, out of the funds or property of such corporation. In citing the cases of Guilford v. Supervisors of Chenango, 13 N. Y. 143, and People v. Supervisors of New York, 11 Abb. 114, a distinction is drawn by which the cases are supposed to be reconciled with the one then under decision. " Those cases and many others," say the court, p. 455, " related, not to the right or power of the legislature to compel an individual or corporation to pay a debt or claim, but to the power of the legislature to raise money by tax,

Those cases which hold that the State may raise bounty moneys by taxation, to be paid to persons in the military service, we think stand by themselves, and are supported on different principles from any which can fairly be summoned to the aid of some of the other cases which we have cited. The burden of the public defence unquestionably rests upon the whole community; and the legislature may properly provide for its apportionment and

and apply such money, when so raised, to the payment thereof. We could not, under the decisions of the courts on this point, made in these and other cases, now hold that the legislature had not authority to impose a tax to pay any claim, or to pay it out of the State treasury; and for this purpose to impose a tax upon the property of the State, or upon any portion of the State. This was fully settled in People v. Mayor, &c. of Brooklyn, 4 N. Y. 419; but neither that case nor the case in 13 N. Y. 143, in any manner gave a warrant for the opinion, that the legislature had a right to direct a municipal corporation to pay a claim for damages for breach of a contract, out of the funds or property of the corporation, without a submission of such claim to a judicial tribunal." If by this is meant that the legislature has power to compel a corporation to tax its citizens for the payment of a demand, but has not the authority to make it a charge against the corporation in any other mode, the distinction seems to be one of form rather than of substance. It is no protection to the rights or property of a municipal corporation to hold that the legislature cannot determine upon the claims against it, if at the same time the corporation may be compelled by statute to assume and discharge the obligation through the levy of a tax for its satisfaction. But if it is only meant to declare that the legislature cannot adjudicate upon disputed claims, there can be no good reason to find fault with the decision. It is one thing to determine that the nature of a claim is such as to make it proper to satisfy it by taxation, and another to adjudge how much is justly due upon it. The one is the exercise of legislative power, the other of judicial. But the power to decide upon the breach of a contract by a corporation, and the extent of the damages which have resulted, is less objectionable and less likely to lead to oppression, than the power to impose through taxation a claim upon a corporation which it never was concerned in creating, against which it protests, and which is unconnected with the ordinary functions and purposes of municipal government; as was the case in Thomas v. Leland, 24 Wend. 67. In Borough of Dunmore's Appeal, 52 Penn. St. 374, a decision was made which seems to conflict with that in People v. Hawes, supra; and with the subsequent case of Baldwin v. Mayor, &c. of New York, 42 Barb. 549. The Pennsylvania court decided that the constitutional guaranty of the right to jury trial had no application to municipal corporations, and a commission might be created by the legislature to adjust the demands between them. See also Layton v. New Orleans, 12 La. An. 515. In People v. Power, 25 Ill. 187, it was held competent for the legislature to apportion the taxes collected in a county between a city therein and the remainder of the county, and that the county revenues "must necessarily be within the control of the legislature for political purposes."

discharge in such manner as its wisdom may prescribe. But those cases which hold it competent for the legislature to give its consent to a municipal corporation engaging in works of public improvement outside its territorial limits, and becoming a stockholder in a private corporation, have certainly, as we think, gone to the very limits of constitutional power in this direction; and to hold that the legislature may go even further, and, under its power to control the taxation of the political divisions and organizations of the State, may *compel* them, against the will of their citizens, to raise money for such purposes, and invest their funds in these exterior undertakings, seems to us to be introducing new principles into our system of local self-government, and to be sanctioning a centralization of power not within the contemplation of the makers of the American constitutions. We think if any such forced taxation is resisted by the municipal organization, it will be very difficult to defend it as a proper exercise of legislative authority in a government where power is distributed on the principles which prevail here.

Legislative Control of Corporate Property.

The legislative power of the State controls and disposes of the property of the State. How far it can also control and dispose of the property of those agencies of government which it has created and endowed with corporate powers is a question which happily there has been very little occasion to discuss in the courts. Being a mere agency of government, it is evident that the municipality cannot itself have that complete and absolute control and power of disposition of its property which is possessed by individuals over their own. For it can hold and own property only for corporate purposes, and these purposes are liable at any time to be so modified by legislation as to render the property no longer available. Moreover, the chartered rights may altogether be taken away; and in that case the legislature has deprived the corporation of its property by depriving it of corporate capacity to hold it. And in many ways, while the corporation holds and enjoys property, the legislature must possess power to interfere with its control at least incidentally; for the mere fact that the corporation possesses property cannot deprive the State of its complete authority to mould and change the corporate organization, and enlarge or diminish its powers, which it possessed before. But whether the State can directly intervene and take away the corporate property, or convert it to other uses than those for which it was procured, or whether, on repealing a charter of incorporation, it can take to itself the corporate property, and dispose of it at its discretion, are different questions from any raised by the indirect and incidental interference referred to.

In the leading case, in which it was held by the Supreme Court of the United States that a private charter of incorporation, granted by a State, was a contract between the State and the corporators, not subject to modification or repeal, except in pursuance of a right expressly reserved, but that the charter of a municipal corporation was not such a contract, it was at the same time declared, as the opinion of the judges, that the legislature could not deprive such municipal corporations of their vested rights in property. " It may be admitted," says one of the judges, " that corporations for mere public government, such as towns, cities, and counties, may in many respects be subject to legislative control. But it will hardly be contended, that even in respect to such corporations, the legislative power is so transcendent that it may, at its will, take away the private property of the corporation, or change the uses of its private funds acquired under the public faith. Can the legislature confiscate to its own use the private funds which a municipal corporation holds under its charter, without any default or consent of the corporators? If a municipal corporation be capable of holding devises and legacies to charitable uses, as many municipal corporations are, does the legislature, under our forms of limited government, possess the authority to seize upon those funds and appropriate them to other uses, at its own arbitrary pleasure, against the will of the donors and donees? From the very nature of our government, the public faith is pledged the other way, and that pledge constitutes a valid compact; and that compact is subject only to judicial inquiry, construction, and abrogation." [1] " The government has no power to revoke a grant, even of its own funds, when given to a private person or corporation for special uses. It cannot recall its own endowments, granted to any hospital or college, or city or town, for the use of such cor-

---

[1] Story, J., in Dartmouth College v. Woodward, 4 Wheat. 694, 695.

porations. The only authority remaining to the government* is judicial, to ascertain the validity of the grant, to enforce its proper uses, to suppress frauds, and, if the uses are charitable, to secure their regular administration through the means of equitable tribunals, in cases where there would otherwise be a failure of justice." [1]

" In respect to public corporations," says another judge, " which exist only for public purposes, such as towns, cities, &c., the legislature may, under proper limitations, change, modify, enlarge, or restrain them, securing, however, the property for the use of those for whom and at whose expense it was purchased." [2] These views had been acted upon by the same court in preceding cases.[3] They draw a distinction between the political rights conferred on corporations, and which are not vested rights in any sense implying constitutional protection, and such rights in property as the corporation acquires, and which are protected by the same reasons which shield similar rights in individuals.[4]

When a municipal division of the territory of the State is changed in its boundaries, two or more consolidated in one, or one subdivided, it is conceded that the legislature possesses the power to make such disposition of the corporate property as natural equity would require in view of the altered condition of things. The fact that a portion of the citizens, before entitled to the benefits springing from the use of specific property for public purposes, will now be deprived of that benefit, cannot affect the validity of the legislative act, which is supposed in some other way to compensate them for the incidental loss.[5] And in many

[1] Ibid. 698.

[2] Washington, J., Dartmouth College v. Woodward, 4 Wheat. 663.

[3] Terrett v. Taylor, 9 Cranch, 43; Town of Pawlet v. Clark, Ibid. 292.

[4] " It is an unsound and even absurd proposition that political power conferred by the legislature can become a vested right, *as against the government*, in any individual or body of men. It is repugnant to the genius of our institutions, and the spirit and meaning of the constitution ; for by that fundamental law, all political rights not there defined and taken out of the exercise of legislative discretion were intended to be left subject to its regulation. If corporations can set up a vested right as against the government to the exercise of this species of power, because it has been conferred upon them by the bounty of the legislature, so may any and every officer under the government do the same." Nelson, J., in People v. Morris, 13 Wend. 331. And see Bristol v. New Chester, 3 N. H. 532; Benson v. Mayor, &c. of New York, 10 Barb. 244.

[5] Bristol v. New Chester, 3 N. H. 533. And see ante, 232 – 234, notes.

other cases the legislature exercises a similar power of control in respect to the corporate property, and may direct its partition and appropriation, with a view to accommodate justly and most effectually the purposes for which it was acquired.

The rule upon the subject seems to be this: when corporate powers are conferred, there is an implied compact between the State and the corporators that the property which they have the capacity to acquire under their charter shall not be taken from them and appropriated to other uses. If the State grants property to the corporation, the grant is an executed contract, which cannot be revoked. The rights acquired, either by such grants or by any other legitimate mode in which such a corporation can acquire property, are vested rights, and cannot be taken away. Nevertheless, when the corporate powers are repealed, the corporate ownership ceases; and by modification of corporate powers the legislature may, in other cases, affect and divest the rights of individual corporators, so far as they can be said to have any rights in public property. And in other ways, and by direct intervention, the legislature may exercise control over the disposition and use of the property, subject to this restriction, that it must not be diverted to a use substantially different from that for which it was acquired.[1]

---

[1] " That the State may make a contract with, or a grant to, a public municipal corporation, which it could not subsequently impair or resume, is not denied ; but in such a case the corporation is to be regarded as a private company. A grant may be made to a public corporation for purposes of private advantage; and although the public may also derive a common benefit therefrom, yet the corporation stands on the same footing, as respects such grant, as would any body of persons upon whom like privileges were conferred. Public or municipal corporations, however, which exist only for public purposes, and possess no powers except such as are bestowed upon them for public political purposes, are subject at all times to the control of the legislature, which may alter, modify, or abolish them at pleasure." Trumbull, J., in Richland County v. Lawrence County, 12 Ill. 8. " Public corporations are but parts of the machinery employed in carrying on the affairs of the State; and they are subject to be changed, modified, or destroyed, as the exigencies of the public may demand. The State may exercise a general superintendence and control over them and their rights and effects, so that their property is not diverted from the uses and objects for which it was given or purchased." Trustees of Schools v. Tatman, 13 Ill. 30, per Treat, Ch. J. And see Harrison v. Bridgeton, 16 Mass. 16 ; Montpelier v. East Montpelier, 27 Vt. 704 ; Same v. Same, 29 Vt. 19 ; Benson v. Mayor, &c. of New York, 10 Barb. 223. See also City of Louisville v. University, 15 B. Monr. 642. In State v. St. Louis County Court, 34 Mo. 572, the following remarks are made by the court, in considering

This restriction is equally applicable where corporate powers are taken away, as in other cases; and whatever might be the nature of the public property which the corporation had acquired, and whatever the purpose of the acquisition, the legislature, when by taking away the corporate authority it became vested with the control of the property, would be under obligation to dispose of it in such manner as to give the original corporators the benefit thereof, by putting it to the use designed, or some kindred or equally beneficial use having reference to the altered condition of things. The obligation is one which, from the very nature of the case, must rest for its enforcement in great measure upon the legislative faith and sense of justice; and it could only be in those cases where there had been a clear disregard of the rights of the original corporators, in the use attempted to be made of the property, that relief could be had through judicial action.

No such restriction, however, can rest upon the legislature in regard to the rights and privileges which the State grants to municipal corporations in the nature of franchises, and which must be understood to be granted as aids or conveniences to the municipality in effecting the purposes of its incorporation. These, like the corporate powers, must be understood to be granted during pleasure.[1]

the cause shown by the county in answer to an application to compel it to meet a requisition for the police board of St. Louis: "As to the second cause shown in the return, it is understood to mean, not that there is in fact no money in the treasury to pay this requisition, but that as a matter of law all the money which is in the treasury was collected for specific purposes from which it cannot be diverted. The specific purposes for which the money was collected were those heretofore directed by the legislature; and this act, being a later expression of the will of the legislature, controls the subject, and so far as it conflicts with previous acts, repeals them. The county is not a private corporation, but an agency of the State government; and though as a public corporation it holds property, such holding is subject to a large extent to the will of the legislature. Whilst the legislature cannot take away from a county its property, it has full power to direct the mode in which the property shall be used for the benefit of the county."

[1] East Hartford v. Hartford Bridge Co., 10 How. 535. On this subject, see ch. 9, post. The case of Trustees of Aberdeen Academy v. Mayor, &c. of Aberdeen, 13 S. & M. 645, appears to be contra. By the charter of the town of Aberdeen in 1837, the legislature granted to it the sole power to grant licenses to sell vinous and spirituous liquors within the corporate limits thereof, and to appropriate the money arising therefrom to city purposes. In 1848 an act was passed giving these moneys to the Aberdeen Female Academy. The act was

Towns and Counties.

Thus far we have been considering general rules, applicable to all classes of municipal organizations possessed of corporate powers, by which these powers may be measured, or the duties which they impose defined. In regard to some of these organizations, however, there are other and peculiar rules which require separate mention. Some of them are so feebly endowed with corporate life, and so much hampered, controlled, and directed in the exercise of the functions which they possess, that they are sometimes spoken of as nondescript in character, and as occupying a position somewhere between that of a corporation and a mere voluntary association of citizens. Counties, townships, school districts, and road districts do not usually possess corporate powers under special charters; but they exist under general laws of the State, which apportion the territory of the State into political divisions for convenience of government, and require of the people residing within those divisions the performance of certain public duties as a part of the machinery of the State; and, in order that they may be able to perform these duties, vest them with certain corporate powers. Whether they shall assume those duties or exercise those powers, the political divisions are not allowed the privilege of choice; the legislature assumes this division of the State to be essential in republican government, and the duties are imposed as a part of the proper and necessary burden which the citizens must assume in the process of self-government. Their functions, therefore, are wholly of a public nature, and there is no room to imply any contract between them and the State, in their organization as corporate bodies, except that which springs from the ordinary rules of good faith, — that the property they shall acquire by local taxation or otherwise, for the purposes of their organization, shall not be seized by the State, and appro-

held void, on the ground that the original grant was of a franchise which constituted property, and it could not be transferred to another, though it might be repealed. The case cites Bailey v. Mayor, &c., 3 Hill, 541, and St. Louis v. Russell, 9 Mo. 507, which seem to have little relevancy. Also, 4 Wheat. 663, 698, 699; and 2 Kent, 305, note, for the general rule protecting municipal corporations in their vested rights to property. The case of Benson v. Mayor, &c. of New York, 10 Barb. 223, also holds the grant of a ferry franchise to a municipal corporation to be irrevocable.

priated in other ways. They are, therefore, sometimes called *quasi* corporations,[1] to distinguish them from the corporations in general, which possess more completely the functions of an artificial entity. Chief Justice Parker, of Massachusetts, in speaking of school districts, has said : "That they are not bodies politic and corporate, with the general powers of corporations, must be admitted; and the reasoning advanced to show their defect of power is conclusive. The same may be said of towns and other municipal societies; which, although recognized by various statutes, and by immemorial usage, as persons or aggregate corporations, with precise duties which may be enforced, and privileges which may be maintained by suits at law, yet are deficient in many of the powers incident to the general character of corporations. They may be considered, under our institutions, as *quasi* corporations, with limited powers, coextensive with the duties imposed upon them by statute or usage, but restrained from the general use of authority which belongs to these metaphysical persons by the common law. The same may be said of all the numerous corporations which have been from time to time created by various acts of the legislature; all of them enjoying the power which is expressly bestowed upon them, and perhaps, in all instances where the act is silent, possessing, by necessary implication, the authority which is requisite to execute the purposes of their creation." " It will not do to apply the strict principles of law respecting corporations in all cases to these aggregate bodies which are created by statute in this Commonwealth. By the several statutes which have been passed respecting school districts, it is manifest that the legislature has supposed that a division of towns, for the purpose of maintaining schools, will promote the important object of general education; and this valuable object of legislative care seems to require, in construing their acts, that a liberal view should be had to the end to be effected."[2] Following out this view, the courts of the New England States held, that when judgments are recovered against towns, parishes, and school districts, any of the property of private owners within

---

[1] Riddle *v.* Proprietors, &c., 7 Mass. 186, 187 ; School District *v.* Wood, 13 Mass. 192; Adams *v.* Wiscasset Bank, 1 Greenl. 361 ; Denton *v.* Jackson, 2 Johns. Ch. 325 ; Beardsley *v.* Smith, 16 Conn. 367 ; Eastman *v.* Meredith, 36 N. H. 296 ; Hopple *v.* Brown, 13 Ohio, N. S. 311.

[2] School District *v.* Wood, 13 Mass. 192.

16

the municipal division is liable to be taken for their discharge. The reasons for this doctrine, and the custom upon which it is founded, are thus stated by the Supreme Court of Connecticut: —

" We know that the relation in which the members of municipal corporations in this State have been supposed to stand, in respect to the corporation itself, as well as to its creditors, has elsewhere been considered in some respects peculiar. We have treated them, for some purposes, as parties to corporate proceedings, and their individuality has not been considered as merged in their corporate connection. Though corporators, they have been holden to be parties to suits, by or against the corporation, and individually liable for its debts. Heretofore this has not been doubted as to the inhabitants of towns, located ecclesiastical societies, and school districts.

" From a recurrence to a history of the law on this subject, we are persuaded that the principle and usage here recognized and followed, in regard to the liability of the inhabitants of towns and communities, were very early adopted by our ancestors. And whether they were considered as a part of the common law of England, or originated here, as necessary to our state of society, it is not very material to inquire. We think, however, that the principle is not of domestic origin, but to some extent was operative and applied in the mother country, especially in cases where a statute fixed a liability upon a municipality which had no corporate funds. The same reason and necessity for the application of such a principle and practice existed in both countries. Such corporations are of a public and political character; they exercise a portion of the governing power of the State. Statutes impose upon them important public duties. In the performance of these, they must contract debts and liabilities, which can only be discharged by a resort to individuals, either by taxation or execution. Taxation, in most cases, can only be the result of the voluntary action of the corporation, dependent upon the contingent will of the majority of the corporators, and upon their tardy and uncertain action. It affords no security to creditors, because they have no power over it. Such reasons as these probably operated with our ancestors in adopting the more efficient and certain remedy by execution, which has been resorted to in the present case, and which they had seen to some extent in operation in the country whose laws were their inheritance.

" The plaintiff would apply to these municipal or *quasi* corporations the close principles applicable to private corporations. But inasmuch as they are not, strictly speaking, corporations, but only municipal bodies, without pecuniary funds, it will not do to apply to them literally, and in all cases, the law of corporations.[1]

" The individual liability of the members of *quasi* corporations, though not expressly adjudged, was very distinctly recognized in the case of Russell v. The Men of Devon.[2] It was alluded to as a known principle in the case of the Attorney-General v. The City of Exeter,[3] applicable as well to cities as to hundreds and parishes. That the rated inhabitants of an English parish are considered as the real parties to suits against the parish is now supposed to be well settled; and so it was decided in the case of The King v. The Inhabitants of Woburn,[4] and The King v. The Inhabitants of Hardwick.[5] And in support of this principle, reference was made to the form of the proceedings; as that they are entitled 'against the inhabitants,' &c.

" In the State of Massachusetts, from whose early institutions we have borrowed many valuable specimens, the individual responsibility of the inhabitants of towns for town debts has long been established. Distinguished counsel in the case of the Merchants' Bank v. Cook,[6] referring to municipal bodies, say: ' For a century past the practical construction of the bar has been that, in an action by or against a corporation, a member of the corporation is a party in the suit.' In several other cases in that State the same principle is repeated. In the case of Riddle v. The Proprietors of the Locks and Canals on Merrimack River,[7] Parsons, Ch. J., in an allusion to this private responsibility of corporators remarks: ' And the sound reason is, that having no corporate fund, and no legal means of obtaining one, each corporator is liable to satisfy any judgment obtained against the corporation.' So in Brewer v. Inhabitants of New Gloucester,[8] the court say: ' As the law provides that, when judgment is recovered against the inhabitants of a town, execution may be levied upon the property of any inhabitant, each inhabitant must be considered as a party.' In the case before referred to of the Merchants' Bank v. Cook,

[1] School District v. Wood, 13 Mass. 192.
[2] 2 Term Rep. 660.
[3] 2 Russ. 45.
[4] 10 East, 395.
[5] 11 East, 577.
[6] 4 Pick. 405.
[7] 7 Mass. 187.
[8] 14 Mass. 216.

Parker, Ch. J., expresses the opinion of the court upon this point thus: ' Towns, parishes, precincts, &c., are but a collection of individuals, with certain corporate powers for political and civil purposes, without any corporate fund, from which a judgment can be satisfied ; but each member of the community is liable, in his person and estate, to the execution which may issue against the body ; each individual, therefore, may be well thought to be a party to a suit brought against them by their collective name. In regard to banks, turnpikes, and other corporations, the case is different.' The counsel concerned in the case of Mower v. Leicester,[1] without contradiction, speak of this practice of subjecting individuals as one of daily occurrence. The law on this subject was very much considered in the case of Chase v. The Merrimack Bank,[2] and was applied and enforced against the members of a territorial parish. ' The question is,' say the court, ' whether, on an execution against a town or parish, the body or estate of any inhabitant may be lawfully taken to satisfy it. This question seems to have been settled in the affirmative by a series of decisions, and ought no longer to be considered as an open question.' The State of Maine, when separated from Massachusetts, retained most of its laws and usages, as they had been recognized in the parent State ; and, among others, the one in question. In Adams v. Wiscasset Bank,[3] Mellen, Ch. J., says: ' It is well known that all judgments against quasi corporations may be satisfied out of the property of any individual inhabitant.'

" The courts of this State, from a time beyond the memory of any living lawyer, have sanctioned and carried out this usage, as one of common-law obligation ; and it has been applied, not to towns only, but also, by legal analogy, to territorial ecclesiastical societies and school districts. The forms of our process against these communities have always corresponded with this view of the law. The writs have issued against the *inhabitants* of towns, societies, and districts *as parties.* As early in the history of our jurisprudence as 1805, a statute was enacted authorizing communities, such as towns, societies, &c., to prosecute and defend suits, and for this purpose to appear, either by *themselves*, agents, or attorneys. If the inhabitants were not then considered as parties individually, and liable to the consequences of judgments against such communities as parties, there would have been a glaring

[1] 9 Mass. 247.   [2] 19 Pick. 564.   [3] 1 Greenl. 361.

impropriety in permitting them to appear and defend by themselves; but if parties, such a right was necessary and indispensable. Of course this privilege has been and may be exercised.[1]

"Our statute providing for the collection of taxes enacts that the treasurer of the State shall direct his warrant to the collectors of the State tax in the several towns. If neither this nor the further proceedings against the collectors and the selectmen authorized by the statute shall enforce the collection of the tax, the law directs that then the treasurer shall issue his execution against the inhabitants of such town. Such an execution may be levied upon the estate of the inhabitants; and this provision of the law was not considered as introducing a new principle, or enforcing a novel remedy, but as being only in conformity with the well-known usage in other cases. The levy of an execution under this statute produced the case of Beers v. Botsford.[2] There the execution, which had been issued against the town of Newtown by the treasurer of the State, had been levied upon the property of the plaintiff, an inhabitant of that town, and he had thus been compelled to pay the balance of a State tax due from the town. He sued the town of Newtown for the recovery of the money so paid by him. The most distinguished professional gentlemen in the State were engaged as counsel in that case; and it did not occur, either to them or to the court, that the plaintiff's property had been taken without right: on the contrary, the case proceeded throughout on the conceded principle of our common law, that the levy was properly made upon the estate of the plaintiff. And without this the plaintiff could not have recovered of the town, but must have resorted to his action against the officer for his illegal and void levy. In Fuller v. Hampton,[3] Peters, J., remarked that, if costs are recovered against a town, the writ of execution to collect them must have been issued against the property of the inhabitants of the town; and this is the invariable practice. The case of Atwater v. Woodbridge[4] also grew out of this ancient usage. The ecclesiastical society of Bethany had been taxed by the town of Woodbridge for its moneys at interest, and the warrant for the collection of the tax had been levied upon the property of the plaintiff, and the tax had thus been collected of him, who was an inhabitant of the located society of Bethany. Brainerd, J., who drew up the

[1] 1 Swift's System, 227.
[2] 3 Day, 159.
[3] 5 Conn. 417.
[4] 6 Conn. 223.

opinion of the court, referring to this proceeding, said: ' This practice, with regard to towns, has prevailed in New England, so far as I have been able to investigate the subject, from an early period, — from its first settlement, — a practice brought by our forefathers from England, which had there obtained in corporations similar to the towns incorporated in New England.' It will here be seen that the principle is considered as applicable to territorial societies as to towns, because the object to be obtained was the same in both, — ' that the town or society should be brought to a sense of duty, and make provision for payment and indemnity'; a very good reason, and very applicable to the case we are considering.

" The law on this subject was more distinctly brought out and considered by this court in the late case of McCloud v. Selby,[1] in which this well-known practice, as it had been applied to towns and ecclesiastical societies, was extended and sanctioned as to school districts ; ' else it would be breaking in upon the analogies of the law.' ' They are communities for different purposes, but essentially of the same character.' And no doubt can remain, since the decision of this case, but that the real principle, in all of the cases on this subject, has been, and is, that the inhabitants of *quasi* corporations are parties individually, as well as in their corporate capacities, to all the actions in which the corporation is a party. And to the same effect is the language of the elementary writers." [2]

So far as this rule rests upon the reason that these organizations have no common fund, and that no other mode exists by which demands against them can be enforced, it cannot be considered applicable in those States where express provision is made by law for compulsory taxation to satisfy any judgment recovered against the corporate body,—the duty being imposed upon some officer, who may be compelled by mandamus to perform it. Nor has any usage, so far as we are aware, grown up in any of the newer States, like that which had so early an origin in New Eng-

[1] 10 Conn. 390 – 395.

[2] Beardsley v. Smith, 16 Conn. 375, citing 2 Kent, 221 ; Angell and Ames on Corp. 374 ; 1 Swift's Dig. 72, 794 ; 5 Dane's Abr. 158. It was held constitutional in this case to extend the same principle to incorporated cities ; and an act of the legislature permitting the enforcement of city debts in the same mode was sustained. For a more recent case in Massachusetts than these cited, see Gaskill v. Dudley, 6 Met. 551.

land. More just, convenient, and inexpensive modes of enforcing such demands have been established by statute, and the rules concerning them are conformed more closely to those which are established for other corporations.

On the other hand, it is settled that these corporations are not liable to a private action, at the suit of a party injured by a neglect of its officers to perform a corporate duty, unless such action is given by statute. This doctrine has been frequently applied where suits have been brought against towns, or the highway officers of towns, to recover for damages sustained in consequence of defects in the public ways. The common law gives no such action, and it is therefore not sustainable at all, unless given by statute. A distinction is made between those corporations which are created for their own benefit, or receive special grants of power for the private convenience and benefit of the corporators, and the incorporated inhabitants of a district, who are by statute invested with particular powers, without their consent. In the latter case, the State may impose corporate duties, and compel their performance, under penalties; but the corporators, who are made such whether they will or no, cannot be considered in the light of persons who have voluntarily, and for a consideration, assumed obligations, so as to owe a duty to every person interested in the performance.[1]

The reason which exempts these public bodies from liability to private actions, based upon neglect to perform public duty, does not apply to villages, boroughs, and cities, which accept special

---

[1] Mower v. Leicester, 9 Mass. 250; Bartlett v. Crozier, 17 Johns. 439; Farnum v. Concord, 2 N. H. 392; Adams v. Wiscasset Bank, 1 Greenl. 361; Baxter v. Winooski Turnpike, 22 Vt. 123; Chidsey v. Canton, 17 Conn. 475; Commissioners of Highways v. Martin, 4 Mich. 557; Morey v. Newfane, 8 Barb. 645; Lorillard v. Monroe, 11 N. Y. 392; Galen v. Clyde and Rose Plank Road Co., 27 Barb. 543. These cases follow the leading English case of Russell v. Men of Devon, 2 T. R. 667. In the very carefully considered case of Eastman v. Meredith, 36 N. H. 284, it was decided, on the principle above stated, that if a building erected by a town for a town-house is so imperfectly constructed that the flooring gives way at the annual town-meeting, and an inhabitant and legal voter, in attendance on the meeting, receives thereby a bodily injury, he cannot maintain an action against the town to recover damages for this injury. The case is carefully distinguished from those where corporations have been held liable for the negligent use of their own property by means of which others are injured. The familiar maxim that one shall so use his own as not to injure that which belongs to another is of general application.

charters from the State. The grant of the corporate franchise, in
these cases, is usually made only at the request of the citizens to
be incorporated, and it is justly assumed that it confers a valuable
privilege. This privilege is a consideration for the duties which
the charter imposes. Larger powers of self-government are conferred than are confided to towns or counties; larger privileges in
the acquisition and control of corporate property; and special
authority is given to make use of the public highways for the
special and peculiar convenience of the citizens of the municipality in various modes not permissible elsewhere. The grant by
the State to the municipality of a portion of its sovereign powers,
for these beneficial purposes, is regarded as raising an implied
promise, on the part of the corporation, to perform the corporate
duties; and this implied contract, made with the sovereign power,
enures to the benefit of every individual interested in its performance.[1] In this respect these corporations are regarded as occupying the same position as private corporations, which, having
accepted a valuable franchise, on condition of the performance of
certain public duties, are held to contract by the acceptance for
the performance of these duties. In the case of public corporations, the liability is contingent on the law affording the means
of performing the duty, which, in some cases, by reason of restrictions upon the power of taxation, might not be done. But
assuming the corporation to be clothed with sufficient power by
the charter to that end, the liability of a city or village, vested
with control of its streets, for any neglect to keep them in repair,
or for any improper construction, has been determined in many
cases.[2]

[1] Selden, J., in Weet v. Brockport, 16 N. Y. 161, note. See also Mayor of
Lyme v. Turner, Cowp. 86; Henley v. Lyme Regis, 5 Bing. 91; Same case in
error, 3 B. & Adol. 77, and 1 Bing. N. C. 222; Mayor, &c. of New York v.
Furze, 3 Hill, 612; Rochester White Lead Co. v. Rochester, 3 N. Y. 464; Hut-
son v. Mayor, &c. of New York, 9 N. Y. 163; Conrad v. Ithaca, 16 N. Y. 158;
Clark v. Washington, 12 Wheat. 40; Riddle v. Proprietors of Locks, &c., 7 Mass.
183; Mears v. Commissioners of Wilmington, 9 Ired. 73; Browning v. Springfield, 17 Ill. 143; Pittsburg v. Grier, 22 Penn. St. 54; Scott v. Mayor, &c. of
Manchester, 37 Eng. L. & Eq. 495; Smoot v. Wetumpka; 24 Ala. 112; Detroit
v. Corey, 9 Mich. 165; Rusch v. Davenport, 6 Iowa, 443; Commissioners v. Duckett,
20 Md. 468; Chicago v. Robbins, 2 Black. 418; Nebraska v. Campbell, Ibid. 590.

[2] Weet v. Brockport, 16 N. Y. 161, note; Hickok v. Plattsburg, Ibid. 158;
Morey v. Newfane, 8 Barb. 645; Browning v. Springfield, 17 Ill. 143; Hyatt v.
Rondout, 44 Barb. 385; Lloyd v. Mayor, &c. of New York, 5 N. Y. 369; Rusch

But if the ground of the action is the omission by the corporation to repair a defect, it would seem that notice of the defect should be brought home to the corporation, or to officers charged with some duty respecting the streets, or that facts should appear sufficient to show that, by proper vigilance, it must have been known.[1]

In regard to all those powers which are conferred upon the corporation, not for the benefit of the general public, but of the corporators, — as to construct works to supply a city with water, or gas-works, or sewers, and the like, — the corporation is held to a still more strict liability, and is made to respond in damages to the parties injured by the negligent manner in which the work is constructed, or guarded, even though, under its charter, the agents for the construction are not chosen by the corporation, and even where the work must, by law, be let to the lowest responsible bidder.

In Bailey v. Mayor, &c., of New York,[2] an action was brought against the city by one who had been injured in his property by the careless construction of the Croton dam for the purpose of supplying the city with water. The work was constructed under the control of water commissioners, in whose appointment the city had no voice; and upon this ground, among others, and also on the ground that the city officers were acting in a public capacity, and, like other public agents, not responsible for the misconduct of

---

v. Davenport, 6 Iowa, 443. The cases of Weet v. Brockport, and Hickok v. Plattsburg, were criticised by Mr. Justice Marvin, in the case of Peck v. Batavia, 32 Barb. 634, where, as well as in Cole v. Medina, 27 Barb. 218, he held that a village merely *authorized* to make and repair sidewalks, but not in terms absolutely and imperatively required to do so, had a discretion conferred upon it in respect to such walks, and was not responsible for a refusal to enact ordinances or by-laws in relation thereto ; nor, if it enacted such ordinances or by-laws, was it liable for damages arising from a neglect to enforce them. The doctrine that a power thus conferred is discretionary does not seem consistent with the ruling in some of the other cases cited, and is criticised in Hyatt v. Rondout, 44 Barb. 392. Calling public meetings for political or philanthropic purposes is no part of the business of a municipal corporation, and it is not liable to one who, in lawfully passing by where the meeting is held, is injured by the discharge of a cannon fired by persons concerned in the meeting. Boyland v. Mayor, &c. of New York, 1 Sandf. 27.

[1] Hart v. Brooklyn, 36 Barb. 226 ; Dewey v. City of Detroit, 15 Mich. 309 ; Garrison v. New York, 5 Bosw. 497 ; McGinity v. Mayor, &c. of New York, 5 Duer, 674.

[2] 3 Hill, 531 ; 2 Denio, 433.

those necessarily appointed by them, it was insisted the city could not be held liable. Nelson, Ch. J., examining the position that, ". admitting the water commissioners to be the appointed agents of the defendants, still the latter are not liable, inasmuch as they were acting solely for the State in prosecuting the work in question, and therefore are not responsible for the conduct of those necessarily employed by them for that purpose," says: " We admit, if the defendants are to be regarded as occupying this relation, and are not chargeable with any want of diligence in the selection of agents, the conclusion contended for would seem to follow. They would then be entitled to all the immunities of public officers charged with a duty which, from its nature, could not be executed, without availing themselves of the services of others ; and the doctrine of *respondeat superior* does not apply to such cases. If a public officer authorize the doing of an act not within the scope of his authority, or if he be guilty of negligence in the discharge of duties to be performed by himself, he will be held responsible ; but not for the misconduct or malfeasance of such persons as he is obliged to employ. But this view cannot be maintained on the facts before us. The powers conferred by the several acts of the legislature, authorizing the execution of this great work, are nót, strictly and legally speaking, conferred for the benefit of the public ; the grant is a special, private franchise, made as well for the private emolument and advantage of the city as for public good. The State, in its sovereign character, has no interest in it. It owns no part of the work. The whole investment, under the law, and the revenue and profits to be derived therefrom, are a part of the private property of the city, ·as much so as the lands and houses belonging to it situate within its corporate limits.

" The argument of the defendants' counsel confounds the powers in question with those belonging to the defendants in their character as a municipal or public body, — such as are granted exclusively for public purposes to counties, cities, towns, and villages, where the corporations have, if I may so speak, no private estate or interest in the grant.

" As the powers in question have been conferred upon one of these public corporations, thus blending, in a measure, those conferred for private advantage and emolument with those already possessed for public purposes, there is some difficulty, I admit, in separating them in the mind, and properly distinguishing the one class from the other, so as to distribute the responsibility attaching to the exercise of each.

" But the distinction is quite clear and well settled, and the process of separation practicable. To this end, regard should be had, not so much to the nature and character of the various powers conferred, as to the object and purpose of the legislature in conferring them. If granted for public purposes exclusively, they belong to the corporate body in its public, political, or municipal character. But if the grant was for purposes of private advantage and emolument, though the public may derive a common benefit therefrom, the corporation *quo ad hoc* is to be regarded as a private company. It stands on the same footing as would any individual or body of persons upon whom the like special franchises had been conferred.[1]

" Suppose the legislature, instead of the franchise in question, had conferred upon the defendants banking powers, or a charter for a railroad leading into the city, in the usual manner in which such powers are conferred upon private companies, could it be doubted that they would hold them in the same character, and be subject to the same duties and liabilities? It cannot be doubted but they would. These powers, in the eye of the law, would be entirely distinct and separate from those appertaining to the defendants as a municipal body. So far as related to the charter thus conferred, they would be regarded as a private company, and be subject to the responsibilities attaching to that class of institutions. The distinction is well stated by the Master of the Rolls, in Moodalay *v.* East India Co.,[2] in answer to an objection made by counsel. There the plaintiff had taken a lease from the company, granting him permission to supply the inhabitants of Madras with tobacco for ten years. Before the expiration of that period, the company dispossessed him, and granted the privilege to another. The plaintiff, preparatory to bringing an action against the company, filed a bill of discovery. One of the objections

---

[1] Dartmouth College *v.* Woodward, 4 Wheat. 668, 672; Phillips *v.* Bury, 1 Ld. Raym. 8; 2 T. R. 352, S. C. ; Allen *v.* McKeen, 1 Sumn. 297 ; People *v.* Morris, 13 Wend. 331 – 338 ; 2 Kent's Com. 275 (4th ed.) ; United States Bank *v.* Planters' Bank, 9 Wheat. 907; Clark *v.* Corp. of Washington, 12 Ibid. 40 ; Moodalay *v.* East India Co., 1 Brown's Ch. R. 469.

[2] 1 Brown's Ch. R. 469.

taken by the defendant was, that the removal of the plaintiff was incident to their character as a sovereign power, the exercise of which could not be questioned in a bill or suit at law. The Master of the Rolls admitted that no suit would lie against a sovereign power for anything done in that capacity; but he denied that the defendants came within the rule. 'They have rights,' he observed, 'as a sovereign power; they have also duties as individuals; if they enter into bonds in India, the sums secured may be recovered here. So in this case, as a private company, they have entered into a private contract, to which they must be liable.' It is upon the like distinction that municipal corporations, in their private character as owners and occupiers of lands and houses, are regarded in the same light as individual owners and occupiers, and dealt with accordingly. As such, they are bound to repair bridges, highways, and churches; are liable to poor-rates; and, in a word, to the discharge of any other duty or obligation to which an individual owner would be subject." [1]

In Stoors *v.* City of Utica,[2] it was held that a city, owing to the public the duty of keeping its streets in a safe condition for travel, was liable to persons receiving injury from the neglect to keep proper lights and guards at night around an excavation which had been made for the construction of a sewer, notwithstanding it had contracted for all proper precautions with the persons executing the work. And in the City of Detroit *v.* Corey [3] the corporation was held liable in a similar case, notwithstanding the work was required by the charter to be let to the lowest bidder. Manning, J., in speaking to the point whether the contractors were to be considered as the agents of the city, so that the maxim *respondeat superior* should apply, says: "It is to be observed that the

---

[1] 2 Inst. 703 ; Thursfield *v.* Jones, Sir T. Jones, 187 ; Rex *v.* Gardner, Cowp. 79 ; Mayor of Lyme *v.* Turner, Ibid. 87 ; Henley *v.* Mayor of Lyme, 5 Bing. 91 ; 1 Bing. N. C. 222, S. C. in House of Lords. See also Lloyd *v.* Mayor, &c. of New York, 5 N. Y. 369. "The corporation of the city of New York possesses two kinds of powers, — one governmental and public, and, to the extent they are held and exercised, is clothed with sovereignty ; the other private, and, to the extent they are held and exercised, is a legal individual. The former are given and used for public purposes, the latter for private purposes. While in the exercise of the former, the corporation is a municipal government, and while in the exercise of the latter is a corporate, legal individual." Ibid. per Foot, J.

[2] 17 N. Y. 104.

[3] 9 Mich. 165.

power under which they acted, and which made that lawful which would otherwise have been unlawful, was not a power given to the city for governmental purposes, or a public municipal duty imposed on the city, as to keep its streets in repair, or the like, but a special legislative grant to the city for private purposes. The sewers of the city, like its works for supplying the city with water, are the private property of the city; they belong to the city. The corporation and its corporators, the citizens, are alone interested in them; the outside public or people of the State at large have no interest in them, as they have in the streets of the city, which are public highways.

" The donee of such a power, whether the donee be an individual or a corporation, takes it with the understanding — for such are the requirements of the law in the execution of the power — that it shall be so executed as not unnecessarily to interfere with the rights of the public, and that all needful and proper measures will be taken, in the execution of it, to guard against accidents to persons lawfully using the highway at the time. He is individually bound for the performance of these obligations; he cannot accept the power divested of them, or rid himself of their performance by executing them through a third person as his agent. He may stipulate with the contractor for their performance, as was done by the city in the present case, but he cannot thereby relieve himself of his personal liability, or compel an injured party to look to his agent, instead of himself, for damages." And in answer to the objection that the contract was let to the lowest bidder, as the law required, it is shown that the provision of law to that effect was introduced for the benefit of the city, to protect it against frauds, and that it should not, therefore, relieve it from any liability.[1]

---

[1] See also Rochester White Lead Co. v. City of Rochester, 3 N. Y. 463; Grant v. City of Brooklyn, 41 Barb. 381; City of Buffalo v. Holloway, 14 Barb. 101, and 7 N. Y. 493; Lloyd v. Mayor, &c. of New York, 5 N. Y. 369; Delmonico v. Mayor, &c. of New York, 1 Sandf. 222; Barton v. Syracuse, 37 Barb. 292. For further illustration of the rules of liability to which municipal corporations are subject for the negligent discharge of corporate duties or the improper construction of corporate works, see Wallace v. Muscatine, 4 Greene (Iowa), 373; Creal v. Keokuk, Ibid. 47; Cotes v. Davenport, 9 Iowa, 227; Walcott v. Swampscott, 1 Allen, 101; Buttrick v. Lowell, Ibid. 172; Munn v. Pittsburg, 40 Penn. St. 364; Pekin v. Newell, 26 Ill. 320; Weightman v. Washington, 1 Black, 39; Kavanaugh v. Brooklyn, 38 Barb. 232; Wendell v. Troy, 39 Barb. 329; Ross v.

We have not deemed it important, in considering the subject embraced within this chapter, to discuss the various questions which might be suggested in regard to the validity of the proceedings by which it is assumed in any case that a municipal corporation has become constituted. These questions are generally questions between the corporators and the State, with which private individuals have no concern. In proceedings where the question whether a corporation exists or not arises collaterally, the courts will not permit its corporate character to be questioned, if it appear to be acting under color of law, and recognized by the State as such. Such a question should be raised by the State itself, by *quo warranto* or other direct proceeding.[1] And the rule, we apprehend, would be nó different, if the constitution itself prescribed the manner of incorporation. Even in such a case, proof that the corporation was acting as such, under legislative action, would be sufficient evidence of right, except as against the State; and private parties could not enter upon any question of regularity. And the State itself may justly be precluded, on the principle of estoppel, from raising such an objection, where there has been long acquiescence and recognition.[2]

Madison, 1 Ind. 281 ; Mayor, &c. of New York *v.* Bailey, 2 Denio, 433; Rochester White Lead Co. *v.* Rochester, 3 N. Y. 463 ; Wheeler *v.* City of Worcester, 10 Allen, 591 ; Burnham *v.* Boston, Ibid. 290 ; Boom *v.* City of Utica, 2 Barb. 104 ; Martin *v.* Mayor, &c. of Brooklyn, 1 Hill, 545 ; Howell *v.* Buffalo, 15 N. Y. 512 ; Lacour *v.* Mayor, &c. of New York, 3 Duer, 406.

[1] State *v.* Carr, 5 N. H. 367 ; President, &c. of Mendota *v.* Thompson, 20 Ill. 200 ; Hamilton *v.* President, &c. of Carthage, 24 Ill. 22. These were prosecutions by municipal corporations for recovery of penalties imposed by by-laws, and where the plea of *nul tiel* corporation was interposed and overruled.

[2] In People *v.* Maynard, 15 Mich. 470, where the invalidity of an act organizing a county, passed several years before, was suggested on constitutional grounds, Campbell, J., says: " If this question had been raised immediately, we are not prepared to say that it would have been altogether free from difficulty. But inasmuch as the arrangement there indicated had been acted upon for ten years before the recent legislation, and had been recognized as valid by all parties interested, it cannot now be disturbed. Even in private associations the acts of parties interested may often estop them from relying on legal objections, which might have availed them if not waived. But in public affairs, where the people have organized themselves under color of law into the ordinary municipal bodies, and have gone on year after year raising taxes, making improvements, and exercising their usual franchises, their rights are properly regarded as depending quite as much on the acquiescence as on the regularity of their origin, and no *ex post facto* inquiry can be permitted to undo their corporate existence. What-

ever may be the rights of individuals before such general acquiescence, the corporate standing of the community can no longer be open to question. See Rumsey *v.* People, 19 N. Y. 41; and Lanning *v.* Carpenter, 20 N. Y. 474, where the effect of the invalidity of an original county organization is very well considered in its public and private bearings. There have been direct legislative recognitions of the new division on several occasions. The exercise of jurisdiction being notorious and open in all such cases, the State as well as county and town taxes being all levied under it, there is no principle which could justify any court, at this late day, in going back to inquire into the regularity of the law of 1857."

CHAPTER IX.

PROTECTION TO PERSON AND PROPERTY UNDER THE CONSTITUTION OF
THE UNITED STATES.

As the government of the United States was one of enumerated powers, it was not deemed important by the framers of its Constitution that a bill of rights should be incorporated among its provisions. If, among the powers conferred, there was none which would authorize or empower the government to deprive the citizen of any of those fundamental rights which it is the object and the duty of the government to protect and defend, and to insure which is the sole purpose of bills of rights, it was thought to be at least unimportant to insert negative clauses in that instrument, inhibiting the government from assuming any such powers, since the mere failure to confer them would leave all such powers beyond the sphere of its constitutional authority. And, as Mr. Hamilton argued, it might seem even dangerous to do so. "For why declare that things shall not be done which there is no power to do? Why, for instance, should it be said that the liberty of the press shall not be restrained, when no power is given by which restrictions may be imposed? I will not contend that such a provision would confer a regulating power; but it is evident that it would furnish, to men disposed to usurp, a plausible pretence for claiming that power. They might urge, with a semblance of reason, that the Constitution ought not to be charged with the absurdity of providing against the abuse of an authority which was not given, and that the provision against restraining the liberty of the press afforded a clear implication that a right to prescribe proper regulations concerning it was intended to be vested in the national government. This may serve as a specimen of the numerous handles which would be given to the doctrine of constructive powers, by the indulgence of an injudicious zeal for bills of rights." [1]

It was also thought that bills of rights, however important

---

[1] Federalist, No. 84.

under a monarchical government, were of no moment in an instrument framed by the people for their own government, by means of agencies selected by the popular choice, and subject to frequent change by popular action. " It has been several times truly remarked, that bills of rights are, in their origin, stipulations between kings and their subjects, abridgments of prerogative in favor of privilege, reservations of rights not surrendered to the prince. Such was Magna Charta, obtained by the barons, sword in hand, from King John. Such were the subsequent confirmations of that charter by succeeding princes. Such was the Petition of Right, assented to by Charles the First, in the beginning of his reign. Such also was the Declaration of Right presented by the Lords and Commons to the Prince of Orange in 1688, and afterwards thrown into the form of an act of Parliament, called the Bill of Rights. It is evident, therefore, that, according to their primitive signification, they have no application to constitutions professedly founded upon the power of the people, and executed by their immediate representatives and servants. Here, in strictness, the people surrender nothing ; and, as they retain everything, they have no need of particular reservations. ' WE, THE PEOPLE OF THE UNITED STATES, to secure the blessings of liberty to ourselves and our posterity, do *ordain* and *establish* this Constitution for the United States of America.' This is a better recognition of popular rights than volumes of those aphorisms which make the principal figure in several of our State bills of rights, and which would sound much better in a treatise of ethics than in a constitution of government." [1]

Reasoning like this was specious, but it was not satisfactory to many of the leading statesmen of that day, who believed that " the purposes of society do not require a surrender of all our rights to our ordinary governors ; that there are certain portions of right not necessary to enable them to carry on an effective government, and which experience has nevertheless proved they will be constantly encroaching on, if submitted to them ; that there are also certain fences which experience has proved peculiarly efficacious against wrong, and rarely obstructive of right, which yet the governing powers have ever shown a disposition to weaken and remove." [2] And these governing powers will be no less dis-

[1] Federalist, No. 84.
[2] Jefferson's Works, vol. 3, 201.

posed to be aggressive when chosen by majorities than when selected by the accident of birth, or at the will of privileged classes. Indeed if, during the long struggle for constitutional liberty in England, covering the whole of the seventeenth century, importance was justly attached to a distinct declaration and enumeration of individual rights on the part of the government, when it was still in the power of the governing authorities to infringe upon or to abrogate them at any time, and when, consequently, the declaration could possess only a moral force, a similar declaration would appear to be of even more value in the Constitution of the United States, where it would constitute authoritative law, and be subject to no modification or repeal, except by the people themselves, whose rights it was designed to protect, and in the manner by the Constitution provided.[1]

---

[1] Mr. Jefferson sums up the objections to a bill of rights in the Constitution of the United States, and answers them as follows: "1. That the rights in question are reserved by the manner in which the Federal powers are granted. Answer. A constitutive act may certainly be so formed as to need no declaration of rights. The act itself has the force of a declaration, as far as it goes; and if it goes to all material points, nothing more is wanting. In the draft of a constitution which I had once a thought of proposing in Virginia, and printed afterwards, I endeavored to reach all the great objects of public liberty, and did not mean to add a declaration of rights. Probably the object was imperfectly executed; but the deficiencies would have been supplied by others in the course of discussion. But in a constitutive act which leaves some precious articles unnoticed, and raises implications against others, a declaration of rights becomes necessary by way of supplement. This is the case of our new Federal Constitution. This instrument forms us into one State, as to certain objects, and gives us a legislative and executive body for those objects. It should therefore guard us against their abuses of power, within the field submitted to them. 2. A positive declaration of some essential rights could not be obtained in the requisite latitude. Answer. Half a loaf is better than no bread. If we cannot secure all our rights, let us secure what we can. 3. The limited powers of the Federal government, and jealousy of the subordinate governments, afford a security, which exists in no other instance. Answer. The first member of this seems resolvable into the first objection before stated. The jealousy of the subordinate governments is a precious reliance. But observe that those governments are only agents. They must have principles furnished them whereon to found their opposition. The declaration of rights will be the text whereby they will try all the acts of the Federal government. In this view it is necessary to the Federal government also; as by the same text they may try the opposition of the subordinate governments. 4. Experience proves the inefficacy of a bill of rights. True. But though it is not absolutely efficacious, under all circumstances, it is of great potency always, and rarely inefficacious. A brace the more will often keep up the building which

The want of a bill of rights was, therefore, made the ground of a decided, earnest, and formidable opposition to the confirmation of the national Constitution by the people ; and its adoption was only secured in some of the leading States in connection with the recommendation of amendments which should cover the ground.[1]

The clauses inserted in the original instrument, for the protection of person and property, had reference mainly to the action of the State governments, and were made limitations upon their power. The exceptions embraced a few cases only, in respect to which the experience of both English and American history had forcibly demonstrated the tendency of power to abuse, not when wielded by a prince only, but also when administered by the agencies of the people themselves.

Bills of attainder were prohibited to be passed, either by the Congress[2] or by the legislatures of the several States.[3] Attainder, in a strict sense, means an extinction of civil and political rights and capacities; and at the common law it followed, as of course, on conviction and sentence to death for treason ; and, in greater or less degree, on conviction and sentence for the different classes of felony.

A bill of attainder was a legislative conviction for alleged crime, with judgment of death. Such convictions have not been uncommon under other governments, and the power to pass these bills has been exercised by the Parliament of England at some periods in its history, under the most oppressive and unjustifiable

would have fallen with that brace the less. There is a remarkable difference between the characters of the inconveniences which attend a declaration of rights and those which attend the want of it. The inconveniences of the declaration are, that it may cramp government in its useful exertions. But the evil of this is short-lived, moderate, and reparable. The inconveniencies of the want of a declaration are permanent, afflictive, and irreparable. They are in constant progression from bad to worse. The executive, in our governments, is not the sole, it is scarcely the principal, object of my jealousy. The tyranny of the legislatures is the most formidable dread at present, and will be for many years. That of the executive will come in its turn ; but it will be at a remote period." Letter to Madison, March 15, 1789, 3 Jefferson's Works, p. 4. See also same volume, pp. 13 and 101 ; vol. 2, pp. 329, 358.

[1] For the various recommendations by Massachusetts, South Carolina, New Hampshire, Virginia, New York, North Carolina, and Rhode Island, see 1 Elliott: Debates, 322 – 334.

[2] Constitution of United States, art. 1, § 9.

[3] Constitution of United States, art. 1, § 10.

circumstances, greatly aggravated by an arbitrary course of procedure, which scarcely took the form of a proceeding for the investigation of an alleged crime. Of late years in England no one had attempted to defend it as a legitimate exercise of power; and if it would be unjustifiable anywhere, there were many reasons why it would be specially obnoxious under a free government, and which rendered its prohibition, under the existing circumstances of our country, a matter of more than ordinary importance. Every one must concede that a legislative body, from its numbers and organization, and from the very intimate dependence of its members upon the people, so that they are liable to be peculiarly susceptible to popular clamor, is not properly constituted to try with coolness, caution, and impartiality a criminal charge, especially when it relates to some subject upon which the popular feeling is excited, and which would be the very class of cases likely to be prosecuted by this mode. And although, if such bills were allowable, they should properly be presented only for offences against the general laws of the land, and be proceeded with on the same full opportunity for investigation and defence which is afforded in the courts of the common law, yet it was remembered that in practice it was often resorted to because an obnoxious person was not subject to punishment under the general law,[1] or because, in proceeding against him by this mode, some rule of the common law requiring a particular species or degree of evidence might be evaded, and a conviction secured on proofs that a jury would not be suffered to accept as overcoming the legal presumption of innocence. Whether the accused should necessarily be served with process; what degree or species of evidence should be required; whether the rules of law should be

[1] Cases of this description were most numerous during the reign of Henry VIII., and among the victims was Cromwell, who is said to have first advised that monarch to resort to this objectionable proceeding. Even the dead were attainted, as in the case of Richard III., and later, of the heroes of the Commonwealth. The most atrocious instance in history, however, only relieved by its weakness and futility, was the great act of attainder passed in 1688 by the Parliament of James II., assembled in Dublin, by which between two and three thousand persons were attainted, their property confiscated, and themselves sentenced to death if they failed to appear at a time named. And, to render the whole proceeding as horrible in barbarity as possible, the list of the proscribed was carefully kept secret until after the time fixed for their appearance! Macaulay's History of England, ch. 12.

followed, either in determining what constituted a crime, or in dealing with the accused after conviction, — were all questions which would necessarily address themselves to the legislative discretion and sense of justice; and the very qualities which are essential in a court to protect individuals on trial before them against popular clamor, or the hate of those in power, were precisely those which were likely to prove weak or wanting in the legislative body at such a time.[1] And what could be more obnoxious in a free government than the exercise of such a power by a popular body, controlled by a mere majority,.fresh from the contests of exciting elections, and quite too apt, under the most favorable circumstances, to suspect the motives of their adversaries, and to resort to measures of doubtful propriety to secure party ends?

Legislative punishments of this severe character, however, were not the only ones known to parliamentary history; but there were others of a milder form, which were only less obnoxious in that the consequences were less terrible. Those legislative convictions which imposed punishments less than that of death were called bills of pains and penalties, as distinguished from bills of attainder; but the constitutional provision was undoubtedly aimed at any and every species of legislative punishment for criminal or supposed criminal offences; and the term "bill of attainder" is used in a generic sense, which would include bills of pains and penalties also.[2]

---

[1] This was equally true, whether the attainder was at the command of the king, as in the case of Cardinal Pole's mother, or at the instigation of the populace, as in the case of Wentworth, Earl of Strafford. The last infliction of capital punishment in England, under a bill of attainder, was upon Sir John Fenwick, in the reign of William and Mary. It is worthy of note that in the preceding reign Sir John had been prominent in the attainder of the unhappy Monmouth. Macaulay's History of England, ch. 5.

[2] Fletcher v. Peck, 6 Cranch, 138; Story on Constitution, § 1344; Cummings v. Missouri, 4 Wal. 277; Ex parte Garland, Ibid. 333. "I think it will be found that the following comprise those essential elements of bills of attainder, in addition to those I have already mentioned [which were that they declared certain persons attainted and their blood corrupted, so that it had lost all heritable property], which distinguish them from other legislation, and which made them so obnoxious to the statesmen who organized our government: 1. They were convictions and sentences pronounced by the legislative department of the government, instead of the judicial. 2. The sentence pronounced and the punishment inflicted were determined by no previous law or fixed rule. 3. The investigation

The thoughtful reader will not fail to discover, in the acts of the American States during the Revolutionary period, sufficient reason for this constitutional provision, even if the still more monitory history of the English attainders had not been so freshly remembered. Some of these acts provided for the forfeiture of the estates, within the Commonwealth, of those British subjects who had withdrawn from the jurisdiction because not satisfied that grievances existed sufficiently serious to justify the last resort of an oppressed people, or because of other reasons not satisfactory to the existing authorities; and the only investigation provided for was an inquiry into the desertion. Others mentioned particular persons by name, adjudged them guilty of adhering to the enemies of the State, and proceeded to inflict punishment upon them, so far as the presence of property within the Commonwealth would enable the government to do so.[1] These were the resorts of a time of extreme peril; and if possible to justify them in a period of revolution, when everything was staked on success, and when the public safety would not permit too much weight to scruples concerning the private rights of those who were not aiding the popular cause, the power to repeat such acts under any possible circumstances in which the country could be placed again was felt to be too dangerous to be left in the legislative hands. So far as proceedings had been completed under those acts, before the treaty of 1783, by the actual transfer of property, they remained valid and effectual afterwards; but so far as they were then incomplete, they were put an end to by that treaty.[2]

The conviction of the propriety of this constitutional provision has been so universal, that it has never been questioned, either in legislative bodies or elsewhere. Nevertheless, cases have recently arisen, growing out of the attempt to break up and destroy the government of the United States, in which the Supreme Court of

into the guilt of the accused, if any such were made, was not necessarily or generally conducted in his presence or that of his counsel, and no recognized rule of evidence governed the inquiry." Per Miller, J., in Ex parte Garland, 4 Wal. 388.

[1] See Belknap's History of New Hampshire, ch. 26; 2 Ramsay's History of South Carolina, 351; 8 Rhode Island Colonial Records, 609; 2 Arnold's History of Rhode Island, 360, 449; Thompson v. Carr, 5 N. H. 510; Sleght v. Kane, 2 Johns. Cas. 236.

[2] Jackson v. Munson, 3 Caines, 137.

the United States has adjudged certain action of Congress void as in violation of this provision.[1] The action referred to was designed to exclude from practice in the United States courts all persons who had taken up arms against the government during the recent rebellion, or who had voluntarily given aid and encouragement to its enemies ; and the mode adopted to effect the exclusion was to require of all persons, before they should be admitted to the bar or allowed to practise, an oath negativing any such disloyal action. This decision has not been universally accepted as sound ; and the Supreme Courts of West Virginia and of the District of Columbia have since refused to follow it, insisting that permission to practise in the courts is not a right, but a privilege, and that the withholding

[1] On the 2d of July, 1862, Congress, by "an act to prescribe an oath of office, and for other purposes," enacted that "hereafter every person elected or appointed to any office of honor or profit under the government of the United States, either in the civil, military, or naval departments of the public service, excepting the President of the United States, shall, before entering upon the duties of such office, take and subscribe the following oath or affirmation: I, A B, do solemnly swear or affirm that I have never voluntarily borne arms against the United States since I have been a citizen thereof; that I have voluntarily given no aid, countenance, counsel, or encouragement to persons engaged in armed hostility thereto; that I have neither sought nor accepted, nor attempted to exercise, the functions of any office whatever, under any authority or pretended authority in hostility to the United States; that I have not yielded a voluntary support to any pretended government, authority, power, or constitution within the United States, hostile or inimical thereto. And I do further swear or affirm that, to the best of my knowledge and ability, I will support and defend the Constitution of the United States against all enemies, foreign and domestic ; that I will bear true faith and allegiance to the same ; that I take this obligation freely, without any mental reservation or purpose of evasion ; and that I will well and faithfully discharge the duties of the office on which I am about to enter, so help me God." On the 24th of January, 1865, Congress passed a supplementary act as follows : "No person after the date of this act shall be admitted to the bar of the Supreme Court of the United States, or at any time after the 4th of March next shall be admitted to the bar of any Circuit or District Court of the United States, or of the Court of Claims, as an attorney or counsellor of such court, or shall be allowed to appear and to be heard in any such court, by virtue of any previous admission, or any special power of attorney, unless he shall have first taken and subscribed the oath " aforesaid. False swearing, under each of the acts, was made perjury. See 12 Statutes at Large, 502; 13 Ibid. 424. In Ex parte Garland, 4 Wal. 333, a majority of the court held the second of these acts void, as partaking of the nature of a bill of pains and penalties, and also as being an *ex post facto* law. The act was looked upon as inflicting a punishment for past conduct ; the exaction of the oath being the mode provided for ascertaining the parties upon whom the act was intended to operate.

it for any reason of state policy or personal unfitness could not be regarded as the infliction of criminal punishment.[1]

The Supreme Court of the United States have also, upon the same reasoning, held a clause in the constitution of Missouri, which, among other things, excluded all priests and clergymen from practising or teaching unless they should first take a similar oath of loyalty, to be void, overruling in so doing a decision of the Supreme Court of that State.[2]

The same provisions of the national Constitution which we have cited[3] also forbid the passage either by the States or by Congress of any *ex post facto* law.

At an early day it was settled by authoritative decision, in opposition to what might seem the more natural and obvious meaning of the term *ex post facto*, that in their scope and purpose these provisions were confined to laws respecting criminal punishments, and had no relation whatever to retrospective legislation, of any other description. And it has, therefore, been repeatedly held, that retrospective laws, when not of a criminal nature, do not come in conflict with the national Constitution, unless obnoxious to its provisions on other grounds than their retrospective character.

" The prohibition in the letter," says Chase, J., in the leading case,[4] " is not to pass any law concerning or after the fact ; but the plain and obvious meaning and intention of the prohibition is this : that the legislatures of the several States shall not pass laws after a fact done by a subject or citizen, which shall have relation to such fact, and punish him for having done it. The prohibition,

---

[1] See the cases of Ex parte Magruder, American Law Register, vol. 6, N. S. p. 292 ; and Ex parte Hunter, Ibid. 410. See also Ex parte Yale, 24 Cal. 241.

[2] Cummings v. Missouri, 4 Wal. 277. The Missouri oath of loyalty was a very stringent one, and applied to electors, State, county, city, and town officers, officers in any corporation, public or private, professors and teachers in educational institutions, attorneys and counsellors, bishops, priests, deacons, ministers, elders, or other clergymen of any denomination. The Supreme Court of Missouri had held this provision valid in the following cases : State v. Garesche, 36 Mo. 256, case of an attorney ; State v. Cummings, 36 Mo. 263, case of a minister, reversed as above stated ; State v. Bernoudy, 36 Mo. 279, case of the recorder of St. Louis ; State v. McAdoo, 36 Mo. 452, where it is held that a certificate of election issued to one who failed to take the oath as required by the constitution was void.

[3] Constitution of United States, art. 1, §§ 9 and 10.

[4] Calder v. Bull, 3 Dall. 390.

considered in this light, is an additional bulwark in favor of the personal security of the subject, to protect his person from punishment by legislative acts having a retrospective operation. I do not think it was inserted to secure the citizen in his private rights of either property or contracts. The prohibitions not to make anything but gold and silver coin a tender in payment of debts, and not to pass any law impairing the obligation of contracts, were inserted to secure private rights; but the restriction not to pass any *ex post facto* law was to secure the person of the subject from injury or punishment, in consequence of such law. If the prohibition against making *ex post facto* laws was intended to secure personal rights from being affected or injured by such law, and the prohibition is sufficiently extensive for that object, the other restraints I have enumerated were unnecessaro, and therefore improper, for both of them are retrospective.

" I will state what laws I consider *ex post facto* laws, within the words and the intent of the prohibition.   1st. Every law that makes an action done before the passing of the law, and which was innocent when done, criminal, and punishes such action. 2d. Every law that aggravates a crime, or makes it greater than it was when committed.   3d. Every law that changes the punishment, and inflicts a greater punishment than the law annexed to the crime when committed.   4th. Every law that alters the legal rules of evidence, and receives less or different testimony than the law required at the time of the commission of the offence, in order to convict the offender.   All these and similar laws are manifestly unjust and oppressive.   In my opinion, the true distinction is between *ex post facto* laws and retrospective laws. Every *ex post facto* law must necessarily be retrospective, but every retrospective law is not an *ex post facto* law; the former only are prohibited.   Every law that takes away or impairs rights vested, agreeably to existing laws, is retrospective and is generally unjust, and may be oppressive; and there is a good general rule, that a law should have no retrospect; but there are cases in which laws may justly, and for the benefit of the community, and also of individuals, relate to a time antecedent to their commencement; as statutes of oblivion or of pardon.   They are certainly retrospective, and literally both concerning and after the facts committed.   But I do not consider any law *ex post facto*, within the prohibition, that mollifies the rigor of the criminal law; but only those that create or aggravate the crime, or increase the punishment, or change the rules of evidence for the purpose of conviction. Every law that is to have an operation before the making thereof, as to commence at an antecedent time, or to save time from the statute of limitations, or to excuse acts which were unlawful, and before committed, and the like, is retrospective. But such acts may be proper and necessary, as the case may be. There is a great and apparent difference between making an unlawful act lawful, and the naking an innocent act criminal, and punishing it as a crime. The expressions *ex post facto* are technical; they had been in use long before the Revolution, and had acquired an appropriate meaning, by legislators, lawyers, and authors." [1]

Assuming this construction of the constitutional provision to be correct, — and it has been accepted and followed as correct by the courts ever since, — it would seem that little need be said relative to the first, second, and fourth classes of *ex post facto* laws, as enumerated in the opinion quoted. It is not essential, however, in order to render a law invalid on these grounds, that it should expressly assume the action to which it relates to be criminal, or provide for its punishment on that ground. If it should subject an individual to a pecuniary penalty for an act which, when done, involved no responsibility,[2] or if it deprived a party of any valuable right — like the right to follow a lawful calling — for acts which were innocent, or at least not punishable by law when committed,[3] the law will be *ex post facto* in the constitutional sense, notwithstanding it does not in terms declare the acts to which the penalty is attached criminal. But how far a law may change the punishment for a criminal offence, and make the change applicable to past offences, is certainly a question of great

---

[1] See also Fletcher *v.* Peck, 6 Cranch, 87; Ogden *v.* Saunders, 12 Wheat. 266; Satterlee *v.* Mathewson, 2 Pet. 380; Watson *v.* Mercer, 8 Pet. 110; Charles River Bridge *v.* Warren Bridge, 11 Pet. 421; Carpenter *v.* Pennsylvania, 17 How. 463; Cummings *v.* Missouri, 4 Wal. 277; Ex parte Garland, Ibid. 333; Baugher *v.* Nelson, 9 Gill, 299; Woart *v.* Winnick, 3 N. H. 475; Locke *v.* Dane, 9 Mass. 363; Dash *v.* Van Kleek, 7 Johns. 497; Evans *v.* Montgomery, 4 W. & S. 218; Tucker *v.* Harris, 13 Geo. 1; Perry's case, 3 Grat. 632; Municipality No. 1 *v.* Wheeler, 10 La. An. 745; New Orleans *v.* Poutz, 14 La. An. 853.

[2] Falconer *v.* Campbell, 2 McLean, 212.

[3] Cummings *v.* Missouri, 4 Wal. 277; Ex parte Garland, Ibid. 333.

difficulty, which has been increased by the decisions made concerning it. As the constitutional provision is made for the protection and security of accused parties against arbitrary and oppressive legislative action, it is evident that any change in the law which goes in mitigation of the punishment is not liable to this objection.[1] But what does go in mitigation of the punishment? If the law makes a fine less in amount, or imprisonment shorter in point of duration, or relieves it from some oppressive incident, or if it dispenses with some severable portion of the legal penalty, no embarrassment would be experienced in reaching a conclusion that the law was favorable to the accused, and therefore not *ex post facto*. But who shall say, when the nature of the punishment is altogether changed, and a fine is substituted for the pillory, or imprisonment for whipping, or imprisonment at hard labor for life for the death penalty, that the punishment is diminished, or at least not increased by the change made? What test of severity does the law or reason furnish in these cases? and must the judge decide upon his own view of the pain, loss, ignominy, and collateral consequences usually attending the punishment? or may he take into view the peculiar condition of the accused, and upon that determine whether, in his particular case, the punishment prescribed by the new law is more severe than that under the old or not?

In State *v.* Arlin,[2] the respondent was charged with a robbery, which, under the law as it existed at the time it was committed, was liable to be punished by solitary imprisonment not exceeding six months, and confinement for life at hard labor in the State prison. As incident to this severe punishment, he was entitled by the same law to have counsel assigned him by the government, to process to compel the attendance of witnesses, to a copy of his indictment, a list of the jurors who were to try him, &c. Before he was brought to trial, the punishment for the offence was reduced to solitary imprisonment not exceeding six months, and confinement at hard labor in the State prison for not less than seven nor more than thirty years. By the new act, the court, *if they thought proper*, were to assign the respondent counsel, and

[1] Strong *v.* State, 1 Blackf. 193 ; Keen *v.* State, 3 Chand. 109 ; Boston *v.* Cummins, 16 Geo. 102 ; Woart *v.* Winnick, 3 N. H. 473 ; State *v.* Arlin, 39 N. H. 180 ; Clarke *v.* State, 23 Miss. 261.

[2] 39 N. H. 179.

furnish him with process to compel the attendance of witnesses in his behalf; and, acting under this discretion, the court assigned the respondent counsel, but declined to do more; while the respondent insisted that he was entitled to all the privileges to which he would have been entitled had the law remained unchanged. The court held this claim to be unfounded in the law. "It is contended," they say, " that, notwithstanding the severity of the respondent's punishment was mitigated by the alteration of the statute, he is entitled to the privileges demanded, as incidents to the offence with which he is charged, at the date of its commission; in other words, it seems to be claimed, that, by committing the alleged offence, the respondent acquired a vested right to have counsel assigned him, to be furnished with process to procure the attendance of witnesses, and to enjoy all the other privileges to which he would have been entitled if tried under laws subjecting him to imprisonment for life upon conviction. This position appears to us wholly untenable. We have no doubt the privileges the respondent claims were designed and created solely as incidents of the severe punishment to which his offence formerly subjected him, and not as incidents of the offence. When the punishment was abolished, its incidents fell with it; and he might as well claim the right to be punished under the former law as to be entitled to the privileges connected with a trial under it." [1]

In Strong v. State,[2] the plaintiff in error was indicted and con-

---

[1] With great deference it may be suggested whether this case does not overlook the important circumstance, that the new law, by taking from the accused that absolute right to defence by counsel, and to the other privileges by which the old law surrounded the trial, — all of which were designed as securities against unjust convictions, — was directly calculated to increase the party's peril, and was in consequence brought within the reason of the rule which holds a law *ex post facto* which changes the rules of evidence after the fact, so as to make a less amount or degree sufficient. Could a law be void as *ex post facto* which made a party liable to conviction for perjury in a previous oath on the testimony of a single witness, and another law unobjectionable on this score which deprived a party, when put on trial for a previous act, of all the usual opportunities of exhibiting the facts and establishing his innocence? Undoubtedly if the party accused was always guilty, and certain to be convicted, the new law must be regarded as mitigating the offence; but, assuming every man to be innocent until he is proved to be guilty, could such a law be looked upon as "mollifying the rigor" of the prior law, or as favorable to the accused, when its mollifying circumstance is more than counterbalanced by others of a contrary character?

[2] 1 Blackf. 193.

victed of perjury, which, under the law as it existed at the time
it was committed, was punishable by not exceeding one hundred
stripes.   Before the trial, this punishment was changed to imprisonment in the penitentiary not exceeding seven years.   The court
held this amendatory law not to be *ex post facto*, as applied to
the case.   "The words *ex post facto* have a definite, technical
signification.   The plain and obvious meaning of this prohibition
is, that the legislature shall not pass any law, after a fact done by
any citizen, which shall have relation to that fact, so as to punish
that which was innocent when done, or to add to the punishment
of that which was criminal, or to increase the malignity of a
crime, or to retrench the rules of evidence so as to make conviction more easy."   "Apply this definition to the act under consideration.   Does this statute make a new offence?   It does not.
Does it increase the malignity of that which was an offence before?   It does not.   Does it so change the rules of evidence as to
make conviction more easy?   This cannot be alleged.   Does it
then increase the punishment of that which was criminal before
its enactment?   We think not."[1]

So in Texas it has been held that the infliction of stripes, from
the peculiarly degrading character of the punishment, was worse
than the death penalty.   "Among all nations of civilized man,
from the earliest ages, the infliction of stripes has been considered
more degrading than death itself."[2]   While, on the other hand,
in South Carolina, where, at the time of the commission of a forgery, the punishment was death, but it was changed before final
judgment to fine, whipping, and imprisonment, the new law was
applied to the case in passing the sentence.[3]   These cases illus-

[1] Mr. Bishop says of this decision: "But certainly the court went far in this
case."   1 Bishop, Crim. Law, § 219 (108).

[2] Herber v. State, 7 Texas, 69.

[3] State v. Williams, 2 Rich. 418.   In Clark v. State, 23 Miss. 261, defendant
was convicted of a mayhem.   Between the commission of the act and his conviction, a statute had been passed, changing the punishment for this offence from
the pillory and a fine to imprisonment in the penitentiary, but providing further,
that "no offence committed and no penalty and forfeiture incurred previous to
the time when this act shall take effect shall be affected by this act, except
that when any punishment, forfeiture, or penalty should have been mitigated by it,
its provisions should be applied to the judgment to be pronounced for offences
committed before its adoption."   In regard to this statute the court say: "We
think that in every case of offence committed before the adoption of the penitentiary code, the prisoner has the option of selecting the punishment prescribed

trate the difficulty of laying down any rule which will be readily and universally accepted as to what is a mitigation of punishment, where its character is changed, and when from the very nature of the case there can be no common standard, by which all minds, however educated, can measure the relative severity and ignominy.

In Hartung v. People,[1] the law providing for the infliction of capital punishment had been so changed as to require the party liable to this penalty to be sentenced to confinement at hard labor in the State prison until the punishment of death should be inflicted ; and it further provided that such punishment should not be inflicted under one year, nor until the governor should issue his warrant for the purpose. The act was evidently designed for the benefit of parties convicted, and, among other things, to enable advantage to be taken, for their benefit, of any circumstances subsequently coming to light which might show the injustice of the judgment, or throw any more favorable light on the action of the accused. Nevertheless, the court held the act inoperative as to offences before committed. " In my opinion," says Denio, J., " it would be perfectly competent for the legislature, by a general law, to remit any separable portion of the prescribed punishment. For instance, if the punishment were fine and imprisonment, a law which should dispense with either the fine or the imprisonment might, I think, be lawfully applied to existing offences ; and so, in my opinion, the term of imprisonment might be reduced, or the number of stripes diminished, in cases punishable in that manner. Anything which, if applied to an individual sentence, would fairly fall within the idea of a remission of a part of the sentence, would not be liable to objection. And any change which should be referable to prison discipline or penal administration as its primary object might also be made to take effect upon past as well as future offences ; as changes in the manner or kind of employment of convicts sentenced to hard labor, the system of supervision, the means of restraint, or the like. Changes of this

in that code in lieu of that to which he was liable before its enactment." But inasmuch as the record did not show that the defendant claimed a commutation of his punishment, the court confirmed a sentence imposed according to the terms of the old law. On this subject, see further the cases of Holt v. State, 2 Texas, 363 ; Dawson v. State, 6 Texas, 347.

[1] 22 N. Y. 105.

sort might operate to increase or mitigate the severity of the punishment of the convict, but would not raise any question under
the constitutional provision we are considering.   The change
wrought by the act of 1860, in the punishment of existing offences
of murder, does not fall within either of these exceptions.   If
it is to be construed to vest in the governor a discretion to determine whether the convict should be executed or remain a perpetual prisoner at hard labor, this would only be equivalent to what
he might do under the authority to commute a sentence.   But he
can, under the Constitution, only do this once for all.   If he refuses the pardon, the convict is executed according to sentence.
If he grants it, his jurisdiction of the case ends.   The act in question places the convict at the mercy of the governor in office at
the expiration of one year from the time of the conviction, and of
all of his successors during the lifetime of the convict.   He may
be ordered to execution at any time, upon any notice, or without
notice.   Under one of the repealed sections of the Revised Statutes, it was required that a period should intervene between the
sentence and execution of not less than four, nor more than eight
weeks.   If we stop here, the change effected by the statute is between an execution within a limited time, to be prescribed by the
court, or a pardon or commutation of the sentence during that
period, on the one hand, and the placing the convict at the mercy
of the executive magistrate for the time, and his successors, to be
executed at his pleasure at any time after one year, on the other.
The sword is indefinitely suspended over his head, ready to fall at
any time.   It is not enough to say, if even that can be said, that
most persons would probably prefer such a fate to the former capital sentence.   It is enough to bring the law within the condemnation of the Constitution, that it changes the punishment after
the commission of the offence, by substituting for the prescribed
penalty a different one.   We have no means of saying whether
one or the other would be the most severe in a given case.   That
would depend upon the disposition and temperament of the convict.   The legislature cannot thus experiment upon the criminal
law.   *The law, moreover, prescribes one year's imprisonment, at
hard labor in the State prison, in addition to the punishment of
death.*   In every case of the execution of a capital sentence, it
must be preceded by the year's imprisonment at hard labor.
True, the concluding part of the punishment cannot be executed

unless the governor concurs by ordering the execution. But as both parts may, in any given case, be inflicted, and as the convict is consequently, under this law, exposed to the double infliction, it is, within both the definitions which have been mentioned, an *ex post facto* law. It changes the punishment, and inflicts a greater punishment than that which the law annexed to the crime when committed. It is enough, in my opinion, that it changes it *in any manner* except by dispensing with divisible portions of it; but upon the other definition announced by Judge Chase, where it is implied that the change must be from a less to a greater punishment, this act cannot be sustained." This decision has since been several times followed in the State of New York,[1] and it must now be regarded as the settled law of that State, that "a law changing the punishment for offences committed before its passage is *ex post facto* and void, under the Constitution, unless the change consists in the remission of some separable part of the punishment before prescribed, or is referable to prison discipline or penal administration as its primary object."[2] And this rule seems to us a sound and sensible one, with perhaps this single qualification, — that the substitution of any other punishment for that of death must be regarded as a mitigation of the penalty.[3]

But so far as mere modes of procedure are concerned, a party has no more right, in a criminal than in a civil action, to insist that his case shall be disposed of under the law in force when the act to be investigated is charged to have taken place. Remedies must always be under the control of the legislature, and it would create endless confusion in legal proceedings if every case was to be conducted only in accordance with the rules of practice, and heard only by the courts, in existence when its facts arose. The legislature may abolish courts and create new ones, and it may prescribe altogether different modes of procedure in its discretion, subject only, as we think, that, in so doing, they must not dispense with any of those substantial protections with which the existing law surrounds the person accused of crime. A law giving the government additional challenges,[4] and another which authorized

---

[1] Shepherd *v.* People, 25 N. Y. 406; Ratzky *v.* People, 29 N. Y. 124; Kuckler *v.* People, 5 Park. Cr. Rep. 212.

[2] Per Davies, J., in Ratzky *v.* People, 29 N. Y. 124.

[3] See 1 Bishop, Crim. Law, § 219 (108).

[4] Walston *v.* Commonwealth, 16 B. Monr. 15.

the amendment of indictments,[1] have both been sustained as applicable to past transactions, as any similar law, tending only to improve the remedy, but working no injustice to the defendant, and depriving him of no substantial right, doubtless would be.

And a law is not objectionable as *ex post facto* which, in providing for the punishment of future offences, authorizes the offender's conduct in the past to be taken into the account, and the punishment to be graduated accordingly. Heavier penalties are often provided by law for a second or any subsequent offence than for the first; and it has not been deemed objectionable that, in providing for such heavier penalties, the prior conviction authorized to be taken into the account may have taken place before the law was passed.[2] In such case, it is the second or subsequent offence that is punished, not the first;[3] and the act would be void if the offence to be actually punished had been committed before it had taken effect, even though it was after its passage.[4]

Laws impairing the Obligation of Contracts.

The Constitution of the United States also forbids the States passing any law impairing the obligation of contracts.[5] It is remarkable that this very important clause was passed over almost without comment during the discussions preceding the adoption of that instrument, though since its adoption no clause which the Constitution contains has been more prolific of litigation, or given rise to more animated and at times angry controversy. It is but twice alluded to in the papers of the Federalist;[6] and though its great importance is assumed, it is evident that the writer had no conception of the prominence it was afterwards to assume in constitutional discussions, or of the very numerous cases to which it has since been applied.

The first question that arises under this provision is, What is a

---

[1] State *v.* Manning, 14 Texas, 402. The defendant in any case must be proceeded against and punished under the law in force when the proceeding is had. State *v.* Williams, 2 Rich. 418; Keene *v.* State, 2 Chand. 109; People *v.* Phelps, 5 Wend. 9; Rand *v.* Commonwealth, 9 Grat. 738.

[2] Rand *v.* Commonwealth, 9 Grat. 738; Ross's case, 2 Pick. 165; People *v.* Butler, 3 Cow. 347.

[3] Rand *v.* Commonwealth, 9 Grat. 738.

[4] Riley's case, 2 Pick. 172.   [5] Const. art. 1, § 10.

[6] Federalist, Nos. 7 and 44.

contract in the sense in which the word is here employed? In the leading case upon this subject, it appeared that the legislature of Georgia had made a grant of land, but afterwards, on an allegation that the grant had been obtained by fraud, a subsequent legislature had passed another act annulling and rescinding the first conveyance, and asserting the right of the State to the land it covered. " A contract," says Ch. J. Marshall, " is a compact between two or more parties, and is either executory or executed. An executory contract is one in which a party binds himself to do or not to do a particular thing. Such was the law under which the conveyance was made by the governor. A contract executed is one in which the object of the contract is performed; and this, says Blackstone, differs in nothing from a grant. The contract between Georgia and the purchasers was executed by the grant. A contract executed, as well as one which is executory, contains obligations binding on the parties. A grant, in its own nature, amounts to an extinguishment of the right of the grantor, and implies a contract not to reassert that right. A party is, therefore, always estopped by his own grant. Since then, in fact, a grant is a contract executed, the obligation of which still continues, and since the Constitution uses the general term ' contract,' without distinguishing between those which are executory and those which are executed, it must be construed to comprehend the latter as well as the former. A law annulling conveyances between individuals, and declaring that the grantors should stand seised of their former estates, notwithstanding those grants, would be as repugnant to the Constitution as a law discharging the vendors of property from the obligation of executing their contracts by conveyances. It would be strange if a contract to convey was secured by the Constitution, while an absolute conveyance remained unprotected. If, under a fair construction of the Constitution, grants are comprehended under the term ' contracts,' is a grant from the State excluded from the operation of the provision? Is the clause to be considered as inhibiting the State from impairing the obligation of contracts between two individuals, but as excluding from that inhibition contracts made with itself? The words themselves contain no such distinction. They are general, and are applicable to contracts of every description. If contracts made with the State are to be exempted from their operations, the exception must arise from the character of the contracting party, not from the words which are employed." And the court proceed to give reasons for their decision, that violence should not " be done to the natural meaning of words, for the purpose of leaving to the legislature the power of seizing, for public use, the estate of an individual, in the form of a law annulling the title by which he holds that estate." [1]

It will be seen that this leading decision settles two important points : first, that an executed contract is within the provision ; and second, that it protects from violation the contracts of States equally with those entered into between private individuals.[2] And it has since been held that compacts between two States are in like manner protected.[3] These decisions, however, do not fully

[1] Fletcher v. Peck, 6 Cranch, 133.

[2] This decision has been repeatedly followed. In the founding of the Colony of Virginia, the religious establishment of England was adopted, and before the Revolution the churches of that denomination had become vested, by grants of the crown or Colony, with large properties, which continued in their possession after the constitution of the State had forbidden the creation or continuance of any religious establishment, possessed of exclusive rights or privileges, or the compelling the citizens to worship under a stipulated form or discipline, or to pay taxes to those whose creed they could not conscientiously believe. By statute in 1801, the legislature asserted their right to all the property of the Episcopal churches in the respective parishes of the State ; and, among other things, directed and authorized the overseers of the poor and their successors in each parish, wherein any glebe land was vacant or should become so, to sell the same and appropriate the proceeds to the use of the poor of the parish. By this act, it will be seen, the State sought in effect to resume grants made by the sovereignty, — a practice which had been common enough in English history, and of which precedents were not wanting in the history of the American Colonies. The Supreme Court of the United States held the grant not revocable, and that the legislative act was therefore unconstitutional and void. Terrett v. Taylor, 9 Cranch, 43. See also Town of Pawlet v. Clark, 9 Cranch, 335; People v. Platt, 17 Johns. 195; Montgomery v. Kasson, 16 Cal. 189; Grogan v. San Francisco, 18 Cal. 590; Rehoboth v. Hunt, 1 Pick. 224; Lowry v. Francis, 2 Yerg. 534; University of North Carolina v. Foy, 2 Hayw. 310. The lien of a bondholder, who has loaned money to the State on a pledge of property by legislative act, cannot be divested or postponed by a subsequent legislative act. Wabash, &c. Co. v. Beers, 2 Black, 448.

[3] On the separation of Kentucky from Virginia a compact was entered into between the proposed new and the old State, by which it was agreed " that all private grants and interests of lands, within the said district, derived from the laws of Virginia, shall remain valid and secure under the laws of the proposed State, and shall be determined by the laws now existing in this State." After the admission of the new State to the Union, " occupying claimant " laws were passed by its legislature, such as were not in existence in Virginia, and by the

determine what is to be regarded as a contract under all circumstances. A grant of land by a State is a contract, because in making it the State deals with the purchaser precisely as any other vendor might ; and if its mode of conveyance is any different, it is only because, by virtue of its sovereignty, it has power to convey by other modes than those which the general law opens to private individuals. But many things done by the State may seem to hold out promises to individuals, which after all cannot be treated as contracts without hampering the legislative power of the State in a manner that would soon leave it without the means of performing its essential functions. The State creates offices, and appoints persons to fill them ; it establishes municipal corporations, with large and valuable privileges for its citizens ; by its general laws it holds out inducements to immigration ; it passes exemption laws, and laws for the encouragement of trade and agriculture ; and under all these laws a greater or less number of citizens expect to derive profit and emolument. But can these laws be regarded as contracts between the State and the officers and corporations who are benefited, or the citizens of the State who expect to be, by their passage, so as to preclude their being repealed ?

On these points it would seem that there could be no difficulty. When the State employs officers or creates municipal corporations as the mere agencies of government, it must have the power to discontinue the agency whenever it is no longer important. " The framers of the Constitution did not intend to restrain the States in the regulation of their civil institutions, adopted for internal government." [1] They may, therefore, discontinue offices and abolish or change the organization of municipal corporations at any time, according to the existing legislative view of state policy, unless forbidden by their own constitutions from doing so. [2] And al-

force of which, under certain circumstances, the owner might be deprived of his title to land, unless he would pay the value of lasting improvements made upon it by an adverse claimant. These acts were also held void; the compact was held inviolable under the Constitution, and it was deemed no objection to its binding character, that its effect was to restrict, in some directions, the legislative power of the State entering into it. Green v. Biddle, 8 Wheat, 1. See also Hawkins v. Barney's Lessee, 5 Pet. 457.

[1] Dartmouth College v. Woodward, 4 Wheat, 629, per Marshall, Ch. J.

[2] Butler v. Pennsylvania, 10 How. 402 ; Warner v. People, 2 Denio, 272 ; Commonwealth v. Bacon, 6 S. & R. 322 ; Commonwealth v. Mann, 5 W. & S.

though municipal corporations, as respects the property which they hold, control, and manage for the benefit of their citizens, are governed by the same rules and subject to the same liabilities as individuals, yet this property, so far as it has been derived from the State, or obtained by the exercise of the ordinary powers of government, must be held subject to control by the State, but under the restriction that it is not to be appropriated to uses foreign to those for which it has been acquired. And the franchises conferred upon such a corporation, for the benefit of its citizens, must be liable to be resumed at any time by the authority which may mould the corporate powers at its will, and even revoke them altogether. The greater power will comprehend the less.[1] If, however, a grant is made to a municipal corporation

418 ; Conner v. New York, 2 Sandf. 355, and 5 N. Y. 285. " Where an office is created by statute, it is wholly within the control of the legislature. The term, the mode of appointment, and the compensation may be altered at pleasure, and the latter may be even taken away without abolishing the office. Such extreme legislation is not to be deemed probable in any case. But we are now discussing the legislative power, not its expediency or propriety. Having the power, the legislature will exercise it for the public good, and it is the sole judge of the exigency which demands its interference." Per Sandford, J., 2 Sandf. 369. " The selection of officers who are nothing more than public agents for the effectuating of public purposes is matter of public convenience or necessity, and so, too, are the periods for the appointment of such agents, but neither the one nor the other of these arrangements can constitute any obligation to continue such agents, or to reappoint them, after the measures which brought them into being shall have been found useless, shall have been fulfilled, or shall have been abrogated as even detrimental to the well-being of the public. The promised compensation for services actually performed and accepted, during the continuance of the particular agency, may undoubtedly be claimed, both upon principles of compact and of equity ; but to insist beyond this upon the perpetuation of a public policy either useless or detrimental, and upon a reward for acts neither desired nor performed, would appear to be reconcilable with neither common justice nor common sense." Daniel, J., in 10 How. 416. See also Territory v. Pyle, 1 Oregon, 149 ; Bryan v. Cattell, 15 Iowa, 538. As to control of municipal corporations, see, further, Marietta v. Fearing, 4 Ohio, 427 ; Bradford v. Cary, 5 Greenl. 339 ; Bush v. Shipman, 4 Scam. 186 ; Trustees, &c. v. Tatman, 13 Ill. 27 ; People v. Morris, 13 Wend. 325 ; Mills v. Williams, 11 Ired. 558.

[1] In East Hartford v. Hartford Bridge Co., 10 How. 533, Mr. Justice Woodbury, in speaking of the grant of a ferry franchise to a municipal corporation, says : " Our opinion is . . . . that the parties to this grant did not by their charter stand in the attitude towards each other of making a contract by it, such as is contemplated by the Constitution, and as could not be modified by subsequent legislation. The legislature was acting here on the one part, and public muni-

charged with a trust in favor of an individual, private corporation,

cipal and political corporations on the other. They were acting, too, in relation to a public object, being virtually a highway across the river, over another highway up and down the river. From this standing and relation of these parties, and from the subject-matter of their action, we think that the doings of the legislature as to this ferry must be considered rather as public laws than as contracts. They related to public interests. They changed as those interests demanded. The grantees, likewise, the towns being mere organizations for public purposes, were liable to have their public powers, rights, and duties modified or abolished at any moment by the legislature. They are incorporated for public, and not private objects. They are allowed to hold privileges or property only for public purposes. The members are not shareholders nor joint partners in any corporate estate, which they can sell or devise to others, or which can be attached and levied on for their debts. Hence, generally, the doings between them and the legislature are in the nature of legislation rather than compact, and subject to all the legislative conditions just named, and therefore to be considered not violated by subsequent legislative changes. It is hardly possible to conceive the grounds on which a different result could be vindicated, without destroying all legislative sovereignty, and checking most legislative improvements, as well as supervision over its subordinate public bodies." A different doctrine was advanced by Mr. Justice Barculo, in Benson v. Mayor, &c. of New York, 10 Barb. 234, who cites in support of his opinion, that ferry grants to the city of New York could not be taken away by the legislature, what is said by Chancellor Kent (2 Kent's Com. 275), that "public corporations . . . . may be empowered to take and hold private property for municipal uses; and such property is invested with the security of other private rights. So corporate franchises, attached to public corporations, are legal estates, coupled with an interest, and are protected as private property." This is true in a general sense, and it is also true that, in respect to such property and franchises, the same rules of responsibility are to be applied as in the case of individuals. Bailey v. Mayor, &c. of New York, 3 Hill, 531. But it does not follow that the legislature, under its power to administer the government, of which these agencies are a part, and for the purposes of which the grant has been made, may not at any time modify the municipal powers and privileges, by transferring the grant to some other agency, or revoking it when it seems to have become unimportant. In People v. Power, 25 Ill. 190, Breese, J., in speaking of a law which provided that three fourths of the taxes collected in the county of Sangamon, with certain deductions, should be paid over to the city of Springfield, which is situated therein, says: "While private corporations are regarded as contracts, which the legislature cannot constitutionally impair, as the trustee of the public interests it has the exclusive and unrestrained control over public corporations; and as it may create, so it may modify or destroy, as public exigency requires or the public interests demand. Coles v. Madison County, Breese, 115. Their whole capacities, powers, and duties are derived from the legislature, and subordinate to that power. If, then, the legislature can destroy a county, they can destroy any of its parts, and take from it any one of its powers. The revenues of a county are not the property of the county, in the sense in which revenue of a private person or corporation is regarded. The whole State

or charity, the interest which the *cestui que trust* has under the grant will sustain it against legislative revocation.[1]

Those charters of incorporation, however, which are granted, not as a part of the machinery of the government, but for the private benefit or purposes of the corporators, are held to be contracts between the legislature and the corporators, based, for their consideration, on the liabilities and duties which the corporators assume by accepting them; and the grant of the franchise can no more be resumed by the legislature, or its benefits diminished or impaired without the consent of the grantees, than any other grant of property or valuable thing, unless the right to do so is reserved in the charter itself.[2]

has an interest in the revenue of a county, and for the public good the legislature must have the power to direct its application. The power conferred upon a county to raise a revenue by taxation is a political power, and its application when collected must necessarily be within the control of the legislature for political purposes. The act of the legislature nowhere proposes to take from the county of Sangamon, and give to the city of Springfield, any property belonging to the county, or revenues collected for the use of the county. *But if it did, it would not be objectionable.* But, on the contrary, it proposes alone to appropriate the revenue which may be collected by the county, by taxes levied on property both in the city and county, in certain proportions ratably to the city and county." And see Bush *v.* Shipman, 4 Scam. 190; Richland County *v.* Lawrence County, 12 Ill. 1; Borough of Dunmore's Appeal, 52 Penn. St. 374; Guilford *v.* Supervisors of Chenango, 18 Barb. 615, and 13 N. Y. 143.

[1] See Town of Pawlet *v.* Clark, 9 Cranch, 292, and Terrett *v.* Taylor, 9 Cranch, 43. The municipal corporation holding property or rights in trust might even be abolished without affecting the grant; but the Court of Chancery might be empowered to appoint a new trustee to take charge of the property and to execute the trust. Montpelier *v.* East Montpelier, 29 Vt. 12.

[2] Dartmouth College *v.* Woodward, 4 Wheat. 519; Trustees of Vincennes University *v.* Indiana, 14 How. 268; Planters' Bank *v.* Sharp, 6 How. 301; Piqua Bank *v.* Knoop, 16 How. 369; Binghamton Bridge Case, 3 Wal. 51; Norris *v.* Trustees of Abingdon Academy, 7 G. & J. 7; Grammar School *v.* Burt, 11 Vt. 632; Brown *v.* Hummel, 6 Penn. St. 86; State *v.* Heyward, 3 Rich. 389; People *v.* Manhattan Co., 9 Wend. 351; Commonwealth *v.* Cullen, 13 Penn. St. 133; Commercial Bank of Natchez *v.* State, 14 Miss. 599; Backus *v.* Lebanon, 11 N. H. 19; Michigan State Bank *v.* Hastings, 1 Doug. Mich. 225; Bridge Co. *v.* Hoboken Co., 2 Beas. 81; Miners' Bank *v.* United States, 1 Greene (Iowa), 553; Edwards *v.* Jagers, 19 Ind. 407; State *v.* Noyes, 47 Me. 189; Bruffett *v.* G. W. R. R. Co., 25 Ill. 353; People *v.* Jackson and Michigan Plank Road Co., 9 Mich. 285; Bank of the State *v.* Bank of Cape Fear, 13 Ired. 75; Mills *v.* Williams, 11 Ired. 558; Hawthorne *v.* Calef, 2 Wal. 10; Wales *v.* Stetson, 2 Mass. 146; Nichols *v.* Bertram, 3 Pick. 342; King *v.* Dedham Bank, 15 Mass. 447; State *v.* Tombeckbee Bank, 2 Stew. 30. In Mills *v.* Williams, 11 Ired. 561, Pearson, J. states the dif-

Perhaps the most interesting question which arises in this discussion is, whether it is competent for the legislature to so bind up its own hands by a grant as to preclude it from exercising for the future any of the essential attributes of sovereignty in regard to any of the subjects within its jurisdiction; whether, for instance, it can agree that it will not exercise the power of taxation, or the police power of the State, or the right of eminent domain, as to certain specified property or persons; and whether, if it shall undertake to do so, the agreement is not void on the general principle that the legislature cannot diminish the power of its successors by irrepealable legislation, and that any other rule might cripple and eventually destroy the government itself. If the legislature has power to do this, it is certainly a very dangerous power, exceedingly liable to abuse, and may possibly come in time to make the constitutional provision in question as prolific of evil as it ever has been, or is likely to be, of good.

So far as the power of taxation is concerned, it has been so often decided by the Supreme Court of the United States, though not without remonstrance on the part of State courts,[1] that an agreement by a State, for a consideration received or supposed to be received, that certain property, rights, or franchises shall be exempt from taxation, or be taxed only at a certain

ference between the acts of incorporation of public and private corporations as follows: "The substantial distinction is this. Some corporations are created by the mere will of the legislature, there being no other party interested or concerned. To this party a portion of the power of the legislature is delegated, to be exercised for the general good, and subject at all times to be modified, changed, or annulled. Other corporations are the result of contract. The legislature is not the only party interested; for, although it has a public purpose to be accomplished, it chooses to do it by the instrumentality of a second party. These two parties make a contract. The legislature, for and in consideration of certain labor and outlay of money, confers upon the party of the second part the privilege of being a corporation, with certain power and capacities. The expectation of benefit to the public is the moving consideration on one side, that of expected remuneration for the outlay is the consideration on the other. It is a *contract*, and therefore cannot be modified, changed, or annulled, without the consent of both parties." An incorporated academy, whose endowment comes exclusively from the public, is a public corporation. Dart v. Houston, 22 Geo. 506.

[1] Mechanics & Traders' Bank v. Debolt, 1 Ohio, N. S. 591; Toledo Bank v. Bond, Ibid. 622; Knoop v. Piqua Bank, Ibid. 603; Milan & R. Plank Road Co. v. Husted, 3 Ohio, N. S. 578; Piscataqua Bridge v. N. H. Bridge, 7 N. H. 69; Brewster v. Hough, 10 N. H. 143; Backus v. Lebanon, 11 N. H. 24; Thorpe v. R. & B. R. R. Co., 27 Vt. 140; Brainard v. Colchester, 31 Conn. 410.

agreed rate, is a contract protected by the Constitution, that the question can no longer be considered an open one.[1] In any case, however, there must be a consideration, so that the State can be supposed to have received a beneficial equivalent; and if the exemption is made as a privilege only, it may be revoked at any time.[2]

The power of the legislature to preclude itself in any case from exercising the power of eminent domain is not so clear. It must be conceded, under the authorities, that the State may grant exclusive franchises, — like the right to construct the only railroad which shall be built between certain termini; or the only bridge which shall be permitted over a river between specified limits; or to own the only ferry which shall be permitted at a certain point,[3] — but the grant of an exclusive privilege will not prevent the legislature from exercising the power of eminent domain in respect thereto. Franchises, like every other thing of value, and in the nature of property, within the State, are subject to this power, and any of their incidents may be taken away, or themselves altogether annihilated by means of its exercise.[4] And it is believed that an express agreement in the charter, that the power of eminent domain should not be so exercised as to impair or affect the franchise granted, if not void as an agreement beyond the power of the legislature to make, must be considered as only a valuable portion of the privileges secured by the grant, and as such liable to be appropriated under the power of eminent domain. The exclusive-

[1] New Jersey v. Wilson, 7 Cranch, 164; Gordon v. Appeal Tax Court, 3 How. 133; Piqua Bank v. Knoop, 16 How. 369; Ohio Life & Trust Co. v. Debolt, Ibid. 416; Dodge v. Woolsey, 18 How. 331; Mechanics & Traders' Bank v. Debolt, 18 How. 380; Mechanics & Traders' Bank v. Thomas, Ibid. 384; McGee v. Mathis, 4 Wal. 143. See also Atwater v. Woodbridge, 6 Conn. 223; Osborne v. Humphrey, 7 Conn. 335; Parker v. Redfield, 10 Conn. 495; Landon v. Litchfield, 11 Conn. 251; Herrick v. Randolph, 13 Vt. 525; Armington v. Barnet, 15 Vt. 751.

[2] Christ's Church v. Philadelphia, 24 How. 300; Brainard v. Colchester, 31 Conn. 410.

[3] West River Bridge Co. v. Dix, 16 Vt. 446, and 6 How. 507; Binghampton Bridge case, 3 Wal. 51; Shorter v. Smith, 9 Geo. 529; Piscataqua Bridge v. N. H. Bridge, 7 N. H. 35; Boston Water Power Co. v. Boston & Worcester R. R. Co., 23 Pick. 360; Boston & Lowell R. R. v. Salem & Lowell R. R., 2 Gray, 9.

[4] Matter of Kerr, 42 Barb. 119; Endfield Toll Bridge Co. v. Hartford & N. H. R. R. Co., 17 Conn. 40, 454; West River Bridge Co. v. Dix, 16 Vt. 446, and 6 How. 507.

ness of the grant, and the agreement against interference with it, if valid, constitute elements in its value to be taken into account in assessing compensation; but appropriating the franchise in such a case no more violates the obligation of the contract than does the appropriation of land which the State has granted under an express or implied agreement for quiet enjoyment by the grantee, but which may nevertheless be taken when the public need requires. All grants are subject to this implied condition; and it may well be worthy of inquiry, whether the agreement that a franchise granted shall not afterwards be appropriated can have any other or greater force than words which would make it an exclusive franchise, but which, notwithstanding, would not preclude a subsequent grant on making compensation.[1] The words of the grant are as much in the way of the grant of a conflicting franchise in the one case as in the other.

It has also been intimated in a very able opinion that the

---

[1] Mr. Greenleaf, in a note to his edition of Cruise on Real Property, vol. 2, p. 67, says upon this subject: " In regard to the position that the grant of the franchise of a ferry, bridge, turnpike, or railroad is in its nature exclusive, so that the State cannot interfere with it by the creation of another similar franchise, tending materially to impair its value, it is with great deference submitted that an important distinction should be observed between those powers of government which are essential attributes of sovereignty, indispensable to be always preserved in full vigor, such as the power to create revenues for the public purposes, to provide for the common defence, to provide safe and convenient ways for the public necessity and convenience, and to take private property for public uses, and the like, and those powers which are not thus essential, such as the power to alienate the lands and other property of the State, and to make contracts of service, and of purchase and sale, or the like. Powers of the former class are essential to the constitution of society, as without them no political community can well exist; and necessity requires that they should continue unimpaired. They are intrusted to the legislature to be exercised, not to be bartered away; and it is indispensable that each legislature should assemble with the same measure of sovereign power which was held by its predecessors. Any act of the legislature disabling itself from the future exercise of powers intrusted to it for the public good must be void, being in effect a covenant to desert its paramount duty to the whole people. It is therefore deemed not competent for a legislature to covenant that it will not, under any circumstances, open another avenue for the public travel within certain limits, or in a certain term of time; such covenant being an alienation of sovereign powers, and a violation of public duty." See also Redfield on Railways (3d ed.), vol. 1, p. 258. That the intention to relinquish the right of eminent domain is not to be presumed in any legislative grant, see People v. Mayor, &c. of N. Y., 32 Barb. 113; Illinois & Michigan Canal v. Chicago & R. I. Railroad Co., 14 Ill. 321.

police power of the State could not be alienated even by express grant.[1] And this opinion is supported by those cases where it has been held that licenses to make use of property in certain modes may be revoked by the State, notwithstanding they may be connected with grants and based upon a consideration.[2] But this subject we shall recur to hereafter.

It would seem, therefore, to be the prevailing opinion, and based upon sound reason, that the State could not barter away, or in any manner abridge or weaken, any of those essential powers which are inherent in all governments, and the existence of which in full vigor is important to the well-being of organized society; and that any contracts to that end cannot be enforced under the provision of the national Constitution now under consideration. If the tax cases are to be regarded as an exception to this statement, the exception is perhaps to be considered a nominal rather than a real one, since taxation is for the purpose of providing the State a revenue, and the State laws which have been enforced as contracts in these cases have been supposed to be based upon con-

---

[1] " We think the power of the legislature to control existing railways in this respect may be found in the general control over the police of the country, which resides in the law-making power in all free states, and which is, by the fifth article of the Bill of Rights in this State, expressly declared to reside perpetually and inalienably in the legislature, which is, perhaps, no more than the enunciation of a general principle applicable to all free states, and which cannot therefore be violated so as to deprive the legislature of the power, even by express grant, to any mere public or private corporation. And when the regulation of the police of a city or town, by general ordinances, is given to such cities or towns, and the regulation of their own internal police is given to railroads, to be carried into effect by their by-laws and other regulations, it is, of course, always, in all such cases, subject to the superior control of the legislature.   That is a responsibility which legislatures cannot divest themselves of, if they would." Thorpe v. R. & B. R. R. Co., 27 Vt. 149, per Redfield, Ch. J. See also Indianapolis, &c. R. R. Co. v. Kercheval, 16 Ind. 84 ; Ohio, &c. R. R. Co. v. M'Clelland, 25 Ill. 140. See State v. Noyes, 47 Me. 189, on the same subject.

[2] See, upon this subject, Brick Presbyterian Church v. Mayor, &c. of New York, 5 Cow. 538 ; Vanderbilt v. Adams, 7 Cow. 349 ; Hirn v. State, 1 Ohio, N. S. 15 ; Calder v. Kurby, 5 Gray, 597. Whether a State, after granting licenses to sell liquors for which a fee is received, can revoke them by a general law forbidding sales, quære. See Freleigh v. State, 8 Mo. 606 ; State v. Sterling, Ibid. 697 ; State v. Hawthorn, 9 Mo. 389 ; State v. Phalen, 3 Harr. 441 ; Calder v. Kurby, 5 Gray, 597 ; Adams v. Hacket, 7 Fost. 294. If it has the power, it would seem an act of bad faith to exercise it, without refunding the money received for the license. Hirn v. State, 1 Ohio, N. S. 21.

sideration, by which the State receives the benefit which would have accrued from an exercise of the relinquished power in the ordinary mode.

We have said in another place that citizens have no vested right in the existing general laws of the State which can preclude their amendment or repeal, and there is no implied promise on the part of the State to protect its citizens against incidental injury occasioned by changes in the law. Nevertheless there may be laws which amount to propositions on the part of the State, which, if accepted by individuals, will become binding contracts. Of this class are perhaps to be considered bounty laws, by which the State promises the payment of a gratuity to any one who will do any particular act supposed to be for the State interest. Unquestionably the State may repeal such an act at any time; but when the proposition has been accepted by the performance of the act before the law is repealed, the contract would seem to be complete, and the promised gratuity becomes a legal debt.[1] So where a State was owner of the stock of a bank, and by the law its bills and notes were to be received in payment of all debts due to the State, it was held that this law constituted a contract with those who should receive the bills before its repeal, and that a repeal of the law could not deprive these holders of the right which it assured.[2] Such a law, with the acceptance of the bills under it, " comes within the definition of a contract. It is a contract founded upon a good and valuable consideration, — a consideration beneficial to the State, as its profits are increased by sustaining the credit, and consequently extending the circulation of the paper of the bank."

That laws permitting the dissolution of the contract of marriage are not within the intention of the clause of the Constitution under discussion seems to be the prevailing opinion.[3] It has been intimated, however, that, so far as property rights are concerned, the contract must stand on the same footing as any other, and that a law passed after the marriage, vesting the property in the wife for her sole use, would be void, as impairing the obligation of con-

---

[1] People v. Auditor-General, 9 Mich. 327. See Montgomery v. Kasson, 16 Cal. 189.

[2] Woodruff v. Trapnall, 10 How. 190. See Winter v. Jones, 10 Geo. 190.

[3] Per Marshall, Ch. J., Dartmouth College v. Woodward, 4 Wheat. 629; Maguire v. Maguire, 7 Dana, 183; Clark v. Clark, 10 N. H. 385.

tracts.[1] But certainly there is no such contract embraced in the marriage as would prevent the legislature changing the law, and vesting in the wife solely all property which she should acquire thereafter ; and if the property had already become vested in the husband, it would be protected in him, against legislative transfer to the wife, on other grounds than that here indicated.

" *The obligation of a contract,*" it is said, " consists in its binding force on the party who makes it. This depends upon the laws in existence when it is made ; these are necessarily referred to in all contracts, and forming a part of them as the measure of the obligation to perform them by the one party, and the right acquired by the other. There can be no other standard by which to ascertain the extent of either, than that which the terms of the contract indicate, according to their settled legal meaning ; when it becomes consummated, the law defines the duty and the right, compels one party to perform the thing contracted for, and gives the other a right to enforce the performance by the remedies then in force. If any subsequent law affect to diminish the duty, or to impair the right, it necessarily bears on the obligation of the contract, in favor of one party, to the injury of the other ; hence any law which, in its operations, amounts to a denial or obstruction of the rights accruing by a contract, though professing to act only on the remedy, is directly obnoxious to the prohibition of the Constitution." [2] " It is the civil obligation of contracts which [the Constitution] is designed to reach ; that is, the obligation which is recog-

---

[1] Holmes v. Holmes, 4 Barb. 295.

[2] McCracken v. Hayward, 2 How. 612.   " The obligation of a contract . . . . is the law which binds the parties to perform their agreement. The law, then, which has this binding obligation, must govern and control the contract, in every shape in which it is intended to bear upon it, whether it affects its validity, construction, or discharge. It is, then, the municipal law of the State, whether that be written or unwritten, which is emphatically the law of the contract made within the State, and must govern it throughout, whenever its performance is sought to be enforced." Washington, J., in Ogden v. Saunders, 12 Wheat. 259. " As I understand it, the law of the contract forms its obligation." Thompson, J., Ibid. 302. " The obligation of the contract consists in the power and efficacy of the law which applies to, and enforces performance of, the contract, or the payment of an equivalent for non-performance. The obligation does not inhere and subsist in the contract itself, *proprio vigore*, but in the law applicable to the contract. This is the sense, I think, in which the Constitution uses the term ' obligation.' "   Trimble, J., Ibid. 318. And see Van Baumbach v. Bade, 9 Wis. 577 ; Johnson v. Higgins, 3 Met. (Ky.) 566.

nized by, and results from, the law of the State in which it is made. If, therefore, a contract when made is by the law of the place declared to be illegal, or deemed to be a nullity, or a *nude pact*, it has no civil obligation, because the law, in such cases, forbids its having any binding efficacy or force. It confers no legal right on the one party and no correspondent legal duty on the other. There is no means allowed or recognized to enforce it; for the maxim is *ex nudo pacto non oritur actio*. But when it does not fall within the predicament of being either illegal or void, its obligatory force is coextensive with its stipulations." [1]

Such being the obligation of a contract, it is obvious that the rights of the parties in respect to it are liable to be affected in many ways by changes in the laws, which it could not have been the intention of the constitutional provision to preclude. "There are few laws which concern the general police of a State, or the government of its citizens, in their intercourse with each other or with strangers, which may not in some way or other affect the contracts which they have entered into or may thereafter form. For what are laws of evidence, or which concern remedies, frauds, and perjuries, laws of registration, and those which affect landlord and tenant, sales at auction, acts of limitation, and those which limit the fees of professional men, and the charges of tavern-keepers, and a multitude of others which crowd the codes of every State, but laws which affect the validity, construction, or duration, or discharge of contracts." [2] But the changes in these laws are not regarded as necessarily affecting the obligation of contracts." Whatever belongs merely to the remedy may be altered according to the will of the State, provided the alteration does not impair the obligation of the contract; [3] and it does not impair it, provided it leaves the parties a substantial remedy, according to the course of justice as it existed at the time the contract was made. [4]

---

[1] Story on Const. § 1380.

[2] Washington, J., in Ogden v. Saunders, 12 Wheat. 259.

[3] Bronson v. Kinzie, 1 How. 316, per Taney, Ch. J.

[4] Stocking v. Hunt, 3 Denio, 274; Van Baumbach v. Bade, 9 Wis. 578; Bronson v. Kinzie, 1 How. 316; McCracken v. Hayward, 2 How. 608; Butler v. Palmer, 1 Hill, 324; Van Renselaer v. Snyder, 9 Barb. 302, and 13 N. Y. 299; Conkey v. Hart, 14 N. Y. 22; Guild v. Rogers, 8 Barb. 502; Story v. Furman, 25 N. Y. 214; Coriell v. Ham, 4 Greene (Iowa), 455; Heyward v. Judd, 4 Minn. 483; Swift v. Fletcher, 6 Minn. 550; Maynes·v. Moor, 16 Ind. 116; Smith v.

It has accordingly been held that laws changing remedies for the enforcement of legal contracts will be valid, notwithstanding the new remedy is less convenient than the old, or less prompt and speedy.[1]

" Without impairing the obligation of the contract, the remedy may certainly be modified as the wisdom of the nation shall direct." [2]   And although the law at the time the contract is made permits the creditor to take the body of his debtor in execution, there can be no doubt of the right to abolish all laws for this purpose.   " Confinement of the debtor may be a punishment for not performing his contract, or may be allowed as a means of inducing him to perform it.   But the State may refuse to inflict this punishment, or may withhold this means, and leave the contract in full force.   Imprisonment is no part of the contract, and simply to release the prisoner does not impair the obligation." [3]   Nor is there any constitutional objection to those laws which except certain portions of a debtor's property from execution being so modified as to increase the exemptions, and the modifications made applicable to contracts previously entered into.   The State " may, if it thinks proper, direct that the necessary implements of agriculture, or the tools of the mechanic, or articles of necessity in household furniture, shall, like wearing apparel, not be liable to execution on judgments.   Regulations of this description have always been considered, in every civilized community, as properly belonging to the remedy, to be exercised or not, by every sovereignty, according to its own views of policy and humanity.   It

---

Packard, 12 Wis. 371 ; Grosvenor v. Chesley, 48 Me. 369 ; Van Renselaer v. Ball, 19 N. Y. 100 ; Van Renselaer v. Hays, Ibid. 68 ; Litchfield v. McComber, 42 Barb. 288 ; Paschal v. Perez, 7 Texas, 365 ; Auld v. Butcher, 2 Kansas, 155 ; Kenyon v. Stewart, 44 Penn. St. 179 ; Clark v. Martin, 49 Penn. St. 299 ; Rison v. Farr, 24 Ark. 161 ; Sanders v. Hillsborough Insurance Co., 44 N. H. 238 ; Huntzinger v. Brock, 3 Grant's Cases, 243 ; Mechanics', &c. Bank Appeal, 31 Conn. 63.

[1] Ogden v. Saunders, 12 Wheat. 270 ; Beers v. Haughton, 9 Pet. 359 ; Bumgardner v. Circuit Court, 4 Mo. 50 ; Tarpley v. Hamer, 17 Miss. 310 ; Quackenbush v. Danks, 1 Dénio, 128, 3 Denio, 594, and 1 N. Y. 129 ; Bronson v. Newberry, 2 Doug. Mich. 38 ; Rockwell v. Hubbell's Adm's, Ibid. 197 ; Evans v. Montgomery, 4 W. & S. 218 ; Holloway v. Sherman, 12 Iowa, 282 ; Sprecker v. Wakeley, 11 Wis. 432 ; Smith v. Packard, 12 Wis. 371 ; Morse v. Goold, 11 N. Y. 281.

[2] Sturges v. Crowninshield, 4 Wheat. 122, per Marshall, Ch. J.

[3] Sturges v. Crowninshield, 4 Wheat. 122, per Marshall, Ch. J. ; Mason v. Haile, 12 Wheat. 370 ; Bronson v. Newberry, 2 Doug. (Mich.) 38.

must reside in every State to enable it to secure its citizens from unjust and harassing litigation, and to protect them in those pursuits which are necessary to the existence and well-being of every community." [1]

And laws which change the rules of evidence relate to the remedy only; and while, as we have elsewhere shown, such laws may, on general principles, be applied to existing causes of action, so, too, it is plain that they are not precluded from such application by the constitutional clause we are considering.[2] And it has been held that the legislature may even take away a common-law remedy altogether, without substituting any in its place, if another and efficient remedy remains. Thus, a law abolishing distress for rent has been sustained as applicable to leases in force at its passage; [3] and it was also held that an express stipulation in the lease, that the lessor should have this remedy, would not prevent the legislature from abolishing it, because this was a subject concerning which it was not competent for the parties to contract in such manner as to bind the hands of the State. In the language of the court: "If this is a subject on which parties can contract, and if their contracts when made become by virtue of the Constitution of the United States superior to the power of the legislature, then it follows that whatever at any time exists as part of the machinery for the administration of justice may be perpetuated, if parties choose so to agree. That this can scarcely have been within the contemplation of the makers of the Constitution, and that if it prevail as law it will give rise to grave inconveniences, is quite obvious. Every such stipulation is in its own nature conditional upon the lawful continuance of the process. The State is no party to

---

[1] Bronson v. Kinzie, 1 How. 311, per Taney, Ch. J.: Rockwell v. Hubbell's Adm's, 2 Doug. (Mich.) 197; Quackenbush v. Danks, 1 Denio, 128, 3 Denio, 594, and 1 N. Y. 129; Morse v. Goold, 11 N. Y. 281; Sprecker v. Wakeley, 11 Wis. 432. "Statutes pertaining to the remedy are merely such as relate to the course and form of proceedings, but do not affect the substance of a judgment when pronounced." Per Merrick, Ch. J., in Morton v. Valentine, 15 La. An. 153.

[2] Neass v. Mercer, 15 Barb. 318. On this subject see the discussions in the Federal courts; Sturges v. Crowninshield, 4 Wheat. 122; Ogden v. Saunders, 12 Wheat. 213; Bronson v. Kinzie, 1 How. 311; McCracken v. Hayward, 2 How. 608.

[3] Van Renselaer v. Snyder, 9 Barb. 302, and 13 N. Y. 299; Guild v. Rogers, 8 Barb. 502; Conkey v. Hart, 14 N. Y. 22.

their contract. It is bound to afford adequate process for the enforcement of rights; but it has not tied its own hands as to the modes by which it will administer justice. Those from necessity belong to the supreme power to prescribe; and their continuance is not the subject of contract between private parties. In truth, it is not at all probable that the parties made their agreement with reference to the possible abolition of distress for rent. The first clause of this special provision is, that the lessor may distrain, sue, re-enter, or resort to any other legal remedy, and the second is, that in cases of distress the lessee waives the exemption of certain property from the process, which by law was exempted. This waiver of exemption was undoubtedly the substantial thing which the parties had in view; but yet perhaps their language cannot be confined to this object, and it may therefore be proper to consider the contract as if it had been their clear purpose to preserve their legal remedy, even if the legislature should think fit to abolish it. In that aspect of it the contract was a subject over which they had no control." [1]

But a law which deprives a party of all legal remedy must necessarily be void. " If the legislature of the State were to undertake to make a law preventing the legal remedy upon a contract lawfully made, and binding on the party to it, there is no question that such legislature would, by such act, exceed its legitimate powers. Such an act must necessarily impair the obligation of the contract within the meaning of the Constitution." [2] And a law which takes from certain classes of persons the right to maintain suits, because of having participated in rebellion against the government, is void on the same ground. [3] And where a statute does not leave a party a substantial remedy according to the course of justice as it existed at the time the contract was made, but shows upon its face an intention to clog, hamper, or embarrass the proceedings to enforce the remedy, so as to destroy it entirely, and thus impair the contract so far as it is in the

---

[1] Conkey v. Hart, 14 N. Y. 30; citing Handy v. Chatfield, 23 Wend. 35; Mason v. Haile, 12 Wheat. 370; Stocking v. Hunt, 3 Denio, 274; and Van Rensselaer v. Snyder, 13 N. Y. 299.

[2] Call v. Hagger, 8 Mass. 430. See Griffin v. Wilcox, 21 Ind. 370.

[3] Rison v. Farr, 24 Ark. 161; McFarland v. Butler, 8 Minn. 116; Jackson v. Same, Ibid. 117.

19

power of the legislature to do it, such statute cannot be regarded as a regulation of the remedy, and is void.[1]

And where a statute dividing a town and incorporating a new one enacted that the new town should pay its proportion towards the support of paupers then constituting a charge against the old town, it was held that a subsequent statute exonerating the new town from this liability was void as impairing the contract created by the first-mentioned statute.[2] And in any case the lawful repeal of a statute cannot constitutionally be made to destroy contracts which have been entered into under it.[3]

So where, by its terms, a contract provides for the payment of money by one party to another, and, by the law then in force, property would be liable to be seized, and sold on execution to the highest bidder, to satisfy any judgment recovered on such contract, a subsequent law, forbidding property from being sold on execution for less than two thirds the valuation made by appraisers, pursuant to the directions contained in the law, though professing to act only on the remedy, amounts to a denial or obstruction of the rights accruing by the contract, and is directly obnoxious to the prohibition of the Constitution.[4] So a law which takes away from .mortgagees the right to possession under their mortgages until after foreclosure is void, because depriving them of the right to the rents and profits, which was a valuable portion of the right secured by the contract. " By this act the mortgagee is required to incur the additional expense of foreclosure, before obtaining possession, and is deprived of the right to add to his security, by the perception of the rents and profits of the premises, during the time required to accomplish this and the time of redemption, and during that time the rents and profits are given to another, who may or may not appropriate them to the payment of the debt, as he chooses, and the mortgagee in the

---

[1] Oatman v. Bond, 15 Wis. 28.

[2] Bowdoinham v. Richmond, 6 Greenl. 12.

[3] Tuolumne Redemption Co. v. Sedgwick, 15 Cal. 515; McCauley v. Brooks, 16 Cal. 11; Commonwealth v. New Bedford Bridge, 2 Gray, 339; State v. Phalen, 3 Harr. 441; State v. Hawthorn, 9 Mo. 389.

[4] McCracken v. Hayward, 2 How. 608; Willard v. Longstreet, 2 Doug. Mich. 172; Rawley v. Hooker, 21 Ind. 144. So a law which, as to existing mortgages foreclosable by sale, prohibits the sale for less than half the appraised value of the land, is void for the same reason. Gantley's Lessee v. Ewing, 3 How. 707; Bronson v. Kinzie, 1 How. 311.

mean time is subjected to the risk, often considerable, of the depreciation in the value of the security." [1] So a law which extends the time for the redemption of lands sold on execution, or for delinquent taxes, after the sales have been made; for in such a case the contract with the purchaser, and for which he has paid his money, is, that he shall have title at the time then provided by the law; and to extend the time for redemption is to alter the substance of the contract, as much as would be the extension of the time for payment of a promissory note. [2] So a law which shortens the time for redemption from a mortgage, after a foreclosure sale has taken place, is void; the rights of the party being fixed by the foreclosure and the law then in force, and the mortgagor being entitled, under the law, to possession of the land until the time of redemption expires. [3] And where by statute a purchaser of lands from the State had the right, upon the forfeiture of his contract of purchase for the non-payment of the sum due upon it, to revive it at any time before a public sale of the lands, by the payment of all sums due upon the contract, with a penalty of five per cent, it was held that this right could not be taken away by a subsequent change in the law which subjected the forfeited lands to private entry and sale. [4] And a statute which

---

[1] Mundy v. Monroe, 1 Mich. 76; Blackwood v. Vanvleet, 11 Mich. 252. Compare Dikeman v. Dikeman, 11 Paige, 484, and James v. Stull, 9 Barb. 482. In the last case it was held that a statute shortening the notice to be given on foreclosure of a mortgage under the power of sale, from twenty-four to twelve weeks, was valid as affecting the remedy only; and that a stipulation in a mortgage that on default being made in payment the mortgagee might sell "according to law," meant according to the law as it should be when sale was made.

[2] Robinson v. Howe, 13 Wis. 341; Dikeman v. Dikeman, 11 Paige, 484; Goenen v. Schroeder, 8 Minn. 387. But see Stone v. Basset, 4 Minn. 298; Heyward v. Judd, Ibid. 483; Freeborn v. Pettibone, 5 Minn. 277.

[3] Cagill v. Power, 1 Mich. 369. The contrary ruling was made in Butler v. Palmer, 1 Hill, 324, by analogy to the statute of limitations. The statute, it was said, was no more in effect than saying: "Unless you redeem within the shorter time prescribed, you shall have no action for a recovery of the land, nor shall your defence against an action be allowed, provided you get possession." And in Robinson v. Howe, 13 Wis. 346, the court, speaking of a similar right in a party, say: "So far as his right of redemption was concerned, it was not derived from any contract, but was given by the law only; and the time within which he might exercise it might be shortened by the legislature, provided a reasonable time was left in which to exercise it, without impairing the obligation of any contract." And see Smith v. Packard, 12 Wis. 371, to the same effect.

[4] State v. Commissioners of School and University Lands, 4 Wis. 414.

authorizes stay of execution, for an unreasonable or indefinite
period, on judgments rendered on pre-existing contracts, is void, as
postponing payment, and taking away all remedy during the continuance of the stay.[1] And a law is void on this ground which
declares a forfeiture of the charter of a corporation for that which
was no cause of forfeiture before.[2] And it has been held that
where a statute authorized a municipal corporation to issue bonds,
and to exercise the power of local taxation in order to pay them,
and persons bought and paid value for bonds issued accordingly,
the power of taxation thus given is a contract which cannot be
withdrawn until the bonds are satisfied ; and that an attempt to
repeal or restrict it by statute is void, and unless the corporation
imposes and collects the tax in all respects as if the subsequent
statute had not been passed, it will be compelled to do so by mandamus.[3] And it has also been held that a statute repealing a
former statute, which made the stock of stockholders in a corporation liable for its debts, was, in respect to creditors existing at
the time of the repeal, a law impairing the obligation of contracts.[4] In each of these cases it is evident that substantial rights

---

[1] Chadwick v. Moore, 8 W. & S. 49; Bunn v. Gorgas, 41 Penn. St. 441;
Stevens v. Andrews, 31 Mo. 205; Hasbrouck v. Shipman, 16 Wis. 296. In Brei-
tenbach v. Bush, 44 Penn. St. 313, and Coxe v. Martin, Ibid. 322, it was held that
an act staying all civil process against volunteers who had enlisted in the national
service for three years or during the war was valid, — "during the war" being
construed to mean unless the war should sooner terminate. See also State v.
Carew, 13 Rich. 498. A general law that all suits pending should be continued
until peace between the Confederate States and the United States, was held void
in Burt v. Williams, 24 Ark. 94. But see McCormick v. Rusch, 15 Iowa, 127.
So was a law staying all proceedings against volunteers who had enlisted "during
the war," this period being indefinite. Clark v. Martin, 3 Grant's Cas. 393. In
Johnson v. Higgins, 3 Met. (Ky.) 566, it was held that the act of the Kentucky
legislature of May 24, 1861, which forbade the rendition, in all the courts of the
State, of any judgment from date till January 1st, 1862, was valid. It related, it
was said, not to the remedy for enforcing a contract, but to the courts which administer the remedy ; and those courts, in a legal sense, constitute no part of the
remedy. A law exempting soldiers from civil process until thirty days after their
discharge from military service was held valid as to all contracts subsequently
entered into, in Bruns v. Crawford, 34 Mo. 330.

[2] People v. Jackson & Michigan Plank Road Co., 9 Mich. 285, per Christiancy,
J.; State v. Tombeckbee Bank, 2 Stew. 30.

[3] Van Hoffman v. Quincy, 4 Wal. 535. See also Soutter v. Madison, 15 Wis.
30; Smith v. Appleton, 19 Wis. 468.

[4] Hawthorne v. Calef, 2 Wal. 10.

were affected ; and where the laws which were held void operated upon the remedy, they either had an effect equivalent to importing some new stipulation into the contract, or they failed to leave the party a substantial remedy such as was assured to him by the law in force when the contract was made.   In Pennsylvania it has been held that a statute authorizing a stay of execution on contracts in which the debtor had waived the right was unconstitutional ;[1] but it seems to us that an agreement to waive a legal privilege which the law gives as a matter of state policy cannot be binding upon a party, unless the law itself provides for the waiver.[2]

Where, however, by the operation of existing laws, a contract cannot be enforced without some new action of a party to fix his liability, it is as competent to prescribe by statute the requisites to the legal validity of such act as it would be in any case to prescribe the legal requisites of a contract to be thereafter made.   Thus, though a verbal promise is sufficient to revive a debt barred by the statute of limitations or by bankruptcy, yet this rule may be changed by a statute making all such future promises void unless in writing.[3]   It is also equally true that where a legal impediment exists to the enforcement of a contract which parties have entered into, the constitutional provision in question will not preclude the legislature from removing such impediment and validating the contract.   A statute of that description would not impair the obligation of contracts, but would perfect and enforce it.[4]   And the obligation of contracts is not impaired by continuing the charter of a corporation for three years, for the purpose of closing its business.[5]

One other topic remains to be mentioned in this connection, and that is, as to the power of the States to pass insolvent laws, and the classes of contracts to which they may be made to apply. As this whole subject has been gone over very often and very fully by the Supreme Court of the United States, and the important questions seem at last to be finally set at rest, we shall

---

[1] Billmeyer v. Evans, 40 Penn. St. 324; Lewis v. Lewis, 44 Penn. St. 127.

[2] See Conkey v. Hart, 14 N. Y. 30 ; Handy v. Chatfield, 23 Wend. 35.

[3] Joy v. Thompson, 1 Doug. (Mich.) 373 ; Kingsley v. Cousins, 47 Me. 91.

[4] As where the defence of usury to a contract is taken away by statute. Welch v. Wadsworth, 30 Conn. 149 ; Curtis v. Leavitt, 15 N. Y. 9. And see Wood v. Kennedy, 19 Ind. 68, and the cases cited, post, ch. 11.

[5] Foster v. Essex Bank, 16 Mass. 245.

content ourselves with giving what we understand to be the conclusions of the court.

1. The several States have power to legislate on the subject of
bankrupt and insolvent laws, subject, however, to the authority
conferred upon Congress by the Constitution to adopt a uniform
system of bankruptcy, which authority, when exercised, is paramount, and State enactments in conflict with those of Congress
upon the subject must give way.[1]

2. Such State laws, however, discharging the person or the
property of the debtor, and thereby terminating the legal obligation of the debts, cannot constitutionally be made to apply to
contracts entered into before they were passed, but they may be
made applicable to such future contracts as can be considered as
having been made in reference to them.[2]

3. Contracts made within a State where an insolvent law exists,
between citizens of that State, are to be considered as made in
reference to the law, and are subject to its provisions. But the
law cannot apply to a contract made in one State between a
citizen thereof and a citizen of another State,[3] nor to contracts
not made within the State, even though made between citizens of
the same State,[4] except, perhaps, where they are citizens of the
State passing the law.[5] And where the contract is made between
a citizen of one State and a citizen of another, the circumstance
that the contract is made payable in the State where the insolvent
law exists will not render such contract subject to be discharged
under the law.[6] If, however, the creditor in any of these cases
makes himself a party to proceedings under the insolvent law, he
will be bound thereby like any other party to judicial proceedings,
and is not to be heard afterwards to object that his debt was
excluded by the Constitution from being affected by the law.[7]

[1] Sturges v. Crowninshield, 4 Wheat. 122; Farmers & Mechanics' Bank v. Smith,
6 Wheat. 131; Ogden v. Saunders, 12 Wheat. 213; Baldwin v. Hale, 1 Wal.
229.

[2] Ogden v. Saunders, 12 Wheat. 213.

[3] Ogden v. Saunders, 12 Wheat. 213; Springer v. Foster, 2 Story, 387; Boyle v.
Zacharie, 6 Pet. 348; Woodhull v. Wagner, Baldw. 300; Suydam v. Broadnax,
14 Pet. 75; Cook v. Moffat, 5 How. 310; Baldwin v. Hale, 1 Wal. 231.

[4] McMillan v. McNeill, 4 Wheat. 209.

[5] Marsh v. Putnam, 3 Gray, 551.

[6] Baldwin v. Hale, 1 Wal. 223; Baldwin v. Bank of Newberry, Ibid. 234; Gilman v. Lockwood, 4 Wal. 409.

[7] Clay v. Smith, 3 Pet. 411; Baldwin v. Hale, 1 Wal. 223; Gilman v. Lockwood, 4 Wal. 409.

CHAPTER X.

OF THE CONSTITUTIONAL PROTECTIONS TO PERSONAL LIBERTY.

ALTHOUGH the people from whom we derive our laws now possess a larger share of civil and political liberty than any other in Europe, there was a period in their history when a considerable proportion were villeins or slaves. Of the servile classes, one portion were *villeins regardant*, or serfs attached to the soil and transferable with it, but not otherwise; while the other portion were *villeins in gross*, whose condition resembled that of the slaves known to the modern law in America.[1] How these people became reduced to this unhappy condition, it may not be possible at this distance of time to determine with entire accuracy; but in regard to the first class, we may suppose that, when a conqueror seized the territory upon which he found them living, he seized also the people as a part of the lawful prize of war, granting them life on condition of their cultivating the soil for his use; and that the second class were more often persons whose lives had been spared on the field of battle, and whose ownership, in accordance with the customs of barbarous times, would pertain to the persons of their captors. Many other causes also contributed to this condition.[2] At the beginning of the reign of John it has been estimated that one half of the Anglo-Saxons were in a condition of servitude. Their treatment was such as might have been expected from masters trained to war and violence, accustomed to think lightly of human life and human suffering, and who knew little and cared less for any doctrine of the rights of man which was applicable to any other than the governing classes.[3]

It would be idle to attempt to follow the imperceptible steps by

---

[1] Co. Lit. § 181 ; 2 Bl. Com. 92.

[2] Hallam's Middle Ages, ch. 2, part 2 ; Vaughan's Revolutions in English History, Book 2, ch. 8.

[3] For a view of the condition of the servile classes, see Wright's Domestic Manners and Sentiments, 101, 102; Crabbe's History of English Law (ed. of 1829), pp. 8, 78, 365 ; Hallam's Middle Ages, ch. 2, part 2 ; Vaughan's Revolutions in English History, Book 2, ch. 8.

which slavery at length ceased to exist in England. It was never abolished by statute;[1] and the time when serfdom ceased altogether cannot be accurately determined.[2] The causes were at work silently for centuries; the historian did not at the time note them; the statesman did not observe them; they were not the subject of agitation or controversy; but the time came when the philanthropist could look over the laws of his country, and declare that slavery had ceased to be recognized by them, though at what precise point in legal history the condition became unlawful he might not be able to determine. Among the causes for its abolition he might be able to enumerate: 1. That the slaves were of the same race with their masters. There was therefore not only an absence of that antipathy which is so often found existing when the ruling and the ruled are of different race, and especially of different color, but instead thereof an active sympathy might often be supposed to exist, which would lead to frequent emancipations. 2. The common law presumed every man to be free until proved to be otherwise; and this presumption, when the slave was of the same race as his master, and had no natural badge of servitude, must often have rendered it extremely difficult to recover the fugitive who denied his thraldom. 3. A residence for a year and a day in a corporate town rendered the villein legally free;[3] so that to him the towns constituted cities of

[1] Barrington on the Statutes (3d ed.), 272.

[2] Mr. Hargrave says, at the commencement of the seventeenth century. 20 State Trials, 40; May's Const. Hist. ch. 11. And Mr. Barrington, p. 278, cites from Rymer a commission from Queen Elizabeth, in the year 1574, directed to Lord Burghley and Sir Walter Mildmay, for inquiring into the lands, tenements, and other goods of all her bondmen and bondwomen in the counties of Cornwall, Devonshire, Somerset, and Gloucester, such as were by blood in a slavish condition, by being born in any of her manors, and to compound with any or all of such bondmen or bondwomen for their manumission and freedom. And this commission, he says, in connection with other circumstances, explains why we hear no more of this kind of servitude. And see Crabbe's History of English Law, 574 (ed. of 1829). This author says that villeinage had disappeared by the time of Charles II. Hurd says in 1661. Law of Freedom and Bondage, vol. 1, p. 136. And see 2 Bl. Com. 96. Macaulay says there were traces of slavery under the Stuarts. History of England, ch. 1. Hume thinks there was no law recognizing it after the time of Henry VII., and that it had ceased before the death of Elizabeth. History of England, ch. 23.

[3] Crabbe's History of English Law (ed. of 1829), p. 79. But this was only as to third persons. The claim of the lord might be made within three years. Ibid. And see Mackintosh's History of England, ch. 4.

refuge.   4. The lord treating him as a freeman, as by receiving homage from him as tenant, or entering into a contract with him under seal, thereby emancipated him, by recognizing in him a capacity to perform those acts which a freeman only can perform. 5. Even the lax morals of the times were favorable to liberty, since the condition of the child followed that of the father; [1] and in law the *nullius filius* had no father.   And 6. The influence of the priesthood was generally against slavery, and must often have shielded the fugitive, and influenced emancipations by appeals to the conscience, especially when the master was near the close of life, and when the conscience would naturally be most sensitive.[2]   And with all these influences there was the further fact that a class of freemen was always near to the slaves in condition and suffering, with whom they were in association, and between whom and themselves there were frequent intermarriages,[3] and that from thence to the highest order in the state there were successive grades; the children of the highest gradually finding their way into those below them, and ways being open by which the children of the lowest might advance themselves by native intellect, energy, or thrift, through the successive grades above them, until the descendants of dukes and earls might be found cultivating the soil, and the man of obscure birth winning his place among the hereditary aristocracy of the realm, through his successful exertions at the bar, or his services to the state in some other capacity.   Inevitably these influences must overthrow the

---

[1] Barrington on Statutes (3d ed.), 276, note; 2 Bl. Com. 93.   But in the very quaint account of "villeinage and niefty," in Mirror of Justices, § 28, it is said, among other things, that "those are villeins who are begotten of a freeman and a nief, and born out of matrimony."   The ancient rule seems to have been that the condition of the child followed that of the mother, but this was changed in the time of Henry I.   Crabbe's History of English Law (ed. of 1829), p. 78; Hallam's Middle Ages, ch. 2, part 2.

[2] In 1514, Henry VIII. manumitted two of his villeins in the following words: "Whereas God created all men free, but afterwards the laws and customs of nations subjected some under the yoke of servitude, we think it *pious and meritorious with God* to manumit Henry Knight, a tailor, and John Herle, a husbandman, our natives, as being born within the manor of Stoke Clymerceysland, in our county of Cornwall, together with all their issue born or to be born, and all their goods, lands, and chattels acquired, so as the said persons and their issue shall from henceforth by us be free and of free condition."   Barrington on Statutes (3d ed.), 275.   See also Mackintosh's England, ch. 4.

[3] Wright's Domestic Manners and Sentiments, 112.

slavery of white men that existed in England,[1] and no other ever became established within the realm. Slavery was permitted, and, indeed, fostered, in the Colonies; in part because a profit was made of the trade, and in part also because it was supposed that the peculiar products of some of them could not be profitably cultivated with free labor; and at times masters brought their slaves with them to England and removed them again without question, until in Sommersett's case, in 1771, it was ruled by Lord Mansfield that slavery was repugnant to the common law, and to bring a slave to England was to emancipate him.[2] The same opinion had been previously expressed by Lord Holt, but without authoritative decision.[3]

In Scotland a condition of servitude continued to a later period. The holding of negroes in slavery was, indeed, held to be illegal

[1] Macaulay says the chief instrument of emancipation was the Christian religion. History of England, ch. 1. Mackintosh also attributes great influence to the priesthood in this reform, not only by their direct appeals to the conscience, but by the judges, who were ecclesiastics, multiplying presumptions and rules of evidence consonant to the equal and humane spirit which breathes throughout the morality of the Gospel. History of England, ch. 4. Hume seems to think emancipation was brought about by selfish considerations on the part of the barons, and from a conviction that the returns from their lands would be increased by changing villeinage into socage tenures. History of England, ch. 23.

[2] Lofft's Rep. 18; 20 Howell's St. Trials, 1; Life of Granville Sharp, by Hoare, ch. 4; Hurd's Law of Freedom and Bondage, vol. 1, 189.

[3] Smith v. Brown, 2 Salk. 666. "The plaintiff declared in *indebitatus assumpsit* for 20*l.* for a negro sold by the plaintiff to the defendant, namely, in *Parochia beatæ Mariæ de Arcubus in Warda de Cheape,* and verdict for plaintiff, and on motion in arrest of judgment Holt, Ch. J., held, that as soon as a negro comes into England he becomes free : one may be a villein in England, but not a slave. And per Powell, J., in a villein the owner has property, but it is an inheritance ; in a word he has property, but it is a chattel real : the law took no notice of a negro. Holt, Ch. J. : You should have averred in your declaration that the sale was in Virginia, and by the laws of that country negroes are salable: for the laws of England do not extend to Virginia : being a conquered country, their law is what the king pleases; and we cannot take notice of it but as set forth: wherefore he directed the plaintiff should amend, and the declaration should be made, that the defendant was indebted to the plaintiff for a negro sold here in London, but that the said negro at the time of the sale was in Virginia, and that negroes by the laws and statutes of Virginia are salable as chattels. Then the attorney-general, coming in, said they were inheritances, and transferable by deed, and not without. And nothing was done." See also Smith v. Gould, Ld. Raym. 1274, S. C., Salk. 666. There is a learned note in Quincy's Rep. p. 94, collecting the English authorities on the subject of slavery.

soon after the Sommersett case ; but the salters and colliers did not acquire their freedom until 1799, nor without an act of Parliament.[1] A previous statute for their enfranchisement through judicial proceedings had proved ineffectual.[2]

The history of slavery in this country pertains rather to general history than to a work upon constitutional law. Throughout the land involuntary servitude is abolished by constitutional amendment, except in the punishment of crime. Nor will the exception permit the convict to be subjected to other servitude than such as is under the control and direction of the public authorities, in the manner heretofore customary. The laws of the various States permit the letting of the services of the convicts, either singly or in gross, to contractors who are to employ them in mechanical trades within or near the prison, and under the surveillance of its officers ; but it might well be doubted if a law which should allow the convict to be placed upon the auction-block and sold to the highest bidder, either for life or for a less period, was in harmony with the spirit of the constitutional prohibition. It is certain that it would be open to very grave abuses, and it is so inconsistent with the general sentiment in countries where slavery does not exist, that it may well be believed not to have been within the understanding of the people in incorporating the exception with the prohibitory amendment.

Unreasonable Searches and Seizures.

Near in importance to exemption from any arbitrary control of the person is that maxim of the common law which secures to the citizen immunity in his home against the prying eyes of the government, and protection in person, property, and papers even against the process of the law, except in a few specified cases. The maxim that " every man's house is his castle "[3] is made a

---

[1] 39 Geo. III. ch. 56.

[2] May's Const. Hist. ch. 11.

[3] Broom's Maxims, 321. Every one remembers the eloquent passage from Chatham : " The poorest man may, in his cottage, bid defiance to all the forces of the crown. It may be frail ; its roof may shake ; the wind may blow through it ; the storm may enter ; the rain may enter ; but the king of England may not enter ; all his force dares not cross the threshold of the ruined tenement." Speech on General Warrants. And see Lieber, Civil Liberty and Self-Government, ch. 6.

part of our constitutional law in the clause prohibiting unreasonable searches and seizures; and in the protection it affords, it is worthy of all the encomiums which have been bestowed upon it.

If in English history we inquire into the original occasion for these constitutional provisions, we shall probably find that they had their origin in the abuse of executive authority, and in the unwarrantable intrusion of executive agents into the houses and among the private papers of individuals, in order to obtain evidence of political or intended political offences. The final overthrow of this practice is so clearly and succinctly stated in a recent work on the constitutional history of England, that we cannot refrain from copying therefrom in the note.[1]

[1] " Among the remnants of a jurisprudence which had favored prerogative at the expense of liberty was that of the arrest of persons under general warrants, without previous evidence of their guilt or identification of their persons. This practice survived the revolution, and was continued without question, on the ground of usage, until the reign of Geo. III., when it received its death-blow from the boldness of Wilkes and the wisdom of Lord Camden. This question was brought to an issue by No. 45 of the 'North Briton,' already so often mentioned. There was the libel, but who was the libeller? Ministers knew not, nor waited to inquire, after the accustomed forms of law; but forthwith Lord Halifax, one of the secretaries of state, issued a warrant, directing four messengers, taking with them a constable, to search for the authors, printers, and publishers; and to apprehend and seize them, together with their papers, and bring them in safe custody before him. No one having been charged or even suspected, — no evidence of crime having been offered, — no one was named in this dread instrument. The offence only was pointed at, not the offender. The magistrate who should have sought proofs of crime deputed this office to his messengers. Armed with their roving commission, they set forth in quest of unknown offenders; and, unable to take evidence, listened to rumors, idle tales, and curious guesses. They held in their hands the liberty of every man whom they were pleased to suspect. Nor were they triflers in their work. In three days they arrested no less than forty-nine persons on suspicion, — many as innocent as Lord Halifax himself. Among the number was Dryden Leach, a printer, whom they took from his bed at night. They seized his papers, and even apprehended his journeymen and servants. He had printed one number of the 'North Briton,' and was then reprinting some other numbers; but as he happened not to have printed No. 45, he was released without being brought before Lord Halifax. They succeeded, however, in arresting Kearsley the publisher, and Balfe the printer, of the obnoxious number, with all their workmen. From them it was discovered that Wilkes was the culprit of whom they were in search; but the evidence was not on oath; and the messengers received verbal directions to apprehend Wilkes under the general warrant. Wilkes, far keener than the crown lawyers, not seeing his own name there, declared it 'a ridiculous warrant against the whole English nation,' and refused to obey it. But after being in custody of the messengers for some hours, in his

The history of this controversy should be read in connection with that in America immediately previous to the American Revo-

own house, he was taken away in a chair, to appear before the Secretaries of State. No sooner had he been removed than the messengers, returning to his house, proceeded to ransack his drawers; and carried off all his private papers, including even his will and his pocket-book. When brought into the presence of Lord Halifax and Lord Egremont, questions were put to Wilkes which he refused to answer: whereupon he was committed close prisoner to the Tower, denied the use of pen and paper, and interdicted from receiving the visits of his friends or even of his professional advisers. From this imprisonment, however, he was shortly released on a writ of habeas corpus, by reason of his privilege as a member of the House of Commons.

"Wilkes and the printers, supported by Lord Temple's liberality, soon questioned the legality of the general warrant. First, several journeymen printers brought action against the messengers. On the first trial, Lord Chief Justice Pratt — not allowing bad precedents to set aside the sound principles of English law — held that the general warrant was illegal; that it was illegally executed; and that the messengers were not indemnified by statute. The journeymen recovered three hundred pounds damages; and the other plaintiffs also obtained verdicts. In all these cases, however, bills of exceptions were tendered and allowed. Mr. Wilkes himself brought an action against Mr. Wood, under-secretary of state, who had personally superintended the execution of the warrant. At this trial it was proved that Mr. Wood and the messengers, after Wilkes's removal in custody, had taken entire possession of his house, refusing admission to his friends; had sent for a blacksmith, who opened the drawers of his bureau; and having taken out the papers, had carried them away in a sack, without taking any list or inventory. All his private manuscripts were seized, and his pocket-book filled up the mouth of the sack. Lord Halifax was examined, and admitted that the warrant had been made out three days before he had received evidence that Wilkes was the author of the 'North Briton.' Lord Chief Justice Pratt thus spoke of the warrant: 'The defendant claimed a right, under precedents, to force persons' houses, break open escritoires, and seize their papers upon a general warrant, where no inventory is made of the things thus taken away, and where no offenders' names are specified in the warrant, and therefore a discretionary power given to messengers to search wherever their suspicions may chance to fall. If such a power is truly invested in a secretary of state, and he can delegate this power, it certainly may affect the person and property of every man in this kingdom, and is totally subversive of the liberty of the subject.' The jury found a verdict for the plaintiff with one thousand pounds damages.

"Four days after Wilkes had obtained his verdict against Mr. Wood, Dryden Leach, the printer, gained another verdict, with four hundred pounds damages against the messengers. A bill of exceptions, however, was tendered and received in this as in other cases, and came on for hearing before the Court of King's Bench in 1765. After much argument, and the citing of precedents showing the practice of the secretary of state's office ever since the revolution, Lord Mansfield pronounced the warrant illegal, saying: 'It is not fit that the judging of the information should be left to the discretion of the officer. The magistrate

lution, in regard to writs of assistance issued by the courts to the revenue officers, empowering them, at their discretion, to search

should judge, and give certain directions to the officer.' The other three judges agreed that the warrant was illegal and bad, ' believing that no degree of antiquity can give sanction to an usage bad in itself.' The judgment was therefore affirmed.

"Wilkes had also brought actions for false imprisonment against both the secretaries of state. Lord Egremont's death put an end to the action against him ; and Lord Halifax, by pleading privilege, and interposing other delays unworthy of his position and character, contrived to put off his appearance until after Wilkes had been outlawed, when he appeared and pleaded the outlawry. But at length, in 1769, no further postponement could be contrived ; the action was tried, and Wilkes obtained no less than four thousand pounds damages. Not only in this action, but throughout the proceedings, in which persons aggrieved by the general warrant had sought redress, the government offered an obstinate and vexatious resistance. The defendants were harassed by every obstacle which the law permitted, and subjected to ruinous costs. The expenses which government itself incurred in these various actions were said to have amounted to one hundred thousand pounds.

"The liberty of the subject was further assured at this period by another remarkable judgment of Lord Camden. In November, 1762, the Earl of Halifax, as secretary of state, had issued a warrant directing certain messengers, taking a constable to their assistance, to search for John Entinck, clerk, the author or one concerned in the writing of several numbers of the ' Monitor, or British Freeholder,' and to seize him, together with his books and papers, and bring him in safe custody before the secretary of state. In execution of this warrant, the messengers apprehended Mr. Entinck in his house, and seized the books and papers in his bureau, writing-desk, and drawers. This case differed from that of Wilkes, as the warrant specified the name of the person against whom it was directed. In respect of the person, it was not a general warrant ; but as regards the papers, it was a general search-warrant, — not specifying any particular papers to be seized, but giving authority to the messengers to take all his books and papers according to their discretion.

"Mr. Entinck brought an action of trespass against the messengers for the seizure of his papers, upon which a jury found a special verdict, with three hundred pounds damages. This special verdict was twice learnedly argued before the Court of Common Pleas, where, at length, in 1765, Lord Camden pronounced an elaborate judgment. He even doubted the right of the secretary of state to commit persons at all, except for high treason ; but in deference to prior decisions, the court felt bound to acknowledge the right. The main question, however, was the legality of a search-warrant for papers. ' If this point should be determined in favor of the jurisdiction,' said Lord Camden, ' the secret cabinets and bureaus of every subject in this kingdom will be thrown open to the search and inspection of a messenger, whenever the secretary of state shall see fit to charge, or even to suspect, a person to be the author, printer, or publisher of a seditious libel.' ' This power, so assumed by the secretary of state, is an execution upon all the party's papers in the first instance. His house is rifled ; his most valuable papers are taken out of his possession, before the paper, for which he is

suspected places for smuggled goods, and which Otis pronounced " the worst instrument of arbitrary power, the most destructive of English liberty and the fundamental principles of law, that ever was found in an English law-book "; since they placed " the liberty of every man in the hands of every petty officer." [1] All these matters are now a long way in the past; but it has not been deemed unwise to repeat in the State constitutions, as well as in the national,[2] the principles already settled in the common law upon this vital point in civil liberty.

For the service of criminal process, the houses of private persons are subject to be broken and entered under circumstances which are fully explained in the works on criminal law, and need not be restated here. And there are also cases where search-warrants are allowed to be issued, under which an officer may be protected in the like action. But as search-warrants are a species of process exceedingly arbitrary in character, and not to be resorted to except for very urgent and satisfactory reasons, the rules of law which pertain to them are of more than ordinary strictness; and if the party acting under them expects legal protection, it is essential that these rules be carefully observed.

charged, is found to be criminal by any competent jurisdiction, and before he is convicted either of writing, publishing, or being concerned in the paper.' It had been found by the special verdict that many such warrants had been issued since the revolution; but he wholly denied their legality. He referred the origin of the practice to the Star Chamber, which in pursuit of libels had given search-warrants to their messenger of the press; a practice which, after the abolition of the Star Chamber, had been revived and authorized by the licensing act of Charles II., in the person of the secretary of state. And he conjectured that this practice had been continued after the expiration of that act, — a conjecture shared by Lord Mansfield and the Court of King's Bench. With the unanimous concurrence of the other judges of his court, this eminent magistrate now finally condemned this dangerous and unconstitutional practice." May's Constitutional History of England, ch. 11. See also Semayne's case, 5 Coke, 91; 1 Smith's Lead. Cas. 183; Entinck v. Carrington, 2 Wils. 275, and 19 State Trials, 1030; Money v. Leach, Burr. 1742; Wilkes's case, 2 Wils. 151, and 19 State Trials, 1405. For debates in Parliament on the same subject, see Hansard's Debates, vol. 15, p. 1393 to 1418, vol. 16, pp. 6 and 209. In further illustration of the same subject, see De Lolme on the English Constitution, ch. 18; Story on Const. §§ 1901, 1902; Bell v. Clapp, 10 Johns. 263; Sailly v. Smith, 11 Johns. 500.

[1] Works of John Adams, Vol. 2, 523 and 524; 2 Hildreth's U. S. 499; 4 Bancroft's U. S. 414; Quincy's Massachusetts Reports, 51. See also the Appendix to these Reports, p. 395, for a history of writs of assistance.

[2] U. S. Const. 4th amendment.

In the first place, they are only to be granted in the cases where they are expressly authorized by law, and not until after a showing made before a magistrate, under oath, that a crime has been committed, and that the party complaining has reasonable cause to suspect that the offender or the property which was the subject or the instrument of the crime is concealed in some specified house or place.[1] And where the law requires a showing of reasonable cause for suspicion, it intends that evidence shall be given which shall seem to the magistrate to warrant such suspicion; for the suspicion itself is no ground for the warrant, except as the facts justify it.[2]

In the next place, the warrant which the magistrate issues must particularly specify the place to be searched, and the object for which the search is to be made. If a building is to be searched, the name of the owner or occupant should be given,[3] or, if not occupied, it should be particularly described, so that the officer will be left to no discretion in respect to the place ; and a misdescription in regard to the ownership,[4] or a description so general that it applies equally to several buildings or places, would render the warrant void in law.[5] Search-warrants are obnoxious to very serious objections, and the law requires the utmost particularity in these cases before the privacy of a man's premises is allowed to be invaded by the minister of the law.[6] And describing goods to be searched for as " goods, wares, and merchandises," without more particular description, is also bad, even in the case of goods supposed to be smuggled,[7] and where there is usually greater difficulty in giving description, and consequently should be more latitude permitted than in the case of stolen property.

[1] 2 Hale, P. C. 149 ; Bish. Cr. Pro. § 716 – 719 ; Arch. Cr. L. 147.

[2] Commonwealth v. Lottery Tickets, 5 Cush. 369.

[3] Stone v. Dana, 5 Met. 98.

[4] Sandford v. Nichols, 13 Mass. 286 ; Allen v. Staples, 6 Gray, 491.

[5] A warrant to search the "houses and buildings of Hiram Ide and Henry Ide " is too general. Humes v. Tabor, 1 R. I. 464. See McGlinchey v. Barrows, 41 Me. 74. So a warrant for the arrest of an unknown person under the designation of John Doe, without further description, is void. Commonwealth v. Crotty, 10 Allen, 403.

[6] A warrant for searching a dwelling-house will not warrant a forcible entry into a barn adjoining the dwelling-house. Jones v. Fletcher, 41 Me. 254 ; Downing v. Porter, 8 Gray, 539 ; Bish. Cr. Pro. § 716 – 719.

[7] Sandford v. Nichols, 13 Mass. 286 ; Arch. Cr. L. 143.

Lord Hale says: " It is fit that such warrants to search do express that search be made in the daytime; and though I do not say they are unlawful without such restriction, yet they are very inconvenient without it; for many times, under pretence of searches made in the night, robberies and burglaries have been committed, and at best it creates great disturbance." [1] And the statutes upon the subject will very generally be found to provide for searches in the daytime only, except in very special cases.

The warrant should also be directed to the sheriff or other proper officer, and not to private persons; though the party complainant may be present for the purposes of identification,[2] and other assistance can lawfully be called in, if necessary.

The warrant must also command that the goods or other articles to be searched for, if found, together with the party in whose custody they are found, be brought before the magistrate, to the end that, upon further examination into the facts, the goods and the party in whose custody they were may be disposed of according to law.[3] And it is a fatal objection to such a warrant, that it leaves the disposition of the goods searched for to the ministerial officer, instead of requiring them to be brought before the magistrate, that he may pass his judgment upon the charge of violation of law; as it also would be a fatal objection to the law authorizing such warrant, if it allowed a condemnation, or other final disposition of the goods, without notice to the claimant, and an opportunity for a hearing afforded him.[4]

The warrant is not allowed to obtain evidence of an intended crime; but only after lawful evidence of an offence actually committed. Nor even then is it allowable to invade one's privacy for the purpose of obtaining evidence against him,[5]

---

[1] 2 Hale, P. C. 150. Arch. Cr. Law, 7th ed. 145.

[2] 2 Hale, P. C. 150. Arch. Cr. Law, 7th ed. 145.

[3] 2 Hale, P. C. 150; Bell v. Clapp, 10 Johns. 263; Hibbard v. People, 4 Mich. 126; Fisher v. McGirr, 1 Gray, 1.

[4] The "search and seizure" clause in some of the prohibitory liquor laws, authorized a warrant to search for liquors illegally kept for sale, which, if found, might be destroyed without the owner being charged with any offence, and being notified and an opportunity afforded for making defence; and these clauses were held void, as well as the process issued under them, even when the proceedings were so conducted as to avoid the constitutional objection. Fisher v. McGirr, 1 Gray, 1; Hibbard v. People, 4 Mich. 126; Green v. Briggs, 1 Curtis, 311. See also Matter of Morton, 10 Mich. 208, for a somewhat similar principle.

[5] The fourth amendment to the Constitution of the United States, found also

except in a few special cases where that which is the subject of the crime is supposed to be concealed, and the public or the complainant has an interest in it or in its destruction. Those special cases are familiar and well understood in the law. Search-warrants have heretofore been allowed to search for stolen goods, for goods supposed to be smuggled, for implements of gaming or counterfeiting, for lottery tickets or prohibited liquors kept for sale contrary to law, for obscene books and papers kept for sale or circulation, and for powder or other dangerous or explosive material, so kept as to endanger the public safety.[1] A statute which should permit the breaking and entering of a man's house, the examination of books and papers with a view to discover the evidence of crime, might possibly not be void on constitutional grounds in some other cases; but the power of the legislature to authorize a resort to this process is one which can properly be exercised only in extreme cases, and it is better oftentimes that crime should go unpunished than that the citizen should be liable to have his premises invaded, his trunks broken open, his private books, papers, and letters exposed to prying curiosity, and to the misconstructions of ignorant and suspicious persons, and this under the direction of a mere ministerial officer, who brings with him such assistants as he pleases, and who will more often select them with reference to physical strength and courage than to their sensitive regard to the rights and feelings of others. To incline against such laws is to incline to the side of safety.[2] They are

in many State constitutions, is very specific in its protection. " The right of the people to be secure in their persons, houses, papers, and effects, against unreasonable searches and seizures, shall not be violated; and no warrants shall issue but upon probable cause, supported by oath or affirmation, and particularly describing the place to be searched, and the persons or things to be seized." It is believed that under this amendment, the seizure of one's papers, in order to obtain evidence against him, is clearly forbidden; and the spirit of the fifth amendment, that no person shall be compelled, in a criminal case, to be a witness against himself, would also forbid such seizure.

[1] In addition to these, a few cases, sometimes provided for by statute, may be referred to. For books and papers of a public character, retained from their lawful custody; for females, supposed to be concealed in houses of ill-fame; for children, enticed or kept away from parents and guardians; for concealed weapons; and for counterfeit money, and forged bills or papers.

[2] Instances sometimes occur in which ministerial officers take such liberties, in endeavoring to discover and punish offenders, as are even more criminal than the offences they seek to punish. The employment of spies and decoys, to

obnoxious in principle, necessarily odious in the mode of execution, and tend to invite abuse and to cover the commission of crime. We think it would generally be safe for the legislature to regard all those searches and seizures " unreasonable " which have hitherto been unknown to the law, and on that ground to abstain from authorizing them, leaving parties and the public to the accustomed remedies.[1]

We have said that if the officer follows the command of his warrant, he is justified, and this is so even if the complaint proves to have been unfounded.[2] But if he exceed the command by

lead men on to the commission of crime, on the pretence of bringing criminals to justice, cannot be too often or too strongly condemned ; and the prying into private correspondence by officers, which has sometimes been permitted by postmasters, is directly in the face of the law, and utterly unjustifiable. The importance of public confidence in the inviolability of correspondence, through the post-office, cannot well be overrated ; and the proposition to permit letters to be opened at the discretion of a ministerial officer, would be met with general indignation. The same may be said of private correspondence by telegraph; the public are not entitled to it for any purpose ; and a man's servants might, with the same propriety, be subpœned to bring into court his private letters and journals, as a telegraph operator to bring in his private correspondence. In either case, it would be equivalent to an unlawful and unjustifiable seizure of his papers, — such an " unreasonable seizure " as is directly condemned by the Constitution. In England, the Secretary of State sometimes issues his warrant for opening a particular letter, where he is possessed of such facts as he is satisfied would justify him with the public ; but no American officer or body possesses such authority, and its usurpation should not be permitted. See May's Constitutional History, ch. 11, for an account of the former and present English practice on this subject.

[1] A search-warrant for libels and other papers of a suspected party was illegal at the common law. See 11 State Trials, 313, 321 ; Arch. Cr. Law (7th ed.), 141. " Search-warrants were never recognized by the common law as processes which might be availed of by individuals in the course of civil proceedings, or for the maintenance of any mere private right ; but their use was confined to cases of public prosecutions instituted and pursued for the suppression of crime, and the detection and punishment of criminals. Even in those cases, if we may rely on the authority of Lord Coke, their legality was formerly doubted ; and Lord Camden said that they crept into the law by imperceptible practice. But their legality has long been considered to be established, on the ground of public necessity ; because without them felons and other malefactors would escape detection." Merrick, J., in Robinson v. Richardson, 13 Gray, 456. " To enter a man's house," said Lord Camden, " by virtue of a nameless warrant, in order to procure evidence, is worse than the Spanish inquisition ; a law under which no Englishman would wish to live an hour." See Entick v. Carrington, 19 State Trials, 1029 ; S. C. 2 Wils. 275 ; Huckle v. Money, 2 Wils. 205.

[2] Barnard v. Bartlett, 10 Cush. 501.

searching in places not described therein, or by seizing persons and articles not commanded, he is not protected by the warrant, and can only justify himself as in other cases where he assumes to act without process.[1] Obeying strictly the command of his warrant, he may break open outer or inner doors, and his justification does not depend upon his discovering that for which he is to make search.[2]

In other cases than those to which we have referred, the law favors the complete and undisturbed dominion of every man in his own premises, and protects him in it with such jealousy that he may defend his possessions against intruders in person, or by his servants or guests, even to the extent of taking the life of the intruder, if that seem essential to the defence.[3]

Quartering Soldiers in Private Houses.

A provision is found incorporated in the constitution of nearly every State, that " no soldier shall in time of peace be quartered in any house without the consent of the owner, nor in time of war but in a manner to be prescribed by law."   To us, after four fifths of a century have passed away since occasion has existed for complaint of the action of government in this particular, the repetition of this declaration seems to savor of idle form and ceremony ; but " a frequent recurrence to the fundamental principles of the Constitution" can never be unimportant, and, indeed, may well be regarded as " absolutely necessary to preserve the advantages of liberty, and to maintain a free government." [4] It is difficult to imagine a more terrible engine of oppression than the power in an executive to fill the house of an obnoxious person with a company of soldiers, who are to be fed and warmed at his expense, under the direction of an officer accustomed to the exercise of arbitrary power, and in whose presence the ordinary laws of courtesy, not less than the civil restraints which protect person and property, must give way to unbridled will ; who is sent as an instrument of

---

[1] Crozier v. Cundey, 9 D. & R. 224 ; Same case, 6 B. & C. 232 ; State v. Brennan's Liquors, 25 Conn. 278.

[2] 2 Hale P. C. 151 ; Barnard v. Bartlett, 10 Cush. 501.

[3] 1 Hale P. C. 481 ; Curtis v. Hubbard, 4 Hill, 437 ; Pond v. People, 8 Mich. 150.

[4] Constitutions of Massachusetts, New Hampshire, Vermont, Florida, Illinois, and North Carolina. See also constitutions of Virginia, Nebraska, and Wisconsin, for a similar declaration.

punishment, and with whom insult and outrage may appear quite in the line of his duty. However contrary to the spirit of the age such a proceeding may be, it can never be impossible that it will be resorted to in times of great excitement and violent party action; and "the *dragonades* of Louis XIV. in France, of James II. of Scotland, and those of more recent and present date, furnish sufficient justification for this specific guaranty."[1] The clause, as we find it in the National and State constitutions, has come down to us through the Petition of Rights, the Bill of Rights of 1688, and the Declaration of Independence, and it is but a branch of the constitutional principle, that the military shall in time of peace be in strict subordination to the civil power.[2]

Criminal Accusations.

Perhaps the most important protection to personal liberty consists in the mode of trial which is secured to every person accused of crime. At the common law, accusations of felony must be made by grand-jury, by bill of indictment; and this process is still retained in most of the States, while others have substituted in its stead an information filed by the prosecuting officer of the State. The mode of trial, however, is the same in all; and this is a trial by jury, surrounded by certain safeguards which are understood to be a part of the system, and which the government cannot dispense with.

And first, the party must be presumed to be innocent until he is proved to be guilty. This is a presumption which attends all the proceedings against him, from their initiation until they result in a verdict, which either finds the party guilty or changes the presumption of innocence into an adjudged fact.

If there was any mode short of confinement which would in all cases insure the attendance of the accused to answer the accusation, it would not be justifiable to submit him to that indignity, since the effect is to subject him to the punishment of a guilty person before it has yet been determined that he has committed any crime.. If the punishment on conviction cannot exceed in severity the forfeiture of a large sum of money, then it is apparent that such a sum of money, or an agreement by responsible

---

[1] Lieber's Civil Liberty and Self-Government, ch. 11.

[2] Story on the Constitution, §§ 1899, 1900; Rawle on Const. 126.

parties to pay it to the government in the event that the accused
should fail to appear, would be sufficient security for his attendance ; and therefore, at the common law, it was customary to
take security of this character in all cases of misdemeanors ; one
or more friends of the prisoner undertaking for his presence on
trial, and agreeing that a certain sum of money should be levied
of their goods and chattels, lands and tenements, if he failed to
appear.   But in the case of felonies, the privilege of giving bail
before trial was not a matter of right; and in this country, although the practice is much more merciful than it was formerly
in England, there are some cases where it is deemed almost a
matter of course, and in others where it is discretionary with the
magistrate to allow it or not, and where it will sometimes be refused if the proof of guilt is strong or the presumption great.
Capital offences are not generally regarded as bailable ; at least
after indictment, or when the party is charged upon the finding
of a coroner's jury ;[1] and this upon the supposition that one who
may be subjected to the terrible punishment that would follow a
conviction would not for any mere pecuniary considerations remain to abide the judgment.[2]   And where the death penalty is
abolished and imprisonment for life substituted, it is not doubted
that the rule would notwithstanding be the same, and bail would
still be denied in the case of the highest offences, except under
very peculiar circumstances.[3]   In the case of other felonies, it is
not usual to refuse bail, and in some of the State constitutions
it has been deemed important to make it a matter of right in
all cases except on capital charges, " when the proof is evident or
the presumption great." [4]

 Wherever bail is allowed, *unreasonable bail* is not to be re-

[1] Matter of Barronet, 1 Ellis & Bl. 1 ; *Ex parte* Tayloe, 5 Cow. 39.

[2] State *v.* Summons, 19 Ohio, 139.

[3] Nevertheless, the court has the power to bail, even in capital cases.   United
States *v.* Hamilton, 3 Dall. 18; State *v.* Rockafellow, 1 Halst. 332; Common-
wealth *v.* Semmes, 11 Leigh, 665 ; People *v.* Smith, 1 Cal. 9 ; People *v.* Van
Horne, 8 Barb. 158 ; United States *v.* Jones, 3 Wash. 224 ; Commonwealth *v.*
Archer, 6 Grat. 705.   In England, all felonies were once capital, but it was always
discretionary with the courts to allow bail.

[4] See, to this effect, provisions in the constitutions of Mississippi, Illinois, Ken-
tucky, Missouri.   And see *Ex parte* Wray, 30 Miss. 673 ; Moore *v.* State, 36
Miss. 137 ; Foley *v.* People, Breese, 31 ; Ullery *v.* Commonwealth, 8 B. Monr. 3 ;
Shore *v.* State, 6 Mo. 640 ; *Ex parte* Banks, 28 Ala. 89 ; State *v.* Summons, 19
Ohio, 139.

quired; but the constitutional principle to this effect is one which, from the very nature of the case, can only be enforced by appeal to the judgment and sense of justice of the court or magistrate who is empowered to fix upon the amount. That bail is reasonable which, in view of the nature of the offence, the penalty which the law attaches to it, and the probabilities that guilt will be established on trial, seems sufficient to secure his attendance. This will depend somewhat upon the prisoner's circumstances; that which is reasonable bail to a man of wealth being equivalent to a denial of the right if exacted of a poor man charged with the like offence. When a court or magistrate requires more than the bail sufficient to secure attendance, and keeps the prisoner in confinement for failure to give it, the constitutional privileges of the accused are invaded, and his right in this particular set at naught; and it is but poor excuse for the act that the wrong is without remedy.

The presumption of innocence is an absolute protection against conviction and punishment, except either, *first*, on confession in open court; or, *second*, on proof which places the guilt beyond any reasonable doubt. Formerly, if a prisoner arraigned for felony stood mute wilfully, or refused to plead on being arraigned, a terrible mode was resorted to for the purpose of compelling him to do so, which might even end in his death,[1] and this because without plea there could be neither trial nor judgment; but a more merciful proceeding is substituted, the court entering a plea of not guilty for a party who, for any reason, fails to plead for himself.

It is again required that the trial be *speedy;* and here also the injunction is addressed to the justice and sound judgment of the court. In this country, where officers are specially appointed or elected to represent the people in these prosecutions, their position gives them an immense power for oppression, which it is to be feared they do not always sufficiently appreciate and wield with due regard to the rights and protection of the accused. When a person charged with crime is willing to proceed at once to trial, no delay on the part of the prosecution is reasonable, except only that which is necessary to secure the attendance of

---

[1] 4 Bl. Com. 325. Poor Giles Corey, accused of witchcraft, was, perhaps, the only person ever pressed to death for refusal to plead in America. 3 Bancroft, 93; 2 Hildreth, 160.

witnesses. Very much, however, must be left to the judgment of the prosecuting officer in these cases; and the court would not compel the government to proceed to trial at the first term after indictment or information filed, if the officer who represents it should state, under the responsibility of his official oath, that he was not and could not be ready at that time.[1] But further delay would not generally be allowed without a more specific showing of the causes which prevent the State proceeding to trial, including the names of the witnesses, the steps taken to procure them, and the facts expected to be proved by them, in order that the court might judge of the reasonableness of the application, and that the prisoner might, if he saw fit to take that course, secure an immediate trial by admitting that the witnesses, if present, would swear to the facts which the prosecution have claimed could be proved by them.[2]

It is also requisite that the trial be *public*. By this it is not meant that every person who sees fit shall in all cases be permitted to attend criminal trials, because there are many cases where, from the character of the charge, and the nature of the evidence by which it is to be supported, the motives to attend the trial on the part of portions of the community would be of the worst character, and where a regard to public morals and public decency would demand the exclusion at least of the young from hearing and witnessing the evidences of human depravity which the trial must necessarily bring to light. The requirement of a public trial is for the benefit of the accused, that the public may see that he is fairly dealt by and not unjustly condemned, and that the presence of interested spectators may keep his triers keenly alive to a sense of their responsibility and to the importance of their functions; and the requirement is fairly met if, without partiality or favoritism, a reasonable proportion of the public is suffered to be present, notwithstanding those persons whose presence could be of no service to the accused, and who would only be drawn thither by a prurient curiosity, are excluded altogether.

[1] Watts *v.* State, 26 Geo. 231.

[2] The Habeas Corpus Act, 31 Ch. 2, c. 2, § 1, required a prisoner charged with crime to be released on bail, if not indicted the first term after their commitment, unless the king's witnesses could not be obtained, and that he should be brought to trial as early as the second term after commitment. The principles of this statute are considered as having been adopted into the American common law.

But a far more important requirement is, that the proceeding to establish guilt shall not be inquisitorial. A peculiar excellence of the common-law system of trial over that which has prevailed in other civilized countries consists in the fact that the accused is never compelled to give evidence against himself. Much as there was in that system that was heartless and cruel, it was not subject to the reproach that it gave judgment upon extorted confessions, than which, as all experience shows, nothing can be more dangerous or more utterly untrustworthy.[1]

It is the law in some of the States, that, when a person is charged with crime, and is brought before an examining magistrate, and the witnesses in support of the charge have been heard, the prisoner may also make a statement concerning the transaction charged against him, and that this may be used against him on the trial if it is believed to have a tendency to establish guilt. But the prisoner is to be first cautioned that he is under no obligation to answer any question put to him unless he chooses, and whatever he says and does must be entirely voluntary.[2] He is also to be allowed the presence and advice of counsel; and if that privilege is denied him, it may be sufficient reason for discrediting any statements that he may have made.[3] When, however, the statute has been complied with, and no species of coercion appears to have been employed, the statement the prisoner may have made is evidence which may be used against him on his trial, and is entitled to great weight.[4] And in any other case,

---

[1] See Lieber's paper on Inquisitorial Trials, Appendix to Civil Liberty and Self-Government. See also article on Criminal Procedure in Scotland and England, Edinb. Rev., Oct. 1858. Judge Foster relates, from Whitelocke, that the Bishop of London, having said to Felton, who had assassinated the Duke of Buckingham, "It you will not confess, you must go to the rack," the man replied, "If it must be so, I know not whom I may accuse, in the extremity of my torture, — Bishop Laud, perhaps, or any lord of this board." "Sound sense," adds Foster, "in the mouth of an enthusiast and ruffian." Laud, having proposed the rack, the matter was shortly debated at the board, and it ended in a reference to the judges, who unanimously resolved that the rack could not be legally used. De Lolme on Constitution of England (ed. of 1807), p. 181, note.

[2] See Rev. Stat. of New York, part 4, ch. 2, tit. 2, § 14 – 16.

[3] Rex v. Ellis, Ry. & Mood. 432. There is no absolute right to the presence of counsel, or to publicity in these preliminary examinations, unless given by statute. Cox v. Coleridge, 1 B. & C. 37.

[4] It should not, however, be taken on oath, and if it is, that will be sufficient reason for rejecting it. Rex v. Smith, 1 Stark. 242; Rex v. Webb, 4 C. & P. 564;

except treason, the confession of the accused may be received in evidence against him, provided no circumstance accompanies the making of it which should detract from its weight in producing conviction on the minds of the hearer.

But to make it admissible in any case, it ought to appear that it was made voluntarily, and that no motives of hope or fear were employed to induce the accused to make it. The evidence ought to be clear and satisfactory that the prisoner was neither threatened nor cajoled into confessing what very possibly was untrue. Under the excitement of a charge of crime, coolness and self-possession are to be looked for in very few persons; and however strongly we may reason with ourselves that no one will confess a heinous offence of which he is not guilty, the records of criminal courts bear abundant testimony to the contrary. If confessions could prove a crime beyond doubt, no act which was ever punished criminally would be better established than witchcraft;[1] and the judicial murders which have been based on such confessions ought to be a warning against the ready admission of confessions in proof of guilt in any case. As "Mr. Justice Parke several times observed" while holding one of his circuits, "too great weight ought not be attached to evidence of what a party has been supposed to have said, as it very frequently happens, not only that the witness has misunderstood what the party has said, but that by unintentionally altering a few of the expressions really used, he gives an effect to the statement completely at variance with what the party really did say."[2] And when the admission is full and positive, it perhaps quite as often happens that it has been made under the influence of the terrible fear caused by the charge, and in the hope that confession may ward

---

Rex v. Lewis, 6 C. & P. 161; Rex v. Rivers, 7 C. & P. 177; Regina v. Pikesley, 9 C. & P. 124. "The view of the English judges, that an oath, even where a party is informed he need answer no questions unless he pleases, would, with most persons, overcome that caution, is, I think, founded on good reason and experience. I think there is no country, — certainly there is none from which any of our legal notions are borrowed, — where a prisoner is ever examined on oath." People v. Thomas, 9 Mich. 318, per Campbell, J.

[1] See Mary Smith's case, 2 Howell's State Trials, 1049; Case of Essex witches, 4 Ibid. 817; Case of Suffolk witches, 6 Ibid. 647; Case of Devon witches, 8 Ibid. 1017.

[2] Note to Earle v. Picken, 5 C. & P. 542. And see 1 Greenl. Ev. § 214, and note.

off some of the consequences which would follow a conviction if guilt was persistently denied.

A confession alone ought not to be sufficient evidence of the *corpus delicti.* There should be other proof that a crime has been committed, and the confession should only be allowed for the purpose of connecting the defendant with the offence.[1] Any solicitations employed to obtain it by working upon the party's hopes or fears will be sufficient to preclude its being received; and even saying to the prisoner that it will be better for him to confess has been decided to be such holding out of inducements to confession, especially when it is said by the person having him in custody, as should exclude the evidence.[2] If, however, counter-

---

[1] Stringfellow v. State, 26 Miss. 157. In this case, it was held, that a confession of murder was not sufficient to warrant conviction, unless the death of the person supposed to be murdered was shown by other evidence. So, in People v. Hennessey, 15 Wend. 147, it was held, that a confession by a clerk, of embezzlement, would not warrant a conviction, where that constitutes the sole evidence that an embezzlement had been committed. See also State v. Guild, 5 Halst. 163; Long's case, 1 Hayw. 524; People v. Lambert, 5 Mich. 349. So in People v. Porter, 2 Park. Cr. R. 14, Walworth, Circuit Judge, held the admission, by the defendant, that he had spoken certain blasphemous words, was not sufficient evidence of the uttering.

[2] Rex v. Enoch, 5 C. & P. 539; State v. Bostick, 4 Harr. 563; Commonwealth v. Taylor, 5 Cush. 605; Morehead v. State, 9 Humph. 635; Regina v. Garner, 1 Den. C. C. 329. Mr. Phillips states the rule thus: " A promise of benefit or favor, or threat or intimation of disfavor, connected with the subject of the charge, held out by a person having authority in the matter, will be sufficient to exclude a confession made in consequence of such inducements, either of hope or fear. The prosecutor or prosecutor's wife or attorney, or the prisoner's master or mistress, or a constable, or a person assisting him in the apprehension or custody, or a magistrate acting in the business, or other magistrate, has been respectively looked upon as having authority in the matter; and the same principle applies, if the inducement has been held out by a person without authority, in the presence of a person who has such authority, and with his sanction, either express or implied." 1 Phil. Ev. by Cowen, Hill, & Edwards, 544, and cases cited. But we think the better reason is in favor of excluding confessions, where inducements have been held out by any person, whether acting by authority or not. King v. Simpson, 1 Mood. C. C. R. 410; State v. Guild, 5 Halst. 163; Spears v. State, 2 Ohio, N. S. 583; Commonwealth v. Knapp, 9 Pick. 496; Rex v. Clewes, 4 C. & P. 221; Rex v. Kingston, Ibid. 387; Rex v. Dunn, Ibid. 543; Rex v. Walkley, 6 C. & P. 175; Rex v. Thomas, 6 C. & P. 353. There are not wanting many opposing authorities, which proceed upon the idea, that " a promise made by an indifferent person, who interfered officiously, without any kind of authority, and promised without the means of performance, can scarcely be deemed sufficient to produce any effect, even on the weakest mind, as an inducement to confess." 1 Greenl.

statements have been made before the confession which were likely to do away with the effect of the inducements, so that the accused cannot be supposed to have acted under their influence, the confession may be received in evidence.[1] But the evidence ought to be very satisfactory on this point, before the court should presume that the prisoner's hope did not still cling to, or his fears dwell upon, the first inducements.[2]

Before prisoners were allowed the benefit of assistance from counsel on trial for high crimes, it was customary for them to make such statements as they saw fit concerning the charge against them, during the progress of the trial, or after the evidence of the prosecution had been put in ; and upon these statements the prosecuting officer or the court would sometimes ask questions, which the accused might answer or not at his option. And although this practice has now become obsolete, yet if the accused in any case should assist in his own defence, and should claim the right of addressing the jury, it would be difficult to confine him to " the record," as a counsel may be confined in his

Ev. § 223. No supposition could be more fallacious; and, in point of fact, a case can scarcely occur in which some one, from age, superior wisdom, or experience, or from his relations to the accused, or to the prosecutor, would not be likely to exercise more influence upon his mind than some of the persons who are regarded as "in authority," under the rule as stated by Mr. Phillips. Mr. Greenleaf thinks that while, as a rule of law, all confessions made to persons in authority should be rejected, " promises and threats by private persons, not being found so uniform in their operation, perhaps may, with more propriety, be treated as mixed questions of law and fact ; the principle of law, that a confession must be voluntary, being strictly adhered to, and the question, whether the promises or threats of the private individuals who employed them were sufficient to overcome the mind of the prisoner, being left to the discretion of the judge, under all the circumstances of the case." 1 Greenl. Ev. § 223. This is a more reasonable rule than that which admits such confessions under all circumstances; but it is impossible for a judge to say whether inducements, in a particular case, *have* influenced the mind or not ; if their nature was such that they were calculated to have that effect, it is safer, and more in accordance with the humane principles of criminal law, to presume, in favor of life and liberty, that the confessions were " forced from the mind by the flattery of hope, or by the torture of fear" (per Eyre, C. B., Warickshall's case, 1 Leach, C. C. 299), and exclude them altogether. The whole subject of evidence of confession is very fully considered in note to 2 Leading Criminal Cases, 182. And see People v. McMahon, 15 N. Y. 383.

[1] State v. Guild, 5 Halst. 163 ; Commonwealth v. Harman, 4 Penn. State, 269 ; State v. Vaigneur, 5 Rich. 391 ; Rex v. Cooper, 5 C. & P. 535 ; Rex v. Howes, 6 C. & P. 404 ; Rex v. Richards, 5 C. & P. 318.

[2] State v. Roberts, 1 Dev. 259 ; Rex v. Cooper, 5 C. & P. 535.

argument. A disposition has been manifested of late to allow the accused to give evidence on his own behalf; and statutes to that effect are in existence in some of the States, which are believed to have had a salutary operation. These statutes, however, cannot be so construed as to authorize compulsory process against an accused to compel him to disclose more than he chooses; they do not so far change the old system as to establish an inquisitorial process for obtaining evidence; they confer a privilege, which the defendant may use at his option; if he does not choose to avail himself of it, unfavorable inferences are not to be drawn against him from that circumstance; and if he does testify, he is at liberty to stop at any point he chooses, and it must be left to the jury to give to a statement which he declines to make a full one such weight as, under the circumstances, they think it entitled to; otherwise the statute must have overruled and overthrown the constitutional maxim, that an accused party is not compelled to testify against himself, and the privilege becomes a snare and a danger.[1]

[1] The statute of Michigan of 1861, p. 169, removed the common-law disabilities of parties to testify, and added: " Nothing in this act shall be construed as giving the right to compel a defendant in criminal cases to testify; but any such defendant shall be at liberty to make a statement to the court or jury, and may be cross-examined on any such statement." It has been held that this statement should not be under oath. People v. Thomas, 9 Mich. 314. That its purpose was to give every person on trial for crime an opportunity to make full explanation to the jury, in respect to the circumstances given in evidence which are supposed to have a bearing against him. Annis v. People, 13 Mich. 511. That the statement is *evidence* in the case, to which the jury can attach such weight as they think it entitled to. Maher v. People, 10 Mich. 212. That the court has no right to instruct the jury that, when it conflicts with the testimony of an unimpeached witness, they must believe the latter in preference. Durant v. People, 13 Mich. 351. And that the prisoner, while on the stand, is entitled to the assistance of counsel in directing his attention to any branch of the charge, that he may make explanations concerning it if he desires. Annis v. People, 13 Mich. 511. The prisoner does not cease to be a defendant by becoming a witness, or forfeit rights by accepting a privilege. And in People v. Thomas, Campbell, J., in speaking of the right which the statute gives to cross-examine a defendant who has made his statement, says: " And while his constitutional right of declining to answer questions cannot be removed, yet a refusal by a party to answer any fair question, not going outside of what he has offered to explain, would have its proper weight with the jury." 9 Mich. 321.

The statement in the text, that the fact that the prisoner does not avail himself of his privilege to make a statement is not to be the subject of comment before the jury, is borne out by a decision on an analogous point under the statute above

The testimony for the people in criminal cases can only be given, as a general rule, by witnesses who are present in court. The defendant is entitled to be confronted with the witnesses against him; and if any of them be absent from the Commonwealth, so that their attendance cannot be compelled, or be dead, or have become incapable of being sworn, there is no mode by which their statements against the prisoner can be used for his conviction. The exceptions to this rule are of cases which are excluded from its reasons from their peculiar circumstances; but they are far from numerous. If the witness was sworn before the examining magistrate, and the accused had an opportunity then to cross-examine him, or before a coroner, or if there was a former trial on which he was sworn, it seems allowable to make use of his deposition, or of the minutes of his examination, if the witness has since deceased, or is out of the jurisdiction, or cannot be found after diligent search, or is insane, or sick and unable to testify, or has been summoned, but appears to have been kept away by the opposite party.[1] So also if a party is on trial for homicide, the declarations of the party whom he is charged with having killed, if made under the solemnity of a conviction that he was at the point of death, and relating to matters of fact concerning the homicide, which passed under his own observation, may be given in evidence against him, — the condition of the party who made them being such that every motive to falsehood must be supposed to be silenced, and the mind to be induced by the most powerful considerations to speak the truth.[2] Not that such evidence is of very conclusive character; it is not always easy to determine, when the declaration is repeated, how much relates to what was seen and positively known, and how much is surmise

referred to. Under that statute the wife may be sworn as a witness for the husband with his assent; but it has been held that his failure to call upon her was not to subject him to inferences of guilt, even though the case was such that, if his defence was true, his wife must have been cognizant of the facts. Knowles v. People, 15 Mich. 408.

For considerations concerning the working of a system which allows the evidence of defendants in criminal cases to be received, see Am. Law Register, N. S. vol. 5, pp. 129 and 705.

[1] 1 Greenl. Ev. § 163 to 166; Bish. Cr. Pro. § 520 to 527.

[2] 1 Greenl. Ev. § 156; Phil. Ev. by Cowen, Hill, & Edwards, vol. 1, 285 to 289; Donnelley v. State, 2 Dutch. 463; Hills's case, 2 Grat. 594; State v. Freeman, 1 Spears, 57.

and suspicion only; but it is admissible from the necessity of the case, and the jury must judge of the weight to be attached to it.

The Traverse Jury.

The trial of the guilt or innocence of the accused must be by jury;[1] and wherever this right is preserved by the constitution, it must be understood as retained in all those cases which were triable by jury at the common law, and with all the common-law incidents to a jury trial, so far as they can be regarded as tending to the protection of the accused.

A petit, petty, or traverse jury is a body of twelve men, who are sworn to try the facts of a case as they are delivered from the evidence placed before them. Any less than this number of twelve would not be a common-law jury, and not such a jury as the constitution preserves to accused parties; and unless that instrument allows a less number in express terms, a full panel could not be waived by consent.[2] The trial of a criminal case by a jury of less than twelve by consent would be void, because the tribunal would be one unknown to the law, the mere voluntary creation of the parties; and it would in effect be an attempt to submit to a species of arbitration the question whether the accused has been guilty of an offence against the State. But in those cases which were formerly not triable by jury, if the legislature should provide for such a trial now, it might doubtless create a statutory tribunal, composed of any number of persons for the purpose, and no question of constitutional law would arise.

The mode of trial by jury is an essential part of the right. The jury must be indifferent between the prisoner and the commonwealth; and to secure this, *challenges* are allowed, both for cause, and peremptory without cause. The jury must be sum-

[1] All that is extant of the legislation of the Plymouth Colony for the first five years consists of the single regulation, " that all criminal facts, and also all manner of trespasses and debts between man and man, shall be tried by the verdict of twelve honest men, to be impanelled by authority in form of a jury, upon their oath." 1 Palfrey's New England, 340.

[2] Work *v.* State, 2 Ohio, N. S. 296; Cancemi *v.* People, 18 N. Y. 128; Brown *v.* State, 8 Blackf. 561; Hill *v.* People, 16 Mich. 351; 2 Lead. Cr. Cas. 337. In Commonwealth *v.* Dailey, 12 Cush. 80, it was held that in a case of misdemeanor, the consent of the defendant, that a verdict might be received from eleven jurors, was binding upon him, and the verdict was valid. See also State *v.* Cox, 3 Eng. 436.

moned from the vicinage where the crime is supposed to have been committed; and the accused will thus have the benefit of his own good character and standing with his fellows, — if these he has preserved, — and also of such knowledge as the jurors may possess of the witnesses who may give evidence against him. He will also be able with more certainty to secure the attendance of his own witnesses. The jury must unanimously concur in the verdict.[1] And they must be left *free to act*. The final decision upon the facts is to rest with them, and any interference by the court to coerce them into a verdict against their will is irregular and unconstitutional. . A judge is not justified in expressing his opinion to the jury that the defendant is guilty upon the evidence adduced.[2] Still less would he be justified in refusing to receive and record the verdict of the jury, because, in his opinion, it is rendered in favor of the prisoner when it ought not to have been.

---

[1] Work *v.* State, 2 Ohio, N. S. 296.

[2] Better far to dispense with jury trial altogether, than for the judge to urge his opinion of the facts upon the jury; for under such a practice he decides the cause while avoiding the responsibility. How often would a jury be found bold enough to declare their opinion in opposition to that of the judge upon the bench, whose words would fall upon their ears with all the weight which experience, learning, and commanding station must always carry with them? What lawyer would care to sum up his case, if he knew the judge, whose words would be so much more powerful, was to declare in his favor, or who would be bold enough to argue the facts to the jury if he knew the judge was to declare against him? Blackstone has justly remarked that, " in settling and adjusting a question of fact, where intrusted to any single magistrate, partiality and injustice have an ample field to range in; either by boldly asserting that to be proved which is not so, or by more artfully distinguishing away the remainder." 3 Bl. Com. 380. These are evils which jury trial is designed to prevent; but vain the effort if the judge is to control by his opinion where the law has given him no power to command. In Campbell's Lives of the Chancellors, ch. 181, the author justly condemns the practice with some judges, in libel cases, of expressing to the jury their belief in the defendant's guilt. On the trial of parties charged with a libel on the Empress of Russia, Lord Kenyon, sneering at the late Libel Act, said : " I am bound by my oath to declare my own opinion, and I should forget my duty were I not to say to you that it is a gross libel." Upon this the author remarks: " Mr. Fox's act only requires the judges to give their opinion on matters of law in libel cases as in other cases. But did any judge ever say, ' Gentlemen, I am of opinion that this is a wilful, malicious, and atrocious murder' ? For a considerable time after the act passed against the unanimous opposition of the judges, they almost all spitefully followed this course. I myself heard one judge say : ' As the legislature requires me to give my own opinion in the present case, I am of opinion that this is a diabolically atrocious libel.'" And see M'Guffie *v.* State, 17 Geo. 497.

He discharges his duty, in giving instructions to the jury, when he has informed them what the law is which is applicable to the case, and what facts will constitute the offence charged; and the jury should be left free and unbiassed by his opinion to determine for themselves whether the facts in evidence against the accused are such as, under the instructions of the judge, show, beyond any reasonable doubt, that he is guilty of the charge.[1]

How far the jury are to judge of the law as well as of the facts, in criminal cases, is a question a full discussion of which we should enter upon with much reluctance. If it be their choice to do so, they may return specially what facts they find established by the evidence, and submit to the court to apply the law to these facts, and thereby determine whether the party is proved to be guilty or not. But they are not obliged in any case to find a special verdict; they have a right for themselves to apply the law to the facts, and to express their own opinion, upon the whole evidence, of the defendant's guilt. Where a general verdict is thus given, the jury necessarily determine in their own mind what the law of the case is;[2] and if their determination is favorable to the prisoner, no mode is known to the law in which it can be reviewed or reversed. A writ of error does not lie on behalf of the Commonwealth to reverse an acquittal, unless expressly given by statute,[3] nor can a new

[1] The independence of the jury, so far as matters of fact are concerned, was settled by Penn's case, 6 Howell's State Trials, 951, and by Bushell's case, which grew out of it, and is reported in Vaughan's Rep. 135. A very full account of the case is also found in Forsyth on Trials by Jury, 397. Bushell was foreman of the jury which refused to find a verdict of guilty at the dictation of the court, and he was punished as for contempt of court for his refusal, but was released on *habeas corpus.*

[2] " As the main object of the institution of the trial by a jury is to guard accused persons against all decisions whatsoever by men intrusted with any permanent official authority, it is not only a settled principle that the opinion which the judge delivers has no weight but such as the jury choose to give it, but their verdict must besides [unless they see fit to return a special finding] comprehend the whole matter in trial, and decide as well upon the fact as upon the point of law which may arise out of it; in other words they must pronounce both on the commission of a certain fact, and on the reason which makes such fact to be contrary to law." De Lolme on the Constitution of England, ch. 13.

[3] See State *v.* Reynolds, 4 Hayw. 110; United States *v.* More, 3 Cranch, 174; People *v.* Dill, 1 Scam. 257; People *v.* Royal, Ibid. 557; Commonwealth *v.* Cummings, 3 Cush. 212; People *v.* Corning, 2 N. Y. 9. A constitutional provision saving " to the defendant the right of appeal," in criminal cases, does not, by im-

trial be granted in such a case ;[1] but neither a writ of error nor a
motion for a new trial could reach an erroneous determination by
the jury, since, as they do not give reasons for their verdict, it can
never be legally known what were the precise grounds for it, and
it is always presumable that it was given in favor of the accused
because the evidence was not sufficient in degree or satisfactory in
character ; and no one is at liberty to allege or suspect that they
have disregarded the law.

Nevertheless, as it is the duty of the court to charge the jury
upon the law applicable to the case, it is still an important question
whether the jury are bound to receive and act upon the law as
given to them by the judge, or whether, on the other hand, his
opinion is advisory only, so that they are at liberty to follow it if it
accords with their own convictions, or to disregard it if it does not.

In one class of cases — that is to say, in criminal prosecutions
for libel — it is now very generally provided by the State constitutions or by statute that the jury shall determine the law and the
facts.[2] How great a change is made in the common law by these

plication, preclude the legislature from giving to the State the same privilege.
State v. Tait, 22 Iowa, 142, 143.

[1] People v. Comstock, 8 Wend. 549 ; State v. Brown, 16 Conn. 54 ; State v.
Kanouse, 1 Spencer, 115 ; State v. Burris, 3 Texas, 118 ; State v. Taylor, 1
Hawks, 462.

[2] See constitutions of Missouri, Alabama, Arkansas, Illinois, Kentucky, Pennsylvania, Texas, Maine, Tennessee, Michigan, and New York. The constitution
of Maryland makes the jury the judges of the law in all criminal cases, and the
same rule is established by constitution or statute in some other States. In
Holder v. State, 5 Geo. 444, the following view was taken of such a statute :
" Our penal code declares : ' On every trial of a crime or offence contained in this
code, or for any crime or offence, the jury shall be judges of the law and the fact,
and shall in every case give a general verdict of guilty or not guilty, and on the
acquittal of any defendant or prisoner no new trial shall on any account be
granted by the court.' Juries were at common law in some sense judges of the
law. Having the right of rendering a general verdict, that right involved a judgment on the law as well as the facts, yet not such a judgment as necessarily to
control the court. The early commentators on the common law, notwithstanding
they concede this right, yet hold that it is the duty of the jury to receive the law
from the court. Thus Blackstone equivocally writes : ' And such public or open
verdict may be either general, *guilty* or *not guilty*, or special, setting forth all the
circumstances of the case, and praying the judgment of the court whether, for
instance, on the facts stated, it be murder, or manslaughter, or no crime at all.
This is where they *doubt* the matter of law, and therefore *choose* to leave it to the
determination of the court, though they have an unquestionable right of determining upon all the circumstances, and of finding a general verdict, *if they think*

provisions, it is difficult to say, because the rule of the common law was not clear upon the authorities ; but for that very reason, and because the law of libel was sometimes administered with great harshness, it was certainly proper and highly desirable that a definite and liberal rule should be thus established.[1]

In all other cases the jury have the clear legal right to return a verdict of guilty or not guilty, and in so doing they necessarily decide such questions of law as well as of fact as are involved in the general question of guilt. If their view conduce to an acquittal, there is no mode known to the law by which their decision can be reviewed or set aside. In such a case, therefore, it appears that they judge of the law as well as of the facts, and that their judgment is final. If, on the other hand, their view lead them to a verdict of guilty, and it is the opinion of the court that such verdict is against law, the verdict will be set aside and a new trial granted. In such a case, although they have judged of the law, the court sets aside their conclusion as improper and unwarranted. But it is clear that the jury are no more the judges of the law when they acquit than when they condemn, and the different result in the two cases arises from the merciful maxim in the common law, which will not suffer an accused party to be twice put in jeopardy, however erroneous may have been the first acquittal. In theory therefore the rule of law would seem to be, that it is the duty of the

---

proper so to hazard a breach of their oath,' &c. 4 Bl. Com. 361 ; Co. Lit. 228 *a* ; 2 Hale, P. C. 313. Our legislature have left no doubt about this matter. The juries in Georgia can find no special verdict at law. They are declared to be judges of the law and the facts, and are required in every case to give a general verdict of guilty or not guilty ; so jealous, and rightfully jealous, were our ancestors of the influence of the State upon the trial of a citizen charged with crime. We are not called upon in this case to determine the relative strength of the judgment of the court, and the jury, upon the law in criminal cases, and shall express no opinion thereon. We only say, it is the right and duty of the court to declare the law in criminal cases as well as civil, and that it is at the same time the right of the jury to judge of the law as well as of the facts in criminal cases. I would not be understood as holding that it is not the province of the court to give the law of the case distinctly in charge to the jury : it is unquestionably its privilege and its duty to instruct them as to what the law is, and officially to direct their finding as to the law, yet at the same time in such way as not to limit the range of their judgment." See also M'Guffie *v.* State, 17 Geo. 497.

[1] For a condensed history of the struggle in England on this subject, see May's Constitutional History, ch. 9. See also Lives of the Chancellors, by Lord Campbell, ch. 178.

jury to receive and follow the law as delivered to them by the court: and such is the current of authority.[1] There are, however, opposing decisions,[2] and it is evident that the prerogative of the court to direct conclusively upon the law cannot be carried very far or insisted upon with much pertinacity, when the jury have the complete power to disregard it, without its action degenerating into mere scolding. Upon this subject the remarks of Mr. Justice Baldwin, of the Supreme Court of the United States, to a jury assisting him in the trial of a criminal charge, and which are given in the note, seem peculiarly dignified and appropriate, and at the same time to embrace about all that can properly be said to a jury on this subject.[3]

[1] United States v. Battiste, 2 Sum. 240; Stittinus v. United States, 5 Cranch, C. C. 573; United States v. Morris, 1 Curtis, 53; Montgomery v. State, 11 Ohio, 427; Commonwealth v. Porter, 10 Met. 263; State v. Peace, 1 Jones, 251; Handy v. State, 7 Mo. 607; Nels v. State, 2 Texas, 280; People v. Pine, 2 Barb. 566; Carpenter v. People, 8 Barb. 603; McGowen v. State, 9 Yerg. 184; Pleasant v. State, 13 Ark. 360; Montee v. Commonwealth, 3 J. J. Marsh, 132; Commonwealth v. Van Tuyl, 1 Met. (Ky.) 1. "As the jury have the right, and if required by the prisoner are bound to return a general verdict of guilty or not guilty, they must necessarily, in the discharge of their duty, decide such questions of the law as well as of fact as are involved in the general question, and there is no mode in which their opinions on questions of law can be reviewed by this court or any other tribunal. But this does not diminish the obligation of the court to explain the law. The instructions of the court in matters of law may safely guide the consciences of the jury, unless they know them to be wrong; and when the jury undertake to decide the law (as they undoubtedly have the power to do), in opposition to the advice of the court, they assume a high responsibility, and should be very careful to see clearly that they are right." Commonwealth v. Knapp, 10 Pick. 496. Cited with approval in McGowan v. State, 9 Yerg. 195; and Dale v. State, 10 Yerg. 555.

[2] See especially State v. Croteau, 23 Vt. 14, which is a very full and carefully considered opinion, holding that at the common law the jury are the judges of the law in criminal cases. See also State v. Wilkinson, 2 Vt. 280; Doss v. Commonwealth, 1 Grat. 557; State v. Jones, 5 Ala. 666; State v. Snow, 6 Shep. 346; State v. Allen, 1 McCord, 525; Armstrong v. State, 4 Blackf. 247; Warren v. State, Ibid. 150; Stocking v. State, 7 Ind. 326; Lynch v. State, 9 Ind. 541; Nelson v. State, 2 Swan, 482.

[3] "In repeating to you what was said on a former occasion to another jury, that you have the power to decide on the law, as well as the facts of this case, and are not bound to find according to our opinion of the law, we feel ourselves constrained to make some explanations not then deemed necessary, but now called for from the course of the defence. You may find a general verdict of guilty or not guilty, as you think proper, or you may find the facts specially, and leave the guilt or innocence of the prisoner to the judgment of the court. If your verdict

One thing more is essential to the complete protection of jury trial, and that is, that the accused shall not be twice put in jeop-

acquit the prisoner, we cannot grant a new trial, however much we may differ with you as to the law which governs the case ; and in this respect a jury are the judges of the law, if they choose to become so. Their judgment is final, not because they settle the law, but because they think it not applicable or do not choose to apply it to the case.

" But if a jury find a prisoner guilty against the opinion of the court on the law of the case, a new trial will be granted. No court will pronounce a judgment on a prisoner against what they believe to be the law. On an acquittal there is no judgment ; and the court do not act, and cannot judge, there remaining nothing to act upon.

" This, then, you will understand to be what is meant by your power to decide on the law, but you will still bear in mind that it is a very old, sound, and valuable maxim in law, that the court answers to questions of law, and the jury to facts. Every day's experience evinces the wisdom of this rule." United States v. Wilson, Baldw. 108. We quote also from an Alabama case : " When the power of juries to find a general verdict, and consequently their right to determine without appeal both law and fact, is admitted, the abstract question whether it is or is not their duty to receive the law from the court becomes rather a question of casuistry or conscience than one of law ; nor can we think that anything is gained in the administration of criminal justice by urging the jury to disregard the opinion of the court upon the law of the case. It must, we think, be admitted, that the judge is better qualified to expound the law, from his previous training, than the jury ; and in practice unless he manifests a wanton disregard of the rights of the prisoner, — a circumstance which rarely happens in this age of the world and in this country, — his opinion of the law will be received by the jury as an authoritative exposition, from their conviction of his superior knowledge of the subject. The right of the jury is doubtless one of inestimable value, especially in those cases where it may be supposed that the government has an interest in the conviction of the criminal; but in this country where the government in all its branches, executive, legislative, and judicial, is created by the people, and is in fact their servant, we are unable to perceive why the jury should be invited or urged to exercise this right contrary to their own convictions of their capacity to do so, without danger of mistake. It appears to us that it is sufficient that it is admitted that it is their peculiar province to determine facts, intents, and purposes ; that it is their right to find a general verdict, and consequently that they must determine the law ; and whether in the exercise of this right, they will distrust the court as expounders of the law, or whether they will receive the law from the court, must be left to their own discretion under the sanction of the oath they have taken." State v. Jones, 5 Ala. 672.

It cannot be denied that discredit is sometimes brought upon the administration of justice by juries acquitting parties who are sufficiently shown to be guilty, and where, had the trial been by the court, a conviction would have been sure to follow. In such cases it must be supposed that the jury have been controlled by their prejudices or their sympathies. However that may be, it by no means follows that because the machinery of jury trial does not work satisfactorily in

ardy upon the same charge. One trial and verdict must, as a general rule, protect him against any subsequent accusation, whether the verdict be for or against him, and whether the courts are satisfied with the verdict or not. We shall not attempt at this point to collect together the great number of legal decisions bearing upon the question of legal jeopardy, and the exceptions to the general rule above stated; for these the reader must be referred to the treatises on criminal law, where the subject will be found extensively treated. It will be sufficient for our present purpose to indicate very briefly the general rules.

A person is once in jeopardy when he is put upon trial, before a court of competent jurisdiction, upon an indictment or infor-

every case, we must therefore condemn and abolish the system, or, what is still worse, tolerate it, and yet denounce it as being unworthy of public confidence. Jury trial, when considered in all its aspects, — as an instrument in the administration of justice; as an educator of the people in law and politics; and as a means of making them feel their responsibility in the government, and the important part they bear in its administration, — is by far the best system of trial yet devised; and we must take it with all its concomitants, among which is a due sense of independence in the jurors. The institution loses its value when the jury becomes a mere instrument for receiving and echoing back the opinions of the judge on the case in trial. Concede its defects, and the truth still remains, that its benefits are indispensable. The remarks of the most distinguished jury lawyer known to English history may be quoted as peculiarly appropriate in this connection : " It is of the nature of everything that is great and useful, both in the animate and inanimate world, to be wild and irregular, and we must be content to take them with the alloys which belong to them, or live without them. . . . . Liberty herself, the last and best gift of God to his creatures, must be taken just as she is. You might pare her down into bashful regularity, shape her into a perfect model of severe, scrupulous law; but she would then be Liberty no longer; and you must be content to die under the lash of this inexorable justice which you had exchanged for the banners of freedom." Erskine on trial of Stackpole for libel on Hastings.

The province of the jury is sometimes invaded by instructions requiring them to adopt, as absolute conclusions of law, those deductions which they are at liberty to draw from a particular state of facts, if they regard them as reasonable : such as that a homicide must be presumed malicious, unless the defendant proves the contrary : which is a rule contradictory of the results of common observation ; or that evidence of a previous good character in the defendant ought to be disregarded, unless the other proof presents a doubtful case : which would deprive an accused party of his chief protection in many cases of false accusations and conspiracies. Upon the presumption of malice in homicide, the reader is referred to the Review of the Trial of Prof. Webster, by Hon. Joel Parker, in the North American Review, No. 72, p. 178. See also upon the functions of judge and jury respectively, the case of Maher v. People, 10 Mich. 212.

mation which is so far valid as to be sufficient to sustain a conviction, and a jury has been charged with his deliverance.[1] And a jury is said to be thus charged when they have been impanelled and sworn.[2] The defendant then becomes entitled to a verdict which shall constitute a bar to a new prosecution, and he cannot be deprived of this bar by a *nolle prosequi* entered by the prosecuting officer against his will, or by a discharge of the jury and a continuance of the cause.[3]

If, however, the court had no jurisdiction of the case,[4] or if the indictment was so far defective that it constituted no legal charge of crime, and no valid judgment could be rendered upon it,[5] or if by any overruling necessity the jury are discharged without a verdict,[6] which might happen from the sickness or death of the judge holding the court,[7] or of a juror,[8] or the inability of the jury to agree upon a verdict after reasonable time for deliberation and effort;[9] or if the term of the court comes to an end before the trial is finished,[10] or the jury are discharged without verdict with the consent of the defendant, express or implied,[11] or if, after verdict against the accused, it has been set aside on

---

[1] Commonwealth *v.* Cook, 6 S. & R. 586 ; State *v.* Norvell, 2 Yerg. 24 ; People *v.* McGowan, 17 Wend. 386 ; Price *v.* State, 19 Ohio, 423 ; Wright *v.* State, 5 Ind. 292 ; People *v.* Cook, 10 Mich. 164 ; State *v.* Ned, 7 Port. 217 ; State *v.* Ephraim, 2 Dev. & Bat. 162. It cannot be said, however, that a party is in legal jeopardy in a prosecution brought about by his own procurement ; and a former conviction or acquittal is consequently no bar to a second indictment, if the former trial was brought about by the procurement of the defendant, and the conviction or acquittal was the result of fraud or collusion on his part. State *v.* Green, 16 Iowa, 239.

[2] McFadden *v.* Commonwealth, 23 Penn. St. 12.

[3] People *v.* Barrett, 2 Caines, 304 ; Commonwealth *v.* Tuck, 20 Pick. 365 ; Mounts *v.* State, 14 Ohio, 295.

[4] Commonwealth *v.* Goddard, 13 Mass. 455 ; People *v.* Tyler, 7 Mich. 161.

[5] People *v.* Cook, 10 Mich. 164.

[6] United States *v.* Perez, 9 Wheat. 579 ; State *v.* Ephraim, 2 Dev. & Bat. 166 ; Commonwealth *v.* Fells, 9 Leigh, 620 ; People *v.* Goodwin, 18 Johns. 205.

[7] Nugent *v.* State, 4 Stew. & Port. 72.

[8] Hector *v.* State, 2 Mo. 166 ; State *v.* Curtis, 5 Humph. 601 ; Mahala *v.* State, 10 Yerg. 532.

[9] People *v.* Goodwin, 18 Johns. 187 ; Miller *v.* State, 8 Ind. 325.

[10] State *v.* Brooks, 3 Humph. 70 ; State *v.* Battle, 7 Ala. 259 ; Mahala *v.* State, 10 Yerg. 532; State *v.* Spier, 1 Dev. 491.

[11] State *v.* Slack, 6 Ala. 676 ; Elijah *v.* State, 1 Humph. 103 ; Commonwealth *v.* Stowell, 9 Met. 572.

his motion for a new trial, or on writ of error, or the judgment thereon been arrested ;[1] in any of these cases the accused may again be put upon trial upon the same facts before charged against him, and the proceedings had will constitute no protection. But where the legal bar has once attached, the government cannot avoid it by varying the form of the charge in a new accusation ; if the first indictment or information were such that the accused might have been convicted under it on proof of the facts by which the second is sought to be sustained, then the jeopardy which attached upon the first must constitute a protection against a trial on the second.[2] And if a prisoner is acquitted on some of the counts in an indictment, and convicted on others, and a new trial is granted on his motion, he can only be put upon trial the second time on those counts on which he was before convicted, and is forever discharged from the others.[3]

Excessive Fines and Cruel and Unusual Punishments.

It is also a constitutional requirement that excessive fines shall not be imposed, nor cruel and unusual punishments inflicted.

Within such bounds as may be prescribed by law, the question what fine shall be imposed is one addressed to the discretion of the court. But it is a discretion to be judicially exercised, and it would be error in law to inflict a punishment clearly excessive.[4] A fine should have some reference to the party's ability to pay it.

---

[1] Casborus v. People, 13 Johns. 351. But where the indictment was good, and the judgment was erroneously arrested, the verdict was held to be a bar. State v. Norvell, 2 Yerg. 24. So, if the error was in the judgment, and not in the prior proceedings, if the judgment is reversed, the prisoner must be discharged. Lowenberg v. People, 27 N. Y. 336. But it is competent for the legislature to provide that, on reversing the erroneous judgment in such a case, the court, if the prior proceedings are regular, shall remand the case for the proper sentence. McKee v. People, 32 N. Y. 239.

[2] State v. Cooper, 1 Green. 360 ; Commonwealth v. Roby, 12 Pick. 504 ; People v. McGowen, 17 Wend. 386 ; Price v. State, 19 Ohio, 423 ; State v. Benham, 7 Conn. 414.

[3] Campbell v. State, 9 Yerg. 333 ; State v. Kittle, 2 Tyler, 471 ; Morris v. State, 8 S. & M. 762 ; Esmon v. State, 1 Swan, 14 ; Guenther v. People, 24 N. Y. 100.

[4] See Barker v. People, 3 Cow. 686. See this case, on the subject of cruel and unusual punishments generally. See also Done v. People, 5 Parker, 364.

By Magna Charta a freeman was not to be amerced for a small fault, but according to the degree of the fault, and for a great crime in proportion to the heinousness of it, *saving to him his contenement;* and after the same manner a merchant, *saving to him his merchandise.* And a villein was to be amerced after the same manner, *saving to him his wainage.* The merciful spirit of these provisions addresses itself to the criminal courts of the American States through the provisions of their constitutions.

It has been decided by the Supreme Court of Connecticut that it was not competent, in the punishment of a common-law offence, to inflict fine and imprisonment without limitation. The precedent it was said, cited by counsel contending for the opposite doctrine, of a punishment for a libel published against the Lord Chancellor Bacon, was deprived of all force of authority by the circumstances attending it; the extravagance of the punishment was clearly referable to the temper of the times. " The common law can never require a fine to the extent of the offender's goods and chattels, or sentence of imprisonment for life. The punishment is both uncertain and unnecessary. It is no more difficult to limit the imprisonment of an atrocious offender to an adequate number of years than to prescribe a limited punishment for minor offences. And when there exists no firmly established practice, and public necessity or convenience does not imperiously demand the principle contended for, it cannot be justified by the common law, as it wants the main ingredients on which that law is founded. Indefinite punishments are fraught with danger, and ought not to be admitted unless the written law should authorize them."[1]

It is somewhat difficult to determine precisely what is meant by cruel and unusual punishments. Probably a punishment declared by statute for an offence which was punishable in the same way at the common law could not be regarded as cruel or unusual in the constitutional sense. And probably any new statutory offence may be made punishable to the extent permitted by the common law for similar offences. But those degrading punishments which in any State had become obsolete before its existing constitution was adopted, we think may well be held to be forbidden by it as cruel and unusual. We may well doubt the right to establish the whipping-post and the pillory in

[1] State *v.* Danforth, 3 Conn. 115.

States where they were never recognized as instruments of punishment, or in States whose constitutions, revised since public opinion had banished them, had forbidden cruel and unusual punishments. In such a case the public sentiment had condemned them as cruel, and they had not merely become unusual, but altogether ceased to be inflicted.

A defendant, however, in any case, is entitled to have the precise measure of punishment meted out to him which the law provides, and no other. A different punishment cannot be substituted, on the ground of its being less in severity. Sentence to transportation for a capital offence is void, and the prisoner is entitled to his discharge, because, the error being in the judgment, he cannot be tried again.[1] If, however, the legal punishment consists of two distinct and severable things, — as fine and imprisonment, — the imposition of either is legal, and the defendant cannot be heard to complain that the other was not imposed also.[2]

The Right of Counsel.

Perhaps the most important privilege of the person accused of crime, connected with his trial, is to be defended by counsel. From very early days a class of men, who have made the laws of their country their special study, and who have been accepted for the confidence of the court in their learning and integrity, have been set apart as officers of the court, whose special duty it was to render aid to the parties and the court,[3] in the application of the law to legal controversies. These persons, before entering upon their employment, were to take an oath of fidelity to the courts whose officers they were, and to their clients,[4] and it was their special

[1] Bourne v. The King, 7 Ad. & Ellis, 58. See also Whitebread v. Queen, 7 Q. B. 582; Rex v. Fletcher, Rus. & Ry. 58. In this case, the court was equally divided on the question, whether the omission, in a sentence to death, of the subsequent directions which the law provided for, rendered the sentence void. See Hartung v. People, 26 N. Y. 167; Elliott v. People, 13 Mich. 365.

[2] See Kane v. People, 8 Wend. 203.

[3] In Commonwealth v. Knapp, 9 Pick. 498, the court refused, on the application of the defendant, to assign Mr. Rantoul as his counsel, because, though admitted to the Common Pleas, he was not yet an attorney of the Supreme Court, and that court, therefore, had not the usual control over him; and besides, counsel was to give aid to the court, as well as to the prisoner, and therefore it was proper that a person of more legal experience should be assigned.

[4] " Every countor is chargeable by the oath that he shall do no wrong nor

duty to see that no wrong was done their clients, by means of false or partial witnesses, or through the perversion or misapplication of law by the court. Strangely enough, however, the aid of this profession was denied in the very cases when it was needed most, and it has cost a long struggle, continuing even into the present century, to rid the English criminal law of one of its most horrible features. In civil causes and on charges for misdemeanor, the parties were entitled to the aid of counsel in eliciting the facts and in presenting both the facts and the law to the court and jury; but when the government charged a party with treason or felony, he was denied this privilege.[1] Only such

falsity, contrary to his knowledge, but shall plead for his client the best he can, according to his understanding." Mirror of Justices, ch. 2, § 5. The oath in Pennsylvania, on the admission of an attorney to the bar, " to behave himself in the office of an attorney, according to the best of his learning and ability, and with all good fidelity, as well to the court as to the client; that he will use no falsehood, nor delay any man's cause, for lucre or malice," is said, by Mr. Sharswood, to present a comprehensive summary of his duties as a practitioner. Sharswood's Legal Ethics, p. 3. The advocate's oath, in Geneva, was as follows : " I solemnly swear, before Almighty God, to be faithful to the Republic, and to the canton of Geneva ; never to depart from the respect due to the tribunals and authorities ; never to counsel or maintain a cause which does not appear to be just or equitable, unless it be the defence of an accused person ; never to employ, knowingly, for the purpose of maintaining the causes confided to me, any means contrary to truth, and never seek to mislead the judges by any artifice or false statement of facts or law ; to abstain from all offensive personality, and to advance no fact contrary to the honor and reputation of the parties, if it be not indispensable to the cause with which I may be charged ; not to encourage either the commencement or continuance of a suit from any motives of passion or interest ; nor to reject, for any consideration personal to myself, the cause of the weak, the stranger, or the oppressed." In " The Lawyer's Oath, its Obligations, and some of the Duties springing out of them," by D. Bethune Duffield, Esq., a masterly analysis is given of this oath ; and he well says of it : " Here you have the creed of an upright and honorable lawyer. The clear, terse, and lofty language in which it is expressed needs no argument to elucidate its principles, no eloquence to enforce its obligations. It has in it the sacred savor of divine inspiration, and sounds almost like a restored reading from Sinai's original, but broken, tablets."

[1] When an ignorant person, unaccustomed to public assemblies, and perhaps feeble in body or in intellect, was put on trial on a charge which, whether true or false, might speedily consign him to an ignominious death, with able counsel arrayed against him, and all the machinery of the law ready to be employed to produce the evidence of circumstances indicating guilt, it is painful to contemplate the barbarity which could deny him professional aid. Especially when in most cases he would be imprisoned immediately on being apprehended, and

legal questions as he could suggest was counsel allowed to argue for him ;[1] and this is but a poor privilege to one who is himself unlearned in the law, and who, as he cannot fail to perceive the monstrous injustice of the whole proceeding, will be quite likely to accept any perversion of the law that occurs in the course of it as quite regular, because entirely in the spirit that denies him a defence. Only after the Revolution of 1688 was a full defence allowed on trials for treason,[2] and not until 1836 was

would thereby be prevented from making even the feeble preparations for defence that might otherwise have been within his power. A " trial " under such circumstances would frequently be only a judicial murder. The spirit in which the old law was administered may be judged by the case of Sir William Parkins, tried for high treason before Lord Holt and his associates in 1695, after the statute 7 William III. ch. 3, allowing counsel to prisoners indicted for treason, but *one day* before it was to take effect. He prayed to be allowed counsel, and quoted the preamble to the statute, that such allowance was just and reasonable. His prayer was denied, Lord Holt declaring that he must administer the law as he found it, and could not anticipate the operation of an act of Parliament even by a single day. The accused was convicted and executed. See Lieber's Hermeneutics, ch. 4, § 15 ; Sedgwick on Stat. & Const. Law, 81.

[1] Probably few prisoners were learned enough to suggest a question like the following : —

On trial of Francis Francia, for high treason, in 1716, Sir Dennis Dutry was called as a juror, and challenged.

" *Prisoner.* His name is Dennis, and they have given me a panel with barbarous Latin. In my copy of the panel, he is returned by the name of Dyonisius. That is not the same name.

" *Sir J. Jekyll*, for the crown. He is to have a copy of the panel, but it is not to be put into English for him.

" *Lord Ch. Baron.* You offer no cause for challenge.

" *Prisoner.* I hope I prove his name is returned, in the panel, Dyonisius.

" *Lord Ch. Baron.* It is so, and that is the Latin for Dennis.

" *Prisoner.* No, it is not : Dennis is a saint in France, and Dyonisius is a saint in Italy. They are two different names, and of different countries.

" *Lord Ch. Baron.* Dyonisius is the Latin for Dennis. If they don't challenge him peremptorily, he must be sworn."

So the prisoner was compelled to challenge peremptorily. 6 Hargrave's State Trials, 59.

[2] See an account of the final passage of this bill in Macaulay's " England," vol. 4, ch. 21. It is surprising, that the effort to extend the same right to all persons accused of felony was so strenuously resisted afterwards, and that, too, notwithstanding the best lawyers in the realm admitted its importance and justice. " I have myself," said Mr. Scarlett, " *often* seen persons I thought innocent convicted, and the guilty escape, for want of some acute and intelligent counsel to show the bearings of the different circumstances on the conduct and situation of the prisoner." House of Commons' Debates, April 25, 1826. " It has lately been

the same privilege extended to persons accused of other felonies.[1]

my lot," said Mr. Denman, on the same occasion, " to try two prisoners who were deaf and dumb, and who could only be made to understand what was passing by the signs of their friends. The cases were clear and simple; but if they had been circumstantial cases, in what a situation would the judge and jury be placed, when the prisoner could have no counsel to plead for him." The cases *looked* clear and simple, to Mr. Denman ; but how could he know they would not have looked otherwise, had the coloring of the prosecution been relieved by a counter-presentation for the defence ? See Sidney Smith's article on Counsel for Prisoners, 45 Edinb. Rev. p. 74 ; Works, vol. 2, p. 353. The plausible objection to extending the right was, that the judge would be counsel for the prisoner, — a pure fallacy at the best, and, with some judges, a frightful mockery. Baron Garrow, in a charge to a grand-jury, said, " It has been truly said that, in criminal cases, judges were counsel for the prisoners. So, undoubtedly, they were, as far as they could be, to prevent undue prejudice, to guard against improper influence being excited against prisoners ; but it was impossible for them to go further than this, for they could not suggest the course of defence prisoners ought to pursue ; for judges only saw the depositions so short a time before the accused appeared at the bar of their country, that it was quite impossible for them to act fully in that capacity."

If one would see how easily, and yet in what a shocking manner, a judge might pervert the law and the evidence, and act the part of both prosecutor and king's counsel, while assuming to be counsel for the prisoner, he need not go further back than the early trials in our own country, and he is referred for a specimen to the trials of Robert Tucker and others for piracy, before Chief Justice Trott, at Charleston, S. C., in 1718, as reported in 6 Hargrave's State Trials, 156 *et seq.* Especially may he there see how the statement of prisoners in one case, to which no credit was given for their exculpation, was used as hearsay evidence to condemn a prisoner in another case. All these abuses would have been checked, perhaps altogether prevented, had the prisoners had able and fearless counsel. But without counsel for the defence, and under such a judge, the witnesses were not free to testify, the prisoners could not safely make even the most honest explanation, and the jury, when they retired, could only feel that returning a verdict in accordance with the opinion of the judge was only matter of form. Sidney Smith's lecture on " The judge that smites contrary to the law " is worthy of being carefully pondered in this connection. " If ever a nation was happy, if ever a nation was visibly blessed by God, if ever a nation was honored abroad, and left at home under a government (which we can now conscientiously call a liberal government) to the full career of talent, industry, and vigor, we are at this moment that people, and this is our happy lot. First, the Gospel has done it, and then justice has done it ; and he who thinks it his duty that this happy condition of existence may remain must guard the piety of these times, and he must watch over the spirit of justice which exists in these times. First, he must take care that the altars of God are not polluted, that the

[1] By statute, 6 and 7 William IV. ch. 114.

With us it is a universal principle of constitutional law, that the prisoner shall be allowed a defence by counsel. The humanity of the law has generally provided that, when the prisoner is unable to employ counsel, the court may designate some one to defend him, who shall be paid by the government; but when no such provision is made, it is a duty which counsel so designated owes to his profession, to the court engaged in the trial, and to the cause of justice, not to withhold his best exertions in the defence of one who has the double misfortune to be stricken by poverty and accused of crime. No one is at liberty to decline such an appointment,[1] and it is to be hoped that few would be disposed to do so.

When the Constitution secures this right, it secures it with all its accustomed privileges and protections. Among these is a shield of protection that is thrown around the confidence the relation of counsel and client requires, and that does not permit the disclosure by the former, even in the courts of justice, of whatever may have been communicated to him by the latter with a view to pending or anticipated litigation. This is the client's privilege; the counsel cannot waive it; and the court would not permit the disclosure, even if the client were not present to take the objection.[2]

Christian faith is retained in purity and in perfection; and then, turning to human affairs, let him strive for spotless, incorruptible justice; praising, honoring, and loving the just judge, and abhorring as the worst enemy of mankind him who is placed there to 'judge after the law, and who smites contrary to the law.'"

[1] Vise v. Hamilton County, 19 Ill. 18. It has been held that, in the absence of express statutory provisions, counties were not liable to compensate counsel assigned by the court to defend poor prisoners. Bacon v. Wayne Co., 1 Mich. 461; but there are several cases to the contrary. Webb v. Baird, 6 Ind. 13; Hall v. Washington Co., 2 Greene (Iowa), 473; Carpenter v. Dane Co., 9 Wis. 277. But we think a court has a right to require the service, whether compensation is made or not; and that counsel who should decline to perform it, for no other reason than that the law does not provide pecuniary compensation, is unfit to be an officer of a court of justice. Said Chief Justice Hale, in one case: " Although sergeants have a monopoly of practice in the Common Pleas, they have a right to practise, and do practise, at this bar; and if we were to assign one of them as counsel, and he was to refuse to act, we should make bold to commit him to prison." Life of Chief Justice Hale, in Campbell's Lives of the Chief Justices, vol. 2.

[2] For a very good case, giving the history and the reason of the exemption of counsel from disclosing professional communications, see Whiting v. Barney, 30 N. Y. 330. The privilege would not cover communications made, not with a view

Once engaged in a cause, the counsel is not afterwards at liberty to withdraw from it, without consent of his client and of the court; and even though he may believe his client guilty, he should endeavor to protect him against a conviction contrary to the law. The cause of public justice will suffer far more through the conviction of a guilty person by means of a perversion of the law, than by his escaping punishment altogether.[1]

But how far the counsel may go in pressing for the acquittal of his client, and to what extent he may be justified in throwing his own personal character as a weight in the scale of justice, are questions of ethics rather than of law. No man is justifiable who defends even a just cause with the weapons of fraud and falsehood, and no man can excuse himself for accepting the confidence of the accused, and then betraying it by a feeble and heartless defence. And in these cases we think the court may sometimes have a duty to perform in seeing that the prisoner suffers nothing

to professional assistance, but in order to induce the attorney to aid in a criminal act. People *v.* Blakeley, 4 Park, Cr. R. 176 ; Bank of Utica *v.* Mersereau, 3 Barb. Ch. R. 598. It has been intimated, in New York, that the statute making parties witnesses, had done away this rule. Mitchell's case, 12 Abb. Pr. Rep. 249. *Sed quære.* If this be so, the protection would still be the same, in criminal cases; for a party accused of crime cannot be compelled to give evidence against himself, and the reason for protecting professional confidence is the same as formerly.

[1] It may even become necessary sometimes for the lawyer to interpose himself between the court and the accused, and to fearlessly brave all consequences, when in no other mode can the law be vindicated and justice done; but the cases are so rare, that doubtless they will always stand out, in judicial history, as prominent exceptions to the ready obedience which the bar should yield to the commands of the court. The famous scene between Mr. Justice Buller and Mr. Erskine, on the trial of the Dean of St. Asaphs, for libel, — 5 Campbell's Lives of Chancellors, ch. 158, — will readily occur to the reader as one of these exceptional cases. Lord Campbell says of Erskine's conduct : " This noble stand, for the independence of the bar, would alone have entitled Erskine to the statue which the profession affectionately erected, to his memory, in Lincoln's Inn Hall. We are to admire the decency and propriety of his demeanor, during the struggle, no less than its spirit, and the felicitous precision with which he meted out the requisite and justifiable portion of defiance. His example has had a salutary effect, in illustrating and establishing the relative duties of judge and advocate in England." And again, in speaking of Mr. Fox's libel bill : " I have said, and I still think, that this great constitutional triumph is mainly to be ascribed to Lord Camden, who had been fighting in the cause for half a century, and uttered his last words in the House of Lords in its support; but had he not received the invaluable assistance of Erskine, as counsel for the Dean of St. Asaphs, *the Star Chamber might have been re-established in this country.*"

from inattention or haste on the part of his counsel, or impatience on the part of the prosecuting officer, or of the court itself. Time may be precious to the court, but it is vastly more so to him whose life or whose liberty may depend upon the careful and patient consideration of the evidence, when the counsel for the defence is endeavoring to submit it to logical analysis, and to show that, how suspicious soever it may be, it is still consistent with innocence. Often, indeed, it must happen that the impression of the prisoner's guilt which the judge and the jury unavoidably receive when the case is first opened to them by the prosecuting officer will, insensibly to themselves, color all the evidence in the case, and only a sense of duty will make them give due attention to the summing up for the prisoner, which after all may prove unexpectedly convincing. Doubtless the privilege of counsel is sometimes abused in these cases; we cannot think an advocate of high standing and character has a right to endeavor to rob the jury of their opinion by asseverating his own belief in the innocence of his client; and there will be cases where the court will feel compelled to impose some reasonable restraints upon the address to the jury;[1] but it is better in these cases to err on the side of liberality, and restrictions that do not leave to counsel, who were apparently acting in good faith, such reasonable time and opportunity as they deemed necessary for presenting their client's case fully, might be regarded as legally so far erroneous as to warrant setting aside a verdict of guilty.[2]

Whether counsel are to address the jury on questions of law, in criminal cases, is a question not free from difficulty. If the jury in the particular case, by the constitution or laws of the State, are judges of the law, it would seem that counsel should be at liberty to address them fully upon it;[3] though the contrary seems to have been held in Maryland;[4] while in Massachusetts, where it is

---

[1] Murphy v. State, 6 Ind. 590; Lynch v. State, 9 Ind. 541.

[2] In People v. Keenan, 13 Cal. 581, a verdict, in a capital case, was set aside on this ground.

[3] Lynch v. State, 9 Ind. 541; Murphy v. State, 6 Ind. 590.

[4] Franklin v. State, 12 Md. 236. What was held in this case was, that counsel should not be allowed to argue the constitutionality of a statute to the jury; and that the constitution, making the jury judges of the law as well as of the facts, would not empower them to decide a statute invalid. This ruling corresponds with that of Judge Chase in United States v. Callendar, Whart. State Trials, 688.

expected that the jury will receive the law from the court, it is nevertheless held that counsel has a right to argue the law to them.[1] It is unquestionably more decorous and more respectful to the bench, that argument upon the law should always be addressed to the court; and such we believe is the general practice. The jury hear the argument, and they have a right to give it such weight as it seems to them properly to be entitled to.

For misconduct in their profession, the members of the bar are more directly and summarily amenable to the courts, who will not fail, in all proper cases, to use their power to protect clients or the public, or to preserve the profession from the contamination and disgrace of a vicious associate.[2] A man of bad reputation may be expelled for that alone;[3] and a counsel who has once taken part in litigation, and become the adviser or intrusted with the secrets of one party, will not afterwards be suffered to engage for an opposing party, notwithstanding the original employment has ceased, and he is not chargeable with intentional wrong.[4] And, on the

[1] Commonwealth v. Porter, 10 Met. 263; Commonwealth v. Austin, 7 Gray, 51.

[2] "As a class, attorneys are supposed to be, and in fact have always been, the vindicators of individual rights, and the fearless asserters of the principles of civil liberty, existing where alone they can exist, in a government, not of parties nor of men, but of laws. On the other hand, to declare them irresponsible to any power but public opinion and their consciences, would be incompatible with free government. Individuals of the class may, and sometimes do, forfeit their professional franchise by abusing it; and a power to exact the forfeiture must be lodged somewhere. Such a power is indispensable to protect the court, the administration of justice, and themselves. Abuses must necessarily creep in; and having a deep stake in the character of their profession, they are vitally concerned in preventing it from being sullied by the misconduct of unworthy members of it. No class of community is more dependent on its reputation for honor and integrity. It is indispensable to the purposes of its creation to assign it a high and honorable standing; but to put it above the judiciary, whose official tenure is good behavior, and whose members are removable from office by the legislature, would render it intractable; and it is therefore necessary to assign it but an equal share of independence. In the absence of specific provision to the contrary, the power of removal is, from its nature, commensurate with the power of appointment, and it is consequently the business of the judges to deal with delinquent members of the bar, and withdraw their faculties when they are incorrigible." Gibson, Ch. J., in re Austin et al. 5 Rawle, 203.

[3] For example, one whose reputation for truth and veracity is so bad that his neighbors would not believe him on oath. Matter of Mills, 1 Mich. 393.

[4] In Gaulden v. State, 11 Geo. 47, it was held that the late solicitor-general, who had instituted a prosecution with which he was no longer connected, could not be suffered to assist in the defence.

22

other hand, the court will not allow counsel to be made the instrument of injustice, or permit the client to exact of him services which are inconsistent with the obligation he owes to the courts and to public justice, which obligation is higher and more sacred than any which can rest upon him to gratify the client's whims or to assist his revenge.[1]

The Writ of Habeas Corpus.

One of the principal protections to personal liberty still remains

[1] In Rush v. Cavenaugh, 2 Penn. St. 189, a prosecutor in a criminal case refused to pay the charges of the counsel employed by him to prosecute in the place of the attorney-general, because the counsel, after a part of the evidence had been put in, had consented that the charge should be withdrawn. In considering whether this was a sufficient reason for the refusal, Chief Justice Gibson says: " The material question is, did the plaintiff violate his professional duty to his client in consenting to withdraw his charge of forgery against Crean when before the alderman, instead of lending himself to the prosecution of one whom he then and has since believed to be an innocent man?

" It is a popular but gross mistake to suppose that a lawyer owes no fidelity to any one except his client; and that the latter is the keeper of his professional conscience. He is expressly bound by his official oath to behave himself in his office of attorney with all due fidelity to the court as well as to the client; and he violates it when he consciously presses for an unjust judgment; much more so when he presses for the conviction of an innocent man. But the prosecution was depending before an alderman, to whom, it may be said, the plaintiff was bound to no such fidelity. Still, he was bound by those obligations which, without oaths, rest upon all men. The high and honorable office of a counsel would be degraded to that of a mercenary, were he compelled to do the bidding of his client against the dictates of his conscience. The origin of the name proves the client to be subordinate to the counsel as his patron. Besides, had the plaintiff succeeded in having Crean held to answer, it would have been his duty to abandon the prosecution at the return of the recognizance. As the office of attorney-general is a public trust which involves, in the discharge of it, the exercise of an almost boundless discretion, by an officer who stands as impartial as a judge, it might be doubted whether counsel retained by a private prosecutor can be allowed to perform any part of his duty; certainly not unless in subservience to his will and instructions. With that restriction usage has sanctioned the practice of employing professional assistants, to whom the attorney-general or his regular substitute may, if he please, confide the direction of the particular prosecution; and it has been beneficial to do so where the prosecuting officer has been overmatched or overborne by numbers. In that predicament the ends of justice may require him to accept assistance. But the professional assistant, like the regular deputy, exercises not his own discretion, but that of the attorney-general, whose locum tenens at sufferance he is; and he consequently does so under the obligations of the official oath."

to be mentioned. But before calling attention to that, it may be important to consider what is meant by personal liberty in the law, that we may the better understand the application of what may be said concerning its guaranties.

Blackstone says personal liberty consists in the power of locomotion, of changing situation, or removing one's person to whatever place one's inclination may direct, without imprisonment or restraint, unless by due course of law.[1] The definition implies that certain qualifications and limitations rest upon this power, which are known to the law and enforced by it, without infringing upon constitutional liberty. Of these qualifications and limitations there are two classes,— those of a public and those of a private nature.

The first class are those which spring from the relative duties and obligations of man to society and his fellow-man, and they may be arranged into sub-classes: as, 1. Those imposed to prevent the commission of crime which is threatened ; 2. Those in punishment of crime committed ; 3. Those in punishment of contempts of courts or legislative bodies, or to render their jurisdiction effectual ; 4. Those necessary to enforce the duty citizens owe in defence of the State ; 5. Those which may become important to protect community against the acts of those who, by reason of mental infirmity, are incapable of self-control. All these limitations are well recognized and understood, but their particular discussion does not belong to our subject. The second class are those which spring from the helpless or dependent condition of individuals in the various relations of life.

1. The husband, at the common law, is recognized as having legal custody of, and power of control over, the wife, with the right to direct as to her labor, and insist upon its performance. The precise nature of the restraints which may be imposed by the husband upon the wife's actions, it is not easy, from the nature of the case, to point out and define ; but they can only be such gentle restraints on her liberty as her improper conduct may seem to require ;[2] and the general tendency of public sentiment, as well as of the modern decisions, has been to do away with the arbitrary power which the husband was formerly supposed to possess, and to place the two sexes in the married state more upon

[1] 1 Bl. Com. 134.
[2] 2 Kent, 181 ; see Cochran's case, 8 Dowl. P. C. 630.

a footing of equality. It is believed that the right of the husband to chastise his wife, under any circumstances, would not be recognized in this country, and in any case his right to control would be gone if he should conduct himself towards the wife in a way not warranted by the relation, and which should render it improper for her to cohabit with him, or if he should be guilty of such conduct as would entitle her, under the laws of the State, to a divorce.[1] His right of control is also gone when the parties live apart, under articles of separation.[2]

2. The father of an infant, being obliged by law to support his child, has a corresponding right to control his actions and employ his services during the continuance of legal infancy. The child may be emancipated from this control before coming of age, either by the express assent of the father, or by being turned away from his father's home and left to care for himself; though in neither case would the father be released from an obligation which rests upon him to prevent the child becoming a public charge, and which the State may enforce whenever necessary. The mother during the father's life has a power of control, subordinate to his; but on his death,[3] or conviction and sentence to imprisonment for felony,[4] she succeeds to the relative rights which the father possessed before.

3. The guardian has a power of control over his ward, corresponding in the main with that which the father has over his child, though in some respects more restricted, while in others it is broader. The appointment of guardian when made by the courts is of local force only, being confined to the State in which it is made, and the guardian would have no power to change the domicile of the ward to another State or country. But the appointment commonly has some reference to the possession of property by the ward, and over this property the guardian possesses a power of control which is not possessed by the father over the property owned by the child.

4. The relation of master and apprentice is founded on a contract between the two, generally with the consent of the parent or party standing in *loco parentis* to the latter, by which the

---

[1] Hutcheson *v.* Peck, 5 Johns. 196 ; Love *v.* Moynahan, 16 Ill. 277.

[2] Saunders *v.* Rodway 13 E. L. & E. 463 ; 16 Jur. 1005.

[3] Dedham *v.* Natick, 16 Mass. 135.

[4] Bailey's case, 6 Dowl. P. C. 311.

master is to teach the apprentice some specified trade or means of living. This relation is also statutory and local, and for power to control or punish against the opposition of the apprentice the statute must be examined.

5. The power of the master to impose restraints upon the action of the servant he employs is of so limited a nature that practically it rests upon voluntary assent. If the servant misconducts himself, or refuses to submit to proper control, the master may discharge him, but cannot resort to confinement or personal chastisement.

6. The relation of teacher and scholar places the former more nearly in place of the parent than either of the two preceding relations places the master. While the pupil is under his care, he has a right to enforce obedience to his commands lawfully given in his capacity of teacher, even to the extent of bodily chastisement or confinement. And in deciding questions of discipline, he acts judicially and is not to be made liable, either civilly or criminally, unless he has acted with express malice, or been guilty of such excess in punishment that malice must be implied.[1] All presumptions favor the correctness of his action.

7. Where parties bail another, in legal proceedings, they are regarded in law as his jailers, selected by himself, and with the right to his legal custody, for the purpose of seizing and delivering him up to the officers of the law at any time before the liability of the bail has become fixed by a forfeiture being judicially declared on his failure to comply with the conditions of the bond.[2] This is a right which they may exercise in person or by agent,[3] and without resort to judicial process.

8. The control of the creditor over the person of his debtor through legal process to enforce payment of his demand is now nearly abolished, thanks to the humane provisions of recent statutory and constitutional provisions. In cases of torts, and where debts were fraudulently contracted, or where there is an attempt at a fraudulent disposition of property with the intent to deprive the creditor of payment, the body of the debtor may be seized and confined; but the reader is referred to the constitution and statutes of his State for information on this subject.

---

[1] State v. Pendergrass, 2 Dev. & Bat. 365; Cooper v. McJunkin, 4 Ind. 290; Commonwealth v. Randall, 4 Gray, 38.

[2] Harp v. Osgood, 2 Hill, 216; Commonwealth v. Brickett, 8 Pick. 138.

[3] Parker v. Bidwell, 3 Conn. 84.

These, then, are the legal restraints upon personal liberty. For any other restraint, or for any abuse of the legal rights which have been specified, the party restrained is entitled to immediate process from the courts, and to speedy relief.

The right to personal liberty did not depend in England on any statute, but it was the birthright of every freeman. As slavery ceased, it became universal, and the judges were bound to protect it by proper writ when infringed. But in those times when the power of the Parliament was undefined and in dispute, and the judges held their offices only during the king's pleasure, it was a matter of course that rights should be violated, and that legal redress should be impracticable, however clear those rights might be. But in other cases it was not so clear what the legal rights of the parties were. The courts which proceeded according to the course of the common law, as well as the courts of chancery, had limits to their authority which could be understood, and a definite course of proceeding marked out by statute or by custom; so that if they exceeded their jurisdiction and invaded the just liberty of the subject, the illegality of the process would generally appear in the proceedings. But there were two tribunals unknown to the common law, but exercising a most fearful authority, against whose abuses it was not easy for the most upright and conscientious judge at all times to afford relief. These were, 1. The *Court of Star Chamber*, which became fully recognized and established in the time of Henry VII., though originating long before. Its jurisdiction extended to all sorts of offences, contempts, and disorders, the punishment of which was not supposed to be adequately provided for by the common law; like slanders of persons in authority, the propagation of seditious news, refusal to lend money to the king, disregard of executive proclamations, &c. It imposed fines without limit, and inflicted any punishment in the discretion of its judges short of death. Even jurors were punished by this court for verdicts in state trials not satisfactory to the authorities. Although the king's chancellor and judges were entitled to seats in this court, its actual administration seems to have fallen into the hands of the king's privy council, which sat as a species of inquisition, and exercised almost any power it saw fit to assume.[1] The court was abolished by the Long Parliament in 1641. 2. The *Court of High Commission*, estab-

---

[1] See Hallam's Constitutional History, chs. 1 and 8.

lished in the time of Elizabeth, exercised a similar power in ecclesiastical matters which the Star Chamber assumed in other cases, and in an equally absolute and arbitrary manner. This court was also abolished in 1641, but was afterwards revived for a short time in the reign of James II.

It is evident that while these tribunals existed there could be no effectual security to liberty. A brief reference to the remarkable struggle during the reign of Charles I. will perhaps the better enable us to understand the importance of the common-law protections to personal liberty to which we shall have occasion to refer, as well as the statutory securities which have since been added.

When the king in 1625 dissolved the Parliament and resorted to forced loans, monopolies, and ship-money as the means of replenishing a treasury that could only lawfully be supplied by taxes voted by the Parliament, the privy council was his convenient means of enforcing compliance with his will. Those who refused to contribute to the loans as demanded were committed to prison. When they petitioned the Court of King's Bench for their discharge, the warden of the Fleet made reply to the writ of *habeas corpus*, that they were detained by a warrant from the privy council, informing him of no particular cause of imprisonment, but that they were committed by the special command of his Majesty. This presented for the decision of the court the question, "Is such a warrant, which does not specify the cause for detention, valid by the laws of England?" The court held that it was, justifying their decision upon supposed precedents, although, as Mr. Hallam says, "it was evidently the consequence of this decision that every statute from the time of Magna Charta, designed to protect the personal liberties of Englishmen, became a dead letter, since the insertion of four words in a warrant (*per speciale mandatum regis*), which might become matter of form, would control their remedial efficacy. And this wound was the more deadly in that the notorious cause of these gentlemen's imprisonment was their withstanding an illegal exaction of money. Everything that distinguished our constitutional laws, all that rendered the name of England valuable, was at stake in this issue."[1] This decision, among other violent acts, led to the Petition of Rights, one of the principal charters of English liberty, but which was not approved by the king until the judges had

---

[1] Hallam's Constitutional History, ch. 7.

intimated that if he saw fit to violate it by arbitrary commitments they would take care that it should not be enforced by their aid against his will. And four years later, when the king committed members of Parliament for words spoken in debate offensive to the royal prerogative, the judges evaded the performance of their duty on *habeas corpus*, and the members were only discharged when the king gave his consent to that course.[1]

The Habeas Corpus Act was passed in 1679, mainly to prevent such abuses, and other evasions of duty by the judges and other officers, and to compel prompt action in any case where illegal imprisonment was alleged. It gave no new rights, but it furnished the means of enforcing those which existed before.[2] The preamble recited that, " whereas great delays have been used by sheriffs, jailers, and other officers, to whose custody any of the king's subjects have been committed for criminal or supposed criminal matters, in making returns of writs of *habeas corpus*, to them directed, by standing out on *alias* or *pluries habeas corpus*, and sometimes more, and by other shifts, to avoid their yielding obedience to such writs, contrary to their duty and the known laws of the land, whereby many of the king's subjects have been and hereafter may be long detained in prison in such cases where by law they are bailable, to their great charge and vexation. For the prevention whereof, and the more speedy relief of all persons imprisoned for any such criminal or supposed criminal matters," the act proceeded to make elaborate and careful provisions for the future. These provisions may be summed up as follows: That the writ of *habeas corpus* might be issued by any court of record or judge thereof, either in term time or vacation, on the application of any person confined or of any other person for him, the application to be in writing and on oath, and with a copy of the warrant of commitment, if any, attached, if procurable ; the writ to be returnable either in court or at chambers ; the person detaining the applicant to make return to the writ by bringing up the prisoner with the cause of his detention, and the court or judge to discharge him, unless the imprisonment appeared to be legal, and in that case to take bail, if the case was bailable ; and performance of all these duties was made compulsory, under heavy penalties.

---

[1] Hallam's Constitutional History, ch. 8.

[2] Hallam's Constitutional History, ch. 13 ; Beeching's case, 4 B. & C. 136 ; Matter of Jackson, 15 Mich. 436.

Thus the duty which the judge or other officer might before evade with impunity, he must now perform or suffer punishment. The act also provided for punishing severely a second commitment for the same cause, after a party had once been discharged on *habeas corpus*, and also made the sending of inhabitants of England, Wales, and Berwick-upon-Tweed abroad for imprisonment illegal, and subject to penalty.[1] Important as this act was, it was less broad in its scope than the remedy had been before, being confined to imprisonment for criminal or supposed criminal matters ;[2] and the contest in Parliament, nearly a century later, to extend its provisions to other cases, was defeated by the opposition of Lord Mansfield, on the ground that it was unnecessary,[3] as it clearly would have been if officers had always been disposed to perform their duty. Another attempt in 1816 was successful.

The Habeas Corpus Act did not, by its terms, extend to the American Colonies, but it was in some expressly, and in others by silent acquiescence adopted, and all the subsequent legislation in the American States has been based upon it, and has consisted of little more than a re-enactment of its essential provisions.

What Courts issue the Writ.

As a general rule the protection of personal liberty rests with the States, and to the State courts the party must apply for relief on *habeas corpus* when his liberty is restrained. The jurisdiction of the national courts is much circumscribed, and is confined to those cases where the unlawful confinement is under pretence of national authority, and to other cases where this process seems important to the enforcement of the national authority.

1. The Judiciary Act of 1789 provided that each of the several Federal courts should have power to issue the writ of *habeas corpus*, and that either of the justices of the Supreme Court, as well as District judges, should have power to grant writs of *habeas corpus* for the purposes of an inquiry into the cause of commitment. Provided, that in no case should such writs extend to

---

[1] Mr. Hurd, in the Appendix to his excellent treatise on the Writ of Habeas Corpus, gives a complete copy of the act.

[2] Mayor of London's case, 3 Wils. 198 ; Wilson's case, 7 Q. B. 984.

[3] Life of Mansfield by Lord Campbell ; 2 Lives of Chief Justices, ch. 35 ; 15 Hansard's Debates, 897 *et seq.*

prisoners in jail, unless where they were in·custody under or by color of the authority of the United States, or were committed to trial before some court of the same, or were necessary to be brought into court to testify.[1]

2. During the South Carolina troubles a further provision was thought necessary, and an act was passed providing that either of the justices of the Supreme Court, or a judge of any District Court of the United States, should have power to grant writs of *habeas corpus* in all cases of a prisoner or prisoners in jail or confinement, for any act done or omitted to be done in pursuance of a law of the United States, or any order, process, or decree of any judge or court thereof, — the purpose of the provision being to protect officers and others acting under the national authority from being prosecuted and imprisoned for so doing, under pretence of State authority.[2]

3. In 1842 a further provision seemed to become necessary to prevent the government being embroiled with foreign nations, and an act was passed growing out of McLeod's case,[3] which provided that, either of the justices of the Supreme Court, or any judge of any District Court of the United States in which a prisoner is confined, in addition to the authority previously conferred by law, should have power to grant writs of *habeas corpus* in all cases of any prisoner or prisoners in jail or confinement, where he, she, or they, being subjects or citizens of a foreign state, and domiciled therein, shall be committed, or confined, or in custody, under or by any authority or law or process founded thereon, of the United States or of any one of them, for or on account of any act done or omitted under any alleged right, title, authority, privilege, protection, or exemption, set up or claimed under the commission or order or sanction of any foreign state or sovereignty, the validity or effect whereof depends upon the law of nations, or under color thereof.[4]

These are the cases in which the national courts and judges have authority ; in other cases the party must be remitted to his remedy in the State courts.[5] And although the State courts for-

---

[1] 1 Statutes at Large, 81.

[2] 4 Statutes at Large, 634. See Robinson's case, 6 McLean, 355.

[3] 25 Wend. 482. See review of this case by Judge Talmadge, 26 Wend. 663 ; and reply to the review, 3 Hill, 635.

[4] 5 Statutes at Large, 539.   [5] Barry *v.* Mercein, 5 How. 103.

merly claimed and exercised the right to inquire into the lawfulness of restraint under the national authority, it is now settled by the decisions of the Supreme Court of the United States, that the determination of that question must rest exclusively with the national courts; and that when a writ of *habeas corpus*, issued by a State court, is served upon any officer or other person who retains another in custody under national authority, it is his duty by proper return to make known to the State court the authority by which he holds such person, but not further to obey the process, and that the State court has no jurisdiction to proceed further with the case.[1]

The State constitutions recognize the writ of *habeas corpus*, and designate the courts which may issue it, but they do not point out the cases in which it may be employed as a remedy. For this we are referred to the common law; and where statutes have been passed making specific provision for particular cases, it is believed that in no case has there been any intention to restrict the remedy, and make it less broad than it was at the common law.[2]

We have elsewhere referred to the rules which determine the validity of judicial proceedings. In the great anxiety, on the part of our legislators, to make the most ample provision for speedy relief from unlawful confinement, authority to issue the writ of *habeas corpus* has been conferred upon inferior judicial officers, who make use of it sometimes as if it were a writ of error, under which they might correct the errors and irregularities of other judges and courts, whatever their relative jurisdiction and dignity. Any such employment of the writ is an abuse.[3] Where a

---

[1] Ableman *v.* Booth, 21 How. 506; Norris *v.* Newton, 5 McLean, 92; Spangler's case, 11 Mich. 298; In re Hopson, 40 Barb. 34.

[2] See Matter of Jackson, 15 Mich. 417, where this whole subject is fully considered. The application for the writ is not necessarily made by the party in person, but may be made by any other person on his behalf, if a sufficient reason is stated for its not being made by him personally. The Hottentot Venus case, 13 East, 195; Child's case, 29 Eng. L. & Eq. R. 259. A wife may have the writ to release the husband from unlawful imprisonment, and may herself be heard on the application. Cobbett's case, 15 Q. B. 181, note; Cobbett *v.* Hudson, 10 Eng. L. & Eq. R. 318; Same case, 15 Q. B. 988. Lord Campbell in this case cites the case of the wife of John Bunyan, who was heard on his behalf when he was in prison.

[3] It is worthy of serious consideration whether, in those States where the whole judicial power is by the constitution vested in certain specified courts, it is competent by law to give to judges at chambers or to inferior officers authority to review the decisions of the courts, and to discharge persons committed under their

party who is in confinement under judicial process is brought up on *habeas corpus*, the court or judge before whom he is returned will inquire : 1. Whether the court or officer issuing the process under which he is confined had jurisdiction to issue it. If so, mere irregularities or errors of judgment in the exercise of that jurisdiction must be disregarded on this process, and must be corrected by regular appellate proceedings.[1] 2. If the process is not void for want of jurisdiction, the further inquiry will be made, whether the case is by law bailable ; and if so, bail will be taken if the party offers it ; otherwise he will be remanded to the former custody.

This writ is also sometimes employed to enable a party to enforce a right to control, growing out of one of the domestic relations ; especially to enable a parent to obtain the custody and control of his child, where it is detained from him by some other person. The courts, however, do not go further in these cases than to inquire what is for the best interest of the child, and they do not feel compelled to remand him to any custody where it appears not to be for the child's interest. The theory of the writ is, that it relieves from improper restraint ; and if the child is of an age to render it proper to consult his feelings and wishes, this may be done in any case,[2] and is especially proper where the parents are living in separation, and both desire his custody. The right of the father, in these cases, is generally recognized as best ; but it is not an absolute right, and must yield to what appears to be for the interest of the child. The courts have a large discretion in these cases, and the tendency of modern decisions has been to extend rather than to limit it.[3]

judgments. Such officers could exercise only a special statutory authority. Yet its exercise in such cases is not only judicial, but it is in the nature of appellate judicial power. The jurisdiction of the Supreme Court of the United States to issue the writ, in cases of confinement under the order of the District Courts, is sustained on the ground that it is appellate. Ex parte Bollman & Swartwout, 4 Cranch, 75 ; Matter of Metzger, 5 How. 190. And see ex parte Kearney, 7 Wheat. 38. Is it competent for the legislature, when the judicial power is all vested in certain courts, to empower a ministerial officer, or even a judicial officer not sitting as a court, to exercise an appellate jurisdiction, however imperfect, over the judgments of such courts ?

[1] People *v.* Cassells, 5 Hill, 164 ; Bushell's case, 9 Ohio, N. S. 183 ; Matter of Metzger, 5 How. 191.

[2] Commonwealth *v.* Aves, 18 Pick. 193.

[3] Barry's case exhausts all the law on this subject. We refer to the various

Right to Discussion and Petition.

The right of the people peaceably to assemble and to petition the government for a redress of grievances is one which "would seem unnecessary to be expressly provided for in a republican government, since it results from the very nature of its structure and institutions. It is impossible that it could be practically denied until the spirit of liberty had wholly disappeared, and the people had become so servile and debased as to be unfit to exercise any of the privileges of freemen."[1]   But it has not been thought unimportant to protect this right by statutory enactments in England, and indeed it will be remembered that one of the most memorable attempts to crush the liberty of the subject in that country made the right of petition the point of attack, and selected for its contemplated victims the chief officers in the episcopal hierarchy.   The trial and acquittal of the seven bishops under James II. constituted one of the decisive battles in English constitutional history, and the right which was then vindicated is "a sacred right which in difficult times shows itself in its full magnitude, frequently serves as a safety-valve if judiciously treated by the recipients, and may give to the representatives or other bodies the most valuable information.   It may right many a wrong, and the deprivation of it would at once be felt by every freeman as a degradation.   The right of petitioning is indeed a necessary consequence of the right of free speech and deliberation, — a simple, primitive, and natural right.   As a privilege, it is not even denied the creature in addressing the Deity."[2]   Happily, the occasions for discussing and defending it have not been numerous in this country, and have been confined to an exciting subject which has now passed away.[3]

---

decisions which are reported in the order in which they were made: 8 Paige, 47; 25 Wend. 64; People v. Mercein, 3 Hill, 399; Barry v. Mercein, 5 How. 108. For the former rule, see King v. De Manneville, 5 East, 221; ex parte Skinner, 9 J. B. Moore, 278.

[1] Story on Const. § 1894.

[2] Lieber, Civil Liberty and Self-Government, ch. 12.

[3] For the discussions on the right of petition in Congress, particularly with reference to slavery, see 2 Benton's Abridgment of Debates, 57 to 60, 182 to 188, 209, 436 to 444; 1 Ibid. 397; 12 Ibid. 660 to 679, 705 to 743; 13 Ibid. 5 to 28, 266 to 290, 557 to 562.   Benton's Thirty Years, vol. 1, ch. 135, vol. 2, ch. 32, 33, 36, 37.   Also the current political histories and biographies.

Right to bear Arms.

Among the other defences to personal liberty should be mentioned the right of the people to keep and bear arms. A standing army is peculiarly obnoxious in any free government, and the jealousy of one has at times been demonstrated so strongly in England as almost to lead to the belief that a standing army recruited from among themselves was more dreaded as an instrument of oppression than a tyrannical king, or any foreign power. So impatient did the English people become of the very army which liberated them from the tyranny of James II., that they demanded its reduction, even before the liberation could be felt to be complete; and to this day, the British Parliament render a standing army practically impossible by only passing a mutiny bill from session to session. The alternative to a standing army is "a well-regulated militia," but this cannot exist unless the people are trained to bearing arms. How far it is in the power of the legislature to regulate this right, we shall not undertake to say, as happily there has been very little 'occasion to discuss that subject by the courts.[1]

[1] In Bliss v. Commonwealth, 2 Lit. 90, the statute "to prevent persons wearing concealed arms" was held unconstitutional, as infringing on the right of the people to bear arms in defence of themselves and of the State. But see Nunn v. State, 1 Kelly, 243. As bearing also upon the right of self-defence, see Ely v. Thompson, 3 A. K. Marsh. 73, where it was held that the statute subjecting free persons of color to corporal punishment for "lifting their hands in opposition" to a white person was held unconstitutional.

CHAPTER XI.

OF THE PROTECTION TO PROPERTY BY "THE LAW OF THE LAND."

THE protection of the subject in the free enjoyment of his life, his liberty, and his property, except as they might be declared, by the judgment of his peers or the law of the land, to be forfeited, was guaranteed by the twenty-ninth chapter of Magna Charta, "which alone," says Blackstone, "would have merited the title that it bears, of the *great* charter." [1] The people of the American States, holding the sovereignty in their own hands, have no occasion to exact pledges for a due observance of individual rights from any one; but the aggressive tendency of power is such, that in framing the instruments under which their governments are to be administered by their agents, they have deemed it important to repeat the guaranty, and thereby adopt it as a principle of constitutional protection. In some form of words it is to be found in each of the State constitutions; [2] and though verbal differences

[1] 4 Bl. Com. 424. The chapter, as it stood in the original charter of John, was: "Ne corpus liberi hominis capiatur nec imprisonetur nec dissaisietur nec utlagetur nec exuletur nec aliquo modo destruatur nec rex eat vel mittat super eum vi nisi per judicium parium suorum vel per legem terre." No freeman shall be taken, or imprisoned, or disseised, or outlawed, or banished, or any ways destroyed, nor will the king pass upon him, or commit him to prison, unless by the judgment of his peers, or the law of the land. In the charter of Henry III., it was varied slightly, as follows: "Nullus liber homo capiatur, vel imprisonetur, aut disseisietur de libero tenemento suo vel libertatibus vel liberis consuetudinibus suis, aut utlagetur, aut exuletur, aut aliquo modo destruatur, nec super eum ibimus nec super eum mittemus, nisi per legale judicium parium suorum vel per legem terræ." See Blackstone's Charters. The Petition of Right — 1 Car. I. ch. 1 — prayed, among other things, "that no man be compelled to make or yield any gift, loan, benevolence, tax, or such like charge, without common consent, by act of Parliament; that none be called upon to make answer for refusal so to do; that freemen be imprisoned or detained only by the law of the land, or by due process of law, and not by the king's special command, without any charge." The Bill of Rights — 1 Wm. & Mary, § 2, ch. 2 — was confined to an enumeration and condemnation of the illegal acts of the preceding reign; but the Great Charter of Henry III. was then, and is still, in force.

[2] The following are the constitutional provisions in the several States: —
Alabama: "That, in all criminal prosecutions, the accused . . . . shall not be

appear in the different provisions, no change in language, it is
thought, has in any case been made with a view to essential

compelled to give evidence against himself, nor be deprived of life, liberty, or
property, but by due course of law." Art. 1, § 7. — *Arkansas:* "That no man
shall be taken or imprisoned, or disseised of his freehold, liberties, or privileges, or
outlawed or exiled, or in any manner destroyed, or deprived of his life, liberty, or
property, but by the judgment of his peers, or the law of the land." Art.
2, § 10. — *California:* Like that of Alabama, substituting "process of law" for
"course of law." Art. 1, § 8. — *Connecticut:* Same as Alabama. Art. 1, § 9. —
Delaware: Like that of Alabama, substituting for "course of law," "the judgment of his peers, or the law of the land." Art. 1, § 7. — *Florida:* "That no
freeman shall be taken, imprisoned, or disseised of his freehold, liberties, or privileges, or outlawed, or exiled, or in any manner destroyed, or deprived of his life,
liberty, or property, but by the law of the land." Art. 1, § 8. — *Georgia:* "No
person shall be deprived of life, liberty, or property, except by due process of
law." Art. 1, § 2. — *Illinois:* "That no freeman shall be imprisoned or disseised
of his freehold, liberties, or privileges, or outlawed, or exiled, or in any manner
deprived of his life, liberty, or property, but by the judgment of his peers, or the
law of the land." Art. 13, § 8. — *Iowa:* "No person shall be deprived of life,
liberty, or property, without due process of law." Art. 1, § 9. — *Kentucky:* "Nor
can he be deprived of his life, liberty, or property, unless by the judgment of his
peers, or the law of the land." Art. 13, § 12. — *Maine:* "Nor be deprived
of his life, liberty, property, or privileges, but by the judgment of his peers, or the
law of the land." Art. 1, § 6. — *Maryland:* "That no man ought to be taken, or
imprisoned, or disseised of his freehold, liberties, or privileges, or outlawed, or
exiled, or in any manner destroyed, or deprived of his life, liberty, or property,
but by the judgment of his peers, or by the law of the land." Declaration of
Rights, § 23. — *Massachusetts:* "No subject shall be arrested, imprisoned, de-
spoiled, or deprived of his property, immunities, or privileges, put out of the protection of the law, exiled or deprived of his life, liberty, or estate, but by the
judgment of his peers, or the law of the land." Declaration of Rights, Art. 12. —
Michigan: "No person shall . . . . be deprived of life, liberty, or property, without due process of law." Art. 6, § 32. — *Minnesota:* "No member of this State
shall be disfranchised, or deprived of any of the rights or privileges secured to
any citizen thereof, unless by the law of the land, or the judgment of his peers."
Art. 1, § 2. — *Mississippi:* "Nor can he be deprived of his life, liberty, or property,
but by due course of law." Art. 1, § 10. — *Missouri:* Same as Delaware. Art.
1, § 18. — *Nevada:* "Nor be deprived of life, liberty, or property, without due
process of law." Art. 1, § 8. — *New Hampshire:* Same as Massachusetts. Bill of
Rights, § 17. — *New York:* Same as Nevada. Art. 1, § 6. — *North Carolina:* "That
no freeman ought to be taken, imprisoned, or disseised of his freehold, liberties, or privileges, or outlawed, or exiled, or in any manner destroyed, or deprived
of his life, liberty, or property, but by the law of the land." Declaration of Rights,
§ 12. — *Pennsylvania:* Like Delaware. Art. 9, § 9. — *Rhode Island:* Like Delaware. Art. 1, § 10. — *South Carolina:* "No person shall be taken, imprisoned, or
disseised of his freehold, liberties, or privileges, or outlawed or exiled, or in any
manner deprived of his life, liberty, or property, but by due process of law." Art.

change in legal effect, and the precise form which the guaranty assumes is therefore unimportant to our discussion. Indeed, the language employed is always nearly identical, except that the phrase " due process [or course] of law " is sometimes employed, and sometimes " the law of the land," and sometimes both ; but the meaning is the same in every case.[1]

What then is meant by " due process of law," and " the law of the land," in the constitutional provisions which we have referred to, as they are applied to the protection of rights in property, and in what cases can legislative action be annulled as not being " the law of the land," or judicial or ministerial action set aside as not being " due process of law " in the constitutional sense?

The definitions of these terms to be found in the reported cases are so various that some difficulty arises in fixing upon one which shall be accurate, complete in itself, and at the same time applicable to all cases. The diversity of definition is not surprising, when we consider the diversity of cases in which it has been attempted, and reflect that a definition which is sufficient for one case, and applicable to its facts, may be altogether insufficient or entirely inapplicable in another.

No definition, perhaps, is more often quoted than that by Mr. Webster in the Dartmouth College case:[2] " By the law of the land is most clearly intended the general law, which hears before it condemns, which proceeds upon inquiry, and renders judgment only after trial. The meaning is, that every citizen shall hold his life, liberty, property, and immunities under the protection of

9, § 2. — *Tennessee:* Same as Florida. Art. 1, § 8. — *Texas:* " No citizen of this State shall be deprived of life, liberty, property, or privileges, outlawed, exiled, or in any manner disfranchised, except by due course of the law of the land." Art. 1, § 16. — *West Virginia:* " No person, in time of peace, shall be deprived of life, liberty, or property, without due process of law." . Art. 2, § 6. In the remaining constitutions, a phrase of similar import is not found ; but it is believed equivalent protection is afforded under provisions to be found in all.

[1] 2 Inst. 50 ; Bouv. Law Dic., " Due process of law," " Law of the land " ; State *v.* Simons, 2 Spears, 767 ; Vanzant *v.* Waddell, 2 Yerg. 260 ; Wally's Heirs *v.* Kennedy, Ibid. 554 ; Matter of John and Cherry Streets, 19 Wend. 659 ; Greene *v.* Briggs, 1 Curt. 311 ; Murray's Lessee *v.* Hoboken Land Co., 18 How. 276, per Curtis, J. ; Parsons *v.* Russell, 11 Mich. 129, per Manning, J. ; Ervine's Appeal, 16 Penn. St. 256.

[2] 4 Wheat. 519.

general rules which govern society. Everything which may pass under the form of an enactment is not the law of the land."

The definition here given is apt and suitable as applied to judicial proceedings, which cannot be valid unless they " proceed upon inquiry," and " render judgment only after trial." It is entirely correct, also, in assuming that a legislative enactment is not necessarily the law of the land. The words " by the law of the land," as used in the Constitution, do not mean a statute passed for the purpose of working the wrong. That construction would render the restriction absolutely nugatory, and turn this part of the Constitution into mere nonsense. The people would be made to say to the two houses : " You shall be vested with the legislative power of the State, but no one shall be disfranchised or deprived of any of the rights or privileges of a citizen, unless you pass a statute for that purpose. In other words, you shall not do the wrong, unless you choose to do it." [1] But there are many cases where the title to property may pass from one person to another, without the intervention of judicial proceedings, properly so called, and we have already seen that special legislative acts designed to accomplish the same end have also been held valid in

[1] Taylor *v.* Porter, 4 Hill, 140, per Bronson, J. See also Jones *v.* Perry, 10 Yerg. 59; Ervine's Appeal, 16 Penn. St. 256; Arrowsmith *v.* Burlingim, 4 McLean, 498; Lane *v.* Dorman, 3 Scam. 238; Reed *v.* Wright, 2 Greene (Iowa), 15; Woodcock *v.* Bennett, 1 Cow. 740; Kinney *v.* Beverley, 2 H. & M. 536. " Those terms, ' law of the land,' do not mean merely an act of the General Assembly. If they did, every restriction upon the legislative authority would be at once abrogated. For what more can the citizen suffer than to be ' taken, imprisoned, disseised of his freehold, liberties, and privileges; be outlawed, exiled, and destroyed, and be deprived of his property, his liberty, and his life,' without crime ? Yet all this he may suffer if an act of the Assembly simply denouncing those penalties upon particular persons, or a particular class of persons, be in itself a law of the land within the sense of the Constitution : for what is in that sense the law of the land must be duly observed by all, and upheld and enforced by the courts. In reference to the infliction of punishment, and divesting the rights of property, it has been repeatedly held in this State, and it is believed in every other of the Union, that there are limitations upon the legislative power, notwithstanding these words; and that the clause itself means that such legislative acts as profess in themselves directly to punish persons, or to deprive the citizen of his property without trial before the judicial tribunals, and a decision upon the matter of right, as determined by the laws under which it vested, according to the course, mode, and usages of the common law, as derived from our forefathers, are not effectually ' laws of the land ' for those purposes." Hoke *v.* Henderson, 4 Dev. 15.

some cases. The necessity for "general rules," therefore, does not preclude the legislature from establishing special rules for particular cases, provided the particular cases range themselves under some general rule of legislative power; nor does the requirement of judicial action demand, in every case, a hearing in court.[1]

On the other hand, we think we shall find that general rules may sometimes be as obnoxious as special, when in their results they deprive parties of vested rights. While every man has a right to require that his own controversies shall be judged by the same rules which settle those of his neighbors, the whole community is also entitled at all times to demand the protection of the ancient principles which shield private rights against arbitrary interference, even though such interference may be under a rule impartial in its application. It is not the partial character of the rule, so much as its arbitrary and unusual nature, which condemns it as unknown to the law of the land. Mr. Justice Edwards says:[2] "Due process of law undoubtedly means, in the due course of legal proceedings, according to those rules and forms which have been established for the protection of private rights." And we know of no single sentence that embodies more tersely and accurately the legal view of the principle we are considering, than the following from an opinion by Mr. Justice Johnson of the Supreme Court of the United States: "As to the words from Magna Charta incorporated in the constitution of Maryland, after volumes spoken and written with a view to their exposition, the good sense of mankind has at length settled down to this, that they were intended to secure the individual from the arbitrary exercise of the powers of government, unrestrained by the established principles of private rights and distributive justice."[3]

---

[1] See Wynehamer v. People, 13 N. Y. 432, per Selden, J. In Janes v. Reynolds, 2 Texas, 251, Chief Justice Hemphill says: "The terms 'law of the land' . . . . are now, in their most usual acceptation, regarded as general public laws, binding upon all the members of the community, under all circumstances, and not partial or private laws, affecting the rights of private individuals or classes of individuals." And see Vanzant v. Waddell, 2 Yerg. 269, per Peck, J.; Hard v. Nearing, 44 Barb. 472.

[2] Westervelt v. Gregg, 12 N. Y. 209.

[3] Bank of Columbia v. Oakley, 4 Wheat. 235. "What is meant by the law of the land? In this State, taking as our guide Zylstra's case, 1 Bay, 384; White v. Kendrick, 1 Brev. 471; State v. Coleman & Maxy, 1 McMull. 502, there can

The principles, then, upon which the process is based are to determine whether it is " due process " or not, and not any considerations of mere form. Administrative and remedial process may change from time to time, but only with due regard to the old landmarks established for the protection of the citizen. When the government, through its established agencies, interferes with the title to one's property, or with his independent enjoyment of it, and its act is called in question as not in accordance with the law of the land, we are to test its validity by those principles of civil liberty and constitutional defence which have become established in our system of law, and not by any rules that pertain to forms of procedure merely. In judicial proceedings the law of the land requires a hearing before condemnation, and judgment before dispossession;[1] but when property is appropriated by the government to public uses, or the legislature attempts to control it through remedial statutes, different considerations prevail from those which relate to controversies between man and man, different proceedings are required, and we have only to see whether the interference can be justified by the established rules applicable to the case. Due process of law in each particular case means, such an exertion of the powers of government as the settled maxims of law sanction, and under such safeguards for the protection of individual rights as those maxims prescribe for the class of cases to which the one in question belongs.[2]

Private rights to property may be interfered with by either the legislative, the executive, or the judicial department of the government. The executive department in every instance must show authority of law for its action ; and occasion does not often arise

be no hesitation in saying that these words mean the common law and the statute law existing in this State at the adoption of our constitution. Altogether they constitute the body of law prescribing the course of justice to which a free man is to be considered amenable in all time to come." Per O'Neill, J., State v. Simons, 2 Speers, 767.

[1] Vanzant v. Waddell, 2 Yerg. 260.

[2] See Wynehamer v. People, 13 N. Y. 432, per Selden, J. In State v. Allen, 2 McCord, 56, the court, in speaking of process for the collection of taxes, say : " We think that any legal process which was originally founded in necessity, has been consecrated by time, and approved and acquiesced in by universal consent, must be considered an exception to the right of trial by jury, and is embraced in the alternative, 'law of the land.'" And see. Hard v. Nearing, 44 Barb. 472 ; Sears v. Cottrell, 5 Mich. 251.

for an examination of the limits which circumscribe its powers. The legislative department may in some cases constitutionally authorize interference, and in others may interpose by direct action. Elsewhere we shall consider the police power of the State, and endeavor to point out how completely all the property of the State, and every person, are subject to control under it, within certain limits, and for the purposes for which that power exists. The right of eminent domain and the right of taxation will also be discussed separately, and it will appear that under each the law of the land sanctions divesting individuals of their property against their will. In every government there is inherent authority to appropriate the property of the citizen for the necessities of the State, and constitutional provisions do not confer the power, though they often surround it with safeguards to prevent abuse. The restraints are, that when specific property is taken, a pecuniary compensation agreed upon or determined by judicial inquiry must be paid; and in other cases it can only be taken for the support of the government, and each citizen can only be required to contribute his just proportion to that end. But there is no rule or principle known to our system under which private property can be taken from one man and transferred to another for the private use and benefit of such other person, whether by general laws or by special enactment. The purpose must be public, and must have reference to the needs of the government. No reason of general public policy will be sufficient to protect such transfers where they operate upon existing vested rights.[1]

Nevertheless, in many cases and ways, remedial legislation may affect the control and disposition of property, and, in some cases may change rights, give remedies where none existed before, and even divest titles in case the legal and equitable rights do not concur in the same person.

The chief restriction is that vested rights must not be dis-

---

[1] Taylor *v.* Porter, 4 Hill, 140. In Matter of Albany St. 11 Wend. 149, it is intimated that the clause in the constitution withholding private property from public use except upon compensation made, of itself implies that it is not to be taken for individual use. And see Matter of John and Cherry Streets, 19 Wend. 676. A different opinion seems to have been held by the Supreme Court of Pennsylvania, when they decided, in Harvey *v.* Thomas, 10 Watts, 63, that the legislature might authorize the laying out of private ways over the lands of unwilling owners, to connect the coal-beds with the works of public improvement; the constitution not in terms prohibiting it.

turbed ; but in its application as a shield of protection, the term
" vested rights " is not used in any narrow or technical sense,
as importing a power of legal control merely, but rather as implying
a vested interest which it is equitable the government should recognize, and of which the individual cannot be deprived without
injustice.

And before proceeding further, it may be well to consider, in the
light of the reported cases, what is a vested right in the constitutional sense, that we may the better judge how far the general
laws of the State may be changed, and how far special provisions
may be made without coming under condemnation. Every man
holds all he possesses, and looks forward to all he hopes for,
through the aid and protection of the laws ; but as changes of circumstances and of public opinion, as well as other reasons of public policy, are all the time calling for changes in the laws, and
these changes must more or less affect the value and stability of
private possessions, and strengthen or destroy well-founded hopes ;
and as the power to make very many of them must be conceded,
it is apparent that many rights, privileges, and exemptions which
usually pertain to ownership under a particular state of the law,
and many reasonable expectations, cannot be regarded as vested
rights in any legal sense.   In many cases the courts, in the exercise of their ordinary jurisdiction, cause the property vested in one
person to be transferred to another, either through a statutory
power, or by the force of their judgments or decrees, or by compulsory conveyances.   If in these cases the court has jurisdiction,
they proceed in accordance with the law of the land, and the right
of one man is divested by way of enforcing a higher and better
right in another.   Of these cases we do not propose to speak ; as
constitutional questions cannot well arise in regard to them, unless they be attended by circumstances of irregularity which are
supposed to take them out of the operation of the general rule.
All vested rights are held subject to the laws for the enforcement
of public duties and private contracts, and for the punishment of
wrongs ; and if they become divested through the operation of
these laws, it is only by way of enforcing the obligations of justice and good order.   What we desire to arrive at now, is the
meaning of the term " vested rights," when employed by way of
indicating the interests of which one cannot be deprived by the
mere force of legislative enactment, or by any other than the

recognized modes of transferring title against the consent of the owner, to which we have alluded.

Interests in Expectancy.

And it would seem that a right cannot be considered a vested right, unless it is something more than a mere expectation, and has already become a title, legal or equitable, to the present or future enjoyment of property, or the present or future enforcement of a demand, or a legal exemption from a demand made by another.   As Mr. Justice Woodbury expresses it, acts of the legislature cannot be regarded as opposed to fundamental axioms of legislation, " unless they impair rights which are vested ; because most civil rights are derived from public laws ; and if, before the rights become vested in particular individuals, the convenience of the State procures amendments or repeals of those laws, those individuals have no cause of complaint.   The power that authorizes or proposes to give may always revoke before an interest is perfected in the donee." [1]   And Chancellor Kent, speaking of retrospective statutes, says, that such a statute, " affecting and changing vested rights, is very generally considered in this country as founded on unconstitutional principles, and consequently inoperative and void.   But this doctrine is not understood to apply to remedial statutes, which may be of a retrospective nature, provided they do not impair contracts, or disturb absolute vested rights, and only go to confirm rights already existing, and in furtherance of the remedy by curing defects and adding to the means of enforcing existing obligations.   Such statutes have been held valid when clearly just and reasonable, and conducive to the general welfare, even though they might operate in a degree upon vested rights." [2]

To particularize : a *mere expectation of property in the future is not a vested right.*   On this ground it is that the rules of descent may be changed, and the changes made applicable to all estates not already passed to the heir by the death of the owner. No one is heir to the living ; and the heir presumptive has no other reason to rely upon succeeding to the property than the promise held out by the statute of descents.   But this promise is no

[1] Merrill *v.* Sherburne, 1 N. H. 213.

[2] 1 Kent, 455.

more than a legislative declaration of its present view of public policy in regard to the order of succession, — a view which may at any time change, and the promise be withdrawn, and a new course of descent declared. The expectation is not property; it cannot be sold or mortgaged; and it is not in any way taken notice of by the law until the moment of the ancestor's death, when the law of descents comes in, and for reasons of general policy transfers his estate to certain persons to the exclusion of others. It is not until that moment that there is a vested right in the person who becomes heir, to be protected by the constitution. A future interest in property cannot be said to be vested in any person, so long as the owner of the interest in possession has full power, by virtue of his ownership, to cut off the expectant right by grant or devise.[1]

The nature of estates is therefore, to a certain extent, subject to legislative control.[2] In this country estates tail are very generally changed to estates in fee simple by statutory provisions, the validity of which is not disputed.[3] Such statutes operate to increase and render more valuable the interest which the tenant in tail possessed, and are not therefore open to objection by him.[4] But no other person in these cases has any vested right, either in possession or reversion; and the expectation of the heir presumptive must be subject to the same control as in other cases.[5]

The cases of rights in property to result from the marriage relation may be referred to the same principle. At the common law the husband, immediately on the marriage, succeeded to certain rights in the real and personal estate which the wife then possessed. These rights were at once vested, and could not be divested by any subsequent change in the law.[6] But other inter-

---

[1] In re Lawrence, 1 Red. Sur. Rep. 310.

[2] Smith on Stat. & Const. Construction, 412.

[3] De Mill v. Lockwood, 3 Blatch. 56.

[4] On the same ground it has been held in Massachusetts that statutes changing existing estates in joint tenancy into estates in common were unobjectionable. They did not impair vested rights, but rendered the tenure more beneficial. Holbrook v. Finney, 4 Mass. 567; Miller v. Miller, 16 Mass. 59; Anable v. Patch, 3 Pick. 363; Burghardt v. Turner, 12 Pick. 534.

[5] 1 Wash. Real Pr. 81 to 84 and notes. The exception to this rule, if any, must be in case of tenant in tail after possibility of issue extinct; where the estate of the tenant has ceased to be an inheritance, and a reversionary right has become vested.

[6] Westervelt v. Gregg, 12 N. Y. 208.

ests were merely in expectancy. He could have a right as tenant by the curtesy initiate, in the wife's estates of inheritance, the moment a child was born of the marriage, who might by possibility become heir to them. The right would be property, subject to conveyance and to be taken for debts; and must therefore be regarded as a vested right not subject to legislative interference. But while it remains in mere expectancy, — that is, before it becomes initiate, — the legislature has full power to modify or abolish it.[1] And the same rule will apply to dower, with this distinction, that the inchoate right is not regarded as property, or anything but a mere expectancy, at any time before it is consummated by the husband's death.[2] In neither of these cases does the marriage alone give a vested right. It gives only a capacity to acquire a right. The same thing may be said with regard to the husband's expectant interest in the after-acquired personalty of the wife ; that it is subject to any changes in the law made before his right becomes vested by the acquisition.[3]

Change of Remedies.

Again, *the right to a particular remedy is not a vested right.* This is the general rule ; and the exceptions are of those peculiar cases where the remedy is a part of the right itself, and which we have considered in another place. As a general rule every State has complete control over the remedies which it shall afford to parties in its courts.[4] It may abolish one class of courts and create another. It may give a new and additional remedy for a right already in existence.[5] And it may abolish old remedies and

[1] Hathorn v. Lyon, 2 Mich. 93 ; Tong v. Marvin, 15 Mich. 60.

[2] Barbour v. Barbour, 46 Me. 9 ; Lucas v. Sawyer, 17 Iowa, 517 ; Moore v. Mayor, &c. of N. Y., 4 Sandf. 456 & 8 N. Y. 110 ; Pratt v. Tefft, 14 Mich. 191 ; Reeve, Dom. Rel. 103, note ; Noel v. Ewing, 9 Ind. 57.

[3] Westervelt v. Gregg, 12 N. Y. 208 ; Norris v. Beyea, 13 N. Y. 273 ; Kelly v. McCarthy, 3 Bradf. 7. And see Plumb v. Sawyer, 21 Conn. 351 ; Clark v. McCreary, 12 S. & M. 347 ; Jackson v. Lyon, 9 Cow. 664.

[4] Lord v. Chadbourne, 42 Me. 429 ; Rosier v. Hale, 10 Iowa, 470 ; Holloway v. Sherman, 12 Iowa, 282 ; McCormick v. Rusch, 15 Iowa, 127 ; Rockwell v. Hubbell's Admrs., 2 Doug. Mich. 197 ; Cusie v. Douglas, 3 Kansas, 123 ; Smith v. Bryan, 34 Ill. 377.

[5] Hope v. Jackson, 2 Yerg. 125 ; Foster v. Essex Bank, 16 Mass. 245 ; Paschall v. Whitsett, 11 Ala. 472 ; Commonwealth v. Commissioners, &c., 6 Pick. 508 ; Whipple v. Farrar, 3 Mich. 436 ; U. S. v. Samperyac, 1 Hemp. 118 ; Sutherland

substitute new. If a statute providing a remedy is repealed while
proceedings are pending, the proceedings will thereby be determined ; [1] and any rule or regulation in regard to the remedy,
which does not, under pretence of regulating it, impair the right
itself, cannot be regarded as beyond the proper province of legislation.

But a vested right of action is property in the same sense in
which tangible things are property, and is equally protected
against arbitrary interference. Where it springs from contract
or from the principles of the common law, it is not competent for
the legislature to take it away.[2] Nor can a party by his misconduct forfeit such a right unless steps are taken to have the forfeiture declared in due judicial proceedings. Forfeitures of rights or
property cannot be adjudged by legislative act, and confiscations
without a judicial hearing and judgment after due notice would
be void as not due process of law. Even Congress has no authority
to protect the executive officers of the government for their acts
during the existence of a civil war, by depriving parties who were
illegally arrested by such officers of all redress in the courts.[3]

---

v. De Leon, 1 Texas, 250 ; Anonymous, 2 Stew. 228. See Lewis *v.* McElvain, 16
Ohio, 347 ; Trustees, &c., *v.* McCaughey, 2 Ohio, N. S. 152 ; Hepburn *v.* Curts,
7 Watts, 300 ; Schenley *v.* Commonwealth, 36 Penn. St. 29 ; Bacon *v.* Callender,
6 Mass. 303 ; Brackett *v.* Norcross, 1 Greenl. 92 ; Ralston *v.* Lothain, 18 Ind.
303.

[1] Bank of Hamilton *v.* Dudley, 2 Pet. 492 ; Ludlow *v.* Jackson, 3 Ohio, 553 ;
Yeaton *v.* U. S., 5 Cranch, 281 ; Schooner Rachel *v.* United States, 6 Cranch, 329.
That where the law has been changed pending the proceedings, judgment must be
pronounced according to the law as it then is, see these cases. Also Commonwealth
v. Duane, 1 Binney, 601 ; United States *v.* Passmore, 4 Dall. 372 ; Commonwealth *v.* Marshall, 11 Pick. 350 ; Commonwealth *v.* Kimball, 21 Pick. 373 ; Hartung *v.* People, 21 N. Y. 99 ; State *v.* Daley, 29 Conn. 272.

[2] Dash *v.* Vankleek, 7 Johns. 477 ; Streubel *v.* Milwaukee & M. R. R. Co., 12
Wis. 67 ; Clark *v.* Clark, 10 N. H. 386 ; Westervelt *v.* Gregg, 12 N. Y. 211 ;
Thornton *v.* Turner, 11 Minn. 339 ; Ward *v.* Brainerd, 1 Aik. 121 ; Keith *v.*
Ware, 2 Vt. 174 ; Lyman *v.* Mower, Ibid. 517 ; Kendall *v.* Dodge, 3 Vt. 360 ; State
v. Auditor, &c., 33 Mo. 287 ; Griffin *v.* Wilcox, 21 Ind. 370 ; Norris *v.* Doniphan,
4 Met. (Ky.) 385. But that which is given as a penalty may be taken away at
any time before recovery of judgment. Oriental Bank *v.* Freeze, 6 Shep. 109.

[3] In Griffin *v.* Wilcox, 21 Ind. 370, the act of Congress of March 3, 1863,
which assumed to indemnify parties who, during the existence of the Rebellion, had
made arrests without legal process, was held unconstitutional and void. In Norris *v.* Doniphan, 4 Met. (Ky.) 385, the act of Congress of July 17, 1862, "to suppress insurrection, to punish treason and rebellion, to seize and confiscate the

And if the legislature cannot confiscate property or rights, neither can it authorize individuals to assume at their option powers of police, which they may exercise in the condemnation and sale of property offending against their regulations, or for the satisfaction of their charges for services and expenses in its management and control, rendered without the consent of its owners.[1]   And a stat-

property of rebels, and for other purposes," was held to be unconstitutional, because it attempted to authorize the confiscation of the property of citizens as a punishment for treason and other crimes, without due process of law, by proceedings *in rem*, in any district in which the property might be, without presentment and indictment by a grand-jury, without arrest or summons of the owner, and upon such evidence of his guilt as would be proof of any fact in admiralty or revenue cases.   And the act being thus void, Congress had no power to prohibit the State courts from giving to the owners the relief they would be entitled to by State laws.   See also Rison *v.* Farr, 24 Ark. 161 ; and Hodgson *v.* Millward, 3 Grant's Cas. 406.

[1] The log-driving and booming corporations, which were authorized to be formed under a general law in Michigan, were empowered, whenever logs or lumber were put into navigable streams without adequate force and means provided for preventing obstructions, to take charge of the same, and cause it to be run, driven, boomed, &c., at the owner's expense, and it gave them a lien on the same to satisfy all just and reasonable charges, with power to sell the property for those charges and for the expenses of sale, on notice, either served personally on the owner, or posted as therein provided.   In Ames *v.* Port Huron Log-Driving and Booming Co., 11 Mich. 147, it was held that the power which this law assumed to confer was in the nature of a public office ; and Campbell, J., says : " It is difficult to perceive by what process a public office can be obtained or exercised without either election or appointment.   The powers of government are parcelled out by the constitution, which certainly contemplates some official responsibility.   Every officer not expressly exempted is required to take an oath of office as a preliminary to discharging his duties.   It is absurd to suppose that any official power can exist in any person by his own assumption, or by the employment of some other private person ; and still more so to recognize in such an assumption a power of depriving individuals of their property.   And it is plain that the exercise of such a power is an act in its nature public, and not private.   The case, however, involves more than the assumption of control.   The corporation, or rather its various agents, must of necessity determine when the case arises justifying interference ; and having assumed possession, it assesses its own charges ; and having assessed them, proceeds to sell the property seized to pay them, with the added expenses of such sale.   These proceedings are all *ex parte*, and are all proceedings *in invitum*.   Their validity must therefore be determined by the rules applicable to such cases.   Except in those cases where proceedings to collect the public revenue may stand upon a peculiar footing of their own, it is an inflexible principle of constitutional right that no person can legally be divested of his property without remuneration, or against his will, unless he is allowed a hearing before an impartial tribunal, where he may contest the claim set up against him, and be

ute which authorizes a party to seize the property of another, without process or warrant, and to sell it without notification to the owner, for the mere punishment of a private trespass, and to enforce a penalty against the owner, is unwarranted and void.[1]

Limitation Laws.

In this connection it may be proper to speak of *limitation laws*, which sometimes result in depriving a person altogether of his property, and yet are in strict conformity with the law of the land,

allowed to meet it on the law and the facts. When his property is wanted *in specie* for public purposes, there are methods assured to him whereby its value can be ascertained. Where a debt or penalty or forfeiture may be set up against him, the determination of his liability becomes a judicial question ; and all judicial functions are required by the constitution to be exercised by courts of justice, or judicial officers regularly chosen. He can only be reached through the forms of law upon a regular hearing, unless he has by contract referred the matter to another mode of determination."

[1] A statute of New York authorized any person to take into his custody and possession any animal which might be trespassing upon his lands, and give notice of the seizure to a justice or commissioner of highways of the town, who should proceed to sell the animal after posting notice. From the proceeds of the sale, the officer was to retain his fees, pay the person taking up the animal fifty cents, and also compensation for keeping it, and the balance to the owner if he should claim it within a year. In Rockwell *v.* Nearing, 35 N. Y. 307, 308, Porter, J., says of this statute : " The legislature has no authority either to deprive the citizen of his property for other than public purposes, or to authorize its seizure without process or warrant, by persons other than the owner, for the mere punishment of a private trespass. So far as the act in question relates to animals trespassing on the premises of the captor, the proceedings it authorizes have not even the mocking semblance of due process of law. The seizure may be privately made ; the party making it is permitted to conceal the property on his own premises ; he is protected, though the trespass was due to his own connivance or neglect ; he is permitted to take what does not belong to him without notice to the owner, though that owner is near and known ; he is allowed to sell, through the intervention of an officer, and without even the form of judicial proceedings, an animal in which he has no interest by way either of title, mortgage, pledge, or lien ; and all to the end that he may receive compensation for detaining it without the consent of the owner, and a fee of fifty cents for his services as an informer. He levies without process, condemns without proof, and sells without execution." And he distinguishes these proceedings from those in distraining cattle *damage feasant*, which are always remedial, and under which the party was authorized to detain the property in pledge for the payment of his damages. See also opinion by Morgan, J., in same case, p. 314 – 317, and the opinions of the several judges in Wynehamer *v.* People, 13 N. Y. 395, 419, 434, and 468.

and quite unobjectionable in principle.[1] A limitation law fixes upon a reasonable time within which a party is allowed to bring suit to recover his rights, and, if he fails to do so, establishes a legal presumption against him that he has no rights in the premises. It is a statute of repose. Every government is bound in good faith to furnish its citizens all needful legal remedies ;[2] but it is not bound to keep its courts open indefinitely for one who neglects or refuses to apply for redress until it may fairly be presumed that the means by which the other party might disprove the claim are lost in the lapse of time.[3]

When the period prescribed by statute has already run, so as to extinguish a claim which one might have made to property in the possession of another, the title to the property, irrespective of the original right, will be regarded as vested in the possessor, so as to entitle him to the same protection that the owner is entitled to in other cases. A subsequent repeal of the limitation law could not be given a retroactive effect, so as to disturb this title.[4] " The right being gone, of course the remedy fell with it ; and as there could be no remedy without a corresponding right, it was useless for the legislature to restore the former, so long as it was prohibited by the constitution from interfering or meddling with the latter." [5]

All limitation laws, however, must proceed upon the idea that the party, by lapse of time and omissions on his part, has forfeited his right to assert his title in the law.[6] Where they relate to

[1] That they should receive a favorable construction, see Leffingwell v. Warren, 2 Black, 599 ; Bell v. Morrison, 1 Pet. 360.

[2] Call v. Hagger, 8 Mass. 430.

[3] Stearns v. Gittings, 23 Ill. 387 ; Beal v. Nason, 2 Shep. 344 ; Bell v. Morrison, 1 Pet. 360.

[4] Brent v. Chapman, 5 Cranch, 358 ; Newby's Admrs. v. Blakey, 3 H. & M. 57 ; Parish v. Eager, 15 Wis. 532 ; Bagg's Appeal, 43 Penn. St. 512 ; Leffingwell v. Warren, 2 Black, 599. But see Swichard v. Bailey, 3 Kansas, 507.

[5] Knox v. Cleveland, 13 Wis. 249 ; Sprecker v. Wakelee, 11 Wis. 432 ; Hill v. Kricke, 11 Wis. 442 ; McKinney v. Springer, 8 Blackf. 506 ; Stipp v. Brown, 2 Ind. 647 ; Wires v. Farr, 25 Vt. 41 ; Davis v. Minor, 1 How. (Miss.) 183 ; Holden v. James, 11 Mass. 396 ; Lewis v. Webb, 3 Greenl. 326 ; Woart v. Winnick, 3 N. H. 473 ; Martin v. Martin, 35 Ala. 560 ; Briggs v. Hubbard, 19 Vt. 86 ; Thompson v. Caldwell, 3 Lit. 137 ; Wright v. Oakley, 5 Met. 400 ; Couch v. McKee, 1 Eng. 495 ; Atkinson v. Dunlap, 50 Me. 111.

[6] Stearns v. Gittings, 23 Ill. 389, per Walker, J. ; Sturgis v. Crowninshield, 4 Wheat. 207, per Marshall, Ch. J. ; Pearce v. Patton, 7 B. Monr. 162 ; Griffin v. McKenzie, 7 Geo. 163.

property, it seems not to be essential that the adverse claimant should be in actual possession;[1] but one who is himself in the legal enjoyment of his property cannot have his rights forfeited to another by failure to bring suit against that other within a time specified, to test the validity of a claim which the latter may make, but has yet taken no steps to enforce. It was therefore held that a statute which, after the lapse of five years, made a tax deed conclusive evidence of a good title, could not be valid as a limitation law against the original owner in possession of the land. Limitation laws cannot compel a resort to legal proceedings by one who is already in the complete enjoyment of all he claims.[2]

All statutes of limitations, also, must proceed on the idea that the party has had opportunity to try his right in the courts. A statute which should bar the existing right of claimants without affording this opportunity, after the time when the statute should take effect, would not be a statute of limitations, but an unlawful attempt to extinguish rights, whatever it might purport to be by its terms. It is essential that they allow a reasonable time after they are passed for the commencement of suits upon existing causes of action;[3] though what shall be considered a reasonable time must be determined by the legislature, into the wisdom of

---

[1] Stearns v. Gittings, 23 Ill. 389 ; Hill v. Kricke, 11 Wis. 442.

[2] Groesbeck v. Seeley, 13 Mich. 329. In Case v. Dean, 16 Mich. 12, it was held that this statute could not be enforced as a limitation law in favor of the holder of the tax title in possession, inasmuch as it did not proceed on the idea of limiting the right to bring suit, but by a conclusive rule of evidence sought to pass over the property to the tax claimant in all cases. The case of Leffingwell v. Warren, 2 Black, 599, is contra. That case purports to be based on Hill v. Kricke, 11 Wis. 442 ; but there the holder of the original title was not in possession, and it was only held not necessary for the holder of the tax title to be in possession in order to claim the benefit of the statute ; ejectment against a claimant being permitted by law when the lands were unoccupied. This circumstance — that the person whose right is to be extinguished is not in possession — seems to us very important. How can a man be justly held guilty of laches in not asserting claims to property when he already possesses and enjoys the property ? The maxim should apply here, " That which was originally void does not by mere lapse of time become valid."

[3] Price v. Hopkin, 13 Mich. 318 ; Call v. Hagger, 8 Mass. 423 ; Proprietors, &c. v. Laboree, 2 Greenl. 294 ; Society, &c. v. Wheeler, 2 Gall. 141 ; Blackford v. Peltier, 1 Blackf. 36 ; Thornton v. Turner, 11 Minn. 339 ; Berry v. Ramsdell, 4 Met. (Ky.) 292. In the last case, it was held that a statute which only allowed thirty days in which to bring action on an existing demand, was unreasonable and void. See also Auld v. Butcher 2 Kansas, 135.

whose decision in establishing a legal bar it does not pertain to the jurisdiction of the courts to inquire.[1]

Alterations in the Rules of Evidence.

It appears also that *a right to be governed by existing rules of evidence is not a vested right.* These rules pertain to the remedies which the State gives to its citizens, and are not regarded as entering into or constituting a part of a contract, or as being of the essence of a right. They are therefore at all times subject to modification and control by the legislature, like other rules affecting the remedy;[2] and the changes which are enacted may be made applicable to existing causes of action, even in those States where retrospective laws are forbidden. For the law as changed would only prescribe rules for presenting the evidence in legal controversies in the future, and it could not therefore be called retrospective, even though some of the subjects upon which it will act were in existence before. It has therefore been held in New Hampshire, that a statute which removed the disqualification of interest, and allowed parties to suits to testify, was not objectionable as applied to existing causes of action.[3] So of a statute which modifies the common-law rule excluding parol evidence to vary the terms of a written contract.[4] So of a statute making the protest of a promissory note evidence of the facts therein stated.[5] These and the like cases will sufficiently illustrate the general rule, that the whole subject is under the control of the legislature, which prescribes such rules for the determination, as well of existing as of future rights, as in its judgment will most completely subserve the ends of justice.[6]

---

[1] Stearns *v.* Gittings, 23 Ill. 387; Call *v.* Hagger, 8 Mass. 430; Price *v.* Hopkin, 13 Mich. 318. But see Berry *v.* Ramsdell, 4 Met. (Ky.) 292.

[2] Kendall *v.* Kingston, 5 Mass. 533; Ogden *v.* Saunders, 12 Wheat. 349; Per Marshall, Ch. J.; Fales *v.* Wadsworth, 23 Me. 533; Karney *v.* Paisley, 13 Iowa, 89; Commonwealth *v.* Williams, 6 Gray, 1; Hickox *v.* Tallman, 38 Barb. 608.

[3] Rich *v.* Flanders, 39 N. H. 323. A very full and satisfactory examination of the whole subject will be found in this case.

[4] Gibbs *v.* Gale, 7 Md. 76.

[5] Fales *v.* Wadsworth, 23 Me. 553.

[6] Per Marshall, Ch. J., in Ogden *v.* Saunders, 12 Wheat. 249; Webb *v.* Den, 17 How. 577; Delaplaine *v.* Cook, 7 Wis. 54; Kendall *v.* Kingston, 5 Mass. 534; Fowler *v.* Chatterton, 6 Bing. 258.

A strong instance in illustration of legislative control over evidence will be found in the laws of some of the States in regard to conveyances of lands upon sales to satisfy delinquent taxes. Independent of special statutory rule on the subject, such conveyances would not be evidence of title. They are executed under a statutory power; and it devolves upon the claimant under them to show that the steps prescribed by statute have been regularly taken. But it cannot be doubted that this rule may be so changed as to make the deed *prima facie* evidence that all the proceedings have been regular, and that the purchaser has thereby acquired a complete title.[1] The burden of proof is thereby changed from one party to the other; the legal presumption which the statute creates in favor of the purchaser being sufficient, in connection with the deed, in the absence of countervailing testimony, to establish his case. Statutes making defective records evidence of valid conveyances are of a similar character, and these usually, perhaps always, have reference to records before made, and provide for making them competent evidence where before they were in law merely void.[2] But they divest no title, and are not even retrospective. They establish what the legislature regard as a reasonable and just rule for the presentation by the parties of their rights before the courts in the future.

But there are fixed bounds to the power of the legislature over this subject, which must not be exceeded. As to what shall be evidence, and who shall assume the burden of proof, its power is unrestricted, so long as its rules are impartial and uniform; but it has no power to establish rules which, under pretence of regulating evidence, altogether preclude a party from exhibiting his rights. Except in those cases which fall within the familiar doctrine of estoppel at the common law, or other cases resting upon similar reasons, it would not be in the power of the legislature to declare that a particular item of evidence should preclude a party from establishing his rights in opposition to it. In judicial investigations, the law of the land requires a trial; and there

---

[1] Hand *v.* Ballou, 12 N. Y. 543; Delaplaine *v.* Cook, 7 Wis. 54; Allen *v.* Armstrong, 16 Iowa, 508; Adams *v.* Beale, 19 Iowa, 61; Amberg *v.* Rogers, 9 Mich. 332; Lumsden *v.* Cross, 10 Wis. 289; Lacey *v.* Davis, 4 Mich. 140; Wright *v.* Dunham, 13 Mich. 414. The rule once established may be repealed, even as to existing deeds. Hickox *v.* Tallman, 38 Barb. 608.

[2] Webb *v.* Den, 17 How. 577.

is no trial if only one party is suffered to produce his evidence. A statute making a tax deed conclusive evidence of a complete title, and precluding the original owner from showing its invalidity, would therefore be void as not a law regulating evidence, but an unconstitutional confiscation of property.[1] And a law which should make the opinion of an officer conclusive evidence of the illegality of an existing contract would be equally nugatory,[2] though perhaps, if parties should enter into a contract while such a law was in force, its provisions might properly be regarded as assented to and binding upon them.

Retrospective Laws.

As to the circumstances under which a man may be said to have a vested right to a defence, it is somewhat difficult to lay down a comprehensive rule. He who has satisfied a demand cannot have it revived against him, and he who has become released from a demand by the operation of the statute of limitations is equally protected. In both cases the right is gone; and to restore it would be to create a new contract for the parties, — a thing quite beyond the power of legislation. So he who was never bound, either legally or equitably, cannot have a demand created against him by mere legislative enactment.[3] But there are many cases under existing laws where defences are allowed upon contracts, or in respect to legal proceedings, which are based upon mere informalities, and where strict justice would sometimes justify the legislature in interfering to take away the defence, if it has the power to do so.

[1] Groesbeck v. Seeley, 13 Mich. 329; Case v. Dean, 16 Mich. 13; White v. Flynn, 23 Ind. 46. As to how far the legislature may make the tax deed conclusive evidence that mere irregularities have not intervened in the proceedings, see Smith v. Cleveland, 17 Wis. 556; and Allen v. Armstrong, 16 Iowa, 508. Undoubtedly the legislature may dispense with mere matters of form in the proceedings, as well after they have been taken as before; but this is quite a different thing from making tax deeds conclusive upon points material to the interest of the property owner. See, further, Wantlan v. White, 19 Ind. 470; People v. Mitchell, 45 Barb. 212.

[2] Young v. Beardsley, 11 Paige, 93.

[3] Medford v. Learned, 16 Mass. 215. In this case it was held that where a pauper had received support from the parish, to which under the law he was entitled, a subsequent legislative act could not make him liable by suit to refund the cost of the support.

24

In regard to these cases, we think investigation will show that *a party has no vested right in a defence based upon an informality not affecting his substantial interests.* And this brings us to a more particular examination of a class of statutes which are constantly coming under the consideration of the courts, and which are known as *retrospective laws.*

There are numerous cases which hold that retrospective laws are not obnoxious to constitutional objection, while in others they have been held to be void. The different decisions have been based upon facts making the different rulings applicable. There is no doubt of the right of the legislature to make laws which reach back to and change or modify the effect of prior transactions, provided retrospective laws are not forbidden, *eo nomine*, by the State constitution, and provided further that no other objection exists than their retrospective character. But legislation of this description is exceedingly liable to abuse ; and it is a sound rule of construction to give a statute a prospective operation only, unless its terms show a legislative intent that it should have retrospective effect.[1] And some of the States have deemed it important to forbid such laws altogether by their constitutions.[2]

---

[1] Dash *v.* Vankleek, 7 Johns. 477 ; Norris *v.* Beyea, 13 N. Y. 273 ; Plumb *v.* Sawyer, 21 Conn. 351 ; Whitman *v.* Hapgood, 13 Mass. 464 ; Medford *v.* Learned, 16 Mass. 215 ; Ray *v.* Gage, 36 Barb. 447 ; Watkins *v.* Haight, 18 Johns. 138 ; Garrett *v.* Beaumont, 24 Miss. 377 ; Briggs *v.* Hubbard, 19 Vt. 86 ; Perkins *v.* Perkins, 7 Conn. 558 ; Hastings *v.* Lane, 3 Shep. 134 ; Guard *v.* Rowan, 2 Scam. 499 ; Sayre *v.* Wisner, 8 Wend. 661 ; Quackenbos *v.* Danks, 1 Denio, 128 ; Garrett *v.* Doe, 1 Scam. 335 ; Thompson *v.* Alexander, 11 Ill. 54 ; State *v.* Barbee, 3 Ind. 258 ; Allbyer *v.* State, 10 Ohio, N. S. 588 ; State *v.* Atwood, 11 Wis. 422 ; Bartruff *v.* Remey, 15 Iowa, 257 ; Tyson *v.* School Directors, 51 Penn. St. 9. And see Broom's Maxims, p. 33, and cases cited ; Atkinson *v.* Dunlap, 50 Me. 111 ; Smith on Stat. & Const. Construction, ch. 7.

[2] See the provision in the constitution of New Hampshire, considered in Woart *v.* Winnick, 3 N. H. 481 ; Clark *v.* Clark, 10 N. H. 386 ; and Rich *v.* Flanders, 39 N. H. 304 ; and that in the constitution of Texas, in De Cordova *v.* Galveston, 4 Texas, 470. The constitution of Ohio provides that " the General Assembly shall have no power to pass retroactive laws, or laws impairing the obligation of contracts ; provided, however, that the General Assembly may, by general laws, authorize the courts to carry into effect the manifest intention of parties and officers, by curing omissions, defects, and errors in instruments and proceedings, arising out of their want of conformity with the laws of this State, and upon such terms as shall be just and equitable." Under this clause it was held competent for the General Assembly to pass an act authorizing the courts to correct mistakes in deeds of married women previously executed, whereby they were rendered

A retrospective statute curing defects in legal proceedings, where they are of the nature of irregularities only, and do not extend to matters of jurisdiction, is not void on constitutional grounds. Of this class are the statutes to cure irregularities in the assessment of property for taxation, and the levy of taxes thereon ;[1] irregularities in the organization or elections of corporations ;[2] irregularities in the votes or other action by municipal corporations, or the like, where a statutory power has failed of due execution, through carelessness of officers or other cause ; irregular sessions of courts, &c.

We know of no better rule to apply to cases of this description than this : If the thing wanting, or which failed to be done, and which constitutes the defect in the proceedings, is something which the legislature might have dispensed with the necessity of by prior statute, then a subsequent statute dispensing with it retrospectively must be sustained. And so if the defect consists in doing something which the legislature might have made immaterial by prior law, it may also be made immaterial by subsequent law.

In Kearney v. Taylor,[3] a sale of real estate belonging to infant tenants in common was made by order of court in a partition suit, and the land bid off by a company of persons who proposed subdividing and selling it in parcels. The sale was confirmed in their names ; but by mutual arrangement the deed was made to one only, for convenience in selling and conveying. This deed failed to convey the title, because not following the sale. The legislature then passed an act providing that, on proof being made to the satisfaction of the court or jury before which such deed was offered in evidence, that the land was sold fairly and without fraud,

ineffectual. Goshorn v. Purcell, 11 Ohio, N. S. 641. The constitution of Tennessee provides that no retrospective law shall be passed. It was held that a law authorizing a bill to be filed by slaves, by their next friend, to emancipate them, although it applied to cases which arose before its passage, was not a retrospective law within the meaning of this clause. Fisher's Negroes v. Dobbs, 6 Yerg. 119.

[1] Butler v. Toledo, 5 Ohio, N. S. 225 ; Strauch v. Shoemaker, 1 W. & S. 175 ; McCoy v. Michew, 7 W. & S. 390 ; Montgomery v. Meredith, 17 Penn. St. 42 ; Dunden v. Snodgrass, 18 Penn. St. 151 ; Williston v. Colkett, 9 Penn. St. 38 ; Boardman v. Beckwith, 18 Iowa, 292. And see Walter v. Bacon, 8 Mass. 472 ; Locke v. Dane, 9 Mass. 360 ; Patterson v. Philbrook, 9 Mass. 153 ; Trustees v. McCaughy, 2 Ohio, N. S. 152.

[2] Syracuse Bank v. Davis, 16 Barb. 188.

[3] 15 How. 494.

and the deed executed in good faith and for a sufficient consideration, and with the consent of the persons reported as purchasers, the deed should have the same effect as though it had been made to the purchasers. The act was conceded to be unobjectionable, and it cannot be doubted that a prior statute, authorizing the deed to be made to one of the purchasers for the benefit of all, and with their assent, would have been open to no objection.[1]

In certain Connecticut cases, transfers of real estate on execution were assailed as void, because the officer had included in his return several small items of fees not allowed by law. Subsequently the legislature passed an act providing that no levy should be deemed void by reason of the officer having included in his return greater fees than were by law allowable, but that all such levies, not in other respects defective, should be valid and effectual to transmit the title of the real estate levied upon. The liability of the officer for receiving more than his legal fees was at the same time left unaffected. In the leading case the court say : " The law, undoubtedly, is retrospective ; but is it unjust? All the charges of the officer on the execution in question are perfectly reasonable, and for necessary services in the performance of his duty ; of consequence they are eminently just ; and so is the act confirming the levies. A law although it be retrospective, if conformable to entire justice, this court has repeatedly decided is to be recognized and enforced." [2]

In another Connecticut case it appeared that certain marriages had been celebrated by persons in the ministry who were not empowered to perform that ceremony by the State law, and that the marriages were consequently void. The legislature afterwards passed an act declaring all such marriages valid ; and the court sustained the act. It was assailed as an exercise of the judicial power, which it clearly was not as, it purported to settle no controversies, but merely to give effect to the desire of the parties, which they had already attempted to carry out through the invalid ceremony. And while it was admitted that the act might be valid to effectu-

---

[1] See Davis v. State Bank, 7 Ind. 316, and Lucas v. Tucker, 17 Ind. 41, for decisions under statutes curing irregular sales by guardians and executors.

[2] Beach v. Walker, 6 Conn. 197 ; Booth v. Booth, 7 Conn. 350. And see Mather v. Chapman, 6 Conn. 54 ; Norton v. Pettibone, 7 Conn. 319 ; Welch v. Wadsworth, 30 Conn. 149. See also Underwood v. Lilly, 10 S. & R. 97 ; Bleakney v. Bank of Greencastle, 17 S. & R. 64 ; Weister v. Hade, 52 Penn. St. 474 ; Ahl v. Gleim, 52 Penn. St. 432.

ate a marriage between the parties, it was insisted that it was void as to the rights of property affected by the marriage relation, because as to them it would have retroactive operation. The court, in disposing of the case, are understood to express the opinion that, if the legislature can have the power to make the marriage valid, still more clearly must they have power to affect incidental rights. " The man and the woman were unmarried, notwithstanding the formal ceremony which passed between them, and free in point of law to live in celibacy, or contract matrimony with any other persons at pleasure. It is a strong exercise of power to compel two persons to marry without their consent, and a palpable perversion of strict legal right. At the same time, the retrospective law thus far directly operating on vested rights is admitted to be unquestionably valid, because manifestly just." [1]

It is not to be inferred from this language that the court understood the legislature to possess power to marry parties against their will. The complete control which the legislature possesses over the domestic relations can hardly extend so far. The legislature may perhaps divorce parties, with or without cause, according to its own good judgment; but for the legislature to marry parties against their consent, we conceive to be decidedly against " the law of the land." And the court must here be understood as speaking with exclusive reference to the case before them, where the legislature were merely, by retrospective act, removing a formal impediment to the marriage to which the parties had consented, and which they had attempted to form. In a case in Pennsylvania it appeared that certain assessments for the expense of grading and paving streets were void for the reason that the city ordinance under which the same were made was inoperative by reason of not having been recorded as required by law. The legislature then passed an act validating the ordinance, and declared therein that the omission to record the ordinance should not affect or impair the lien of the assessments against the lot owners. In passing upon the validity of this act, the court say: " Whenever there is a right, though imperfect, the constitution does not prohibit the legislature from giving a remedy. In Hepburn v. Curts,[2] it was said, 'the legislature, provided it does not violate the constitutional provisions, may pass retrospective laws,

---

[1] Goshen v. Stonington, 4 Conn. 224, per Hosmer, J.

[2] 7 Watts, 300.

such as in their operation may affect suits pending, and give to a
party a remedy which he did not previously possess, or modify an
existing remedy, or remove an impediment in the way of legal
proceedings.' What more has been done in this case? . . . .
While [the ordinance] was in force, contracts to do the work were
made in pursuance of it, and the liability of the city was incurred.
But it was suffered to become of no effect by the failure to record
it. Notwithstanding this, the grading and paving were done, and
the lots of the defendants received the benefit at the public expense. Now can the omission to record the ordinance diminish
the equitable right of the public to reimbursement? It is at
most but a formal defect in the remedy provided, — an oversight.
That such defects may be cured by retroactive legislation need not
be argued." [1]

On the same principle legislative acts validating invalid contracts
have been sustained. When these acts go no further than to bind
a party by a contract which he has attempted to enter into, but
which was invalid by reason of personal disability on his part to
make it, or through neglect of some legal formality, or in consequence of some ingredient in the contract forbidden by law, they
cannot well be obnoxious to constitutional objection.

By a law of Ohio, all bonds, notes, bills, or contracts, negotiable
or payable at any unauthorized bank, or made for the purpose of
being discounted at such bank, were declared to be void. While
this law was in force, a note was made for the purpose of being
discounted at one of these institutions, and was actually discounted
by it. Afterwards the legislature passed an act, reciting that many
persons were indebted to such bank, by bonds, bills, notes, &c., and
that owing, among other things, to doubts of its right to recover its
debts, it was unable to meet its own obligations, and had ceased
business, and for the purpose of winding up its affairs had made
an assignment to a trustee ; therefore the act authorized the said
trustee to bring suits on the said bonds, bills, notes, &c., and declared it should not be lawful for the defendants in such suits
" to plead, set up, or insist upon, in defence, that the notes, bonds,
bills, or other written evidences of such indebtedness are void on
account of being contracts against or in violation of any statute

---

[1] Schenley v. Commonwealth, 36 Penn. St. 29, 57. See also State v. Newark, 3
Dutch. 185 ; Den v. Downam, 1 Green (N. J.), 135 ; People v. Seymour, 16
Cal. 332.

law of this State, or on account of their being contrary to public policy." The law was sustained as a law "that contracts may be enforced," and as in furtherance of equity and good morals.[1] The original invalidity was only because of the statute, and was founded upon a principle of public policy which the legislature had seen fit to abrogate. Under these circumstances the defendant could not be permitted to rely upon it.[2]

By a statute of Connecticut, where loans of money were made, and a bonus paid by the borrower over and beyond the interest and bonus permitted by law, the demand was subject to a deduction from the principal of all the interest and bonus paid. A construction appears to have been put upon this statute by business men different from that which was afterwards given by the courts; and a large number of contracts of loan were in consequence subject to a deduction. The legislature then passed a "healing act," which provided that such loans theretofore made should not be held, by reason of the taking of such bonus, usurious, illegal, or in any respect void; but that, if otherwise legal, they were thereby confirmed, and declared to be valid, as to principal, interest, and

[1] Lewis v. McElvain, 16 Ohio, 347.

[2] Trustees v. McCaughy, 2 Ohio, N. S. 155; Johnson v. Bentley, 16 Ohio, 97. See also Syracuse Bank v. Davis, 16 Barb. 188. By statute, notes issued by unincorporated banking associations were declared void. This statute was afterwards repealed, and action was brought against bankers on notes previously issued. Objection being taken that the legislature could not validate the void contracts, the Judge says: "I will consider this case on the broad ground of the contract having been void when made, and of no new contract having arisen since the repealing act. But by rendering the contract void it was not annihilated. The object of the [original] act was not to vest any right in any unlawful banking association, but directly the reverse. The motive was not to create a privilege, or shield them from the payment of their just debts, but to restrain them from violating the law by destroying the credit of their paper, and punishing those who received it. How then can the defendants complain? As unauthorized bankers they were violators of the law, and objects not of protection but of punishment. The repealing act was a statutory pardon of the crime committed by the receivers of this illegal medium. Might not the legislature pardon the crime, without consulting those who committed it? . . . . How can the defendants say there was no contract, when the plaintiff produces their written engagement for the performance of a duty, binding in conscience if not in law? Although the contract, for reasons of policy, was so far void that an action could not be sustained on it, yet a moral obligation to perform it, whenever those reasons ceased, remained; and it would be going very far to say that the legislature may not add a legal sanction to that obligation, on account of some fancied constitutional restriction." Hess v. Werts, 4 S. & R. 361.

bonus. The case of Goshen v. Stonington was regarded as
sufficient authority to support this law ; and the principle derived
from that case is stated to be, " that where a statute is expressly
retroactive, and the object and effect of it is to correct an innocent
mistake, remedy a mischief, execute the intention of the parties,
and promote justice, then both as a matter of right and of public
policy affecting the peace and welfare of the community, the law
should be sustained.[1]

By a decision in the State of Pennsylvania, it was held that the
relation of landlord and tenant could not exist in that State under
a Connecticut title. A statute was afterwards passed providing
that the relation of landlord and tenant " shall exist and be held
as fully and effectually between Connecticut settlers and Pennsylvania claimants as between other citizens of this Commonwealth,
on the trial of any case now pending or hereafter to be brought
within this Commonwealth, any law or usage to the contrary
notwithstanding." In a suit which was pending and had been
once tried before the statute was passed, the statute was sustained
by the Supreme Court of the State, and afterwards by the Supreme
Court of the United States, to which last-mentioned court it had
been removed on the allegation that it violated the obligation of
contracts. As its only effect was to remove from contracts which
the parties had made a legal impediment to their enforcement,
there seems no room for doubt, in the light of the other authorities we have referred to, that the decision was correct.[2]

In the State of Ohio, certain deeds made by married women
were ineffectual for the purposes of record and evidence, by reason
of the omission on the part of the officer taking the acknowledgment to state in his certificate that, before and at the time of the
grantor making the acknowledgment, he made the contents known
to her, by reading or otherwise. An act was afterwards passed
which provided that " any deed heretofore executed pursuant to

---

[1] Savings Bank v. Allen, 28 Conn. 97. See also Savings Bank v. Bates, 8
Conn. 505 ; Andrews v. Russell, 7 Blackf. 474 ; Grimes v. Doe, 8 Blackf. 371 ;
Thompson v. Morgan, 6 Minn. 292. In Curtis v. Leavitt, 17 Barb. 309, and 15
N. Y. 9, a statute forbidding the interposition of the defence of usury was treated
as a statute repealing a penalty. See also Wilson v. Hardesty, 1 Md. Ch. 66 ;
Welch v. Wadsworth, 30 Conn. 149 ; Washburn v. Franklin, 35 Barb. 599.

[2] Satterlee v. Matthewson, 16 S. & R. 169, and 2 Pet. 380. And see Watson
v. Mercer, 8 Pet. 88 ; Lessee of Dulany v. Tilghman, 6 Gill & J. 461 ; Payne v.
Treadwell, 16 Cal. 220.

law, by husband and wife, shall be received in evidence, in any of the courts of this State, as conveying the estate of the wife, although the magistrate taking the acknowledgment of such deed shall not have certified that he read or made known the contents of such deed before or at the time she acknowledged the execution thereof." It was held that this statute was unobjectionable. The deeds with the defective acknowledgments were regarded by the court, and by the statute, as sufficient for the purpose of conveying the grantor's estate, and no vested rights were disturbed or wrong done by giving them effect as evidence.[1]

Other cases go much further than this, and hold that, although the deed was originally ineffectual for the purpose of conveying the title, the healing statute may accomplish the intent of the parties by giving it effect.[2] At first sight these cases might seem to go beyond the mere confirmation of a contract, and to be at least technically objectionable, as depriving a party of property

---

[1] Chestnut v. Shane's Lessee, 16 Ohio, 599, overruling Connell v. Connell, 6 Ohio, 358 ; Good v. Zercher, 12 Ohio, 364 ; Meddock v. Williams, 12 Ohio, 377 ; and Silliman v. Cummins, 13 Ohio, 116. Of the dissenting opinion in the last case, which the court approve in 16 Ohio, 609, 610, they say : " That opinion stands upon the ground that the act operates only upon that class of deeds where enough had been done to show that a court of chancery ought, in each case, to render a decree for a conveyance, assuming that the certificate was not such as the law required. And that where a title in equity was such that a court of chancery ought to interfere and decree a good legal title, it was within the power of the legislature to confirm the deed, without subjecting an indefinite number to the useless expense of unnecessary litigation." See also Lessee of Dulany v. Tilghman, 6 Gill & J. 461. But the legislature has no power to legalize and make valid the deed of an insane person. Routsong v. Wolf, 35 Mo. 174.

[2] Lessee of Walton v. Bailey, 1 Binney, 477 ; Underwood v. Lilly, 10 S. & R. 101 ; Barnet v. Barnet, 15 S. & R. 72 ; Tate v. Stooltzfoos, 16 S. & R. 35 ; Watson v. Mercer, 8 Pet. 88 ; Carpenter v. Pennsylvania, 17 How. 456 ; Davis v. State Bank, 7 Ind. 316 ; Goshorn v. Purcell, 11 Ohio, N. S. 641. In the last case the court say : " The act of the married woman may, under the law, have been void and inoperative ; but in justice and equity it did not leave her right to the property untouched. She had capacity to do the act in a form prescribed by law for her protection. She intended to do the act in the prescribed form. She attempted to do it, and her attempt was received and acted on in good faith. A mistake subsequently discovered invalidates the act ; justice and equity require that she should not take advantage of the mistake ; and she has therefore no just right to the property. She has no right to complain if the law which prescribed forms for her protection shall interfere to prevent her reliance upon them to resist the demands of justice." Similar language is employed in the Pennsylvania cases.

without due process of law; since they proceeded upon the assumption that the title still remained in the grantor, and that the healing act was required for the purpose of divesting him of it, and passing it over to the grantee. There is some apparent force, therefore, in the objection that such a statute deprives a party of vested rights. But the objection is more specious than sound. If all that is wanting to a valid contract or conveyance is the observance of some legal formality, the party may have a legal right to avoid it; but this right is coupled with no equity, even though the case be such that no remedy could be afforded the other party in the courts. The right which the healing act takes away in such case is *the right in the party to avoid his contract,* — a naked legal right, which it is usually unjust to insist upon, and which no constitutional provision was ever designed to protect.[1] As put by Chief Justice Parker of Massachusetts, a party cannot have a vested right to do wrong;[2] or as stated by the Supreme Court of New Jersey, " laws curing defects which would otherwise operate to frustrate what must be presumed to be the desire of the party affected, cannot be considered as taking away vested rights. Courts do not regard rights as vested contrary to the justice and equity of the case." [3]

The operation of these cases, however, must be carefully confined to the parties to the original contract, and to such other persons as only occupy the same position with no greater equities. Subsequent *bona fide* purchasers cannot be divested of the property which they have acquired, by a retrospective act changing the legal position of their grantor in regard to the thing purchased. While an invalid deed may be made good as between the parties, yet if, while it remained invalid, and the grantor still retained the legal title to the land, a third person had purchased and received a conveyance of the land, with no notice of any fact which should

---

[1] Gibson *v.* Hibbard, 13 Mich. 215 ; State *v.* Norwood, 12 Md. 195. In the first of. these cases a check, void at the time it was given for want of a revenue stamp, was held valid after being stamped under a subsequent act of Congress permitting it. And see Harris *v.* Rutledge, 19 Iowa, 389, where the same ruling was made. The Maryland case was still stronger, as there the curative statute was passed after judgment had been rendered against the right claimed under the defective instrument, and it was held that it must be applied by the appellate court.

[2] Foster *v.* Essex Bank, 16 Mass. 245.

[3] State *v.* Newark, 3 Dutch. 197.

preclude his acquiring an equitable as well as a legal title thereby, it would not be in the power of the legislature to divest him of his title through confirmation of the original deed. The position of the case is altogether changed by this purchase. The legal title is no longer separated from equities, but in the hands of the second purchaser is united with an equity as strong as that which exists in favor of him who purchased first. Under such circumstances even the courts of equity must recognize the right of the second purchaser as best, and it is secure against legislative interference.[1]

We have already referred to the case of contracts by municipal corporations which, when made, were in excess of their authority, but subsequently have been confirmed by legislative action. If the contract was one which the legislature might originally have authorized, the case falls within the rule we have laid down, and the legislative action is to be sustained.[2] Some of the cases where municipal subscriptions in aid of railroads were held valid were cases where the original undertaking was without authority of law, and was confirmed by retrospective act of legislation.[3]

It has not commonly been regarded as a matter of importance whether the enabling act was before or after the corporation had entered into the contract; and if the legislature possesses that complete control over the subject of taxation by municipal corporations which has been declared in many cases, it is difficult to see how such a corporation can successfully contest the validity of a special statute which only sanctions a contract before made by the

---

[1] Brinton v. Seevers, 12 Iowa, 389 ; Southard v. Central R. R. Co., 2 Dutch. 22; Thompson v. Morgan, 6 Minn. 292 ; Meighen v. Strong, 6 Minn. 177. These cases must not be understood as establishing any·different principle from that laid down in Goshen v. Stonington, 4 Conn. 209, where it was held competent to validate a marriage, notwithstanding the rights of third parties would be incidentally affected. Rights of third parties are liable to be incidentally affected in any case where a defective contract is made good ; but this is no more than might happen in enforcing a contract or decreeing a divorce. Such incidental injuries give no right to complain. It is only one who has acquired vested rights who can claim the protection of the law.

[2] Shaw v. Norfolk Co. R. R. Corp., 5 Gray, 180.

[3] McMillan v. Boyles, 6 Iowa, 330 ; Gould v. Sterling, 23 N. Y. 457 ; Thompson v. Lee County, 3 Wal. 327 ; Bridgeport v. Housatonic R. R. Co., 15 Conn. 475 ; Board of Commissioners v. Bright, 18 Ind. 93.

corporation — and which, though *ultra vires*, was for a public object — and compels its performance through taxation.[1]

[1] In Hasbrouck *v.* Milwaukee, 13 Wis. 37, it appeared that the city of Milwaukee had been authorized to contract for the construction of a harbor, at an expense not to exceed $100,000. A contract was entered into by the city providing for a larger expenditure; and a special legislative act was afterwards obtained to ratify it. The court held that the subsequent legislative ratification was not sufficient, *proprio vigore*, and without evidence that such ratification was procured with the assent of the city, or had been subsequently acted upon or confirmed by it, to make the contract obligatory upon the city. The court say, per *Dixon*, Ch. J.: "The question is, can the legislature, by recognizing the existence of a previously void contract, and authorizing its discharge by the city, or in any other way, coerce the city against its will into a performance of it, or does the law require the assent of the city as well as of the legislature in order to make the obligation binding and efficacious? I must say that, in my opinion, the latter act, as well as the former, is necessary for that purpose, and that without it the obligation cannot be enforced. A contract void for want of capacity in one or both of the contracting parties to enter into it is as no contract; it is as if no attempt at an agreement had ever been made. And to admit that the legislature, of its own choice, and against the wishes of either or both of the contracting parties, can give it life and vigor, is to admit that it is within the scope of legislative authority to divest settled rights of property, and to take the property of one individual or corporation and transfer it to another." This reasoning, it seems to us, would have required a different decision in many of the cases which we have heretofore cited. The cases of Guilford *v.* Supervisors of Chenango, 18 Barb. 615, and 13 N. Y. 143; Brewster *v.* Syracuse, 19 N. Y. 116; and Thomas *v.* Leland, 24 Wend. 65, especially go much further than is necessary to sustain legislation of the character we are now considering. In Brewster *v.* Syracuse, parties had constructed a sewer for the city at a stipulated price, which had been fully paid to them. The charter of the city forbade the payment of extra compensation to contractors in any case. The legislature afterwards passed an act empowering the Common Council of Syracuse to assess, collect, and pay over the further sum of $600 in addition to the contract price; and this act was held constitutional. In Thomas *v.* Leland, certain parties had given bond to the State, conditioned to pay into the treasury a certain sum of money as an inducement to the State to connect the Chenango Canal with the Erie at Utica, instead of at Whitestown as originally contemplated, — the sum mentioned being the increased expense in consequence of the change. Afterwards the legislature, deeming the debt thus contracted by individuals unreasonably partial and onerous, passed an act, the object of which was to levy the amount on the owners of real estate in Utica. This act seemed to the court unobjectionable. "The general purpose of raising the money by tax was to construct a canal, a public highway, which the legislature believed would be a benefit to the city of Utica as such; and independently of the bond, the case is the ordinary one of local taxation to make or improve a highway. If such an act be otherwise constitutional, we do not see how the circumstance that a bond had before been given securing the same money can detract from its validity. Should an individual volunteer to secure a sum of money, in itself properly leviable

In none of the cases to which we have referred is it of any importance that the legislative act which cures the defect was passed after suit brought in which the invalidity was sought to be taken advantage of. The bringing of suit vests no right to a particular decision;[1] and the case must be determined on the law as it stands when the judgment is rendered.[2] It has been held that a statute allowing amendments to indictments in criminal cases might constitutionally be applied to cases then pending;[3] and it has also been decided that a statute changing the rules of evidence might be applied to pending suits, even under a constitution which forbade retrospective laws.[4] And if a case is appealed, and the law is changed pending the appeal, the appellate court must decide according to the law in force when their decision is rendered.[5]

But the healing statute must in all cases be confined to validating acts which the legislature might previously have authorized.

by way of tax on a town or county, there would be nothing in the nature of such an arrangement which would preclude the legislature from resorting, by way of tax, to those who are primarily and more justly liable. Even should he pay the money, what is there in the constitution to preclude his being reimbursed by a tax?" Here, it will be perceived, the corporation was compelled to assume an obligation which it had not even attempted to incur, but which private persons, for considerations which seemed to them sufficient, had taken upon their own shoulders. And while we think the case of Hasbrouck v. Milwaukee is not in harmony with the current of authority on this point, we also think the case of Thomas v. Leland may be considered as going to the opposite extreme.

[1] Bacon v. Callender, 6 Mass. 309; Butler v. Palmer, 1 Hill, 324.

[2] Watson v. Mercer, 8 Pet. 88; Mather v. Chapman, 6 Conn. 54.

[3] State v. Manning, 11 Texas, 402.

[4] Rich v. Flanders, 39 N. H. 304.

[5] State v. Norwood, 12 Md. 195. But see Hedger v. Rennaker, 3 Met. (Ky.) 255. In Yeaton v. United States, 5 Cranch, 281, a vessel had been condemned in admiralty, and, pending an appeal, the act under which the condemnation was declared was repealed. The court held that the cause must be considered as if no sentence had been pronounced; and if no sentence had been pronounced, it has long been settled on general principles that, after the expiration or repeal of a law, no penalty can be enforced nor punishment inflicted for violation of the law committed while it was in force, unless some special provision be made for that purpose by statute. See also Schooner Rachel v. United States, 6 Cranch, 329; Commonwealth v. Duane, 1 Binney, 601; United States v. Passmore, 4 Dall. 372; Commonwealth v. Marshall, 11 Pick. 350; Commonwealth v. Kimball, 21 Pick. 373; Hartung v. People, 22 N. Y. 100. See also People v. Seymour, 16 Cal. 332, for a decision sustaining a law which precluded parties from taking advantage of informalities in a tax.

It cannot make good retrospectively acts which it had previously no power to permit. There lies before us at this time a volume of statutes of one of the States, in which are contained laws declaring certain tax-rolls valid and effectual, notwithstanding the following irregularities and imperfections: a failure in the supervisor to carry out separately opposite each parcel of land on the roll the taxes charged upon such parcel, as required by law; a failure in the supervisor to sign the certificate attached to the roll; a failure in the voters of the township to designate, as required by law, in a certain vote by which they had assumed the payment of bounty moneys, whether they should be raised by tax or loan; corrections made in the roll by the supervisor after it had been delivered to the collector; the including by the supervisor of a sum to be raised for township purposes without the previous vote of the township, as required by law; adding to the roll a sum to be raised which could not be lawfully levied by taxation without previous legislative authority; the failure of the supervisor to make out the roll within the time required by law; and the accidental omission of a parcel of land which should have been embraced by the roll. In each of these cases, except the last, the act required by law which failed to be performed might by previous legislation have been dispensed with; and perhaps in the last case there might be question whether the roll was avoided by the omission referred to, and, if it was, whether the subsequent act could cure it.[1] But if township officers should assume to do acts under the power of taxation which could not lawfully be justified as an exercise of that power, no subsequent legislation could make them good. If a part of the property or persons of a township were assessed at one rate and a part at another, there would be no such apportionment as is essential to taxation, and the roll would be beyond the reach of a curative act. And if persons or property were assessed for tax-

---

[1] See Billings v. Detten, 15 Ill. 218, and Thames Manufacturing Co. v. Lathrop, 7 Conn. 550, for cases where curative statutes were held not effectual to reach defects in tax proceedings. As to what defects may and what may not be cured by subsequent legislation, see Allen v. Armstrong, 16 Iowa, 508, and Smith v. Cleveland, 17 Wis. 556. In Tallman v. Janesville, 17 Wis. 71, the constitutional authority of the legislature to cause an irregular tax to be reassessed in a subsequent year, where the rights of *bona fide* purchasers had intervened, was disputed; but the court sustained the authority as " a salutary and highly beneficial feature of our systems of taxation," and " not to be abandoned because in some instances it produces individual hardships."

ation in a jurisdiction where they were not, a healing statute would be equally ineffectual to charge them. In such a case there would be a fatal defect of jurisdiction ; and even in judicial proceedings, if there was originally a failure of jurisdiction, no subsequent law can confer it.[1]

A Statutory Privilege is not a Vested Right.

Of this class are exemptions from the performance of public duty, upon juries, or in the militia, and the like ; exemptions of property or person from assessment for taxation ; exemptions of property from being seized by attachment or execution, or for the payment of taxes ; exemption from highway labor, and the like. The State requires the performance of military duty by those persons only who are within certain specified ages ; but if, in the opinion of the legislature, the public exigencies should demand military service from all other persons capable of bearing arms, the privilege of exemption would be recalled without violation of any constitutional principle. The fact that a party had passed the legal age under an existing law could not protect him when public policy or public necessity demanded a change.[2] In like manner exemptions from taxation are always subject to be recalled, when they have been granted as a mere privilege, and not for a consideration ; as in the case of exemption of buildings for religious or educational purposes, and the like. So also are exemptions of property from execution.[3] So, as we have already seen, a penalty given by statute may be taken away by statute at any time before judgment is recovered.[4] But if a bounty is offered, and the party

---

[1] So held in McDaniel v. Correll, 19 Ill. 228, where a statute had been passed to make valid certain proceedings in court which were void for want of jurisdiction of the persons interested. See also Denny v. Mattoon, 2 Allen, 361. In Walpole v. Elliott, 18 Ind. 259, it was held competent to confirm the proceedings of a court not held pursuant to law ; but in that case there was not a failure of jurisdiction, but only an irregular exercise of it.

[2] Commonwealth v. Bird, 12 Mass. 443.

[3] Bull v. Conroe, 13 Wis. 238.

[4] Oriental Bank v. Freeze, 6 Shep. 109. The statute authorized the plaintiff, when there had been a breach of a prison bond, to recover upon it the amount of his judgment and costs. This was regarded by the court as in the nature of a penalty ; and it was therefore held competent for the legislature, notwithstanding a breach might have occurred, to so change the law as to limit the plaintiff's

has actually earned it, the offer, and its acceptance by earning it, must be regarded as a contract, and a subsequent repeal of the statute cannot deprive the party of the moneys.[1] A franchise granted by the State, with a reservation of a right to repeal, must be regarded as a mere privilege while it continues, and the legislature may recall it at any time, without affording any ground to claim redress. A mill-dam act, which gives to the owner of the dam the right to maintain it on payment to owners of lands flowed the assessed damages, may be repealed, even as to dams already erected.[2]

Consequential Injuries.

It is also a rule that a party has no vested right to be protected against consequential injuries arising from the exercise of rights by others. Under the police power the State sometimes destroys for the time being, and perhaps permanently, the value of property to the owner, without affording him any redress. The construction of a new way, or the discontinuance of an old one, may very seriously affect the value of property; the removal of a county or State capital will often reduce very largely the value of all the property of the place from whence it was moved: but in neither case can the party injured enjoin the act, or claim compensation from the public. The granting of a charter to a new corporation may sometimes render valueless the franchise of an existing corporation, without constituting any breach of contract between the State and the first grantees. The State of Massachusetts granted to a corporation the right to construct a toll-bridge across the Charles River, under a charter which was to continue for forty years, afterwards extended to seventy, at the end of which time the bridge was to belong to the Commonwealth. During the term the corporation was to pay two hundred pounds annually to Harvard College. Forty-two years after the bridge was opened for passengers, the State incorporated a company for the purpose of erecting another bridge over the same river a short distance only from the first, and which would accommodate the same passengers. The necessary effect would be to decrease greatly the

recovery to his actual damages. See also Welch v. Wadsworth, 30 Conn. 149; Washburn v. Franklin, 35 Barb. 599.

[1] People v. State Auditors, 9 Mich. 327.

[2] Pratt v. Brown, 3 Wis. 603.

value of the first franchise, if not to render it altogether worthless. The terms of the first charter, however, did not make it exclusive ; no contract was violated in granting the second ; the injury which resulted was incidental to the exercise of an undoubted right by the State, and all the vested rights of the first corporation still remained, though less valuable in consequence of the new grant. It was therefore a case of damage without legal injury.[1]

Having thus endeavored to point out what are and what are not to be regarded as vested rights, and to indicate the cases in which such rights are shielded from legislative interference, it may be well now to speak of other cases in which legislation has endeavored to control parties as to the manner in which they should make use of their property, or to create claims against it through the action of other parties against the will of the owners. We do not allude now to the control which the State may exercise through the police power, and which is merely a power of regulation with a view to the best interests and the most complete enjoyment of rights by all ; but to that which, under a claim of State policy, and without any reference to wrongful act or omission by the owner, would exercise a supervision over his enjoyment of undoubted rights, or in other cases would compel him to recognize and satisfy demands upon his property which have been created without his assent.

The first class of cases must be so few and so baseless in principle as to make it unnecessary to spend time in discussing them. The State of Kentucky at one time passed an act to compel the owners of lands to make certain improvements upon them within a specified time, and declared them forfeited to the State in case the improvements were not made. It would be difficult to frame, from the general principles of government, any reasonable argument in support of such a statute. It was not the exercise of the right of eminent domain, for that appropriates property to some specific public use on making compensation. It was not taxation, for that is simply an apportionment of the burden of supporting the government. It was not a police regulation, for that could not go beyond preventing an improper use of the land with reference to

---

[1] Charles River Bridge v. Warren Bridge, 11 Pet. 420. For the doctrine of *damnum absque injuria*, see Broom's Maxims, 185. See also Turnpike Co. v. State, 3 Wal. 210 ; Piscataqua Bridge v. New Hampshire Bridge, 7 N. H. 35 ; English v. New Haven, &c. Co., 32 Conn. 240.

25

the due exercise of rights and enjoyment of legal privileges by others. It was purely and simply a law to forfeit a man's property if he failed to improve it to the legislative satisfaction. To such a power, if possessed by the government, there could be no limit but the legislative discretion, and it could no more be defended on principle than the regulation which should authorize the officer to enter a man's dwelling and seize his furniture if it fell below, or his food if it exceeded, an established legal standard.[1] Sumptuary laws are confessedly obnoxious, and on principle indefensible ; and laws of the class we have referred to come under the same condemnation.

But different considerations arise when one man has been in possession of the land of another, and made improvements upon it in good faith, and in the expectation that he was to reap the benefit of them. If this has been done with the assent of the owner, express or implied, or if it has been suffered through his negligence, and he afterwards recovers the lands and appropriates the improvements, there will exist against him at least a strong equitable claim for reimbursement, and perhaps no sufficient reason why it should not be changed by legislation into a lien upon the land.

The statute of Vermont upon this subject will illustrate the whole class of statutes in regard to what are known as *betterments*. It provided, in substance, that after recovery against a defendant in ejectment, where he or those through whom he claimed had purchased or taken a lease of the land, supposing at the time that the title purchased was good, or the lease valid to convey and secure the title and interest therein expressed, the defendant should be entitled to recover of the plaintiff the full value of the improvements made by him or by those through whom he claimed, to be assessed by jury, and to be enforced against the land, and not otherwise. The value was ascertained by estimating the increased value of the land in consequence of the improvements ; but the plaintiff, at his election, might have the value of the land without the improvements assessed, and the defendant should purchase the same at that price within four years, or lose the benefit of his claim for improvements. But the benefit of the law was not given to one who had entered on land

---

[1] See Gaines *v.* Buford, 1 Dana, 499, where the act was declared unconstitutional. Also Violett *v.* Violett, 2 Dana, 326.

by virtue of a contract with the legal owner, unless it should appear that the owner had failed to fulfil such contract on his part.[1]

This statute, and similar ones which preceded it, have frequently been enforced by the Supreme Court of Vermont, and adjudged constitutional. In an early case the court explained the principle of these statutes as follows: " The action for betterments, as they are now termed in the statute, is given on the supposition that the legal title is found to be in the plaintiff in ejectment, and is intended to secure to the defendant the fruit of his labor, and to the plaintiff all that he is justly entitled to, which is his land in as good a situation as it would have been had no labor been bestowed thereon. The statute is highly equitable in all its provisions, and would do exact justice if the value either of the improvements or of the land was always correctly estimated. The principles on which it is founded are taken from the civil law, where ample provision was made for reimbursing to the *bona fide* possessor the expense of his improvements, if he was removed from his possession by the legal owner. It gives to the possessor not the expense which he has laid out on the land, but the amount which he has increased the value of the land by his *betterments* thereon ; or, in other words, the difference between the value of the land as it is when the owner recovers it and the value if no improvement had been made. If the owner take the land, together with the improvements, at the advanced value which it has from the labor of the possessor, what can be more just than that he should pay the difference ? But if he is unwilling to pay this difference, by giving a deed as the statute provides, he receives the value as it would have been if nothing had been done thereon. The only objection which can be made is, that it is sometimes compelling the owner to sell when he may have been content with the property in its natural state. But this, when weighed against the loss to the *bona fide* possessor, and against the injustice of depriving him of the fruits of his labor, and giving it to another, who, by his negligence in not sooner enforcing his claim, has in some measure contributed to the mistake under which he has labored, is not entitled to very great consideration." [2]

[1] Revised Statutes of Vermont, 216.
[2] Brown *v.* Storm, 4 Vt. 37.

The last circumstance stated in this opinion — the negligence
of the owner in asserting his claim — is evidently deemed important in some States, whose statutes only allow a recovery for
improvements by one who has been in possession a certain number of years. But a later Vermont case dismisses it from consideration as a necessary ground upon which to base the right of
recovery. " The right of the occupant to recover the value of his
improvements," say the court, " does not depend upon the question whether the real owner has been vigilant or negligent in the
assertion of his rights. It stands upon a principle of natural
justice and equity, viz., that the occupant in good faith, believing
himself to be the owner, has added to the permanent value of the
land by his labor and his money ; is in equity entitled to such
added value ; and that it would be unjust that the owner of the
land should be enriched by acquiring the value of such improvements, without compensation to him who made them. This
principle of natural justice has been very widely, we may say
universally, recognized." [1]

[1] Whitney v. Richardson, 31 Vt. 306. For other cases in which similar laws
have been held constitutional, see Armstrong v. Jackson, 1 Blackf. 374 ; Fowler
v. Halbert, 4 Bibb, 54 ; Withington v. Corey, 2 N. H. 115 ; Bacon v. Callender,
6 Mass. 303 ; Ross v. Irving, 14 Ill. 171 ; Pacquette v. Pickness, 19 Wis. 219 ;
Childs v. Shower, 18 Iowa, 261 ; Saunders v. Wilson, 19 Texas, 194 ; Brackett v.
Norcross, 1 Greenl. 92 ; Hunt's Lessee v. M'Mahan, 5 Ohio, 132. For a contrary
ruling, see Nelson v. Allen, 1 Yerg. 376. Mr. Justice *Story*, in Society, &c. v.
Wheeler, 2 Gall. 105, held that such a law could not constitutionally be made to
apply to improvements made before its passage ; but this decision was made under
the New Hampshire constitution, which forbade retrospective laws. The principles of equity upon which such legislation is sustained would seem not to depend
upon the time when the improvements were made. In Childs v. Shower, 18
Iowa, 261, it was held that the legislature could not constitutionally make the
value of the improvements a personal charge against the owner of the land, and
authorize a personal judgment against him. The same ruling was had in M'Coy
v. Grandy, 3 Ohio, N. S. 463. A statute had been passed authorizing the occupying claimant, at his option, after judgment rendered against him for the recovery
of the land, to demand payment from the successful claimant of the full value of
his lasting and valuable improvements, or to pay to the successful claimant the
value of the land without the improvements, and retain it. The court say : " The
occupying claimant act, ... in securing to the occupant a compensation for his
improvements as a condition precedent to the restitution of the lands to the owner,
goes to the utmost stretch of the legislative power touching this subject. And the
statute . . . . providing for the transfer of the fee in the land to the occupying
claimant, without the consent of the owner, is a palpable invasion of the right of
private property, and clearly in conflict with the constitution."

Betterment laws, then, recognize the existence of an equitable right, and give a remedy for it where none had been given before. It is true that they make a man pay for improvements which he has not directed to be made, but the case presents no feature of officious interference by the government with private property. The improvements have been made by one person in good faith, and are now to be appropriated by another. The parties cannot be placed in *statu quo*, and the statute therefore accomplishes justice as near as the circumstances of the case will admit, by compelling the owner, who, if he declines to sell, must necessarily appropriate the betterments made by another, to pay for their value. The case is peculiar, but a statute cannot be void as an unconstitutional interference with private property which adjusts the rights of parties as near as possible according to natural justice.[1]

Unequal and Partial Legislation.

In the course of our discussion of this subject, it has been seen that some statutes are void, though general in their scope, while others are valid, though establishing rules for single cases only. An enactment may therefore be the law of the land, without being a general law. And this being so, it may be important to consider in what cases constitutional principles will require a statute to be general in its application, and in what cases it may be valid without being so.

The cases relating to municipal corporations stand upon peculiar grounds, from the fact that those corporations are mere agencies of government, and as such subject to complete legislative control. Statutes authorizing the sale of property of minors, and other persons under disability, are also exceptional, in that they are applied for by parties representing the interest of the owners, and are remedial in their character. Such statutes are supported by the presumption that the party in interest would consent if capable of doing so, and in law is to be considered as assenting in

[1] A town which, against the owner's will, illegally takes a lot of land for a school-house lot, and erects a school-house thereon, cannot be allowed anything for betterments. The betterment law, it is said, does not apply " where a party is taking land by force of the statute, and is bound to see that all the steps are regular. If it did, the party taking the land might in fact compel a sale of the land, or compel the party to buy the school-house, or any other building erected upon it." Harris *v.* Inhabitants of Marblehead, 10 Gray, 44.

the person of the guardian of his interest. And perhaps in any other case, if a party petitions for legislation and avails himself of it, he may be justly held estopped from disputing its validity ; so that the great bulk of private legislation which is being procured from year to year may be at once dismissed from this discussion.

Laws public in their objects may be general or local in their application ; they may embrace many subjects or one, and they may extend to all the citizens or be confined to particular classes, as minors, or married women, bankers or traders, and the like. The power that legislates for the State at large must determine whether particular rules shall extend to the whole State and all its citizens, or to a part of the State or a class of its citizens only. The circumstances of a particular locality, or the prevailing public opinion in that section of the State, may require or make acceptable different police regulations from those demanded in another, or call for different taxation, and a different application of the public moneys. The legislature may, therefore, prescribe or authorize different laws of police, allow the right of eminent domain to be exercised in different cases and through different modes, and prescribe peculiar restrictions upon taxation in each distinct municipality, provided the State constitution does not forbid. This is done constantly, and the fact that the laws are local in their operation is not supposed to render them objectionable in principle. The legislature may also deem it desirable to establish peculiar rules for the several occupations, and distinctions in the rights, obligations, and legal capacities of different classes of citizens. The business of common carriers, for instance, or of bankers, may require special statutory regulations for the general benefit, and it may be desirable to give one class of laborers a special lien for their wages, while it would be impracticable or impolitic to do the same by persons engaged in some other employments. If otherwise unobjectionable, all that can be required in these cases is, that they be general in their application to the class or the locality to which they apply, and they are then *general laws* in the constitutional sense.

But a statute would not be constitutional which should proscribe a class or a party for opinion's sake,[1] or which should select partic-

---

[1] The sixth section of the Metropolitan Police Law of Baltimore (1859) provided that " no Black Republican, or indorser or supporter of the Helper book, shall be appointed to any office " under the Board of Police which it established. This

ular individuals from a class or locality, and subject them to peculiar rules, or impose upon them special obligations or burdens, from which others in the same locality or class are exempt.[1])

The legislature may suspend the operation of the general laws of the State ; but when it does so, the suspension must be general, and cannot be made in individual cases, or for particular localities.[2] Privileges may be granted to individuals, when by so doing the rights of other persons are not injuriously affected ; disabilities may be removed ; the legislature as *parens patriæ* may grant authority to the guardians of incompetent persons to exercise a statutory authority over their estate for their assistance, comfort, or support, and for the discharge of legal or equitable liens upon it ; but every one has a right to demand that he be governed by general rules, and a special statute that singles his case out as one to be regulated by a different law from that which is applied in

was claimed to be unconstitutional, as introducing into legislation the principle of proscription for the sake of political opinion, which was directly opposed to the cardinal principles on which the constitution was founded. The court dismissed the objection in the following words: " That portion of the sixth section which relates to Black Republicans, &c. is obnoxious to the objection urged against it, if we are to consider that class of persons as proscribed on account of their political or religious opinions. But we cannot understand, officially, who are meant to be affected by the proviso, and therefore cannot express a judicial opinion on the question." Baltimore *v.* State, 15 Md. 468. See also p. 484. This does not seem to be a very satisfactory disposition of so grave a constitutional objection to a legislative act. That courts may take judicial notice of the fact that the electors of the country are divided into parties with well-known designations cannot be doubted ; and when one of these is proscribed by a name familiarly applied to it by its opponents, the inference that it is done because of political opinion seems to be too conclusive to need further support than that which is found in the act itself. And we know no reason why courts should decline to take notice of those facts of general notoriety, which, like the names of political parties, are a part of the public history of the times.

¹ Lin Sing *v.* Washburn, 20 Cal. 534. The constitution of Michigan forbids legislative divorces. The legislature passed an act authorizing the Circuit Court for St. Joseph County to grant a divorce from the bonds of matrimony to James M. Teft, provided it should be made to appear to the court that his wife for five years had been, and still was, hopelessly insane. Insanity was not a ground for divorce under the general law, and the act was held void. Teft *v.* Teft, 3 Mich. 67.

² That the statute of limitations cannot be suspended in particular cases, while allowed to remain in force generally, see Holden *v.* James, 11 Mass. 396 ; Davison *v.* Johonnot, 7 Met. 393. And that the general exemption laws of the State cannot be varied for particular cases or localities, see Bull *v.* Conroe, 13 Wis. 238, 244.

all similar cases would not be legitimate legislation, but an arbitrary mandate, unrecognized in free government. Mr. Locke has said of those who make the laws: " They are to govern by promulgated, established laws, not to be varied in particular cases, but to have one rule for rich and poor, for the favorite at court and the countryman at plough " ; [1] and this may be justly said to have become a maxim in the law, by which may be tested the authority and binding force of legislative enactments.[2]

Special courts could not be created for the trial of the rights and obligations of particular individuals; [3] and those cases in which legislative acts granting new trials or other special relief in judicial proceedings, while they have been regarded as usurpations of judicial authority, have also been considered obnoxious to the objection that they undertook to suspend general laws in special

---

[1] Locke on Civil Government, § 142.

[2] In Lewis v. Webb, 3 Greenl. 326, the validity of a statute granting an appeal from a decree of the Probate Court in a particular case came under review. The court say: " On principle it can never be within the bounds of legitimate legislation to enact a special law, or pass a resolve dispensing with the general law in a particular case, and granting a privilege and indulgence to one man, by way of exemption from the operation and effect of such general law, leaving all other persons under its operation. Such a law is neither just nor reasonable in its consequences. It is our boast that we live under a government of laws, and not of men; but this can hardly be deemed a blessing, unless those laws have for their immovable basis the great principles of constitutional equality. Can it be supposed for a moment that, if the legislature should pass a general law, and add a section by way of proviso, that it never should be construed to have any operation or effect upon the persons, rights, or property of Archelaus Lewis or John Gordon, such a proviso would receive the sanction or even the countenance of a court of law? And how does the supposed case differ from the present? A resolve passed after the general law can produce only the same effect as such proviso. In fact, neither can have any legal operation." See also Durham v. Lewiston, 4 Greenl. 140; Holden v. James, 11 Mass. 396; Piquet, Appellant, 5 Pick. 64; Budd v. State, 3 Humph. 483; Wally's Heirs v. Kennedy, 2 Yerg. 554. In the last case it is said: " The rights of every individual must stand or fall by the same rule or law that governs every other member of the body politic, or land, under similar circumstances; and every partial or private law, which directly proposes to destroy or affect individual rights, or does the same thing by affording remedies leading to similar consequences, is unconstitutional and void. Were it otherwise, odious individuals and corporations would be governed by one law; the mass of the community and those who made the law by another; whereas the like general law affecting the whole community equally could not have been passed."

[3] As, for instance, the debtors of a particular bank. Bank of the State v. Cooper, 2 Yerg. 599.

cases. The doubt might also arise whether a regulation made for any one class of citizens, entirely arbitrary in its character, and restricting their rights, privileges, or legal capacities in a manner before unknown to the law, could be sustained, notwithstanding its generality. Distinctions in these respects should be based upon some reason which renders them important, — like the want of capacity in infants, and insane persons; but if the legislature should undertake to provide that persons following some specified lawful trade or employment should not have capacity to make contracts, or to receive conveyances, or to build such houses as others were allowed to erect, or in any other way to make such use of their property as was permissible to others, it can scarcely be doubted that the act would transcend the due bounds of legislative power, even if it did not come in conflict with express constitutional provisions. The man or the class forbidden the acquisition or enjoyment of property in the manner permitted to the community at large would be deprived of *liberty* in particulars of primary importance to his or their " pursuit of happiness." [1]

Equality of rights, privileges, and capacities unquestionably should be the aim of the law; and if special privileges are granted, or special burdens or restrictions imposed in any case, it must be presumed that the legislature designed to depart as little as possible from this fundamental maxim of government. The State, it is to be presumed, has no favors to bestow, and designs to inflict no arbitrary deprivation of rights. Special privileges are obnoxious, and discriminations against persons or classes are still more so, and as a rule of construction are always to be leaned against as probably not contemplated or designed. It has been held that a statute requiring attorneys to render services in suits for poor persons 'without fee or reward was to be confined strictly to the cases therein prescribed; and if by its terms it

---

[1] Burlamiqui (c. 3, § 15) defines *natural liberty* as the right which nature gives to all mankind of disposing of their persons and property after the manner they judge most consonant to their happiness, on condition of their acting within the limits of the law of nature, and so as not to interfere with an equal exercise of the same rights by other men. See 1 Bl. Com. 125. Lieber says: "Liberty of social man consists in the protection of unrestrained action in as high a degree as the same claim of protection of each individual admits of, or in the most efficient protection of his rights, claims, interests, as a man or citizen, or of his humanity manifested as a social being." Civil Liberty and Self-Government.

expressly covered civil cases only, it could not be extended to embrace defences of criminal prosecutions.[1] So where a constitutional provision confined the elective franchise to " *white* male citizens," and it appeared that the legislation of the State had always treated of negroes, mulattoes, and *other colored persons*, in contradistinction to white, it was held that although quadroons, being a recognized class of colored persons, must be excluded, yet that the rule of exclusion would not be carried further.[2] So a statute making parties witnesses against themselves cannot be construed to compel them to disclose facts which would subject them to criminal punishment.[3] And a statute which authorizes a summary process in favor of a bank against debtors who have by express contract made their obligations payable at such bank, being in derogation of the ordinary principles of private rights, must be subjected to a strict construction.[4]

There are unquestionably cases in which the State may grant privileges to specified individuals without violating any constitutional principle, because, from the nature of the case, it is impossible they should be possessed and enjoyed by all; and if it is important that they should exist, the proper State authority must be left to select the grantees. Of this class are grants of the franchise to be a corporation. Such grants, however, which confer upon a few persons what cannot be shared by the many, and which, though supposed to be made on public grounds, are nevertheless frequently of great value to the corporators and therefore sought with avidity, are never to be extended by construction beyond the plain terms in which they are conferred. No rule is better settled than that charters of incorporation are to be construed strictly against the corporators.[5] The just presumption in

---

[1] Webb *v.* Baird, 6 Ind. 13.

[2] People *v.* Dean, 14 Mich. 406. In Ohio it has been held that the term " white " might be held to include all persons having a preponderance of white blood. Gray *v.* State, 4 Ohio, 354 ; Jeffries *v.* Ankeny, 11 Ohio, 372 ; Thacker *v.* Hawk, Ibid. 376 ; Anderson *v.* Millikin, 9 Ohio, N. S. 568. The decisions elsewhere are different, as they probably would be now in Ohio, if the question were new. See Van Camp *v.* Board of Education, 9 Ohio, N. S. 406.

[3] Broadbent *v.* State, 7 Md. 416. See People *v.* Thomas, 9 Mich. 314 ; Knowles *v.* People, 15 Mich. 408.

[4] Bank of Columbia *v.* Okely, 4 Wheat. 241.

[5] Providence Bank *v.* Billings, 4 Pet. 514 ; Charles River Bridge *v.* Warren Bridge, 11 Pet. 544 ; Perrine *v.* Chesapeake & Delaware Canal Co. 9 How. 172 ;

every such case is, that the State has granted in express terms
all that it designed to grant at all. " When a State," says the
Supreme Court of Pennsylvania, " means to clothe a corporate
body with a portion of her own sovereignty, and to disarm herself to that extent of the power that belongs to her, it is so easy
to say so, that we will never believe it to be meant when it is not
said. . . . In the construction of a charter, to be in doubt is to
be resolved; and every resolution which springs from doubt is
against the corporation. If the usefulness of the company would
be increased by extending [its privileges], let the legislature see
to it, but remember that nothing but plain English words will
do it." [1]

Richmond, &c., R. R. Co. v. Louisa R. R. Co., 13 How. 71; Bradley v. N. Y. &
N. H. R. R. Co., 21 Conn. 294; Parker v. Sunbury & Erie R. R. Co., 19 Penn.
St. 211; Wales v. Stetson, 2 Mass. 143; Chenango Bridge Co. v. Binghamton
Bridge Co., 27 N. Y. 87, and 3 Wal. 51.

[1] Pennsylvania R. R. Co. v. Canal Commissioners, 21 Penn. St. 22. And see
Commonwealth v. Pittsburg, &c. R. R. Co., 24 Penn. St. 159; Chenango Bridge
Co. v. Binghamton Bridge Co., 27 N. Y. 93, per Wright, J. We quote from the
Supreme Court of Connecticut in Bradley v. N. Y. & N. H. R. R. Co., 21 Conn.
306 : " The rules of construction which apply to general legislation, in regard to
those subjects in which the public at large are interested, are essentially different
from those which apply to private grants to individuals, of powers or privileges
designed to be exercised with special reference to their own advantage, although
involving in their exercise incidental benefits to the community generally. The
former are to be expounded largely and beneficially for the purposes for which
they were enacted; the latter liberally, in favor of the public, and strictly as
against the grantees. The power in the one case is original and inherent in the
State or sovereign power, and is exercised solely for the general good of the community; in the other it is merely derivative, is special if not exclusive in its character, and is in derogation of common right, in the sense that it confers privileges
to which the members of the community at large are not entitled. Acts of the
former kind, being dictated solely by a regard to the benefit of the public generally, attract none of that prejudice or jealousy towards them which naturally would
arise towards those of the other description, from the consideration that the latter
were obtained with a view to the benefit of particular individuals, and the apprehension that their interests might be promoted at the sacrifice or to the injury of
those of others whose interests should be equally regarded. It is universally understood to be one of the implied and necessary conditions upon which men enter
into society and form governments, that sacrifices must sometimes be required of
individuals for the general benefit of the community, for which they have no
rightful claim to specific compensation; but, as between the several individuals
composing the community, it is the duty of the State to protect them in the enjoyment of just and equal rights. A law, therefore, enacted for the common good,
and which there would ordinarily be no inducement to pervert from that purpose,

And this rule is not confined to the grant of a corporate franchise, but it extends to all grants of franchises or privileges by
the State to individuals, in the benefits of which the people at
large cannot participate. " Private statutes," says Parsons, Ch.
J., " made for the accommodation of particular citizens or corporations, ought not to be construed to affect the rights or privileges
of others, unless such construction results from express words
or from necessary implication." [1] And the grant of ferry rights,
or the right to erect a toll-bridge, and the like, is not only to be
construed strictly against the grantees, but it will not be held to
exclude the grant of a similar and competing privilege to others,
unless the terms of the grant render such construction imperative.[2]

is entitled to be viewed with less jealousy and distrust than one enacted to promote the interests of particular persons, and which would constantly present a
motive for encroaching on the rights of others."

[1] Coolidge v. Williams, 4 Mass. 140.   See also Dyer v. Tuscaloosa Bridge Co.,
2 Port. (Ala.) 296. In Sprague v. Birdsall, 2 Cow. 419, it was held that one
embarking upon the Cayuga Lake six miles from the bridge of the Cayuga Bridge
Co., and crossing the lake in an oblique direction so as to land within sixty rods of
the bridge, was not liable to pay toll under a provision in the charter of said company which made it unlawful for any person to cross within three miles of the
bridge without paying toll. In another case arising under the same charter,
which authorized the company to build a bridge across the lake or the outlet
thereof, and to rebuild in case it should be destroyed or carried away by the ice,
and prohibited all other persons from erecting a bridge within three miles of the
place where a bridge should be erected by the company, it was held, after the
company had erected a bridge across the lake and it had been carried away by
the ice, that they had no authority afterwards to rebuild across the *outlet* of the
lake, two miles from the place where the first bridge was built, and that the restricted limits were to be measured from the place where the first bridge was
erected. Cayuga Bridge Co. v. Magee, 2 Paige, 116 ; Same case, 6 Wend. 85.
In Chapin v. The Paper Works, 30 Conn. 461, it was held that statutes giving a
preference to certain creditors over others should be construed with reasonable
strictness, as the law favored equality. In People v. Lambier, 5 Denio, 9, it appeared
that an act of the legislature had authorized a proprietor of lands lying in the
East River, which is an arm of the sea, to construct wharves and bulkheads in the
river, in front of his land, and there was at the time a public highway through
the land, terminating at the river. Held, that the proprietor could not, by filling
up the land between the shore and the bulkhead, obstruct the public right of passage
from the land to the water, but that the street was, by operation of law, extended
from the former terminus over the newly made land to the water.

[2] Mills v. St. Clair County, 8 How. 569; Mohawk Bridge Co. v. Utica & S. R.
R. Co., 6 Paige, 554 ; Chenango Bridge Co. v. Binghamton Bridge Co. 27 N.
Y. 87 ; Same case, 3 Wal. 51.

The Constitution of the United States contains a provision that is important in this connection ; which is, that the citizens of each State shall be entitled to all the privileges and immunities of citizens of the several States.[1] Although the precise meaning of "privileges and immunities" is not very definitely settled as yet, it appears to be conceded that this provision secures in each State to the citizens of all other States the right to remove to and carry on business therein ; the right by the usual modes to acquire and hold property, and to protect and defend the same in the law ; the right to the usual remedies for the collection of debts and the enforcement of other personal rights, and the right to be exempt, in property and person, from taxes or burdens which the property or persons of citizens of the same State are not subject to.[2] To this extent, at least, discriminations could not be made by State laws against them. But it is unquestionable that many other rights and privileges may be made — as they usually are — to depend upon actual residence : such as the right to vote, to have the benefit of exemption laws, to take fish in the waters of the State, and the like. And the constitutional provision is not violated by a statute which allows process by attachment against a debtor not a resident of the State, notwithstanding such process is not admissible against a resident.[3]

Judicial Proceedings.

Individual citizens require protection against judicial action as well as against legislative ; and perhaps the question, what constitutes due process of law, is as often made in regard to judicial proceedings as in any other cases. But it is not so difficult here to arrive at satisfactory conclusions, since the bounds of the judicial authority are much better defined than those of the legislative, and each case can generally be brought to a definite and well-settled test.

The proceedings in any court are void if it wants jurisdiction of the case in which it has assumed to act. Jurisdiction is, *first,* of

---

[1] Const. of U. S. art. 4, § 2. See ante, p. 15, 16.

[2] Corfield *v.* Coryell, 4 Wash. 380 ; Campbell *v.* Morris, 3 H. & McH. 554 ; Crandall *v.* State, 10 Conn. 343 ; Oliver *v.* Washington Mills, 11 Allen, 281.

[3] Campbell *v.* Morris, 3 H. & McH. 554 ; State *v.* Medbury, 3 R. I. 141. And see generally the cases cited, ante, p. 16, note.

the subject-matter; and, *second*, of the persons whose rights are to be passed upon.[1]

A court has jurisdiction of any subject-matter, if, by the law of its organization, it has authority to take cognizance of, try, and determine cases of that description. If it assumes to act in a case over which the law does not give it authority, the proceeding and judgment will be altogether void, and rights of property cannot be divested by means of it.

And on this point there is an important maxim of the law, that consent will not confer jurisdiction:[2] by which is meant that the consent of parties cannot empower a court to act upon subjects which are not submitted to its judgment by the law. The law creates courts, and with reference to considerations of general public policy defines and limits their jurisdiction; and this can neither be enlarged nor restricted by the act of the parties.

Accordingly, where a court by law has no jurisdiction of the subject-matter of a controversy, a party whose rights are sought to be affected by it is at liberty to repudiate its proceedings and refuse to be bound by them, notwithstanding he may once have consented to its action, either by voluntarily commencing the proceeding as plaintiff, or as defendant by appearing and pleading to the merits, or by any other formal or informal action. This right he may avail himself of at any stage of the case; and the maxim that requires one to move promptly who would take advantage of an irregularity does not apply here, since this is not mere irregular action, but a total want of power to act at all. Consent is sometimes implied from failure to object; but there can be no

---

[1] Bouvier defines jurisdiction thus : " Jurisdiction is a power constitutionally conferred upon a court, a single judge, or a magistrate, to take cognizance and decide causes according to law, and to carry their sentence into execution. The tract of land within which a court, judge, or magistrate has jurisdiction is called his *territory;* and his power in relation to his territory is called his *territorial jurisdiction.*" 3 Bouv. Inst. 71.

[2] Coffin *v.* Tracy, 3 Caines, 129; Blin *v.* Campbell, 14 Johns. 432; Cuyler *v.* Rochester, 12 Wend. 165; Dudley *v.* Mayhew, 3 N. Y. 9; Preston *v.* Boston, 12 Pick. 7; Chapman *v.* Morgan, 2 Greene (Iowa), 374; Thompson *v.* Steamboat Morton, 2 Ohio, N. S. 26; Gilliland *v.* Administrator of Sellers, Ibid. 223; Dicks *v.* Hatch, 10 Iowa, 380; Overstreet *v.* Brown, 4 McCord, 79; Green *v.* Collins, 6 Ired. 139; Bostwick *v.* Perkins, 4 Geo. 47; Georgia R. R. &c. *v.* Harris, 5 Geo. 527; State *v.* Bonney, 34 Me. 223; Little *v.* Fitts, 33 Ala. 343; Ginn *v.* Rogers, 4 Gilm. 131 ; Neill *v.* Keese, 5 Texas, 23; Ames *v.* Boland, 1 Minn. 365; Brady *v.* Richardson, 18 Ind. 1.

waiver of rights by laches in a case where consent would be altogether nugatory.[1]

In regard to private controversies, the law always encourages arrangements;[2] and the settlements which the parties may make for themselves, it allows to be made for them by arbitrators mutually chosen. But the courts of a country cannot have those controversies referred to them by the parties which the law-making power has seen fit to exclude from their cognizance. If the judges should sit to hear such controversies, they would not sit as a court; at the most they would be arbitrators only, and their action could not be sustained on that theory, unless it appeared that the parties had designed to make the judges their arbitrators, instead of expecting from them valid judicial action as an organized court. Even then the decision could not be binding as a judgment, but only as an award; and a mere neglect by either party to object the want of jurisdiction could not make the decision binding upon him either as a judgment or as an award. Still less could consent in a criminal case bind the defendant; since criminal charges are not the subject of arbitration, and any infliction of criminal punishment upon an individual, except in pursuance of the law of the land, is a wrong done to the State, whether the individual assented or not. Those cases in which it has been held that the constitutional right of trial by jury cannot be waived are strongly illustrative of the legal view of this subject.[3]

If the parties cannot confer jurisdiction upon a court by consent, neither can they by consent empower any individual other than the judge of the court to exercise its powers. Judges are chosen in such manner as shall be provided by law; and a stipulation by parties that any other person than the judge shall exercise his functions in their case would be nugatory, even though the judge should vacate his seat for the purposes of the hearing.[4]

Sometimes jurisdiction of the subject-matter will depend upon considerations of locality, either of the thing in dispute or of the parties. At law certain actions are local, and others are transi-

---

[1] Hill v. People, 16 Mich. 351.

[2] Moore v. Detroit Locomotive Works, 14 Mich. 266.

[3] Brown v. State, 8 Blackf. 561; Work v. Ohio, 2 Ohio, N. S. 296; Cancemi v. People, 18 N. Y. 128; Smith v. People, 9 Mich. 193; Hill v. People, 16 Mich. 351. See also State v. Turner, 1 Wright, 20.

[4] Winchester v. Ayres, 4 Greene (Iowa), 104.

tory. The first can only be tried where the property is which is the subject of the controversy, or in respect to which the controversy has arisen. The United States courts take cognizance of certain causes by reason only of the fact that the parties are residents of different States or countries.[1] The question of jurisdiction in these cases is sometimes determined by the common law, and sometimes is matter of statutory regulation. But there is a class of cases in respect to which the courts of the several States of the Union are constantly being called upon to exercise authority, and in which, while the jurisdiction is conceded to rest on considerations of locality, there has not, unfortunately, at all times been entire harmony of action as to what shall confer jurisdiction. We refer now to suits for divorce from the bonds of matrimony.

The courts of one State or country have no general authority to grant divorces, unless for some reason they have control over the particular marriage contract which is sought to be annulled. But what circumstance gives such control? Is it the fact that the marriage was entered into in such country or State? Or that the alleged breach of the marriage bond was within that jurisdiction? Or that the parties resided within it either at the time of the marriage or at the time of the offence? Or that the parties now reside in such State or country, though both marriage and offence may have taken place elsewhere? Or must marriage, offence, and residence, all or any two of them, combine to confer the authority? These are questions which have frequently demanded the thoughtful attention of the courts, who have sought to establish a rule at once sound in principle, and that shall protect as far as possible the rights of the parties, one or the other of whom, unfortunately, under the operation of any rule which can be established, it will frequently be found has been the victim of gross injustice.

We conceive the true rule to be that the actual, *bona fide* residence of either husband or wife within a State will give to that

---

[1] See a case where a judgment of a United States court was treated as of no force, because the court had not jurisdiction in respect to the plaintiff. Vose *v.* Morton, 4 Cush. 27. As to third persons, a judgment against an individual may sometimes be treated as void, when he was not suable in that court or in that manner, notwithstanding he may have so submitted himself to the jurisdiction as to be personally bound. See Georgia R. R. &c. *v.* Harris, 5 Geo. 527; Hinchman *v.* Town, 10 Mich. 508.

State authority to determine the *status* of such party, and to pass upon any questions affecting his or her continuance in the marriage relation, irrespective of the locality of the marriage, or of any alleged offence ; and that any such court in that State as the legislature may have authorized to take cognizance of the subject may lawfully pass upon such questions, and annul the marriage for any cause allowed by the local law.   But if a party goes to a jurisdiction other than that of his domicile for the purpose of procuring a divorce, and has residence there for that purpose only, such residence is not *bona fide*, and does not confer upon the courts of that State or country jurisdiction over the marriage relation, and any decree they may assume to make would be void as to the other party.[1]

[1] There are a number of cases in which this subject has been considered.   In Inhabitants of Hanover *v.* Turner, 14 Mass. 227, instructions to a jury were sustained, that if they were satisfied the husband, who had been a citizen of Massachusetts, removed to Vermont merely for the purpose of procuring a divorce, and that the pretended cause for divorce arose, if it ever did arise, in Massachusetts, and that the wife was never within the jurisdiction of the court of Vermont, then and in such case the decree of divorce which the husband had obtained in Vermont must be considered as fraudulently obtained, and that it could not operate so as to dissolve the marriage between the parties.   See also Vischer *v.* Vischer, 12 Barb. 640 ; and McGiffert *v.* McGiffert, 31 Barb. 69.   In Chase *v.* Chase, 6 Gray, 157, the same ruling was had as to a foreign divorce, notwithstanding the wife appeared in and defended the foreign suit.   In Clark *v.* Clark, 8 N. H. 21, the court refused a divorce on the ground that the alleged cause of divorce (adultery), though committed within the State, was so committed while the parties had their domicile abroad.   This decision was followed in Greenlaw *v.* Greenlaw, 12 N. H. 200.   The court say : " If the defendant never had any domicile in this State, the libellant could not come here, bringing with her a cause of divorce over which this court had jurisdiction.   If at the time of the [alleged offence] the domicile of the parties was in Maine, and the facts furnished no cause for a divorce there, she could not come here and allege those matters which had already occurred, as a ground for a divorce under the laws of this State.   Should she under such circumstances obtain a decree of divorce here, it must be regarded as a mere nullity elsewhere."   In Frary *v.* Frary, 10 N. H. 61, importance was attached to the fact that the *marriage* took place in New Hampshire, and it was held that the court had jurisdiction of the wife's application for a divorce, notwithstanding the offence was committed in Vermont, but during the time of the wife's residence in New Hampshire.   See also Kimball *v.* Kimball, 13 N. H. 225 ; Bachelder *v.* Bachelder, 14 N. H. 380 ; Payson *v.* Payson, 34 N. H. 518 ; Hopkins *v.* Hopkins, 35 N. H. 474.   In Wilcox *v.* Wilcox, 10 Ind. 436, it was held that the residence of the libellant at the time of the application for a divorce was sufficient to confer jurisdiction, and a decree dismissing the bill because the cause

26

But to render the jurisdiction of a court effectual in any case, it is necessary that the thing in controversy, or the parties interested, be subjected to the process of the court. Certain cases are said to proceed *in rem*, because they take notice rather of the thing in controversy than of the persons concerned; and the process is served upon that which is the object of the suit, without

for divorce arose out of the State was reversed. And see Tolen *v.* Tolen, 2 Blackf. 407. See also Jackson *v.* Jackson, 1 Johns. 424; Barber *v.* Root, 10 Mass. 263; Borden *v.* Fitch, 15 Johns. 121; Bradshaw *v.* Heath, 13 Wend. 407. In any of these cases the question of actual residence will be open to inquiry wherever it becomes important, notwithstanding the record of proceedings is in due form, and contains the affidavit of residence required by the practice. Leith *v.* Leith, 39 N. H. 20. And see McGiffert *v.* McGiffert, 31 Barb. 69; Todd *v.* Kerr, 42 Barb. 317. The Pennsylvania cases agree with those of New Hampshire, in holding that a divorce should not be granted unless the cause alleged occurred while the complainant had domicile within the State. Dorsey *v.* Dorsey, 7 Watts, 349; Hollister *v.* Hollister, 6 Penn. St. 449; McDermott's appeal, 8 W. & S. 251. For cases supporting to a greater or less extent the doctrine stated in the text, see Harding *v.* Alden, 9 Greenl. 140; Ditson *v.* Ditson, 4 R. I. 87; Pawling *v.* Bird's Exrs., 13 Johns. 192; Harrison *v.* Harrison, 19 Ala. 499; Thompson *v.* State, 28 Ala. 12; Cooper *v.* Cooper, 7 Ohio, 594; Mansfield *v.* McIntyre, 10 Ohio, 28; Smith *v.* Smith, 4 Greene (Iowa), 266; Yates *v.* Yates, 2 Beasley, 280; Maguire *v.* Maguire, 7 Dana, 181; Waltz *v.* Waltz, 18 Ind. 449; Hull *v.* Hull, 2 Strob. Eq. 174; Manley *v.* Manley, 4 Chand. 97; Hubbell *v.* Hubbell, 3 Wis. 662; Gleason *v.* Gleason, 4 Wis. 64; Hare *v.* Hare, 15 Texas, 355. And see Story, Confl. Laws, § 230 *a*; Bishop on Mar. & Div. 727 et seq.; Ibid. (4th ed.) vol. 2, § 155 et seq. A number of the cases cited hold that the wife may have a domicile separate from the husband, and may therefore be entitled to a divorce, though the husband never resided in the State. These cases proceed upon the theory that, although in general the domicile of the husband is the domicile of the wife, yet that if he be guilty of such act or dereliction of duty in the relation as entitles her to have it partially or wholly dissolved, she is at liberty to establish a separate jurisdictional domicile of her own. Ditson *v.* Ditson, 4 R. I. 87; Harding *v.* Alden, 9 Greenl. 140; Maguire *v.* Maguire. 7 Dana, 181; Hollister *v.* Hollister, 6 Penn. St. 449. The doctrine in New York seems to be, that a divorce obtained in another State, without personal service of process or appearance of the defendant, is absolutely void. Vischer *v.* Vischer, 12 Barb. 640; McGiffert *v.* McGiffert, 31 Barb. 69; Todd *v.* Kerr, 42 Barb. 317.

Upon the whole subject of jurisdiction in divorce suits, no case in the books is more full and satisfactory than that of Ditson *v.* Ditson, *supra*, which reviews and comments upon a number of the cases cited, and particularly upon the Massachusetts cases of Barber *v.* Root, 10 Mass. 265; Inhabitants of Hanover *v.* Turner, 14 Mass. 227; Harteau *v.* Harteau, 14 Pick. 181; and Lyon *v.* Lyon, 2 Gray, 367. The divorce of one party divorces both. Cooper *v.* Cooper, 7 Ohio, 594. And will leave both at liberty to enter into new marriage relations, unless the local statute expressly forbids the guilty party from contracting a second marriage.

specially noticing the interested parties ; while in other cases the parties themselves are brought before the court by process.   Of the first class admiralty proceedings are an illustration ; the court acquiring jurisdiction by seizing the vessel or other thing to which the controversy relates.   In cases within this class, notice to all concerned is required to be given either personally or by some species of publication or proclamation ; and if not given, the court which had jurisdiction of the property will have none to render judgment.[1]   Suits at the common law, however, proceed against the parties whose interests are sought to be affected ; and only those persons are concluded by the adjudication who are served with process, or who voluntarily appear.[2]   Some cases also partake of the nature of both proceedings *in rem* and of personal actions, since, although they proceed by seizing property, they also contemplate the service of process on defendant parties.   Of this class are the proceedings by foreign attachment, in which the property of a non-resident or concealed debtor is seized and retained by the officer as security for the satisfaction of any judgment that may be recovered against him, but at the same time process is issued to be served upon the defendant, and which must be served, or some substitute for service had before judgment can be rendered.

In such cases, as well as in divorce suits, it will often happen that the party proceeded against cannot be found in the State, and personal service upon him is therefore impossible, unless it is allowable to make it wherever he may be found abroad.   But any such service would be ineffectual.   No State has authority to invade the jurisdiction of another, and by service of process compel parties there resident or being to submit their controversies to the determination of its courts ; and those courts will consequently be sometimes unable to enforce a jurisdiction which the State possesses in respect to the subjects within its limits, unless

---

[1] Doughty *v.* Hope, 3 Denio, 594.   See Matter of Empire City Bank, 18 N. Y. 199 ; Nations *v.* Johnson, 24 How. 204 – 205 ; Blackwell on Tax Titles, 213.

[2] Where, however, a statute provides for the taking of a certain security, and authorizes judgment to be rendered upon it on motion, without process, the party entering into the security must be understood to assent to the condition, and to waive process and consent to judgment. Lewis *v.* Garrett's Admr., 6 Miss. 434 ; People *v.* Van Eps, 4 Wend. 390 ; Chappee *v.* Thomas, 5 Mich. 53 ; Gildersleeve *v.* People, 10 Barb. 35 ; People *v.* Lott, 21 Barb. 130 ; Pratt *v.* Donovan, 10 Wis. 378.

a substituted service is admissible. A substituted service is provided by statute for many such cases; generally in the form of a notice, published in the public journals, or posted, as the statute may direct; the mode being chosen with a view to bring it, if possible, home to the knowledge of the party to be affected, and to give him an opportunity to appear and defend. The right of the legislature to prescribe such notice, and to give it effect as process, rests upon the necessity of the case, and has been long recognized and acted upon.[1]

But such notice is restricted in its legal effect, and cannot be made available for all purposes. It will enable the court to give effect to the proceeding so far as it is one *in rem*, but when the *res* is disposed of the authority of the court ceases. The statute may give it effect so far as the subject-matter of the proceeding is within the limits, and therefore under the control, of the State; but the notice cannot be made to stand in the place of process, so as to subject the defendant to a valid judgment against him personally. In attachment proceedings, the published notice may be sufficient to enable the plaintiff to obtain a judgment which he can enforce by sale of the property attached, but for any other purpose such judgment would be ineffectual. The defendant could not be followed into another State or country, and there have recovery against him upon the judgment as an established demand. The fact that process was not personally served is a conclusive objection to the judgment as a personal claim, unless the defendant caused his appearance to be entered in the attachment proceedings.[2] Where a party has property in a State, and

---

[1] " It may be admitted that a statute which authorized any debt or damages to be adjudged against a person upon purely *ex parte* proceedings, without pretence of notice, or any provision for defending, would be a violation of the constitution, and void; but when the legislature has provided a kind of notice by which it is reasonably probable that the party proceeded against will be apprised of what is going on against him, and an opportunity is afforded him to defend, I am of opinion that the courts have not the power to pronounce the proceedings illegal." Denio, J., in Matter of Empire City Bank, 18 N. Y. 200. See also, per Morgan, J., in Rockwell *v.* Nearing, 35 N. Y. 314; Nations *v.* Johnson, 24 How. 195; Beard *v.* Beard, 21 Ind. 321; Mason *v.* Messenger, 17 Iowa, 261.

[2] Pawling *v.* Willson, 13 Johns. 192; Heirs of Holman *v.* Bank of Norfolk, 12 Ala. 369; Curtis *v.* Gibbs, 1 Penn. 399; Miller's Exr. *v.* Miller, 1 Bailey, 242; Cone *v.* Cotton, 2 Blackf. 82; Kilburn *v.* Woodworth, 5 Johns. 37; Robinson *v.* Ward's Exr., 8 Johns. 86; Hall *v.* Williams, 6 Pick. 232; Bartlet *v.* Knight, 1 Mass. 401; St. Albans *v.* Bush, 4 Vt. 58; Fenton *v.* Garlick, 8 Johns.

resides elsewhere, his property is justly subject to all valid claims that may exist against him there ; but beyond this, due process of law would require appearance or personal service before the defendant could be personally bound by any judgment rendered.

The same rule applies in divorce cases. The courts of the State where the complaining party resides have jurisdiction of the subject-matter ; and if the other party is a nonresident, they must be authorized to proceed without personal service of process. The publication which is permitted by the statute is sufficient to justify a decree in these cases changing the *status* of the complaining party, and thereby terminating the marriage ;[1] and it might be sufficient also to empower the court to pass upon the question of the custody and control of the children of the marriage, if they were then within its jurisdiction. But a decree on this subject could only be absolutely binding on the parties while the children remained within the jurisdiction ; if they acquire a domicile in another State or country, the judicial tribunals of that State or country would have authority to determine the question of their guardianship there.[2]

194 ; Bissell v. Briggs, 9 Mass. 462 ; Denison v. Hyde, 6 Conn. 508 ; Aldrich v. Kinney, 4 Conn. 380 ; Hoxie v. Wright, 2 Vt. 263 ; Newell v. Newton, 10 Pick. 470 ; Starbuck v. Murray, 5 Wend. 161 ; Armstrong v. Harshaw, 1 Dev. 188 ; Bradshaw v. Heath, 13 Wend. 407 ; Bates v. Delavan, 5 Paige, 299 ; Webster v. Reid, 11 How. 460 ; Gleason v. Dodd, 4 Met. 333 ; Green v. Custard, 23 How. 486. In Ex parte Heyfron, 7 How. (Miss.) 127, it was held that an attorney could not be stricken from the rolls without notice of the proceeding, and opportunity to be heard. Leaving notice with one's family is not equivalent to personal service. Rape v. Heaton, 9 Wis. 329. And see Bimeler v. Dawson, 4 Scam. 536.

[1] Hull v. Hull, 2 Strob. Eq. 174 ; Manley v. Manley, 4 Chand. 97 ; Hubbell v. Hubbell, 3 Wis. 662 ; Mansfield v. McIntyre, 10 Ohio, 28 ; Ditson v. Ditson, 4 R. I. 87 ; Harrison v. Harrison, 19 Ala. 499 ; Thompson v. State, 28 Ala. 12 ; Harding v. Alden, 9 Greenl. 140 ; Maguire v. Maguire, 7 Dana, 181 ; Todd v. Kerr, 42 Barb. 317. It is immaterial in these cases whether notice was actually brought home to the defendant or not. And see Heirs of Holman v. Bank of Norfolk, 12 Ala. 369.

[2] This must be so on general principles, as the appointment of guardian for minors is of local force only. See Monell v. Dickey, 1 Johns. Ch. 156 ; Woodworth v. Spring, 4 Allen, 321 ; Potter v. Hiscox, 30 Conn. 508 ; Kraft v. Wickey, 4 G. & J. 322. The case of Townsend v. Kendall, 4 Minn. 412, appears to be contra, but some reliance is placed by the court on the statute of the State which allows the foreign appointment to be recognized for the purposes of a sale of the real estate of a ward.

But in divorce cases, no more than in any other, can the court make a decree for the payment of money by a defendant not served with process, and not appearing in the case, which shall be binding upon him personally. It must follow, in such a case, that the wife, when complainant, cannot obtain a valid decree for alimony, nor a valid judgment for costs. If the defendant had property within the State, it would be competent to provide by law for the seizure and appropriation of such property, under the decree of the court, to the use of the complainant; but the legal tribunals elsewhere would not recognize a decree for alimony or for costs not based on personal service or appearance. The remedy of the complainant must generally, in these cases, be confined to a dissolution of the marriage, with the incidental benefits springing therefrom, and to an order for the custody of the children, if within the State.[1]

When the question is raised whether the proceedings of a court may not be void for want of jurisdiction, it will sometimes be important to note the grade of the court and the extent of its authority. Some courts are of general jurisdiction, by which is meant that their authority extends to a great variety of matters; while others are only of special and limited jurisdiction, by which it is understood that they have authority extending only to certain specified cases. The want of jurisdiction is equally fatal in the proceedings of each; but different rules prevail in showing it. It is not to be assumed that a court of general jurisdiction has in any case proceeded to adjudge upon matters over which it had no authority; and its jurisdiction is to be presumed, whether there are recitals in its records to show it or not. On the other hand, no such intendment is made in favor of the judgment of a court of limited jurisdiction, but the recitals contained in the minutes of proceedings must be sufficient to show that the case was one which the law permitted the court to take cognizance of, and that the parties were subjected to its jurisdiction by proper process.[2]

---

[1] See Jackson v. Jackson, 1 Johns. 424; Harding v. Alden, 9 Greenl. 140; Holmes v. Holmes, 4 Barb. 295; Crane v. Meginnis, 1 Gill & J. 463; Maguire v. Maguire, 7 Dana, 181; Townsend v. Griffin, 4 Harr. 440.

[2] See Dakin v. Hudson, 6 Cow. 221; Cleveland v. Rogers, 6 Wend. 438; People v. Koeber, 7 Hill, 39; Sheldon v. Wright, 1 Seld. 511; Clark v. Holmes, 1 Doug. (Mich.) 390; Cooper v. Sunderland, 3 Iowa, 114; Wall v. Trumbull, 16 Mich. 228; Denning v. Corwin, 11 Wend. 647; Bridge v. Ford, 6 Mass. 641; Smith v. Rice, 11 Mass. 511; Barrett v. Crane, 16 Vt. 246; Teft v. Griffin, 5 Geo.

There is also another difference between these two classes of tribunals in this, that the jurisdiction of the one may be disproved under circumstances where it would not be allowed in the case of the other. A record is not commonly suffered to be contradicted by parol evidence; but wherever a fact showing want of jurisdiction in a court of general jurisdiction can be proved without contradicting its recitals, it is allowable to do so, and thus defeat its effect.[1] But in the case of a court of special and limited authority, it is permitted to go still further, and to show a want of jurisdiction even in opposition to the recitals contained in the record.[2] This we conceive to be the general rule, though there are apparent exceptions of those cases where the jurisdiction may be said to depend upon the existence of a certain state of facts, which must be passed upon by the courts themselves, and in respect to which the decision of the court once rendered, if there was any evidence whatever on which to base it, must be held final and conclusive in all collateral inquiries, notwithstanding it may have erred in its conclusions.[3]

185; Jennings v. Stafford, 1 Ired. 404; Hershaw v. Taylor, 3 Jones, 513; Perrine v. Farr, 2 Zab. 356; State v. Metzger, 26 Mo. 65.

[1] See this subject considered at some length in Wilcox v. Kassick, 2 Mich. 165. And see Rape v. Heaton, 9 Wis. 329; Bimelar v. Dawson, 4 Scam. 536; Webster v. Reid, 11 How. 437.

[2] Sheldon v. Wright, 5 N. Y. 497; Dyckman v. Mayor, &c. of N. Y. 5 N. Y. 434; Clark v. Holmes, 1 Doug. (Mich.) 390; Cooper v. Sunderland, 3 Iowa, 114; Sears v. Terry, 26 Conn. 273; Brown v. Foster, 6 R. I. 564; Fawcett v. Fowliss, 1 Man. & R. 102. But see Facey v. Fuller, 13 Mich. 527, where it was held that the entry in the docket of a justice that the parties appeared and proceeded to trial was conclusive. And see Selin v Snyder, 7 S. & R. 72.

[3] Britain v. Kinnard, 1 B. & B. 432. Conviction under the Bumboat Act. The record was fair on its face, but it was insisted that the vessel in question was not a "boat" within the intent of the act. Dallas, Ch. J. : " The general principle applicable to cases of this description is perfectly clear: it is established by all the ancient, and recognized by all the modern decisions; and the principle is, that a conviction by a magistrate, who has jurisdiction over the subject-matter, is, if no defects appear on the face of it, conclusive evidence of the facts stated in it. Such being the principle, what are the facts of the present case? If the subject-matter in the present case were a boat, it is agreed that the boat would be forfeited; and the conviction stated it to be a boat. But it is said that, in order to give the magistrate jurisdiction, the subject-matter of his conviction must be a boat; and that it is competent to the party to impeach the conviction by showing that it was not a boat. I agree, that if he had not jurisdiction, the conviction signifies nothing. Had he then jurisdiction in this case? By the act of Parliament he is empowered to search for and seize gunpowder in any boat on the

When it is once made to appear that a court has jurisdiction
both of the subject-matter and of the parties, the judgment which

river Thames. Now, allowing, for the sake of argument, that 'boat' is a word
of technical meaning, and somewhat different from a vessel, still, it was a matter
of fact to be made out before the magistrate, and on which he was to draw his own
conclusion. But it is said that a jurisdiction limited as to person, place, and subject-
matter is stinted in its nature, and cannot be lawfully exceeded. I agree: but
upon the inquiry before the magistrate, does not the person form a question to be
decided upon the evidence? Does not the place, does not the subject-matter,
form such a question? The possession of a boat, therefore, with gunpowder on
board, is part of the offence charged; and how could the magistrate decide, but
by examining evidence in proof of what was alleged? The magistrate, it is
urged, could not give himself jurisdiction by finding that to be a fact which did
not exist. But he is bound to inquire as to the fact, and when he has inquired
his conviction is conclusive of it. The magistrates have inquired in the present
instance, and they find the subject of conviction to be a boat. Much has been
said about the danger of magistrates giving themselves jurisdiction; and extreme
cases have been put, as of a magistrate seizing a ship of seventy-four guns, and
calling it a boat. Suppose such a thing done, the conviction is still conclusive, and
we cannot look out of it. It is urged that the party is without remedy; and so
he is, without civil remedy, in this and many other cases; his remedy is by proceeding criminally; and if the decision were so gross as to call a ship of seventy-four
guns a boat, it would be good ground for a criminal proceeding. Formerly the rule
was to intend everything against a stinted jurisdiction: that is not the rule now;
and nothing is to be intended but what is fair and reasonable, and it is reasonable
to intend that magistrates will do what is right." Richardson, J., in the same case,
states the real point very clearly: "Whether the vessel in question were a boat
or no was a fact on which the magistrate was to decide; and the fallacy lies in
assuming that the fact which the magistrate has to decide is that which constitutes
his jurisdiction. If a fact decided as this has been might be questioned in a civil
suit, the magistrate would never be safe in his jurisdiction. Suppose the case for
a conviction under the game laws of having partridges in possession: could the
magistrate, in an action of trespass, be called on to show that the bird in question
was really a partridge? and yet it might as well be urged, in that case, that the
magistrate had no jurisdiction unless the bird were a partridge, as it may be urged
in the present case that he has none unless the machine be a boat. So in the case
of a conviction for keeping dogs for the destruction of game without being duly
qualified to do so: after the conviction had found that the offender kept a dog of
that description, could he, in a civil action, be allowed to dispute the truth of
the conviction? In a question like the present we are not to look at the inconvenience, but at the law; but surely if the magistrate acts *bona fide*, and comes
to his conclusion as to matters of fact according to the best of his judgment, it
would be highly unjust if he were to have to defend himself in a civil action; and
the more so, as he might have been compelled by a mandamus to proceed on the
investigation. Upon the general principle, therefore, that where the magistrate
has jurisdiction his conviction is conclusive evidence of the facts stated in it, I
think this rule must be discharged." See also Mather v. Hodd, 8 Johns, 44;

it pronounces must be held conclusive and binding upon the parties thereto and their privies, notwithstanding the court may have proceeded irregularly, or erred in its application of the law to the case before it. It is a general rule that irregularities in the course of judicial proceedings do not render them void.[1] An irregularity may be defined as the failure to observe that particular course of proceeding which, conformably with the practice of the court, ought to have been observed in the case ;[2] and if a party claims to be aggrieved by this, he must apply to the court in which the suit is pending to set aside the proceedings, or to give him such other redress as he thinks himself entitled to ; or he must take steps to have the judgment reversed by removing the case for review to an appellate court, if any such there be. Wherever the question of the validity of the proceedings arises in any collateral suit, he will be held bound by them to the same extent as if in all respects the court had proceeded according to law. An irregularity cannot be taken advantage of collaterally ; that is to say, in any other suit than that in which the irregularity occurs, or on appeal or process in error therefrom. And even in the same proceeding an irregularity may be waived, and will commonly be held to be waived if the party entitled to complain of it shall take any subsequent step in the case inconsistent with an intent on his part to take advantage of it.[3]

We have thus briefly indicated the cases in which judicial action may be treated as void because not in accordance with the

Mackaboy v. Commonwealth, 2 Virg. Cas. 268; Ex parte Kellogg, 6 Vt. 509; State v. Scott, 1 Bailey, 294 ; Facey v. Fuller, 13 Mich. 527; Wall v. Trumbull, 16 Mich. 228 ; Sheldon v. Wright, 5 N. Y. 512.

[1] Ex parte Kellogg, 6 Vt. 509; Edgerton v. Hart, 8 Vt. 208; Carter v. Walker, 2 Ohio, N. S. 339.

[2] " The doing or not doing that in the conduct of a suit at law which, conformably to the practice of the court, ought or ought not to be done." Bouv. Law Dic.

[3] Robinson v. West, 1 Sandf. 19; Malone v. Clark, 2 Hill, 657; Wood v. Randall, 5 Hill, 285; Baker v. Kerr, 13 Iowa, 384; Loomis v. Wadhams, 8 Gray, 557; Warren v. Glynn, 37 N. H. 340. A strong instance of waiver is where, on appeal from a court having no jurisdiction of the subject-matter to a court having general jurisdiction, the parties going to trial without objection are held bound by the judgment. Randolph Co. v. Ralls, 18 Ill. 29; Wells v. Scott, 4 Mich. 347; Tower v. Lamb, 6 Mich. 362. In Hoffman v. Locke, 19 Penn. St. 57, objection was taken on constitutional grounds to a statute which allowed judgment to be entered up for the plaintiff in certain cases, if the defendant failed to make and file an affidavit of merits; but the court sustained it.

law of the land. The design of the present work does not permit an enlarged discussion of the topics which suggest themselves in this connection, and which, however interesting and important, do not specially pertain to the subject of constitutional law.

But a party in any case has a right to demand that the judgment of the court be given upon his suit, and he cannot be bound by a delegated exercise of judicial power, whether the delegation be by the courts or by legislative act devolving judicial duties on ministerial officers.[1] Proceedings in any such case would be void ; but they must be carefully distinguished from those cases in which the court has itself acted, though irregularly. Even the denial of jury trial, in cases where that privilege is reserved by the Constitution, does not render the proceedings void, but only makes them liable to be reversed for the error.[2]

There is also a maxim of law regarding judicial action which may have an important bearing upon the constitutional validity of judgments in some cases. No one ought to be a judge in his own cause ; and so inflexible and so manifestly just is this rule, that Lork Coke has laid it down that " even an act of Parliament made against natural equity, as to make a man a judge in his own case, is void in itself ; for *jura naturæ sunt immutabilia,* and they are *leges legum.*" [3]

---

[1] Hall *v.* Marks, 34 Ill. 363 ; Chandler *v.* Nash, 5 Mich. 409. For the distinction between judicial and ministerial acts, see Flournoy *v.* Jeffersonville, 17 Ind. 173.

[2] The several State constitutions preserve the right of trial by jury, with permission in some for the parties to waive the right in civil cases. Those cases which before the constitution were not triable by jury need not be made so now. Dane Co. *v.* Dunning, 20 Wis. 210 ; Crandall *v.* James, 6 R. I. 104 ; Lake Erie &c. R. R. Co. *v.* Heath, 9 Ind. 558 ; Backus *v.* Lebanon, 11 N. H. 19 ; 'Cabor *v.* Cook, 15 Mich. 322 ; Stilwell *v.* Kellogg, 14 Wis. 461 ; Sands *v.* Kimbark, 27 N. Y. 147. And where a new tribunal is created without common-law powers, jury trial need not be given. Rhines *v.* Clark, 51 Penn. St. 96 ; Haines *v.* Levin, Ibid. 412. But the legislature cannot deprive a party of a common-law right, — e. g. a right of navigation, — and compel him to abide the estimate of commissioners upon his damages. Haines *v.* Levin, 51 Penn. St. 412. Where the constitution gives the right, it cannot be made by statute to depend upon any condition. Greene *v.* Briggs, 1 Curt. 311. Though it has been held that, if a trial is given in one court without a jury, with a right to appeal and to have a trial by jury in the appellate court, that is sufficient. Beers *v.* Beers, 4 Conn. 535 ; Stewart *v.* Mayor, &c., 7 Md. 500 ; Morford *v.* Barnes, 8 Yerg. 444 ; Jones *v.* Robbins, 8 Gray, 329.

[3] Co. Lit. § 212. It is now well understood, however, that even in a case of

This maxim applies in all cases where judicial functions are to be exercised, and excludes all who are interested, however remotely, from taking part in their exercise. It is not left to the discretion of a judge, or to his sense of decency, to decide whether he shall act or not; all his powers are subject to this absolute limitation; and when his own rights are in question, he has no authority to determine the cause.[1] Nor is it essential that the judge be a party named in the record; if the suit is brought or defended in his interest, or if he is a corporator in a corporation which is a party, or which will be benefited or damnified by the judgment, he is equally excluded as if he were the party named.[2] Accordingly, where the Lord Chancellor, who was a shareholder in a company in whose favor the Vice-Chancellor had rendered a decree, affirmed this decree, the House of Lords reversed the decree on this ground, Lord Campbell observing: " It is of the last importance that the maxim that ' no man is to be a judge in his own cause' should be held sacred. And that is not to be confined to a cause in which he is a party, but applies to a cause in which he has an interest." " We have again and again set aside proceedings in inferior tribunals, because an individual who had an interest in a cause took a part in the decision. And it will have a most salutary effect on these tribunals, when it is known that this high court of last resort, in a case in which the Lord Chancellor of England had an interest, considered that his decree was on that account a decree not according to law, and should be set aside. This will be a lesson to all inferior tribunals to take care, not only that in their decrees they are not influenced by their personal interest, but to avoid the appearance of laboring under such an influence." [3]

It is matter of some interest to know whether the legislatures of the American States can set aside this maxim of the common law, and by express enactment permit one to act judicially when

this kind, if one could be imagined to exist, the courts could not declare the act of Parliament void; though they would never find such an intent in the statute, if any other could possibly be made consistent with the words.

[1] Washington Insurance Co. v. Price, Hopk. Ch. 2.

[2] Washington Insurance Co. v. Price, Hopk. Ch. 2; Dimes v. Proprietors of Grand Junction Canal, 3 House of Lords Cases, 759; Pearce v. Atwood, 13 Mass. 340; Peck v. Freeholders of Essex, Spencer, 457; Commonwealth v. McLane, 4 Gray, 427.

[3] Dimes v. Proprietors of Grand Junction Canal, 3 House of Lords Cases, 759.

interested in the controversy. The maxim itself, it is said, in some cases, does not apply where, from necessity, the judge must proceed in the case, there being no other tribunal authorized to act;[1] but we prefer the opinion of Chancellor Sandford of New York, that in such a case it belongs to the power which created such a court to provide another in which this judge may be a party; and whether another tribunal is established or not, he at least is not intrusted with authority to determine his own rights or his own wrongs.[2]

It has been held that where the interest was that of corporator in a municipal corporation, the legislature might provide that it should constitute no disqualification where the corporation was a party. But the ground of this ruling appears to be, that the interest is so remote, trifling, and insignificant, that it may fairly be supposed to be incapable of affecting the judgment or of influencing the conduct of an individual.[3] And where penalties are imposed, to be recovered only in a municipal court, the judges or jurors in which would be interested as corporators in the recovery, the law providing for such recovery must be regarded as precluding the objection of interest.[4] And it is very common, in a certain class of cases, for the law to provide that certain township and county officers shall audit their own accounts for services rendered the public; but in such case there is no adversary party, unless the State, which passes the law, or the municipalities which are its component parts and subject to its control, can be regarded as such.

But except in cases resting upon such reasons, we do not see how the legislature can have any power to abolish a maxim which is among the fundamentals of judicial authority. The people, indeed, when framing their constitution, may establish so great an anomaly, if they see fit;[5] but if the legislature is intrusted with apportioning and providing for the exercise of the judicial power, we cannot understand them to be authorized, in the execution of this trust, to do that which has never been recognized as

[1] Ranger v. Great Western R., 5 House of Lords Cases, 88; Stewart v. Mechanics & Farmers' Bank, 19 Johns. 501.

[2] Washington Insurance Co. v. Price, Hopk. Ch. 2.

[3] Commonwealth v. Reed, 1 Gray, 475.

[4] Commonwealth v. Ryan, 5 Mass. 90; Hill v. Wells, 6 Pick. 104; Commonwealth v. Emery, 11 Cush. 406.

[5] Matter of Leefe, 2 Barb. Ch. 39.

being within the province of the judicial authority. To empower one party to a controversy to decide it for himself is not within the legislative authority, because it is not the establishment of any rule of action or decision, but is a placing of the other party, so far as that controversy is concerned, out of the protection of the law, and submitting him to the control of one whose interest it will be to decide arbitrarily and unjustly.[1]

Nor do we see how the objection of interest can be waived by the other party. If not taken before the decision is rendered, it will avail in an appellate court; and the suit may there be dismissed on that ground.[2] The judge acting in such a case is not simply proceeding irregularly, but he is acting without jurisdiction. And if one of the judges constituting a court is disqualified on this ground, the judgment will be void, even though the proper number may have concurred in the result, not reckoning the interested party.[3]

Mere formal acts necessary to enable the case to be brought before a proper tribunal for adjudication, an interested judge may do;[4] but that is the extent of his power.

[1] See Ames v. Port Huron Log-Driving & Booming Co., 11 Mich. 139.

[2] Richardson v. Welcome, 6 Cush. 332; Dimes v. Proprietors of Grand Junction Canal, 3 House of Lords Cases, 787. And see Sigourney v. Sibley, 21 Pick. 106; Oakley v. Aspinwall, 3 N. Y. 547.

[3] In Queen v. Justices of Hertfordshire, 6 Queen's Bench, 753, it was decided that, if any one of the magistrates hearing a case at sessions was interested, the court was improperly constituted, and an order made in the case should be quashed. It was also decided that it was no answer to the objection, that there was a majority in favor of the decision without reckoning the interested party, nor that the interested party withdrew before the decision, if he appeared to have joined in discussing the matter with the other magistrates. See also the Queen v. Justices of Suffolk, 18 Q. B. 416; The Queen v. Justices of London, Ibid. 421.

[4] Richardson v. Boston, 1 Curtis, C. C. 251; Washington Insurance Co. v. Price, Hopk. Ch. 1; Buckingham v. Davis, 9 Md. 324; Heydenfeldt v. Towns, 27 Ala. 430.

CHAPTER XII.

LIBERTY OF SPEECH AND OF THE PRESS.

THE first amendment to the Constitution of the United States provides, among other things, that Congress shall make no law abridging the freedom of speech or of the press. With jealous care of what is almost universally regarded a sacred right, essential to the existence and perpetuity of free government, a provision of similar import has been embodied in each of the State constitutions, and a constitutional principle is thereby established which is supposed to form a shield of protection to the free expression of opinion in every part of our land.[1]

[1] The following are the constitutional provisions: *Maine:* Every citizen may freely speak, write, and publish his sentiments on any subject, being responsible for the abuse of this liberty. No law shall be passed regulating or restraining the freedom of the press; and, in prosecutions for any publication respecting the official conduct of men in public capacity, or the qualifications of those who are candidates for the suffrages of the people, or where the matter published is proper for public information, the truth thereof may be given in evidence; and in all indictments for libel, the jury, after having received the direction of the court, shall have a right to determine, at their discretion, the law and the fact. Declaration of Rights, § 4.—*New Hampshire:* The liberty of the press is essential to the security of freedom in a State; it ought, therefore, to be inviolably preserved. Bill of Rights, § 22. — *Vermont:* That the people have a right to freedom of speech, and of writing and publishing their sentiments concerning the transactions of government; therefore the freedom of the press ought not to be restrained. Declaration of Rights, Art. 13. — *Massachusetts:* The liberty of the press is essential to the security of freedom in a State; it ought not, therefore, to be restrained in this Commonwealth. Declaration of Rights, Art. 16. — *Rhode Island:* The liberty of the press being essential to the security of freedom in a State, any person may publish his sentiments on any subject, being responsible for the abuse of that liberty; and in all trials for libel, both civil and criminal, the truth, unless published from malicious motives, shall be sufficient defence to the person charged. Art. 1, § 20. — *Connecticut:* No law shall ever be passed to curtail or restrain the liberty of speech or of the press. In all prosecutions or indictments for libel, the truth may be given in evidence, and the jury shall have the right to determine the law and the facts, under the direction of the court. Art. 1, §§ 6 and 7. — *New York:* Every person may freely speak, write, and publish his sentiments on all subjects, being responsible for the abuse of that right; and no law shall be passed to restrain or abridge the liberty of speech or the press. In all criminal prosecu-

It is to be observed of these several provisions, that they recognize certain rights as now existing, and seek to protect and perpet-

tions or indictments for libels, the truth may be given in evidence to the jury, and if it shall appear to the jury that the matter charged as libellous is true, and was published with good motives and for justifiable ends, the party shall be acquitted, and the jury shall have the right to determine the law and the fact. Art. 1, § 8.
— *New Jersey:* Every person may freely speak, write, and publish his sentiments on all subjects, being responsible for the abuse of that right. No law shall be passed to restrain or abridge the liberty of speech or of the press. In all prosecutions or indictments for libel, the truth may be given in evidence to the jury; and if it shall appear to the jury that the matter charged as libellous is true, and was published with good motives, and for justifiable ends, the party shall be acquitted; and the jury shall have the right to determine the law and the fact. Art 1, § 5. — *Pennsylvania:* That the printing-presses shall be free to every person who undertakes to examine the proceedings of the legislature, or any branch of government, and no law shall ever be made to restrain the right thereof. The free communication of thoughts and opinions is one of the invaluable rights of man, and every citizen may freely speak, write, and print on any subject, being responsible for the abuse of the liberty. In prosecutions for the publication of papers, investigating the official conduct of officers or men in public capacity, or where the matter published is proper for public information, the truth thereof may be given in evidence; and in all indictments for libels, the jury shall have a right to determine the law and the facts, under the direction of the court, as in other cases. Art. 9, § 7. — *Delaware:* The press shall be free to every citizen who undertakes to examine the official conduct of men acting in public capacity, and any citizen may print on any such subject, being responsible for the abuse of that liberty. In prosecutions for publications investigating the proceedings of officers, or where the matter published is proper for public information, the truth thereof may be given in evidence; and in all indictments for libels, the jury may determine the facts and the law, as in other cases. Art. 1, § 5. — *Maryland:* That the liberty of the press ought to be inviolably preserved; that every citizen of the State ought to be allowed to speak, write, and publish his sentiments on all subjects, being responsible for the abuse of that liberty. Declaration of Rights, Art. 40.
— *West Virginia:* No law abridging the freedom of speech or of the press shall be passed; but the legislature may provide for the restraint and punishment of the publishing and vending of obscene books, papers, and pictures, and of libel and defamation of character, and for the recovery in civil action, by the aggrieved party, of suitable damages for such libel or defamation. Attempts to justify and uphold an armed invasion of the State, or an organized insurrection therein during the continuance of such invasion or insurrection, by publicly speaking, writing, or printing, or by publishing or circulating such writing or printing, may be by law declared a misdemeanor, and punished accordingly. In prosecutions and civil suits for libel, the truth may be given in evidence; and if it shall appear to the jury that the matter charged as libellous is true, and was published with good motives, and for justifiable ends, the verdict shall be for the defendant. Art. 2, §§ 4 and 5. — *Tennessee:* Nearly the same as Pennsylvania. Art. 1, § 19. — *Ohio:* Every citizen may freely speak, write, and publish his sentiments on all subjects,

uate them, by declaring that they shall not be abridged, or that they shall remain inviolate. They do not create new rights, but

being responsible for the abuse of the right; and no law shall be passed to restrain or abridge liberty of speech or of the press. In all criminal prosecutions for libel, the truth may be given in evidence to the jury; and if it shall appear to the jury that the matter charged as libellous is true, and was published with good motives and for justifiable ends, the party shall be acquitted. Art. 1, § 11. — *Iowa*, Art. 1, § 7, and *Nevada*, Art. 1, § 9. Substantially same as Ohio. — *Illinois*: Nearly the same as Pennsylvania. Art. 13, §§ 23 and 24. — *Indiana*: No law shall be passed restraining the free interchange of thought and opinion, or restricting the right to speak, write, or print freely on any subject whatever; but for the abuse of that right every person shall be responsible. In all prosecutions for libel, the truth of the matters alleged to be libellous may be given in justification. Art. 1, §§ 9 and 10. — *Michigan*: In all prosecutions for libels, the truth may be given in evidence to the jury; and if it shall appear to the jury that the matter charged as libellous is true, and was published with good motives and for justifiable ends, the party shall be acquitted. The jury shall have the right to determine the law and the fact. Art. 6, § 25. — *Wisconsin*: Same as New York. Art. 1, § 3. — *Minnesota*: The liberty of the press shall forever remain inviolate, and all persons may freely speak, write, and publish their sentiments on all subjects, being responsible for the abuse of such right. Art. 1, § 3. — *Oregon*: No law shall be passed restraining the free expression of opinion, or restricting the right to speak, write, or print freely on any subject whatever; but every person shall be responsible for the abuse of this right. Art. 1, § 8. — *California*: Same as New York. Art. 1, § 9. — *Kansas*: The liberty of the press shall be inviolate, and all persons may freely speak, write, or publish their sentiments on all subjects, being responsible for the abuse of such right; and in all civil or criminal actions for libel, the truth may be given in evidence to the jury, and if it shall appear that the alleged libellous matter was published for justifiable ends, the accused party shall be acquitted. Bill of Rights, § 11. — *Missouri*: That the free communication of thoughts and opinions is one of the invaluable rights of man; and that every person may freely speak, write, and print on any subject, being responsible for the abuse of that liberty; that in all prosecutions for libel, the truth thereof may be given in evidence, and the jury may determine the law and the facts, under the direction of the court. Art. 1, § 27. — *Nebraska*: Same as New York. Art. 1, § 3. — *Arkansas*: That printing-presses shall be free to every person; and no law shall ever be made to restrain the rights thereof. The free communication of thoughts and opinions is one of the invaluable rights of man; and every citizen may freely speak, write, and print on any subject, being responsible for the abuse of that liberty. In prosecutions for the publication of papers investigating the official conduct of officers or men in public capacity, or where the matter published is proper for public information, the truth thereof may be given in evidence, and in all indictments for libels the jury shall have the right to determine the law and the facts. Art. 2, §§ 7 and 8. — *Florida*: That every citizen may freely speak, write, and publish his sentiments on all subjects, being responsible for the abuse of that liberty; and no law shall be passed to curtail, abridge, or restrain the liberty of speech or of the press.

their purpose is to protect the citizen in the enjoyment of those already possessed. We are at once, therefore, turned back from these provisions to the common law, in order that we may ascertain what the rights are which are thus protected, and what is the extent of the privileges they assure.

At the common law, however, it will be found that liberty of the press was neither well protected nor well defined: The art of printing, in the hands of private persons, has, until within a comparatively recent period, been regarded rather as an engine of mischief, which required the restraining hand of the government, than as a power for good, to be encouraged as such. Like a vicious beast it might be made useful if properly harnessed and fettered. The government assumed to itself the right to determine what books might be published, and censors were appointed

Art. 1, § 5. — *Georgia:* Freedom of speech and freedom of the press are inherent elements of political liberty. But while every citizen may freely speak, or write, or print on any subject, he shall be responsible for the abuse of the liberty. Art. 1, § 6. — *Louisiana:* The press shall be free; every citizen may freely speak, write, and publish his sentiments on all subjects, being responsible for an abuse of this liberty. Title 7, Art. 111. — *North Carolina:* That the freedom of the press is one of the great bulwarks of liberty, and therefore ought never to be restrained. Declaration of Rights, § 15. — *South Carolina:* The trial by jury, as heretofore used in this State, and the liberty of the press, shall be forever inviolably preserved. Art. 9, § 7. — *Alabama:* That in prosecutions for the publication of papers investigating the official conduct of officers or men in public capacity, or when the matter published is proper for public information, the truth thereof may be given in evidence, and that in all indictments for libels the jury shall have the right to determine the law and the facts, under the direction of the court. Art. 1, § 13. — *Mississippi:* No law shall ever be passed to curtail or restrain the liberty of speech or of the press. In all prosecutions or indictments for libel, the truth may be given in evidence; and if it shall appear to the jury that the matter charged as libellous is true, and was published with good motives and for justifiable ends, the party shall be acquitted; and the jury shall have the right to determine the law and the facts. Art. 1, §§ 7 and 8. — *Texas:* Every citizen shall be at liberty to speak, write, or publish his opinions on any subject, being responsible for the abuse of that privilege; and no law shall ever be passed curtailing the liberty of speech or of the press. In prosecutions for the publication of papers investigating the official conduct of officers, or men in a public capacity, or when the matter published is proper for public information, the truth thereof may be given in evidence; and in all indictments for libels, the jury shall have the right to determine the law and the facts, under the direction of the court, as in other cases. Art. 1, §§ 5 and 6. — *Virginia:* That the freedom of the press is one of the great bulwarks of liberty, and can never be restrained but by despotic governments. Bill of Rights, § 12.

27

without whose permission it was criminal to publish a book upon any subject. Through all the changes of government this censorship was continued until after the revolution of 1688, and there are no instances in English history of more cruel and relentless persecution than for the publication of books which now would pass unnoticed. To a much later day the press was not free to publish even the current news of the day where the government could imagine itself to be interested in concealment. Many matters, the publication of which now seems important to the harmonious working of free institutions and to the proper observation of public officers by those interested in the discharge of their duties, were treated by the public authorities as offences against good order, and contempts of their authority. By a fiction not very far removed from the truth, the Parliament was supposed to sit with closed doors. No official publication of its debates was provided for, and no other allowed.[1] The brief sketches which found their way into print were usually disguised under the garb of discussions in a fictitious parliament, in a foreign country. Several times the Parliament resolved that any such publication, or any intermeddling by letter-writers, was a breach of their privileges, and should be punished accordingly on discovery of the offenders. For such a publication in 1747 the editor of the " Gentleman's Magazine " was brought to the bar of the House of Commons for reprimand, and only discharged on expressing his contrition. The general publication of Parliamentary debates dates only from the American Revolution, and even then was still considered a technical breach of privilege.[2]

The American Colonies followed the practice of the parent country. Even the laws were not at first published for general circulation, and it seemed to be thought desirable by the magistrates to keep the people in ignorance of the precise boundary

---

[1] In 1641, Sir Edward Deering was expelled and imprisoned for publishing a collection of his own speeches, and the book was ordered to be burned by the common hangman. See May's Const. Hist. ch. 7.

[2] See May's Constitutional History, chs. 7, 9, and 10, for a complete account of the struggle between the government and the press, resulting at last in the complete enfranchisement and protection of the latter in the publication of all matters of public interest, and in the discussion of public affairs. Freedom to report proceedings and debates was due at last to Wilkes, who, worthless as he was, proved a great public benefactor in his obstinate defence of liberty of the press and security from arbitrary search and arrest.

between that which was lawful and that which was prohibited, as more likely to make them avoid all doubtful actions. The magistrates of Massachusetts, when compelled by public opinion to suffer the publication of general laws in 1649, sent them forth with their protest, as a hazardous experiment. For publishing the laws of one session in Virginia, in 1682, the printer was arrested and put under bonds until the king's pleasure could be known, and the king's pleasure was that no printing should be allowed in the Colony.[1] There were not wanting instances of the public burning of books, as offenders against good order. Such was the fate of Elliot's book in defence of unmixed principles of popular freedom,[2] and Calef's book against Cotton Mather, which was given to the flames at Cambridge.[3] A single printing-press was introduced into the Colony so early as 1640, but the publications even of State documents did not become free until 1719, when, after a quarrel between Governor Shute and the House, he directed that body not to print one of their remonstrances, and, on their disobeying, sought in vain to procure the punishment of their printer.[4] When Dongan was sent out as Governor of New York in 1683, he was expressly instructed to suffer no printing,[5] and that Colony obtained its first press in 1692, through a Philadelphia printer being driven thence for publishing an address from a Quaker, in which he accused his brethren in office of being inconsistent with their principles in exercising political authority.[6] So late as 1671, Governor Berkley of Virginia expressed his thankfulness that neither free schools nor printing were introduced in the Colony, and his trust that these breeders of disobedience, heresy, and sects would long be unknown.[7]

The public bodies of the united nation did not at once invite publicity to their deliberations. The Constitutional Convention of 1787 sat with closed doors, and although imperfect reports of the debates have since been published, the injunction of secrecy upon its members was never removed.

The Senate for a time followed this example, and the first open

---

[1] 1 Hildreth, History of the United States, 561.
[2] 2 Bancroft, 73 ; 1 Hildreth, 452 ; 2 Palfrey's New England, 511, 512.
[3] 1 Bancroft, 97 ; 2 Hildreth, 166.
[4] 2 Hildreth, 298.
[5] 2 Hildreth, 77.
[6] 2 Hildreth, 171.
[7] 1 Hildreth, 526.

debate was had in 1793, on the occasion of the controversy over the right of Mr. Gallatin to a seat in that body. The House of Representatives sat with open doors from the first, tolerating the presence of reporters — over whose admission, however, the Speaker assumed control — and refusing in 1796 the pittance of two thousand dollars for full publication of debates.

It must be evident from these brief references that liberty of the press, as now exercised, is of modern origin,[1] and commentators seem to be agreed in the opinion that the term itself means only that liberty of publication without the previous permission of the government, which was obtained by the abolition of the censorship. In a strict sense, Mr. Hallam says, it consists merely in exemption from a licenser.[2] A similar view is expressed by De Lolme. "Liberty of the press," he says, "consists in this: that neither courts of justice, nor any other judges whatever, are authorized to take notice of writings *intended* for the press, but are confined to those which are actually printed."[3] Blackstone also adopts the same opinion,[4] and it has been followed by American commentators of standard authority as embodying correctly the idea incorporated in the constitutional law of the country by the provisions in the American Bills of Rights.[5]

It is conceded on all sides that the common-law rules that subjected the libeller to responsibility for the private injury, or the public scandal occasioned by his conduct, are not abolished by the protection afforded to the press in our constitutions. The words of Ch. J. Parker of Massachusetts on this subject have been frequently quoted, generally recognized as sound in principle, and accepted as authority. "Nor does our constitution or declaration of rights," he says, speaking of his own State, "abrogate the common law in this respect, as some have insisted. The sixteenth article declares that ' liberty of the press is essential to the security of freedom in a State : it ought not therefore to be restrained in this Commonwealth.' The *liberty* of the press, not its licentious-

---

[1] It is mentioned neither in the English Petition of Rights nor in the Bill of Rights; of so little importance did it seem to those who were seeking to redress grievances in those days.

[2] Hallam's Const. Hist. of England, ch. 15.

[3] De Lolme, Const. of England, 254.

[4] 4 Bl. Com. 151.

[5] Story on Const. § 1889 ; 2 Kent, 17 et seq. ; Rawle on Const. ch. 10.

ness: this is the construction which a just regard to the other parts of that instrument, and to the wisdom of those who founded it, requires. In the eleventh article it is declared that every subject of the Commonwealth ought to find a certain remedy, by having recourse to the laws, for all injuries or wrongs which he, may receive in his person, property, or character; and thus the general declaration in the sixteenth article is qualified. Besides, it is well understood and received as a commentary on this provision for the liberty of the press, that it was intended to prevent all such *previous restraints* upon publications as had been practised by other governments, and in early times here, to stifle the efforts of patriots towards enlightening their fellow-subjects upon their rights and the duties of rulers. The liberty of the press was to be unrestrained, but he who used it was to be responsible in case of its abuse; like the right to keep fire-arms, which does not protect him who uses them for annoyance or destruction." [1]

Conceding, however, that liberty of speech and of the press does not imply complete exemption from responsibility for everything a citizen may say or publish, and complete immunity to ruin the reputation or business of others so far as falsehood and detraction may be able to accomplish that end, it is still believed that the mere exemption from previous restraints cannot be all that is secured by the constitutional provisions, inasmuch as of words to be uttered orally there can be no previous censorship, and the liberty of the press might be rendered a mockery and a delusion, and the phrase itself a byword if, while every man was at liberty to publish what he pleased, the public authorities might nevertheless punish him for harmless publications.

An examination of the controversies which have grown out of the repressive measures resorted to for the purpose of restraining the free expression of opinion will sufficiently indicate the purpose of the guaranties which have since been secured against such restraints in the future. Except so far as those guaranties relate to the mode of trial, and are designed to secure to every accused person the right to be judged by the opinion of a jury upon the criminality of his act, their purpose has evidently been to protect parties in the free publication of matters of public concern, to

---

[1] Commonwealth *v.* Blanding, 3 Pick. 313. See charge of Chief Justice McKean of Penn., 5 Hildreth, 166; Wharton's State Trials, 323; State *v.* Lehre, 2 Rep. Const. Court, 809.

secure their right to free discussion of public events and public measures, and to enable every citizen at any time to bring the government and any person in authority to the bar of public opinion by any just criticism upon their conduct in the exercise of the authority which the people have conferred upon them. To guard against repressive measures by the several departments of the government, by means of which persons in power might secure themselves and their favorites from just scrutiny and condemnation, was the general purpose ; and there was no design or desire to enlarge the rules of the common law which protected private character from detraction and abuse, except so far as seemed necessary to secure to accused parties a fair trial. The evils to be guarded against were not the censorship of the press merely, but any action of the government by means of which it might prevent such free and general discussion of public matters as seems absolutely essential to prepare the people for an intelligent exercise of their rights as citizens.

The constitutional liberty of speech and of the press, as we understand it, implies a right to freely utter and publish whatever the citizen may please, and to be protected against any responsibility for the publication, except so far as such publications, from their blasphemy, obscenity, or scandalous character, may be a public offence, or as by their falsehood and malice they may injuriously affect the private character of individuals. Or, to state the same thing in somewhat different words, we understand liberty of speech and of the press to imply not only liberty to publish, but complete immunity for the publication, so long as it is not harmful in its character, when tested by such standards as the law affords. For these standards we must look to the common-law rules which were in force when the constitutional guaranties were established.

At the common law an action would lie against any person publishing a false and malicious communication tending to disgrace or injure another. Falsehood, malice, and injury were the elements of the action ; but as the law presumed innocence of crime or misconduct until the contrary was proved, the falsity of an injurious publication was presumed until its truth was averred and substantiated by the defendant ; and if false, malice in the publication was also presumed unless the publication was privileged under rules to be hereafter stated. There were many cases, also, where the law presumed injury, and did not call upon the complaining party to make any other showing that he was damnified than such implication as arose from the character of the communication itself. If it accused him of a criminal offence, involving moral turpitude, and such as would subject a party proved guilty of it to punishment by imprisonment,[1] if it charged him with insanity,[2] or with an infectious disease, the effect of the charge, if believed, being to exclude him from the society of his fellows ;[3] if the charge affected the party in his business, office, or means of livelihood, like charging a trader with insolvency, and the like ;[4] or if any injurious charge holding a party up to public contempt, scorn, or ridicule is propagated by printing, writing, signs, burlesques, &c.,[5] — the law presumed injury, and the charge was said to be actionable *per se*. And although it was formerly held that to charge a female with want of chastity was not actionable without proof of special damage,[6] yet of late a disposition has been exhibited to

---

[1] Alexander *v.* Alexander, 9 Wend. 141 ; Wagaman *v.* Byers, 17 Md. 183 ; Castlebery *v.* Kelly, 26 Geo. 606 ; Redway *v.* Gray, 31 Vt. 292 ; Hoag *v.* Hatch, 23 Conn. 585 ; Burton *v.* Burton, 3 Greene (Iowa), 316 ; Wright *v.* Paige, 36 Barb. 438. But the charge must be unequivocal. Van Rensselaer *v.* Dole, 1 Johns. Cas. 279 ; Dexter *v.* Taber, 12 Johns. 239 ; Hopkins *v.* Beedle, 1 Caines, 347 ; Butterfield *v.* Buffam, 9 N. H. 156 ; Holt *v.* Scolefield, 6 T. R. 691 ; Jacobs *v.* Fyler, 3 Hill, 572 ; Crone *v.* Angell, 14 Mich. 340 ; Bonner *v.* McPhail, 31 Barb. 106 ; Mower *v.* Watson, 11 Vt. 536. Though it is not necessary that technical words be employed ; if the necessary inference, taking the words together, is a charge of crime, it is sufficient. Morgan *v.* Livingston, 2 Rich. 573 ; True *v.* Plumley, 36 Me. 466 ; Curtis *v.* Curtis, 10 Bing. 477. It is not essential that the charge should be such as, if true, to subject the party *now* to punishment. It is the disgrace attending the charge that gives the right of action, and therefore to say that the person is a returned convict is actionable. Baum *v.* Clause, 5 Hill, 196 ; Smith *v.* Stewart, 5 Penn. St. 372 ; Utley *v.* Campbell, 5 T. B. Monr. 396 ; Holley *v.* Burgess, 9 Ala. 728. Or to accuse him of a crime for which prosecution would be barred by statute of limitations would be actionable. Van Ankin *v.* Westfall, 14 Johns. 233 ; Poe *v.* Grever, 3 Sneed, 664 ; Stewart *v.* Howe, 17 Ill. 71.

[2] Perkins *v.* Mitchell, 31 Barb. 461. But see Joannes *v.* Burt, 6 Allen 236.

[3] Carlslake *v.* Mapledorum, 2 T. R. 473.

[4] Lindsey *v.* Smith, 7 Johns. 360 ; Thomas *v.* Croswell, 7 Johns. 264 ; Riggs *v.* Denniston, 3 Johns. Cas. 198 ; Fonvard *v.* Adams, 7 Wend. 204.

[5] Janson *v.* Stuart, 1 T. R. 748 ; Van Ness *v.* Hamilton, 19 Johns. 367 ; Clegg *v.* Laffer, 10 Bing. 250 ; Steele *v.* Southwick, 9 Johns. 214.

[6] Gascoign *v.* Ambler, 2 Ld. Raym. 1004 ; Graves *v.* Blanchet, 2 Salk. 696 ; Wilby *v.* Elston, 8 C. B. 142 ; Buys *v.* Gillespie, 2 Johns. 115 ; Brooker *v.* Coffin, 5 Johns. 188 ; Bradt *v.* Towsley, 13 Wend. 253 ; Dyer *v.* Morris, 4 Mo. 214 ; Stanfield *v.* Boyer, 6 H. & J. 248 ; Woodbury *v.* Thompson, 3 N. H. 194.

break away from this rule in favor of one more just and sensible,[1] and the statutes of several of the States have either made adultery and incontinence punishable as crimes, whereby to charge them becomes actionable *per se* under the common-law rule, or else in express terms have declared such a charge actionable without proof of special damage.[2]

But in any other case a party complaining of a false, malicious, and disparaging communication might maintain an action therefor, on averment and proof of special damage.[3] But in any of these cases the truth of the charge, if pleaded and established, was generally a complete defence.[4]

In those cases in which the injurious charge was propagated by printing, writing, signs, burlesques, &c., there might also be a criminal prosecution, as well as a suit for private damages. The criminal prosecution was based upon the idea that the tendency of such publications was to excite to a breach of the public peace ;[5] and on similar grounds to publish injurious charges against a for-

---

[1] See the cases of Sexton *v.* Todd, Wright, 317 ; Wilson *v.* Runyan, Ibid. 671 ; Malone *v.* Stewart, 15 Ohio, 319 ; Moberly *v.* Preston, 8 Mo. 462 ; Sidgreaves *v.* Myatt, 22 Ala. 617 ; Terry *v.* Bright, 4 Md. 430.

[2] See Frisbie *v.* Fowler, 2 Conn. 707 ; Miller *v.* Parish, 8 Pick. 384 ; Pledger *v.* Hitchcock, 1 Kelley, 550 ; Smally *v.* Anderson, 2 T. B. Monr. 56 ; Williams *v.* Bryant, 4 Ala. 44 ; Dailey *v.* Reynolds, 4 Greene (Iowa), 354 ; Symonds *v.* Carter, 32 N. H. 458 ; McBrayer *v.* Hill, 4 Ired. 136 ; Morris *v.* Barkley, 1 Lit. 64 ; Phillips *v.* Wiley, 2 Lit. 153 ; Watts *v.* Greenlee, 2 Dev. 115 ; Drummond *v.* Leslie, 5 Blackf. 453 ; Worth *v.* Butler, 7 Blackf. 251 ; Richardson *v.* Roberts, 23 Geo. 215 ; Buford *v.* Wible, 32 Penn. St. 95 ; Freeman *v.* Price, 2 Bailey, 115 ; Regnier *v.* Cabot, 2 Gil. 34 ; Ranger *v.* Goodrich, 17 Wis. 78. The injustice of the common-law rule is perceived from those cases where it has been held that an allegation that, in consequence of the charge, the plaintiff had fallen into disgrace, contempt, and infamy, and lost her credit, reputation, and peace of mind (Woodbury *v.* Thompson, 3 N. H. 194), and that she is shunned by her neighbors (Beach *v.* Ranney, 2 Hill, 310), was not a sufficient allegation of special damage to maintain the action.

[3] Kelley *v.* Partington, 3 Nev. & M. 116 ; Steele *v.* Southwick, 9 Johns. 214 ; Hallock *v.* Miller, 2 Barb. 630 ; Powers *v.* Dubois, 17 Wend. 63 ; Weed *v.* Foster, 11 Barb. 203 ; Cooper *v.* Greeley, 1 Denio, 347 ; Stone *v.* Cooper, 2 Denio, 293. The damage, however, must be of a pecuniary character. Beach *v.* Ranney, 2 Hill, 309. But very slight damage has been held sufficient to support considerable recoveries. Williams *v.* Hill, 19 Wend. 305 ; Bradt *v.* Towsley, 13 Wend. 253 ; Olmsted *v.* Miller, 1 Wend. 506 ; Moore *v.* Meagher, 1 Taunt. 39 ; Knight *v.* Gibbs, 1 Ad. & El. 43.

[4] See 1 Hilliard on Torts, 410 ; Heard on Libel and Slander, § 151.

[5] Commonwealth *v.* Clap, 4 Mass. 168.

eign prince or ruler was also held punishable as a public offence, as tending to embroil the two nations, and disturb the peace of the world.[1]

We are not so much concerned, however, with the general rules pertaining to the punishment of injurious publications, as with those special cases where, for some reason of general public policy, the publication is claimed to be privileged, and where, consequently, it may be supposed to be within the constitutional protection. It has always been held, notwithstanding the general rule that malice is to be inferred from a false and injurious publication, that there were some cases to which the presumption would not apply, and where a private action could not be maintained without proof of express malice. These are the cases which are said to be privileged. The term "privileged," as applied to a communication alleged to be libellous, means generally that the circumstances under which it was made were such as to rebut the legal inference of malice, and to throw upon the plaintiff the burden of offering some evidence of its existence beyond the mere falsity of the charge.[2] The cases falling within this classification are those in which a party has a duty to discharge which requires that he should be allowed to speak freely and fully that which he believes; where he is himself directly interested in the subject-matter of the communication, and makes it with a view to the protection or advancement of his own interest, or where he is communicating confidentially with a person interested in the communication, and by way of advice or admonition.[3] Many such cases suggest themselves which are purely of private concern; such as answers to inquiries into the character or conduct of one formerly employed by the person to whom the inquiry is addressed, and of whom the information is sought with a view to guiding the inquirer in his own action in determining upon employing the same person;[4] answers to inquiries by one tradesman of another

---

[1] 27 State Trials, 627; 2 May's Const. Hist. of England, ch. 9.

[2] Lewis v. Chapman, 16 N. Y. 373, per Selden, J.

[3] "When a communication is made in confidence, either by or to a person interested in the communication, supposing it to be true, or by way of admonition or advice, it seems to be a general rule that malice (i. e. express malice) is essential to the maintenance of an action." 1 Stark. on Slander, 321. See Harrison v. Bush, 5 El. & Bl. 344; Somerville v. Hawkins, 10 C. B. 589.

[4] Pattison v. Jones, 8 B. & C. 578; Elam v. Badger, 23 Ill. 498; Bradley v. Heath, 12 Pick. 163.

as to the solvency of a person whom the inquirer has been desired to trust;[1] answers by a creditor to inquiries regarding the conduct and dealings of his debtor, made by one who had become surety for the debt;[2] communications from an agent to his principal, reflecting injuriously upon the conduct of a third person in a matter connected with the agency;[3] communications to a near relative respecting the character of a person to whom the relative is in negotiation for marriage;[4] and as many more like cases as would fall within the same reasons.[5] The rules of law applicable to these cases are very well settled, and are not likely to be changed with a view to greater stringency.[6]

Libels upon the Government.

At the common law it was indictable to publish anything against the constitution of the country, or the established system of government. The basis of such a prosecution was the tendency of the publications to excite disaffection with the government, and thus induce a revolutionary spirit. The law always,

---

[1] Smith v. Thomas, 2 Bing. (N. C.) 372.

[2] Dunman v. Bigg, 1 Campb. 269, note.

[3] Washburn v. Cooke, 3 Denio, 110.

[4] Todd v. Hawkins, 8 C. & P. 88. But there is no protection to such a communication from a stranger. Johannes v. Bennet, 5 Allen, 170.

[5] As to whether a stranger volunteering to give information injurious to another, to one interested in the knowledge, is privileged in so doing, see Coxhead v. Richards, 2 M. G. & S. 569; and Bennett v. Deacon, Ibid. 628. Where a confidential relation of any description exists between the parties, the communication is privileged; as where the tenant of a nobleman had written to inform him of his gamekeeper's neglect of duty. Cockagne v. Hodgkisson, 5 C. & P. 543. Where a son-in-law wrote to warn his mother-in-law of the bad character of a man she was about to marry. Todd v. Hawkins, 8 C. & P. 88. Where a banker communicated with his correspondent concerning a note sent to him for collection; the court saying that " all that is necessary to entitle such communication to be privileged is, that the relation of the parties should be such as to afford reasonable ground for supposing an innocent motive for giving the information, and to deprive the act of the appearance of officious intermeddling with the affairs of others." Lewis v. Chapman, 16 N. Y. 375. Where one communicated to an employer his suspicions of dishonest conduct in a servant towards himself. Amann v. Damm, 8 C. B. (N. S.) 597.

[6] See further, Lawler v. Earle, 5 Allen, 22; Grimes v. Coyle, 6 B. Monr. 301; Rector v. Smith, 11 Iowa, 302; Gosslin v. Cannon, 1 Harr. 3; Joannes v. Bennett, 5 Allen, 169; State v. Burnham, 9 N. H. 34.

however, allowed a calm and temperate discussion of public events
and measures, and the right of every man to give every public
matter a candid, full, and free discussion was recognized. It was
only when a publication went beyond this, and tended to excite
tumult, that it became criminal.[1] It cannot be doubted, however,
that the common-law rules on this subject were administered in
many cases with great harshness, and quite beyond any reasonable
construction which those rules would bear. This was especially
true during the long and bloody struggle with France, at the close
of the last and beginning of the present century, and for a few
subsequent years, until a rising public discontent with the prosecutions began to lead to acquittals, and finally to abandonment of
all such attempts to restrain the free expression of sentiments on
public affairs. Such prosecutions have now altogether ceased in
England. Like the censorship of the press, they have fallen out
of the British constitutional system.

" When the press errs, it is by the press itself that its errors are
left to be corrected. Repression has ceased to be the policy of
rulers, and statesmen have at length realized the wise maxim of
Lord Bacon, that ' the punishing of wits enhances their authority,
and a forbidden writing is thought to be a certain spark of truth
that flies up in the faces of them that seek to tread it out.' "[2]
We shall venture to express a doubt if the common-law principles
on this subject can be considered as having been practically
adopted in the American States. It is certain that no prosecutions could now be maintained in the United States courts for
libels on the general government, since those courts have no common-law jurisdiction,[3] and there is now no statute, and never was
except during the brief existence of the Sedition Law, which
assumed to confer any such power.

The Sedition Law was passed during the administration of the
elder Adams, when the fabric of government was still new and
untried, and when many men seemed to think that the breath of
heated party discussions might tumble it about their heads. Its
constitutionality was always disputed by a large party, and its
impolicy was without question. Its direct tendency was to produce the very state of things it sought to repress; the prosecu-

---

[1] Regina v. Collins, 9 C. & P. 456, per Littledale, J.*
[2] May's Constitutional Hist. ch. 10.
[3] United States v. Hudson, 7 Cranch, 32.

tions under it were instrumental, among other things, in the final overthrow and destruction of the party by which it was adopted, and it is impossible to conceive, at the present time, of any such state of things as would be likely to bring about its re-enactment, or the passage of any similar repressive statute.[1]

When it is among the fundamental principles of the government that the people frame their own constitution, and that in doing so they reserve to themselves the power to amend it from time to time, as the public sentiment may change, it is difficult to conceive any sound basis on which prosecutions for libel on the system of government can be based, except when their evident intent and purpose is to excite rebellion and civil war. It is very easy to lay down a rule for the discussion of constitutional questions; that they are privileged, if conducted with calmness and temperance, and that they are not indictable unless they go beyond the bounds of fair discussion. But what is calmness and temperance, and what is fair in the discussion of supposed evils in the government? And if something is to be allowed " for a little feeling in men's minds,"[2] how great shall be the allowance? The heat of the discussion will generally be in proportion to the magnitude of the evil, as it appears to the party discussing it: must the question, whether he has exceeded due bounds or not, be tried by judge and jury, who may sit under different circumstances from those under which he has spoken, or at least after the heat of the occasion has passed away, and who, feeling none of the excitement themselves, may think it unreasonable that any one else should ever have felt it? The dangerous character of such prosecutions would be the more glaring if aimed at those classes who, not being admitted to a share in the government, attacked the constitution in the point which excluded them. Sharp criticism, ridicule, and the exhibition of such feeling as a sense of injustice engenders, is to be expected from any discussion in these cases; but when the very classes who have established the exclusion as proper and reasonable are to try as judges and jurors the assaults made upon it, they will be very likely to enter upon the examina-

---

[1] For prosecutions under this law, see Lyon's case, Wharton's State Trials, 333; Cooper's case, Ibid. 659; Haswell's case, Ibid. 684; Callender's case, Ibid. 688. And see 2 Randall's Life of Jefferson, 417 – 421; 5 Hildreth's Hist. of U. S. 247, 365.

[2] Regina v. Collins, 9 C. & P. 460, per Littledale, J.

tion with a preconceived notion that such assaults upon their reasonable regulations must necessarily be unreasonable. The great danger, however, of recognizing any such principle in the common law of America, is, that in times of high party excitement, it may lead to prosecutions by the party in power, to bolster up wrongs and sustain abuses and oppressions by crushing adverse criticism and discussion. The evil, indeed, could not be of long continuance ; for, judging· from experience, the reaction would be speedy, thorough, and effectual ; but it would be no less a serious evil while it lasted, the direct tendency of which would be to excite discontent and to breed a rebellious spirit. Repression of full and free discussion is dangerous in any government resting upon the will of the people. The people cannot fail to feel that they are deprived of rights, and will be certain to become discontented, when their discussion of public measures is sought to be circumscribed by the judgment of others upon their temperance or fairness. They must be left at liberty to speak with the freedom which the magnitude of the supposed wrongs appears in their minds to demand ; and if they exceed all the proper bounds of moderation, the consolation must be, that the evil likely to spring from the violent discussion will probably be less, and its correction by public sentiment more speedy, than if the terrors of the law were brought to bear to prevent the discussion.

The English common-law rule which made libels on the constitution or the government indictable, as it was administered by the courts, seems to us unsuited to the condition and circumstances of the people of America, and therefore to have never been adopted in the several states. If so, it would not be in the power of the State legislatures to pass laws which should make mere criticism of the constitution or of the measures of government a crime, however sharp, unreasonable, and intemperate it might be. The constitutional freedom of speech and of the press must mean a freedom as broad as existed when the constitution which guarantees it was adopted, and it would not be in the power of the legislature to restrict it, except in those cases of publications injurious to private character, or public morals or safety, which come strictly within the reasons of civil or criminal liability at the common law, but where, nevertheless, the common law as we have adopted it failed to provide a remedy. It certainly could not be said that freedom of speech was violated by a law which should make imputing the want of chastity to a female actionable without proof of special damage; for the charge is one of grievous wrong, without any reason in public policy demanding protection to the communication, and the case is strictly analogous to many other cases where the common law made the party responsible for his false accusations. The constitutional provisions do not prevent the modification of the common-law rules of liability for libels and slanders, but they would not permit bringing new cases within those rules when they do not rest upon the same reasons.[1]

---

[1] In Respublica v. Dennie, 4 Yeates, 267, the defendant was indicted in 1805 for publishing the following in a public newspaper: "A democracy is scarcely tolerated at any period of national history. Its omens are always sinister, and its powers are unpropitious. With all the lights of experience blazing before our eyes, it is impossible not to discover the futility of this form of government. It was weak and wicked at Athens, it was bad in Sparta, and worse in Rome. It has been tried in France, and terminated in despotism. It was tried in England, and rejected with the utmost loathing and abhorrence. It is on its trial here, and its issue will be civil war, desolation, and anarchy. No wise man but discerns its imperfections, no good man but shudders at its miseries, no honest man but proclaims its fraud, and no brave man but draws his sword against its force. The institution of a scheme of polity so radically contemptible and vicious is a memorable example of what the villany of some men can devise, the folly of others receive, and both establish in spite of reason, reflection, and sensation." Judge Yeates charged the jury, among other things, as follows: "The seventh section of the ninth article of the constitution of the State must be our guide upon this occasion; it forms the solemn compact between the people and the three branches of the government, — the legislative, executive, and judicial powers. Neither of them can exceed the limits prescribed to them respectively. To this exposition of the public will every branch of the common law and of our municipal acts of assembly must conform; and if incompatible therewith, they must yield and give way. Judicial decisions cannot weigh against it when repugnant thereto. It runs thus: 'The printing-presses shall be free to every person who undertakes to examine the proceedings of the legislature, or any branch of the government; and no law shall ever be made to restrain the right thereof. The free communication of thoughts and opinions is one of the invaluable rights of man; and every citizen may freely speak, write, and print on any subject, being responsible for the abuse of that liberty. In prosecutions for the publication of papers, investigating the official conduct of officers or men in a public capacity, or where the matter published is proper for public information, the truth thereof may be given in evidence; and in all indictments for libels, the jury shall have a right to determine the law and the facts under the direction of the court, as in other cases.' Thus it is evident that legislative acts, or of any branch of the government, are open to public discussion; and every citizen may freely speak, write, or print on any subject, but is accountable for the abuse of that privilege. There shall be no licenses of the press. Publish as you please in the first instance,

Criticism upon Officers and Candidates for Office.

There are certain cases where criticism upon public officers, their actions, character, and motives, is not only recognized as

without control ; but you are answerable both to the community and the individual if you proceed to unwarrantable lengths. No alteration is hereby made in the law as to private men affected by injurious publications, unless the discussion be proper for public information. But 'if one uses the weapon of truth wantonly for disturbing the peace of families, he is guilty of a libel.' Per General Hamilton, in Croswell's Trial, p. 70. The matter published is not proper for public information. The common weal is not interested in such a communication, except to suppress it.

" What is the meaning of the words, ' being responsible for the abuse of that liberty,' if the jury are interdicted from deciding on the case ? Who else can constitutionally decide on it ? The expressions relate to and pervade every part of the sentence. The objection that the determinations of juries may vary at different times, arising from their different political opinions, proves too much. The same matter may be objected against them when party spirit runs high, in other criminal persecutions. But we have no other constitutional mode of decision pointed out to us, and we are bound to use the method described.

" It is no infraction of the law to publish temperate investigations of the nature and forms of government. The day is long past since Algernon Sidney's celebrated treatise on government, cited on this trial, was considered as a treasonable libel. The enlightened advocates of representative republican government pride themselves in the reflection that the more deeply their system is examined, the more fully will the judgments of honest men be satisfied that it is the most conducive to the safety and happiness of a free people. Such matters are ' proper for public information.' But there is a marked and evident distinction between such publications, and those which are plainly accompanied with a criminal intent, deliberately designed to unloosen the social band of union, totally to unhinge the minds of the citizens, and to produce popular discontent with the exercise of power by the known constituted authorities. These latter writings are subversive of all government and good order. ' The liberty of the press consists in publishing the truth, from good motives and for justifiable ends, though it reflects on government or on magistrates.' Per General Hamilton, in Croswell's Trial, pp. 63, 64. It disseminates political knowledge, and, by adding to the common stock of freedom, gives a just confidence to every individual. But the malicious publications which I have reprobated infect insidiously the public mind with a subtle poison, and produce the most mischievous and alarming consequences by their tendency to anarchy, sedition, and civil war. We cannot, consistently with our official duty, declare such conduct dispunishable. We believe that it is not justified by the words or meaning of our constitution. It is true it may not be easy in every instance to draw the exact distinguishing line. To the jury it peculiarly belongs to decide on the intent and object of the writing. It is their duty to judge candidly and fairly, leaning to the favorable side when the criminal intent is not clearly and evidently ascertained.

legitimate, but large latitude and great freedom of expression permitted, so long as good faith inspires the communication.   There are cases where it is clearly the duty of every one to speak freely what he may have to say concerning public officers, or those who may present themselves for public positions.   Through the ballot-box the electors approve or condemn those who ask their suffrages ; and however emphatic the condemnation, and upon whatever grounds, no action will lie therefor.   Some officers, however, are not chosen by the people directly, but designated through some other•mode of appointment.   But the public have a right to be

" It remains, therefore, under our most careful consideration of the ninth article of the constitution, for the jury to divest themselves of all political prejudices (if any such they have), and dispassionately to examine the publication which is the ground of the present prosecution. They must decide on their oaths, as they will answer to God and their country, whether the defendant, as a factious and seditious person, with the criminal intentions imputed to him, in order to accomplish the objects stated in the indictment, did make and publish the writing in question. Should they find the charges laid against him in the indictment to be well founded, they are bound to find him guilty. They must judge for themselves on the plain import of the words, without any forced or strained construction of the meaning of the author or editor, and determine on the correctness of the innuendoes. To every word they will assign its natural sense, but will collect the true intention from the context, the whole piece. They will accurately weigh the probabilities of the charge against a literary man. Consequences they will wholly disregard, but firmly discharge their duty. Representative republican governments stand on immovable bases, which cannot be shaken by theoretical systems. Yet if the consciences of the jury shall be clearly satisfied that the publication was seditiously, maliciously, and wilfully aimed at the independence of the United States, the Constitution thereof or of this State, they should convict the defendant. If, on the other hand, the production was honestly meant to inform the public mind, and warn them against supposed dangers in society, though the subject may have been treated erroneously, or that the censures on democracy were bestowed on pure unmixed democracy, where the people *en masse* execute the sovereign power without the medium of their representatives (agreeably to our forms of government), as have occurred at different times in Athens, Sparta, Rome, France, and England, then, however the judgments of the jury may incline them to think individually, they should acquit the defendant. In the first instance the act would be criminal; in the last it would be innocent. If the jury should doubt of the criminal intention, then also the law pronounces that he should be acquitted. 4 Burr. 2552, per Ld. Mansfield." Verdict, not guilty. The fate of this prosecution was the same that would attend any of a similar character in this country, admitting its law to be sound, except possibly in cases of violent excitement, and when a jury could be made to believe that the defendant contemplated and was laboring to produce a change of government, not by contitutional means, but by rebellion and civil war.

heard on the question of their selection ; and they have the right, for such reasons as seem to their minds sufficient, to ask for their dismissal afterwards.   They have also the right to complain of official conduct affecting themselves, and to petition for a redress of grievances.   A principal purpose in perpetuating and guarding the right of petition is to insure to the public a right to be heard in these and the like cases.

In a case in the Court for the Correction of Errors of the State of New York, a party was prosecuted for a libel contained in a petition signed by him and a number of other citizens of his county, and presented to the council of appointment, praying for the removal of the plaintiff from the office of district attorney of the county, which, the petition charged, he was prostituting to private purposes.   The defendant did not justify the truth of this allegation, and the plaintiff had judgment.   On error, the sole question was, whether the communication was to be regarded as privileged, that character having been denied it by the court below.   The prevailing opinion in the court of review character-ized this as " a decision which violates the most sacred and un-questionable rights of free citizens ; rights essential to the very ex-istence of a free government ; rights necessarily connected with the relations of constituent and representative ; the right of petitioning for a redress of grievances, and the right of remonstrating to the competent authority against the abuse of official functions."   And it was held that the communication was privileged, and could not support an action for libel, unless the plaintiff could show that the petition was malicious and groundless, and presented for the pur-pose of injuring his character.[1]   Such a petition, it was said, although containing false and injurious aspersions, did not *prima facie* carry with it the presumption of malice.[2]   A similar ruling was made by the Supreme Court of Pennsylvania, where a party was prosecuted for charges against a justice of the peace, con-tained in a deposition made to be presented to the governor.[3] The subsequent case of Howard *v.* Thompson[4] has enlarged this rule somewhat, and has required of the plaintiff, in order to sus-tain his action in any such case, to prove not only malice in the

[1] Thorn *v.* Blanchard, 5 Johns. 528, per Clinton, Senator.
[2] Ibid. p. 526, per L'Hommedieu, Senator.
[3] Gray *v.* Pentland, 2 S. & R. 23.
[4] 21 Wend. 319.

defendant, but also a want of probable cause for believing the injurious charges which the petition contained. The action for libel, in such a case, it was said, was in the nature of an action for malicious prosecution ; and in that action malice and want of probable cause are both necessary ingredients. And it has also been held that in such a case the court will neither compel the officer to whom it was addressed to produce the petition in evidence, nor will they suffer its contents to be proved by parol.[1]

The rule of protection in these cases does not appear to be disputed, and has been laid down in other cases coming within the same reasons.[2] The rule, however, is subject to this qualification, that the petition or remonstrance must be addressed to the body or officer having the power of appointment or removal, or the authority to give the redress or grant the relief which is sought ; or at least that the petitioner should really and in good faith believe he is addressing himself to an authority possessing power in the premises.[3]

[1] Gray v. Pentland, 2 S. & R. 23.

[2] In Kershaw v Bailey, 1 Exch. 743, the defendant was prosecuted for slander in a communication made by him to the vestry, imputing perjury to the plaintiff as a reason why the vestry should not return him on the list of persons qualified to serve as constables. The defendant was a parishioner, and his communication was held privileged. In O'Donaghue v. McGovern, 23 Wend. 26, a communication from a member of a church to his bishop, respecting the character, moral conduct, and demeanor of a clergyman of the church, was placed upon the same footing of privilege. And see Reid v. Delorme, 2 Brev. 76 ; Chapman v. Calder, 14 Penn. St. 365. A remonstrance to the board of excise, against the granting of a license to the plaintiff, comes under the same rule of protection. Vanderzee v. McGregor, 12 Wend. 545. See also Kendillon v. Maltby, 1 Car. & Marsh. 402 ; Streety v. Wood, 15 Barb. 105 ; Bradley v. Heath, 12 Pick. 163.

[3] This principle is recognized in all the cases referred to. See also Fairman v. Ives, 5 B. & Ald. 642. In that case a petition addressed by a creditor of an officer in the army to the Secretary of War, bona fide and with a view of obtaining through his interference the payment of a debt due, and containing a statement of facts which, though derogatory to the officer's character, the creditor believed to be true, was held not to support an action. A letter to the Postmaster-General complaining of the conduct of a postmaster, with a view to the redress of grievances, is privileged. Woodward v. Lander, 6 C. & P. 548 ; Cook v. Hill, 3 Sandf. 341. And a complaint to a master, charging a servant with a dishonest act which had been imputed to the complaining party, has also been held privileged. · Coward v. Wellington, 7 C. & P. 531. And see further, Hosmer v. Loveland, 19 Barb. 111. A petition is privileged while being circulated. Venderzee v. McGregor, 12 Wend. 545 ; Streety v. Wood, 15 Barb. 105. If, however, a petition is circulated and exhibited, but never presented, the fact that the libellous charge has

Such being the rule of privilege when one interested in the discharge of powers of a public nature is addressing himself to the body having the authority of appointment, supervision, or removal, the question arises whether the same reasons do not require the like privilege when the citizen addresses himself to his fellow-citizens in regard to the conduct of persons elevated to office by their suffrages, or in regard to the character, capacity, or fitness of those who may present themselves, or be presented by their friends — which always assumes their assent — as candidates for public positions.

When Morgan Lewis was Governor of the State of New York, and was a candidate for re-election, a public meeting of his opponents was called, at which an address was adopted condemning his conduct in various particulars. Among other things, he was charged with want of fidelity to his party, pursuing a system of family aggrandizement in his appointments, signing the charter of a bank with notice that it had been procured by fraudulent practices, publishing doctrines unworthy of a chief magistrate and subversive of the dearest interests of society, attempting to destroy the liberty of the press by vexatious prosecutions, and calling out the militia without occasion, thereby putting them to unnecessary trouble and expense. These seem to have been the more serious charges. The chairman of the meeting signed the address, and he was prosecuted by the governor for the libel contained therein. No justification was attempted upon the facts, and the Supreme Court held the circumstances to constitute no protection in the law. We quote from the opinion delivered by Mr. Justice Thompson : —

" Where the act is in itself unlawful, the proof of justification or excuse lies on the defendant, and on failure thereof the law implies a criminal intent.[1] If a libel contains an imputation of a crime, or is actionable without showing special damage, malice is, *prima facie,* implied ; and if the defendant claims to be exonerated, on the ground of want of malice, it lies on him to show it was published under such circumstances as to rebut this presumption of law.[2] The manner and occasion of the publication have been relied on for this purpose, and in justification of the libel. It has

assumed the form of a petition will not give it protection. State *v.* Burnham, 9 N. H. 34.   And see Hunt *v.* Bennett, 19 N. Y. 173 ; Van Wyck *v.* Aspinwall, 17 N. Y. 190.

[1] 5 Burr. 2667 ; 4 T. R. 127.   [2] 1 T. R. 110.

not been pretended but that the address in question would be
libellous if considered as the act of an individual ; but its being
the act of a public meeting, of which the defendant was a member,
and the publication being against a candidate for a public office,
have been strenuously urged as affording a complete justification.
The doctrine contended for by the defendant's counsel results in
the position that every publication ushered forth under the sanction of a public political meeting, against a candidate for an elective office, is beyond the reach of legal inquiry.   To such a proposition I can never yield my assent.   Although it was urged by the
defendant's counsel, I cannot discover any analogy whatever between the proceedings of such meetings and those of courts of
justice, or any other organized tribunals known in our law for the
redress of grievances.   That electors should have a right to assemble, and freely and openly to examine the fitness and qualifications of candidates for public offices, and communicate their
opinions to others, is a position to which I most cordially accede.
But there is a wide difference between this privilege, and a right
irresponsibly to charge a candidate with direct specific and unfounded crimes.   It would, in my judgment, be a monstrous
doctrine to establish, that, when a man becomes a candidate for an
elective office, he thereby gives to others a right to accuse him of
any imaginable crimes with impunity.   Candidates have rights as
well as electors ; and those rights and privileges must be so
guarded and protected as to harmonize one with the other.   If
one hundred or one thousand men, when assembled together,
undertake to charge a man with specific crimes, I see no reason
why it should be less criminal than if each one should do it individually, at different times and places.   All that is required, in the
one case or the other, is, not to transcend the bounds of truth.   If
a man has committed a crime, any one has a right to charge him
with it, and is not responsible for the accusation ; and can any one
wish for more latitude than this ?   Can it be claimed a privilege
to accuse *ad libitum* a candidate with the most base and detest-
able crimes ?   There is nothing upon the record showing the least
foundation or pretence for the charges.   The accusations, then,
being false, the *prima facie* presumption of law is, that the publication was malicious ; and the circumstance of the defendant being
associated with others does not *per se* rebut this presumption.
How far this circumstance ought to affect the measure of damages

is a question not arising on the record. It may in some cases mitigate, in others enhance them. Every case must necessarily, from the nature of the action, depend upon its own circumstances, which are to be submitted to the sound discretion of a jury. It is difficult, and perhaps impossible, to lay down any general rule on the subject." [1]

The difficulty one meets with in the examination of this opinion is in ascertaining in what manner the privileges of electors, of which it speaks, are protected by it. It is not discovered that the citizen who publicly discusses the qualifications and fitness of the candidate for public office who challenges his suffrage, is, by this decision, so far as suits for recovery of private damages are concerned, placed on any different footing in the law from that occupied by one who drags before the public the character of a private individual. In either case, if the publication proves to be false, the law attaches to it a presumption of malice. Nothing in the occasion justifies or excuses the act in either case. It is true it is intimated that it may lie in the sound discretion of a jury to be moderate in the imposition of damages, but it is also intimated that the jury would be at liberty to consider the circumstances of the public meeting an aggravation. There is absolutely no privilege of discussion to the elector under such a rule; no right to canvass the fitness of candidates beyond what exists in other cases. Whatever reasons he may give his neighbors for voting against a candidate, he must be prepared to support by evidence in the courts. In criminal prosecutions, if he can prove the truth of his charges, he may be protected in some cases where he would not be if the person assailed was only a private individual; because in the latter case he must make a showing of a justifiable occasion for uttering even the truth. But in all cases where the matter is proper for the public information, the truth justifies its publication.

The case above quoted is sustained by a subsequent decision of the Court for the Correction of Errors, which in like manner repudiated the claim of privilege.[2] The office then in question was that of Lieutenant-Governor, and the candidate was charged in public newspapers with habits of intoxication which unfitted him for the position. And this last decision has since been followed as authority by the Superior Court of New York, in a case, however, which does not seem to be analogous, since there the general pub-

[1] Lewis v. Few, 5 Johns. 1, 35.   [2] King v. Root, 4 Wend. 113.

lic was addressed in regard to a candidate for an office which was not elective, but was to be filled by an appointing board.[1]

The case of King v. Root[2] is certainly a very remarkable one, when the evidence given in the case is considered. The Lieutenant-Governor was charged in the public press with intoxication in the Senate Chamber, exhibited as he was proceeding to take his seat as presiding officer of that body. When prosecuted for libel, the publishers justified the charge as true, and brought a number of witnesses who were present on the occasion, and who testified to the correctness of the statement. There was therefore abundant reason for supposing the charge to have been published in the full belief in its truth. If it was true, there was abundant reason, on public grounds, for making the publication. Nevertheless, the jury were of opinion that the preponderance of evidence was against the truth of the charge, and being instructed that the only privilege the defendants had was " simply to publish the truth and nothing more," and that the unsuccessful attempt at justification — which in fact was only the forming of such an issue and putting in such evidence as showed the defendants had reason for making the charge — was in itself an aggravation of the offence, they returned a verdict for the plaintiff with large damages. Throughout his instructions to the jury by the judge presiding at the trial, no privilege of discussion whatever is conceded to the elector, springing from the relation of elector and candidate, or of citizen and representative, but the case is considered as one where the accusation was to be defended precisely as if no public considerations had in any way been involved.[3]

The law of New York is not placed by these decisions on a footing very satisfactory to those who claim the utmost freedom of discussion in public affairs. The courts have considered the subject as if there were no middle ground between absolute immunity for falsehood and the application of the same strict rules which prevail in other cases. Whether they have duly considered the importance of publicity and discussion on all matters of general concern in a representative government must be left to the consideration of the courts as these questions shall come before them in the future. It is perhaps safe to say that the general public

---

[1] Hunt v. Bennett, 4 E. D. Smith, 647; Same case, 19 N. Y. 173.

[2] 4 Wend. 113. See the same case in the Supreme Court, 7 Cow. 613.

[3] See also Onslow v. Hone, 3 Wils. 177 ; Harwood v. Astley, 1 New Rep. 47.

sentiment and the prevailing customs allow a greater freedom of discussion, and hold the elector less strictly to what he may be able to justify as true than is done by these decisions.

A much more reasonable rule — though still, we think, not sufficiently comprehensive — was indicated by Pollock, C. B., in a case where it was urged upon the court that a sermon, preached but not published, was the subject of criticism in the enlarged style of commentary which that word seems to introduce according to the decided cases; and that the conduct of a clergy-man with reference to the parish charity, and especially the rules of it, justified any *bona fide* remarks, whether founded in truth in point of fact, or justice in point of commentary, provided only they were an honest and *bona fide* comment. " My brother Wilde," he says, " urged upon the court the importance of this question; and I own I think it is a question of very grave and deep impor-tance. He pressed upon us that, whenever the public had an in-terest in such a discussion, the law ought to protect it, and work out the public good by permitting public opinion, through the medium of the public press, to operate upon such transactions. I am not sure that so extended a rule is at all necessary to the pub-lic good. I do not in any degree complain; on the contrary, I think it quite right that all matters that are entirely of a public nature — conduct of ministers, conduct of judges, the proceedings of all persons who are responsible to the public at large — are deemed to be public property; and that all *bona fide* and honest remarks upon such persons, and their conduct, may be made with perfect freedom, and without being questioned too nicely for either truth or justice." [1]   But these remarks were somewhat aside from the case then before the learned judge, and though supported by similar remarks from his associates, yet one of those associates deemed it important to draw such a distinction as to detract very much from the value of this privilege. " It seems," he says, " that there is a distinction, although I must say I really can hardly tell what the limits of it are, between the comments on a man's public conduct and on his private conduct. I can understand that you have a right to comment on the public acts of a minister, upon the public acts of a general, upon the public judgments of a judge, upon the public skill of an actor; I can understand that; but I do not know where the limit can be drawn distinctly between where the

---

[1] Gathercole *v.* Miall, 15 M. & W. 331 – 333.

comment is to cease, as being applied solely to a man's public conduct, and where it is to begin as applicable to his private character;
because, although it is quite competent for a person to speak of a
judgment of a judge as being an extremely erroneous and foolish
one, — and no doubt comments of that sort have great tendency to
make persons careful of what they say, — and although it is perfectly competent for persons to say of an actor that he is a remark-
ably bad actor, and ought not to be permitted to perform such and
such parts, because he performs them so ill, yet you ought not to
be allowed to say of an actor that he has disgraced himself in private
life, nor to say of a judge or a minister that he has committed felony, or anything of that description, which is in no way connected
with his public conduct or public judgment; and therefore there
must be some limits, although I do not distinctly see where those
limits are to be drawn. No doubt, if there are such limits, my
brother Wilde is perfectly right in saying that the only ground on
which the verdict and damages can go is for the excess, and not
for the lawful exercise of the criticism." [1]

The narrowness of any such rule consists in its assumption,
that the private character of a public officer is something aside
from, and not entering into or influencing, his public conduct,
and that a thoroughly dishonest man may be a just minister, and
that a judge who is corrupt and debauched in private life may be
pure and upright in his judgments; in other words, that an evil
tree is as likely as any other to bring forth good fruits. Any such
assumption is false to human nature, and the public have a right
to assume that a corrupt life will influence public conduct, however plausibly it may be glossed over. They are, therefore, interested in knowing what the character of their public servants is, as
well as that of persons offering themselves for their suffrages. If
so, it would seem that there should be some privilege of comment; that that privilege could only be limited by good faith and
just intention; and of these a jury might judge, taking into account the nature of the charges made, and the reasons which existed for making them.

Recent English cases give considerable latitude of comment to
publishers of public journals, upon subjects in the discussion of
which the public have an interest, and hold the discussions privi-

---

[1] Alderson, B., same case, p. 338.

leged if conducted within the bounds of moderation and reason.[1] And in this country it has been held that where a charge against an officer or a candidate respects only his qualifications for the office, and does not impugn his character, it forms no basis for a recovery of damages. To address to the electors of a district letters charging that a candidate for office is of impaired understanding, and his mind weakened by disease, is presenting that subject to " the proper and legitimate tribunal to try the question." " Talents and qualifications for office are mere matters of opinion, of which the electors are the only competent judges." [2]

Statements in the Course of Judicial Proceedings.

There are some cases which are so absolutely privileged on reasons of public policy, that no inquiry into motives is permitted in an action for slander or libel. Of these, the case of a party who is called upon to give evidence in the course of judicial proceedings is a familiar illustration. No action will lie against a witness at the suit of a party aggrieved by his false testimony, even though malice be charged. The remedy against a dishonest witness is confined to the criminal prosecution for perjury.[3] False accusations, however, contained in the affidavits or other proceedings, by which a prosecution is commenced for supposed crime,

[1] In Kelley v. Sherlock, 1 Law Rep. Q. B. 686, it was held that a sermon commenting upon public affairs — e. g. the appointment of chaplains for prisons and the election of a Jew for mayor — was a proper subject for comment in the papers. And in Kelley v. Tinling, 1 Law Rep. Q. B. 699, a church-warden, having written to the plaintiff, the incumbent, accusing him of having desecrated the church by allowing books to be sold in it during service, and by turning the vestry-room into a cooking-apartment, the correspondence was published without the plaintiff's permission in the defendant's newspaper, with comments on the plaintiff's conduct. Held, that this was a matter of public interest, which might be made the subject of public discussion; and that the publication was therefore not libellous, unless the language used was stronger than, in the opinion of the jury, the occasion justified.

[2] Mayrant v. Richardson, 1 Nott & McCord, 348.

[3] But a qualification of this rule is made where what is said by the witness is not pertinent or material to the cause, and he has been actuated by malice in stating it. He is not, however, to be himself the judge of what is pertinent or material when questions are put to him, and no objection or warning comes to him from court or counsel. Calkins v. Sumner, 13 Wis. 193. See also Warner v. Paine, 2 Sandf. 195; Garr v. Selden, 4 N. Y. 91; Jennings v. Paine, 4 Wis. 358; Perkins v. Mitchell, 31 Barb. 461; Revis v. Smith, 18 C. B. 126.

or in any other papers in the course of judicial proceedings, are not so absolutely protected. They are privileged,[1] but the party making them is liable to action, if actual malice be averred and proved.[2] Preliminary information, furnished with a view to set on foot an inquiry into an alleged offence, or to institute a criminal prosecution, is, in like manner, privileged;[3] but the protection only extends to those communications which are in the course of the proceedings to bring the supposed offender to justice, or are designed for the purpose of originating or forwarding such proceedings; and communications not of that character are not protected, even although judicial proceedings may be pending for the investigation of the offence which the communication refers to.[4] Still less would a party be justified in repeating a charge of crime, after the person charged has been examined on his complaint, and acquitted of all guilt.[5]

Privilege of Counsel.

One of the most important cases of privilege, in a constitutional point of view, is that of counsel employed to represent a party in

[1] Astley v. Younge, Burr. 807.

[2] Padmore v. Lawrence, 11 Ad. & El. 380; Kine v. Sewell, 3 M. & W. 297; Burlingame v. Burlingame, 8 Cow. 141; Kidder v. Parkhurst, 3 Allen, 393; Doyle v. O'Doherty, 1 Car. & Marsh. 418; Wilson v. Collins, 5 C. & P. 373; Home v. Bentinck, 2 Brod. & Bing. 130; Jarvis v. Hatheway, 3 Johns. 180. In Goslin v. Cannon, 1 Harr. 3, it was held that where a crime had been committed, expressions of opinion founded upon facts within the knowledge of the party, or communicated to him, made prudently and in confidence, to discreet persons, and made obviously in good faith with a view only to direct their watchfulness and enlist their aid in recovering the money stolen, and detecting and bringing to justice the offender, were privileged. The cause, occasion, object, and end, it was said, was justifiable, proper, and legal, and such as should actuate every good citizen.

[3] Grimes v. Coyle, 6 B. Monr. 301.

[4] Dancaster v. Hewson, 2 M. & Ry. 176.

[5] Burlingame v. Burlingame, 8 Cow. 141. In Mower v. Watson, 11 Vt. 536, an action was brought for slander in saying to a witness who was giving his testimony on a material point in a cause then on trial to which defendant was a party, "That's a lie," and for repeating the same statement to counsel for the opposite party afterwards. The words were held not to be privileged. To the same effect are the cases of McClaughry v. Wetmore, 6 Johns. 82, and Kean v. McLaughlin, 2 S. & R. 469. See also Torrey v. Field, 10 Vt. 353; Gilbert v. People, 1 Denio, 41. A report made by a grand-jury upon a subject which they conceive to be within their jurisdiction, but which is not, is nevertheless privileged. Rector v. Smith, 11 Iowa, 302.

judicial proceedings. The benefit of the constitutional right to counsel depends very greatly on the freedom with which he is allowed to act, and to comment on the facts appearing in the case, and on the inferences deducible therefrom. The character, conduct, and motives of parties and their witnesses, as well as of other persons more remotely connected with the proceedings, enter very largely into any judicial inquiry, and must form the subject of comment, if they are to be sifted and weighed. To make the comment of value, there must be the liberty of examination in every possible light, and of suggesting any view of the circumstances of the case, and of the motives surrounding it, which seems legitimate to the person discussing them. It will often happen, in criminal proceedings, that, while no reasonable doubt can exist that a crime has been committed, there may be very great doubt whether the prosecutor or the accused is the guilty party; and to confine the counsel for the defence to such remarks concerning the prosecutor as he might defend, if he had made them without any occasion, would render the right to counsel, in many cases, of no value. The law justly and necessarily, in view of the importance of the privilege, allows very great liberty in these cases, and surrounds them with a protection that is a complete shield in all cases, except those where the privilege of counsel has been plainly and palpably abused.

The rule upon this subject was laid down in these words in an early English case: " A counsellor hath privilege to enforce anything which is informed him by his client, and to give it in evidence, it being pertinent to the matter in question, and not to examine whether it be true or false; for a counsellor is at his peril to give in evidence that which his client informs him, being pertinent to the matter in question; but matter not pertinent to the issue, or the matter in question, he need not deliver; for he is to discern in his discretion what he is to deliver, and what not; and although it be false, he is excusable, it being pertinent to the matter. But if he give in evidence anything not material to the issue, which is scandalous, he ought to aver it to be true; otherwise he is punishable; for it shall be considered as spoken maliciously and without cause; which is a good ground for the action. . . . . So if counsel object matter against a witness which is slanderous, if there be cause to discredit his testimony, and it be pertinent to the matter in question, it is justifiable, what he delivers by information, although it be false." [1] The privilege of counsel in these cases is the same with that of the party himself,[2] and the limitation upon it is concisely suggested in a Pennsylvania case, " that if a man should abuse his privilege, and under pretence of pleading his cause, designedly wander from the point in question, and maliciously heap slander upon his adversary, I will not say that he is not responsible in an action at law." [3] Chief Justice Shaw has stated the rule very fully and clearly : " We take the rule to be well settled by the authorities that words spoken in the course of judicial proceedings, though they are such as impute crime to another, and therefore if spoken elsewhere would import malice and be actionable in themselves, are not actionable, if they are applicable and pertinent to the subject of the inquiry. The question, therefore, in such cases is, not whether the words spoken are true, not whether they are actionable in themselves, but whether they were spoken in the course of judicial proceedings, and whether they are relevant or pertinent to the cause or subject of the inquiry. And in determining what is pertinent, much latitude must be allowed to the judgment and discretion of those who are intrusted with the conduct of a cause in court, and a much larger allowance made for the ardent and excited feelings with which a party, or counsel who naturally and almost necessarily identifies himself with his client, may become animated, by constantly regarding one side only of an interesting and animated controversy, in which the dearest rights of such party may become involved. And if these feelings sometimes manifest themselves in strong invectives, or exaggerated expressions, beyond what the occasion would strictly justify, it is to be recollected that this is said to a judge who hears both sides, in whose mind the exaggerated statement may be at once controlled and met by evidence and argument of a contrary tendency from the other party, and who, from the impartiality of his position, will naturally give to an exaggerated assertion, not warranted by the occasion, no more weight than it deserves. Still, this privilege must be restrained by some limit, and we consider that limit to be this: that a party or counsel shall not avail himself of his situation to

---

[1] Brook v. Montagne, Cro. Jac. 90. See this case approved and applied in Hodgson v. Scarlett, 1 B. & Ald. 232.

[2] Hoar v. Wood, 3 Met. 194, per Shaw, Ch. J.

[3] McMillian v. Birch, 1 Binney, 178, per Tilghman, Ch. J.

gratify private malice by uttering slanderous expressions, either against a party, witness, or third person, which have no relation to the cause or subject-matter of the inquiry. Subject to this restriction, it is, on the whole, for the public interest and best calculated to subserve the purposes of justice to allow counsel full freedom of speech, in conducting the cases and advocating and sustaining the rights of their constituents; and this freedom of discussion ought not to be impaired by numerous and refined distinctions." [1]

Privileges of Legislators.

The privileges of a legislator in the use of language in debate is made broader and more complete than that of the counsel or party in judicial proceedings by constitutional provisions, which give him complete immunity, by forbidding his being questioned in any other place for anything said in speech or debate.[2] In an early case in Massachusetts, the question of the extent of this constitutional privilege came before the Supreme Court, and was largely discussed as well by counsel as by the court. The constitutional provision then in force in that State was as follows : " The freedom of deliberation, speech, and debate in either house cannot be the foundation of any accusation or prosecution, action or complaint, in any other court or place whatsoever." The defendant was a member of the General Court, and was prosecuted for uttering slanderous words to a fellow-member, in relation to the plaintiff. The member to whom the words were uttered had moved a resolution, on the suggestion of the plaintiff, for the appointment of an additional notary-public in the county where the plaintiff

---

[1] Hoar v. Wood, 3 Met. 197. See also Padmore v. Lawrence, 11 Ad. & El. 380; Ring v. Wheeler, 7 Cow. 725; Mower v. Watson, 11 Vt. 536; Gilbert v. People, 1 Denio, 41; Hastings v. Lusk, 22 Wend. 410; Bradley v. Heath, 12 Pick. 163. In Hastings v. Lusk, it is said that the privilege of counsel is as broad as that of a legislative body; however false and malicious may be the charge made by him affecting the reputation of another, an action of slander will not lie provided what is said be pertinent to the question under discussion. And see Warner v. Paine, 2 Sandf. 195; Garr v. Selden, 4 N. Y. 91; Jennings v. Paine, 4 Wis. 358.

[2] There are provisions to this effect in every State constitution except those of Virginia, North Carolina, South Carolina, Mississippi, Texas, California, and Nevada. Mr. Cushing, in his work on the Law and Practice of Legislative Assemblies, § 602, has expressed the opinion that these provisions were unnecessary, and that the protection was equally complete without them.

resided. The mover, in reply to an inquiry privately made by defendant, as to the source of his information that such appointment was necessary, had designated the plaintiff, and the defendant had replied by a charge against the plaintiff of a criminal offence. The question before the court was, whether this reply was privileged. The house was in session at the time, but the remark was not made in course of speech or debate, and had no other connection with the legislative proceedings than is above shown.

Referring to the constitutional provision quoted, the learned judge who delivered the opinion of the court in this case thus expressed himself: " In considering this article, it appears to me that the privilege secured by it is not so much the privilege of the house as an organized body, as of each individual member composing it, who is entitled to this privilege even against the declared will of the house. For he does not hold this privilege at the pleasure of the house, but derives it from the will of the people expressed in the constitution, which is paramount to the will of either or both branches of the legislature. In this respect, the privilege here secured resembles other privileges attached to each member by another part of the constitution, by which he is exempted from arrest on mesne (or original) process, during his going to, returning from, or attending the General Court. Of these privileges, thus secured to each member, he cannot be deprived by a resolve of the house, or by an act of the legislature.

" These privileges are thus secured, not with the intention of protecting the members against prosecutions for their own benefit, but to support the rights of the people, by enabling their representatives to execute the functions of their office without fear of prosecution, civil or criminal. I therefore think the article ought not to be construed strictly, but liberally, that the full design of it may be answered. I will not confine it to delivering an opinion, uttering a speech, or haranguing in debate, but will extend it to the giving of a vote, to the making of a written report, and to every other act, resulting from the nature and in the execution of the office ; and I would define the article as securing to every member exemption from prosecution for everything said or done by him, as a representative, in the exercise of the functions of that office, without inquiring whether the exercise was regular according to the rules of the house, or irregular and against their rules. I do

not confine the member to his place in the house, and I am satisfied that there are cases in which he is entitled to this privilege
when not within the walls of the representatives' chamber.   He
cannot be exercising the functions of his office as member of a
body, unless the body is in existence.   The house must be in session
to enable him to claim this privilege, and it is in session notwithstanding occasional adjournments for short intervals for the convenience of the members.   If a member, therefore, be out of the
chamber, sitting in committee, executing the commission of the
house, it appears to me that such member is within the reason of
the article, and ought to be considered within the privilege.   The
body of which he is a member is in session, and he, as a member
of that body, is in fact discharging the duties of his office.   He
ought therefore to be protected from civil or criminal prosecutions
for everything said or done by him in the exercise of his functions
as a representative, in a committee, either in debating or assenting to or draughting a report.   Neither can I deny the member
his privilege when executing the duties of the office, in a convention of both houses, although the convention may be holden in the
Senate Chamber."   And after considering the hardships that
might result to individuals in consequence of this privilege, he proceeds : " A more extensive construction of the privilege of the
members secured by this article I cannot give, because it could
not be supported by the language or the manifest intent of the
article.   When a representative is not acting as a member of the
house, he is not entitled to any privilege above his fellow-citizens ;
nor are the rights of the people affected if he is placed on the same
ground on which his constituents stand."   And coming more particularly to the facts then before the court, it was shown that the
defendant was not in the discharge of any official duty at the time
of uttering the obnoxious words ; that they had no connection or
relevancy to the business then before the house, but might with
equal pertinency have been uttered at any other time or place,
and consequently could not, even under the liberal rule of protection which the court had laid down, be regarded as within the
privilege.[1]

[1] Coffin v. Coffin, 4 Mass. 1.   See Jefferson's Manual, § 3 ; Hosmer v. Loveland, 19 Barb. 111 ; State v. Burnham, 9 N. H. 34.

Publication of privileged Communications through the Press.

If now we turn from the rules of law which protect communications because of the occasion on which they are made and the duty resting upon the person making them, to those rules which concern the spreading before the world the same communications, we shall discover a very remarkable difference. It does not follow because a counsel may freely speak as he believes or is instructed in court, that therefore he may publish his speech through the public press. The privilege in court is necessary to the complete discharge of his duty to his client; but when the suit is ended, that duty is discharged, and he is not called upon to appeal from the court and the jury to the general public. Indeed such an appeal, while it could not generally have benefit to the client in view, would be unfair and injurious to the parties reflected upon by the argument, inasmuch as it would take only a partial and one-sided view of the case, and the public would not have, as the court and jury did, all the facts of the case as given in evidence before them, so that they might be in position to weigh the arguments fairly and understandingly, and reject injurious inferences not warranted by the evidence.

The law, however, favors publicity in legal proceedings, so far as that object can be attained without injustice to parties. The public are permitted to attend nearly all judicial inquiries, and there appears to be no sufficient reason why they should not also be allowed to see in print the reports of trials, if they can thus have them presented as fully as they are in court, or at least all the material portion of the proceedings stated impartially, so that one shall not, by means of them, derive erroneous impressions, which he would not have received from hearing the case in court.

It seems to be a settled rule of law, that a fair and impartial account of judicial proceedings, which have not been *ex parte*, but in the hearing of both parties, is, generally speaking, a justifiable publication.[1] But it is said that, if a party is to be allowed to publish what passes in a court of justice, he must publish the whole case, and not merely state the conclusion which he himself draws from the evidence.[2] A plea that the supposed libel was *in*

---

[1] Hoare *v.* Silverlock, 9 C. B. 20.   And see Stanley *v.* Webb, 4 Sandf. 21; Cincinnati Gazette Co. *v.* Timberlake, 10 Ohio, N. S. 548.   But not if the matter published is indecent or blasphemous.   Rex *v.* Carlisle, 3 B. & Ald. 167; Rex *v.* Creevey, 1 M. & S. 273.

[2] Lewis *v.* Walter, 4 B. & Ald. 611.

substance, a true account and report of a trial has been held bad ;[1] and a statement of the circumstances of a trial as from counsel in the case has been held not privileged.[2]   The report must also be strictly confined to the actual proceedings in court, and must contain no defamatory observations or comments from any quarter whatsoever, in addition to what forms strictly and properly the legal proceedings.[3]   And if the nature of the case is such as to make it improper that the proceedings should be spread before the public, because of their immoral tendency, or of the blasphemous or indecent character of the evidence exhibited, the publication, though impartial and full, will be a public offence, and punishable accordingly.[4]

It has, however, been held, that the publication of *ex parte* proceedings, or mere preliminary examinations, though of a judicial character, is not privileged ; and when they reflect injuriously upon individuals, the publisher derives no protection from their having already been delivered in court.[5]   The reason for distin-

[1] Flint *v.* Pike, 4 B. & C. 473.

[2] Saunders *v.* Mills, 6 Bing. 213; Flint *v.* Pike, 4 B. & C. 473.   And see Stanley *v.* Webb, 4 Sandf. 26 ; Lewis *v.* Walter, 4 B. & Ald. 605.

[3] Stiles *v.* Nokes, 7 East, 493; Delegal *v.* Highley, 3 Bing. (N. C.) 950.   And see Lewis *v.* Clement, 3 B. & Ald. 702.

[4] Rex *v.* Carlile, 3 B. & Ald. 167; Rex *v.* Creevey, 1 M. & S. 273.

[5] Duncan *v.* Thwaites, 3 B. & C. 556; Flint *v.* Pike, 4 B. & C. 473 ; Stanley *v.* Webb, 4 Sandf. 21; Charlton *v.* Watton, 6 C. & P. 385; Cincinnati Gazette Co. *v.* Timberlake, 10 Ohio, N. S. 548; Mathews *v.* Beach, 5 Sandf. 256; Huff *v.* Bennett, 4 Sandf. 120.   It seems, however, that if the proceeding has resulted in the discharge of the person accused, or in a decision that no cause exists for proceeding against him, a publication of an account of it is privileged.   In Curry *v.* Walter, 1 B. & P. 525, the Court of Common Pleas held that, in an action for libel, it was a good defence, under the plea of not guilty, that the alleged libel was a true account of what had passed upon a motion in the Court of King's Bench for an information against two magistrates for corruption in refusing to license an inn; the motion having been refused for want of notice to the magistrates.   In Lewis *v.* Levy, El. Bl. & El. 537, the publisher of a newspaper gave a full report of an examination before a magistrate on a charge of perjury, resulting in the discharge of the defendant; and the Court of Queen's Bench sustained the claim of privilege; distinguishing the case from those where the party was held for trial, and where the publication of the charges and evidence might tend to his prejudice on the trial.   The opinion of Lord Campbell in the case, however, seems to go far towards questioning the correctness of the decisions above cited.   See especially his quotation from the opinion of Lord Denman, delivered before a committee of the House of Lords in the year 1843, on the law of libel. " I have no doubt that [police reports] are extremely useful for the detection of

29

guishing these cases from those where the parties are heard is thus stated by Lord Ellenborough, in the early case of The King v. Fisher : [1] " Jurors and judges are still but men ; they cannot always control feeling excited by inflammatory language. If they are exposed to be thus warped and misled, injustice must sometimes be done. Trials at law, fairly reported, although they may occasionally prove injurious to individuals, have been held to be privileged. Let them continue so privileged. The benefit they produce is great and permanent, and the evil that arises from them is rare and incidental. But these preliminary examinations have no such privilege. Their only tendency is to prejudge those whom the law still presumes to be innocent, and to poison the sources of justice. It is of infinite importance to us all, that whatever has a tendency to prevent a fair trial should be guarded against. Every one of us may be questioned in a court of law, and called upon to defend his life and character. We would then wish to meet a jury of our countrymen with unbiassed minds. But for this there can be no security, if such publications are permitted." And in another case it has been said : " It is our boast that we are governed by that just and salutary rule upon which security of life and character often depends, that every man is presumed innocent of crimes charged upon him, until he is proved guilty. But the circulation of charges founded upon *ex parte* testimony, of statements made, often under excitement, by persons smarting under real or fancied wrongs, may prejudice the public mind, and cause the judgment of conviction to be passed long before the day of trial has arrived. When that day of trial comes, the rule has been

guilt by making facts notorious, and for bringing those facts more correctly to the knowledge of all parties interested in unravelling the truth. The public, I think, are perfectly aware that those proceedings are *ex parte*, and they become more and more aware of it in proportion to their growing intelligence ; they know that such proceedings are only in course of trial, and they do not form their opinion until the trial is had. Perfect publicity in judicial proceedings is of the highest importance in other points of view, but in its effects on character I think it desirable. The statement made in open court will probably find its way to the ears of all in whose good opinion the party assailed feels an interest, probably in an exaggerated form, and the imputation may often rest upon the wrong person; both these evils are prevented by correct reports." In the case of Lewis v. Levy, it was insisted that the privilege of publication only extended to the proceedings of the superior courts of law and equity; but the court gave no countenance to any such distinction.

[1] 2 Camp. 563.

reversed, and the presumption of guilt has been substituted for the presumption of innocence. The chances of a fair and impartial trial are diminished. Suppose the charge to be utterly groundless. If every preliminary *ex parte* complaint which may be made before a police magistrate may, with entire immunity, be published and scattered broadcast over the land, then the character of the innocent, who may be the victim of a conspiracy, or of charges proved afterwards to have arisen entirely from misapprehension, may be cloven down, without any malice on the part of the publisher. The refutation of slander, in such cases, generally follows its propagation at distant intervals, and brings often but an imperfect balm to wounds which have become festered, and perhaps incurable. It is not to be denied, that occasionally the publication of such proceedings is productive of good, and promotes the ends of justice: But, in such cases, the publisher must find his justification, not in privilege, but in the truth of the charges." [1]

Privilege of Publishers of News.

Among the inventions of modern times, by which the world has been powerfully influenced, and civilization advanced with wonderful celerity, must be classed the newspaper. Beginning with a small sheet, insignificant alike in matter and appearance, published at considerable intervals, and including but few in its visits, it has become the daily vehicle, to almost every family in the land, of information from all quarters of the globe, and upon every subject. Through it, and by means of the electric telegraph, the public proceedings of every civilized country, the debates of the leading legislative bodies, the events of war, the triumphs of peace, the storms in the physical world, and the agitations in the moral and mental, are brought home to the knowledge of every reading person, and, to a very large extent, before the day is over on which the events have taken place. And not public events merely are discussed and described, but the actions and words of public men are made public property; and any person sufficiently notorious

[1] Stanley *v.* Webb, 4 Sandf. 30. See this case approved and followed in Cincinnati Gazette Co. *v.* Timberlake, 10 Ohio, N. S. 548, where, however, the court are careful not to express an opinion whether a publication of the proceedings on preliminary examinations may not be privileged, where the accused is present, with full opportunity of defence.

to become an object of public interest will find his movements chronicled in this index of the times. Every party has its newspaper organs; every shade of opinion on political, religious, literary, moral, industrial, or financial questions has its representative; every locality has its press to advocate its claims, and advance its interests, and even the days regarded as sacred have their special papers to furnish reading suitable for the time. The newspaper is also the medium by means of which all classes of the people communicate with each other concerning their wants and desires, and through which they offer their wares, and seek bargains. As it has gradually increased in value, and in the extent and variety of its contents, so the exactions of the community upon its conductors have also increased, until it is demanded of the newspaper publisher, that he shall daily spread before his readers a complete summary of the events transpiring in the world, public or private, so far as those readers can reasonably be supposed to take an interest in them; and he who does not comply with this demand must give way to him who will.

The newspaper is also one of the chief means for the education of the people. The highest and the lowest in the scale of intelligence resort to its columns for information; it is read by those who read nothing else, and the best minds of the age make it the medium of communication with each other on the highest and most abstruse subjects. Upon politics it may be said to be the chief educator of the people; its influence is potent in every legislative body; it gives tone and direction to public sentiment on each important subject as it arises; and no administration in any free country ventures to overlook or disregard an element so pervading in its influence, and withal so powerful.

And yet it may be doubted if the newspaper, as such, has ever influenced at all the current of the common law in any particular important to the protection of the publishers. The railway has become the successor of the king's highway, and the plastic rules of the common law have accommodated themselves to the new condition of things; but the changes accomplished by the public press seem to have passed unnoticed in the law, and, save only where modifications have been made by constitution or statute, the publisher of the daily paper occupies to-day the position in the courts that the village gossip and retailer of scandal occupied two hundred years ago, with no more privilege and no more protection.

We quote from an opinion by the Supreme Court of New York, in a case where a publisher of a newspaper was prosecuted for libel, and where the position was taken by counsel that the publication was privileged: " It is made a point in this case, and was insisted upon in argument, that the editor of a public newspaper is at liberty to copy an item of news from another paper, giving at the same time his authority, without subjecting himself to legal responsibility, however libellous the article may be, unless express malice is shown.   It was conceded that the law did not, and ought not, to extend a similar indulgence to any other class of citizens ; but the counsel said that a distinction should be made in favor of editors, on the ground of the peculiarity of their occupation. That their business was to disseminate useful information among the people ; to publish such matters relating to the current events of the day happening at home or abroad as fell within the sphere of their observation, and as the public curiosity or taste demanded ; and that it was impracticable for them at all times to ascertain the truth or falsehood of the various statements contained in other journals.   We were also told that if the law were not thus indulgent, some legislative relief might become necessary for the protection of this class of citizens.   *Undoubtedly if it be desirable to pamper a depraved public appetite or taste*, if there be any such, by the republication of all the falsehoods and calumnies upon private character that may find their way into the press, — to give encouragement to the widest possible circulation of these vile and defamatory publications by protecting the retailers of them, — some legislative interference will be necessary, for no countenance can be found for the irresponsibility claimed in the common law.   That reprobates the libeller, whether author or publisher, and subjects him to both civil and criminal responsibility.   His offence is there ranked with that of the receiver of stolen goods, the perjurer and suborner of perjury, the disturber of the public peace, the conspirator, and other offenders of like character."   And again: " The act of publication is an adoption of the original calumny, which must be defended in the same way as if invented by the defendant. The republication assumes and indorses the truth of the charge, and when called on by the aggrieved party, the publisher should be held strictly to the proof.   If he chooses to become the indorser and retailer of private scandal, without taking the trouble to inquire into the truth of what he publishes, there is no ground for complaint if the law, which is as studious to protect the character as the property of a citizen, holds him to this responsibility.   The rule is not only just and wise in itself, but, if steadily and inflexibly adhered to and applied by courts and juries, will greatly tend to the promotion of truth, good morals, and common decency on the part of the press, by inculcating caution and inquiry into the truth of charges against private character before they are published and circulated throughout the community." [1]

If this strong condemnatory language were confined to the cases where private character is dragged before the public for detraction and abuse, to pander to a depraved appetite for scandal, its propriety and justice and the force of its reasons would be at once conceded.   But a very large proportion of what the newspapers spread before the public relates to matters of public concern, but in which, nevertheless, individuals figure, and must therefore be mentioned in any account.   To a great extent, also, the information comes from abroad ; the publisher can have no knowledge concerning it, and no inquiries which he could make would be likely to give him more definite information, unless he delays the publication until it ceases to be of value to his readers.   Whatever view the law may take, the public sentiment does not brand the publisher of a newspaper as libeller, conspirator, or villain, because the telegraph despatches transmitted to him from all parts of the world, without any knowledge on his part concerning them, are published in his paper, in reliance upon the prudence, care, and honesty of those who have charge of the lines of communication, and whose interest it is to be vigilant and truthful.   The public demand and expect accounts of every important meeting, of every important trial, and of all the events which have a bearing upon trade and business, or upon political affairs.   It is impossible that these shall be given in all cases without matters being mentioned derogatory to individuals ; and if the question were a new one in the law, it might be worthy of inquiry whether some line of distinction could not be drawn which would protect the publisher when giving in good faith such items of news as would be proper, if true, to spread before the public, and which he gives in the regular course of his employment, in pursuance of a public demand, and without any negligence, as they come to him from the

[1] Hotchkiss v. Oliphant, 2 Hill, 513, per Nelson, Ch. J.   And see King v. Root, 4 Wend. 138, per Walworth, Chancellor.

usual and legitimate sources, which he has reason to rely upon; at the same time leaving him liable when he makes his columns the vehicle of private gossip, detraction, and malice.

The question, however, is not new, and the authorities have generally held the publisher of a paper to the same rigid responsibility with any other person who makes injurious communications. Malice on his part is conclusively inferred, if the communications are false. It is no defence that they have been copied with or without comment from another paper;[1] or that the source of the information was stated at the time of the publication;[2] or that the publication was made in the paper without the knowledge of the proprietor, as an advertisement or otherwise;[3] or that it consists in a criticism on the course and character of a candidate for public office;[4] or that it is a correct and impartial account of a public

---

[1] Hotchkiss v. Oliphant, 2 Hill, 510. Even though they be preceded by the statement that they are so copied. Sanford v. Bennett, 24 N. Y. 20.

[2] Dole v. Lyon, 10 Johns. 447; Mapes v. Weeks, 4 Wend. 659; Inman v. Foster, 8 Wend. 602; Hotchkiss v. Oliphant, 2 Hill, 514.

[3] Andres v. Wells, 7 Johns. 260; Huff v. Bennett, 4 Sandf. 120; Same case, 6 N. Y. 337; Marten v. Van Schaick, 4 Paige, 479; Commonwealth v. Nichols, 10 Met. 259.

[4] King v. Root, 4 Wend. 113. The action was for a libel, published in the New York American, reflecting upon Root, who was candidate for lieutenant-governor. We quote from the opinion of the chancellor: "It is insisted that this libel was a privileged communication. If so, the defendants were under no obligation to prove the truth of the charge, and the party libelled had no right to recover, unless he established malice in fact, or showed that the editors knew the charge to be false. The effect of such a doctrine would be deplorable. Instead of protecting, it would be destroying the freedom of the press, if it were understood that an editor could publish what he pleased against candidates for office, without being answerable for the truth of such publications. No honest man could afford to be an editor, and no man who had any character to lose would be a candidate for office under such a construction of the law of libel. The only safe rule to adopt in such cases, is to permit editors to publish what they please in relation to the character and qualifications of candidates for office, but holding them responsible for the truth of what they publish." Notwithstanding the deplorable consequences here predicted from too great license to the press, it is matter of daily observation that the press, in its comments upon public events and public men, proceeds in all respects as though it were privileged; public opinion would not sanction prosecutions by candidates for office for publications amounting to technical libels, but which were nevertheless published without malice in fact; and the man who has a "character to lose" presents himself for the suffrages of his fellow-citizens in the full reliance that detraction by the public press will be corrected through the same instrumentality, and that unmerited abuse will react on the

meeting,[1] or of any proceedings in which the public have an interest, unless they were legislative or judicial in their character, and where both parties had opportunity to be heard.[2] Criticisms on

public opinion in his favor. Meantime the press is gradually becoming more just, liberal, and dignified in its dealings with political opponents, and vituperation is much less common, reckless, and bitter now than it was at the beginning of the century, when repression was more often resorted to as a remedy.

[1] Dawson v. Duncan, 7 El. & Bl. 229.

[2] Sanford v. Bennett, 24 N. Y. 20. Bennett was sued for publishing in the New York Herald the speech of a person convicted of murder, made upon the scaffold as he was about to be executed, and reflecting upon the counsel who had defended him. The principal question in the case was, whether a statute of the State, passed after the publication but before the trial, was applicable. The statute privileged any fair and true report in a newspaper, of a judicial, legislative, or other public official proceeding, or statement, speech, argument, or debate in the course of the same. The court held the statute not applicable, both because it was not retrospective in its provisions, and therefore could not apply to publications previously made, and also because this was not any such proceeding as the statute contemplated. Upon the question whether the publication was not privileged, independent of the statute, Denio, J., says: "The want of legal connection between the words spoken and the proceeding which was going forward at the same time and place, which has led me to the conclusion that the statute does not apply, shows that it is not within the reason upon which the common-law rule is based. That rule assumes that the public may have a legitimate interest in being made acquainted with the proceedings of courts of justice and of legislative bodies. The free circulation of such intelligence is of vast advantage in every country, and particularly here, where all reforms in legal or administrative polity must proceed from the people at large. But neither the reason of the rule, nor, as I believe, the rule itself has any application to a proceeding in which neither forensic debate nor legislative or administrative deliberations or determinations have any place. Where the proceeding is a mere act, with which neither oral nor written communications have anything more than an accidental or fortuitous connection, there is no room for the application of the doctrine of privilege to whatever may be spoken or written at the time and place where and when it is transpiring. Such transactions are subject to be reported, described, and published in newspapers or otherwise, like other affairs in which individuals and communities feel a curiosity, and with the same liability attaching to the publisher to answer for any injury which may happen to the character of individuals if, in the course of such publications, libellous imputations are applied to any one. It is of course perfectly lawful to publish all the circumstances attending a public execution, including the dying speech of the malefactor; but it is a necessary condition of that right, that if scandalous imputations are used by the culprit or any one else which are untrue, he who publishes them afterwards must be responsible for the wrong and injury thereby occasioned to the person attacked." Mason, J., in the same case gives a reason for concurring in the conclusion of the court, which seems to us to possess some force, independent of the question of privilege. It is

works of art and literary productions are allowable, if fair, reasonable, and temperate ; but the artist or author is not to be criticised
through his works, and his personal character is not made the
property of the public by his publications.[1] For further privilege
it would seem that publishers of news must appeal to the protection of public opinion, or to the legislature for such modification
of the law as may seem important to their just protection.

The publisher of a newspaper, however, though responsible for
all the actual damage which a party may suffer in consequence of
injurious publications in his paper, cannot be properly made liable
for exemplary or vindictive damages, where the article complained of was inserted in his paper without his personal knowledge, and he has been guilty of no negligence in the selection of
agents, or of personal misconduct, and is not shown habitually to
make his paper the vehicle of detraction and malice.[2]

Publication of Legislative Proceedings.

Although debates, reports, and other proceedings in legislative
bodies are privileged, it does not seem to follow that the publication
of them is always equally privileged. The English decisions do not
place such publications on any higher ground of right than any
other communication through the public press. A member of
Parliament, it is said, has a right to publish his speech, but it
must not be made the vehicle of slander against any individual,
and if it is, it is a libel.[3] And in another case: " A member of

that the provisions of law then in force, requiring capital executions to be within
the walls of the prison, or in an adjoining inclosure, and excluding all spectators
with limited exceptions, must be regarded as indicating a legislative policy adverse to the publicity of what passes on such occasions.

[1] The libel suits brought by J. Fennimore Cooper may be usefully consulted
in this connection. Cooper v. Stone, 24 Wend. 434; Cooper v. Barber, 24
Wend. 105 ; Cooper v. Greeley, 1 Denio, 347; Stone v. Cooper, 2 Denio, 293.
As to criticisms on public entertainments, see Fry v. Bennett, 5 Sandf. 54, and
28 N. Y. 324; Dibdin v. Swan, 1 Esp. 28 ; Green v. Chapman, 4 Bing. (N. C.)
92.   As to how far sermons, preached but not otherwise published, form a proper
subject for comment and criticism by the public press, see Gathercole v. Miall,
15 M. & W. 318.

[2] Daily Post Co. v. McArthur, and Detroit Free Press v. Same, 16 Mich. 447.

[3] Rex v. Lord Abington, 1 Esp. 226. In this case the defendant was fined,
imprisoned, and required to find security for his good behavior, for a
libel contained in a speech made by him in Parliament, and afterwards published.

[the House of Commons] has spoken what he thought material, and what he was at liberty to speak, in his character as a member of that house. So far he is privileged; but he has not stopped there, but, unauthorized by the house, has chosen to publish an account of that speech, in what he has pleased to call a corrected form, and in that publication has thrown out reflections injurious to the character of an individual." And he was convicted and fined for the libel.[1]

The circumstance that the publication was unauthorized by the house was alluded to in this opinion, but the rule of law would seem to be unaffected by it, since it was afterwards held that an order of the house directing a report made to it to be published did not constitute any protection to the official printer, who had published it in the regular course of his duty, in compliance with such order. All the power of the house was not sufficient to protect its printer in obeying the order to make this publication; and a statute was therefore passed to protect in the future persons publishing parliamentary reports, votes, or other proceedings by order of either house.[2]

[1] Rex v. Creevey, 1 M. & S. 278.

[2] Stat. 3 and 4 Victoria, c. 9. The case was that of Stockdale v. Hansard, very fully reported in 9 Al. & El. 1. See also 11 Al. & El. 253. The Messrs. Hansard were printers to the House of Commons, and had printed by order of that house the report of the inspectors of prisons, in which a book, published by Stockdale, and found among the prisoners in Newgate, was described as obscene and indecent. Stockdale brought an action against the printers for libel, and recovered judgment. Lord Denman, presiding on the trial, said that " the fact of the House of Commons having directed Messrs. Hansard to publish all their parliamentary reports is no justification for them, or for any bookseller who publishes any parliamentary report containing a libel against any man." The house resented this opinion and resolved, " that the power of publishing such of its reports, votes, and proceedings as it shall deem necessary or conducive to the public interests is an essential incident to the constitutional functions of Parliament, more especially of this house as the representative portion of it." They also resolved that for any person to institute a suit in order to call its privileges in question, or for any court to decide upon matters of privilege inconsistent with the determination of either house, was a breach of privilege. Stockdale, however, brought other actions and again recovered. When he sought to enforce these judgments by executions, his solicitor and himself were proceeded against for contempt of the house, and imprisoned. While in prison, Stockdale commenced a further suit. The sheriffs who had been ordered by the House of Commons to restore the money which they had collected were, on the other hand, compelled by attachments from the Queen's Bench to pay it over to Stockdale. In this complicated state of affairs, the proper and dignified mode of relieving the

It has been intimated, however, that what a representative is privileged to address to the house of which he is a member, he is also privileged to address to his constituents; and that the *bona fide* publication for that purpose of his speech in the house is protected.[1] And the practice in this country appears to proceed on difficulty by the passage of a statute making such publications privileged for the future was adopted. For an account of this controversy, in addition to what appears in the law reports, see May's Law and Practice of Parliament, 156 – 159, 2d ed.; May's Constitutional History, ch. 7. A case in some respects similar to that of Stockdale v. Hansard is that of Popham v. Pickburn, 7 Hurl. & Nor. 891. The defendant, the proprietor of a newspaper, was sued for publishing a report made by a medical officer of health to a vestry board, in pursuance of the statute, and which reflected severely upon the conduct of the plaintiff. The publication was made without any comment, and as a part of the proceedings of the vestry board. It was held not to be privileged, notwithstanding the statute provided for the publication of the report by the vestry board, — which, however, had not yet been made. Wilde, B., delivering the opinion of the court, said : " The defendant has published that of the plaintiff which is undoubtedly a libel, and which is untrue. He seeks to protect himself on the ground that the publication is a correct report of a document read at a meeting of the Clerkenwell vestry, which document must have been published and sold at a small price by the vestry in a short time. But we are of opinion this furnishes no defence. Undoubtedly the report of a trial in a court of justice in which this document had been read would not make the publisher thereof liable to an action for libel, and reasonably, for such reports only extend that publicity which is so important a feature of the administration of the law in England, and thus enable to be witnesses of it not merely the few whom the court can hold, but the thousands who can read the reports. But no case has decided that the reports of what takes place at the meeting of such a body as this vestry are so privileged; indeed the case cited in the argument [Rex v. Wright, 8 T. R. 293] is an authority that they are not. Then, is the publication justified by the statute ? It is true that the document would have been accessible to the public in a short time, though not published by the defendant; but this cannot justify his anticipating the publication, and giving it a wider circulation, and possibly without an answer which the vestry might have received in some subsequent report or otherwise, and which would then have been circulated with the libel. This defence therefore fails.

" It was further contended that this libel might be justified as a matter of public discussion on a subject of public interest. The answer is : This is not a discussion or comment. It is the statement of a fact. To charge a man incorrectly with a disgraceful act is very different from commenting on a fact relating to him truly stated; there the writer may, by his opinion, libel himself rather than the subject of his remarks.

" It is to be further observed that this decision does not determine or affect the question whether, after the statutory publication, it might or might not be competent to others to republish these reports, with or without reasonable comments."

[1] Lives of Chief Justices, by Lord Campbell, vol. 3, p. 167; Davison v. Duncan, 7 El. & Bl. 229, 233.

this idea; the speeches and proceedings in Congress being fully reported by the press, and the exemption of the member from being called to account for his speech being apparently supposed to extend to its publication also. When complete publicity is thus practised, perhaps every speech published should be regarded as addressed *bona fide* by the representative, not only to the house, but also to his constituents. But whether that view be taken or not, if publication is provided for by law, as in the case of Congressional debates, the publishing must be considered as privileged.

The Jury as Judges of the Law.

In a considerable number of the State constitutions it provided that, in prosecutions for libel, the jury shall have a right to determine the law and the fact. In some it is added, " as in other cases "; in others, " under the direction of the court." For the necessity of these provisions we must recur to the rulings of the English judges in the latter half of the last century, and the memorable contest in the courts and in Parliament, resulting at last in the passage of Mr. Fox's Libel Act, declaratory of the rights of juries in prosecutions for libel.

In the year 1770, Woodfall, the printer of the Morning Adver- tiser, was tried before Lord Mansfield for having published in his paper what was alleged to be a libel on the king; and his lordship told the jury that all they had to consider was, whether the defend- ant had published the paper set out in the information, and whether the innuendoes, imputing a particular meaning to particu- lar words were true, as that " the K—— " meant his Majesty King George III. ; but that they were not to consider whether the publication was, as alleged in the information, false and malicious, those being mere formal words ; and that whether the letter was libellous or innocent was a pure question of law, upon which the opinion of the court might be taken by a demurrer or a motion in arrest of judgment. His charge obviously required the jury, if satisfied the publication was made, and had the meaning attrib- uted to it, to render a verdict of guilty, whether they believed the publication false and malicious or not ; in other words, to convict the party of guilt, notwithstanding they might believe the essen- tial element of criminality to be wanting. The jury, dissatisfied with these instructions, and unwilling to make their verdict cover matters upon which they were not at liberty to exercise their judgment, returned a verdict of " guilty of printing and publishing *only*," but this the court afterwards rejected as ambiguous, and ordered a new trial.[1]

In Miller's case, which was tried the same year, Lord Mansfield instructed the jury as follows : " The direction I am going to give you is with a full conviction and confidence that it is the language of the law.   If you by your verdict find the defendant not guilty, the fact established by that verdict is, he did not publish a paper of that meaning ; that fact is established, and there is an end of the prosecution.   You are to try the fact, because your verdict establishes that fact, that he did not publish it.   If you find that, according to your judgment, your verdict is final, and if you find it otherwise, it is between God and your consciences, for that is the basis upon which all verdicts ought to be founded ; then the fact finally established by your verdict, if you find him guilty, is, that he printed and published a paper of the tenor and of the meaning set forth in the information ; that is the only fact finally established by your verdict ; and whatever fact is finally established never can be controverted in any shape whatever.   But you do not by that verdict give an opinion, or establish whether it is or not lawful to print or publish a paper of the tenor and meaning in the information ; for, supposing the defendant is found guilty, and the paper is such a paper as by the law of the land may be printed and published, the defendant has a right to have judgment respited, and to have it carried to the highest court of judicature." [2]

Whether these instructions were really in accordance with the law of England, it would be of little importance now to inquire. They were assailed as not only destructive to the liberty of the press, but as taking from the jury that right to cover by their verdict all the matter charged and constituting the alleged offence, which was conceded to be their right in all other cases.   In no other case could the jury be required to find a criminal intent which they did not believe to exist.   In the House of Lords they were assailed by Lord Chatham ; and Lord Camden, the Chief Justice of the Common Pleas, in direct contradiction to Lord Mansfield, declared his instructions not to be the law of England.

---

[1] 20 State Trials, 895.   [2] 20 State Trials, 870.

Nevertheless, with the judges generally the view of Lord Mansfield prevailed, and it continued to be enforced for more than twenty years, so far as juries would suffer themselves to be controlled by the directions of the courts.

The act known as Fox's Libel Act was passed in 1792 against the protest of Lord Thurlow and five other lords, who predicted from it " the confusion and destruction of the law of England." It was entitled " An act to remove doubts respecting the functions of juries in cases of libel," and it declared and enacted that the jury might give a general verdict of guilty or not guilty, upon the whole matter put in issue upon the indictment or information, and should not be required or directed by the court or judge before whom it should be tried to find the defendant guilty, merely on the proof of the publication of the paper charged to be a libel, and of the sense ascribed to the same in the indictment or information : *Provided*, that on every such trial the court or judge before whom it should be tried should, according to their discretion, give their opinion and direction to the jury on the matter in issue, in like manner as in other criminal cases : *Provided also*, that nothing therein contained should prevent the jury from finding a special verdict in their discretion, as in other criminal cases : *Provided also*, that in case the jury should find the defendant guilty, he might move in arrest of judgment on such ground and in such manner as by law he might have done before the passing of the act.

Whether this statute made the jury the rightful judges of the law as well as of the facts in libel cases, or whether, on the other hand, it only placed these cases on the same footing as other criminal prosecutions, leaving it the duty of the jury to accept and follow the instructions of the judge upon the criminal character of the publication, are questions upon which there are still differences of opinion. Its friends have placed the former construction upon it, while others adopt the opposite view.[1]

In the United States the disposition of the early judges was to adopt the view of Lord Mansfield as a correct exposition of the respective functions of court and jury in cases of libel ; and on the memorable trial of Callendar, which led to the impeachment of Judge Chase of the United States Supreme Court, the right of the

---

[1] Compare Forsyth on Trial by Jury, ch. 12, with May's Constitutional History of England, ch. 9.

jury to judge of the law was the point in dispute upon which that judge first delivered his opinion, and afterwards invited argument. The charge there was of libel upon President Adams, and was prosecuted under the Sedition Law so called, which expressly provided that the jury should have the right to determine the law and the fact, under the direction of the court, as in other cases. The defence insisted that the Sedition Law was unconstitutional and void, and proposed to argue that question to the jury, but were stopped by the court. The question of the constitutionality of a statute, it was said by Judge Chase, was a judicial question, and could only be passed upon by the court; the jury might determine the law applicable to the case under the statute, but they could not inquire into the validity of the statute by which that right was given.[1]

Whatever may be the true import of Mr. Fox's Libel Act, it would seem clear that a constitutional provision which allows the jury to determine the law refers the questions of law to them for their rightful decision. Wherever such provisions exist, the jury, we think, are the judges of the law; and the argument of counsel upon it is rightfully addressed to both the court and the jury. Nor can the distinction be maintained which was taken by Judge Chase, and which forbids the jury considering questions affecting the constitutional validity of statutes. When the question before them is, what is the law of the case, the highest and paramount law of the case cannot be shut from view. Nevertheless, we conceive it to be proper and indeed the duty of the judge to instruct the jury upon the law in these cases, and it is to be expected that they will generally adopt and follow his opinion.

Where, however, the constitution provides that they shall be judges of the law " as in other cases," or may determine the law and the fact " under the direction of the court," we must perhaps conclude that the intention has been simply to put libel cases on the same footing with any other criminal prosecutions,[2] and that the jury will be expected to receive the law from the court.

[1] Wharton's State Trials, 688.

[2] " By the last clause of the sixth section of the eighth article of the constitution of this State, it is declared that, in all indictments for libel, the jury shall have the right to determine the law and the facts under the direction of the court as in other cases. It would seem from this that the framers of our Bill of Rights did not imagine that juries were rightfully judges of the law and fact in criminal cases, independently of the directions of courts. Their right to judge of the law is a

" Good Motives and Justifiable Ends."

In civil suits to recover damages for slander or libel, the truth is generally a complete defence, if pleaded and established.[1] In criminal prosecutions it was formerly not so. The basis of the prosecution being that the libel was likely to disturb the peace and order of society, that liability was supposed to be all the greater if the injurious charges were true, as a man would be more likely to commit a breach of the peace when the matters alleged against him were true than if they were false, in which latter case he might, perhaps, afford to treat them with contempt. Hence arose the common maxim, " The greater the truth the greater the libel," which subjected the law on this subject to a great deal of ridicule and contempt. The constitutional provisions we have quoted generally make the truth a defence if published with good motives and for justifiable ends. Precisely what showing shall establish good motives and justifiable occasion must be settled by future decisions. In one case the suggestion was thrown out that proof of the truth of the charge alone might be sufficient,[2] but this was not an authoritative decision, and it could not be true in any case where the matter published was not fit to be spread before the public, whether true or false. It must be held, we think, that where the defendant justifies in a criminal prosecution, the burden is upon him to prove, not only the truth of the charge, but also the " good motives and justifiable ends" of the publication. These might appear from the very character of the publication itself, if it was true; as where it exhibited the misconduct or unfitness of a candidate for public office; but where it related to a

---

right to be exercised only under the direction of the courts; and if they go aside from that direction and determine the law incorrectly, they depart from their duty and commit a public wrong; and this in criminal as well as in civil cases." Montgomery v. State, 11 Ohio, 427. See also State v. Allen, 1 McCord, 525.

[1] Foss v. Hildreth, 10 Allen, 76. See ante, 455.

[2] Charge of Judge Betts to the jury in King v. Root, 4 Wend. 121 : " Should the scope of proofs and circumstances lead you to suppose the defendants had no good end in contemplation, that they were instigated to these charges solely to avenge personal and political resentments against the plaintiff, still, if they have satisfactorily shown the charges to be true, they must be acquitted of all liability to damage in a private action on account of the publication. Indeed, if good motives and justifiable ends must be shown, they might well be implied from the establishment of the truth of a charge, for the like reason that malice is inferred from its falsity."

person in private life, and who was himself taking no such action as should put his character in issue before the public, some further showing would generally be requisite after the truth had been proved.[1]

[1] In Commonwealth *v.* Bonner, 9 Met. 410, the defendant was indicted for a libel on one Oliver Brown, in the following words: "However, there were few who, according to the old toper's dictionary, were drunk; yea, in all conscience, drunk as a drunken man; and who and which of you desperadoes of the town got them so? Was it you whose groggery was open, and the rat soup measured out at your bar to drunkards, while a daughter lay a corpse in your house, and even on the day she was laid in her cold and silent grave, a·victim of God's chastening rod upon your guilty drunkard-manufacturing head? Was it you who refused to close your drunkery on the day that your aged father was laid in the narrow house appointed for all the living, and which must erelong receive your recreant carcass? We ask again, Was it you? Was it you?" On the trial the defendant introduced evidence to prove, and contended that he did prove, all the facts alleged in his publication. The court charged the jury that the burden was upon the defendant to show that the matter charged to be libellous was published with good motives and for justifiable ends; that malice is the wilful doing of an unlawful act, and does not necessarily imply personal ill-will towards the person libelled. The defendant excepted to the ruling of the court as applied to the facts proved, contending that, having proved the truth of all the facts alleged in the libel, and the publication being in reference to an illegal traffic, a public nuisance, the jury should have been instructed that it was incumbent on the government to show that defendant's motives were malicious, in the popular sense of the word, as respects said Brown. By the court, Shaw, Ch. J.: "The court are of opinion that the charge of the judge of the Common Pleas was strictly correct. If the publication be libellous, that is, be such as to bring the person libelled into hatred, contempt, and ridicule amongst the people, malice is presumed from the injurious act. But by Rev. Stat. c. 133, § 6, 'in every prosecution for writing or publishing a libel, the defendant may give in evidence, in his defence upon the trial, the truth of the matter contained in the publication charged as libellous: provided, that such evidence shall not be deemed a sufficient justification, unless it shall be further made to appear, on the trial, that the matter charged to be libellous was published with good motives and for justifiable ends.' Nothing can be more explicit. The judge therefore was right in directing the jury that, after the publication had been shown to have been made by the defendant, and to be libellous and malicious, the burden was on the defendant, not only to prove the truth of the matter charged as libellous, but likewise that it was published with good motives and for justifiable ends. We are also satisfied that the judge was right in his description or definition of legal malice, that it is not malice in its popular sense, viz. that of hatred and ill-will to the party libelled, but an act done wilfully, unlawfully, and in violation of the just rights of another." And yet it would seem as if, conceding the facts published to be true, the jury ought to have found the occasion a proper one for correcting such indecent conduct by public exposure. See further on this subject, Regina *v.* New-

man, 1 El. & Bl. 268 and 558; Same case, 18 E. L. & Eq. 113; Barthelemy v. People, 2 Hill, 248; State v. White, 7 Ired. 180; Commonwealth v. Snelling, 15 Pick. 337. The fact that the publication is copied from another source is clearly no protection, if it is not true in fact. Regina v. Newman, *ub sup.* Neither are the motives or good character of the defendant, if he has published libellous matter which is false. Barthelemy v. People, 2 Hill, 248; Commonwealth v. Snelling, 15 Pick. 337.

CHAPTER XIII.

RELIGIOUS LIBERTY.

HE who shall examine with care the American constitutions will find nothing more fully or more plainly expressed than the desire of their framers to preserve and perpetuate religious liberty, and to guard against the slightest approach towards inequality of civil or political rights based upon difference of religious belief. The American people came to the work of framing their fundamental laws, after centuries of oppression and persecution, sometimes by one religious party and sometimes by another, had taught them the utter futility of attempting to propagate religious opinions by the terrors of human laws. They could not fail to perceive also that the union of Church and State was, if not wholly impracticable in America, certainly opposed to the spirit of our institutions, and that any domineering of one sect over another was repressing to the energies of the people, and must necessarily tend to discontent and disorder. Whatever, therefore, may have been their individual sentiments upon religious questions, or upon the propriety of the State assuming any supervision of religious affairs under other circumstances, the general voice has been to make all persons equal before the law, and to leave questions of religious belief and religious worship to be questions between every man and his Maker, which human tribunals are not to take cognizance of, so long as the public order is not disturbed, except as the person himself, by voluntary action in associating himself with a religious organization, may have conferred upon such organization a jurisdiction over him in ecclesiastical matters. These constitutions, therefore, have not established religious toleration merely, but religious equality; in that particular being far in advance not only of the mother country, but also of much of the colonial legislation, which, though more liberal than that of other civilized countries, was still connected with features of discrimination based upon religious belief.[1]

---

[1] It was not easy two centuries ago to make men understand how there could be complete religious liberty, and at the same time order and due subordination

In completeness and phraseology the provisions in the State constitutions on the subject of religious liberty differ very greatly, some of them being confined to declarations and prohibitions designed to secure the most perfect equality before the law of all shades of religious belief, while some exhibit a jealousy of ecclesiastical authority by making persons who exercise the functions of a clergyman, priest, or teacher of any religious persuasion, society, or sect, ineligible to civil office,[1] and still others show some traces of the old notion, that truth and a sense of duty are inconsistent with scepticism in religion.[2]   These are exceptional

to authority in the State. Roger Williams explained and defended his own views and illustrated the subject thus: " There goes many a ship to sea, with many hundred souls in one ship, whose weal and woe is common, and is a true picture of a commonwealth, or human combination or society.   It hath fallen out sometimes that both Papists and Protestants, Jews and Turks, may be embarked in one ship; upon which supposal, I affirm that all the liberty of conscience I ever pleaded for turns upon these two hinges, that none of the Papists, Protestants, Jews, or Turks be forced to come to the ship's prayers, or worship, nor compelled from their own particular prayers or worship, if they practise any. I further add, that I never denied that, notwithstanding this liberty, the commander of this ship ought to command the ship's course, yea, and also command that justice, peace, and sobriety be kept and practised, both among the seamen and all the passengers. If any of the seamen refuse to perform their service, or passengers to pay their freight; if any refuse to help, in person or purse, towards the common charges or defence; if any refuse to obey the common laws and orders of the ship, concerning their common peace or preservation; if any shall mutiny and rise up against their commanders and officers; if any should preach or write that there ought to be no commanders or officers, because all are equal in Christ, therefore no masters nor officers, no laws nor orders, no corrections nor punishments; I say I never denied but in such cases, whatever is pretended, the commander or commanders may judge, resist, compel, and punish such transgressors according to their deserts and merits."   Arnold's History of Rhode Island, vol. 1, 254; citing Knowles, 279, 280.

   [1] There are provisions to this effect, more or less broad, in the constitutions of Tennessee, Louisiana, North Carolina, Virginia, South Carolina, Texas, Delaware, and Kentucky.

   [2] The constitution of Pennsylvania provides "that no person who acknowledges the being of God, and a future state of rewards and punishments, shall on account of his religious sentiments be disqualified to hold any office or place of trust or profit under this commonwealth." Art. 9, § 4.   The constitution of North Tennessee: " No person who denies the being of a God, or a future state of rewards and punishments, shall hold any office in the civil department of this State." Art. 9, § 2.   The constitution of Arkansas: " No person who denies the being of a God shall hold any office in the civil department of this State, nor be allowed his oath in any court." Art. 8, § 3.   The constitution of Mississippi: " No per-

clauses, however, and not great in number, and it is believed they are not often made use of to deprive any person of the civil or political rights or privileges which are placed within the reach of his fellows.

Those things which are not lawful under any of the American constitutions may be stated thus : —

1. Any law respecting an establishment of religion. The legislatures have not been left at liberty to effect a union of Church and State, or to establish preferences by law in favor of any one religious denomination or mode of worship. There is not religious liberty where any one sect is favored by the State and given an advantage by law over other sects. Whatever establishes a distinction against one class or sect is, to the extent to which the distinction operates unfavorably, a persecution ; and, if based on religious grounds, is religious persecution. It is not toleration which is established in our system, but religious equality.

2. Compulsory support, by taxation or otherwise, of religious instruction. Not only is no one denomination to be favored at the expense of the rest, but all support of religious instruction must be entirely voluntary.

3. Compulsory attendance upon religious worship. Whoever is not led by choice or a sense of duty to attend upon the ordinances of religion is not to be compelled to do so by the State. The State will seek, so far as practicable, to enforce the obligations and duties which the citizen may owe to his fellow-citizen, but those which he owes to his Maker are to be enforced by the admonitions of the conscience, and not by the penalties of human laws.

4. Restraints upon the free exercise of religion according to the dictates of the conscience. No external authority is to place itself

son who denies the being of a God, or a future state of rewards and punishments, shall hold any office in the civil department of this State." On the other hand, the constitutions of Alabama, Kansas, Virginia, West Virginia, Maine, Delaware, Illinois, Indiana, Iowa, Oregon, Ohio, New Jersey, Nebraska, Texas, and Wisconsin, expressly forbid religious tests as a qualification for office or public trust. The constitution of Tennessee also, by its bill of rights, forbids any such test, but afterwards establishes one. The constitution of Maryland provides • " that no other test or qualification ought to be required on admission to any office of trust or profit than such oath of allegiance and fidelity to this State and the United States as may be prescribed by this constitution, and such oath of office and qualification as may be prescribed by this constitution, or by the laws of the State, and a declaration of belief in the Christian religion, or in the existence of God, and in a future state of rewards and punishments." Declaration of Rights, art. 37.

between the finite being and the Infinite, when the former is seeking to render that homage which is due, and in a mode which commends itself to his belief as suitable for him to render and acceptable to its object.

5. Restraints upon the expression of religious belief. An earnest believer usually regards it his duty to propagate his opinions. To deprive him of this right is to take from him the power to perform what he considers a most sacred obligation.

These are the prohibitions which in some form of words are to be found in the American constitutions, and which secure freedom of conscience and of religious worship. No man in religious matters is to be subjected to the censorship of the State or of any public authority; and the State is not to inquire into or take notice of religious belief, when the citizen performs his duty to the State and to his fellows.[1]

But while thus careful to establish religious freedom and equality, the American constitutions contain no provisions which prohibit the authorities from such solemn recognition of a superintending Providence in public transactions and exercises as the general religious sentiment of mankind inspires, and as seems meet in finite and dependent beings. Whatever may be the shades

---

[1] Congress is forbidden, by the first amendment to the Constitution of the United States, from making any law respecting an establishment of religion, or prohibiting the free exercise thereof. Mr. Story says of this provision : "It was under a solemn consciousness of the dangers from ecclesiastical ambition, the bigotry of spiritual pride, and the intolerance of sects, exemplified in our domestic, as well as in foreign annals, that it was deemed advisable to exclude from the national government all power to act upon the subject. The situation, too, of the different States equally proclaimed the policy, as well as the necessity, of such an exclusion. In some of the States Episcopalians constituted the predominant sect ; in others, Presbyterians; in others, Congregationalists ; in others, Quakers; and in others again there was a close numerical rivalry among contending sects. It was impossible that there should not arise perpetual strife and perpetual jealousy on the subject of ecclesiastical ascendancy, if the national government were left free to create a religious establishment. The only security was in extirpating the power. But this alone would have been an imperfect security, if it had not been followed up by a declaration of the right of the free exercise of religion, and a prohibition (as we have seen) of all religious tests. Thus, the whole power over the subject of religion is left exclusively to the State governments, to be acted upon according to their own sense of justice, and the State constitutions; and the Catholic and the Protestant, the Calvinist and the Armenian, the Jew and the Infidel, may sit down at the common table of the national councils, without any inquisition into their faith or mode of worship." Story on the Constitution, § 1879.

of religious belief, all must acknowledge the fitness of recognizing in important human affairs the superintending care and control of the great Governor of the universe, and of acknowledging with thanksgiving his boundless favors, at the same time that we bow in contrition when visited with the penalties of his broken laws. No principle of constitutional law is violated when thanksgiving or fast days are appointed ; when chaplains are designated for the army and navy ; when legislative sessions are opened with prayer or the reading of the Scriptures, or when religious teaching is encouraged by exempting houses of religious worship from taxation for the support of the State government. Undoubtedly the spirit of the constitution will require, in all these cases, that care be taken to avoid discrimination in favor of any one denomination or sect ; but the power to do any of these things will not be unconstitutional, simply because of being susceptible of abuse. This public recognition of religious worship, however, is not based entirely, perhaps even mainly, upon a sense of what is due to the Supreme Being himself, as the author of all good and of all law ; but the same reasons of state policy which induce the government to aid institutions of charity and seminaries of instruction will also incline it to foster religious worship and religious institutions, as conservators of the public morals, and valuable, if not indispensable assistants to the preservation of the public order.

Nor, while recognizing a superintending Providence, are we always precluded from recognizing also, in the rules prescribed for the conduct of citizens, the patent fact that the prevailing religion in the States is Christian. Some acts would be offensive to public sentiment in a Christian community, and would tend to public disorder, which, in a Mahometan or Pagan country, might be passed without notice, or even be regarded as meritorious. The criminal laws of every country have reference in great degree to the prevailing public sentiment, and punish those acts as crimes which disturb the peace and order, or tend to shock the moral sense, of the community. The moral sense is measurably regulated and controlled by the religious belief ; and therefore it is that those things which, estimated by a Christian standard, are profane and blasphemous are. properly punished as offences, since they are offensive in the highest degree to the general public sense, and have a direct tendency to undermine the moral support of the laws and corrupt the community.

It is frequently said that Christianity is a part of the law of the land. In a certain sense, and for certain purposes, this is true. The best features of the common law, and especially those which relate to the family and social relations; which compel the parent to support the child, and the husband the wife; which make the marriage tie permanent, and forbid polygamy, have either been derived from, or have been improved and strengthened by, the prevailing religion and the teachings of its sacred book. But the law does not attempt to enforce the precepts of Christianity, on the ground of their sacred character or divine origin. Some of those precepts are universally recognized as being incapable of enforcement by human laws, notwithstanding they are of continual and universal obligation. Christianity, therefore, is not a part of the law of the land, in the sense that would entitle the courts to take notice of and base their judgments upon it, except so far as they should find that its precepts had been incorporated in, and thus become a component part of, the law.[1]

Mr. Justice Story has said, in the Girard will case, that although Christianity is a part of the common law of the state, it is only so in this qualified sense, *that its divine origin and truth are admitted*, and therefore it is not to be maliciously and openly reviled and blasphemed against, to the annoyance of believers or to the injury of the public.[2] It may be doubted, however, if the punishment of blasphemy is based necessarily upon an admission of the divine origin and truth of the Christian religion.

Blasphemy has been defined as consisting in speaking evil of the Deity with an impious purpose to derogate from the divine majesty, and to alienate the minds of others from the love and reverence of God. It is purposely using words concerning God calculated and designed to impair and destroy the reverence, respect, and confidence due to him, as the intelligent Creator, Governor, and Judge of the world. It embraces the idea of detraction when used toward the Supreme Being, as calumny usually carries the same idea when applied to an individual. It is a wilful and malicious attempt to lessen men's reverence of God, by denying his existence, or his attributes as an intelligent Creator, Governor, and Judge of men, and to prevent their having confidence in him

---

[1] Andrew *v.* Bible Society, 4 Sandf. 182; Ayres *v.* Methodist Church, 3 Sandf. 377.

[2] Vidal *v.* Girard Ex'rs, 2 How. 198.

as such.[1] Contumelious reproaches and profane ridicule of Christ
or of the Holy Scriptures have the same evil effect in sapping the
foundations of society and of public order, and are classed under
the same head.[2]

In an early case when a prosecution for blasphemy came before
Lord Hale, he is reported to have said: " Such kind of wicked,
blasphemous words are not only an offence to God and religion,
but a crime against the laws, state, and government, and therefore
punishable in the Court of King's Bench. For to say religion is
a cheat, is to subvert all those obligations whereby civil society is
preserved; that Christianity is a part of the laws of England, and
to reproach the Christian religion is to speak in subversion of the
law." [3] Eminent judges in this country have adopted this language, and applied it to prosecutions for blasphemy, where the
charge consisted in malicious ridicule of the Author and Founder
of the Christian religion. The early cases in New York and Massachusetts [4] are particularly marked by clearness and precision on
this point, and Mr. Justice Clayton of Delaware has also adopted
and followed the ruling of Lord Chief Justice Hale, with such explanations of the true basis of these prosecutions as to give us a
clear understanding of the maxim that Christianity is a part of the
law of the land, as applied in these cases.[5] Taken with the expla-

---

[1] Shaw, Ch. J., in Commonwealth v. Kneeland, 20 Pick. 213.

[2] People v. Ruggles, 8 Johns. 290 ; Commonwealth v. Kneeland, 20 Pick. 213 ;
Updegraph v. Commonwealth, 11 S. & R. 394 ; State v. Chandler, 2 Harr. 553 ;
Rex v. Waddington, 1 B. C. 26 ; Rex v. Carlile, 3 B. & Ald. 161.

[3] King v. Taylor, 3 Keb. 607 ; Vent. 293.

[4] People v. Ruggles, 8 Johns. 291 ; Commonwealth v. Kneeland, 20 Pick. 203.

[5] State v. Chandler, 2 Harr. 555. The case is very full, clear, and instructive,
and cites all the English and American authorities. The conclusion at which it
arrives is, that " Christianity was never considered a part of the common law, so
far as that for a violation of its injunctions, independent of the established laws of
man, and without the sanction of any positive act of Parliament made to enforce
those injunctions, any man could be drawn to answer in a common-law court. It
was a part of the common law, 'so far that any person reviling, subverting, or
ridiculing it might be prosecuted at common law,' as Lord Mansfield has declared ;
because, in the judgment of our English ancestors and their judicial tribunals, he
who reviled, subverted, or ridiculed Christianity did an act which struck at the
foundation of their civil society, and tended by its necessary consequences to
disturb that common peace of the land of which (as Lord Coke had reported) the
common law was the preserver. The common law . . . . adapted itself to the
religion of the country just so far as was necessary for the peace and safety of
civil institutions ; but it took cognizance of offences against God only when, by

nation given, there is nothing in the maxim of which the believer in any creed can justly complain. The language which the Christian regards as blasphemous, no man in sound mind can feel under a sense of duty to make use of under any circumstances. No person is therefore deprived of a right when he is prohibited, under penalties, from uttering it.

But it does not follow, because blasphemy is punishable as a crime, that therefore one is not at liberty to dispute and argue against the truth of the Christian religion, or of any accepted dogma. Its " divine origin and truth " are not so far admitted in the law as to preclude their being controverted. To forbid discussion upon this subject, except by the various sects of believers, would be to abridge the liberty of speech and of the press in a point which, with many, would be regarded as most important of all. Blasphemy implies something more than a denial of any of the truths of religion, even of the highest and most vital. A bad motive must exist; there must be a wilful and malicious attempt to lessen men's reverence for the Deity, or for the accepted religion. But outside of such wilful and malicious attempt, there is a broad field for candid investigation and discussion, which is as much open to the Jew and the Mahometan as to the professors of the Christian faith. " No author or printer who fairly and conscientiously promulgates the opinions with whose truths he is impressed, for the benefit of others, is answerable as a criminal. A malicious and mischievous intention is, in such a case, the broad boundary between right and wrong; it is to be collected from the offensive levity, scurrilous and opprobrious language, and other circumstances, whether the act of the party was malicious." [1] Legal blasphemy implies that the words were uttered in a wanton manner, " with a wicked and malicious disposition, and not in a serious discussion upon any controverted point in religion." [2] The courts have always been careful, in administering the law, to say that they did not intend to include in blasphemy, disputes between learned men upon particular controverted points.[3] The consti-

---

their inevitable effects, they became offences against man and his temporal security."

[1] Updegraph v. Commonwealth, 11 S. & R. 394.

[2] People v. Ruggles, 8 Johns. 293, per Kent, Ch. J.

[3] Rex v. Woolston, Strange, 834, Fitzg. 64 ; People v. Ruggles, 8 Johns. 293, per Kent, Ch. J.

tutional provisions for the protection of religious liberty not only include within their protecting power all sentiments and professions concerning or upon the subjects of religion, but they guarantee to every one a perfect right to form and to promulgate such opinions and doctrines upon religious matters, and in relation to the existence, power, and providence of a Supreme Being, as to himself shall seem just. In doing this, he acts under an awful responsibility, but it is not to any human tribunal.[1]

[1] Per Shaw Ch. J., in Commonwealth v. Kneeland, 20 Pick. 234. The language of the courts has perhaps not always been as guarded as it should have been on this subject. In The King v. Waddington, 1 B. & C. 26, the defendant was on trial for blasphemous libel in saying that Jesus Christ was an impostor, and a murderer in principle. One of the jurors asked the Lord Chief Justice (Abbott) whether a work which denied the divinity of our Saviour was a libel. The Lord Chief Justice replied that " a work speaking of Jesus Christ in the language used in the publication in question was a libel, Christianity being a part of the law of the land." This was doubtless true, as the wrong motive was apparent; but it did not answer the juror's question. On motion for a new trial, the remarks of Best, J., are open to a construction which answers the question in the affirmative : " My Lord Chief Justice reports to us that he told the jury that it was an indictable offence to speak of Jesus Christ in the manner that he is spoken of in the publication for which this defendant is indicted. It cannot admit of the least doubt that this direction was correct. The 53 G. 3, ch. 160, has made no alteration in the common law relative to libel. If, previous to the passing of that statute, it would have been a libel to deny, in any printed book, the divinity of the second person in the Trinity, the same publication would be a libel now. The 53 G. 3, ch. 160, as its title expresses, is an act to relieve persons who impugn the doctrine of the Trinity from certain penalties. If we look at the body of the act to see from what penalties such parties are relieved, we find that they are the penalties from which the 1 W. & M. Sess. 1, ch. 18, exempted all Protestant dissenters, except such as denied the Trinity, and the penalties or disabilities which the 9 & 10 W. 3, imposed on those who denied the Trinity. The 1 W. & M. Sess. 1, ch. 18, is, as it has been usually called, an act of toleration, or one which allows dissenters to worship God in the mode that is agreeable to their religious opinions, and exempts them from punishment for non-attendance at the Established Church, and nonconformity to its rites. The legislature, in passing that act, only thought of easing the conscience of dissenters, and not of allowing them to attempt to weaken the faith of the members of the Church. The 9 & 10 W. 3 was to give security to the government, by rendering men incapable of office who entertained opinions hostile to the established religion. The only penalty imposed by that statute is exclusion from office, and that penalty is incurred by any manifestations of the dangerous opinion, without proof of intention in the person entertaining it either to induce others to be of that opinion, or in any manner to disturb persons of a different persuasion. This statute rested on the principle of the test laws, and did not interfere with the common law relative to blasphemous

Other forms of profanity, besides that of blasphemy, are also made punishable by statute in the several States. These cases are of a character which no one can justify, and which involve no question of religious liberty. The right to use profane and indecent language is recognized by no religious creed, and the practice is reprobated by right-thinking men of every nation and every belief. The statutes for the punishment of public profanity require no further defence than the natural impulses of every man who believes in a Supreme Being, and recognizes his right to our reverence.

Laws against the desecration of the Christian Sabbath, by labor or sports, are not so readily defensible by arguments the force of which will be felt by all. It is no hardship to any one to compel him to abstain from profanity or blasphemy, and none can complain that his rights of conscience are invaded by this enforced respect to a prevailing religious sentiment. But the Jew, who is forced to observe the first day of the week, when his conscience requires of him the observance of the seventh also, may plausibly urge that the law discriminates against his religion, and, by forcing him to keep a second Sabbath in each week, unjustly, though by indirection, punishes him for his belief.

The laws which prohibit ordinary employments on Sunday are to be defended either on the same grounds which justify the punishment of blasphemy, or as a sanitary regulation based upon the demonstration of experience that one day's rest in seven is needful to recuperate the exhausted energies of body and mind. If

libels. It is not necessary for me to say whether it be libellous to argue from the Scriptures against the divinity of Christ; that is not what the defendant professes to do; he argues against the divinity of Christ by denying the truth of the Scriptures. A work containing such arguments, published maliciously (which the jury in this case have found), is by the common law a libel, and the legislature has never altered this law, nor can it ever do so while the Christian religion is considered the basis of that law." It is a little difficult, perhaps, to determine precisely how far this opinion was designed to go in holding that the law forbids the public denial of the truth of the Scriptures. That arguments against it, made in good faith by those who do not accept it, are legitimate and rightful, we think there is no doubt; and the learned judge doubtless meant to admit as much when he required a malicious publication as an ingredient in the offence.

In People v. Porter, 2 Park, Cr. R. 14, the defence of *drunkenness* was made to a prosecution for a blasphemous libel. Walworth, Circuit Judge, presiding at the trial, declared the intoxication of defendant at the time of uttering the words to be an aggravation of the offence, rather than an excuse.

sustained on the first ground, it must be held that, to the Jew or the Seventh-day Baptist, such a law is not to be regarded as a violation of religious liberty, but rather as an enforced deference which one differing from the common belief pays to the public conscience. The Supreme Court of Pennsylvania have preferred to defend such legislation upon the second ground, rather than the first ;[1] but it appears to us that, if the benefit to the individual is alone to be considered, the argument against the law which he may make who has already observed the seventh day of the week is unanswerable. But on the other ground, it is clear that these laws are supportable on authority, notwithstanding the inconvenience which they occasion to those whose religious sentiments do not recognize the sacred character of the first day of the week.[2]

Whatever deference the Constitution or the laws may require to be paid in some cases to the conscientious scruples or religious convictions of the majority, the general policy always is to care-

---

[1] "It intermeddles not with the natural and indefeasible right of all men to worship Almighty God according to the dictates of their own consciences; it compels none to attend, erect, or support any place of worship; or to maintain any ministry against his consent; it pretends not to control or to interfere with the rights of conscience, and it establishes no preference for any religious establishment or mode of worship. It treats no religious doctrine as paramount in the State; it enforces no unwilling attendance upon the celebration of divine worship. It says not to the Jew or Sabbatarian, 'You shall desecrate the day you esteem as holy, and keep sacred to religion that *we* deem to be so.' It enters upon no discussion of rival claims of the first and seventh days of the week, nor pretends to bind upon the conscience of any man any conclusion upon a subject which each must decide for himself. It intrudes not into the domestic circle to dictate when, where, or to what god its inmates shall address their orisons; nor does it presume to enter the synagogue of the Israelite, or the church of the seventh-day Christian, to command or even persuade their attendance in the temples of those who especially approach the altar on Sunday. It does not in the slightest degree infringe upon the Sabbath of any sect, or curtail their freedom of worship. It detracts not one hour from any period of time they may feel bound to devote to this object, nor does it add a moment beyond what they may choose to employ. Its sole mission is to inculcate a temporary weekly cessation from labor, but it adds not to this requirement any religious obligation." Specht *v.* Commonwealth, 8 Penn. St. 312.

[2] Commonwealth *v.* Wolf, 3 S. & R. 50; Commonwealth *v.* Lisher, 17 S. & R. 160; Shover *v.* State, 5 Eng. 529; Voglesong *v.* State, 9 Ind. 112; State *v.* Ambs, 20 Mo. 214; Cincinnati *v.* Rice, 15 Ohio, 225. In Simonds's Ex'rs *v.* Gratz, 2 Pen. & Watts, 416, it was held that the conscientious scruples of a Jew to appear and attend a trial of his cause on Saturday was not sufficient cause for a continuance. But *quære* of this.

fully avoid any compulsion which infringes on the religious scruples of any, however little reason may seem to other persons to underlie them. Even in the important matter of bearing arms for the public defence, those who cannot in conscience do so are excused, and their proportion of this great and sometimes necessary burden is borne by the rest of the community.[1]

Some of the State constitutions have also done away with the distinction which the common law had established in the credibility of witnesses. All religions were recognized by the law to the extent of allowing all persons to be sworn and to give their evidence, who believed in a supreme superintending Providence who rewards and punishes, and that an oath was binding upon their conscience.[2] But the want of such belief rendered the person incompetent. Wherever the common law remains unchanged, it must be held no violation of religious liberty to recognize and enforce its distinctions; but the tendency is to do away with them entirely, or to allow one's unbelief to go to his credibility only, if taken into account at all.[3]

[1] There are constitutional provisions to this effect in New Hampshire, Alabama, Texas, Illinois, Indiana, Vermont, Tennessee.

[2] See upon this point the leading case of Ormichund v. Barker, Willes, 538, and 1 Smith's Leading Cases, 535, where will be found a full discussion of this subject. Some of the earlier American cases required of a witness that he should believe in the existence of God, and of a state of rewards and punishments after the present life. See especially Atwood v. Welton, 7 Conn. 66. But this rule did not generally obtain; belief in a Supreme Being who would punish false swearing, whether in this world or the world to come, being regarded sufficient. Cubbison v. McCreary, 7 W. & S. 262; Blocker v. Burness, 2 Ala. 354; Jones v. Harris, 1 Strob. 160; Shaw v. Moore, 4 Jones, 25; Hunscom v. Hunscom, 15 Mass. 184; Brock v. Milligan, 10 Ohio, 121; Bennett v. State, 1 Swan, 411; Central R. R. Co. v. Rockafellow, 17 Ill. 541; Arnold v. Arnold, 13 Vt. 362. But one who lacked this belief was not sworn, because there was no mode known to the law by which it was supposed an oath could be made binding upon his conscience. Arnold v. Arnold, 13 Vt. 362.

[3] The States of Iowa, Minnesota, Michigan, Oregon, Wisconsin, and New York have constitutional provisions expressly doing away with incompetency from want of religious belief. Perhaps the general provisions in some of the other constitutions declaring complete equality of civil rights, privileges, and capacities are sufficiently broad to accomplish the same purpose. Perry's case, 3 Grat. 632. In Michigan, a witness is not to be questioned concerning his religious belief. People v. Jenness, 5 Mich. 305.

CHAPTER XIV.

THE POWER OF TAXATION.

THE power to impose taxes is one so unlimited in force and so searching in extent, that the courts scarcely venture to declare that it is subject to any restrictions whatever, except such as rest in the discretion of the authority which exercises it. It reaches to every trade or occupation; to every object of industry, use, or enjoyment; to every species of possession; and it imposes a burden which, in case of failure to discharge it, may be followed by seizure and sale or confiscation of property. No attribute of sovereignty is more pervading, and at no point does the power of the government affect more constantly and intimately all the relations of life than through this power.

Taxes are defined to be burdens or charges imposed by the legislative power upon persons or property, to raise money for public purposes.[1] The power to tax rests upon necessity, and is inherent in every sovereignty. The legislature of every free State will possess it under the general grant of legislative power, whether particularly specified in the constitution among the powers to be exercised by it or not. No constitutional government can exist without it, and no arbitrary government without regular and steady taxation could be anything but an oppressive and vexatious despotism, since the only alternative to taxation would be a forced extortion for the needs of government from such persons or objects as the men in power might select as victims. In the language of Chief Justice Marshall: " The power of taxing the people and their property is essential to the very existence of government, and may be legitimately exercised on the objects to which it is applicable to the utmost extent to which the government may choose to carry it. The only security against the abuse of this power is found in the structure of the government itself. In imposing a

---

[1] Blackwell on Tax Titles, 1. A tax is a contribution imposed by government on individuals for the service of the State. It is distinguished from a subsidy as being certain and orderly, which is shown in its derivation from Greek, τάξις, *ordo*, order or arrangement. Jacob, Law Dic.; Bouvier, Law Dic.

tax, the legislature acts upon its constituents. This is, in general, a sufficient security against erroneous and oppressive taxation. The people of a State, therefore, give to their government a right of taxing themselves and their property ; and as the exigencies of the government cannot be limited, they prescribe no limits to the exercise of this right, resting confidently on the interest of the legislator, and on the influence of the constituents over their representative, to guard them against its abuse." [1]

And the same high authority has said in another case : " The power of legislation, and consequently of taxation, operates on all persons and property belonging to the body politic. This is an original principle, which has its foundation in society itself. It is granted by all for the benefit of all. It resides in the government as part of itself, and need not be reserved where property of any description, or the right to use it in any manner, is granted to individuals or corporate bodies. However absolute the right of any individual may be, it is still in the nature of that right that it must bear a portion of the public burdens, and that portion must be determined by the legislature. This vital power may be abused ; but the interest, wisdom, and justice of the representative body, and its relations with its constituents, furnish the only security against unjust and excessive taxation, as well as against unwise taxation." [2] And again, the same judge says it is " unfit for the judicial department to inquire what degree of taxation is the legitimate use, and what degree may amount to the abuse, of the power." [3] And the same general views have been frequently expressed in other cases. [4]

And it is upon the ground that the power of taxation is so unlimited, so far as those objects are concerned which are subjected to it, that the national courts have held that all the agencies of the general government were, by necessary implication, excepted from the taxing power of the States. Otherwise the States might impose taxation to an extent that might cripple, if not wholly defeat,

---

[1] McCulloch v. Maryland, 4 Wheat. 428.

[2] Providence Bank v. Billings, 4 Pet. 561.

[3] McCulloch v. Maryland, 4 Wheat. 430.

[4] Kirby v. Shaw, 19 Penn. St. 260; Sharpless v. Mayor, &c. 21 Penn. St. 168 ; Weister v. Hade, 52 Penn. St. 478 ; Wingate v. Sluder, 6 Jones, Law, 552 ; Herrick v. Randolph, 13 Vt. 529 ; Armington v. Barnet, 15 Vt. 745 ; Thomas v. Leland, 24 Wend. 65 ; People v. Mayor, &c. of Brooklyn, 4 N. Y. 425 ; Portland Bank v. Apthorp, 12 Mass. 252.

the operations of the national authorities within their proper sphere of action. "That the power to tax," says Chief Justice Marshall, "involves the power to destroy; that the power to destroy may defeat and render useless the power to create; that there is a plain repugnance in conferring on one government a power to control the constitutional measures of another, which other, with respect to those very measures, is declared to be supreme over that which exerts the control, — are propositions not to be denied." And referring to the argument that confidence in the good faith of the State governments must forbid our indulging the anticipation of such consequences, he adds: "But all inconsistences are to be reconciled by the magic word, — confidence. Taxation, it is said, does not necessarily and unavoidably destroy. To carry it to the excess of destruction would be an abuse, to presume which would banish that confidence which is essential to all government. But is this a case of confidence? Would the people of any one State trust those of another with a power to control the most insignificant operations of their State government? We know they would not. Why then should we suppose that the people of any one State would be willing to trust those of another with a power to control the operations of a government to which they have confided their most important and most valuable interests? In the legislature of the Union alone are all represented. The legislature of the Union alone, therefore, can be trusted by the people with the power of controlling measures which concern all, in the confidence that it will not be abused. This, then, is not a case of confidence." [1]

[1] McCulloch v. Maryland, 4 Wheat. 431. The case involved the right of the State of Maryland to impose taxes upon the operations, within its limits, of the Bank of the United States, created by authority of Congress. "If," continues the Chief Justice, "we apply the principle for which the State of Maryland contends to the Constitution generally, we shall find it capable of changing totally the character of that instrument. We shall find it capable of arresting all the measures of the government, and of prostrating it at the foot of the States. The American people have declared their Constitution, and the laws made in pursuance thereof, to be supreme; but this principle would transfer the supremacy in fact to the States. If the States may tax one instrument employed by the government in the execution of its powers, they may tax any and every other instrument. They may tax the mail; they may tax the mint; they may tax patent rights; they may tax the papers of the custom-house; they may tax judicial process; they may tax all the means employed by the government to an excess which would defeat all the ends of government. This was not intended by the

If, therefore, the Congress of the Union may constitutionally create a Bank of the United States, and such bank is to be considered an agency of the national government in the accomplishment of its constitutional purposes, the power of the States to tax such bank, or its property, or the means of performing its functions, is prohibited by necessary implication.[1] In like manner a State is prohibited from taxing an officer of the general government for his office or its emoluments, since such a tax, having the effect to reduce the compensation for the services provided by the act of Congress, would to that extent conflict with such act, and tend to neutralize its purpose.[2] So the States may not impose taxes upon the obligations or evidences of debt issued by the general government upon the loans made to it, unless such taxation is permitted by law of Congress, and then only in the manner such law shall prescribe, — any such tax being an impediment to the operations of the government in negotiating loans, and in greater or less degree, in proportion to its magnitude, tending to cripple and embarrass the national power.[3] The tax upon the national securities is a tax upon the exercise of the power of Congress " to borrow money on the credit of the United States." The exercise of this power is interfered with to the extent of the tax imposed under State authority, and the liability of the certificates of stock or other securities to taxation by a State, in the hands of individuals, would necessarily affect their value in market, and therefore affect the free and unrestrained exercise of the power: " If the right to impose a tax exists, it is a right which, in its nature, acknowledges no limits. It may be carried to any extent within the jurisdiction of the State or corporation which imposes it, which the will of such State or corporation may prescribe." [4]

American people. They did not design to make their government dependent on the States."

[1] McCulloch v. Maryland, 4 Wheat. 316; Osborn v. United States Bank, 9 Wheat. 738; Dobbins v. Commissioners of Erie Co., 16 Pet. 435.

[2] Dobbins v. Commissioners of Erie Co., 16 Pet. 435.

[3] Weston v. Charleston, 2 Pet. 449; Bank of Commerce v. New York City, 2 Black, 620; Bank Tax Case, 2 Wal. 200; Van Allen v. Assessors, 3 Wal. 573; People v. Commissioners, 4 Wal. 244; Bradley v. People, Ibid. 459.

[4] Weston v. Charleston, 4 Pet. 449; Bank of Commerce v. New York City, 2 Black, 631. This principle is unquestionably sound, but a great deal of difficulty has been experienced in consequence of it, under the law of Congress establishing the National Banking System, which undertakes to subject the National Banks

If the States cannot tax the means by which the national government performs its functions, neither, on the other hand, and for the same reasons, can the latter tax the agencies of the State governments. " The same supreme power which established the departments of the general government determined that the local governments should also exist for their own purposes, and made it impossible to protect the people in their common interests without them. Each of these several agencies is confined to its own sphere, and all are strictly subordinate to the Constitution which limits them, and independent of other agencies, except as thereby made dependent. There is nothing in the Constitution [of the United States] which can be made to admit of any interference by Congress with the secure existence of any State authority within its lawful bounds. And any such interference by the indirect means of taxation, is quite as much beyond the power of the national legislature, as if the interference were direct and extreme." [1] It has therefore been held that the law of Congress requiring judicial process to be stamped could not constitutionally be applied to the process of the State courts ; since otherwise Congress might impose such restrictions upon the State courts as would put an end to their effective action, and be equivalent practically to abolishing them altogether.[2]

to State taxation, but at the same time to guard those institutions against unjust discriminations, by providing that their shares shall only be taxed at the place where the bank is located, and in the same manner as shares in the State banks are taxed. The difficulty is in harmonizing the State and national laws on the subject, and it will be illustrated in a measure by some of the cases above cited ; though the full extent of the difficulty is only perceived in other cases where the taxation of State banks is fixed by constitutional provisions, which provide modes that cannot be harmonized at all with the law of Congress.

   [1] Fifield v. Close, 15 Mich. 509.

   [2] Warren v. Paul, 22 Ind. 279 ; Jones v. Estate of Keep, 19 Wis. 369 ; Fifield v. Close, 15 Mich. 505 ; Union Bank v. Hill, 3 Cold. (Tenn.) 325. " State governments," it is said in the Indiana case, " are to exist with judicial tribunals of their own. This is manifest all the way through the Constitution. This being so, these tribunals must not be subject to be encroached upon or controlled by Congress. This would be incompatible with their free existence. It was held, when Congress created a United States Bank, and is now decided, when the United States has given bonds for borrowed money, that as Congress had rights to create such fiscal agents, and issue such bonds, it would be incompatible with the full and free enjoyment of those rights to allow that the States might tax the bank or bonds ; because, if the right to so tax them was conceded, the States might exercise the right to the destruction of Congressional power. The argu-

Strong as is the language employed to characterize the taxing power in some of the cases which have considered this subject, subsequent events have demonstrated that it was by no means extravagant. An enormous national debt has not only made

ment applies with full force to the exemption of State governments from Federal legislative interference.

"There must be some limit to the power of Congress to lay stamp taxes. Suppose a State to form a new, or to amend her existing constitution; could Congress declare that it should be void, unless stamped with a Federal stamp? Can Congress require State legislatures to stamp their bills, journals, laws, &c. in order that they shall be valid? Can it require the executive' to stamp all commissions? If so, where is he to get the money? Can Congress compel the State legislatures to appropriate it? Can Congress thus subjugate a State by legislation? We think this will scarcely be pretended. Where, then, is the line of dividing power in this particular? Could Congress require voters in State and corporation elections to stamp their tickets to render them valid? Under the old Confederation, Congress legislated upon States, not upon the citizens of the State. The most important change wrought in the government by the Constitution was that legislation operated upon the citizens directly, enforced by Federal tribunals and agencies, not upon the States. Another established constitutional principle is, that the government of the United States, while sovereign within its sphere, is still limited in jurisdiction and power to certain specified subjects. Taking these three propositions then as true, — 1. States are to exist with independent powers and institutions within their spheres; 2. The Federal government is to exist with independent powers and institutions within its sphere; 3. The Federal government operates within its sphere upon the people in their individual capacities, as citizens and subjects of that government, within its sphere of power, and upon its own officers and institutions as a part of itself, — taking these propositions as true, we say, it seems to result as necessary to harmony of operation between the Federal and State governments, that the Federal government must be limited, in its right to lay and collect stamp taxes, to the citizens and their transactions as such, or as acting in the Federal government, officially or otherwise; and cannot be laid upon and collected from individuals or their proceedings when acting, not as citizens transacting business with each other as such, but officially or in the pursuit of rights and duties in and through State official agencies and institutions. When thus acting, they are not acting under the jurisdiction nor within the power of the United States; not acting as subjects of that government, not within its sphere of power over them; and neither they nor their proceedings are subject to interference from the United States. Can Congress regulate or prescribe the taxation of costs in a State court? The Federal government may tax the Governor of a State, or the clerk of a State court, and his transactions as an individual, but not as a State officer. This must be so, or the State may be annihilated at the pleasure of the Federal government. The Federal government may perhaps take by taxation most of the property in a State, if exigencies require; but it has not a right, by direct or indirect means, to annihilate the functions of the State government."

imposts necessary which in some cases reach several hundred per cent of the original cost of the articles upon which they are imposed, but the systems of State banking which were in force when the necessity for contracting that debt first arose have been literally taxed out of existence by burdens avowedly imposed for that very purpose. If taxation is thus unlimited in extent upon the objects within its reach, it cannot be extravagant to say that the agencies of government are excepted from it, or otherwise its exercise might altogether destroy the government through the destruction of its agencies. That which was predicted as a possible event has been demonstrated by actual facts to be within the compass of the power; and if considerations of policy were important, it might be added that, if the States possessed the authority to tax the agencies of the national government, they would hold within their hands a constitutional weapon which factions and disappointed parties would be able to wield with terrible effect when the policy of the national government did not accord with their views; while, on the other hand, if the national government possessed a corresponding power over the agencies of the State governments, there would not be wanting men who, in times of strong party excitement, would be willing and eager to resort to this power as a means of coercing the States in their legislation upon the subjects remaining under their control.

There are other subjects which are or may be removed from the sphere of State taxation by force of the Constitution of the United States, or of the legislation of Congress under it. That instrument declares that "no State shall, without the consent of Congress, lay any imposts or duties on imports or exports, except what may be absolutely necessary for executing its inspection laws." Under this prohibition some difficulty has been experienced in indicating with sufficient accuracy for practical purposes the point of time at which articles brought into the country from abroad cease to be regarded as imports in the sense of constitutional protection, and become liable to State taxation; but it has been said generally, that when the importer has so acted upon the thing imported that it has become incorporated and mixed up with the mass of property in the country, it has perhaps lost its distinctive character as an import, and has become subject to the taxing power of the State; but while remaining the property of the importer, in his warehouse, in the original form or package in which it was

imported, a tax upon it is too plainly a duty on imports to escape
the prohibition in the Constitution.[1] And it was also declared in
the same case, that a State law which, for revenue purposes,
required an importer to take a license and pay fifty dollars before
he should be permitted to sell a package of imported goods, was
equivalent to laying a duty upon imports. And it has been held
in another case, that a stamp duty imposed by the legislature of
California upon bills of lading for gold or silver, transported from
that State to any port or place out of the State, was in effect a tax
upon exports, and the law was consequently void.[2]

Congress also is vested with power to regulate commerce; but
this power is not so far exclusive as to prevent regulations by the
States also, when they do not conflict with those established by
Congress.[3] The States may unquestionably tax the subjects of
commerce; and no necessary conflict with that complete control
which is vested in Congress appears until the power is so exercised
as to defeat or embarrass the congressional legislation. Where
Congress has not acted at all upon the subject, the State taxation
cannot be invalid on this ground; but when national regulations
exist, under which rights are established or privileges given, the
State can impose no burdens which shall in effect make the enjoyment of those rights and privileges contingent upon the payment
of tribute to the State.[4]

It is also believed that that provision in the Constitution of the

---

[1] Brown v. Maryland, 12 Wheat. 441, per Marshall, Ch. J.

[2] Almy v. People, 24 How. 169. See also Brumagim v. Tillinghast, 18 Cal.
265; Garrison v. Tillinghast, Ibid. 404.

[3] Cooley v. Board of Wardens, 12 How. 299. See also Wilson v. Blackbird
Creek Marsh Co., 2 Pet. 245.

[4] In Brown v. Maryland, it was held that a license fee of fifty dollars, required
by the State of an importer before he should be permitted to sell imported goods,
was unconstitutional, as coming directly in conflict with the regulations of Congress over commerce. For further discussion of this subject in the United States
courts, see New York v. Miln, 11 Pet. 102; License Cases, 5 How. 504. See
also Lin Sing v. Washburn, 20 Cal. 534; Erie Railway Co. v. New Jersey, 4
Am. Law Reg. N. S. 238, reversing same case in 1 Vroom; Pennsylvania R. R.
Co. v. Commonwealth, 3 Grant, 128; and the full discussion of the subject in the
two opinions in Wolcott v. People, 17 Mich. In the recent case of Crandall v.
Nevada, to appear in 6 Wallace, and which is reported in 2 Western Jurist, 89,
it was held that a State law imposing a tax of one dollar on each person leaving
the State by public conveyance was not void as coming in conflict with the
control of Congress over commerce.

United States, which declares that " the citizens of each State
shall be entitled to all the privileges and immunities of the citizens
of the several States,"[1] will preclude any State from imposing
upon the property within its limits belonging to citizens of other
States any higher burdens by way of taxation than are imposed
upon the like property of its own citizens. This is the express
decision of the Supreme Court of Alabama,[2] following in this
particular the *dictum* of an eminent Federal judge at an early
day.[3]

Having thus indicated the extent of the taxing power, it is
necessary to add that certain elements are essential in all taxation,
and that it will not necessarily follow because the power is so vast,
that everything which may be done under pretence of its exercise will leave the citizen without redress, notwithstanding there
be no conflict with constitutional provisions. Everything that may
be done under the name of taxation is not necessarily a tax ; and
it may happen that an oppressive burden imposed by the government, when it comes to be carefully scrutinized, will prove, instead
of a tax, to be an unlawful confiscation of property, unwarranted
by any principle of constitutional government.

In the first place, taxation having for its only legitimate object
the raising of money for public purposes and the proper needs
of government, the exaction of moneys from the citizens for
other purposes is not a proper exercise of this power, and
must therefore be unauthorized. In this, however, we do not
use the word *public* in any narrow and restricted sense, nor do
we mean to be understood that whenever the legislature shall
overstep the legitimate bounds of their authority, the courts can
interfere to arrest their action. There are many cases of unconstitutional action by the representatives of the people which can
be reached only through the ballot-box ; and there are other
cases where the line of distinction between that which is allowable
and that which is not is so faint and shadowy that the decision of
the legislature must be accepted as final, even though the judicial
opinion might be different. But there are still other cases where

---

[1] Art. 4, § 2.

[2] Wiley *v.* Parmer, 14 Ala. 627.

[3] Washington J. in Corfield *v.* Coryell, 4 Wash. C. C. 380. And see Camp
bell *v.* Morris, 3 H. & McH. 554 ; Ward *v.* Morris, 4 H. & McH. 340 ; and other
cases cited, ante, p. 16, note. See also Oliver *v.* Washington Mills, 11 Allen, 268.

it is entirely possible for the legislature so clearly to exceed the bounds of due authority that we cannot doubt the right of the courts to interfere to check what can only be looked upon as ruthless extortion, provided the nature of the case is such that judicial process can afford relief. An unlimited power to make any and everything lawful which the legislature might see fit to call taxation, would be, when plainly stated, an unlimited power to plunder the citizen.[1]

It must always be conceded that the proper authority to determine what should and what should not properly constitute a public burden is the legislative department of the State. This is not only true for the State at large, but it is true also in respect to each municipality or political division of the State; these inferior corporate existences having only such authority in this regard as the legislature shall confer upon them. And in determining this question, the legislature cannot be held to any narrow or technical rule. Certain expenditures are not only absolutely necessary to the continued existence of the government, but as a matter of policy it may sometimes be proper and wise to assume other burdens which rest entirely on considerations of honor, gratitude, or charity. The officers of government must be paid, the laws printed, roads constructed, and public buildings erected; but with a view to the general well-being of society, it may also be important that the children of the State should be educated, the poor kept from starvation, losses in the public service indemnified, and incentives held out to faithful and fearless discharge of duty in the future, by the payment of pensions to those who have been faithful public servants in the past. There will therefore be necessary expenditures, and expenditures which rest upon considerations of policy alone; and in regard to the one as much as to the other, the decision of that department to which alone questions of State policy are addressed must be accepted as conclusive.

Very strong language has been used by the courts, in some of the cases on this subject. In a case where was questioned the

---

[1] Tyson v. School Directors, 51 Penn. St. 9; Morford v. Unger, 8 Iowa, 92. "It is the clear right of every citizen to insist that no unlawful or unauthorized exaction shall be made upon him under the guise of taxation. If any such illegal encroachment is attempted, he can always invoke the aid of the judicial tribunals for his protection, and prevent his money or other property from being taken and appropriated for a purpose and in a manner not authorized by the Constitution and laws." Per Bigelow, Ch. J., in Freeland v. Hastings, 10 Allen, 575.

validity of the State law confirming township action which granted gratuities to persons enlisting in the military service of the United States, the Supreme Court of Connecticut assigned the following reasons in its favor : —

" In the first place, if it be conceded that it is not competent for the legislative power to make a gift of the common property, or of a sum of money to be raised by taxation, where no possible public benefit, direct or indirect, can be derived therefrom, such exercise of the legislative power must be of an extraordinary character to justify the interference of the judiciary ; and this is not that case.

" Second. If there be the least possibility that making the gift will be promotive in any degree of the public welfare, it becomes a question of policy, and not of natural justice, and the determination of the legislature is conclusive. And such is this case. Such gifts to unfortunate classes of society, as the indigent blind, the deaf and dumb, or insane, or grants to particular colleges or schools, or grants of pensions, swords, or other mementoes for past services, involving the general good indirectly and in slight degree, are frequently made and never questioned.

" Third. The government of the United States was constituted by the people of the State, although acting in concert with the people of the other States, and the general good of the people of this State is involved in the maintenance of that general government. In many conceivable ways the action of the town might not only mitigate the burdens imposed upon a class, but render the service of that class more efficient to the general government, and therefore it must be presumed that the legislature found that the public good would be thereby promoted.

" And fourth. It is obviously possible, and therefore to be intended, that the General Assembly found a clear equity to justify their action." [1]

And the Supreme Court of Wisconsin has said : " To justify the court in arresting the proceedings and in declaring the tax void, the absence of all possible public interest in the purposes for which the funds are raised must be clear and palpable ; so clear and palpable as to be perceptible by every mind at the first blush. . . . . It is not denied that claims founded in equity and justice, in the

---

[1] Booth *v.* Woodbury, 32 Conn. 128.　See to the same effect Speer *v.* School Directors of Blairville, 50 Penn. St. 150.

largest sense of those terms, or in gratitude or charity, will support a tax. Such is the language of the authorities." [1]

But we think it clear in the words of the Supreme Court of Wisconsin, that " the legislature cannot . . . . in the form of a tax take the money of the citizen and give to an individual, the public interest or welfare being in no way connected with the transaction. The objects for which money is raised by taxation must be public, and such as subserve the common interest and well-being of the community required to contribute." [2] Or, as stated by the Supreme Court of Pennsylvania, " the legislature has no constitutional right to . . . . levy a tax, or to authorize any municipal corporation to do it, in order to raise funds for a mere private purpose. No such authority passed to the assembly by the general grant of the legislative power. This would not be legislation. Taxation is a mode of raising revenue for public purposes. When it is prostituted to objects in no way connected with the public interest or welfare, it ceases to be taxation and becomes plunder. Transferring money from the owners of it into the possession of those who have no title to it, though it be done under the name and form of a tax, is unconstitutional for all the reasons which forbid the legislature to usurp any other power not granted to them." [3] And by the same court, in a still later case, where the question was whether the legislature could lawfully require a municipality to refund to a bounty association the sums which they had advanced to relieve themselves from an impending military conscription ; " such an enactment would not be legislation at all. It would be in the nature of judicial action, it is true, but wanting the justice of notice to parties to be affected by the hearing, trial, and all that gives sanction and force to regular judicial proceedings ; it would much more resemble an imperial rescript than constitutional legislation: first, in declaring an obligation where none was created or previously existed ; and next, in decreeing payment, by directing the money or property of the people to be sequestered to make the payment. The legislature can exercise no such despotic functions." [4]

---

[1] Brodhead v. City of Milwaukee, 19 Wis. 652.

[2] Per Dixon, Ch. J., in Brodhead v. Milwaukee, 19 Wis. 652. See also Lumsden v. Cross, 10 Wis. 282.

[3] Per Black, Ch. J., in Sharpless v. Mayor, &c., 21 Penn. St. 168.

[4] Tyson v. School Directors of Halifax, 51 Penn. St. 9. The decisions in Miller v. Grandy, 13 Mich. 540, Crowell v. Hopkinton, 45 N. H. 9, and Shack-

The Supreme Court of Michigan has proceeded upon the same
principle in a recent case. The State is forbidden by the consti-

ford v. Newington, 46 N. H. 415, so far as they hold that a bounty law is not to
be held to cover moneys before advanced by an individual without any pledge of
the public credit, must be held referable, we think, to the same principle. We are
aware that there are some cases the doctrine of which seems opposed to those we
have cited, but perhaps a careful examination will enable us to harmonize them
all.   One of these is Guilford v. Supervisors of Chenango, 18 Barb. 615, and 13
N. Y. 143.   The facts in that case were as follows: Cornell and Clark were formerly commissioners of highways of the town of Guilford, and as such, by direction of the voters of the town, had sued the Butternut & Oxford Turnpike Road
Company.   They were unsuccessful in the action, and were, after a long litigation, obliged to pay costs.   The town then refused to reimburse them these costs.
Cornell and Clark sued the town, and, after prosecuting the action to the court of
last resort, ascertained that they had no legal remedy.   They then applied to the
legislature, and procured an act authorizing the question of payment or not by
the town to be submitted to the voters at the succeeding town meeting.   The
voters decided that they would not tax themselves for any such purpose.   Another
application was then made to the legislature, which resulted in a law authorizing
the county judge of Chenango County to appoint three commissioners, whose duty
it should be to hear and determine the amount of costs and expenses incurred by
Cornell and Clark in the prosecution and defence of the suits mentioned.   It
authorized the commissioners to make an award, which was to be filed with the
county clerk, and the board of supervisors were then required, at their next
annual meeting, to apportion the amount of the award upon the taxable property
of the town of Guilford, and provide for its collection in the same manner as
other taxes are collected.   The validity of this act was affirmed.   It was regarded as one of those of which Denio, J., says "the statute book is full, perhaps
too full, of laws awarding damages and compensation of various kinds to be paid
by the public to individuals, who had failed to obtain what they considered equitably
due to them by the decision of administrative officers acting under the provisions
of former laws.   The courts have no power to supervise or review the doings of
the legislature in such cases."   It is apparent that there was a strong equitable
claim upon the township in this case for the reimbursement of moneys expended
by public officers under the direction of their constituents, and perhaps no principle of constitutional law was violated by the legislature thus changing it into a
legal demand, and compelling its satisfaction.   Mr. Sedgwick criticises this act,
and says of it that it "may be called taxation, but in truth it is the reversal of a
judicial decision."   Sedg. on Stat. & Const. Law, 414.   There are very many
claims, however, resting in equity, which the courts would be compelled to reject,
but which it would be very proper for the legislature to recognize, and provide
for by taxation.   Brewster v. City of Syracuse, 19 N. Y. 116.   Another case,
perhaps still stronger than that of Guilford v. The Supervisors, is Thomas v.
Leland, 24 Wend. 65.   Persons at Utica had given bond to pay the extraordinary
expense that would be caused to the State by changing the junction of the
Chenango Canal from Whitesborough to Utica, and the legislature afterwards
passed an act requiring the amount to be levied by a tax on the real property of

tution to engage in works of public improvement, except in the expenditure of grants or other property made to it for this purpose. The State, with this prohibition in force, entered into a contract. with a private party for the construction by such party of an improvement in the Muskegon River, for which the State was to pay

the city of Utica. The theory of this act may be stated thus : The canal was a public way. The expense of constructing all public ways may be properly charged on the community specially or peculiarly benefited by it. The city of Utica was specially and peculiarly benefited by having the canal terminate there ; and as the expense of construction was thereby increased, it was proper and equitable that the property to be benefited should pay this difference, instead of the State at large. The act was sustained by the courts, and it was well remarked that the fact that a bond had been before given securing the same money could not detract from its validity. See on this point, Shaw v. Dennis, 5 Gilm. 416. Whether this case is reconcilable with some others, and especially with that of Hampshire v. Franklin, 16 Mass. 83, we have elsewhere expressed a doubt; but as an exercise of the power of taxation, it does not conflict with the principles stated in the text. Nevertheless, for the legislature in any case to compel a municipality to assume a burden, on the ground of local benefit or local obligation, against the will of the citizens, is the exercise of an arbitrary power little in harmony with the general features of our republican system, and only to be justified in extreme cases. The general idea of our tax system is, that those shall vote the burdens who are to pay them ; and it would be intolerable that a central authority should have power, not only to tax localities for local purposes of a public character which they did not approve, but also, if it so pleased, to compel them to assume and discharge private claims not equitably chargeable upon them. The cases of Cheaney v. Hooser, 9 B. Monr. 330 ; Sharp's Ex. v. Dunavan, 17 B. Mont. 223 ; Mathus v. Shields, 2 Met. (Ky.) 553, will throw some light on this general subject. The case of Cypress Pond Draining Co. v. Hooper, 2 Met. (Ky.) 350, is also instructive. The Cypress Pond Draining Company was incorporated to drain and keep drained the lands within a specified boundary, at the cost of the owners, and was authorized by the act to collect a tax on each acre, not exceeding twenty-five cents per acre, for that purpose, for ten years, to be collected by the sheriff. With the money thus collected the board of managers, six in number, named in the act, was required to drain certain creeks and ponds within said boundary. The members of the board owned in the aggregate 3,840 acres, the larger portion of which was low land, subject to inundation, and of little or no value in its then condition, but which would be rendered very valuable by the contemplated draining. The corporate boundary contained 14,621 acres, owned by sixty-eight persons. Thirty-four of these, owning 5,975 acres, had no agency in the passage of the act, and no notice of the application therefor, gave no assent to its provisions, and a very small portion of their land, if any, would be benefited or improved in value by the proposed draining ; and they resisted the collection of the tax. As to these owners the act of incorporation was held unconstitutional and inoperative. See also The City of Covington v. Southgate, 15 B. Monr. 491.

the contractor fifty thousand dollars, from the Internal Improvement Fund. The improvement was made, but the State officers declined to draw warrants for the amount, on the ground that the fund from which payment was to have been made was exhausted. The State then passed an act for the levying of tolls upon the property passing through the improvement sufficient to pay the contract price within five years. The court held this act void. As the State had no power to construct or pay for such a work from its general fund, and could not constitutionally have agreed to pay the contractors from tolls, there was no theory on which the act could be supported, except it was that the State had misappropriated the Internal Improvement Fund, and therefore ought to provide payment from some other source. But if the State had misappropriated the fund, the burden of reimbursement would fall upon the State at large ; it could not lawfully be imposed upon a single town or district, or upon the commerce of a single town or district. The burden must be borne by those upon whom it justly rests ; and to recognize in the State a power to compel some single district to assume and discharge a State debt would be to recognize its power to make an obnoxious district or an obnoxious class bear the whole burden of the State government. An act to that effect would not be taxation, nor would it be the exercise of any legitimate legislative authority.[1] And it may be said of such an act, that, so far as it would operate to make those who would pay the tolls pay more than their proportion of the State obligation, it

---

[1] Ryerson v. Utley, 16 Mich. 269. " Uniformity in taxation implies equality in the burden of taxation." Bank v. Hines, 3 Ohio, N. S. 15. " This equality in the burden constitutes the very substance designed to be secured by the rule." Weeks v. City of Milwaukee, 10 Wis. 258. " There can be no doubt that, as a general rule, where an expenditure is to be made for a public object, the execution of which will be substantially beneficial to every portion of the Commonwealth alike, and in the benefits and advantages of which all the people will equally participate, if the money is to be raised by taxation, the assessment would be deemed to come within that class which was laid to defray one of the general charges of government, and ought therefore to be imposed as nearly as possible with equality upon all persons resident and estates lying within the Commonwealth. . . . . An assessment for such a purpose, if laid in any other manner, could not in any just or proper sense be regarded as ' proportional ' within the meaning of the constitution." Merrick v. Inhabitants of Amherst, 12 Allen, 504, per Bigelow, Ch. J. Taxation not levied according to the principles upon which the right to tax is based, is an unlawful appropriation of private property to public uses. City of Covington v. Southgate, 15 B. Mon. 498.

was in effect taking their property for the private benefit of other citizens of the State, and was obnoxious to all the objections against the appropriation of private property for private purposes which could exist in any other case.

And the Supreme Court of Iowa has said: "'If there be such a flagrant and palpable departure from equity in the burden imposed; if it be imposed for the benefit of others, or for purposes in which those objecting have no interest, and are therefore not bound to contribute, it is no matter in what form the power is exercised, — whether in the unequal levy of a tax, or in the regulation of the boundaries of the local government, which results in subjecting the party unjustly to local taxes, — it must be regarded as coming within the prohibition of the constitution designed to protect private rights against oppression however made, and whether under color of recognized power or not." [1]

When, therefore, the legislature directs the levy of a tax for a purpose not public, and which cannot properly be made a public burden on any of the grounds above indicated, or which if public cannot properly be made to rest on the district taxed, we must conclude that they are exercising an authority not conferred in the general grant of legislative power, and which is therefore unconstitutional. " The power of taxation," says an eminent writer, " is a great governmental attribute, with which the courts have very wisely, as we shall hereafter see, shown extreme unwillingness to interfere; but if abused, the abuse should share the fate of all other usurpations." [2] In the case of burdens thus assumed by the legislature on behalf of the State, it must be very rare indeed that a remedy can be afforded in the courts. It would certainly be a very dangerous assumption of power for a court to attempt to stay the collection of State taxes because an illegal demand was included in the levy; and indeed, as State taxes are not usually levied for the purpose of satisfying specific demands, but a gross sum is raised which it is calculated will be sufficient for the wants of the year, the question is not one usually of the unconstitutionality of taxation, but of the misappropriation of moneys which have been raised by taxation. But when the State orders a city, township, or village to raise money by taxation for a specified purpose, and that purpose is one in no degree tending to the public benefit, and

[1] Morford v. Unger, 8 Iowa, 92.
[2] Sedgwick on Const. & Stat. Law, 414.

this fact is plain and palpable, the usurpation is also in the same degree plain and palpable, and a court of competent jurisdiction could not feel at liberty to decline to enforce the paramount law.

In the second place, it is of the very essence of taxation that it be equal and uniform ; and to this end, that there should be some system of apportionment. Where the burden is common, there should be common contribution to discharge it.[1] Taxation is the equivalent for the protection which the government affords to the persons and property of its citizens ; and as all are alike protected, so all alike should bear the burden, in proportion to the interests secured. Taxes by the poll are justly regarded as odious, and are seldom resorted to for the collection of revenue ; and when levied upon property there must be an apportionment with reference to a uniform standard, or they degenerate into mere arbitrary exactions. In this particular the State constitutions have been very specific, but in providing for equality and uniformity they have done little more than to state in concise language a principle of constitutional law which is inherent in the power to tax.

Taxes may assume the form of duties, imposts, and excises ; and those collected by the national government are very largely of this character. They may also assume the form of license fees, for permission to carry on particular occupations, or to enjoy special franchises. They may be specific ; such as are often levied upon corporations, in reference to the amount of capital stock, or to the business done, or profits earned by them. Or they may be direct, upon property, in proportion to its value, or upon some other basis of apportionment, which the legislature shall regard as just, and which shall keep in view the general idea of uniformity. The taxes collected by the States are mostly of the latter class, and it is to them that the constitutional principles we shall have occasion to discuss will apply.

As to all taxation apportioned upon property, tnere must be taxing districts, and within these districts the rule of absolute uniformity must apply. A State tax is to be apportioned through the State, a county tax through the county, a city tax through the city ; while in the case of local improvements, benefiting in a peculiar manner some portion of the State or of a county or city, it is competent to arrange a special taxing district, within which the expense shall be apportioned. School districts and road districts are

---

[1] 2 Kent, 231 ; Sanborn *v.* Rice, 9 Minn. 273.

also taxing districts for the peculiar purposes for which they exist, and villages may have special powers of taxation distinct from the townships of which they form a part. Whenever it is made a requirement of the State constitution that taxation shall be upon property according to value, such a requirement implies an assessment of valuation by public officers at such regular periods as shall be provided by law, and a taxation upon the basis of such assessment until the period arrives for making it anew. Thus, the constitutions of Maine and Massachusetts require that there should be a valuation of estates within the Commonwealth to be made at least every ten years ; [1] the constitution of Michigan requires the annual assessments which are made by township officers to be equalized by a State board, which reviews them for that purpose every five years; [2] and the constitution of Rhode Island requires the legislature " from time to time " to provide for new valuations of property for the assessment of taxes in such manner as they may deem best. [3] Some other constitutions contain no provisions upon this subject ; but the necessity for valuation is necessarily implied, though the mode of making it, and the periods at which it shall be made, are left to the legislative discretion.

There are some kinds of taxes, however, that are not usually assessed according to the value of property, and some which could not be thus assessed. And there is probably no State which does not levy other taxes than those which are imposed upon property. Every burden which the State imposes upon its citizens with a view to a revenue, either for itself or for any of the municipal governments, or for the support of the governmental machinery in any of the political divisions, is imposed under the power of taxation, whether imposed under the name of tax, or under some other designation. The license fees which are sometimes required to be paid by those who follow particular employments are, when imposed for purposes of revenue, taxes ; the tolls upon the persons or property making use of the works of public improvement owned and controlled by the State, are a species of tax ; stamp duties when imposed are taxes, and it is very customary to require that corporations shall pay a certain sum annually, in proportion to their

---

[1] Constitution of Maine, art. 9, § 7; Constitution of Mass. Part. 2, ch. 1, § 1, art. 4.

[2] Constitution of Mich. art. 14, § 13.

[3] Constitution of Rhode Island, art. 4, § 15.

capital stock, or by some other standard, and which is the mode regarded by the State as more convenient and suitable for the taxation of such organizations. It would therefore seem that the constitutional requirements, that taxation upon property shall be according to value, do not include every species of taxation ; but all cases like those we have referred to are, by implication, excepted.

But in addition to these cases, there are others where taxes are levied directly upon property, which are nevertheless held not to be within the constitutional provisions. Assessments for the opening, making, improving, or repairing of streets, the draining of swamps, and the like local works, have been generally made upon property, with some reference to the supposed benefits which the property would receive therefrom. Instead, therefore, of making the assessment include all the property of the municipal organization in which the improvement is made, a new and special taxing district is created, whose bounds are confined to the limits within which property receives a special and peculiar benefit, in consequence of the improvement. Even within this district the assessment is sometimes made by some other standard than that of value ; and it is evident that if the taxing district is created with reference to special benefit, it would be equally just and proper to make the taxation within the district have reference to the benefit the property receives, rather than its relative value. The opening or paving a street may increase the value of all property upon or near it ; and it may be just that all such property should contribute to the expense of the improvement: but there is very little proportion between the previous value of such property and the benefit which it will receive. A lot upon the street may be greatly increased in value, another at a little distance may be but slightly benefited ; and if no constitutional provision interferes, it would seem just and proper that the tax levied within the taxing district should have reference, not to value, but to benefit.

Taxation upon this basis, however, has been met by this objection ; that it was appropriating private property for public use without providing compensation, and was therefore in violation of those constitutional principles which declare the inviolability of private property. But those principles have no reference to the taking of property under the right of taxation. When the constitution provides that private property shall not be taken for public use without just compensation made therefor, it has reference to

32

an appropriation thereof under the right of eminent domain. Taxation and eminent domain indeed rest substantially on the same foundation, as each implies the taking of private property for the public use on compensation made ; but the compensation is different in the two cases. When taxation takes money for the public use, the tax-payer receives, or is supposed to receive, his just compensation in the protection which government affords to his life, liberty; and property, and in the increase in the value of his possessions by the use to which the government applies the money raised by the tax.[1]

But if these special local levies are *taxation*, do they come under the general provisions on the subject of taxation to be found in our State constitutions ? The constitution of Michigan provides that " the legislature shall provide an uniform rule of taxation, except on property paying specific taxes ; and taxes shall be levied upon such property as shall be prescribed by law " ;[2] and again : " All assessments hereafter authorized shall be on property at its cash value." [3] The first of these provisions has been regarded as confiding to the discretion of the legislature the establishment of the rule of uniformity by which taxation was to be imposed ; and the second as having reference to the annual valuation of property for the purposes of taxation, which it is customary to make in that State, and not to the actual levy of a tax. And a local tax, therefore, levied in the city of Detroit, to meet the expense of paving a public street, and which was levied, not in proportion to the value of property, but according to an arbitrary scale of supposed benefit, was held not invalid under the constitutional provision.[4]

So the constitution of Illinois provides that " the General Assembly shall provide for levying a tax by valuation, so that every person and corporation shall pay a tax in proportion to the value of his or her property ; such value to be ascertained by some person or persons to be elected or appointed in such manner as the General Assembly shall direct, and not otherwise," [5] &c. The charter of the city of Peoria provided that, when a public street

---

[1] People v. Mayor, &c. of Brooklyn, 4 N. Y. 422; Williams v. Mayor, &c. of Detroit, 2 Mich. 565; Scovills v. Cleveland, 1 Ohio, N. S. 126; Northern Indiana R. R. Co. v. Connelly, 10 Ohio, N. S. 165.

[2] Art. 14, § 11.   [3] Art. 14, § 12.

[4] Williams v. Mayor, &c. of Detroit, 2 Mich. 560. And see Woodbridge v. Detroit, 8 Mich. 274.

[5] Art. 9, § 2.

was opened or improved, commissioners should be appointed by the county court to assess upon the property benefited the expense of the improvement in proportion to the benefit. These provisions were held to be constitutional, on the ground that assessments of this character were not such taxation as was contemplated by the general terms which the constitution employed.[1] And a similar view of these local assessments has been taken in other cases.[2]

But whatever may be the basis of the taxation, the requirement that it shall be uniform is universal. It applies as much to these local assessments as to any other species of taxes. The difference is only in the character of the uniformity, and in the basis on which it is established. But to render taxation uniform in any case, two things are essential. The first of these is that each taxing district should confine itself to the objects of taxation within its limits. Otherwise there is or may be duplicate taxation, and of course inequality. Assessments upon real estate not lying within the taxing districts would be void,[3] and assessments for personal property

[1] City of Peoria v. Kidder, 26 Ill. 357.

[2] People v. Mayor, &c. of Brooklyn, 4 N. Y. 419 ; Matter of Mayor, &c. of New York, 11 Johns. 77 ; Sharp v. Spier, 4 Hill, 76 ; Livingston v. Mayor, &c. of New York, 8 Wend. 85 ; Matter of Furman St., 17 Wend. 649 ; Nichols v. Bridgeport, 23 Conn. 189 ; Schenley v. City of Alleghany, 25 Penn. St. 128 ; McBride v. Chicago, 22 Ill. 574 ; City of Peoria v. Kidder, 26 Ill. 351 ; City of Lexington v. McQuillan's Heirs, 9 Dana, 513 ; Hines v. Leavenworth, 3 Kansas, 186 ; St. Joseph v. O'Donoghue, 31 Mo. 345 ; Egyptian Levee Co. v. Hardin, 27 Mo. 495 ; Burnet v. Sacramento, 12 Cal. 76 ; Yeatman v. Crandell, 11 La. An. 220 ; Wallace v. Shelton, 14 La. An. 498 ; Hill v. Higdon, 5 Ohio, N. S. 243 ; Marion v. Epler, Ibid. 250 ; Reeves v. Treasurer of Wood Co., 8 Ohio, N. S. 333 ; Northern Ind. R. R. Co. v. Connelly, 10 Ohio, N. S. 159; Maloy v. Marietta, 11 Ohio, N. S. 636 ; State v. Dean, 3 Zab. 335 ; State v. Mayor, &c. of Jersey City, 4 Zab. 662 ; Bond v. Kenosha, 17 Wis. 289 ; City of Fairfield v. Ratcliff, 20 Iowa, 396 ; Municipality No. 2 v. White, 9 La. An. 447 ; Cumming v. Police Jury, Ibid. 503 ; Northern Liberties v. St. John's Church, 13 Penn. St. 107. The cases of Weeks v. Milwaukee, 10 Wis. 242, and Lumsden v. Cross, Ibid. 282, recognize the fact that these local burdens are generally imposed under the name of *assessments* instead of *taxes*, and that therefore they are not covered by the general provisions in the constitution of the State on the subject of taxation. An exemption of church property from taxation will not preclude its being assessed for improving streets in front of it. Le Fever v. Detroit, 2 Mich. 586 ; Lockwood v. St. Louis, 24 Mo. 20.

[3] But sometimes, when a parcel of real estate lies partly in two districts, authority is given by law to assess the whole in one of these districts, and the whole parcel may then be considered as having been embraced within the district where taxed, by an enlargement of the district bounds to include it. Saunders v. Springstein, 4 Wend. 429.

made against persons not residing in the district would also be
void, unless made with reference to the actual presence of the
property in such district.[1]

In Wells v. City of Weston,[2] the Supreme Court of Missouri
deny the right of the legislature to subject property located in one
taxing district to taxation in another, upon the express ground
that it is in substance the arbitrary taxation of the property of one
class of citizens for the benefit of another class. The case was
one where the legislature sought to subject real estate lying outside the limits of a city to taxation for city purposes, on the theory
that it received some benefit from the city government, and ought
to contribute to its support. In Kentucky[3] and Iowa[4] decisions
have been made which, while affirming the same principle as the
case above cited, go still further, and declare that it is not competent for the legislature to increase the limits of a city, in order to
include therein farming lands, occupied by the owner for agricultural purposes, and not required for either streets or houses, or
other purposes of a town, and solely for the purpose of increasing
the city revenue by taxation. The courts admit that the extension of the limits of a city or town, so as to include its actual
enlargement, as manifested by houses and population, is to be
deemed a legitimate exercise of the taxing power, but they declare
that an indefinite or unreasonable extension, so as to embrace
lands or farms at a distance from the local government, does not
rest upon the same authority. And although it may be a delicate
as well as a difficult duty for the judiciary to interpose, the court
had no doubt but strictly there are limits beyond which the legislative discretion cannot go. " It is not every case of injustice or
oppression which may be reached; and it is not every case which
will authorize a judicial tribunal to inquire into the minute operation of laws imposing taxes, or defining the boundaries of local
jurisdictions. The extension of the limits of the local authority
may in some cases be greater than is necessary to include the adjacent population, or territory laid out into city lots, without a

---

[1] People v. Supervisors of Chenango, 11 N. Y. 563; Mygatt v. Washburn, 15
N. Y. 316; Brown v. Smith, 24 Barb. 419; Hartland v. Church, 47 Me. 169;
Lessee of Hughey v. Horrell, 2 Ohio, 231.

[2] 22 Mo. 385.

[3] City of Covington v. Southgate, 15 B. Monr. 491.

[4] Morford v. Unger, 8 Iowa, 82.

case being presented in which the courts would be called upon to apply a nice and exact scrutiny as to its practical operation. It must be a case of flagrant injustice and palpable wrong, amounting to the taking of private property without such compensation in return as the tax-payer is at liberty to consider a fair equivalent for the tax." This decision has been subsequently recognized and followed as authority, in the last-named State.[1]

The second essential is that the apportionment of taxes should reach all the objects of taxation within the district. Of the correctness of this as a principle, there can be little doubt, though there may sometimes be difficulty in determining whether in practice it has been applied or not.

" With the single exception of specific taxes," says Christiancy, J., in Woodbridge v. Detroit,[2] " the terms ' tax ' and ' assessment ' both, I think, when applied to property, and especially to lands, always include the idea of some ratio or rule of apportionment, so that of the whole sum to be raised, the part paid by one piece of property shall bear some known relation to, or be affected by, that paid by another. Thus, if one hundred dollars are to be raised from tracts A, B, and C, the amount paid by A will reduce by so much that to be paid by B and C, and so of the others. In the case of specific taxes, as well as duties and imposts, though the amount paid by one is not affected by that paid by another, yet there is a known and fixed relation of one to the other, a uniform rate by which it is imposed upon the whole species or class of property or persons to which the specific tax applies; and this is so of duties and imposts, whether specific or *ad valorem*. To compel individuals to contribute money or property to the use of the public, without reference to any common ratio, and without requiring the sum

---

[1] Langworthy v. Dubuque, 13 Iowa, 86 ; Fulton v. Davenport, 17 Iowa, 404 ; Buell v. Ball, 20 Iowa, 282. These cases, however, do not hold the legislative act which enlarges the city limits to be absolutely void, but only hold that they will limit the exercise of the taxing power as nearly as practicable to the line where the extension of the boundaries ceases to be beneficial to the proprietor in a municipal point of view. For this purpose they enter into an inquiry of fact, whether the lands in question, in view of their relative position to the growing and improved parts of the town, and partaking more or less of the benefits of municipal government, are proper subjects of municipal taxation ; and if not, they enjoin the collection of such taxes. It would seem as if there must be great practical difficulties — if not some of principle — in making this disposition of such a case.

[2] 8 Mich. 301.

paid by one piece or kind of property or by one person to bear any relation whatever to that paid by another is, it seems to me, to lay a forced contribution, not a tax, duty, or impost, within the sense of these terms as applied to the exercise of powers by any enlightened or responsible government."

In the case of Knowlton v. Supervisors of Rock County,[1] an important and interesting question arose, involving the very point now under discussion. The constitution of Wisconsin provides that " the rule of taxation shall be uniform," which, if we are correct in what we have already stated, is no more than an affirmance of a settled principle of constitutional law. The city of Janesville included within its territorial limits, not only the land embraced within the recorded plat of the village of Janesville and its additions, but also a large quantity of the adjacent farming or agricultural lands. Conceiving the owners of these lands, too greatly and unequally burdened by taxation for the support of the city government, the legislature passed an act declaring that " in no case shall the real and personal property within the territorial limits of said city, and not included within the territorial limits of the recorded plat of the village of Janesville, or of any additions to said village, which may be used, occupied, or reserved for agricultural or horticultural purposes, be subject to an annual tax to defray the current expenses of said city exceeding one half of one per cent, nor for the repair and building of roads and bridges, and the support of the poor, more than one half as much on each dollar's valuation shall be levied for such purposes as on the property within such recorded plats, nor shall the same be subject to any tax for any of the purposes mentioned in § 3 of ch. 5 of [the city charter], nor shall the said farming or gardening lands be subject to any tax other than before mentioned for any city purpose whatever." Under the charter the property of the city was liable to an annual tax of one per cent to defray the current expenses of the city ; and also an additional tax of such sum as the common council might deem necessary for the repair and building of roads and bridges, and for the support of the poor. Thus it will be perceived that the legislature, within the same taxing district, undertook to provide that a portion of the property should be taxed at one rate in proportion to value, and another portion at a much lower rate ; while from taxation for certain proper local purposes the latter class was exempted altogether.

[1] 9 Wis. 410.

" It was contended in argument," say the court, " that as those provisions fixed one uniform rate without the recorded plats, and another within them, thus taxing all the property without alike, and all within alike, they do not infringe the Constitution. In other words, that for the purpose of taxation, the legislature have the right arbitrarily to divide up and classify the property of the citizens, and, having done so, they do not violate the constitutional rule of uniformity, provided all the property within a given class is rated alike.

" The answer to this argument is, that it creates different *rules* of taxation to the number of which there is no limit, except that fixed by legislative discretion, while the constitution establishes but one fixed, unbending, uniform rule on the subject. It is believed that if the legislature can by classification thus arbitrarily and without regard to value discriminate in the same municipal corporation between personal and real property within, and personal and real property without, a recorded plat, they can also by the same means discriminate between lands used for one purpose and those used for another, such as lands used for growing wheat and those used for growing corn, or any other crop ; meadow-lands and pasture-lands, cultivated and uncultivated lands ; or they can classify by the description, such as odd-numbered lots and blocks and even-numbered ones, or odd and even numbered sections. Personal property can be classified by its character, use, or description, or. as in the present case, by its location, and thus the rules of taxation may be multiplied to an extent equal in number to the different kinds, uses, descriptions, and locations of real and personal property. We do not see why the system may not be carried further, and the classification be made by the character, trade, profession, or business of the owners. For certainly this rule of uniformity can as well be applied to such a classification as any other, and thus the constitutional provision be saved intact. Such a construction would make the constitution operative only to the extent of prohibiting the legislature from discriminating in favor of particular individuals, and would reduce the people, while considering so grave and important a proposition, to the ridiculous attitude of saying to the legislature, ' You shall not discriminate between single individuals or corporations ; but you may divide the citizens up into different classes, as the followers of different trades, professions, or kinds of business, or as the owners of

different species or descriptions of property, and legislate for one
class, and against another, as much as you please, provided you
serve all of the favored or unfavored classes alike ' : thus affording
a direct and solemn sanction to a system of taxation so manifestly
and grossly unjust that it will not find an apologist anywhere, at
least outside of those who are the recipients of its favor. We do
not believe the framers of that instrument intended such a construction, and therefore cannot adopt it." [1]

The principle to be deduced from the Iowa and Wisconsin cases,
assuming that they do not in any degree conflict, seems to be this :
The legislature cannot arbitrarily include within the limits of a
village, borough, or city, property and persons not properly chargeable with its burdens, and for the sole purpose of increasing the
corporate revenues by the exaction of the taxes. But whenever
the corporate boundaries are established, it is to be understood
that whatever property is included within those limits has been
thus included by the legislature, because it justly belongs there as
being within the circuit which is benefited by the local government, and which ought consequently to contribute to its burdens.
The legislature cannot, therefore, after having already, by including the property within the corporation, declared its opinion that
such property should contribute to the local government, immediately turn about and establish a basis of taxation which assumes
that the property is not in fact urban property at all, but is agricultural lands, and should be assessed accordingly. The rule of
apportionment must be uniform throughout the taxing district,
applicable to all alike; but the legislature have no power to arrange
the taxing districts arbitrarily, and without reference to the great
fundamental principle of taxation, that the burden must be borne
by those upon whom it justly rests. The Kentucky and Iowa decisions hold that, in a case where they have manifestly and unmis-
takably done so, the courts may interfere and restrain the imposition of municipal burdens on property which does not properly
belong within the municipal taxing district at all.

[1] Per Dixon, Ch. J., 9 Wisconsin, 421. Besides the other cases referred to,
see, on this same general subject, Lin Sing v. Washburn, 20 Cal. 534 ; State v. Merchants' Ins. Co., 12 La. An. 802 ; Adams v. Somerville, 2 Head, 363 ; McComb v.
Bell, 2 Minn. 295 ; Attorney-General v. Winnebago Lake & Fox River P. R.
Co., 11 Wis. 35 ; Weeks v. Milwaukee, 10 Wis. 242 ; O'Kane v. Treat, 25 Ill.
557 ; Philadelphia Association, &c. v. Wood, 39 Penn. 73 ; Sacramento v. Crocker,
16 Cal. 119.

This rule of uniformity has perhaps been found most difficult of application in regard to those cases of taxation which are commonly known under the head of assessments, and which are made either for local improvement and repair, or to prevent local causes resulting in the destruction of health or property. In those cases where it has been held that those assessments were not covered by the constitutional provision that taxation should be laid upon property in proportion to value, it has nevertheless been decided that the authority to make them must be referred to the taxing power, and not to the police power of the State, under which sidewalks have been ordered to be constructed. Apportionment of the burden was therefore essential, though it need not be made upon property in proportion to its value. But the question then arises: What shall be the rule of apportionment? Can a street be ordered graded and paved, and the expense assessed exclusively upon the property which, in the opinion of the assessors, shall be peculiarly benefited thereby in proportion to such benefit? Or may a taxing district be created for the purpose, and the expense assessed in proportion to the area of the lots? Or may the street be made a taxing district, and the cost levied in proportion to the frontage? Or may each lot owner be required to grade and pave in front of his lot? These are grave questions, and they have not been found of easy solution.

The case of the People v. The Mayor, &c. of Brooklyn[1] is a leading case, holding that a statute authorizing a municipal corporation to grade and improve streets, and to assess the expense among the owners and occupants of lands benefited by the improvement, in proportion to the amount of such benefit, is a constitutional and valid law. The court in that case concede that taxation cannot be laid without apportionment, but hold that the basis of apportionment in these cases is left by the constitution with the legislature. The application of any one rule or principle of apportionment to all cases would be manifestly oppressive and unjust. Taxation is sometimes regulated by one principle and sometimes by another; and very often it has been apportioned without reference to locality, or to the tax-payer's ability to contribute, or to any proportion between the burden and the benefit. " The excise laws, and taxes on carriages and watches, are among the many examples of

---

[1] 4 N. Y. 419 ; overruling same case, 6 Barb. 209.

this description of taxation. Some taxes affect classes of inhabitants only. All duties on imported goods are taxes on the class of consumers. The tax on one imported article falls on a large class of consumers, while the tax on another affects comparatively a few individuals. The duty on one article consumed by one class of inhabitants is twenty per cent of its value, while on another, consumed by a different class, it is forty per cent. The duty on one foreign commodity is laid for the purpose of revenue mainly, without reference to the ability of its consumers to pay, as in the case of the duty on salt. The duty on another is laid for the purpose of encouraging domestic manufacture of the same article, thus compelling the consumer to pay a higher price to one man than he could otherwise have bought the article for from another. These discriminations may be impolitic, and in some cases unjust; but if the power of taxation upon importations had not been transferred by the people of this State to the Federal government, there could have been no pretence for declaring them to be unconstitutional in State legislation.

"A property tax for the general purposes of the government, either of the State at large or of a county, city, or other district, is regarded as a just and equitable tax. The reason is obvious. It apportions the burden according to the benefit more nearly than any other inflexible rule of general taxation. A rich man derives more benefit from taxation, in the protection and improvement of his property, than a poor man, and ought therefore to pay more. But the amount of each man's benefit in general taxation cannot be ascertained and estimated with any degree of certainty; and for that reason a property tax is adopted, instead of an estimate of benefits. In local taxation, however, for special purposes, the local benefits may in many cases be seen, traced, and estimated to a reasonable certainty. At least this has been supposed and assumed to be true by the legislature, whose duty it is to prescribe the rules on which taxation is to be apportioned, and whose determination of this matter, being within the scope of its lawful power, is conclusive."

The reasoning of this case has been generally accepted as satisfactory, and followed in subsequent cases.[1]

---

[1] Scoville v. Cleveland, 1 Ohio, N. S. 126; Hill v. Higdon, 5 Ohio, N. S. 243; Marion v. Epler, Ibid. 250; Maloy v. Marietta, 11 Ohio, N. S. 636; City of Peoria v. Kidder, 26 Ill. 351; Reeves v. Treasurer of Wood Co., 8 Ohio, N. S.

On the other hand, and on the same reasoning, it has been held equally competent to make the street a taxing district, and assess the expense of the improvement upon the lots in proportion to the frontage.[1] Here also is apportionment by a rule which approximates to what is just, but which, like any other rule that can be applied, is only an approximation to absolute equality. But if, in the opinion of the legislature, it is the proper rule to apply to any particular case, the courts must enforce it.

333 ; Garrett v. St. Louis, 25 Mo. 505. The legislation in Ohio on the subject has authorized the cities and villages, in opening and improving streets, to assess the expense either upon the lots abutting on the street in proportion to the street front, or upon the lands in proportion to their assessed value. In a case where the former mode was resorted to, and an assessment made upon property owned by the Northern Indiana Railroad Company for its corporate purposes, Peck, J. thus states and answers an objection to the validity of the tax : " But it is said that assessments, as distinguished from general taxation, rest solely upon the idea of *equivalents;* a compensation proportioned to the special benefits derived from the improvement, and that, in the case at bar, the railroad company is not, and in the nature of things cannot be, in any degree benefited by the improvement. It is quite true that the right to impose such special taxes is based upon a presumed equivalent; but it by no means follows that there must be in fact such full equivalent in every instance, or that its absence will render the assessment invalid. The rule of apportionment, whether by the front foot or a percentage upon the assessed valuation, must be *uniform,* affecting all the owners and all the property abutting on the street alike. One rule cannot be applied to one owner, and a different rule to another owner. One could not be assessed ten per cent, another five, another three, and another left altogether unassessed because he was not in fact benefited. It is manifest that the actual benefits resulting from the improvement may be as various almost as the number of the owners and the uses to which the property may be applied. No general rule, therefore, could be laid down which would do equal and exact justice to all. The legislature have not attempted so vain a thing, but have prescribed two different modes in which the assessment may be made, and left the city authorities free to adopt either. The mode adopted by the council becomes the statutory equivalent for the benefits conferred, although in fact the burden imposed may greatly preponderate. In such case, if no fraud intervene, and the assessment does not substantially exhaust the owner's interest in the land, his remedy would seem to be to procure, by a timely appeal to the city authorities, a reduction of the special assessment, and its imposition, in whole or in part, upon the public at large." 10 Ohio, N. S. 165.

[1] Williams v. Detroit, 2 Mich. 560 ; Northern Ind. R. R. Co. v. Connelly, 10 Ohio, N. S. 159 ; Lumsden v. Cross, 10 Wis. 282. And see St. Joseph v. O'Donoghue, 31 Mo. 145 ; Burnet v. Sacramento, 12 Cal. 76 ; Scoville v. Cleveland, 1 Ohio, N. S. 133 ; Hill v. Higdon, 5 Ohio, N. S. 246 ; Ernst v. Kunkle, Ibid. 520 ; Hines v. Leavenworth, 3 Kansas, 186.

But a very different case is presented when the legislature undertakes to provide that each lot upon a street shall pay the whole expense of grading and paving the street along its front. For while in such a case there would be something having the outward appearance of apportionment, it requires but slight examination to discover that it is a deceptive semblance only, and that the measure of equality which the constitution requires is entirely wanting. If every lot owner is compelled to construct the street in front of his lot, his tax is neither increased nor diminished by the assessment upon his neighbors; nothing is divided or apportioned between him and them; and each particular lot is in fact arbitrarily made a taxing district, and charged with the whole expenditure therein, and thus apportionment avoided. If the tax were for grading the street simply, those lots which were already at the established grade would escape altogether, while those on either side, which chanced to be above and below, must bear the whole burden, though no more benefited by the improvement than the others.[1] It is evident, therefore, that a law for making assessments on this basis could not have in view such distribution of burdens in proportion to benefits as ought to be a cardinal idea in every tax law. It would be nakedly an arbitrary command of the law to each lot owner to construct the street in front of his lot at his own expense, according to a prescribed standard; and a power to issue such command could never be exercised by a constitutional government, unless we are at liberty to treat it as a police regulation, and place the duty to make the streets upon the same footing as that to keep the sidewalks free from obstruction and fit for passage. But any such idea is clearly inadmissible.[2]

[1] In fact, lots above and below an established grade are usually less benefited by the grading than the others; because the improvement subjects them to new burdens, in order to bring the general surface to the grade of the street, which the others escape.

[2] See City of Lexington v. McQuillan's Heirs, 9 Dana, 513, and opinions of Campbell and Christiancy, JJ. in Woodbridge v. Detroit, 8 Mich. 274. The case of Weeks v. Milwaukee, 10 Wis. 258, seems to be contra. We quote from the opinion of the court by Paine, J. After stating the rule that uniformity in taxation implies equality in the burden, he proceeds: " The principle upon which these assessments rests is clearly destructive of this equality. It requires every lot owner to build whatever improvements the public may require on the street in front of his lot, without reference to inequalities in the value of the lots, in the expense of constructing the improvements, or to the question whether the lot is injured or benefited by their construction. Corner lots are required to construct

In many other cases, besides the construction, improvement, and repair of streets, may special taxing districts be created, with a

and keep in repair three times as much as other lots; and yet it is well known that the difference in value bears no proportion to this difference in burden. In front of one lot the expense of building the street may exceed the value of the lot; and its construction may impose on the owner additional expense, to render his lot accessible. In front of another lot, of even much greater value, the expense is comparatively slight. These inequalities are obvious; and I have always thought the principle of such assessments was radically wrong. They have been very extensively discussed, and sustained upon the ground that the lot should pay because it receives the benefit. But if this be true, that the improvements in front of a lot are made for the benefit of the lot only, then the right of the public to tax the owner at all for that purpose fails; because the public has no right to tax the citizen to make him build improvements for his own benefit merely. It must be for a public purpose; and it being once established that the construction of streets is a public purpose that will justify taxation, I think it follows, if the matter is to be settled on principle, that the taxation should be equal and uniform, and that to make it so the whole taxable property of the political division in which the improvement is made should be taxed by a uniform rule for the purpose of its construction.

" But in sustaining these assessments when private property was wanted for a street, it has been said that the State could take it, because the use of a street was a public use; in order to justify a resort to the power of taxation, it is said the building of a street is a public purpose. But then, having got the land to build it on, and the power to tax by holding it a public purpose, they immediately abandon that idea, and say that it is a private benefit, and make the owner of the lot build the whole of it. I think this is the same in principle as it would be to say that the town, in which the county seat is located, should build the county buildings, or that the county where the capital is should construct the public edifices of the State, upon the ground that, by being located nearer, they derived a greater benefit than others. If the question, therefore, was, whether the system of assessment could be sustained upon principle, I should have no hesitation in deciding it in the negative. I fully agree with the reasoning of the Supreme Court of Louisiana in the case of Municipality No. 2 v. White, 9 La. An. 447, upon this point.

" But the question is not whether this system is established upon sound principles, but whether the legislature has power, under the constitution, to establish such a system. As already stated, if the provision requiring the rule of taxation to be uniform was the only one bearing upon the question, I should answer this also in the negative. But there is another provision which seems to me so important that it has changed the result to which I should otherwise have arrived. That provision is § 3 of art. 11, and is as follows: ' It shall be the duty of the legislature, and they are hereby empowered, to provide for the organization of cities and incorporated villages, and to restrict their power of taxation, *assessment*, borrowing money, contracting debts, and loaning their credit, so as to prevent abuses in assessments and taxation, and in contracting debts by such municipal corporations.'

view to local improvements.   The cases of drains to relieve swamps, marshes, and other low lands of their stagnant water, and of levees to prevent lands being overflowed by rivers, will at once suggest themselves.   In providing for such cases, however, the legislature exercises another power besides the power of taxation.   On the theory that the drainage is for the purpose of benefiting the land, it would be difficult to defend such legislation.   But if the stagnant water causes sickness, it may be a nuisance, which, under its power of police, the State would have authority to abate.   The laws for this purpose, so far as they have fallen under our observation, have proceeded upon this theory.   Nevertheless, when the State incurs

" It cannot well be denied that if the word 'assessment,' as used in this section, had reference to this established system of special taxation for municipal improvements, that then it is a clear recognition of the existence and legality of the power."   And the court, having reached the conclusion that the word *did* have reference to such an established system, sustain the assessment, adding : " The same effect was given to the same clause in the constitution of Ohio, by the Supreme Court of that State, in a recent decision in the case of Hill *v.* Higdon, 5 Ohio, N. S. 243.   And the reasoning of Chief Justice Ranney on the question I think it impossible to answer."

If the State of Wisconsin had any settled and known practice, designated as assessments, under which each lot owner was compelled to construct the streets in front of his lot, then the constitution as quoted may well be held to recognize such practice.   In this view, however, it is still difficult to discover any " restriction " in a law which perpetuates the arbitrary and unjust custom, and which still permits the whole expense of making the street in front of each lot to be imposed upon it.   The only restriction which the law imposes is, that its terms exclude uniformity, equality, and justice, which surely could not be the restriction the constitution designed.   Certainly the learned judge shows very clearly that such a law is unwarranted as a legitimate exercise of the taxing power ; and as it cannot be warranted under any other power known to constitutional government, the authority to adopt it should not be found in doubtful words.   The case of Hill *v.* Higdon, referred to, is different.   There the expense of improving the street was assessed upon the property abutting on the street, in proportion to the foot front.   The decision there was, that the constitutional provision that "laws shall be passed taxing by a uniform rule all moneys, &c., and also all real and personal property, according to its true value in money," had no reference to these local assessments, which might still. be made, as they were before the constitution was adopted, with reference to the benefits conferred.   The case, therefore, showed a rule of apportionment which was made applicable throughout the taxing district, to wit, along the street so far as the improvement extended. The case of State *v.* City of Portage, 12 Wis. 562, holds that a law authorizing the expense of an improvement to be assessed upon the abutting lots, in proportion to their front or size, would not justify and sustain city action which required the owner of each lot to bear the expense of the improvement in front of it.

expense in the exercise of its police power for this purpose, it is proper to assess that expense upon the portion of the community specially and peculiarly benefited. The assessment is usually made with reference to the benefit to property ; and it is difficult to frame or to conceive of any other rule of apportionment that would operate so justly and so equally in these cases. There may be difficulty in the detail ; difficulty in securing just and impartial assessments ; but the principle of such a law would not depend for its soundness upon such considerations.[1]

---

[1] See Reeves *v.* Treasurer of Wood Co., 8 Ohio, N. S. 333 ; French *v.* Kirkland, 1 Paige, 117 ; Philips *v.* Wickham, Ibid. 590. In Woodruff *v.* Fisher, 17 Barb. 224, Hand, J., speaking of one of these drainage laws, says : " If the object to be accomplished by this statute may be considered a public improvement, the power of taxation seems to have been sustained upon analogous principles. [Citing People *v.* Mayor, &c. of Brooklyn, 4 N. Y. 419 ; Thomas *v.* Leland, 24 Wend. 65 ; and Livingston *v.* Mayor, &c. of New York, 8 Wend. 101.] But if the object was merely to improve the property of individuals, I think the statute would be void, although it provided for compensation. The water privileges on Indian River cannot be taken or affected in any way solely for the private advantage of others, however numerous the beneficiaries. Several statutes have been passed for draining swamps, but it seems to me that the principle above advanced rests upon natural and constitutional law. The professed object of this statute is to promote public health. And one question that arises is, whether the owners of large tracts of land in a state of nature can be taxed to pay the expense of draining them, by destroying the dams, &c., of other persons away from the drowned lands, and for the purposes of public health. This law proposes to destroy the water power of certain persons against their will, to drain the lands of others, also, for all that appears, against their will ; and all at the expense of the latter, for this public good. If this taxation is illegal, no mode of compensation is provided, and all is illegal." " The owners of these lands could not be convicted of maintaining a public nuisance because they did not drain them ; even though they were the owners of the lands upon which the obstructions are situated. It does not appear by the act or the complaint that the sickness to be prevented prevails among inhabitants on the wet lands, nor whether these lands will be benefited or injured by draining ; and certainly, unless they will be benefited, it would seem to be partial legislation to tax a certain tract of land, for the expense of doing to it what did not improve it, merely because, in a state of nature, it may be productive of sickness. Street assessments are put upon the ground that the land assessed is improved, and its value greatly enhanced." The remarks of Green, J., in Williams *v.* Mayor, &c. of Detroit, 2 Mich. 567, may be here quoted : " Every species of taxation, in every mode, is in theory and principle based upon an idea of compensation, benefit, or advantage to the person or property taxed, either directly or indirectly. If the tax is levied for the support of the government and general police of the State, for the education and moral instruction of the citizens, or the con-

In certain classes of cases, it has been customary to call upon the citizen to appear in person and perform service for the State, in the nature of police duties. The burden of improving and repairing the common highways of the country, except in the urban districts, is generally laid upon the people in the form of an assessment of labor. The assessment may be upon each citizen, in proportion to his property; or, in addition to the property assessment, there may be one also by the poll. But though the public burden assumes the form of labor, it is still taxation, and must, therefore, be levied on some principle of uniformity. But it is a peculiar species of taxation; and the general terms " tax," or " taxation," as employed in the State constitutions, would not generally be understood to include it. It has been decided that the clause in the constitution of Illinois, that " the mode of levying a tax shall be by valuation, so that every person shall pay a tax in proportion to the value of the property he or she has in his or her possession," did not prevent the levy of poll-taxes in highway labor. " The framers of the constitution intended to direct a uniform mode of taxation on property, and not to prohibit any other species of taxation, but to leave the legislature the power to impose such other taxes as would be consonant to public justice, and as the circumstances of the country might require. They probably intended to prevent the imposition of an arbitrary tax on property, according to kind and quantity, and without reference to value. The inequality of the mode of taxation was the object to be avoided. We cannot believe that they intended that all the public burdens should be borne by those having property in possession, wholly exempting the rest of the community, who, by the

struction of works of internal improvement, he is supposed to receive a just compensation in the security which the government affords to his person and property, the means of enjoying his possessions, and their enhanced capacity to contribute to his comfort and gratification, which constitute their value."

It has been held incompetent, however, for a city which has itself created a nuisance on the property of a citizen, to tax him for the expense of removing or abating it. Weeks v. Milwaukee, 10 Wis. 258.

In Egyptian Levee Co. v. Hardin, 27 Mo. 495, it was held that a special assessment for the purpose of reclaiming a district from inundation might properly be laid upon land in proportion to its area, and that the constitutional provision that taxation should be levied on property in proportion to its valuation did not preclude this mode of assessment. The same ruling was made in Louisiana cases. Crowley v. Copley, 2 La. An. 329; Yeatman v. Crandall, 11 La. An. 220; Wallace v. Shelton, 14 La. An. 498; Bishop v. Marks, 15 La. An. 147.

same constitution were made secure in the exercise of the rights of suffrage, and all the immunities of the citizen." [1]   And in another case, where an assessment of highway labor is compared with one upon adjacent property for widening a street, and which had been held not to be taxation in the constitutional sense of that word, it is said : " An assessment of labor for the repair of roads and streets is less like a tax than is such an assessment. The former is not based upon, nor has it any reference to, property or values owned by the person of whom it is required, whilst the latter is based alone upon the property designated by the law imposing it.   Nor is an assessment a capitation tax, as that is a sum of money levied upon each poll. This rate, on the contrary, is a requisition for so many days' labor, which may be commuted in money. No doubt, the number of days levied, and the sum which may be received by commutation, must be uniform within the limits of the district or body imposing the same. This requisition for labor to repair roads is not a tax, and hence this exemption is not repugnant to the constitution." [2]

It will be apparent from what has already been said, that it is not essential to the validity of taxation that it be levied according to rules of abstract justice. It is only essential that the legislature keep within its proper sphere of action, and not impose burdens under the name of taxation which are not taxes in fact ; and its decision must be final and conclusive. Absolute equality and strict justice are unattainable in tax proceedings. The legislature must be left to decide for itself how nearly it is possible to approximate so desirable a result.   It must happen under any tax law that some property will be taxed twice, while other property will escape taxation altogether. Instances will also occur where persons will be taxed as owners of property which has ceased to exist. The system in vogue for taking valuations of property fixes upon a certain time for that purpose, and a party becomes liable to be taxed upon what he possesses at the time the valuing officer calls upon him. Yet changes of property from person to person are occurring while the valuation is going on, and the same parcel of property is found by the assessor in the hands of two different persons, and is twice assessed, while another parcel for similar reasons is not assessed at all. Then the man who owns property when the assessment is

[1] Sawyer v. City of Alton, 3 Scam. 130.
[2] Town of Pleasant v. Kost, 29 Ill. 494.

taken may have been deprived of it by accident or other misfortune before the tax becomes payable; but the tax is nevertheless a charge against him. And when the valuation is only made once in a series of years, the occasional hardships and inequalities .in consequence of relative changes in the value of property from various causes become sometimes very glaring. Nevertheless, no question of constitutional law is involved in these cases, and the legislative control is complete.[1]

The legislature must also, except when an unbending rule has been prescribed for it by the constitution, have power to select in its discretion the subjects of taxation. The rule of uniformity requires an apportionment among all the subjects of taxation within the districts; but it does not require that everything which the legislature might make taxable shall be made so in fact. Many exemptions are usually made from taxation from reasons the cogency of which is at once apparent. The agencies of the national government, we have seen, are not taxable by the States; and the agencies and property of States, counties, cities, boroughs, towns, and villages are also exempted by law, because, if any portion of the public expenses was imposed upon them, it must in some form be collected from the citizens before it can be paid. No beneficial object could therefore be accomplished by any such assessment. The property of educational and religious institutions is also generally exempted from taxation by law upon very similar considerations, and from a prevailing belief that it is the policy and the interest of the State to encourage them. If the State

---

[1] In Shaw v. Dennis, 5 Gilm. 418, objection was taken to an assessment made for a local improvement under a special statute, that the commissioners, in determining who should be liable to pay the tax, and the amount each should pay, were to be governed by the last assessment of taxable property in the county. It was insisted that this was an unjust criterion, for a man might have disposed of all the taxable property assessed to him in the last assessment before this 'tax was actually declared by the commissioners. The court, however, regarded the objection as more refined than practical, and one that, if allowed, would at once annihilate the power of taxation. "In the imposition of taxes exact and critical justice and equality are absolutely unattainable. If we attempt it, we might have to divide a single year's tax upon a given article of property among a dozen different individuals who owned it at different times during the year, and then be almost as far from the desired end as when we started. The proposition is Utopian. The legislature must adopt some practicable system; and there is no more danger of oppression or injustice in taking a former valuation than in relying upon one to be made subsequently."

may cause taxes to be levied from motives of charity or gratitude, so for the like reasons it may exempt the objects of charity and gratitude from taxation. Property is sometimes released from taxation by contract with the State and corporations, and specified occupations are sometimes charged with specific taxes in lieu of all taxation of their property. A broad field is here opened to legislative discretion. As matter of State policy it might also be deemed proper to make general exemption of sufficient of the tools of trade or other means of support to enable the poor man, not yet a pauper, to escape becoming a public burden. There is still ample room for apportionment after all such exemptions have been made. The constitutional requirement of equality and uniformity only extends to such objects of taxation as the legislature shall determine to be properly subject to the burden.[1] The power to determine the persons and the objects to be taxed is trusted exclusively to the legislative department;[2] but over all those the burden must be spread, or it will be unequal and unlawful as to those who are selected to make the payment.[3]

In some of the States it has been decided that the particular

---

[1] State v. North, 27 Mo. 464 ; People v. Colman, 3 Cal. 46.

[2] Wilson v. Mayor, &c. of New York, 4 E. D. Smith, 675; Hill v. Higdon, 5 Ohio N. S. 245. Notwithstanding a requirement that " the rule of taxation shall be uniform," the legislature may levy specific State taxes on corporations, and exempt them from municipal taxation. So held on the ground of *stare decisis.* Kneeland v. Milwaukee, 15 Wis. 454.

[3] In the case of Weeks v. Milwaukee, 10 Wis. 242, a somewhat peculiar exemption was made. It appears that several lots in the city upon which a new hotel was being constructed, of the value of from $150,000 to $200,000, were purposely omitted to be taxed, under the direction of the Common Council, "in view of the great public benefit which the construction of the hotel would be to the city." Paine, J., in delivering the opinion of the court, says: "I have no doubt this exemption originated in motives of generosity and public spirit. And perhaps the same motives should induce the tax-payers of the city to submit to the slight increase of the tax thereby imposed on each, without questioning its strict legality. But they cannot be compelled to. No man is obliged to be more generous than the law requires, but each may stand strictly upon his legal rights. That this exemption was illegal, was scarcely contested. I shall, therefore, make no effort to show that the Common Council had no authority to suspend or repeal the general law of the State, declaring what property shall be taxable and what exempt. But the important question presented is, whether, conceding it to have been entirely unauthorized, it vitiates the tax assessed upon other property. And upon this question I think the following rule is established, both by reason and authority. Omissions of this character, arising from mistakes of fact, erro-

provisions inserted in their constitutions to insure uniformity are
so worded as to forbid exemptions. Thus the constitution of Illinois provides that " the General Assembly shall provide for levying a tax by valuation, so that every person and corporation shall
pay a tax in proportion to the value of his or her property." [1]
Under this it has been held that exemption by the legislature of
persons residing in a city from a tax levied to repair roads beyond
the city limits, by township authority, — the city being embraced
within the township which, for that purpose, was the taxing district, — was void.[2] It is to be observed of these cases, however,
that they would have fallen within the general principle laid down
in Knowlton v. Supervisors of Rock Co.,[3] and the legislative acts

neous computations, or errors of judgment on the part of those to whom the execution of the taxing laws is intrusted, do not necessarily vitiate the whole tax.
But intentional disregard of those laws, in such manner as to impose illegal taxes
on those who are assessed, does. The first part of the rule is necessary to enable
taxes to be collected at all. The execution of these laws is necessarily entrusted
to men, and men are fallible, liable to frequent mistakes of fact and errors of
judgment. If such errors, on the part of those who are attempting in good faith
to perform their duties, should vitiate the whole tax, no tax could ever be collected. And, therefore, though they sometimes increase improperly the burdens
of those paying taxes, that part of the rule which holds the tax not thereby
avoided is absolutely essential to a continuance of government. But it seems to
me clear that the other part is equally essential to the just protection of the
citizen. If those executing these laws may deliberately disregard them, and
assess the whole tax upon a part only of those who are liable to pay it, and have
it still a legal tax, then the laws afford no protection, and the citizen is at the
mercy of those officers, who, by being appointed to execute the laws, would seem
to be thereby placed beyond legal control. I know of no considerations of public
policy or necessity that can justify carrying the rule to that extent. And the
fact that in this instance the disregard of the law proceeded from good motives
ought not to affect the decision of the question. It is a rule of law that is to be
established; and, if established here because the motives were good, it would
serve as a precedent where the motives were bad, and the power usurped for
purposes of oppression." P. 263 – 265. See also Henry v. Chester, 15 Vt. 460;
State v. Collector of Jersey City, 4 Zab. 108; Insurance Co. v. Yard, 17 Penn.
St. 331; Williams v. School District, 21 Pick. 75; Hersey v. Supervisors of Milwaukee, 16 Wis. 185. But it seems that an omission of property from the tax-
roll by the assessor, unintentionally, through want of judgment and lack of diligence and business habits, will not invalidate the roll. Dean v. Gleason, 16
Wis. 1.

[1] Art. 9, § 2.

[2] O'Kane v. Treat, 25 Ill. 561; Hunsaker v. Wright, 30 Ill. 146. See also
Trustees v. McConnell, 12 Ill. 138.

[3] 9 Wis. 410.

under consideration might perhaps have been declared void on general principles, irrespective of the peculiar wording of the constitution. These cases, notwithstanding, as well as others in Illinois, recognize the power in the legislature to *commute* for a tax, or to contract for its release for a consideration. The constitution of Ohio provides [1] that "laws shall be passed taxing by a uniform rule all moneys, credits, investments in bonds, stocks, joint-stock companies, or otherwise ; and also all real and personal property, according to its true value in money." Under this section it was held not competent for the legislature to provide that lands within the limits of a city should not be taxed for any city purpose, except roads, unless the same were laid off into town lots and recorded as such, or into out lots of not exceeding five acres each.[2] Upon this case we should make the same remark as upon the Illinois cases above referred to.

It is, moreover, essential to valid taxation that the taxing officers be able to show legislative authority for the burden they assume to impose in every instance. Taxes can only be voted by the people's representatives. They are in every instance a gift from the people to the government, which the latter is to expend in furnishing the people protection, security, and such facilities for enjoyment as it properly pertains to government to provide. This principle is a chief corner-stone of Anglo-Saxon liberty ; and it has operated not only as an important check on government, in preventing extravagant expenditures, as well as unjust and tyrannical action, but it has been an important guaranty of the right of private property. Property is secure from the lawless grasp of the government, if the means of existence of the government depend upon the voluntary grants of those who own the property. Our ancestors coupled their grants with demands for the redress of grievances ; but in modern times the surest protection against grievances has been found to be to vote specific taxes for the specific purposes to which the people's representatives are willing they shall be devoted ;[3] and the government must then become petitioner, if it desire money for other objects. And then these grants are only made periodically. Only a few things, such as the salaries of officers, the interest upon the public debt, the support

---

[1] Art. 12, § 2.

[2] Zanesville *v.* Auditor of Muskingum County, 5 Ohio, N. S. 589.

[3] Hoboken *v.* Phinney, 5 Dutch. 65.

of schools, and the like, are provided for by permanent laws; and not always is this done. The government is dependent from year to year on the periodical vote of supplies. And this vote will come from representatives who are newly chosen by the people, and who will be expected to reflect their views regarding the public expenditures. State taxation, therefore, is not likely to be excessive or onerous, except when the people, in times of financial ease, excitement, and inflation, have allowed the incurring of extravagant debts, the burden of which remains after the excitement has passed away.

But it is as true of the political divisions of the State as it is of the State at large, that legislative authority must be shown for every levy of taxes.[1] The power to levy taxes by these divisions comes from the State. The State confers it, and at the same time exercises a parental supervision by circumscribing it. Indeed, on general principles, the power is circumscribed by the rule that the taxation by the local authorities can only be for local purposes.[2] Neither the State nor the local body can authorize the imposition of a tax on the people of a county or town for an object in which the people of the county or town are not concerned. And by some of the State constitutions it is expressly required that the State, in creating municipal corporations, shall restrict their power of taxation over the subjects within their control. These requirements, however, impose an obligation upon the legislature which only its sense of duty can compel it to perform.[3] It is evident that if the legislature fail to enact the restrictive legislation, the courts have no power to compel such action. Whether in any case a charter of incorporation could be held void on the ground that it conferred unlimited powers of taxation, is a question that could not well arise, as a charter is probably never granted which does not impose some restrictions; and where that is the case, it must be inferred that those were all the restrictions the legislature deemed important, and that therefore the constitutional duty of the legislature has been performed.[4]

Clark v. Davenport, 14 Iowa, 494; Burlington v. Kellar, 18 Iowa, 59; Mays Cincinnati, 1 Ohio, N. S. 273.

[2] Foster v. Kenosha, 12 Wis. 616.

[3] In Hill v. Higdon, 5 Ohio, N. S. 248, Ranney, J. says of this provision: "A failure to perform this duty may be of very serious import, but lays no foundation for judicial correction." And see Maloy v. Marietta, 11 Ohio, N. S. 638.

[4] The constitution of Ohio requires the legislature to provide by general laws

When, however, it is said to be essential to valid taxation that there be legislative authority for every tax that is laid, it is not meant that the legislative department of the State must have passed upon the necessity and propriety of every particular tax;

for the organization of cities and incorporated villages, and to restrict their power of taxation, assessment, &c. The general law authorizing the expense of grading and paving streets to be assessed on the grounds bounding and abutting on the street, in proportion to the street front, was regarded as being passed in attempted fulfilment of the constitutional duty, and therefore valid. The chief restriction in the case was, that it did not authorize assessment in any other or different mode from what had been customary. Northern Indiana R. R. Co. v. Connelly, 10 Ohio, N. S. 165. The statute also provided that no improvement or repair of a street or highway, the cost of which was to be assessed upon the owners, should be directed without the concurrence of two thirds of the members elected to the municipal council, or unless two thirds of the owners to be charged should petition in writing therefor. In Maloy v. Marietta, 11 Ohio, N. S. 639, Peck, J. says: "This may be said to be a very imperfect protection; and, in some cases, will doubtless prove to be so; but it is calculated and designed, by the unanimity or the publicity it requires, to prevent any flagrant abuses of the power. Such is plainly its object; and we know of no rights conferred upon courts to interfere with the exercise of a legislative discretion which the constitution has delegated to the law-making power." And see Weeks v. Milwaukee, 10 Wis. 242. The constitution of Michigan requires the legislature, in providing for the incorporation of cities and villages, to "restrict their power of taxation," &c. The Detroit Metropolitan Police Law made it the duty of the Board of Police to prepare and submit to the city controller, on or before the first day of May in each year, an estimate in detail of the cost and expense of maintaining the police department, and the Common Council was required to raise the same by general tax. These provisions, it was claimed, were in conflict with the constitution, because no limit was fixed by them to the estimates that might be made. In People v. Mahaney, 13 Mich. 498, the court say: "Whether this provision of the constitution can be regarded as mandatory in a sense that would make all charters of municipal corporations and acts relating thereto which are wanting in this limitation invalid, we do not feel called upon to decide in this case, since it is clear that a limitation upon taxation is fixed by the act before us. The constitution has not prescribed the character of the restriction which shall be imposed, and from the nature of the case it was impossible to do more than to make it the duty of the legislature to set some bounds to a power so liable to abuse. A provision which, like the one complained of, limits the power of taxation to the actual expenses as estimated by the governing board, after first limiting the power of the board to incur expense within narrow limits, is as much a *restriction* as if it confined the power to a certain percentage upon taxable property, or to a sum proportioned to the number of inhabitants in the city. Whether the restriction fixed upon would as effectually guard the citizen against abuse as any other which might have been established was a question for the legislative department of the government, and does not concern us on this inquiry."

but those who assume to seize the property of the citizen for the satisfaction of the tax must be able to show that that particular tax is authorized, either by general or special law. The power inherent in the government to tax lies dormant until a constitutional law has been passed calling it into action, and is then vitalized only to the extent provided by the law. Those, therefore, who act under such law should be careful to keep within its limits, lest they remove from their acts the shield of its protection. While we do not propose to enter upon any attempt to point out the various cases in which a failure to obey strictly the requirements of the law will render the proceedings void, and in regard to which a diversity of decision would be met with, we think we shall be safe in saying that, in cases of this description, which propose to dispossess the citizen of his property against his will, not only will any excess of taxation beyond what the law allows render the proceedings void, but any failure to comply with such requirements of the laws as are made for the protection of the owner's interest will also render them void.

There are several cases in which taxes have been levied but slightly in excess of legislative power, in which it has been urged in defence of the proceedings that the law ought not to take notice of such unimportant matters; but an excess of jurisdiction is never unimportant. In one case in Maine the excess was eighty-seven cents only in a tax of $225.75, but it was held sufficient to render the proceedings void. We quote from Mellen, Ch. J., delivering the opinion of the court: "It is contended that the sum of eighty-seven cents is such a trifle as to fall within the range of the maxim *de minimis*, &c.; but if not, that still this small excess does not vitiate the assessment. The maxim is so vague in itself as to form a very unsafe ground of proceeding or judging; and it may be almost as difficult to apply it as a rule in pecuniary concerns as to the interest which a witness has in the event of a cause; and in such case it cannot apply. Any interest excludes him. The assessment was therefore unauthorized and void. If the line which the legislature has established be once passed, we know of no boundary to the discretion of the assessors." [1] The same view has been taken by the Supreme Court of Michigan, by which the

---

[1] Huse *v.* Merriam, 2 Greenl. 375. See Joyner *v.* School District, 3 Cush. 567; Kemper *v.* McClelland, 19 Ohio, 324; School District *v.* Merrills, 12 Conn. 437; Elwell *v.* Shaw, 1 Greenl. 335.

opinion is expressed that the maxim *de minimis lex non curat* should be applied with great caution to proceedings of this character, and that the excess could not be held unimportant and overlooked where, as in that case, each dollar of legal tax was perceptibly increased thereby.[1] Perhaps, however, a slight excess, not the result of intention, but of erroneous calculations, may be overlooked, in view of the great difficulty in making all such calculations mathematically correct, and the consequent impolicy of requiring entire freedom from all errors.[2]

Wherever a tax is invalid because of excess of authority, or because the requisites in tax proceedings which the law has provided for the protection of the tax-payer are not complied with, any sale of property based upon it will be void also. The owner is not deprived of his property by " the law of the land," if it is taken to satisfy an illegal tax. And if property is sold for the satisfaction of several taxes, any one of which is unauthorized, or for any reason illegal, the sale is altogether void.[3]

[1] Case *v.* Dean, 16 Mich. 12.

[2] This was the view taken by the Supreme Court of Wisconsin in Kelley *v.* Corson, 8 Wis. 182, where an excess of $ 8.61 in a tax of $ 6,654.57 was held not to be fatal; it appearing not to be the result of intention, and the court thinking that an accidental error no greater than this ought to be disregarded.

[3] This has been repeatedly held. Elwell *v.* Shaw, 1 Greenl. 335 ; Lacy *v.* Davis, 4 Mich. 140 ; Bangs *v.* Snow, 1 Mass. 188 ; Thurston *v.* Little, 3 Mass. 429 ; Dillingham *v.* Snow, 5 Mass. 547 ; Stetson *v.* Kempton, 13 Mass. 283 ; Libby *v.* Burnham, 15 Mass. 144 ; Hayden *v.* Foster, 13 Pick. 492 ; Torrey *v.* Millbury, 21 Pick. 70 ; Alvord *v.* Collin, 20 Pick. 418 ; Drew *v.* Davis, 10 Vt. 506 ; Doe *v.* McQuilkin, 8 Blackf. 335 ; Kemper *v.* McClelland, 19 Ohio, 324. This is upon the ground that the sale being based upon both the legal and the illegal tax, it is manifestly impossible afterwards to make the distinction, so that the act shall be partly a trespass and partly innocent. But when a party asks relief in equity before a sale against the collection of taxes a part of which are legal, he will be required first to pay that part, or at least to so distinguish them from the others that process of injunction can be so framed as to leave the legal taxes to be enforced ; and failing in this, his bill will be dismissed. Conway *v.* Waverley, 15 Mich. 257 ; Palmer *v.* Napoleon, 16 Mich. 176 ; Hersey *v.* Supervisors of Milwaukee, 16 Wis. 182 ; Bond *v.* Kenosha, 17 Wis. 288.

As to the character and extent of the irregularities which should defeat the proceedings for the collection of taxes, we could not undertake to speak here. We think the statement in the text, that a failure to comply with any such requirements of the law as are made for the protection of the owner's interest will prove fatal to a tax sale, will be found abundantly sustained by the authorities, while many of the cases go still further in making irregularities fatal. It appears to us that where the requirement of the law which has failed of observance was one which had regard simply to the due and orderly conduct of the proceedings, or to the protection of the public interest, as against the officer, so that to the taxpayer it is immaterial whether it was complied with or not, a failure to comply ought not to be recognized as a foundation for complaint by him. But those safeguards which the legislature has thrown around the estates of citizens, to protect them against unequal, unjust, and extortionate taxation, the courts are not at liberty to do away with by declaring them non-essential. To hold the requirement of the law in regard to them directory only, and not mandatory, is in effect to exercise a dispensing power over the laws. Mr. Blackwell, in his treatise on tax titles, has collected the cases on this subject industriously, and perhaps we shall be pardoned for saying also with a perceptible leaning against that species of conveyance. As illustrations how far the courts will go, in some cases, to sustain irregular taxation, where officers have acted in good faith, reference is made to Kelley v. Corson, 11 Wis. 1; Hersey v. Supervisors of Milwaukee, 16 Wis. 185. See also Mills v. Gleason, 11 Wis. 497, where the court endeavors to lay down a general rule as to the illegalities which should render a tax roll invalid.

CHAPTER XV.

THE EMINENT DOMAIN.

EVERY sovereignty has or may have buildings, lands, and other property which it holds for the use of its officers and agents in the performance of public functions, or perhaps to increase the State revenues through its improvement, its rents, issues and profits, or its sale. Such property constitutes the ordinary domain of the State. In respect to it the same rules of use, enjoyment, and alienation apply which pertain to the ownership of like property by individuals, and the State is in fact but an individual proprietor, and possesses no greater or other rights than would have pertained to the ownership of the same property by any citizen.

There are also certain rights which are of a nature to exclude altogether the idea of private ownership, and which are peculiarly devoted to the use and enjoyment of the individual citizens who compose the organized society, but the regulation and control of which are vested in the State by virtue of its sovereignty. The State, however, is not so much the owner as the governing and supervisory trustee of such rights, vested with the power and charged with the duty of so regulating, protecting, and controlling them as to secure to each citizen the privilege to make them available for his purposes, so far as may be consistent with an equal enjoyment by every other citizen of the same privileges.[1] Nevertheless, some of these rights are of such a nature that sometimes the most feasible mode of enabling every citizen to participate therein will be for the State to transfer its control, wholly or partially, to individuals, either receiving on behalf of its citizens a compensation therefor, or securing for the citizens generally a release from some burden which would have rested upon them in

---

[1] In The Company of Free Fishers, &c. v. Gann, 20 C. B., N. S. 1, it was held that the ownership of the crown in the bed of navigable waters is for the benefit of the subject, and cannot be used in any manner so as to derogate from or interfere with the right of navigation, which belongs by law to all the subjects of the realm. And that consequently the grantees of a particular portion who occupied it for a fishery could not be lawfully authorized to charge and collect anchorage dues from vessels anchoring therein.

respect to such right had the State retained the usual control in its own hands.

The rights of which we speak are considered as pertaining to the State by virtue of an authority existing in every sovereignty, and which is called *the right of eminent domain*. Some of these are complete without any action on the part of the State ; like the rights of navigation in its lakes and other navigable waters, the rights of fishery in public waters, and the right of the State to the precious metals which may be mined within its limits. Other rights only become complete and are rendered effectual through the State displacing, to a greater or less degree, the rights of private ownership and control ; either by contract with the owner, by accepting his gift, or by appropriating his property against his will by means of its superior power. Of these the common highway furnishes the most frequent example ; the public rights being acquired therein either by the grant or dedication of the owner of the land over which they run, or by a species of forcible dispossession where the public necessity demands the way, and the private owner will neither give nor sell it. All these rights rest upon a principle which in every sovereignty is essential to its existence and perpetuity, and which, so far as when called into action it excludes pre-existing private rights, is sometimes spoken of as based upon an implied reservation by the government when its citizens acquire property from it or under its protection. And as there is not often occasion to speak of the eminent domain except in connection with those cases in which the government is necessitated to appropriate property against the will of the owners, the right itself is generally defined as if it were restricted to such cases, and is said to be that superior right of property pertaining to the sovereignty by which the private property acquired by its citizens under its protection may be taken or its use controlled for the public benefit, without regard to the wishes of the owners. More accurately, it is the rightful authority which must rest in every sovereignty to control and regulate those rights of a public nature which pertain to its citizens in common, and to appropriate and control individual property for the public benefit, as the public safety, convenience, or necessity may demand.[1]

[1] " The right which belongs to the society or to the sovereign of disposing, in case of necessity, and for the public safety, of all the wealth contained in the State, is called the eminent domain.' McKinley, J., in Pollard's Lessee *v.*

When the existence of a particular power in the government is recognized upon the ground of necessity, no delegation of the legislative power by the people can be held to include authority in the legislative department to bargain away such power, or to so tie up the hands of the government as to preclude its repeated exercise, as often and under such circumstances as the needs of the government may require. To hold that it could would be to hold that the authority to make laws for the government of the State might legitimately be so exercised as to prevent the State from performing its ordinary and essential functions. A legislative undertaking to this effect would therefore be unwarranted; and that provision of the Constitution of the United States which forbids the States violating the obligation of contracts could not render that valid and effectual which was originally in excess of proper authority. Upon this subject we shall only refer in this place to what we have already said elsewhere.[1]

As under the peculiar American system the protection and regulation of private rights, privileges, and immunities in general properly pertain to the State governments, and those governments are expected to make provision for those conveniences and necessities which are usually provided for their citizens through exercise of the right of eminent domain, the right itself, it would seem, must pertain to those governments also, rather than to the government of the nation; and such has been the decision of the courts. In the new Territories, however, where the government of the United States possesses the complete sovereignty, it possesses also,

Hogan, 3 How. 223. "Notwithstanding the grant to individuals, the highest and most exact idea of property remains in the government, or in the aggregate body of the people in their sovereign capacity; and they have a right to resume the possession of the property, in the manner directed by the constitution and laws of the State, whenever the public interest requires it. This right of resumption may be exercised, not only where the safety, but also where the interest or even the expediency of the State is concerned; as where the land of the individual is wanted for a road, canal, or other public improvement." Walworth, Chancellor, in Beekman v. Saratoga & Schenectady R. R. Co., 3 Paige, 73. The right is inherent in all governments, and requires no constitutional provision to give it force. Brown v. Beatty, 34 Miss. 227; Taylor v. Porter, 4 Hill, 143. "Title to property is always held upon the implied condition that it must be surrendered to the government, either in whole or in part, when the public necessities, evidenced according to the established forms of law, demand." Hogeboom, J. in People v. Mayor, &c. of New York, 32 Barb. 112.

[1] See ante, p. 281.

as incident thereto, the right of eminent domain ; but this right passes thence to the newly formed State whenever it is admitted into the Union.[1] So far, however, as it may be necessary to appropriate lands or other property for its own purposes, as for forts, light-houses, military posts or roads, and the like, the general government may still exercise the right within the States, and for the same reasons on which the right rests in any case, namely, the absolute necessity that the means in the government for performing its functions and perpetuating its existence should not be subject to be controlled or defeated by the want of consent of private parties, or of any other authority.

What Property subject to the Right.

Every species of property which may become necessary for the public use, and which the government cannot appropriate under any other recognized right, is subject to be seized and appropriated under the right of eminent domain.[2] Lands for the public ways ; timber, stone, and gravel to make and improve the public ways ;[3] a building that stands in the way of a contemplated improvement, or which for any other reason it is necessary to take, remove, or destroy for the public good ;[4] streams of water,[5] corporate franchises,[6] and generally, it may be said, legal and equitable rights of

[1] Pollard's Lessee v. Hogan, 3 How. 212 ; Goodtitle v. Kibbee, 9 How. 471 ; Doe v. Beebe, 13 How. 25 ; United States v. The Railroad Bridge Co., 6 McLean, 517 ; Gilmer v. Lime Point, 18 Cal. 229.

[2] People v. Mayor, &c. of New York, 32 Barb. 102 ; Bailey v. Miltenberger, 31 Penn. St. 37.

[3] Wheelock v. Young, 4 Wend. 647 ; Lyon v. Jerome, 15 Wend. 569 ; Jerome v. Ross, 7 Johns. Ch. 315 ; Bliss v. Hosmer, 15 Ohio, 44 ; Watkins v. Walker Co., 18 Texas, 585. In Eldridge v. Smith, 34 Vt. 484, it was held competent for a railroad company to appropriate lands for piling the wood and lumber used on he road, and brought to it to be transported thereon.

[4] Wells v. Somerset, &c. R. R. Co., 47 Me. 345. But the destruction of a private house during a fire to prevent the spreading of a conflagration is not an appropriation under the right of eminent domain, but an exercise of the police power. Sorocco v. Geary, 3 Cal. 69. " The destruction was authorized by the law of overruling necessity ; it was the exercise of a natural right belonging to every individual, not conferred by law, but tacitly excepted from all human codes." Per Sherman, Senator, in Russell v. Mayor, &c. of New York, 2 Denio, 473. But see Hale v. Lawrence, 1 Zab. 714 ; Same v. Same, 3 Zab. 590.

[5] Gardner v. Newburg, 2 Johns. Ch. 162.

[6] Piscataqua Bridge v. New Hampshire Bridge, 7 N. H. 35 ; Crosby v. Hanover, 36 N. H. 420 ; Boston Water Power Co. v. Boston & Worcester R. R. Co., 23 Pick .

every description — save money, which it cannot be needful to take under this power, and rights of action, which can only be available when made to produce money, — are liable to be appropriated.[1]

Legislative Authority requisite.

The right to appropriate private property to public uses lies

360 ; Central Bridge Corporation v. Lowell, 4 Gray, 474 ; West River Bridge v. Dix, 6 How. 507 ; Richmond R. R. Co. v. Louisa R. R. Co., 13 How. 81, per Girer, J. ; Chesapeake & Ohio Canal Co. v. Baltimore & Ohio R. R. Co., 4 Gill. & J. 1 ; State v. Noyes, 47 Me. 189 ; Red River Bridge Co. v. Clarksville, 1 Sneed, 176 ; Armington v. Barnet, 15 Vt. 745 ; White River Turnpike Co. v. Vermont Central R. R. Co., 21 Vt. 594 ; Newcastle, &c. R. R. Co. v. Peru & Indiana R. R. Co., 3 Ind. 464 ; Springfield v. Connecticut River R. R. Co., 4 Cush. 63 ; Forward v. Hampshire, &c. Canal Co., 22 Pick. 462. "The only true rule of policy as well as of law is, that a grant for one public purpose must yield to another more urgent and important, and this can be effected without any infringement on the constitutional rights of the subject. If in such cases suitable and adequate provision is made by the legislature for the compensation of those whose property or franchise is injured or taken away, there is no violation of public faith or private right. The obligation of the contract created by the original charter is thereby recognized." Per Bigelow, J. in Central Bridge Corporation v. Lowell, 4 Gray, 482.

[1] Property of individuals cannot be appropriated by the State under this power for the mere purpose of adding to the revenues of the State. Thus it has been held in Ohio, that in appropriating the water of streams for the purposes of a canal, more could not be taken than was needed for that object, with a view to raising a revenue by selling or leasing it. "The State, notwithstanding the sovereignty of her character, can take only sufficient water from private streams for the purposes of the canal. So far the law authorizes the commissioners to invade private right as to take what may be necessary for canal navigation, and to this extent authority is conferred by the constitution, provided a compensation be paid to the owner. The principle is founded on the superior claims of a whole community over an individual citizen ; but then in those cases only where private property is wanted for *public use*, or demanded by the *public welfare*. We know of no instances in which it has or can be taken, even by State authority, for the mere purpose of raising a revenue by sale or otherwise ; and the exercise of such a power would be utterly destructive of individual right, and break down all the distinctions between *meum* and *tuum*, and annihilate them forever at the pleasure of the State." Wood, J. in Buckingham v. Smith, 10 Ohio, 296. To the same effect is Cooper v. Williams, 5 Ohio, 392.

Taking money under the right of eminent domain, when it must be compensated in money afterwards, could be nothing more nor less than a forced loan, which could only be justified as a last resort in a time of extreme peril, where neither the credit of the government nor the power of taxation could be made available. It is impossible to lay down rules for such a case, except such as the law of overruling necessity shall prescribe at the time.

dormant in the State until legislative action is adopted pointing out the occasions, the mode, conditions and agencies for its appropriation.   Private property can only be taken pursuant to law ; but a legislative act declaring the necessity is for this purpose " the law of the land," and no further adjudication or finding is essential.[1]   But here is to be kept in view that general, as well as reasonable and just rule, that whenever in pursuance of law the property of an individual is to be divested by proceedings against his will, there must be a strict compliance with all the provisions of the law which are made for his protection and benefit.   Those provisions must be regarded as in the nature of conditions precedent, which must not only be complied with before the right of the property owner is disturbed, but the party claiming authority under the adverse proceeding must affirmatively show such compliance.   For example : if by a statute prescribing the mode of exercising the right of eminent domain, the damages to be assessed in favor of the property owner for the taking of his land are to be so assessed by disinterested freeholders of the municipality, the proceedings will be ineffectual unless they show on their face that the appraisers were such freeholders and inhabitants.[2]   So if the statute only authorizes proceedings *in invitum* after an effort has been made to agree with the owner on the compensation to be made, the fact of such effort and its failure must appear.[3]   So if the statute vests the title to lands appropriated in the State or in

---

[1] " Whatever may be the theoretical foundation for the right of eminent domain, it is certain that it attaches as an incident to every sovereignty, and constitutes a condition upon which all property is holden. When the public necessity requires it, private rights to property must yield to the paramount right of the sovereign power. We have repeatedly held that the character of the work for which the property is taken, and not the means or agencies employed for its construction, determines the question of power in the exercise of this right. It requires no judicial condemnation to subject private property to public uses. Like the power to tax, it resides in the legislative department to whom the delegation is made. It may be exercised directly or indirectly by that body ; and it can only be restrained by the judiciary when its limits have been exceeded, or its authority has been abused or perverted." Kramer *v.* Cleveland & Pittsburg R. R. Co., 5 Ohio, N. S. 146.

[2] Nichols *v.* Bridgeport, 23 Conn. 189 ; Judson *v.* Bridgeport, 25 Conn. 428.

[3] Reitenbaugh *v.* Chester Valley R. R. Co., 21 Penn. St. 100. But it was held in this case that if the owner appears in proceedings taken for the assessment of damages, and contests the amount without objecting the want of any such attempt, the court must presume it to have been made.

a corporation on payment therefor being made, then it is plain
that such payment is a condition precedent which must first be
complied with.[1] So where a general railroad law authorized
routes to be surveyed by associated persons desirous of constructing roads, and if the legislature, on being petitioned for the purpose, should decide by law that a proposed road would be of sufficient utility to justify its construction, then the company, when
organized, might proceed to take land for the way, it was held that,
until the route was approved by the legislature, no authority existed
under the law to appropriate land for the purpose.[2] These cases
will perhaps, sufficiently for our present purposes, illustrate the
general rule, without particularizing further.[3]

[1] Stacy v. Vermont Central R. R. Co., 27 Vt. 44. By the section of the
statute under which the land was appropriated, it was provided that when land
or other real estate was taken by the corporation, for the use of their road, and
the parties were unable to agree upon the price of the land, the same should be
ascertained and determined by the commissioners, together with the costs and
charges accruing thereon, *and upon the payment of the same, or by depositing the
amount in a bank, as should be ordered by the commissioners, the corporation should
be deemed to be seised and possessed of the lands.* Held that, until the payment
was made, the company had no right to enter upon the land to construct the
road, or to exercise any act of ownership over it; and that a court of equity
would enjoin them from exercising any such right, or they might be prosecuted
in trespass at law. This case follows Baltimore & Susquehanna R. R. Co. v.
Nesbit, 10 How. 395, and Bloodgood v. Mohawk & Hudson R. R. Co., 18 Wend.
10, where the statutory provisions were similar. In the case in Howard it is said:
"It can hardly be questioned that without acceptance in the mode prescribed
[i. e. by payment of the damages assessed], the company were not bound; that
if they had been dissatisfied with the estimate placed on the land, or could
have procured a more eligible site for the location of their road, they would have
been at liberty, before such acceptance, wholly to renounce the inquisition. The
proprietors of the land could have no authority to coerce the company into its
adoption." Daniel, J., 10 How. 399.

[2] Gillinwater v. Mississippi, &c. R. R. Co., 13 Ill. 1. "The statute says that,
after a certain other act shall have been passed, the company may then proceed
to take private property for the use of their road; that is equivalent to saying that
that right shall not be exercised without such subsequent act. The right to take
private property for public use is one of the highest prerogatives of the sovereign
power; and here the legislature has, in language not to be mistaken, expressed
its intention to reserve that power until it could judge for itself whether the proposed road would be of sufficient public utility to justify the use of this high
prerogative. It did not intend to cast this power away, to be gathered up and
used by any who might choose to exercise it." Ibid. p. 4.

[3] See also the cases of Atlantic & Ohio R. R. Co. v. Sullivant, 5 Ohio, N. S.
277; Parsons v. Howe, 41 Me. 218; Atkinson v. Marietta & Cincinnati R. R.
Co., 15 Ohio, N. S. 21.

34

So the powers granted by such statutes are not to be extended by intendment, especially when they are being exercised by a corporation by way of appropriation of land for its corporate purposes. " There is no rule more familiar or better settled than this, that grants of corporate power, being in derogation of common right, are to be strictly construed; and this is especially the case where the power claimed is a delegation of the right of eminent domain, one of the highest powers of sovereignty pertaining to the State itself, and interfering most seriously and often vexatiously with the ordinary rights of property." [1]   It was accordingly held that where a railroad company was authorized by law to " enter upon any land to survey, lay down, and construct its road," " to locate and construct branch roads," &c., to appropriate land " for necessary side tracks," and " a right of way over adjacent lands sufficient to enable such company to construct and repair its road," and the company had located and was engaged in the construction of its permanent main road along the north side of a town, it was not authorized under this grant of power to appropriate a temporary right of way, for the term of three years, along the south side of the town, to be used as a substitute for the main track while the latter was in course of construction. [2]

The Purpose.

It is conceded, on all hands, that the purpose for which this right may be exercised must be a *public* purpose; and that the legislature has no power, in any case, to take the property of one individual and pass it over to another without reference to a public use to which it is to be applied. " The right of eminent domain does not imply a right in the sovereign power to take the property of one citizen and transfer it to another, even for a full compensation, where the public interest will be in no way promoted by such transfer." [3]   The legislature, therefore, cannot authorize

[1] Currier v. Marietta & Cincinnati R. R. Co., 11 Ohio, N. S. 231.

[2] Currier v. Marietta & Cincinnati R. R. Co., 11 Ohio, N. S. 228.   And see Gilmer v. Lime Point, 19 Cal. 47 ; Bensley v. Mountain Lake, &c. Co., 13 Cal. 306 ; Brunnig v. N. O. Canal & Banking Co., 12 La. An. 541.

[3] Beekman v. Saratoga & Schenectady R. R. Co., 3 Paige, 73 ; Hepburn's case, 3 Bland, 95 ; Sadler v. Langham, 34 Ala. 311 ; Pittsburg v. Scott, 1 Penn. St. 139 ; Matter of Albany St., 11 Wend. 149 ; Matter of John and Cherry Sts., 19 Wend. 659 ; Cooper v. Williams, 5 Ohio, 393 ; Buckingham v. Smith, 10 Ohio, 296 ; Reeves v. Treasurer of Wood Co., 8 Ohio, N. S. 333.   See this sub-

private roads to be laid across the land of unwilling parties by an exercise of this right. Such ways would be the property of those for whom they were established; and although they would not deprive the owner of his fee, they would take from him to some extent the beneficial use and enjoyment of his property. It would not be material, however, to inquire what quantum of interest would pass from him. It would be enough that some interest, some portion of his estate, no matter how small, had been taken from him without his consent.[1] Nor can it be of importance that the public will be incidentally benefited through the increased improvement of the land, or otherwise. The *public use* implies a possession, occupation, and enjoyment of the land by the public, or public agencies;[2] and there could be no protection whatever to private property, if the right of the government to seize and appropriate it could exist for any other use.

There is still room, however, for much difference of opinion as

ject considered on principle and authority by Senator Tracy in Bloodgood *v.* Mohawk & Hudson R. R. Co., 18 Wend. 55 et seq. See also Embury *v.* Conner, 3 N. Y. 511; Kramer *v.* Cleveland & Pittsburg R. R. Co., 5 Ohio, N. S. 146; Pratt *v.* Brown, 3 Wis. 603; Concord R. R. *v.* Greeley, 17 N. H. 47.

[1] Taylor *v.* Porter, 4 Hill, 142, per Bronson, J.; White *v.* White, 5 Barb. 474; Sadler *v.* Langham, 34 Ala. 311; Pittsburg *v.* Scott, 1 Penn. St. 139. A neighborhood road is only a private road, and taking land for it would not be for a public use. Dickey *v.* Tennison, 27 Mo. 373. To avoid this difficulty it is provided by the constitutions of some of the States that private roads may be laid out under proceedings corresponding to those for the establishment of highways. There are provisions to that effect in the constitutions of New York, Georgia, and Michigan. But in Harvey *v.* Thomas, 10 Watts, 65, it was held that the right might be exercised in order to the establishment of private ways from coal fields to connect them with the public improvements, there being nothing in the constitution forbidding it. See also the Pocopson Road, 16 Penn. St. 15. But this seems a very insufficent reason, and the doctrine is directly opposed to Young *v.* McKenzie, 3 Georgia, 44; Taylor *v.* Porter, 4 Hill, 146; Buffalo & N. Y. R. R. Co. *v.* Brainerd, 9 N. Y. 108; Bradley *v.* N. Y. & N. H. R. R. Co., 21 Conn. 305; Reeves *v.* Treasurer of Wood Co., 8 Ohio, N. S. 344, and many other cases: though possibly convenient access to the great coal fields of the State might be held to be so far a matter of general concern as to support an exercise of the power on the ground of the public benefit. In Eldridge *v.* Smith, 34 Vt. 484, it was held that the manufacture of railroad cars was not so legitimately and necessarily connected with the management of a railroad that the company would be authorized to appropriate lands therefor. So also of land for the erection of dwelling-houses to rent by railroad companies to their employees.

[2] Per Tracy, Senator, in Bloodgood *v.* Mohawk & Hudson R. R. Co., 18 Wend. 60.

to what is a public use. It has been said that " if the public
interest can be in any way promoted by the taking of private
property, it must rest in the wisdom of the legislature to determine whether the benefit to the public will be of sufficient importance to render it expedient for them to exercise the right of
eminent domain, and to authorize an interference with the private
rights of individuals for that purpose.[1] It is upon this principle
that the legislatures of several of the States have authorized the
condemnation of the lands of individuals for mill sites, when from
the nature of the country such mill sites could not be obtained for
the accommodation of the inhabitants without overflowing the lands
thus condemned. Upon the same principle of public benefit, not
only the agents of the government, but also individuals and corporate bodies, have been authorized to take private property for
the purpose of making public highways, turnpike roads, and canals ;
of erecting and constructing wharves and basins, of establishing
ferries ; of draining swamps and marshes ; and of bringing water
to cities and villages. In all such cases the object of the legislative grant of power is the public benefit derived from the contemplated improvement, whether such improvement is to be effected
directly by the agents of the government, or through the medium
of corporate bodies or of individual enterprise." [2]

It would not be safe, however, to apply with much liberality the
language above quoted, that " where the public interest can be in
any way promoted by the taking of private property," the taking
can be considered for a public use. It is certain that there are
many ways in which the property of individual owners can be
better employed or occupied when the general public is considered than it actually is by the owners themselves. It may be for
the public benefit that all the wild lands in the State be improved
and cultivated, all the low lands drained, all the unsightly places
beautified, all dilapidated buildings replaced by new ; because all
these things tend to give an aspect of beauty, thrift, and comfort
to the country, and thereby to invite settlement, increase the value
of lands, and gratify the public taste ; but the common law has
never sanctioned an appropriation of property based upon these
considerations alone ; and any such appropriation must therefore

---

[1] 2 Kent, Com. 340.

[2] Walworth, Chancellor, in Beekman v. Saratoga & Schenectady R. R. Co., 3
Paige, 73. And see Wilson v. Blackbird Creek Marsh Co., 2 Pet. 251.

be held to be forbidden by our constitutions. The settled practice of free governments must be our guide in determining what is a public use; and that only can be regarded as such where the government is supplying its own needs, or is furnishing facilities for its citizens in regard to those matters of public necessity, convenience, or welfare, which, on account of their peculiar character and the difficulty in making provision for them otherwise, it is both proper and usual for the government to provide.

Every government makes provision for the public ways; and for this purpose it may seize and appropriate lands. And as the wants of traffic and travel require facilities beyond those afforded by the common highway, over which every one may pass with his own vehicles, the government may establish the higher grade of highways, upon some of which its own vehicles alone shall run, while others shall be open for use by all on the payment of toll. The common highway is kept in repair by assessments of labor and money; the tolls paid turnpikes, or the fares on railways, are the equivalents to these assessments, and the latter are equally public highways with the others, when open for use to the public impartially. The government provides court-houses for the administration of justice; buildings for its seminaries of instruction;[1] aqueducts to convey pure and wholesome water into large towns;[2] it builds levees to prevent the country being overflowed by the rising streams;[3] it may cause drains to be constructed to relieve swamps and marshes of their stagnant water;[4] and other measures of public utility, in which the public at large are interested, and which require the appropriation of private property, are also within the power, where they fall within the same reasons as the cases mentioned.[5]

[1] Williams v. School District, 33 Vt. 271.

[2] Reddall v. Bryan, 14 Md. 444; Kane v. Baltimore, 15 Md. 240; Gardner v. Newburg, 2 Johns. Ch. 162.

[3] Mithoff v. Carrollton, 12 La. An. 185; Cash v. Whitworth, 13 La. An. 401; Inge v. Police Jury, 14 La. An. 117.

[4] Anderson v. Kerns Draining Co., 14 Ind. 199; Reeves v. Treasurer of Wood County, 8 Ohio, N. S. 344. See a clear statement of the general principle and its necessity in the last-mentioned case. The drains, however, which can be authorized to be cut across the land of unwilling parties, or for which individuals can be taxed, must not be mere private drains, but must have reference to the public health, convenience, or welfare. Reeves v. Treasurer, &c. supra. And see People v. Nearing, 27 N. Y. 306.

[5] Such, for instance, as the construction of a public park, which, in large cities,

Whether the power of eminent domain can rightfully be exercised in the condemnation of lands for manufacturing purposes, where the manufactories are to be owned and occupied by individuals, is a question upon which the authorities are at variance. Saw-mills, grist-mills, and other manufactories are certainly a public necessity; and while the country is new, and capital not over-abundant for such enterprises, it sometimes seems essential that government should offer large inducements to parties who will supply this necessity. Before steam power came into use, water power was almost the sole reliance; and as reservoirs were generally necessary for this purpose, it would frequently happen that the owner of a valuable mill site was unable to render it available, because the owners of lands which must be flowed to obtain a reservoir would neither consent to the construction of a dam, nor sell their lands unless at extravagant and inadmissible prices. The legislature in some of the States has taken the matter in hand, and has surmounted the difficulty, sometimes by authorizing the land to be appropriated, and at others by permitting the erection of the dam, but requiring the mill owner to pay annually to the proprietor of the land the damages caused by the flowing, to be assessed in some impartial mode.[1] There is certainly very much less reason for such statutes now than there was at the beginning of the present century; but their validity has often been recognized in some of the States, and perhaps the same courts would continue to recognize it, notwithstanding the public necessity may no longer demand such laws.[2] The rights granted by these laws to mill owners are said by Chief Justice Shaw of Massachusetts to be " granted for the better use of the water power, upon considerations of general policy and the general good," [3] and in this view, and in order to render a valuable property available which might otherwise be made of little value by narrow, selfish, and

is as much a matter of public utility as a railway or a supply of pure water. See Matter of Central Park Extension, 16 Abb. Pr. Rep. 56; Owners of Ground v. Mayor, &c. of Albany, 15 Wend. 374. Or sewers in cities. Hildreth v. Lowell, 11 Gray, 345.

[1] See Angell on Watercourses, ch. 12, for references to the statutes on this subject.

[2] " The encouragement of mills has always been a favorite object with the legislature; and though the reasons for it may have ceased, the favor of the legislature continues." Wolcott Woollen Manufacturing Co. v. Upham, 5 Pick. 294.

[3] French v. Braintree Manufacturing Co., 23 Pick. 220.

unfriendly conduct on the part of individuals, such laws may perhaps be sustained on the same grounds which support an exercise
of the right of eminent domain to protect, drain, and render valuable lands which, by the overflow of a river, might otherwise be an
extensive and worthless swamp.[1]

[1] Action on the case for raising a dam across the Merrimac River, by which a
mill stream emptying into that river, above the site of said dam, was set back and
overflowed, and a mill of the plaintiff situated thereon, and the mill privilege, were
damaged and destroyed. Demurrer to the declaration. The defendant company were chartered for the purpose of constructing a dam across the Merrimac
River, and constructing one or more locks and canals, in connection with said
dam, to remove obstructions in said river by falls and rapids, and to create a
water power to be used for mechanical and manufacturing purposes. The defendants claimed that they were justified in what they had done, by an act of the
legislature exercising the sovereign power of the State, in the right of eminent
domain; that the plaintiffs' property in the mill and mill privilege was taken and
appropriated under this right; and that his remedy was by a claim of damages
under the act, and not by action at common law as for a wrongful and unwarrantable encroachment upon his right of property. Shaw, Ch. J. : " It is contended that if this act was intended to authorize the defendant company to take
the mill power and mill of the plaintiff, it was void because it was not taken for
public use, and it was not within the power of the government in the exercise of
the right of eminent domain. This is the main question. In determining it, we
must look to the declared purposes of the act; and if a public use is declared, it
will be so held, unless it manifestly appears by the provisions of the act that they
can have no tendency to advance and promote such public use. The declared
purposes are to improve the navigation of the Merrimac River, and to create a
large mill power for mechanical and manufacturing purposes. In general, whether
a particular structure, as a bridge, or a lock, or canal, or road, is for the public
use, is a question for the legislature, and which may be presumed to have been
correctly decided by them. Commonwealth v. Breed, 4 Pick. 463. That the
improvement of the navigation of a river is done for the public use has been too
frequently decided and acted upon to require authorities. And so to create a
wholly artificial navigation by canals. The establishment of a great mill power
for manufacturing purposes, as an object of great public interest, especially since
manufacturing has come to be one of the great industrial pursuits of the Commonwealth, seems to have been regarded by the legislature, and sanctioned by
the jurisprudence of the Commonwealth, and in our judgment rightly so, in determining what is a public use, justifying the exercise of right of eminent domain.
See St. 1825, ch. 148, incorporating the Salem Mill Dam Corporation ; Boston &
Roxbury Mill Dam Corporation v. Newman, 12 Pick. 467. The acts since passed,
and the cases since decided on this ground, are very numerous. That the erection
of this dam would have a strong and direct tendency to advance both these public
objects, there is no doubt. We are therefore of opinion that the powers conferred
on the corporation by this act were so done within the scope of the authority of
the legislature, and were not a violation of the constitution of the Common-

On the other hand, it is said that the legislature of New York has never exercised the right of eminent domain in favor of mills of any kind, and that " sites for steam-engines, hotels, churches, and other public conveniences might as well be taken by the exercise of this extraordinary power.[1] And a similar view has been taken by the Supreme Court of Alabama.[2] It is quite possible that in any State in which this question would be a new one, and where it would not be embarrassed by long acquiescence and judicial as well as legislative precedents, it would be held that these laws are not sound in principle, and that they cannot be sustained by the maxims on which is based the right of eminent domain.[3]

The Taking of Property.

Although property can only be taken for a public use, and the legislature of the State must determine in what cases, it has long been settled that it is not essential that the taking should be to or by the State itself, if by any other agency in the opinion of the legislature the use can be made equally effectual for the public benefit. There are many cases where the appropriation consists simply in throwing the property open to use by such persons as may see fit to avail themselves of it, as in the case of common highways and public parks ; and here the title of the owner is not disturbed except as it is charged with this burden ; and the State defends the easement, not by virtue of any title in the property, but through criminal proceedings when the general right is dis-

---

wealth." Hazen v. Essex Company, 12 Cush. 477. See also Boston & Roxbury Mill Corporation v. Newman, 12 Pick. 467 ; Fiske v. Framingham Manufacturing Co., Ibid. 67 ; Harding v. Goodlett, 3 Yerg. 41. The courts of Wisconsin have sustained such laws. Newcomb v. Smith, 1 Chand. 71 ; Thien v. Voegtlander, 3 Wis. 465 ; Pratt v. Brown, Ibid. 603. And those of Connecticut. Olmstead v. Camp, 33 Conn. 532. And they have been enforced elsewhere without question. Burgess v. Clark, 13 Ired. 109 ; McAfee's Heirs v. Kennedy, 1 Lit. 92 ; Smith v. Connelly, 1 T. B. Monr. 58 ; Shackleford v. Coffey, 4 J. J. Marsh. 40 ; Crenshaw v. Slate River Co., 6 Rand. 245. In Newell v. Smith, 15 Wis. 101, it was held not constitutional to authorize the appropriation of the property, and leave the owner no remedy except to subsequently recover its value in an action of trespass.

[1] Hay v. Cohoes Company, 3 Barb. 47.

[2] Sadler v. Langham, 34 Ala. 311.

[3] See this whole subject discussed in a review of Angell on Watercourses, 2 American Jurist, p. 25.

turbed. But in other cases it seems important to take the title; and in many of these cases it is convenient, if not necessary, that the taking be, not by the State, but by the municipality for which the use is specially designed, and to whose care and government it will be confided. When property is needed for a district school-house, it is proper that the district appropriate it; and it is strictly in accordance with the general theory as well as with the practice of our government for the State to delegate to the district the exercise of the power of eminent domain for this special purpose. So a county may be authorized to take lands for its court-house or jail; a city, for its town hall, its reservoirs of water, its sewers and other public works of like importance. In these cases no question arises; the taking is by the public; the use is by the public; and the benefit to accrue therefrom is shared in greater or less degree by the whole public.

If, however, it be constitutional to appropriate lands for mill dams or mill sites, it ought also to be constitutional that the taking be by individuals instead of by the State or any of its organized political divisions; since it is no part of the business of the government to engage in manufacturing operations which come in competition with private enterprise; and the cases must be very peculiar and very rare where a State or municipal corporation could be justified in any such undertaking. And although the practice is not entirely uniform on the subject, the general sentiment is adverse to the construction of railways by the State, and the opinion is quite prevalent, if not general, that they can be better managed, controlled, and operated for the public benefit in the hands of individuals than by State or municipal officers or agencies.

And while there are unquestionably some objections to compelling a citizen to surrender his property to a corporation, whose corporators, in receiving it, are influenced by motives of private gain and emolument, so that *to them* the purpose of the appropriation is altogether private, yet conceding it to be settled that these highways are a public necessity, if the legislature, reflecting the public sentiment, decide that the general benefit is better promoted by their construction through individuals or corporations, it would clearly be pressing a constitutional maxim to an absurd extreme if it were to be held that the public necessity should only be provided for in the way which is least consistent with the public interest. Accordingly, on the principle of public benefit, not only the State and its political divisions, but also individuals and corporate bodies, have been authorized to take private property for the construction of such highways; and the fact that the members of such corporate bodies have a pecuniary interest, such as will give the corporation the character of private, will not prevent the State from using it to accomplish the public object.[1]

The Necessity for the Taking.

The authority to determine in any case whether it is needful to exercise this power must rest with the State itself; and the question is always one of a strictly political character, not requiring any hearing upon the facts or any judicial determination. Nevertheless, when the improvement is one of local importance only, and must be determined upon a view of the facts which the people of the vicinity may be supposed to best understand, the question of necessity is generally referred to some local tribunal, and it may even be submitted to a jury to decide upon evidence. But parties interested have no constitutional right to be heard upon the question, unless the State constitution clearly and expressly recognizes and provides for it. On general principles, the final decision rests with the legislative department of the State; and if the question is referred to any tribunal for trial, the reference and the opportunity for being heard are matters of favor and not of right. The State is not under any obligation to make provision for a judicial contest upon that question. And where the case is such that it is proper to delegate to individuals or to a corporation the power to appropriate property, it is also competent to delegate the authority to decide upon the necessity for the taking.[2]

[1] Beekman v. Saratoga & Schenectady R. R. Co., 3 Paige, 73; Wilson v. Blackbird Creek Marsh Co., 2 Pet. 251; Buonaparte v. Camden & Amboy R. R. Co., 1 Bald. 205; Bloodgood v. Mohawk & Hudson R. R. Co., 18 Wend. 1; Lebanon v. Olcott, 1 N. H. 339; Petition of Mount Washington Road Co., 35 N. H. 141; Pratt v. Brown, 3 Wis. 603; Swan v. Williams, 2 Mich. 427; Stevens v. Middlesex Canal, 12 Mass. 466; Boston Mill Dam v. Newman, 12 Pick. 467; Gilmer v. Lime Point, 18 Cal. 229; Armington v. Barnet, 15 Vt. 750; White River Turnpike v. Central Railroad, 21 Vt. 590; Raleigh, &c. R. R. Co. v. Davis, 2 Dev. & Bat. 451; Whiteman's Exr. v. Wilmington, &c. R. R. Co., 2 Harr. 514; Bradley v. N. Y. & N. H. R. R. Co., 21 Conn. 294.

[2] People v. Smith, 21 N. Y. 597; Ford v. Chicago & N. W. R. R. Co., 14 Wis.

How much Property may be taken.

The taking of property must always be limited to the necessity of the case, and consequently no more can be appropriated in any

617; Matter of Albany St., 11 Wend. 152; Lyon v. Jerome, 26 Wend. 484 ; Hays v. Risher, 32 Penn. St. 169 ; North Missouri R. R. Co. v. Lackland, 25 Mo. 515 ; Same v. Gott, Ibid. 540.   In the case first cited, Denio, J. says : " The question is, whether the State, in the exercise of the power to appropriate the property of individuals to a public use, where the duty of judging of the expediency of making the appropriation, in a class of cases, is committed to public officers, is obliged to afford to the owners of the property an opportunity to be heard before those officers when they sit for the purpose of making the determination.   I do not speak now of the process for arriving at the amount of compensation to be paid to the owners, but of the determination whether, under the circumstances of a particular case, the property required for the purpose shall be taken or not; and I am of opinion that the State is not under any obligation to make provision for a judicial contest upon that question.   The only part of the constitution which refers to the subject is that which forbids private property to be taken for public use without compensation, and that which prescribes the manner in which the compensation shall be ascertained.   It is not pretended that the statute under consideration violates either of those provisions.   There is therefore no constitutional injunction on the point under consideration.   The necessity for appropriating private property for the use of the public or of the government is not a judicial question.   The power resides in the legislature.   It may be exercised by means of a statute which shall at once designate the property to be appropriated and the purpose of the appropriation ; or it may be delegated to public officers, or, as it has been repeatedly held, to private corporations established to carry on enterprises in which the public are interested.   There is no restraint upon the power, except that requiring compensation to be made.   And where the power is committed to public officers, it is a subject of legislative discretion to determine what prudential regulations shall be established to secure a discreet and judicious exercise of the authority.   The constitutional provision securing a trial by jury in certain cases, and that which declares that no citizen shall be deprived of his property without due process of law, have no application to the case.   The jury trial can only be claimed as a constitutional right where the subject is judicial in its character.   The exercise of the right of eminent domain stands on the same ground with the power of taxation.   Both are emanations from the law-making power.   They are attributes of political sovereignty, for the exercise of which the legislature is under no necessity to address itself to the courts.   In imposing a tax, or in appropriating the property of a citizen, or of a class of citizens, for a public purpose, with a proper provision for compensation, the legislative act is itself due process of law ; though it would not be if it should undertake to appropriate the property of one citizen for the use of another, or to confiscate the property of one person or class of persons, or a particular description of property upon some view of public policy, where it could not be said to be taken for a public use.   It follows from these views that

instance than the proper tribunal shall adjudge to be needed for
the particular use for which the appropriation is made. When a
part only of a man's premises is needed by the public, the need of
that part will not justify the taking of the whole, even though
compensation be made therefor. The moment the appropriation
goes beyond the necessity of the case, it ceases to be justified on
the principles which underlie the right of eminent domain.[1] If,

it is not necessary for the legislature, in the exercise of the right of eminent
domain, either directly, or indirectly through public officers or agents, to invest
the proceedings with the forms or substance of judicial process. It may allow the
owner to intervene and participate in the discussion before the officer or board to
whom the power is given of determining whether the appropriation shall be made
in a particular case, or it may provide that the officers shall act upon their own
views of propriety and duty, without the aid of a forensic contest. The appropriation of the propriety is an act of public administration, and the form and manner of its performance is such as the legislature in its discretion shall prescribe."

[1] By a statute of New York it was enacted that whenever a part only of a lot
or parcel of land should be required for the purposes of a city street, if the
commissioners for assessing compensation should deem it expedient to include the
whole lot in the assessment, they should have power so to do; and the part not
wanted for the particular street or improvement should, upon the confirmation of
the report, become vested in the corporation, and might be appropriated to public
uses, or sold in case of no such appropriation. Of this statute it was said by the
Supreme Court of New York : " If this provision was intended merely to give to
the corporation capacity to take property under such circumstances with the consent of the owner, and then to dispose of the same, there can be no objection to
it ; but if it is to be taken literally, that the commissioners may, against the consent of the owner, take the whole lot, when only a part is required for public use,
and the residue to be applied to private use, it assumes a power which, with all
respect, the legislature did not possess. The constitution, by authorizing the
appropriation of property to public use, impliedly declares that for any other use
private property shall not be taken from one and applied to the private use of
another. It is in violation of natural right ; and if it is not in violation of the
letter of the constitution, it is of its spirit, and cannot be supported. This
power has been supposed to be convenient when the greater part of a lot is
taken, and only a small part left, not required for public use, and that small part
of but little value in the hands of the owner. In such case the corporation has
been supposed best qualified to take and dispose of such parcels, or gores, as they
have sometimes been called ; and probably this assumption of power has been
acquiesced in by the proprietors. I know of no case where the power has been
questioned, and where it has received the deliberate sanction of this court.
Suppose a case where only a few feet, or even inches, are wanted, from one end
of a lot to widen a street, and a valuable building stands upon the other end of
such lot ; would the power be conceded to exist to take the whole lot, whether
the owner consented or not ? The *quantity* of the residue of any lot cannot vary
the principle. The owner may be very unwilling to part with only a few feet ;

however, the statute providing for such appropriation is acted upon, and the property owner accepts the compensation awarded to him under it, he will be precluded by this implied assent from afterwards objecting to the excessive appropriation.[1] And there is nothing in the principle we have stated which, when land is needed for a public improvement, will preclude the appropriation of whatever might be necessary for incidental conveniences ; such as the workshops or depot buildings of a railway company,[2] or materials to be used in the construction of the road, and so on. Express legislative power, however, is needed for these purposes ; it will not follow that, because such things are convenient to the accomplishment of the general object, the public may appropriate them without express authority of law ; but the power to appropriate must be expressly conferred, and the public agencies seeking to exercise this high prerogative must be careful to keep within the authority delegated, since the public necessity cannot be held to extend beyond what has been plainly declared on the face of the legislative enactment.

What constitutes a Taking of Property.

Any proper exercise of the powers of government, which does not directly encroach upon the property of an individual, or disturb him in its possession or enjoyment, will not entitle him to compensation, or give him a right of action.[3] If, for instance, the

and I hold it equally incompetent for the legislature to dispose of private property, whether feet or acres are the subject of this assumed power." Matter of Albany St., 11 Wend. 151, per Savage, Ch. J.

[1] Embury v. Conner, 3 N. Y. 511. There is clearly nothing in constitutional principles which would preclude the legislature from providing that a man's property might be taken with his assent, whether the assent was evidenced by deed or not; and if he accepts payment, he must be deemed to assent. The more recent case of House v. Rochester, 15 Barb. 517, is not, we think, opposed to Embury v. Conner, of which it makes no mention.

[2] Chicago B. & Q. R. R. Co. v. Wilson, 17 Ill. 123 ; Low v. Galena & C. U. R. R. Co., 18 Ill. 324 ; Giesy v. Cincinnati, W. & Z. R. R. Co., 4 Ohio, N. S. 308.

[3] Zimmerman v. Union Canal Co., 1 W. & S. 346 ; Shrunk v. Schuylkill Navigation Co., 14 S. & R. 71 ; Monongahela Navigation Co. v. Coons, 6 W. & S. 101 ; Davidson v. Boston & Maine R. R. Co., 3 Cush. 91 ; Gould v. Hudson River R. R. Co., 12 Barb. 616, and 6 N. Y. 522 ; Radcliff v. Mayor, &c. of Brooklyn, 4 N. Y. 195 ; Murray v. Menifee, 20 Ark. 561 ; Hooker v. New Haven & Northamp-

State, under its power to provide and regulate the public highways, should authorize the construction of a bridge across a navigable river, it is quite possible that all proprietary interests in land
upon the river might be injuriously affected; but such injury could
no more give a valid claim against the State for damages, than
could any change in the general laws of the State, which, while
keeping in view the general good, might injuriously affect particular interests.[1]   So if, by the erection of a dam in order to improve
navigation, the owner of a fishery finds it diminished in value,[2] or
if by deepening the channel of a river to improve the navigation a
spring is destroyed,[3] or by a change in the grade of a city street
the value of adjacent lots is diminished,[4] — in these and similar
cases the law affords no redress for the injury.   So if, in consequence of the construction of a public work, an injury occurs, but
the work was constructed on proper plan and without negligence,
and the injury is caused by accidental and extraordinary circumstances, the injured party cannot demand compensation.[5]

ton Co., 14 Conn. 146; People v. Kerr, 27 N. Y. 193; Fuller v. Eddings, 11
Rich. Law, 239; Eddings v. Seabrook, 12 Rich. Law, 504; Richardson v. Vermont Central R. R. Co., 25 Vt. 465; Kennett's petition, 4 Fost. 139; Alexander
v. Milwaukee, 16 Wis. 247; Richmond, &c. Co. v. Rogers, 1 Duvall, 135; Harvey v. Lackawana, &c. R. R. Co., 47 Penn. St. 428.

[1] Davidson v. Boston & Maine R. R. Co., 3 Cush. 91.

[2] Shrunk v. Schuylkill Navigation Co., 14 S. & R. 71.

[3] Commonwealth v. Richter, 1 Penn. St. 467.

[4] British Plate Manufacturing Co. v. Meredith, 4 T. R. 794; Matter of Furman Street, 17 Wend. 649; Radcliff's Exrs. v. Mayor, &c. of Brooklyn, 4 N. Y.
195; Graves v. Otis, 2 Hill, 466; Wilson v. Mayor, &c. of New York, 1 Denio,
595; Murphy v. Chicago, 29 Ill. 279; Roberts v. Chicago, 26 Ill. 249; Charlton
v. Alleghany City, 1 Grant, 208; La Fayette v. Bush, 19 Ind. 326; Macy v.
Indianapolis, 17 Ind. 267; Green v. Reading, 9 Watts, 382; O'Conner v. Pittsburg, 18 Penn. St. 187; In re Ridge Street, 29 Penn. St. 391; Callendar v. Marsh,
1 Pick. 417; Creal v. Keokuk, 4 Greene (Iowa), 47; Smith v. Washington, 20
How. 135; Skinner v. Hartford Bridge Co., 29 Conn. 523; Benden v. Nashua,
17 N. H. 477; Goszler v. Georgetown, 6 Wheat. 703.   The cases of McComb v.
Akron, 15 Ohio, 474, and 18 Ohio, 229; and Crawford v. Delaware, 7 Ohio, N.
S. 459, are contra.   Those cases, however, admit that a party whose interests
are injured by the original establishment of a street grade can have no claim to
compensation; but they hold that when the grade is once established, and lot
are improved in reference to it, the corporation has no right to change the grade
afterwards, except on payment of the damages.

[5] As in Sprague v. Worcester, 13 Gray, 193, where, in consequence of the
erection of a bridge over a stream on which a mill was situated, the mill was
injured by an extraordinary rise in the stream; the bridge, however, being in all
respects properly constructed.

This principle is peculiarly applicable to those cases where property is appropriated under the right of eminent domain. It must frequently occur that a party will find his rights seriously affected without any property to which he has claim being appropriated. As where a road is laid out along the line of a man's land without appropriating any portion of it, so that in consequence he is compelled to keep up the whole of a fence which before was a partition fence and his neighbor required to support one half.[1] No property being taken in this case, the party has no relief, unless the statute shall give it. The loss is *damnum absque injuria*. So a turnpike company, whose profits will be diminished by the construction of a railroad along the same general line of travel, is not entitled to compensation.[2] So where a railroad company, in constructing their road in a proper manner on their own land, raised a high embankment near to and in front of the plaintiff's house, so as to prevent his passing to and from the same with the same convenience as before, this consequential injury was held to give no claim to compensation.[3] So the owner of dams erected by legislative authority is without remedy, if they are afterwards rendered valueless by the construction of a canal.[4]

[1] Kennett's petition, 4 Fost. 139. And Eddings *v.* Seabrook, 12 Rich. Law 504.

[2] Troy & Boston R. R. Co. *v.* Northern Turnpike Co., 16 Barb. 100. See La Fayette Plank Road Co. *v.* New Albany & Salem R. R. Co., 13 Ind. 90; Richmond, &c. Co. *v.* Rogers, 1 Duvall, 135. So an increased competition with a party's business caused by the construction or extension of a road is not a ground of claim. Harvey *v.* Lackawana, &c. R. R. Co., 47 Penn. St. 428. " Every great public improvement must, almost of necessity, more or less affect individual convenience and property; and when the injury sustained is remote and consequential, it is *damnum absque injuria*, and is to be borne as a part of the price to be paid for the advantages of the social condition. This is founded upon the principle that the general good is to prevail over partial individual convenience." Lansing *v.* Smith, 8 Cow. 149.

[3] Richardson *v.* Vermont Central R. R. Co., 25 Vt. 465. But *quære* if this could be so, if the effect were to prevent access from the lot to the highway. In the same case it was held that an excavation by the company on their own land, so near the line of the plaintiff's that his land, without any artificial weight thereon, slid into the excavation, would render the company liable for the injury; the plaintiff being entitled to the lateral support for his land.

[4] Susquehanna Canal Co. *v.* Wright, 9 W. & S. 9 ; Monongahela Navigation Co. *v.* Coons, 6 W. & S. 101. In any case, if parties exercising the right of eminent domain, shall cause injury to others by a negligent or improper construction of their work, they may be liable in damages. Rowe *v.* Granite Bridge Corpora-

And in New York it has been held that, as the land, where the tide
ebbs and flows, between high and low water mark, belongs to the
public, the State may lawfully authorize a railroad company to
construct their road along the water front below high-water mark,
and that the owner of the adjacent bank could claim no compensation for the consequential injury to his interests.[1] So the granting of a ferry right with a landing on private property within a
highway terminating on a private stream is not an appropriation
of property,[2] the ferry being a mere continuation of the highway,
and the landing-place upon the private property having previously
been appropriated to public uses.

These cases must suffice as illustrations of the principle stated,
though many others might be referred to. On the other hand,
any injury to the property of an individual which deprives the
owner of the ordinary use of it is equivalent to a taking, and
entitles him to compensation.[3] Water front on a stream where
the tide does not ebb and flow is property, and if taken must be
paid for as such.[4] So with an exclusive right of wharfage upon
tide water.[5] So with the right of the owner of land to use an
adjoining street, whether he is owner of the land over which the

tion, 21 Pick. 348 ; Sprague v. Worcester, 13 Gray, 193. And if a public work
is of a character to necessarily disturb the occupation and enjoyment of his estate
by one whose land is not taken, he may have an action on the case for the injury,
notwithstanding the statute makes no provision for compensation. As where the
necessary, and not simply the accidental, consequence was, to flood a man's
premises with water, thereby greatly diminishing their value. Hooker v. New
Haven & Northampton Co., 14 Conn. 146 ; Same case, 15 Conn. 312 ; Evans-
ville, &c. R. R. Co. v. Dick, 9 Ind. 433 ; Robinson v. N. Y. & Erie R. R. Co.,
27 Barb. 512 ; Trustees of Wabash & Erie Canal v. Spears, 16 Ind. 441. So
where, by blasting rock in making an excavation, the fragments are thrown upon
adjacent buildings so as to render their occupation unsafe. Hay v. Cohoes Co.,
2 N. Y. 159 ; Tremain v. Same, Ibid. 163 ; Carman v. Steubenville & Indiana
R. R. Co., 4 Ohio, N. S. 399 ; Sunbury & Erie R. R. Co. v. Hummel, 27 Penn.
St. 99. There has been some disposition to hold private corporations liable for
all incidental damages caused by their exercise of the right of eminent domain.
See Tinsman v. Belvidere & Delaware R. R. Co., 2 Dutch. 148 ; Alexander v.
Milwaukee, 16 Wis. 255.

[1] Gould v. Hudson River R. R. Co., 6 N. Y. 522. But see the dissenting
opinion of Edmonds, J., in this case.

[2] Murray v. Menifee, 20 Ark. 561.

[3] Hooker v. New Haven & Northampton Co., 14 Conn. 146.

[4] Varick v. Smith, 9 Paige, 547.

[5] Murray v. Sharp, 1 Bosw. 539.

street is laid out or not.[1] So with the right of pasturage in streets, which belongs to the owners of the soil.[2] So a partial destruction or diminution of value of property by the act of the government, directly and not merely incidentally affecting it, is to that extent an appropriation.[3]

It sometimes becomes important, where a highway has been laid out and opened, to establish a different and higher grade of way upon the same line, with a view to accommodate an increased public demand. The State may be willing to surrender the control of the streets in these cases, and authorize turnpike, plank-road, or railroad corporations to occupy them for their purposes ; and if it shall give such consent, the control, so far as is necessary to the purposes of the turnpike, plank road or railway, is thereby passed over to the corporation, and their structure in what was before a common highway cannot be regarded as a nuisance. But the municipal organizations in the State have no power to give such consent, without express legislative permission ; the general control of their streets which is commonly given by municipal charters not being sufficient authority for this purpose.[4] When, however, the

---

[1] Lackland v. North Missouri R. R. Co., 31 Mo. 180.

[2] Tonawanda R. R. Co. v. Munger, 5 Denio, 255 ; Woodruff v. Neal, 28 Conn. 165. In this case it was held that a by-law of a town giving liberty to the inhabitants to depasture their cows in the public highways under certain regulations, passed under the authority of a general statute empowering towns to pass such by-laws, was of no validity because it appropriated the pasturage, which was private property, to the public use, without making compensation. The contrary has been held in New York as to all highways laid out while such a statute was in existence ; the owner being held to be compensated for the pasturage as well as for the use of the land for other purposes, at the time the highway was laid out. Griffin v. Martin, 7 Barb. 297 ; Hardenburgh v. Lockwood, 25 Barb. 9. See also Kerwhacker v. Cleveland C. & C. R. R. Co., 3 Ohio, N. S. 177, where it was held that by ancient custom in that State there was a right of pasturage by the public in the highways.

[3] See Glover v. Powell, 2 Stockt. 211.

[4] Lackland v. North Missouri R. R. Co., 31 Mo. 180 ; N. Y. & Harlem R. R. Co. v. Mayor, &c. of New York, 1 Hilt. 562 ; Milhau v. Sharp, 27 N. Y. 611. In Inhabitants of Springfield v. Connecticut River R. R. Co., 4 Cush. 71, it was held that legislative authority to construct a railroad between certain *termini*, without prescribing its precise course and direction, would not *prima facie* confer power to lay out the road on and along an existing public highway. Per Shaw, Ch. J. : " The whole course of legislation on the subject of railroads is opposed to such a construction. The crossing of public highways by railroads is obviously necessary, and of course warranted ; and numerous provisions are industriously made to regulate such

35

public authorities have thus assented, it may be found that the owners of the adjacent lots, who are also owners of the fee in the highway subject to the public easement, may be unwilling to assent to the change, and may find or think their interests seriously and injuriously affected thereby. The question may then arise, Is the owner of the land, who has been once compensated for the injury he has sustained in the appropriation of his land as a highway, entitled to a new assessment for any further injury he may sustain in consequence of the street being subjected to a change in the use not contemplated at the time of the original taking, but nevertheless in furtherance of the same general purpose ?

When a common highway is made a turnpike or a plank road, upon which tolls are collected, there is much reason for holding that the owner of the soil is not entitled to any further compensation. The turnpike or the plank road is still a highway, subject to be used in the same manner as the highway was before, and if properly constructed is generally expected to increase rather than diminish the value of property along its line ; and though the adjoining proprietors are required to pay toll, they are supposed to be, and generally are, fully compensated for this burden by the increased excellence of the road, and by their exemption from highway labor upon it.[1] But it is different when a highway is appropriated for the purposes of a railroad. " It is quite apparent that the use by the public of a highway, and the use thereof by a

---

crossings, by determining when they shall be on the same and when on different levels, in order to avoid collision, and when on the same level what gates, fences, and barriers shall be made, and what guards shall be kept to insure safety. Had it been intended that railroad companies, under a general grant, should have power to lay a railroad over a highway longitudinally, which ordinarily is not necessary, we think that would have been done in express terms, accompanied with full legislative provisions for maintaining such barriers and modes of separation as would tend to make the use of the same road, for both modes of travel. consistent with the safety of travellers on both. The absence of any such provision affords a strong inference that, under general terms, it was not intended that such a power should be given." See also Commonwealth v. Erie & N. E. R. R. Co., 27 Penn. St. 339.

[1] See Commonwealth v. Wilkinson, 16 Pick. 175 ; Benedict v. Goit, 3 Barb. 459 ; Wright v. Carter, 3 Dutch. 76 ; Chagrin Falls & Cleveland Plank Road Co. v. Cane, 2 Ohio, N. S. 419. But see Williams v. Natural Bridge Plank Road Co., 21 Mo. 580. In Murray v. County Commissioners of Berkshire, 12 Met. 455, it was held that owners of lands adjoining a turnpike were not entitled to compensation when the turnpike was changed to a common highway.

railroad company, is essentially different. In the one case every person is at liberty to travel over the highway in any place or part thereof, but he has no exclusive right of occupation of any part thereof except while he is temporarily passing over it. It would be trespass for him to occupy any part of the highway exclusively for any longer period of time than was necessary for that purpose, and the stoppages incident thereto. But a railroad company takes exclusive and permanent possession of a portion of the street or highway. It lays down its rails upon, or imbeds them in, the soil, and thus appropriates a portion of the street to its exclusive use, and for its own particular mode of conveyance. In the one case, all persons may travel on the street or highway in their own common modes of conveyance. In the other, no one can travel on or over the rails laid down, except the railroad company and with their cars specially adapted to the tracks. In one case the use is general and open alike to all. In the other, it is peculiar and exclusive.

" It is true that the actual use of the street by the railroad may not be so absolute and constant as to exclude the public also from its use. With a single track, and particularly if the cars used upon it were propelled by horse-power, the interruption of the public easement in the street might be very trifling and of no practical consequence to the public at large. But this consideration cannot affect the question of the right of property, or of the increase of the burden upon the soil. It would present simply a question of degree in respect to the enlargement of the easement, and would not affect the principle, that the use of a street for the purposes of a railroad imposed upon it a new burden." [1]

[1] Wager v. Troy Union R. R. Co., 25 N. Y. 532, approving Williams v. New York Central R. R. Co., 16 N. Y. 97; Carpenter v. Oswego & Syracuse R. R. Co., 24 N. Y. 655; Mahon v. New York Central R. R. Co., Ibid. 658. In Inhabitants of Springfield v. Connecticut River R. R. Co., 4 Cush. 71, where, however, the precise question here discussed was not involved, Chief Justice Shaw, in comparing railroads with common highways, says: " The two uses are almost, if not wholly, inconsistent with each other, so that taking the highway for a railroad will nearly supersede the former use to which it had been legally appropriated." See also Presbyterian Society of Waterloo v. Auburn & Rochester R. R. Co., 3 Hill, 567; Craig v. Rochester, &c. R. R. Co., 39 Barb. 494. The cases of Philadelphia & Trenton R. R. Co., 6 Whart. 25, and Morris & Essex R. R. Co. v. Newark, 2 Stockt. 352, are opposed to the New York cases. And see Wolfe v. Covington & Lexington R. R. Co., 15 B. Monr. 404; Commonwealth v. Erie & N. E. R. R. Co., 27 Penn. St. 339. The case in narton was questioned in

The case above quoted from is approved in recent cases in Wisconsin, where importance is attached to the different effect the common highway and the railroad will have upon the value of adjacent property. " The dedication to the public as a highway," it is said, " enhances the value of the lot, and renders it more convenient and useful to the owner. The use by the railroad company diminishes its value, and renders it inconvenient and comparatively useless. It would be a most unjust and oppressive rule which would deny the owner compensation under such circumstances.[1]

It is not always the case, however, that the value of a lot of land will be enhanced by the laying out of a common highway across it, or diminished by the construction of a railway over the same line afterwards. The constitutional question cannot depend upon the accidental circumstance that the new road will or will not have an injurious effect ; though that circumstance is properly referred to, since it is difficult to perceive how a change of use which may have an injurious effect not contemplated in the original appropriation can be considered anything else than the imposition of a new burden upon the owner's estate. In Connecticut, where the authority of the legislature to authorize a railroad to be constructed in a common highway without compensation to land owners is also denied, importance is attached to the terms of the statute under which the original appropriation was made, and which are regarded as confining the taking to the purposes of a common highway, and no other. The reasoning of the court appears to us sound ; and it is applicable to the statutes of the States generally.[2]

Monongahela Co. v. Coons, 6 W. & S. 117, and the subsequent case of Miffin v. Railroad Co., 16 Penn. St. 192, appears to be inconsistent with it.

[1] Ford v. Chicago & Northwestern R. R. Co., 14 Wis. 616 ; followed in Pomeroy v. Chicago & M. R. R. Co., 16 Wis. 640.

[2] Imlay v. Union Branch R. R. Co., 26 Conn. 255. " When land is condemned for a special purpose," say the court, " on the score of public utility, the sequestration is limited to that particular use. Land taken for a highway is not thereby converted into a common. As the property is not taken, but the use only, the right of the public is limited to the use, the specific use, for which the proprietor has been divested of a complete dominion over his own estate. These are propositions which are no longer open to discussion. But it is contended that land once taken and still held for highway purposes may be used for a railway without exceeding the limits of the easement already acquired by the public. If this is true, if the new use of the land is within the scope of the original sequestration or

It would appear from the cases cited that the weight of judicial authority is against the power of the legislature to appropriate a

dedication, it would follow that the railway privileges are not an encroachment on the estate remaining in the owner of the soil, and that the new mode of enjoying the public easement will not enable him rightfully to assert a claim to damages therefor. On the contrary, if the true intent and efficacy of the original condemnation was not to subject the land to such a burden as will be imposed upon it when it is confiscated to the uses and control of a railroad corporation, it cannot be denied that in such a case the estate of the owner of the soil is injuriously affected by the supervening servitude; that his rights are abridged, and that in a legal sense his land is again taken for public uses. Thus it appears that the court have simply to decide whether there is such an identity between a highway and a railway, that statutes conferring a right to establish the former include an authority to construct the latter.

" The term ' public highway,' as employed in such of our statutes as convey the right of eminent domain, has certainly a limited import. Although, as suggested at the bar, a navigable river or a canal is, in some sense, a public highway, yet an easement assumed under the name of a highway would not enable the public to convert a street into a canal. The highway, in the true meaning of the word, would be destroyed. But as no such destruction of the highway is necessarily involved in the location of a railroad track upon it, we are pressed to establish the legal proposition that a highway, such as is referred to in these statutes, means or at least comprehends a railroad. Such a construction is possible only when it is made to appear that there is a substantial practical or technical identity between the uses of land for highway and for railway purposes.

" No one can fail to see that the terms ' railway' and ' highway ' are not convertible, or that the two uses, practically considered, although analogous, are not identical. Land as ordinarily appropriated by a railroad company is inconvenient, and even impassable, to those who would use it as a common highway. Such a corporation does not hold itself bound to made or to keep its embankments and bridges in a condition which will facilitate the *transitus* of such vehicles as ply over an ordinary road. A practical dissimilarity obviously exists between a railway and a common highway, and is recognized as the basis of a legal distinction between them. It is so recognized on a large scale when railway privileges are sought from legislative bodies, and granted by them. If the terms ' highway ' and ' railway ' are synonymous, or if one of them includes the other by legal implication, no act could be more superfluous than to require or to grant authority to construct railways over localities already occupied as highways.

" If a legal identity does not subsist between a highway and a railway, it is illogical to argue that, because a railway may be so constructed as not to interfere with the ordinary uses of a highway, and so as to be consistent with the highway right already existing, therefore such a new use is included within the old use. It might as well be urged, that if a common, or a canal, laid out over the route of a public road, could be so arranged as to leave an ample roadway for vehicles and passengers on foot, the land should be held to be originally condemned for a canal or a common, as properly incident to the highway use.

" There is an important practical reason why courts should be slow to recog-

common highway to the purposes of a railroad, unless at the same time provision is made for compensation to the owners of the fee.

nize a legal identity between the two uses referred to. They are by no means the same thing to the proprietor whose land is taken; on the contrary, they suggest widely different standards of compensation. One can readily conceive of cases where the value of real estate would be directly enhanced by the opening of a highway through it; while its confiscation for a railway at the same or a subsequent time would be a gross injury to the estate, and a total subversion of the mode of enjoyment expected by the owner when he yielded his private rights to the public exigency.

" But essential distinctions also exist between highway and railway powers, as conferred by statute, — distinctions which are founded in the very nature of the powers themselves. In the case of the highway, the statute provides that, after the observance of certain legal forms, the locality in question shall be forever subservient to the right of every individual in the community to pass over the thoroughfare so created at all times. This right involves the important implication that he shall so use the privilege as to leave the privilege of all others as unobstructed as his own, and that he is therefore to use the road in the manner in which such roads are ordinarily used, with such vehicles as will not obstruct, or require the destruction of the ordinary modes of travel thereon. He is not authorized to lay down a railway track, and run his own locomotive and car upon it. No one ever thought of regarding highway acts as conferring railway privileges, involving a right in every individual, not only to break up ordinary travel, but also to exact tolls from the public for the privilege of using the peculiar conveyances adapted to a railroad. If a right of this description is not conferred when a highway is authorized by law, it is idle to pretend that any proprietor is divested of such a right. It would seem that, under such circumstances, the true construction of highway laws could hardly be debatable, and that the absence of legal identity between the two uses of which we speak was patent and entire.

" Again, no argument or illustration can strengthen the self-evident proposition that, when a railway is authorized over a public highway, a right is created against the proprietor of the fee, in favor of a person, an artificial person, to whom he before bore no legal relation whatever. It is understood that when such an easement is sought or bestowed, a new and independent right will accrue to the railroad corporation as against the owner of the soil, and that, without any reference to the existence of the highway, his land will forever stand charged with the accruing servitude. Accordingly, if such a highway were to be discontinued according to the legal forms prescribed for that purpose, the railroad corporation would still insist upon the express and independent grant of an easement to itself, enabling it to maintain its own road on the site of the abandoned roadway. We are of opinion, therefore, as was distinctly intimated by this court in a former case (see opinion of Hinman, J., in Nicholson v. N. Y. & N. H. R. R. Co., 22 Conn. 85), that to subject the owner of the soil of a highway to a further appropriation of his land to railway uses is the imposition of a new servitude upon his estate, and is an act demanding the compensation which the law awards when land is taken for public purposes."

These cases, however, have had reference to the common railroad, operated by steam. In one of the New York cases[1] it is intimated, and in another case in the same State it was directly decided, that the ruling should be the same in the case of the street railway operated by horse-power.[2] There is generally, however, a very great difference in the two cases, and some of the considerations to which the courts have attached importance could have no application in many cases of common horse railways. A horse railway, as a general thing, will interfere very little with the ordinary use of the way by the public, even upon the very line of the road ; and in many cases it would be a relief to an overburdened way, rather than an impediment to the previous use. In Connecticut, after it had been decided, as above shown, that the owner of the fee subject to a perpetual highway was entitled to compensation when the highway was appropriated for an ordinary railroad, it was also held that the authority to lay and use a horse-railway track in a public street was not a new servitude imposed upon the land for which the owner of the fee would be entitled to damages, but that it was a part of the public use to which the land was originally subjected when taken for a street.[3] The same distinction between horse railways and those operated by steam is also taken in recent New York cases.[4] But whether the mere difference in the motive-power will make different principles applicable, is a question which the courts will probably have occasion to consider further. Conceding that the interests of individual owners will not generally suffer, or their use of the highway be incommoded by the laying down and use of the track of a horse railway upon it, there are nevertheless cases where it might seriously impede, if not altogether exclude, the general travel and use by the ordinary modes, and very greatly reduce the value of all the property along the line. Suppose, for instance, a narrow street in a city, occupied altogether by wholesale houses, which require constantly the use of the whole street in connection with their business, and suppose this to be turned over to a street-railway company, whose line is such as to make the road a principal avenue of travel, and to require such

---

[1] Wager v. Troy Union R. R. Co., 25 N. Y. 532.

[2] Craig v. Rochester City & Brighton R. R. Co., 39 Barb. 449.

[3] Elliott v. Fair Haven & Westville R. R. Co., 32 Conn. 586.

[4] Brooklyn Central, &c. R. R. Co. v. Brooklyn City R. R. Co., 33 Barb. 422
People v. Kerr, 37 Barb. 357 ; Same case, 27 N. Y. 188.

constant passage of cars as to drive all drayage from the street.
The corporation, under these circumstances, will substantially have
a monopoly in the use of the street; their vehicles will drive the
business from it, and the business property will become comparatively worthless. And if property owners are without remedy in
such case, it is certainly a very great hardship upon them, and a
very striking and forcible instance and illustration of damage without legal injury.

When property is appropriated for a public way, and the proprietor is paid for the public easement, the compensation is generally estimated, in practice, at the value of the land itself.[1] If,
therefore, no other circumstances were to be taken into the
account in these cases, the owner, who has been paid the value of
his land, could not reasonably complain of any use to which it
might afterwards be put by the public. But, as pointed out in the
Connecticut case,[2] the compensation is always liable either to
exceed or to fall below the value of the land taken, in consequence
of incidental injuries or benefits to the owner as proprietor of the
land which remains. These injuries or benefits will be estimated
with reference to the identical use to which the property is appropriated; and if it is afterwards put to another use, which causes
greater incidental injury, and the owner is not entitled to further
compensation, it is very evident that he has suffered a wrong by
the change which could not have been foreseen and provided
against. And if, on the other hand, he is entitled in any case to
an assessment of damages in consequence of such an appropriation
of the street affecting his rights injuriously, then he must be entitled to such an assessment in every case, and the question involved
will be, not as to the right, but only of the *quantum* of damages.
The horse railway either is or is not the imposition of a new burden upon the estate. If it is not, the owner of the fee is entitled
to compensation in no case; if it is, he is entitled to have an assessment of damages in every case.

In New York, where, by law, when a public street is laid out or
dedicated, the fee in the soil becomes vested in the city, it has been
held that the legislature might authorize the construction of a
horse railway in a street, and that neither the city nor the owners
of lots were entitled to compensation, notwithstanding it was

---

[1] Murray v. County Commissioners, 12 Met. 457, per Shaw, Ch. J.

[2] Imlay v. Union Branch R. R. Co., 26 Conn. 257.

found as a fact that the lot owners would suffer injury from the construction of the road. The city was not entitled, because, though it held the fee, it held it in trust for the use of all the people of the State, and not as corporate or municipal property; and the land having been originally acquired under the right of eminent domain, and the trust being *publici juris*, it was under the unqualified control of the legislature, and any appropriation of it to public use by legislative authority could not be regarded as an appropriation of the private property of the city. And so far as the adjacent lot owners were concerned, their interest in the streets, as distinct from that of other citizens, was only as having a possibility of reverter after the public use of the land should cease; and the value of this, if anything, was inappreciable, and could not entitle them to compensation.[1]

So in Indiana, where the title in fee to streets in cities and villages is vested in the public, it is held that the adjacent land owners are not entitled to the statutory remedy for an assessment of damages in consequence of the street being appropriated to the use of a railroad; and this without regard to the motive-power by which the road is operated. At the same time it is also held that the lot owners may maintain an action at law if, in consequence of the railroad, they are cut off from the ordinary use of the street.[2] So in the State of Illinois, in a case where a lot owner had filed a bill in equity to restrain the laying down of the track of a railroad, by consent of the common council, to be operated by steam in one of the streets of Chicago, it was held that the bill could not be maintained; the title to the street being in the city, which might appropriate it to any proper city purpose.[3]

[1] People *v.* Kerr, 37 Barb. 357; Same case, 27 N. Y. 188. And see Brooklyn Central, &c. R. R. Co. *v.* Brooklyn City R. R. Co., 33 Barb. 420; Brooklyn & Newtown R. R. Co. *v.* Coney Island R. R. Co., 35 Barb. 364; New York *v.* Kerr, 38 Barb. 369; Chapman *v.* Albany & Schenectady R. R. Co., 10 Barb. 360. Although, in the case of People *v.* Kerr, the several judges seem generally to have agreed on the principle as stated in the text, it is not very clear how much importance was attached to the fact that the fee to the street was in the city, or that the decision would have been different if that had not been the case.

[2] Protzman *v.* Indianapolis & Cincinnati R. R. Co., 9 Ind. 467; New Albany & Salem R. R. Co. *v.* O'Daily, 13 Ind. 353; Same *v.* Same, 12 Ind. 551.

[3] Moses *v.* Pittsburg, Fort Wayne & Chicago R. R. Co., 21 Ill. 522. We quote from the opinion of Caton, Ch. J.: "By the city charter, the common council is vested with the exclusive control and regulation of the streets of the city, the fee-simple title to which we have already decided is vested in the muni-

It is not easy, as is very evident, to trace a clear line of authority running through the various decisions bearing upon the

cipal corporation. The city charter also empowers the common council to direct and control the location of railroad tracks within the city. In granting this permission to locate the track in Beach Street, the common council acted under an express power granted by the legislature. So that the defendant has all the right which both the legislature and the common council could give it, to occupy the street with its track. But the complainant assumes higher ground, and claims that any use of the street, even under the authority of the legislature and the common council, which tends to deteriorate the value of his property on the street, is a violation of that fundamental law which forbids private property to be taken for public use without just compensation. This is manifestly an erroneous view of the constitutional guaranty thus invoked. It must necessarily happen that streets will be used for various legitimate purposes, which will, to a greater or less extent, incommode persons residing or doing business upon them, and just to that extent damage their property; and yet such damage is incident to all city property, and for it a party can claim no remedy. The common council may appoint certain localities where hacks and drays shall stand waiting for employment, or where wagons loaded with hay or wood, or other commodities, shall stand waiting for purchasers. This may drive customers away from shops or stores in the vicinity, and yet there is no remedy for the damage. A street is made for the passage of persons and property; and the law cannot define what exclusive means of transportation and passage shall be used. Universal experience shows that this can best be left to the determination of the municipal authorities, who are supposed to be best acquainted with the wants and necessities of the citizens generally. To say that a new mode of passage shall be banished from the streets, no matter how much the general good may require it, simply because streets were not so used in the days of Blackstone, would hardly comport with the advancement and enlightenment of the present age. Steam has but lately taken the place, to any extent, of animal power for land transportation, and for that reason alone shall it be expelled the streets? For the same reason camels must be kept out, though they might be profitably employed. Some fancy horse or timid lady might be frightened by such uncouth objects. Or is the objection not in the motive-power, but because the carriages are larger than were formerly used, and run upon iron, and are confined to a given track in the street? Then street railroads must not be admitted; they have large carriages which run on iron rails, and are confined to a given track. Their momentum is great, and may do damage to ordinary vehicles or foot passengers. Indeed we may suppose or assume that streets occupied by them are not so pleasant for other carriages, or so desirable for residences or business stands, as if not thus occupied. But for this reason the property owners along the street cannot expect to stop such improvements. The convenience of those who live at a greater distance from the centre of a city requires the use of such improvements, and for their benefit the owners of property upon the street must submit to the burden, when the common council determine that the public good requires it. Cars upon street railroads are now generally if not universally propelled by horses, but who can say how long it will be before it will be found safe and profitable to propel them with

appropriation of the ordinary highways and streets to the use of railroads of any grade or species; but a strong inclination is apparent to hold that, when the fee in the public way is taken from the former owner, it is taken *for any public use whatever* to which the public authorities, with the legislative assent, may see fit afterwards to devote it, in furtherance of the general purpose of the original appropriation; [1] and if this is so, the owner must be held to be compensated at the time of the original taking for any such possible use; and he takes his chances of that use, or any change in it, proving beneficial or deleterious to any remaining property he may own or business he may be engaged in; and it must also be held that the possibility that the land may, at some future time, revert to him, by the public use ceasing, is too remote and contingent to be considered as property at all. [2] At the same time it must be confessed that it is difficult to determine precisely how far some of the decisions made have been governed by the circumstance that the fee was or was not in the public, or, on the other hand, have proceeded on the theory that a railway was only in furtherance of the original purpose of the appropriation, and not

steam, or some other power besides horses? Should we say that this road should be enjoined, we could advance no reason for it which would not apply with equal force to street railroads; so that consistency would require that we should stop all. Nor would the evil which would result from the rule we must lay down stop here. We must prohibit every use of a street which discommodes those who reside or do business upon it, because their property will else be damaged. This question has been presented in other States, and in some instances, where the public have only an easement in the street, and the owner of the adjoining property still holds the fee in the street, it has been sustained; but the weight of authority, and certainly, in our apprehension, all sound reasoning, is the other way."

All the cases from which we have quoted assume that the use of the street by the railroad company is still a public use; and probably it would not be held that an appropriation of a street, or of any part of it, by an individual or company, for his or their own private use, unconnected with any accommodation of the public, was consistent with the purpose for which it was originally acquired. See Brown *v.* Duplessis, 14 La. An. 842; Green *v.* Portland, 32 Me. 431.

[1] On this subject see, in addition to the other cases cited, West *v.* Bancroft, 32 Vt. 367; Kelsey *v.* King, 32 Barb. 410; Ohio & Lexington R. R. Co. *v.* Applegate, 8 Dana, 289. When, however, land is taken or dedicated specifically for a street, it would seem, although the fee is taken, it is taken for the restricted use only; that is to say, for such uses as streets in cities are commonly put to.

[2] As to whether there is such possibility of reverter, see Heyward *v.* Mayor, &c. of New York, 7 N. Y. 314; People *v.* Kerr, 27 N. Y. 211, per Wright, J.; Plitt *v.* Cox, 43 Penn. St. 486.

to be regarded as the imposition of any new burden, even where an easement only was originally taken.[1]

Perhaps the true distinction in these cases relates, not to the motive-power of the railway, or to the question whether the fee simple or a mere easement was taken in the original appropriation, but depends upon the question whether the railway constitutes a thoroughfare, or on the other hand is a mere local convenience. When land is taken or dedicated for a town street, it is unquestionably appropriated for all the ordinary purposes of a town street; not merely the purposes to which such streets were formerly applied, but those demanded by new improvements and new wants. Among these purposes is the use for carriages which run upon a grooved track; and the preparation of important streets in large cities for their use is not only a frequent necessity, which must be supposed to have been contemplated, but it is almost as much a matter of course as the grading and paving. The appropriation of a country highway for the purposes of a railway, on the other hand, is neither usual nor often important; and it cannot with any justice be regarded as within the contemplation of the parties when

[1] There is great difficulty, as it seems to us, in supporting important distinctions upon the fact that the *fee* was originally taken for the use of the public, instead of a mere easement. If the fee is appropriated or dedicated, it is for a particular use only; and it is a *conditional* fee, — a fee on condition that the land continue to be occupied for that use. The practical difference in the cases is, that when the fee is taken, the possession of the original owner is excluded; and in the case of city streets where there is occasion to devote them to many other purposes besides those of passage, but nevertheless not inconsistent, such as for the laying of water and gas pipes, and the construction of sewers, this exclusion of any private right of occupation is important, and will sometimes save controversies and litigation. But to say that when a man has declared a dedication for a particular use, under a statute which makes a dedication the gift of a fee, he thereby makes it liable to be appropriated to other purposes, when the same could not be done if a perpetual easement had been dedicated, seems to be basing important distinctions upon a difference which after all is more technical than real, and which in any view does not affect the distinction made. The same reasoning which has sustained the legislature in authorizing a railroad track to be laid down in a city street would support its action in authorizing it to be made into a canal; and the purpose of the original dedication or appropriation would thereby be entirely defeated. Is it not more consistent with established rules to hold that a dedication or appropriation to one purpose confines the use to that purpose; and when it is taken for any other, the original owner has not been compensated for the injury he may sustain in consequence, and is therefore entitled to it now?

the highway is first established.   And if this is so, it is clear that the owner cannot be considered as compensated for the new use at the time of the original appropriation.

Although the regulation of a navigable stream will give to the persons incidentally affected no right to compensation, yet if the stream is diverted from its natural course, so that those entitled to its benefits are prevented from making use of it as before, the deprivation of this right is a taking which entitles them to compensation, notwithstanding the taking may be for the purpose of creating another and more valuable channel of navigation.[1] The owners of land over which such a stream flows, although they do not own the flowing water itself, yet have a property in the use of that water as it flows past them, for the purpose of producing mechanical power, or for any of the other purposes for which they can make it available, without depriving those below them of the like use, or encroaching upon the rights of those above; and this property is equally protected with any of a more tangible character.[2]

What Interest in Land can be taken under the Right of Eminent Domain.

Where land is appropriated to the public use under the right of eminent domain, and against the will of the owner, we have seen how careful the law is to limit the public authorities to their precise needs, and not to allow the dispossession of the owner from any portion of his freehold which the public use does not require. This must be so on the general principle that the right being based on necessity cannot be any broader than the necessity which supports it.   For the same reason, it would seem that, in respect to the land actually taken, if there can be any conjoint occupation of the owner and the public, the former should not be altogether excluded, but should be allowed to occupy for his private purposes to any extent not inconsistent with the public use.   As a general rule, the laws for the exercise of the right of eminent domain do not assume to go further than to appropriate the use, and the title

[1] People v. Canal Appraisers, 13 Wend. 355. And see Hatch v. Vermont Central R. R. Co., 25 Vt. 49; Bellinger v. New York Central R. R. Co., 23 N. Y. 42; Gardner v. Newburg, 2 Johns. Ch. 162.

[2] Morgan v. King, 18 Barb. 284; Same case, 35 N. Y. 454; Gardner v. Newburg, 2 Johns. Ch. 162.

in fee still remains in the original owner. In the common high-ways, the public have a perpetual easement, but the soil is the property of the adjacent owner, and he may make any use of it which does not interfere with the public right of passage, and the public can use it only for the purposes usual with such ways.[1] And when the land ceases to be used by the public as a way, the owner will again become restored to his complete and exclusive possession, and the fee will cease to be encumbered with the easement.[2]

It seems, however, to be competent for the State to appropriate the title to the land in fee, and so to altogether exclude any use by the former owner, except that which every individual citizen is entitled to make, if in the opinion of the legislature it is needful that the fee be taken. The judicial decisions to this effect proceed upon the idea that, in some cases, the public purposes cannot be fully accomplished without appropriating the complete title ; and where this is so in the opinion of the legislature, the same reasons which support the legislature in their right to decide absolutely and finally upon the necessity of the taking will also support their decision as to the estate to be taken. The power, it is said in one case, " must of necessity rest in the legislature, in order to secure the useful exercise and enjoyment of the right in question. A case might arise where a temporary use would be all that the public interest required. Another case might require the permanent and apparently the perpetual occupation and enjoyment of the property by the public ; and the right to take it must be coextensive with the necessity of the case, and the measure of compensation should of course be graduated by the nature and the duration of the estate or interest of which the owner is deprived." [3] And it was therefore held, where the statute provided that lands might be compulsorily taken in fee-simple for the purposes of an almshouse extension, and they were taken accordingly, that the title of the original owner was thereby entirely divested, and that when the land ceased to

---

[1] In Adams v. Rivers, 11 Barb. 390, a person who stood in the public way and abused the occupant of an adjoining lot was held liable in trespass as being unlawfully there, because not using the highway for the purpose to which it was appropriated.

[2] Dean v. Sullivan R. R. Co., 2 Fost. 321 ; Blake v. Rich, 34 N. H. 282 ; Henry v. Dubuque & Pacific R. R. Co., 2 Iowa, 288 ; Weston v. Foster, 7 Met. 299 ; Quimby v. Vermont Central R. R. Co., 23 Vt. 387 ; Giesy v. Cincinnati, &c. R. R. Co., 4 Ohio, N. S. 327.

[3] Heyward v. Mayor, &c. of New York, 7 N. Y. 314.

be used for the public purpose, the title remained in the municipality which had appropriated it, and did not revert to the former owner or his heirs.[1] And it does not seem to be uncommon to provide that, in the case of some classes of public ways, and especially of city and village streets, the dedication or appropriation to the public use shall vest the title to the land in the State, county, or city ; the purposes for which the land may be required by the public being so numerous and varied, and so impossible of complete specification in advance, that nothing short of a complete ownership in the public is deemed sufficient to provide for them. In any case, however, an easement only would be taken, unless the statute plainly contemplated and provided for the appropriation of a larger interest.[2]

Compensation for Property taken.

It is a primary requisite, in the appropriation of lands for public purposes, that compensation shall be made therefor. Eminent domain differs from taxation in that, in the former case, the citizen is compelled to surrender to the public something beyond his due proportion for the public benefit. The public seize and appropriate his particular estate, because it has special need for it, and not because it is right, as between him and the government, that he should surrender it.[3] To him, therefore, the benefit and protection he receives from the government are not sufficient compensation ; for those benefits are the equivalent for the taxes he pays, and the other public burdens he assumes in common with the community at large. And this compensation must be pecuniary in its character, because it is in the nature of a payment for a compulsory purchase.[4]

[1] Heyward v. Mayor, &c. of New York, 7 N. Y. 314. And see Baker v. Johnson, 2 Hill, 348 ; Wheeler v. Rochester, &c. R. R. Co., 12 Barb. 227 ; Munger v. Tonawanda R. R. Co., 4 N. Y. 349 ; Rexford v. Knight, 11 N. Y. 308 ; Commonwealth v. Fisher, 1 Pen. & Watts, 462 ; De Varaigne v. Fox, 2 Blatch. 95 ; Coster v. N. J. R. R. Co., 3 Zab. 227 ; Plitt v. Cox, 43 Penn. St. 486.

[2] Barclay v. Howell's Lessee, 6 Pet. 498 ; Rust v. Lowe, 6 Mass. 90 ; Jackson v. Rutland & B. R. R. Co., 25 Vt. 151 ; Jackson v. Hathaway, 15 Johns. 447.

[3] People v. Mayor, &c. of Brooklyn, 4 N. Y. 419 ; Woodbridge v. Detroit, 8 Mich. 278 ; Booth v. Woodbury, 32 Conn. 130.

[4] The effect of the right of eminent domain against the individual " amounts to nothing more than a power to oblige him to sell and convey when the public necessities require it." Johnson, J. in Fletcher v. Peck, 6 Cranch, 145. And see Bradshaw v. Rogers, 20 Johns. 103, per Spencer, Ch. J. ; People v. Mayor,

The *time* when the compensation must be made may depend
upon the peculiar constitutional provisions of the State. In some
of the States, by express constitutional direction, compensation
must be made before the property is taken. No constitutional
principle, however, is violated by a statute which allows private
property to be entered upon and temporarily occupied for the
purpose of a survey and other incipient proceedings, with a view
to judging and determining whether the public needs require the
appropriation or not, and, if so, what the proper location shall be ;
and the party acting under this statutory authority would neither
be bound to make compensation for the temporary possession, nor
be liable to action of trespass.[1] When, however, the land has
been viewed, and a determination arrived at to appropriate it, the
question of compensation is to be considered ; and in the absence of
any express constitutional provision fixing the time and the manner of making it, the question who is to take the property —
whether the State, or one of its political divisions or municipalities, or, on the other hand, some private corporation — may be an
important consideration.

When the property is taken directly by the State, or by any
municipal corporation by State authority, it has been repeatedly
held not to be essential to the validity of a law for the exercise of
the right of eminent domain, that it should provide for making
compensation before the actual appropriation. It is sufficient if
provision is made by the law by which the party can obtain compensation, and that an impartial tribunal is provided for assessing
it.[2] The decisions upon this point assume that, when the State

&c. of Brooklyn, 4 N. Y. 419 ; Carson *v.* Coleman, 3 Stockt. 106 ; United States
v. Minnesota, &c. R. R. Co., 1 Minn. 127 ; Railroad Co. *v.* Ferris, 26 Texas, 603 ;
Curran *v.* Shattuck, 24 Cal. 427 ; State *v.* Graves, 19 Md. 351.

[1] Bloodgood *v.* Mohawk & Hudson R. R. Co., 14•Wend. 51, and 18 Wend. 9 ;
Cushman *v.* Smith, 34 Me. 247 ; Nichols *v.* Somerset, &c. R. R. Co., 43 Me. 356 ;
Mercer *v.* McWilliams, Wright (Ohio), 132 ; Walther *v.* Warner, 25 Mo. 277 ;
Fox *v.* W. P. R. R. Co., 31 Cal. 538.

[2] Bloodgood *v.* Mohawk & Hudson R. R. Co., 18 Wend. 9 ; Rogers *v.* Brad-
shaw, 20 Johns. 744 ; Calking *v.* Baldwin, 4 Wend. 667 ; Case *v.* Thompson, 6
Wend. 634 ; Fletcher *v.* Auburn & Syracuse R. R. Co., 25 Wend. 462 ; Rexford
v. Knight, 11 N. Y. 308 ; Taylor *v.* Marcy, 25 Ill. 518 ; Callison *v.* Hedrick, 15
Grat. 244 ; Jackson *v.* Winn's Heirs, 4 Lit. 323 ; People *v.* Green, 3 Mich. 496 ;
Lyon *v.* Jerome, 26 Wend. 497, per Verplanck, Senator ; Gardner *v.* Newburg,
2 Johns. Ch. 162 ; Charlestown Branch R. R. Co. *v.* Middlesex, 7 Met. 78 ;
Harper *v.* Richardson, 22 Cal. 251 ; Baker *v.* Johnson, 2 Hill, 342 ; People *v.*

has provided a remedy by resort to which the party can have his compensation assessed, adequate means are afforded for its satisfaction ; since the property of the municipality, or of the State, is a fund to which he can resort without risk of loss.[1] It is essential, however, that the remedy be one to which the party can resort on his own motion ; if the provision be such that only the public authorities appropriating the land are authorized to take proceedings for the assessment, it must be held to be void.[2] But if the remedy is adequate, and the party is allowed to pursue it, it is not unconstitutional to limit the period in which he shall resort to it, and to provide that, unless he shall take proceedings for the assessment of damages within a specified time, all right thereto shall be barred.[3] The right to compensation, when property is appropriated by the public, may always be waived ;[4] and a failure to apply for and

Hayden, 6 Hill, 359. " Although it may not be necessary, within the constitutional provision, that the amount of compensation should be actually ascertained and paid before property is thus taken, it is, I apprehend, the settled doctrine, even as against the State itself, that at least certain and adequate provision must first be made by law (except in cases of public emergency), so that the owner can coerce payment through the judicial tribunals or otherwise, without any unreasonable or unnecessary delay ; otherwise the law making the appropriation is no better than blank paper. Bloodgood v. Mohawk & Hudson R. R. Co., 18 Wend. 9. The provisions of the statute prescribing the mode of compensation in cases like the present, when properly understood and administered, come fully up to this great fundamental principle ; and even if any doubt could be entertained about the true construction, it should be made to lean in favor of the one that is found to be most in conformity with the constitutional requisite." People v. Hayden, 6 Hill, 359. " A provision for compensation is an indispensable attendant upon the due and constitutional exercise of the power of depriving an individual of his property." Gardner v. Newburg, 2 Johns. Ch. 168.

[1] In Commissioners, &c. v. Bowie, 34 Ala. 461, it was held that a provision by law that compensation when assessed should be paid to the owner by the county treasurer sufficiently secured its payment.

[2] Shepardson v. Milwaukee & Beloit R. R. Co., 6 Wis. 605 ; Powers v. Bears, 12 Wis. 220. See McCann v. Sierra Co., 7 Cal. 121 ; Colton v. Rossi, 9 Cal. 595 ; Ragatz v. Dubuque, 4 Iowa, 343. But in People v. Hayden, 6 Hill, 359, where the statute provided for appraisers who were to proceed to appraise the land as soon as it was appropriated, the proper remedy of the owner, if they failed to perform this duty, was held to be to apply for a mandamus.

[3] People v. Green, 3 Mich. 496 ; Charlestown Branch R. R. Co. v. Middlesex, 7 Met. 78 ; Rexford v. Knight, 11 N. Y. 308 ; Taylor v. Marcy, 25 Ill. 518 ; Callison v. Hedrick, 15 Grat. 244 ; Gilmer v. Lime Point, 18 Cal. 229 ; Harper v. Richardson, 22 Cal. 251.

[4] Matter of Albany St., 11 Wend. 149 ; Brown v. Worcester, 13 Gray, 31.

have the compensation assessed, when reasonable time and opportunity and a proper tribunal are afforded for the purpose, may
well be considered a waiver.

Where, however, the property is not taken by the State, or by a
municipal corporation, but by a private corporation which, though
for this purpose to be regarded as a public agent, appropriates it
for the benefit and profit of its members, and which may or may
not be sufficiently responsible to make secure and certain the payment, in all cases, of the compensation which shall be assessed, it
is certainly proper, and it has sometimes been questioned whether
it was not absolutely essential, that payment be actually made before the owner could be divested of his freehold.[1] Chancellor
Kent has expressed the opinion, that compensation and appropriation should be concurrent. "The settled and fundamental doctrine is, that government has no right to take private property for
public purposes, without giving just compensation ; and it seems
to be necessarily implied that the indemnity should, in cases which
will admit of it, be previously and equitably ascertained, and be
ready for reception, concurrently in point of time with the actual
exercise of the right of eminent domain." [2] And while this is not
an inflexible rule unless established by the constitution, it is so
just and reasonable that statutory provisions for taking private
property very generally make payment precede or accompany the
appropriation, and by several of the State constitutions this is
expressly required.[3] And on general principles, it is essential that
an adequate fund be provided from which the owner of the property can certainly obtain compensation ; it is not competent to
deprive him of his property, and turn him over to an action at law
against a corporation which may or may not prove responsible,

---

[1] This is the intimation in Shepardson v. Milwaukee & Beloit R. R. Co., 6 Wis.
605 ; Powers v. Bears, 12 Wis. 220 ; State v. Graves, 19 Md. 351 ; Dronberger v.
Reed, 11 Ind. 420. But see Calking v. Baldwin, 4 Wend. 667.

[2] 2 Kent, 339, note.

[3] The constitution of Florida provides "that private property shall not be
taken or applied to public use, unless just compensation be first made therefor."
Art. 1, § 14. See also, to the same effect, Constitution of Georgia, art. 1, § 17 ;
Constitution of Iowa, art. 1, § 18 ; Constitution of Kansas, art. 12, § 4 ; Constitu-
tion of Kentucky, art. 13, § 14 ; Constitution of Minnesota, art. 1, § 13 ; Consti-
tution of Mississippi, art. 1, § 13 ; Constitution of Nevada, art. 1, § 8 ; Constitu-
tion of Ohio, art. 1, § 19. The Constitution of Indiana, art. 1, § 21, and that of
Oregon, art. 1, § 19, require compensation to be first made, except when the property is appropriated by the State.

and to a judgment of uncertain efficacy.[1] For the consequence would be, in some cases, that the party might lose his estate without redress, in violation of the inflexible maxim upon which the right is based.

What the tribunal shall be which is to assess the compensation must be determined either by the constitution or by the statute which provides for the appropriation. The case is not one where, as a matter of right, the party is entitled to a trial by jury, unless the constitution has provided that tribunal for the purpose.[2] Nevertheless, the proceeding is judicial in its character, and the party in interest is entitled to have an impartial tribunal, and the usual rights and privileges which attend judicial investigations. It is not competent for the State itself to fix the compensation through the legislature, for this would make it the judge in its own cause.[3] And, if a jury is provided, the party must have the ordinary opportunity to appear when it is to be empanelled, that he may make any legal objections.[4] And he has the same right to notice of the time and place of assessment as he would have in any other case of judicial proceedings, and the assessment will be invalid if no such notice is given.[5] These are just as well as familiar rules, and they are perhaps invariably recognized in legislation.

It is not our purpose to follow these proceedings, and to attempt to point out the course of practice to be observed, and which is so different under the statutes of different States. An inflexible rule should govern them all, that the interest and exclusive right of the owner is to be regarded and protected so far as may be consistent with a recognition of the public necessity. While the owner is not to be disseized until compensation is provided, neither, on the other hand, when the public authorities have taken such steps as to finally settle upon the appropriation, ought he to be left in a

---

[1] Shepardson v. Milwaukee & Beloit R. R. Co., 6 Wis. 605 ; Walther v. Warner, 25 Mo. 277 ; Curran v. Shattuck, 24 Cal. 427; Memphis & Charleston R. R. Co. v. Payne, 37 Miss. 700 ; Henry v. Dubuque & Pacific R. R. Co., 10 Iowa, 540.

[2] Petition of Mount Washington Co., 35 N. H. 134.

[3] Charles River Bridge v. Warren Bridge, 7 Pick. 344 ; Same case, 11 Pet. 571, per McLean, J.

[4] People v. Tallman, 36 Barb. 222 ; Booneville v. Ormrod, 26 Miss. 193. A jury, without further explanation in the law, must be understood as one of twelve persons. Lamb v. Lane, 4 Ohio, N. S. 167.

[5] Hood v. Finch, 8 Wis. 381 ; Dickey v. Tennison, 27 Mo. 373.

state of uncertainty, and compelled to wait for compensation until some future time, when they may see fit to occupy it. The land should either be his or he should be paid for it. Whenever, therefore, the necessary steps have been taken on the part of the public to select the property to be taken, locate the public work, and declare the appropriation, the owner becomes absolutely entitled to the compensation, whether the public proceed at once to occupy the property or not. If a street is laid out over the land of an individual, he is entitled to demand payment of his damages, without waiting for the street to be opened.[1] And if a railway line is located across his land, and the damages are appraised, his right to payment is complete, and he cannot be required to wait until the railway company shall actually occupy his premises, or enter upon the construction of the road at that point. It is not to be forgotten, however, that the proceedings for the assessment and collection of damages are statutory, and displace the usual remedies ; that the public agents who keep within the statute are not liable to common-law action ;[2] that it is only where they fail to follow the statute that they render themselves liable as trespassers ;[3] though if they construct their work in a careless, negligent, and improper manner, by means of which carelessness, negligence, or improper construction a party is injured in his rights, he may have an action at the common law as in other cases of injurious negligence.[4]

---

[1] Philadelphia v. Dickson, 38 Penn. St. 247 ; Philadelphia v. Dyer, 41 Penn. St. 463 ; Hallock v. Franklin County, 2 Met. 559 ; Harrington v. County Commissioners, 22 Pick. 268 ; Blake v. Dubuque, 13 Iowa, 66 ; Higgins v. Chicago, 18 Ill. 276 ; County of Peoria v. Harvey, Ibid. 364 ; Shaw v. Charlestown, 3 Allen, 538 ; Hampton v. Coffin, 4 N. H. 517 ; Clough v. Unity, 18 N. H. 77. And where a city thus appropriates land for a street, it would not be allowed to set up in defence to a demand for compensation its own irregularities in the proceedings taken to condemn the land. Higgins v. Chicago, 18 Ill. 276 ; Chicago v. Wheeler, 25 Ill. 478.

[2] East & West India Dock, &c. Co. v. Gattke, 15 Jur. 61 ; Kimble v. White Water Valley Canal, 1 Ind. 285 ; Mason v. Kennebec, &c. R. R. Co., 31 Me. 215 ; Aldrich v. Cheshire R. R. Co., 1 Fost. 359 ; Brown v. Beatty, 34 Miss. 227 ; Pettibone v. La Crosse & Milwaukee R. R. Co., 14 Wis. 443 ; Vilas v. Milwaukee & Mississippi R. R. Co., 15 Wis. 233.

[3] Dean v. Sullivan R. R. Co., 2 Fost. 316 ; Furniss v. Hudson River R. R. Co., 5 Sandf. 551.

[4] Lawrence v. Great Northern R. Co., 20 L. J. Rep. Q. B. 293 ; Bagnall v. London & N. W. R., 7 H. & N. 423 ; Brown v. Cayuga & Susquehanna R. R. Co., 12 N. Y. 487.

The principle upon which the damages are to be assessed is always an important consideration in these cases; and the circumstances of different appropriations are sometimes so peculiar that it has been found somewhat difficult to establish a rule that shall always be just and equitable. If the whole of a man's estate is taken, there can generally be little difficulty in fixing upon the measure of compensation; for it is apparent that, in such a case, he ought to have the whole market value of his premises, and he cannot reasonably demand more. The question is reduced to one of market value, to be determined upon the testimony of those who have knowledge upon that subject, or whose business or experience entitles their opinions to weight. It may be that, in such a case, the market value may not seem to the owner an adequate compensation; for he may have reasons peculiar to himself, springing from association, or other cause, which make him unwilling to part with the property on the estimate of his neighbors; but such reasons are incapable of being taken into account in legal proceedings, where the question is one of compensation in money, inasmuch as it is manifestly impossible to measure them by any standard of pecuniary value. Concede to the government a right to appropriate the property on paying for it, and we are at once remitted to the same standards for estimating values which are applied in other cases, and which necessarily measure the worth of property by its value as an article of sale, or as a means of producing pecuniary returns.

When, however, only a portion of a parcel of land is appropriated, just compensation may perhaps depend upon the effect which the appropriation may have on the owner's interest in the remainder, to increase or diminish its value, in consequence of the use to which that taken is to be devoted, or in consequence of the condition in which it may leave the remainder in respect to convenience of use. If, for instance, a public way is laid out through a tract of land which before was not accessible, and if in consequence it is given a front, or two fronts, upon the street, which furnish valuable and marketable sites for building lots, it may be that the value of that which remains is made, in consequence of taking a part, vastly greater than the whole was before, and that the owner is benefited instead of damnified by the appropriation. Indeed, the great majority of streets in cities and villages are dedicated to the public use by the owners of lands, without any other compensation or expectation of compensation than the increased benefit; and this is very often the case with land for other public improvements, which are of peculiar value to the locality where they are made. But where, on the other hand, a railroad is laid out across a man's premises, running between his house and his outbuildings, necessitating, perhaps, the removal of some of them, or upon such a grade as to render deep cuttings or high embankments necessary, and thereby greatly increasing the inconveniences attending the management and use of the land, as well as the risks of accidental injuries, it will often happen that the pecuniary loss which he would suffer by the appropriation of the right of way would greatly exceed the value of the land taken, and to pay him that value only would be to make very inadequate compensation.

It seems clear that, in these cases, it is proper and just that the injuries suffered, and the benefits received, by the proprietor, as owner of the remaining portion of the land, should be taken into account in measuring the compensation. This, indeed, is generally conceded; but what injuries shall be allowed for, or what benefits estimated, is not always so apparent. The question, as we find it considered by the authorities, seems to be, not so much what the value is of that which is taken, but whether what remains is reduced in value by the appropriation, and, if so, to what extent; in other words, what pecuniary injury the owner sustains by a part of his land being appropriated. But, in estimating either the injuries or the benefits, those which the owner sustains or receives in common with the community generally, and which are not peculiar to him and connected with his ownership, use, and enjoyment of the particular parcel of land, should be altogether excluded, as it would be unjust to compensate him for the one, or to charge him with the other, when no account is taken of such incidental benefits and injuries with other citizens who receive or feel them equally with himself, but whose lands do not chance to be taken.[1]

---

[1] In Somerville & Easton R. R. Co. *ads.* Doughty, 2 Zab. 495, a motion was made for a new trial on an assessment of compensation for land taken by a railroad company, on the ground that the judge in his charge to the jury informed them "that they were authorized by law to ascertain and assess the damages sustained by the plaintiff to his other lands not taken and occupied by the defendants; to his dwelling-house, and other buildings and improvements, by reducing their value, changing their character, obstructing their free use, by subjecting his buildings to the hazards of fire, his family and stock to injury and obstruction in their necessary passage across the road, the inconvenience caused by embank-

The question, then, in these cases, relates first to the value of the land appropriated; which is to be assessed with reference to what ments or excavations, and, in general, the effect of the railroad upon his adjacent lands, in deteriorating their value, in the condition they were found, whether adapted for agricultural purposes only, or for dwellings, stores, shops, or other like purposes."

" On a careful review of this charge," says the judge, delivering the opinion of the court, " I cannot see that any legal principle was violated, or any unsound doctrine advanced. The charter provides that the jury shall assess the value of the land and materials taken by the company, and the damages. The damages here contemplated are not damages to the land actually occupied or covered by the road, but such damages as the owner may sustain in his other and adjacent lands not occupied by the company's road. His buildings may be reduced in value by the contiguity of the road, and the use of engines upon it. His lands and buildings, before adapted and used for particular purposes, may, from the same cause, become utterly unfitted for such purposes. The owner may be incommoded by high embankments or deep excavations on the line of the road, his buildings subjected to greater hazard from fire, his household and stock to injury or destruction, unless guarded with more than ordinary care. It requires no special experience or sagacity to perceive that such are the usual and natural effects of railroads upon the adjoining lands, and which necessarily deteriorate not only their marketable but their intrinsic value. The judge, therefore, did not exceed his duty in instructing the jury that these were proper subjects for their consideration in estimating the damages which the plaintiff might sustain by reason of the location of this road upon and across his lands." And in the same case it was held that the jury, in assessing compensation, were to adopt as the standard of value for the lands taken, not such a price as they would bring at a forced sale in the market for money, but such a price as they could be purchased at, provided they were for sale, and the owner asked such prices as, in the opinion of the community, they were reasonably worth; that it was matter of universal experience that land would not always bring at a forced sale what it was reasonably worth, and the owner, not desiring to sell, could not reasonably be required to take less. In Sater v. Burlington & Mount Pleasant Plank Road Co., 1 Iowa, 393, Isbell, J., says: " The terms used in the constitution, 'just compensation,' are not ambiguous. They undoubtedly mean a fair equivalent; that the person whose property is taken shall be made whole. But while the end to be attained is plain, the mode of arriving at it is not without its difficulty. On due consideration, we see no more practical rule than to first ascertain the fair marketable value of the premises over which the proposed improvement is to pass, irrespective of such improvement, and also a like value of the same, in the condition in which they will be immediately after the land for the improvement has been taken, irrespective of the benefit which will result from the improvement, and the difference in value to constitute the measure of compensation. But in ascertaining the depreciated value of the premises after that part which has been taken for public use has been appropriated, regard must be had only to the immediate, and not remote, consequence of the appropriation; that is to say, the value of the remaining premises is not to be depreciated by heaping consequence on conse-

it is worth for sale, in view of the uses to which it may be applied,
and not simply in reference to its productiveness to the owner in the
condition in which he has seen fit to leave it.[1] Second, if less than
the whole estate is taken, then there is further to be considered
how much the portion not taken is increased or diminished in
value in consequence of the appropriation.[2]

quence. While we see no more practical mode of ascertainment than this, yet it
must still be borne in mind that this is but a mode of ascertainment; that after all,
the true criterion is the one provided by the constitution, namely, just compensation for the property taken." See this rule illustrated and applied in Henry *v.*
Dubuque & Pacific R. R. Co., 2 Iowa, 300, where it is said: " That the language
of the constitution means that the person whose property is taken for public use
shall have a fair equivalent in money for the injury done him by such taking; in
other words, that he shall be made whole so far as money is a measure of compensation, we are equally clear. This just compensation should be precisely commensurate with the injury sustained by having the property taken; neither more
nor less." And see the recent Kentucky cases of Richmond, &c. Co. *v.* Rogers,
1 Duvall, 135; Robinson *v.* Robinson, Ibid. 162.

[1] Matter of Furman St., 17 Wend. 669; Tide-Water Canal Co. *v.* Archer, 9
Gill & J. 480; State *v.* Burlington, &c. R. R. Co., 1 Iowa, 386; Parks *v.* Boston,
15 Pick. 206; First Parish, &c. *v.* Middlesex, 7 Gray, 106; Dickenson *v.* Inhabitants of Fitchburg, 13 Gray, 546; Lexington *v.* Long, 31 Mo. 369.

[2] Denton *v.* Polk, 9 Iowa, 594; Parks *v.* Boston, 15 Pick. 198; Dickenson *v.*
Fitchburg, 13 Gray, 546; Newby *v.* Platte County, 25 Mo. 258; Pacific R. R.
Co. *v.* Chrystal, Ibid. 544; Somerville & Easton R. R. Co. *ads.* Doughty, 2 Zab.
495; Carpenter *v.* Landaff, 42 N. H. 218; Troy & Boston R. R. Co. *v.* Lee, 13
Barb. 169; Tide-Water Canal Co. *v.* Archer, 9 Gill & J. 480; Winona & St.
Paul R. R. Co. *v.* Waldron, 11 Minn. 515; Nicholson *v.* N. Y. & N. H. R. R. Co.,
22 Conn. 74; Nichols *v.* Bridgeport, 23 Conn. 189. " Compensation is an equivalent for property taken, or for an injury. It must be ascertained by estimating
the actual damage the party has sustained. That damage is the sum of the
actual value of the property taken, and of the injury done to the residue of the
property by the use of that part which is taken. The benefit is, in part, an
equivalent to the loss and damage. The loss and damage of the defendant is the
value of the land the company has taken, and the injury which the location and
use of the road through his tract may cause to the remainder. The amount
which may be assessed for these particulars the company admits that it is bound
to pay. But as a set-off, it claims credit for the benefit the defendant has received
from the construction of the road. That benefit may consist in the enhanced
value of the residue of his tract. When the company has paid the defendant the
excess of his loss or damage over and above the benefit and advantage he has
derived from the road, he will have received a just compensation. It is objected
that the enhanced salable value of the land should not be assessed as a benefit to
the defendant, because it is precarious and uncertain. The argument admits that
the enhanced value, if permanent, should be assessed. But whether the appreciation is permanent and substantial, or transient and illusory, is a subject about

But in doing this, there must be excluded from consideration those benefits which the owner receives only in common with the community at large in consequence of his ownership of other property,[1]

which the court is not competent to determine. It must be submitted to a jury, who will give credit to the company according to the circumstances. The argument is not tenable, that an increased salable value is no benefit to the owner of land unless he sells it. This is true if it be assumed that the price will decline. The chance of this is estimated by the jury, in the amount which they may assess for that benefit. The sum assessed is therefore (so far as human foresight can anticipate the future) the exponent of the substantial increase of the value of the land. This is a benefit to the owner, by enlarging his credit and his ability to pay his debts or provide for his family, in the same manner and to the same extent as if his fortune was increased by an acquisition of property." Greenville and Columbia R. R. Co. v. Partlow, 5 Rich. 437. And see Pennsylvania R. R. Co. v. Reiley, 8 Penn. St. 445; Matter of Albany St., 11 Wend. 153; Upton v. South Reading Branch R. R., 8 Cush. 600; Proprietors, &c. v. Nashua and Lowell R. R. Co., 10 Cush. 385; Mayor, &c. of Lexington v. Long, 31 Mo. 369. In Newby v. Platte County, 25 Mo. 358, the right to assess benefits was referred to the taxing power; but this seems not necessary, and indeed somewhat difficult on principle. See Sutton's Heirs v. Louisville, 5 Dana, 30 – 34.

[1] Dickenson v. Inhabitants of Fitchburg, 13 Gray, 546; Newby v. Platte County, 25 Mo. 258; Pacific R. R. Co. v. Chrystal, Ibid. 544; Carpenter v. Landaff, 42 N. H. 218; Mount Washington Co.'s Petition, 35 N. H. 134; Penrice v. Wallis, 37 Miss. 172; Palmer Co. v. Ferrill, 17 Pick. 58; Meacham v. Fitchburg R. R. Co., 4 Cush. 291, where the jury were instructed that, if they were satisfied that the laying out and constructing of the railroad had occasioned any benefit or advantage to the lands of the petitioner through which the road passed, or lands immediately adjoining or connected therewith, rendering the part not taken for the railroad more convenient or useful to the petitioner, or giving it some peculiar increase in value compared with other lands generally in the vicinity, it would be the duty of the jury to allow for such benefit, or increase of value, by way of set-off, in favor of the railroad company; but, on the other hand, if the construction of the railroad, by increasing the convenience of the people of the town generally as a place for residence, and by its anticipated and probable effect in increasing the population, business, and general prosperity of the place, had been the occasion of an increase in the salable value of real estate generally near the station, including the petitioner's land, and thereby occasioning a benefit or advantage to him, in common with other owners of real estate in the vicinity, this benefit was too contingent, indirect, and remote to be brought into consideration in settling the question of damages to the petitioner for taking his particular parcel of land. Upton v. South Reading Branch R. R. Co., 8 Cush. 600. It has sometimes been objected, with great force, that it was unjust and oppressive to set off benefits against the loss and damage which the owner of the property sustains, because thereby he is taxed for such benefits, while his neighbors, no part of whose land is taken, enjoy the same benefits without the loss; and

and also those incidental injuries to other property, such as would
not give to other persons a right to compensation,[1] while allowing
those which directly affect the value of the remainder of the land
not taken ; such as the necessity for increased fencing, and the
like.[2] And if an assessment on these principles makes the benefits
equal the damages and awards the owner nothing, he is nevertheless to be considered as having received full compensation, and consequently as not being in position to complain.[3]

The statutory assessment of compensation will cover all consequential damages which the owner of the land sustains by means
of the construction of the work, except such as may result from

the courts of Kentucky have held it to be unconstitutional, and that full compensation for the land taken must be made in money. Sutton v. Louisville, 5 Dana,
28 ; Rice v. Turnpike Co., 7 Dana, 81 ; Jacob v. Louisville, 9 Dana, 114. And
some other States have established, by their constitutions, the rule that benefits
shall not be deducted. See Deaton v. County of Polk, 9 Iowa, 596 ; Giesy v.
Cincinnati, W. & Z. R. R. Co., 4 Ohio, N. S. 308 ; Woodfolk v. Nashville R. R.
Co., 2 Swan, 422. But the cases generally adopt the doctrine stated in the
text; and if the owner is paid his actual damages, he has no occasion to complain because his neighbors are fortunate enough to receive a benefit. Greenville & Columbia R. R. Co. v. Partlow, 5 Rich. 438 ; Mayor, &c. of Lexington v
Long, 31 Mo. 369.

[1] Somerville, &c. R. R. Co. ads. Doughty, 2 Zab. 495 ; Dorlan v. East Brandy-
wine, &c. R. R. Co., 46 Penn. St. 520 ; Proprietors, &c. v. Nashua & Lowell
R. R. Co., 10 Cush. 385 ; Louisville & Nashville R. R. Co. v. Thompson, 18 B.
Monr. 735 ; Winona & St. Peter's R. R. Co. v. Denman, 10 Minn. 267.

[2] Pennsylvania R. R. Co. v. Reiley, 8 Penn. St. 445 ; Greenville & Columbia R. R. Co. v. Partlow, 5 Rich. 439 ; Dearborn v. Railroad Co., 4 Fost. 179 ;
Carpenter v. Landaff, 42 N. H. 220 ; Dorlan v. East Brandywine, &c. R. R. Co.,
46 Penn. St. 520 ; Winona & St. Peter's R. R. Co. v. Denman, 10 Minn. 267 ;
Mount Washington Co.'s Petition, 35 N. H. 134. Where a part of a meeting-
house lot was taken for a highway, it was held that the anticipated annoyance to
worshippers by the use of the way by noisy and dissolute persons on the Sabbath
could form no basis for any assessment of damages. First Parish in Woburn v.
Middlesex County, 7 Gray, 106.

[3] White v. County Commissioners of Norfolk, 2 Cush. 361 ; Whitman v. Boston
& Maine R. R. Co., 3 Allen, 133 ; Nichols v. Bridgeport, 23 Conn. 189. But it
is not competent for the commissioners who assess the compensation to require
that which is to be made to be in whole or in part in anything else than money.
An award of " one hundred and fifty dollars, with a wagon-way and stop for cattle,"
is void, as undertaking to pay the owner in part in conveniences to be furnished
him, and which he may not want, and certainly cannot be compelled to take, instead
of money. Central Ohio R. R. Co. v. Holler, 7 Ohio, N. S. 225.

negligence or improper construction,[1] and for which an action at
the common law will lie, as already stated.

[1] Philadelphia & Reading R. R. Co. v. Yeiser, 8 Penn. St. 366 ; Aldrich v.
Cheshire R. R. Co., 1 Fost. 359 ; Dearborn v. Boston, Concord, & Montreal R. R.
Co., 4 Fost. 179 ; Dodge v. County Commissioners, 3 Met. 380 ; Brown v. Providence, W. & B. R. R. Co., 5 Gray, 35 ; Mason v. Kennebec & Portland R. R. Co.,
31 Me. 215.

CHAPTER XVI.

THE POLICE POWER OF THE STATES.

ON questions of conflict between national and State authority, and on questions whether the State exceeds its just powers in dealing with the property and restraining the actions of individuals, it often becomes necessary to consider the extent and proper bounds of a power in the States, which, like that of taxation, pervades every department of business and reaches to every interest and every subject of profit or enjoyment. We refer to what is known as the police power.

The police of a State, in a comprehensive sense, embraces its system of internal regulation, by which it is sought not only to preserve the public order and to prevent offences against the State, but also to establish for the intercourse of citizen with citizen those rules of good manners and good neighborhood which are calculated to prevent a conflict of rights, and to insure to each the uninterrupted enjoyment of his own, so far as is reasonably consistent with a like enjoyment of rights by others.[1]

In the present chapter we shall have occasion to speak of the police power principally as it affects the use and enjoyment of property; the object being to show the universality of its presence, and to indicate, so far as may be practicable, the limits which settled principles of constitutional law assign to its interference.

" We think it is a settled principle," says Chief Justice Shaw,

---

[1] Blackstone defines the public police and economy as "the due regulation and domestic order of the kingdom, whereby the inhabitants of a State, like members of a well-governed family, are bound to conform their general behavior to the rules of propriety, good neighborhood, and good manners, and to be decent, industrious, and inoffensive in their respective stations." 4 Bl. Com. 162. Jeremy Bentham, in his General View of Public Offences, has this definition: "Police is in general a system of precaution, either for the prevention of crimes or of calamities. Its business may be distributed into eight distinct branches: 1. Police for the prevention of offences; 2. Police for the prevention of calamities; 3. Police for the prevention of endemic diseases; 4. Police of charity; 5. Police of interior communications; 6. Police of public amusements; 7. Police for recent intelligence; 8. Police for registration." Edinburgh Ed. of Works, part ix., p. 157.

" growing out of the nature of well-ordered civil society, that every holder of property, however absolute and unqualified may be his title, holds it under the implied liability that his use of it shall not be injurious to the equal enjoyment of others having an equal right to the enjoyment of their property, nor injurious to the rights of the community. All property in this Commonwealth is . . . . held subject to those general regulations which are necessary to the common good and general welfare. Rights of property, like all other social and conventional rights, are subject to such reasonable limitations in their enjoyment as shall prevent them from being injurious, and to such reasonable restraints and regulations established by law as the legislature, under the governing and controlling power vested in them by the constitution may think necessary and expedient. This is very different from the right of eminent domain, — the right of a government to take and appropriate private property whenever the public exigency requires it, which can be done only on condition of providing a reasonable compensation therefor. The power we allude to is rather the police power ; the power vested in the legislature by the constitution to make, ordain, and establish all manner of wholesome and reasonable laws, statutes, and ordinances, either with penalties or without, not repugnant to the constitution, as they shall judge to be for the good and welfare of the Commonwealth, and of the subjects of the same. It is much easier to perceive and realize the existence and sources of this power than to mark its boundaries, or prescribe limits to its exercise." [1]

" This police power of the State," says another eminent judge, " extends to the protection of the lives, limbs, health, comfort, and quiet of all persons, and the protection of all property within the State. According to the maxim, *Sic utere tuo ut alienum non lædas*, which being of universal application, it must, of course, be within the range of legislative action to define the mode and manner in which every one may so use his own as not to injure others." And again : [By this] " general police power of the State, persons and property are subjected to all kinds of restraints and burdens, in order to secure the general comfort, health, and prosperity of the

---

[1] Commonwealth v. Alger, 7 Cush. 84. See also Commonwealth v. Tewksbury, 11 Met. 57 ; Hart v. Mayor, &c. of Albany, 9 Wend. 571 ; New Albany & Salem R. R. Co. v. Tilton, 12 Ind. 3 ; Indianapolis & Cincinnati R. R. Co. v. Kercheval, 16 Ind. 84 ; Ohio & Mississippi R. R. Co. v. McClelland, 25 Ill. 140 ; People v. Draper, 25 Barb. 374 ; Baltimore v. State, 15 Md. 390.

State; of the perfect right in the legislature to do which, no question ever was, or, upon acknowledged general principles, ever can be made, so far as natural persons are concerned." [1]

One of the most important questions respecting this power, in a constitutional point of view, concerns those cases over which jurisdiction is vested in the national government, whereby, it is sometimes claimed, that the police jurisdiction of the State is necessarily excluded, as otherwise the State would be found operating within the sphere of the national powers, and establishing regulations which would either abridge the rights which the national Constitution undertakes to render inviolable, or burden the privileges which, being conferred by law of Congress, are not properly subject to control by any other authority. It is plain, however, from a statement of the theory upon which the police power rests, that any proper exercise of it by the State cannot come in conflict with the provisions of the Constitution of the United States. If the power only extends to a regulation of rights with a view to the due protection and enjoyment of all, without depriving any one of that which is justly and properly his own, then its possession and exercise by the State, in respect to the persons and property of its citizens, cannot well afford a basis for an appeal to the protection of the national authorities.

This subject has often been considered in its bearings upon the clause of the Constitution of the United States which forbids the States passing any laws violating the obligation of contracts; and it has been invariably held that this clause does not so far remove from State control the rights and properties which depend for their existence or enforcement upon contracts, as to relieve them from the operation of such general regulations for the good government of the State and the protection of the rights of individuals as may be deemed important. All contracts and all rights, it is held, are subject to this power; and regulations which affect them may not only be established by the State, but must also be subject to change from time to time, with reference to the general well-being of the community, as circumstances change, or as experience demonstrates the necessity. [2]

---

[1] Redfield, Ch. J., in Thorpe v. Rutland & Burlington R. R. Co., 27 Vt. 149. See the maxim, " Sic utere," &c., — " Enjoy your own property in such manner as not to injure that of another," — in Broom's Legal Maxims (5th Am. ed.), p. 327.

[2] In the case of Thorpe v. Rutland & Burlington R. R. Co., 27 Vt. 140, a

Perhaps the most striking illustrations of the principle here stated will be found among the judicial decisions which have held

question arose under a provision in the Vermont General Railroad Law of 1849, which required each railroad corporation to erect and maintain fences on the line of their road, and also cattle guards at all farm and road crossings, suitable and sufficient to prevent cattle and other animals from getting upon the railroad, and which made the corporation and its agents liable for all damages which should· be done by their agents or engines to cattle, horses, or other animals thereon, if occasioned by the want of such fences and cattle guards. It was not disputed that this provision would be valid as to such corporations as might be afterwards created within the State; but in respect to those previously in existence, and whose charters contained no such provision, it was claimed that this legislation was inoperative, since otherwise its effect would be to modify, and to that extent to violate, the obligation of the charter-contract. The case, say the court, "resolves itself into the narrow question of the right of the legislature, by general statute, to require all railways, whether now in operation or hereafter to be chartered or built, to fence their roads upon both sides, and provide sufficient cattle guards at all farm and road crossings, under penalty of paying all damages caused by their neglect to comply with such requirements. . . . . We think the power of the legislature to control existing railways in this respect may be found in the general control over the police of the country, which resides in the law-making power in all free States, and which is, by the fifth article of the bill of rights of this State, expressly declared to reside perpetually and inalienably in the legislature; which is, perhaps, no more than the enunciation of a general principle applicable to all free States, and which cannot therefore be violated so as to deprive the legislature of the power, even by express grant to any mere public or private corporation. And when the regulation of the police of a city or town, by general ordinances, is given to such towns and cities, and the regulation of their own internal police is given to railroads to be carried into effect by their by-laws and other regulations, it is of course always, in all such cases, subject to the superior control of the legislature. That is a responsibility which legislatures cannot divest themselves of if they would.

"So far as railroads are concerned, this police power which resides primarily and ultimately in the legislature is twofold: 1. The police of the roads, which, in the absence of legislative control, the corporations themselves exercise over their operatives, and to some extent over all who do business with them, or come upon their grounds, through their general statutes, and by their officers. We apprehend there can be no manner of doubt that the legislature may, if they deem the public good requires it, of which they are to judge, and in all doubtful cases their judgment is final, require the several railroads in the State to establish and maintain the same kind of police which is now observed upon some of the more important roads in the country for their own security, or even such a police as is found upon the English railways, and those upon the Continent of Europe. No one ever questioned the right of the Connecticut legislature to require trains upon all of their railroads to come to a stand before passing draws in bridges; or of the Massachusetts legislature to require the same thing before passing another railroad. And by parity of reasoning may all railways be required so to conduct that the rights insured to private corporations by their charters, and the manner of their exercise, are subject to such new regulations as from time to time may be made by the State with a view to the public protection, health, and safety, and to properly guard the rights of other individuals and corporations. Although these charters are to be regarded as contracts, and the rights assured by them are inviolable, it does not follow that these rights are at once, by force of the charter-contract, removed from the sphere of State regulation, and that the charter implies an undertaking, on the part of the State, that in the same way in which their exercise is themselves as to other persons, natural or corporate, as not unreasonably to injure them or their property. And if the business of railways is specially dangerous, they may be required to bear the expense of erecting such safeguards as will render it ordinarily safe to others, as is often required of natural persons under such circumstances.

"There would be no end of illustrations upon this subject. . . . . It may be extended to the supervision of the track, tending switches, running upon the time of other trains, running a road with a single track, using improper rails, not using proper precaution by way of safety-beams in case of the breaking of axletrees, the number of brakemen upon a train with reference to the number of cars, employing intemperate or incompetent engineers and servants, running beyond a given rate of speed, and a thousand similar things, most of which have been made the subject of legislation or judicial determination, and all of which may be. Hegeman v. Western R. Co., 16 Barb. 353.

" 2. There is also the general police power of the State, by which persons and property are subjected to all kinds of restraints and burdens, in order to secure the general comfort, health, and prosperity of the State ; of the perfect right in the legislature to do which no question ever was, or, upon acknowledged general principles, ever can be made, so far as natural persons are concerned. And it is certainly calculated to excite surprise and alarm that the right to do the same in regard to railways should be made a serious question." And the court proceed to consider the various cases in which the right of the legislature to regulate matters of private concern with reference to the general public good has been acted upon as unquestioned, or sustained by judicial decisions, and quote, as pertinent to the general question of what laws are prohibited on the ground of impairing the obligation of contracts, the language of Chief Justice Marshall in Dartmouth College v. Woodward, 4 Wheat. 518, 629, that " the framers of the Constitution did not intend to restrain the States in the regulation of their civil institutions, adopted for internal government, and that the instrument they have given us is not to be so construed." See to the same effect Suydam v. Moore, 8. Barb. 358 ; Waldron v. Rensselaer & Saratoga R. R. Co., 8 Barb. 390; Galena & Chicago U. R. R. Co. v. Loomis, 13 Ill. 548 ; Fitchburg R. R. v. Grand Junction R. R. Co., 1 Allen, 552 ; Veazie v. Mayo, 45 Me. 560 ; Peters v. Iron Mountain R. R. Co., 23 Mo. 107 ; Grannahan v. Hannibal, &c. R. R. Co., 30 Mo. 546 ; Indianopolis & Cincinnati R. R. Co. v. Kercheval, 16 Ind. 84 ; Galena & Chicago U. R. R. Co. v. Appleby, 28 Ill. 283.

permissible at first, and under the regulations then existing, and those only, may the corporators continue to exercise their rights while the artificial existence continues. The obligation of the contract by no means extends so far ; but on the contrary, the rights and privileges which it confers are only thereby placed upon the same footing with other legal rights and privileges of the citizen in respect to proper rules for their due regulation, protection, and enjoyment.

The limit to the exercise of the police power in these cases must be this : the regulations must have reference to the comfort, safety, or welfare of society ; they must not be in conflict with any of the provisions of the charter ; and they must not, under pretence of regulation, take from the corporation any of the essential rights and privileges which the charter confers. In short, they must be police regulations in fact, and not amendments of the charter in curtailment of the corporate franchise.[1] The maxim, *Sic utere tuo ut alienum non lædas,* is that which lies at the foundation of the power ; and to whatever enactment affecting the management and business of private corporations it cannot fairly be applied, the power itself will not extend. It has accordingly been held that where a corporation was chartered with the right to take toll from passengers over their road, a subsequent statute authorizing a certain class of persons to go toll free was void.[2] This was not a regulation of existing rights, but it took from the corporation that

---

[1] Washington Bridge Co. *v.* State, 18 Conn. 53 ; Bailey *v.* Philadelphia, &c. R. R. Co., 4 Harr. 389 ; State *v.* Noyes, 47 Me. 189 ; Pingrey *v.* Washburn, 1 Aiken, 268 ; Miller *v.* N. Y. & Erie R. R. Co., 21 Barb. 513 ; People *v.* Jackson & Michigan Plank Road Co., 9 Mich. 307. In Benson *v.* Mayor, &c. of New York, 10 Barb. 245, it is said, in considering a ferry right granted to a city : " Franchises of this description are partly of a public and partly of a private nature. So far as the accommodation of passengers is concerned, they are *publici juris ;* so far as they require capital and produce revenue, they are *priviti juris.* Certain duties and burdens are imposed upon the grantees, who are compensated therefor by the privilege of levying ferriage and the security from spoliation arising from the irrevocable nature of the grant. The State may legislate touching them, so far as they are *publici juris.* Thus, laws may be passed to punish neglect or misconduct in conducting the ferries, to secure the safety of passengers from danger and imposition, &c. But the State cannot take away the ferries themselves, nor deprive the city of their legitimate rents and profits." And see People *v.* Mayor, &c. of New York, 32 Barb. 102, 116.

[2] Pingrey *v.* Washburn, 1 Aiken, 268. This decision, and those which follow, assume that there is nothing in the original charter of the corporation which would warrant an amendment of the charter to this effect.

which they before possessed, namely, the right to tolls, and conferred upon individuals that which before they had not, namely, the privilege to pass over the road free of toll. " Powers," it is said in another case, " which can only be justified on this specific ground [that they are police regulations], and which would otherwise be clearly prohibited by the constitution, can be such only as are so clearly necessary to the safety, comfort, and well-being of society, or so imperatively required by the public necessity, as to lead to the rational and satisfactory conclusion that the framers of the constitution could not, as men of ordinary prudence and foresight, have intended to prohibit their exercise in the particular case, notwithstanding the language of the prohibition would otherwise include it." [1] And it was therefore held that an act subsequent to the charter of a plank-road company, and not assented to by the corporators, which subjected them to a total forfeiture of their franchises for that which by the charter was cause for partial forfeiture only, was void as violating the obligation of contracts.[2] And even a provision in a corporate charter, empowering the legislature to alter, modify, or repeal it, would not authorize a subsequent act which, on pretence of amendment or of a police regulation, would have the effect to appropriate a portion of the corporate property to the public use.[3] And where by its charter the corporation is empowered to construct over a river a certain bridge, which must necessarily constitute an obstruction to the navigation of the river, a subsequent amendment making the corporation liable for such obstruction would be void, as in effect depriving the corporation of the very right which the charter assured to it.[4] So where the charter reserved to the legislature the right of modification after the corporators had been reimbursed their expenses in constructing the bridge, with twelve per cent interest thereon,

---

[1] Christiancy, J. in People v. Jackson & Michigan Plank Road Co., 9 Mich. 307.

[2] Ibid. And see State v. Noyes, 47 Me. 189.

[3] The reservation of a right to amend or repeal would not justify an act requiring a railroad company to cause a proposed new street or highway to be taken across their track, and to cause the necessary embankments, excavations, and other work to be done for that purpose at their own expense ; thus not only appropriating a part of their property to another public use, but compelling them to be at the expense of fitting it for such use. Miller v. N. Y. & Erie R. R. Co., 21 Barb. 513.

[4] Bailey v. Philadelphia, &c. R. R. Co., 4 Harr. 389.

an amendment before such reimbursement, requiring the construction of a fifty-foot draw for the passage of vessels in place of one of
thirty-two feet, was held unconstitutional and void.[1] So a power
to a municipal corporation to regulate the speed of railway carriages would not authorize such regulation except in the streets
and public grounds of the city ; such being the fair construction of
the power, and the necessity for this police regulation not extending further.[2]

On the other hand, the right to require existing railroad corporations to fence their track, and to make them liable for all beasts
killed by going upon it, has been sustained on two grounds : first,
as regarding the division fence between adjoining proprietors, and
in that view being but a reasonable provision for the protection of
domestic animals ; and second, and chiefly, as essential to the protection of persons being transported in the railway carriages.[3]
Having this double purpose in view, the owner of beasts killed or
injured may maintain an action for the damage suffered, notwithstanding he may not himself be free from negligence.[4] But it
would, perhaps, require an express legislative declaration that
the corporation should be liable for the beasts thus destroyed to

[1] Washington Bridge Co. v. State, 18 Conn. 53.

[2] State v. Jersey City, 5 Dutch. 170.   In Buffalo & Niagara Falls R. R. Co. v.
Buffalo, 5 Hill, 209, it was held that a statutory power in a city to regulate the
running of cars within the corporate limits would justify an ordinance entirely
prohibiting the use of steam for propelling cars through any part of the city.   And
see Great Western R. R. Co. v. Decatur, 33 Ill. 381.

[3] Thorpe v. Rutland & Burlington R. R. Co., 27 Vt. 156 ; New Albany &
Salem R. R. Co. v. Tilton, 12 Ind. 3 ; Same v. Maiden, Ibid. 10 ; Same v. McNa-
mara, 11 Ind. 543 ; Ohio & Mississippi R. R. Co. v. McClelland, 25 Ill. 145 ;
Madison & Indianapolis R. R. Co. v. Whiteneck, 8 Ind. 230 ; Indianapolis &
Cincinnati R. R. Co. v. Townsend, 10 Ind. 38 ; Same v. Kercheval, 16 Ind. 84 ;
Corwin v. N. Y. & Erie R. R. Co., 13 N. Y. 42 ; Horn v. Atlantic & St. Lawrence R. R. Co., 35 N. H. 169, and 36 Ibid. 440 ; Fawcett v. York & North Midland R. Co., 15 Jur. 173 ; Smith v. Eastern R. R. Co., 35 N. H. 356 ; Bulkley
v. N. Y. & N. H. R. R. Co., 27 Conn. 479.   A subsequent statute making railroad
companies liable for injuries by fire communicated by their locomotive-engines
was sustained in Lyman v. Boston & Worcester R. R. Co., 4 Cush. 288.   And
see Camden & Amboy R. R. Co. v. Briggs, 2 Zab. 623.

[4] Corwin v. N. Y. & Erie R. R. Co., 13 N. Y. 42 ; Indianapolis & Cincinnati
R. R. Co. v. Townsend, 10 Ind. 38 ; Suydam v. Moore, 8 Barb. 358 ; Fawcett v.
York & North Midland R. Co., 15 Jur. 173 ; Waldron v. Rensselaer & Schenectady R. R. Co., 8 Barb. 390 ; Horne v. Atlantic & St. Lawrence R. R. Co.,
35 N. H. 169.

create so great an innovation in the common law. The general rule, where a corporation has failed to obey the police regulations established for its government, would not make the corporation liable to the party injured, if his own negligence contributed with that of the corporation in producing the injury.[1]

The State may also regulate the grade of railways, and prescribe how, and upon what grade, railway tracts shall cross each other; and it may apportion the expense of making the necessary crossings between the corporations owning the roads.[2] And it may establish regulations requiring existing railways to ring the bell or blow the whistle of their engines immediately before passing highways at grade, or other places where their approach might be dangerous to travel.[3] And it has even been intimated that it might be competent for the State to make railway corporations liable as insurers for the safety of all persons carried by them, in the same manner that they are by law liable as carriers of goods; though this would seem to be pushing the police power to an ex-

---

[1] Jackson v. Rutland & Burlington R. R. Co., 25 Vt. 150. And see Marsh v. N. Y. & Erie R. R. Co., 14 Barb. 364; Joliet & N. I. R. R. Co. v. Jones, 20 Ill. 221; Tonawanda R. R. Co. v. Munger, 5 Denio, 255, and 4 N. Y. 255. In Indianapolis & Cincinnati R. R. Co. v. Kercheval, 16 Ind. 84, it was held that a clause in the charter of a railroad corporation which declared that when the corporators should have procured a right of way as therein provided, they should be seised in fee simple of the right to the land, and should have the sole use and occupation of the same, and no person, body corporate or politic should in any way interfere therewith, molest, disturb, or injure any of the rights and privileges thereby granted, &c., would not take from the State the power to establish a police regulation making the corporation liable for cattle killed by their cars.

[2] Fitchburg R. R. Co. v. Grand Junction R. R. Co., 1 Allen, 552, and 4 Allen, 198.

[3] "The legislature has the power, by general laws, from time to time, as the public exigencies may require, to regulate corporations in their franchises, so as to provide for the public safety. The provision in question is a mere police regulation, enacted for the protection and safety of the public, and in no manner interferes with or impairs the powers conferred on the defendants in their act of incorporation." Galena & Chicago U. R. R. Co. v. Loomis, 13 Ill. 548. And see Stuyvesant v. Mayor, &c. of New York, 7 Cow. 604; Benson v. Mayor, &c. of New York, 10 Barb. 240; Bulkley v. N. Y. & N. H. R. R. Co., 27 Conn. 486; Veazie v. Mayo, 45 Me. 560; Same case, 49 Me. 156; Galena & Chicago U. R. R. Co. v. Dill, 22 Ill. 264; Same v. Appleby, 28 Ill. 283; Ohio & Mississippi R. R. Co. v. McClelland, 25 Ill. 145; Clark's Admr. v. Hannibal & St. Jo. R. R. Co. 36 Mo. 202.

treme.[1] But those statutes which have recently become common,
and which give an action to the representatives of persons killed
by the wrongful act, neglect, or default of another, may unquestionably be held applicable to corporations previously chartered,
and may be sustained as only giving a remedy for a wrong for
which the common law had failed to make provision.[2]

Those statutes which regulate or altogether prohibit the sale of
intoxicating drinks as a beverage have also sometimes been supposed to conflict with the Federal Constitution. Such of these,
however, as assume to regulate only, and to prohibit sales by other
persons than those who should be licensed by the public authorities,
have not suggested any serious question of constitutional power.
They are but the ordinary police regulations, such as the State may
make in respect to all classes of trade or employment.[3] But those
which undertake altogether to prohibit the manufacture and sale
of intoxicating drinks as a beverage have been assailed as violating express provisions of the national Constitution, and also as

---

[1] Thorpe v. Rutland & Burlington R. R. Co., 27 Vt. 152. Carriers of goods
are liable as insurers, notwithstanding they may have been guiltless of negligence,
because such is their contract with the shipper when they receive his goods for
transportation ; but carriers of persons assume no such obligations at the common
law ; and where a company of individuals receive from the State a charter which
makes them carriers of persons, and chargeable as such for their own default or
negligence only, it may well be doubted if it be competent for the legislature
afterwards to impose upon their contracts new burdens, and make them respond
in damages where they have been guilty of no default. In other words, whether
that could be a proper police regulation which did not assume to regulate the
business of the carrier with a view to the just protection of the rights and interests of others, but which imposed a new obligation, for the benefit of others, upon
a party guilty of no neglect of duty. But perhaps such a regulation would not go
further than that in Stanley v. Stanley, 26 Me. 191, where it was held competent
for the legislature to pass an act making the stockholders of existing banks liable
for all corporate debts thereafter created ; or in Peters v. Iron Mountain R. R. Co.
23 Mo. 107, and Grannahan v. Hannibal, &c. R. R. Co., 30 Mo. 546, where an
act was sustained which made companies previously chartered liable for the debts
of contractors to the workmen whom they had employed.

[2] Southwestern R. R. Co. v. Paulk, 24 Geo. 356 ; Coosa River Steamboat Co.
v. Barclay, 30 Ala. 120. In Boston, Concord, & Montreal R. R. v. State, 32 N. H.
215, a statute making railroad corporations liable to indictment and fine, in case
of the loss of life by the negligence or carelessness of the proprietors or their servants, was adjudged constitutional, as applicable to corporations previously in
existence.

[3] Bode v. State, 7 Gill, 326 ; Bancroft v. Dumas, 21 Vt. 456 ; Thomasson v.
State, 15 Ind. 449 ; License Cases, 5 How. 504.

subversive of fundamental rights, and therefore not within the grant of legislative power.

That legislation of this character was void, so far as it affected imported liquors, or such as might be introduced from one State into another, because in conflict with the power of Congress over commerce, was strongly urged in the License Cases before the Supreme Court of the United States, but that view did not obtain the assent of the court. The majority of the court expressed the opinion — which, however, was *obiter* in those cases — that the introduction of imported liquors into a State, and their sale in the original packages as imported, could not be forbidden, because to do so would be to forbid what Congress, in its regulation of commerce, and in the levy of imposts, had permitted;[1] but it was conceded by all, that when the orignal package was broken up for use or for retail by the importer, and also when the commodity had passed from his hands into the hands of a purchaser, it ceased to be an import, or a part of foreign commerce, and thereby became subject to the laws of the State, and might be taxed for State purposes, and the sale regulated by the State like any other property.[2] It was also decided, in these cases, that the power of Congress to regulate commerce between the States did not exclude regulations by the States, except so far as they might come in conflict with those established by Congress; and that, consequently, as Congress had not undertaken to regulate commerce in liquors between the States, a law of New Hampshire could not be held void which punished the sale, in that State, of gin purchased in Boston and sold in New Hampshire, notwithstanding the sale was in the cask in which it was imported, but by one not licensed by the selectmen.[3]

It would seem, from the views expressed by the several members of the court in these cases, that the State laws known as Prohibitory Liquor Laws, the purpose of which is to prevent altogether

[1] Taney, Ch. J., 5 How. 574; McLean, J., Ibid. 589; Catron, J., Ibid. 608. And see Brown v. Maryland, 12 Wheat. 419; Lincoln v. Smith, 27 Vt. 335. Bradford v. Stevens, 10 Gray, 379; State v. Robinson, 49 Me. 285.

[2] Daniel, J. held that the right to regulate was not excluded, even while the packages remained in the hands of the importer unbroken (p. 612). See also the views of Grier, J. (p. 631).

[3] See also Bode v. State, 7 Gill, 326; Jones v. People, 14 Ill. 196; State v. Wheeler, 25 Conn. 290; Santo v. State, 2 Iowa, 202; Commonwealth v. Clapp, 5 Gray, 97.

the manufacture and sale of intoxicating drinks as a beverage, so far as legislation can accomplish that object, cannot be held void as in conflict with the power of Congress to regulate commerce, and to levy imposts and duties. And it has been held that they were not void, because tending to prevent the fulfilment of contracts previously made, and thereby violating the obligation of contracts.[1]

The same laws have also been sustained, when the question of conflict with State constitutions, or with general fundamental principles, has been raised. They are looked upon as police regulations established by the legislature for the prevention of intemperance, pauperism, and crime, and for the abatement of nuisances.[2] It has also been held competent to declare the liquor kept for sale a nuisance, and to provide legal process for its condemnation and destruction, and to seize and condemn the building occupied as a dram shop on the same ground.[3] And it is only where, in framing such legislation, care has not been taken to observe those principles of protection which surround the persons and dwellings of individuals, securing them against unreasonable searches and seizures, and giving them a right to trial before condemnation, that the courts have felt at liberty to declare that it exceeded the proper province of police regulation.[4] Perhaps there is no instance in which the power of the legislature to make such regulations as may destroy the value of property, without compensation to the owner, appears in a more striking light than in the case of these statutes. The trade in alcoholic drinks being lawful, and the

[1] People v. Hawley, 3 Mich. 330; Reynolds v. Geary, 26 Conn. 179.

[2] Commonwealth v. Kendall, 12 Cush. 414 ; Commonwealth v. Clapp, 5 Gray, 97 ; Commonwealth v. Howe, 13 Gray, 26 ; Santo v. State, 2 Iowa, 202 ; Our House v. State, 4 Greene (Iowa), 172 ; Zumhoff v. State, Ibid. 526 ; State v. Donehey, 8 Iowa, 396 ; State v. Wheeler, 25 Conn. 290; Reynolds v. Geary, 26 Conn. 179; Oviatt v. Pond, 29 Conn. 479 ; People v. Hawley, 3 Mich. 330 ; People v. Gallagher, 4 Mich. 244 ; Jones v. People, 14 Ill. 196 ; State v. Prescott, 27 Vt. 194 ; Lincoln v. Smith, Ibid. 328 ; Gill v. Parker, 31 Vt. 610. But see Beebe v. State, 6 Ind. 501; Meshmeier v. State, 11 Ind. 484; Wynehamer v. People, 13 N. Y. 378. In Reynolds v. Geary, 26 Conn. 179, it was held that the State law forbidding suits for the price of liquors sold was to be applied to contracts made out of the State, and lawful where made.

[3] Our House v. State, 4 Greene (Iowa), 172. See also Lincoln v. Smith, 27 Vt. 328 ; Oviatt v. Pond, 29 Conn. 479 ; State v. Robinson, 33 Maine, 568 ; License Cases, 5 How. 589. But see Wynehamer v. People, 13 N. Y. 378 ; Welch v. Stowell, 2 Doug. Mich. 332.

[4] Hibbard v. People, 4 Mich. 125 ; Fisher v. McGirr, 1 Gray, 1. But see Meshmeier v. State, 11 Ind. 484 ; Wynehamer v. People, 13 N. Y. 378.

capital employed in it being fully protected by law, the legislature then steps in, and, by an enactment based on general reasons of public utility, annihilates the traffic, destroys altogether the employment, and reduces to a nominal value the property on hand. Even the keeping of that for the purposes of sale becomes a criminal offence, and, without any change whatever in his own conduct or employment, the merchant of yesterday becomes the criminal of to-day, and the very building in which he lives and conducts the business which to that moment was lawful becomes perhaps a nuisance, if the statute shall so declare, and liable to be proceeded against for a forfeiture. A statute which can do this must be justified upon the highest reasons of public benefit; but, whether satisfactory or not, they rest exclusively in the legislative wisdom.

Within the last two or three years, new questions have arisen in regard to these laws, and other State regulations, arising out of the imposition of burdens on various occupations by Congress, with a view to raising revenue for the national government. These burdens are imposed in the form of what are called license fees; and it has been claimed that, when the party paid the fee, he was thereby licensed to carry on the business, despite the regulations which the State government might make upon the subject. This view, however, has not been taken by the courts, who have regarded the congressional legislation imposing a license fee as only a species of taxation, without the payment of which the business could not lawfully be carried on, but which, nevertheless, did not propose to make any business lawful which was not lawful before, or to relieve it from any burdens or restrictions imposed by the regulations of the State. The licenses give no authority, and are mere receipts for taxes.[1]

Numerous other illustrations might be given of the power in the States to make regulations affecting commerce, and which are sustainable as regulations of police. Among these, quarantine regulations and health laws of every description will readily suggest themselves, and these are or may be sometimes carried to the extent of ordering the destruction of private property when infected with disease or otherwise dangerous.[2] These regulations

---

[1] License Tax Cases, 5 Wal. 462; Purvear v. Commonwealth, Ibid. 475; Commonwealth v. Holbrook, 10 Allen, 200.

[2] See remarks of Grier, J. in License Cases, 5 How. 632; Meeker v. Van Rensselaer, 15 Wend. 397.

have generally passed unchallenged. The right to pass inspection laws, and to levy duties so far as may be necessary to render them effectual is also undoubted, and is expressly recognized by the Constitution.[1] But certain powers which still more directly affect commerce may sometimes be exercised where the purpose is not to interfere with congressional legislation, but merely to regulate the times and manner of transacting business with a view to facilitate trade, secure order, and prevent confusion.

An act of the State of New York declared that the harbor-masters appointed under the State laws should have authority to regulate and station all ships and vessels in the stream of the East and North rivers, within the limits of the city of New York, and the wharves thereof, and to remove from time to time such vessels as were not employed in receiving and discharging their cargoes, to make room for such others as required to be more immediately accommodated, for the purpose of receiving and discharging theirs ; and that the harbor-masters or either of them should have authority to determine how far and in what instances it was the duty of the masters and others, having charge of ships or vessels, to accommodate each other in their respective situations ; and it imposed a penalty for refusing or neglecting to obey the directions of the harbor-masters or either of them. In a suit brought against the master of a steam vessel, who had refused to move his vessel a certain distance as directed by one of the harbor-masters, in order to accommodate a new arrival, the act was assailed as an unconstitutional invasion of the power of Congress over commerce, but was sustained as a regulation prescribing the manner of exercising individual rights over property employed in commerce.[2]

[1] Art. 1, § 10, clause 2.

[2] Vanderbilt v. Adams, 7 Cow. 351. Woodworth, J. in this case, states very clearly the principle on which police regulations, in such cases, are sustainable : " It seems to me the power exercised in this case is essentially necessary for the purpose of protecting the rights of all concerned. It is not, in the legitimate sense of the term, a violation of any right, but the exercise of a power indispensably necessary, where an extensive commerce is carried on. If the harbor is crowded with vessels arriving daily from foreign parts, the power is incident to such a state of things. Disorder and confusion would be the consequence, if there was no control. . . . . The right assumed under the law would not be upheld, if exerted beyond what may be considered a necessary police regulation. The line between what would be a clear invasion of right on the one hand, and regulations not lessening the value of the right, and calculated for the benefit of all, must be distinctly marked. . . . . Police regulations are legal and binding, because for the

The line of distinction between that which constitutes an inter-ference with commerce, and that which is a mere police regula-tion, is sometimes exceedingly dim and shadowy, and it is not to be wondered at that learned jurists differ when endeavoring to classify the cases which arise. It is not doubted that Congress has the power to go beyond the general regulations of commerce which it is accustomed to establish, and to descend to the most minute directions, if it shall be deemed advisable; and that to whatever extent ground shall be covered by those directions, the exercise of State power is excluded. Congress may establish police regula-tions, as well as the States; confining their operation to the sub-jects over which it is given control by the Constitution. But as the general police power can better be exercised under the super-vision of the local authority, and mischiefs are not likely to spring therefrom so long as the power to arrest collision resides in the national courts, the regulations which are made by Congress do not often exclude the establishment of others by the State covering very many particulars. Moreover, the regulations of commerce are usually, and in some cases must be, general and uniform for the whole country; while in some localities, State and local policy will demand peculiar regulations with reference to special and peculiar circumstances.

The State of Maryland passed an act requiring all importers of foreign goods, by the bale or package, &c. to take out a license, for which they should pay fifty dollars, and, in case of neglect or refusal to take out such license, subjected them to certain forfeit-ures and penalties. License laws are of two kinds: those which require the payment of a license fee by way of raising a revenue, and are therefore the exercise of the power of taxation; and those

general benefit, and do not proceed to the length of impairing any right, in the proper sense of that term. The sovereign power in a community, therefore, may and ought to prescribe the manner of exercising individual rights over property. It is for the better protection and enjoyment of that absolute dominion which the individual claims. The power rests on the implied right and duty of the supreme power to protect all by statutory regulations; so that, on the whole, the benefit of all is promoted. Every public regulation in a city may, and does, in some sense, limit and restrict the absolute right that existed previously. But this is not con-sidered as an injury. So far from it, the individual, as well as others, is sup-posed to be benefited. It may, then, be said that such a power is incident to every well-regulated society, and without which it could not well exist." See Owners of James Gray v. Owners of The John Frazer, 21 How. 184; Bene-dict v. Vanderbilt, 1 Robertson, 194.

which are mere police regulations, and which require the payment only of such license fee as will cover the expense of the license and of enforcing the regulation.[1]   The Maryland act seems to fall properly within the former of these classes, and it was held void as in conflict with that provision of the Constitution which prohibits a State from laying any impost, &c., and also with the clause which declares that Congress shall have the power to regulate commerce. The reasoning of the court was this : Sale is the object of all importation of goods, and the power to allow importation must therefore imply the power to authorize the sale of the thing imported ; that consequently a penalty inflicted for selling an article in the character of importer was in opposition to the act of Congress, which authorized importation ; that a power to tax an article in the hands of the importer the instant it was landed was the same in effect as a power to tax it whilst entering the port; that consequently the law of Maryland was obnoxious to the charge of unconstitutionality, on the ground of its violating the two provisions referred to.[2]   And a State law which required the master of every vessel engaged in foreign commerce to pay a certain sum to a State officer, on account of every passenger brought from a foreign country into the State, or before landing any alien passenger, was held void for similar reasons.[3]

On the other hand, a law of the State of New York was sustained which required, under a penalty, that the master of every vessel arriving from a foreign port should report to the mayor or recorder of the city of New York an account of his passengers ; the object being to prevent New York from being burdened by an influx of persons brought thither in ships from foreign countries and the other States, and for that purpose to require a report of the names, places of birth, &c. of all passengers, that the necessary steps might be taken by the city authorities to prevent them from becoming chargeable as paupers.[4]   And a State regulation of pilots and pilotage was held unobjectionable, though it was conceded that Congress had full power to make regulations on the same

---

[1] Ash v. People, 11 Mich. 347.   See ante, p. 201.

[2] Brown v. Maryland, 12 Wheat. 419.

[3] Passenger Cases, 7. How. 283 ; see also Lin Sing v. Washburn, 20 Cal. 534, where a State law imposing a special tax on every Chinese person over eighteen years of age for each month of his residence in the State was held unconstitutional, as in conflict with the power of Congress over commerce.

[4] City of New York v. Miln, 11 Pet. 102.

subject, which, however, it had not exercised.[1] These several cases, and the elaborate discussions with which the decisions in each were accompanied, together with the leading case of Gibbons v. Ogden,[2] may be almost said to exhaust the reasoning upon the subject, and to leave little to be done by those who follow beyond the application of such rules for classification as they have indicated.

We have elsewhere referred to cases in which laws requiring all persons to refrain from their ordinary callings on the first day of the week have been held not to encroach upon the religious liberty of those citizens who do not observe that day as sacred. Neither are they unconstitutional as a restraint upon trade and commerce, or because they have the effect to destroy the value of a lease of property to be used on that day, or to make void a contract for Sunday services.[3]

The highways within and through a State are constructed by the State itself, which has full power to provide all proper regulations of police to govern the action of persons using them, and to make from time to time such alterations in these ways as the proper authorities shall deem proper.[4] A very common regulation is that parties meeting shall turn to the right; the propriety of which none will question. So the speed of travel may be regulated with a view to safe use and general protection, and to prevent a public nuisance.[5] So beasts may be prohibited from running at large, under the penalty of being seized and sold.[6] And it has been held competent under the same power to require the owners of urban property to construct and keep in repair and free from obstructions the sidewalks in front of it, and in case of their failure to do so to authorize the public authorities to do it at the expense of the property,[7] the courts distinguishing this from taxation, on the

---

[1] Cooley v. Board of Wardens, 12 How. 299. See Barnaby v. State, 21 Ind. 450.

[2] 9 Wheat. 1.

[3] Lindenmuller v. People, 33 Barb. 576. And see Ex parte Andrews, 18 Cal. 678; Ex parte Bird, 19 Cal. 130.

[4] As to the right to change the grade of a street from time to time without liability to parties incidentally injured, see ante 207.

[5] Commonwealth v. Worcester, 3 Pick. 473; People v. Jenkins, 1 Hill, 469; People v. Roe, Ibid. 470.

[6] McKee v. McKee, 8 B. Monr. 433.

[7] Godard, Petitioner, 16 Pick. 504; Bonsall v. Mayor of Lebanon, 19 Ohio, 418; Paxson v. Sweet, 1 Green, N. J. 196; Lowell v. Hadley, 8 Met. 180;

ground of the peculiar interest which those upon whom the duty is imposed have in its performance, and their peculiar power and ability to perform it with the promptness which the good of the community requires.[1] For the like reasons it has been held competent, where a district of country was liable to be inundated by the overflow of a large river, to require the owners of lands lying upon the river to construct levees on the river front at their own expense, and, on their failure to comply with this regulation, to cause such levees to be constructed under the direction of the public authorities, and the expense assessed upon the land of such owners.[2]

Navigable waters are also a species of public highway, and as such come under the control of the States. The term " navigable," at the common law, was only applied to those waters where the tide ebbed and flowed, but all streams which were of sufficient capacity for useful navigation, though not called navigable, were public, and subject to the same general rights which the public exercised in highways by land.[3] In this country there has been a very general disposition to consider all streams public which are useful as channels for commerce, wherever they are found of sufficient capacity to float the products of the mines, the forests, or the tillage of the country through which they flow, to market.[4] And if a stream is of sufficient capacity for the floating of rafts and logs in the condition in which it generally appears by nature, it will be regarded as public, notwithstanding there may be times when it becomes too dry and

Washington v. Mayor, &c. of Nashville, 1 Swan, 177 ; Mayor, &c. v. Medbury, 6 Humph. 368 ; Woodbridge v. Detroit, 8 Mich. 309, per Christiancy, J. ; Matter of Dorrance St., 4 R. I. 230 ; Deblois v. Barker, Ibid. 445 ; Hart v. Brooklyn, 36 Barb. 226.

[1] See especially the case of Godard, Petitioner, 16 Pick. 504, for a clear and strong statement of the grounds on which such legislation can be supported.

[2] Crowley v. Copley, 2 La. An. 329.

[3] Lorman v. Benson, 8 Mich. 26 ; Morgan v. King, 18 Barb. 283.

[4] Brown v. Chadbourne, 31 Me. 9 ; Shaw v. Crawford, 10 Johns. 236 ; Munson v. Hungerford, 6 Barb. 265 ; Browne v. Scofield, 8 Barb. 239 ; Morgan v. King, 18 Barb. 284, 30 Barb. 9 and 35 N. Y. 454 ; Cates v. Wadlington, 1 McCord, 580 ; Commonwealth v. Chapin, 5 Pick. 199 ; Moore v. Sanbourne, 2 Mich. 519 ; Lorman v. Benson, 8 Mich. 18 ; Depew v. Board of Trustees, &c., 5 Ind. 8 ; Board of Trustees v. Pidge, Ibid. 13 ; Stuart v. Clark, 2 Swan, 9 ; Dalrymple v. Mead, 1 Grant's Cases, 197 ; Commissioners of Homochitto River v. Withers, 29 Miss. 21 ; Rhodes v. Otis, 33 Ala. 578 ; McManus v. Carmichael, 3 Iowa, 1. And see Scott v. Willson, 3 N. H. 321.

shallow for the purpose. " The capacity of a stream, which generally appears by the nature, amount, importance, and necessity of
the business done upon it, must be the criterion. A brook, although it might carry down saw-logs for a few days, during a
freshet, is not therefore a public highway. But a stream upon
which and its tributaries saw-logs to an unlimited amount can be
floated every spring, and for the period of from four to eight weeks,
and for the distance of one hundred and fifty miles, and upon
which unquestionably many thousands will be annually transported for many years to come, if it be legal so to do, has the character
of a public stream *for that purpose.* So far the purpose is useful
for trade and commerce, and to the interests of the community.
The floating of logs is not mentioned by Lord Hale [in De Jure
Maris], and probably no river in Great Britain was, in his day, or
ever will be, put to that use. But here it is common, necessary,
and profitable, especially while the country is new ; and if it be
considered a lawful mode of using the river, it is easy to adapt well-
settled principles of law to the case. And they are not the less
applicable because this particular business may not always continue ; though if it can of necessity last but a short time, and the
river can be used for no other purpose, that circumstance would
have weight in the consideration of the question." [1] But if the
stream was not thus useful in its natural condition, but has been
rendered susceptible of use by the labors of the owner of the soil,
the right of passage will be in the nature of a private way, and the
public do not acquire a right to the benefit of the owner's labor,
unless he sees fit to dedicate it to their use.[2]

All navigable waters are for the use of all the citizens ; and
there cannot lawfully be any exclusive private appropriation of any
portion of them.[3] The question what is a navigable stream would
seem to be a mixed question of law and fact ;[4] and though it is
said that the legislature of the State may determine whether a

---

[1] Morgan v. King, 18 Barb. 288 ; Moore v. Sanborne, 2 Mich. 519.

[2] Wadsworth's Adm'r v. Smith, 11 Me. 278 ; Ward v. Warner, 8. Mich. 521.

[3] Commonwealth v. Charlestown, 1 Pick. 180 ; Kean v. Stetson, 5 Pick. 492 ;
Arnold v. Mundy, 1 Halst. 1 ; Bird v. Smith, 8 Watts, 434. They are equally
for the use of the public in the winter when covered with ice ; and one who cuts
a hole in the ice in an accustomed way, by means of which one passing upon the
ice is injured, is liable to an action for the injury. French v. Camp, 6 Shep. 433.

[4] See Treat v. Lord, 42 Me. 552.

stream shall be considered a public highway or not,[1] yet if in fact it is not one, the legislature cannot make it so by simple declaration, since, if it is private property, the legislature cannot appropriate it to a public use without providing for compensation.[2]

The general right to control and regulate the public use of navigable waters is unquestionably in the State ; but there are certain restrictions upon this right growing out of the power of Congress over commerce. Congress is empowered to regulate commerce with foreign nations and among the several States ; and wherever a river forms a highway upon which commerce is conducted with foreign nations or between States, it must fall under the control of Congress, under this power over commerce. The circumstance, however, that a stream is navigable, and capable of being used for foreign or inter-State commerce, does not exclude regulation by the State, if in fact Congress has not exercised its power in regard to it ;[3] or having exercised it, the State law does not come in conflict with the congressional regulations, or interfere with the rights which are permitted by them.

The decisions of the Federal judiciary in regard to navigable waters seem to have settled the following points : —

1. That no State can grant an exclusive monopoly for the navigation of any portion of the waters within its limits upon which commerce is carried on under coasting licenses granted under the authority of Congress,[4] since such a grant would come directly in conflict with the power which Congress has exercised. But a State law granting to an individual an exclusive right to navigate the upper waters of a river, lying wholly within the limits of the State, separated from tide water by falls impassable for purposes of navi-

---

[1] Glover v. Powell, 2 Stockt. 211 ; American River Water Co. v. Amsden, 6 Cal. 443 ; Baker v. Lewis, 33 Penn. St. 301.

[2] Morgan v. King, 18 Barb. 284 ; Same case, 35 N. Y. 454.

[3] Wilson v. Black Bird Creek Marsh Co., 2 Pet. 245. In this case it was held that a State law permitting a creek navigable from the sea to be dammed so as to exclude vessels altogether was not opposed to the Constitution of the United States, there being no legislation by Congress with which it would come in conflict. And see Wheeling Bridge Case, 13 How. 518.

[4] Gibbons v. Ogden, 9 Wheat. 1. The case was the well-known historical one, involving the validity of the grant by the State of·New York to Robert Fulton and his associates of the exclusive right to navigate the waters of that State with vessels propelled by steam.

gation, and not forming a part of any continuous track of commerce between two or more States, or with a foreign country, does not come within the reason of this decision, and cannot be declared void as opposed to the Constitution of the United States.[1]

2. The States have the same power to improve navigable waters which they possess over other highways;[2] and where money has been expended in making such improvement, it is competent for the State to impose tolls on the commerce which passes through and has the benefit of the improvement, even where the stream is one over which the regulations of commerce extend.[3]

3. The States may authorize the construction of bridges over navigable waters, for railroads as well as for every other species of highway, notwithstanding they may to some extent interfere with the right of navigation.[4] If the stream is not one which is subject to the control of Congress, the State law permitting the erection cannot be questioned on any ground of public inconvenience. The legislature must always have power to determine what public ways are needed, and to what extent the accommodation of travel over one way must yield to the greater necessity of another. But if the stream is one over which the regulations of Congress extend, the question is somewhat complicated, and it becomes necessary to consider whether such bridge will interfere with the regulations or not. But the bridge is not necessarily unlawful, because it may constitute, to some degree, an obstruction to commerce, if it is properly built and upon a proper plan, and if the general traffic of the country will be aided rather than impeded by its construction. There are many cases where a bridge over a river may be vastly more important than the navigation; and there are other cases where, although the traffic upon the river is important, yet an incon-

---

[1] Veazie v. Moor, 14 How. 568. The exclusive right granted in this case was to the navigation of the Penobscot River above Old Town, which was to continue for twenty years, in consideration of improvements in the navigation to be made by the grantees. Below Old Town there were a fall and several dams on the river, rendering navigation from the sea impossible.

[2] The improvement of a stream by State authority will give no right of action to an individual incidentally injured by the improvement. Zimmerman v. Union Canal Co., 1 W. & S. 346.

[3] Palmer v. Cuyahoga Co., 3 McLean, 226; Kellogg v. Union Co., 12 Conn. 7; Thames Bank v. Lovell, 18 Conn. 500.

[4] See Commonwealth v. Breed, 4 Pick. 460; Depew v. Trustees of W. & E. Canal, 5 Ind. 8.

venience caused by a bridge with draws would be much less seriously felt by the public, and be a much lighter burden upon trade and travel than a break in a line of railroad communication necessitating the employment of a ferry. In general terms it may be said that the State may authorize such constructions, provided they do not constitute material obstructions to navigation; but whether they are to be regarded as material obstructions or not is to be determined in each case upon its own circumstances. The character of the structure, the facility afforded for vessels to pass it, the relative amount of traffic likely to be done upon the stream and over the bridge, and whether the traffic by rail would be likely to be more incommoded by the want of the bridge than the traffic by water with it, are all circumstances to be taken into account in determining this question. It is quite evident that the same structure might constitute a material obstruction on the Ohio or the Mississippi, where vessels are constantly passing, which would be unobjectionable on a stream which a boat only enters at intervals of weeks or months. The decision of the State legislature that the erection is not an obstruction is not conclusive; but the final determination will rest with the Federal courts, who have jurisdiction to cause the structure to be abated, if it be found to obstruct unnecessarily the traffic upon the water. Parties constructing the bridge must be prepared to show, not only the State authority, and that the plan and construction are proper, but also that it accommodates more than it impedes the general commerce.[1]

4. The States may lawfully establish ferries over navigable waters, and grant licenses for keeping the same, and forbid unlicensed persons from running boats or ferries without such license. This also is only the establishment of a public way, and it can make no difference whether or not the water is entirely within the State, or, on the other hand, is a highway for inter-State or foreign commerce.[2]

5. The State may also authorize the construction of dams across

---

[1] See this subject fully considered in the Wheeling Bridge Case, 13 How. 518. See also Columbus Insurance Co. v. Peoria Bridge Co., 6 McLean, 72; Same v. Curtenius, Ibid. 209; Jolly v. Terre Haute Draw-Bridge Co., Ibid. 237; U. S. v. New Bedford Bridge, 1 W. & M. 401; Commissioners of St. Joseph Co. v. Pidge, 5 Ind. 8.

[2] Conway v. Taylor's Exr., 1 Black, 603; Chilvers v. People, 11 Mich. 43. In both these cases the State license law was sustained as against a vessel enrolled and licensed under the laws of Congress. And see Fanning v. Gregorie, 16 How. 534. Ferry rights may be so regulated as to rates of ferriage, and ferry franchises

navigable waters ; and where no question of Federal authority is
involved, the legislative permission to erect a dam will exempt the
structure from being considered a nuisance,[1] and it would seem
also that it must exempt the party constructing it from liability to
any private action for injury to navigation, so long as he keeps
within the authority granted, and is guilty of no negligence.[2]

6. To the foregoing it may be added that the State has the same
power of regulating the speed and general conduct of ships or
other vessels navigating its water highways, that it has to regulate
the speed and conduct of persons and vehicles upon the ordinary
highway; subject always to the restriction that its regulations
must not come in conflict with any regulations established by Congress for the foreign commerce or that between the States.[3]

It would be quite impossible to enumerate all the instances in
which this power is or may be exercised, because the various cases
in which the exercise by one individual of his rights may conflict
with a similar exercise by others, or may be detrimental to the
public order or safety, are infinite in number and in variety.   And
there are other cases where it becomes necessary for the public
authorities to interfere with the control by individuals of their
property, and even to destroy it, where the owners themselves have
fully observed all their duties to their fellows and to the State, but
where, nevertheless, some controlling public necessity demands the
interference or destruction.   A strong instance of this description
is where it becomes necessary to take, use, or destroy the private
property of individuals to prevent the spreading of a fire, the rav-
ages of a pestilence, the advance of a hostile army, or any other
great public calamity.[4]   Here the individual is in no degree in

and privileges so controlled in the hands of grantees and lessees, that they shall
not be abused to the serious detriment or inconvenience of the public.   Where
this power is given to a municipality, it may be recalled at any time.   People
v. Mayor, &c. of N. Y., 32 Barb. 102.

[1] Wilson v. Blackbird Creek Marsh Co., 2 Pet. 245 ; Brown v. Commonwealth,
3 S. &. R. 273 ; Bacon v. Arthur, 4 Watts, 437 ; Hogg v. Zanesville Co., 5 Ohio,
410.   And see Flanagan v. Philadelphia, 42 Penn. St. 219 ; Depew v. Trustees of W. & E. Canal, 5 Ind. 8.

[2] See Bailey v. Philadelphia, &c. R. R. Co., 4 Harr. 389 ; Roush v. Walter,
10 Watts, 86 ; Parker v. Cutler Mill Dam Co., 7 Shep. 353 ; Zimmerman v.
Union Canal Co., 1 W. & S. 346 ; Depew v. Trustees of W. & E. Canal, 5 Ind. 8.

[3] People v. Jenkins, 1 Hill, 469 ; People v. Roe, 1 Hill, 470.

[4] Mayor, &c. of New York v. Lord, 18 Wend. 129 ; Russell v. Mayor, &c. of
New York, 2 Denio, 461 ; Sorocco v. Geary, 3 Cal. 69 ; Hale v. Lawrence, 1 Zab.

fault, but his interest must yield to that " necessity " which " knows no law." The establishment of limits within the denser portions of cities and villages, within which buildings constructed of inflammable materials shall not be erected or repaired, may also, in some cases, be equivalent to a destruction of private property ; but regulations for this purpose have been sustained notwithstanding this result.[1] Wharf lines may also be established for the general good, even though they prevent the owners of water-fronts from building out on that which constitutes private property.[2] And, whenever the legislature deem it necessary to the protection of a harbor to forbid the removal of stones, gravel, or sand from the beach, they may establish regulations to that effect under penalties, and make them applicable to the owners of the soil equally with other persons. Such regulations are only " a just restraint of an injurious use of property, which the legislature have authority " to impose.[3]

So a particular use of property may sometimes be forbidden, where, by a change of circumstances, and without the fault of the owner, that which was once lawful, proper, and unobjectionable has now become a public nuisance, endangering the public health or the public safety. Mill dams are sometimes destroyed upon this ground ;[4] and churchyards which, found, by the advance of urban population, to be detrimental to the public health, or in danger of becoming so, are liable to be closed against further use for cemetery purposes.[5] The keeping of gunpowder in unsafe quantities in cities or villages ;[6] the sale of poisonous drugs, unless labelled ; allowing unmuzzled dogs to be at large when danger of hydrophobia is apprehended ;[7] or the keeping for sale unwholesome

714 ; American Print Works v. Lawrence, Ibid. 248 ; Meeker v. Van Rensselaer, 15 Wend. 397.

[1] Respublica v. Duquet, 2 Yeates, 493 ; Wadleigh v. Gilman, 3 Fairf. 403 ; Brady v. Northwestern Ins. Co., 11 Mich. 425 ; Vanderbilt v. Adams, 7 Cow. 352, per Woodworth, J.

[2] Commonwealth v. Alger, 7 Cush. 53. See Hart v. Mayor, &c. of Albany, 9 Wend. 571.

[3] Commonwealth v. Tewksbury, 11 Met. 55.

[4] Miller v. Craig, 3 Stockt. 175.

[5] Brick Presbyterian Church v. Mayor, &c. of New York, 5 Cow. 538 ; Coates v. Mayor, &c. of New York, 7 Cow. 604.

[6] Foote v. Fire Department, 5 Hill, 99. And see License Cases, 5 How. 589, per McLean, J. ; Fisher v. McGirr, 1 Gray, 27, per Shaw, Ch. J.

[7] Morey v. Brown, 42 N. H. 373.

provisions, or other deleterious substances, — are all subject to be forbidden under this power. And, generally, it may be said that each State has complete authority to provide for the abatement of nuisances, whether they exist by the parties' fault or not.[1]

The preservation of the public morals is peculiarly subject to legislative supervision, which may forbid the keeping, exhibition, or sale of indecent books or pictures, and cause their destruction if seized ; or prohibit or regulate the places of amusement that may be resorted to for the purpose of gaming ; [2] or forbid altogether the keeping of implements of gaming for unlawful games ; or prevent the keeping and exhibition of stallions in public places.[3] And the power to provide for the compulsory observance of the first day of the week is also to be referred to the same authority.[4]

So the markets are regulated, and particular articles allowed to be sold in particular places only, or after license ; [5] weights and measures are established, and dealers compelled to conform to the fixed standards under penalty, and the like.[6] These instances are more than sufficient to illustrate the pervading nature of this power, and we need not weary the reader with further enumeration. Many of them have been previously referred to under the head of municipal by-laws.

Whether the prohibited act or omission shall be made a criminal offence, punishable under the general laws, or subject to punishment under municipal by-laws, or, on the other hand, the party be deprived of any remedy for any right which, but for the regu-

---

[1] See Miller v. Craig, 3 Stockt. 175 ; Weeks v. Milwaukee, 10 Wis. 242. But under this power it would not be competent for a city to tax a lot owner for the expense of abating a nuisance on his lot which the city itself had created. Weeks v. Milwaukee, Ibid.

[2] Tanner v. Trustees of Albion, 5 Hill, 121 ; Commonwealth v. Colton, 8 Gray, 488.

[3] Nolin v. Mayor of Franklin, 4 Yerg. 163.

[4] Specht v. Commonwealth, 8 Penn. St. 312 ; State v. Ambs, 20 Mo. 214 ; Adams v. Hamel, 2 Doug. (Mich.) 73 ; Vogelsong v. State, 9 Ind. 112 ; Shover v. State, 5 Eng. 259 ; Bloom v. Richards, 2 Ohio, N. S. 387 ; Lindenmuller v. People, 33 Barb. 548 ; Ex parte Andrews, 18 Cal. 678 ; Ex parte Bird, 19 Cal. 130.

[5] Nightingale's Case, 11 Pick. 168 ; Buffalo v. Webster, 10 Wend. 99 ; Bush v. Seabury, 8 Johns. 418 ; Ash v. People, 11 Mich. 347 ; State v. Leiber, 11 Iowa, 407 ; Le Claire v. Davenport, 13 Iowa, 210 ; White v. Kent, 11 Ohio, N. S. 550.

[6] Guillotte v. New Orleans, 12 La. An. 432 ; Page v. Fazackerly, 36 Barb. 392 ; Mayor, &c. of Mobile v. Yuille, 3 Ala. 139.

lation, he might have had against other persons, are questions which the legislature must decide. It is sufficient for us to have pointed out that, in addition to the power to punish misdemeanors and felonies, the State has also the authority to make extensive and varied regulations as to the time, mode, and circumstances in and under which parties shall assert, enjoy, or exercise their rights, without coming in conflict with any of those constitutional principles which are established for the protection of private rights or private property.

CHAPTER XVII.

THE EXPRESSION OF THE POPULAR WILL.

ALTHOUGH by their constitutions the people have delegated the exercise of sovereign powers to the several departments, they have not thereby divested themselves of the sovereignty, but directly or indirectly complete control of the government is in their hands, and the three departments are responsible to and subject to be changed, directed, controlled, or abolished by them. But this control and direction must be exercised in the legitimate mode. The voice of the people can only be heard when expressed in the times and under the conditions which they themselves have prescribed and pointed out by the Constitution; and if any attempt should be made by any portion of the people, however large, to interfere with the regular working of the agencies of government at any other time or in any other mode than as allowed by existing law, either constitutional or statutory, it would be revolutionary in character, and to be resisted and repressed by the officers of government.

The authority of the people is exercised through *elections*, by means of which they select and appoint the legislative, executive, and judicial officers, to whom shall be entrusted the powers of government. In some cases also they pass upon other questions specially submitted to them, and adopt or reject a measure according as a majority vote for or against it. It is obviously impossible that the people should consider, mature, and adopt their own laws; but when a law has been perfected, or when it is deemed desirable to take the expression of public sentiment upon any one question, the ordinary machinery of elections is adequate to the end, and the expression is easily and without confusion obtained by submitting the law for an affirmative or negative vote. In this manner are constitutions and amendments thereof adopted or rejected, and matters of local importance in many cases, like the location of a county seat, the contracting of a local debt, the erection of a public building, the acceptance of a municipal charter, and the like, are passed upon and determined by the people interested in the question, under constitutional or statutory provisions which provide therefor.

The Right to Participate in Elections.

The conditions for the exercise of the elective franchise are established by every State for itself, and though there is a general uniformity of qualifications, there is also some diversity. Women, minors, and aliens are excluded in all the States from participation in the general elections; though in some the alien becomes qualified after a certain residence, if he has declared his intention to become a citizen; and in some elections also persons are excluded who lack a specified property qualification, or who do not pay taxes, or who have been convicted of infamous crimes. In some States idiots and lunatics are also expressly excluded, and it has been supposed that these unfortunate classes, by the common political law of England and of this country, were excluded with women, minors, and aliens from exercising the right of suffrage, even though not prohibited therefrom by any express constitutional or statutory provision.[1]

Conditions necessary to its Exercise.

One of these is, that the party offering to vote must reside within the district which is to be affected by the exercise of the right. If a State officer is to be chosen, the voter must be a resident of the State; and if a county, city, or township officer, he must reside within such county, city, or township. This is the general rule; and for the more convenient determination of the right to vote, and to prevent fraud, it is now generally required that the elector shall only take part in either local or general elections at the place of

---

[1] See Cushing's Legislative Assemblies, § 24. Also § 27, and notes referring to legislative cases. Drunkenness is regarded as temporary insanity. Ibid. Idiots and lunatics are expressly excluded by the constitutions of Delaware, Iowa, Kansas, Maryland, Minnesota, Nevada, New Jersey, Ohio, Oregon, Rhode Island, West Virginia, and Wisconsin. *Paupers* are excluded in New York, California, Louisiana, Maine, Massachusetts, New Hampshire, New Jersey, Rhode Island, South Carolina, and West Virginia. *Persons under guardianship* are excluded in Kansas, Maine, Massachusetts, Minnesota, and Wisconsin. *Persons under interdiction* are excluded in Louisiania; and *persons excused from paying taxes at their own request*, in New Hampshire. Capacity to read is required in Connecticut, and capacity to read and write in Massachusetts.

his residence, where he will be known and where the opportunities for illegal or fraudulent voting will be less than if allowed to vote at a distance and among strangers. And where this is the requirement of the constitution, any statute permitting voters to deposit their ballots elsewhere must necessarily be void.[1]

A person's residence is the place of his domicile, or the place where his habitation is fixed, without any present intention of removing therefrom.[2] The words "inhabitant," " citizen," and "resident," as employed in different constitutions to define the qualifications of electors, mean substantially the same thing; and one is an inhabitant, resident, or citizen at the place where he has his domicile or home.[3] Every person at all times must be considered as having a domicile somewhere, and that which he has acquired at one place is considered as continuing until another is acquired at a different place. It has been held that a student in an institution of learning, who has residence there for purposes of instruction, may vote at such place, provided he is emancipated from his father's family, and for the time has no home elsewhere.[4]

---

[1] Opinions of Judges, 30 Conn. 591; Hulseman v. Rems, 41 Penn. St. 396; Chase v. Miller, Ibid. 403; Opinions of Judges, 44 N. H. 633; Bourland v. Hildreth, 26 Cal. 161; People v. Blodgett, 13 Mich. 127. There are now constitutional provisions in New York, Michigan, Missouri, Connecticut, Maryland, Nevada, Rhode Island, and Pennsylvania, which permit soldiers in actual service to cast their votes where they may happen to be stationed at the time of voting. The case of Morrison v. Springer, 15 Iowa, 304, is adverse to those above cited.

[2] Putnam v. Johnson, 10 Mass. 488; Rue High's Case, 2 Doug. (Mich.) 523; Story, Confl. Laws, § 43.

[3] Cushing's Law and Practice of Legislative Assemblies, § 36.

[4] Putnam v. Johnson, 10 Mass. 488; Lincoln v. Hapgood, 11 Mass. 350. " The questions of residence, inhabitancy, or domicile — for although not in all respects precisely the same, they are nearly so, and depend much upon the same evidence — are attended with more difficulty than almost any other which are presented for adjudication. No exact definition can be given of domicile; it depends upon no one fact or combination of circumstances; but, from the whole taken together, it must be determined in each particular case. It is a maxim that every man must have a domicile somewhere, and also that he can have but one. Of course it follows that his existing domicile continues until he acquires another; and vice versa, by acquiring a new domicile he relinquishes his former one. From this view it is manifest that very slight circumstances must often decide the question. It depends upon the preponderance of the evidence in favor of two or more places; and it may often occur that the evidence of facts tending to establish the domicile in one place would be entirely conclusive, were it not for the existence of facts and circumstances of a still more conclusive and decisive character, which

In some of the States it is regarded as important that lists of voters should be prepared before the day of election, in which should be registered the name of every person qualified to vote. By this arrangement the officers whose duty it is to administer the election laws are enabled to proceed with more deliberation in the discharge of their duties, and to avoid the haste and confusion that must attend the determination upon election day of the various and sometimes difficult questions concerning the right of individuals to exercise this important franchise. Electors also, by means of this registry, are notified in advance what persons claim the right to vote, and are enabled to make the necessary examination to determine whether the claim is well founded, and to exercise the right of challenge if satisfied any person registered is unqualified. When the constitution has established no such rule, and is entirely silent on the subject, it has been sometimes claimed that the statute requiring voters to be registered before the day of election, and excluding from the right all whose names do not appear upon the list, was unconstitutional and void, as adding another test to the qualifications of electors, which the constitution

fix it beyond question in another. So, on the contrary, very slight circumstances may fix one's domicile, if not controlled by more conclusive facts fixing it in another place. If a seaman, without family or property, sails from the place of his nativity, which may be considered his domicile of origin, although he may return only at long intervals, or even be absent many years, yet if he does not by some actual residence or other means acquire a domicile elsewhere, he retains his domicile of origin." Shaw, Ch. J., Thorndike v. City of Boston, 1 Met. 245. In Inhabitants of Abington v. Inhabitants of North Bridgewater, 23 Pick. 170, it appeared that a town line run through the house occupied by a party, leaving a portion on one side sufficient to form a habitation, and a portion on the other not sufficient for that purpose. Held, that the domicile must be deemed to be on the side first mentioned. It was intimated also that where a house was thus divided, and the party slept habitually on one side, that circumstance should be regarded as a preponderating one to fix his residence there, in the absence of other proof. And see Rex v. St. Olave's, 1 Strange, 51.

By the constitutions of several of the States, it is provided, in substance, that no person shall be deemed to have gained or lost a residence by reason of his presence or absence, while employed in the service of the United States; nor while a student in any seminary of learning; nor while kept at any almshouse or asylum at public expense, nor while confined in any public prison. See Const. of N. Y., art. 2, § 3; Const. of Illinois, art. 6, § 5; Const. of Ind., art. 2, § 4; Const. of California, art. 2, § 4; Const. of Mich., art. 7, § 5; Const. of Rhode Island, art. 2, § 4; Const. of Minnesota, art. 7, § 3; Const. of Missouri, art. 2, § 20; Const. of Nevada, art. 2, § 2; Const. of Oregon, art. 2, §§ 4 and 5; Const. of Wisconsin, art. 3, §§ 4 and 5.

has prescribed, and as having the effect, where electors are not registered, to exclude from voting persons who have an absolute right to that franchise by the fundamental law. This position however has not been accepted as sound by the courts. The provision for a registry deprives no one of his right, but is only a reasonable regulation under which the right may be exercised.[1] Such regulations must always have been within the power of the legislature, unless forbidden. Many resting upon the same principle are always prescribed, and have never been supposed to be open to objection. Although the Constitution provides that all male citizens twenty-one years of age and upwards shall be entitled to vote, it would not be seriously contended that a statute which should require all such citizens to go to the established place for holding the polls, and there deposit their ballots, and not elsewhere, was a violation of the Constitution, because prescribing an additional qualification, namely, the presence of the elector at the polls. All such reasonable regulations of the constitutional right which seem to the legislature important to the preservation of order in elections, to guard against fraud, undue influence, and oppression, and to preserve the purity of the ballot-box, are not only within the constitutional power of the legislature, but are commendable, and at least some of them absolutely essential. And where the law requires such a registry, and forbids the reception of votes from any persons not registered, an election in a township where no such registry has ever been made will be void, and cannot be sustained by making proof that none in fact but duly qualified electors have voted. It is no answer that such a rule may enable the registry officers, by neglecting their duty, to disfranchise the electors altogether; the remedy of the electors is by proceedings to compel the performance of the duty; and the statute, being imperative and mandatory, cannot be disregarded.[2] The danger, however, of any such misconduct on the part of officers is comparatively small, when the duty is entrusted to those who are chosen in the locality where the registry is to be made, and who are consequently immediately responsible to those who are interested in being registered.

In some other cases preliminary action by the public authorities may be requisite before any legal election can be held. If an

---

[1] Capen v. Foster, 12 Pick. 485; People v. Kopplekom, 16 Mich. 342.

[2] People v. Kopplekom, 16 Mich. 342.

election is one which a municipality may hold or not at its option, and the proper municipal authority decides against holding it, it is evident that individual citizens must acquiesce, and that any votes which may be cast by them on the assumption of right must be altogether nugatory.[1] The same would be true of an election to be held after proclamation for that purpose, where no such proclamation has been made.[2] Where, however, both the time and the place of an election are prescribed by law, every voter has a right to take notice of the law, and to deposit his ballot at the time and place appointed, notwithstanding the officer, whose duty it is to give notice of the election, has failed in that duty. The notice to be thus given is only additional to that which the statute itself gives, and is prescribed for the purpose of greater publicity; but the right to hold the election comes from the statute, and not from the official notice. It has therefore been frequently held that when a vacancy exists in an office, which the law requires shall be filled at the next general election, the time and place of which are fixed, and that notice of the general election shall also specify the vacancy to be filled, an election at that time and place to fill the vacancy will be valid, notwithstanding the notice is not given; and such election cannot be defeated by showing that a small portion only of the electors were actually aware of the vacancy or cast their votes to fill it.[3] But this would not be the case if either the time or the place were not fixed by law, so that notice became essential for that purpose.[4]

[1] Opinions of Judges, 7 Mass. 525; Opinions of Judges, 15 Mass. 537.

[2] People v. Porter, 6 Cal. 26; McKune v. Weller, 11 Cal. 49; People v. Martin, 12 Cal. 409; Jones v. State, 1 Kansas, 273.

[3] People v. Cowles, 13 N. Y. 350; People v. Brenahm, 3 Cal. 477; State v. Jones, 19 Ind. 356; People v. Hartwell, 12 Mich. 508; Dishon v. Smith, 10 Iowa, 212.

[4] State v. Young, 4 Iowa, 561. An act had been passed for the incorporation of the city of Washington, and by its terms it was to be submitted to the people on the 16th of the following February, for their acceptance or rejection, at an election to be called and holden in the same manner as township elections under the general law. The time of notice for the regular township elections was, by law, to be determined by the trustees, but for the first township meeting fifteen days' notice was made requisite. An election was holden, assumed to be under the act in question; but no notice was given of it, except by the circulation, on the morning of the election, of an extra newspaper containing a notice that an election would be held on that day at a specified place. It was held that the election was void. The act contemplated *some* notice before any legal vote

The Manner of exercising the Right.

The mode of voting in this country, at all general elections, is almost universally by ballot.[1] " A ballot may be defined to be a piece of paper, or other suitable material, with the name written or printed upon it of the person to be voted for; and where the suffrages are given in this form, each of the electors in person deposits such a vote in the box, or other receptacle provided for the purpose, and kept by the proper officers.[2] The distinguishing feature of this mode of voting is, that every voter is thus enabled to secure and preserve the most complete and inviolable secrecy in regard to the persons for whom he votes, and thus escape the influences which, under the system of oral suffrages, may be brought to bear upon him with a view to overbear and intimidate, and thus prevent the real expression of public sentiment.[3]

could be taken, and that which was given could not be considered any notice at all. This case differs from all of those above cited, where vacancies were to be filled at a general election, and where the law itself would give to the electors all the information which was requisite. In this case, although the time was fixed, the place was not; and, if a notice thus circulated on the morning of election could be held sufficient, it might well happen that the electors generally would fail to be informed, so that their right to vote might be exercised.

[1] The exceptions are in Virginia, Arkansas, Kentucky, Georgia, and possibly by law in some other States.

[2] Cush. Leg. Assemb. § 103.

[3] " In this country, and indeed in every country where officers are elective, different modes have been adopted for the electors to signify their choice. The most common modes have been either by voting *viva voce*, that is, by the elector openly naming the person he designates for the office, or by ballot, which is depositing in a box provided for the purpose a paper on which is the name of the person he intends for the office. The principle object of this last mode is to enable the elector to express his opinion secretly, without being subject to be overawed, or to any ill will or persecution on account of his vote for either of the candidates who may be before the public. The method of voting by tablets in Rome was an example of this manner of voting. There certain officers appointed for that purpose, called Diribitores, delivered to each voter as many tablets as there were candidates, one of whose names was written upon every tablet. The voter put into a chest prepared for that purpose which of these tablets he pleased and they were afterwards taken out and counted: Cicero defines tablets to be little *billets*, in which the people brought their suffrages. The clause in the Constitution directing the election of the several State officers was undoubtedly intended to provide that the election should be made by this mode of voting to the exclusion of any other. In this mode the freemen can individually express their choice, without being under the necessity of publicly declaring the object of their choice; their collective

In order to secure as perfectly as possible the benefits anticipated from this system, statutes have been passed, in some of the
States, which prohibit ballots being received or counted unless the
same are written or printed upon white paper, without any marks
or figures thereon intended to distinguish one ballot from another.[1]
These statutes are simply declaratory of a constitutional principle
that inheres in the system of voting by ballot, and which ought to
be inviolable whether declared or not.   In the absence of such a
statute, all devices by which party managers are enabled to distinguish ballots in the hand of the voter, and thus determine whether
he is voting for or against them, are opposed to the spirit of the
Constitution, inasmuch as they tend to defeat the design for which
voting by ballot is established, and, though they may not render an
election void, they are exceedingly reprehensible, and ought to be
discountenanced by all good citizens.   The system of ballot-voting
rests upon the idea that every elector is to be entirely at liberty to
vote for whom he pleases and with what party he pleases, and that
no one is to have the right, or be in position, to question him for
it, either then or at any subsequent time.[2]   The courts have held
that a voter, even in case of a contested election, cannot be compelled to disclose for whom he voted ; and for the same reason we
think others who may accidentally, or by trick or artifice, have
acquired knowledge on the subject, should not be allowed to tes-

---

voice can be easily ascertained, and the evidence of it transmitted to the place
where their votes are to be counted, and the result declared with as little inconvenience as possible." Temple v. Mead, 4 Vt. 541. In this case it was held that
a *printed* ballot was within the meaning of the constitution which required all
ballots for certain State officers to be "fairly written." To the same effect is
Henshaw v. Foster, 9 Pick. 312.

[1] See People v. Kilduff, 15 Ill. 500. In this case it was held that the common
lines on ruled paper did not render the ballots void.

[2] " The right to vote in this manner has usually been considered an important
and valuable safeguard of the independence of the humble citizen against the
influence which wealth and station might be supposed to exercise. This object
would be accomplished but very imperfectly if the privacy supposed to be secured
was limited to the moment of depositing the ballot. The spirit of the system requires that the elector should be secured then and at all times thereafter against
reproach or animadversion, or any other prejudice on account of having voted
according to his own unbiassed judgment ; and that security is made to consist in
shutting up within the privacy of his own mind all knowledge of the manner in
which he has bestowed his suffrage." Per Denio, Ch. J. in People v. Pease, 27
N. Y. 81.

tify to such knowledge, or to give any information in the courts upon the subject. Public policy requires that the veil of secrecy should be impenetrable, unless the voter himself voluntarily determines to lift it; his ballot is absolutely privileged; and to allow evidence of its contents, when he has not waived the privilege, is to encourage trickery and fraud, and would in effect establish this remarkable anomaly, that, while the law from motives of public policy establishes the secret ballot with a view to conceal the elector's action, it at the same time encourages a system of espionage, by means of which the veil of secrecy may be penetrated and the voter's action disclosed to the public.[1]

Every ballot should be complete in itself, and ought not to require extensive evidence to enable the election officers to deter-

---

[1] See this subject fully considered in People v. Cicotte, 16 Mich. 283. A very loose system prevails in the contests over legislative elections, and it has been held that when a voter refuses to disclose for whom he voted, evidence is admissible of the general reputation of the political character of the voter, and as to the party to which he belonged at the time of the election. Cong. Globe, XVI. App. 456. This is assuming that the voter adheres strictly to party, and always votes the "straight ticket"; an assumption which may not be a very violent one in the majority of cases, but which is scarcely creditable to the manly independence and self-reliance of any free people; and however strongly disposed legislative bodies may be to act upon it, we are not prepared to see any such rule of evidence adopted by the courts. If a voter chooses voluntarily to exhibit his ballot publicly, perhaps there is no reason why those to whom it was shown should not testify to its contents; but in other cases the knowledge of its contents is his own exclusive property, and he can neither be compelled to part with it, nor, as we think, is any one else who accidentally or surreptitiously becomes possessed of it, or to whom the ballot has been shown with a view to information, advice, or alteration, at liberty to make the disclosure. Such third person might be guilty of no legal offence if he should do so; but he is certainly invading the constitutional privileges of his neighbor, and we are aware of no sound principle of law which will justify a court in compelling or even permitting him to testify to what he has seen. And as the law does not compel a voter to testify, "surely it cannot be so inconsistent with itself as to authorize a judicial inquiry upon a particular subject, and at the same time industriously provide for the concealment of the only material facts upon which the results of such an inquiry must depend." Per Denio, Ch. J. in People v. Pease, 27 N. Y. 81. It was held in People v. Cicotte, 16 Mich. 283, that until it was distinctly shown that the elector waived his privilege of secrecy, any evidence as to the character or contents of his ballot was inadmissible. It was also held that where a voter's qualification was in question, but his want of right to vote was not conceded, the privilege was and must be the same; as otherwise any person's ballot might be inquired into by simply asserting his want of qualification.

mine the voter's intention. Perfect certainty, however, is not required in these cases. It is sufficient if an examination leaves no reasonable doubt upon the intention, and technical accuracy is never required in any case. The cardinal rule is to give effect to the intention of the voter, whenever it is not left in uncertainty ;[1] but if an ambiguity appears upon its face, the elector cannot be received as a witness to make it good by testifying for whom or for what office he intended the vote.[2]

The ballot in no case should contain more names than are authorized to be voted for, for any particular office at that election ; and, if it should, it must be rejected for the obvious impossibility of the canvassing officers choosing from among the names on the ballot, and applying the ballot to some to the exclusion of others. The choice must be made by the elector himself, and be expressed by the ballot. Accordingly, where only one supervisor was to be chosen, and a ballot was deposited having upon it the names of two persons for that office, it was held that it must be rejected for ambiguity.[3] It has been held, however, that if a voter shall write a name upon a printed ballot, in connection with the title to an office, this is such a designation of the name written for that office as to sufficiently demonstrate his intention, even though he omit to strike off the printed name of the opposing candidate. The writing in such a case, it is held, ought to prevail as the highest evidence of the voter's intention, and the failure to strike off the printed name will be regarded as an accidental oversight.[4]

[1] People v. Matteson, 17 Ill. 169; People v. Cook, 8 N. Y. 67; State v. Elwood, 12 Wis. 551; People v. Bates, 11 Mich. 362.

[2] People v. Seaman, 5 Denio, 409. The mental purpose of an elector is not provable; it must be determined by his acts. People v. Saxton, 22 N. Y. 309. And where the intent is to be gathered from the ballot, it is a question of law and cannot be submitted to the jury as one of fact. People v. McManus, 34 Barb. 620.

[3] People v. Seaman, 5 Denio, 409. See also Atty.-Genl. v. Ely, 4 Wis. 420; People v. Loomis, 8 Wend. 396; People v. Cook, 14 Barb. 259, and 8 N. Y. 67. Such a vote, however, could not be rejected as to candidates for other offices regularly named upon the ballot; it would be void only as to the particular office for which the duplicate ballot was cast. Atty.-Genl. v. Ely, 4 Wis. 420.

[4] People v. Saxton, 22 N. Y. 309. This ruling suggests this query : Suppose at an election where printed slips containing the names of candidates, with a designation of the office, are supplied to voters, to be pasted over the names of opposing candidates, — as is very common, — a ballot should be found in the box containing the name of a candidate for one office, — say the county clerk, — with

The name on the ballot should be clearly expressed, and ought to be given fully. Errors in spelling, however, will not defeat the ballot if the sound is the same;[1] nor abbreviations,[2] if such as are in common use and generally understood, so that there can be no reasonable doubt of the intent. And it would seem that where a ballot is cast which contains only the initials of the Christian name of the candidate, it ought to be sufficient, as it designates the person voted for with the same certainty which is commonly met with in contracts and other private writings, and the intention of the vote cannot reasonably be open to any doubt.[3] As the law knows only

a designation of the office pasted over the name of a candidate for some other office, — say coroner; so that the ballot would contain the name of two persons for county clerk and of none for coroner. In such a case, is the slip the highest evidence of the intention of the voter as to who should receive his suffrage for county clerk, and must it be counted for that office? And if so, then does not the ballot also show the intention of the elector to cast his vote for the person for coroner whose name is thus accidentally pasted over, and should it not be counted for that person? The case of People v. Saxton would seem to be opposed to People v. Seaman, 5 Denio, 409, where the court refused to allow evidence to be given to explain the ambiguity occasioned by the one name being placed upon the ticket, without the other being erased. "The intention of the elector cannot be thus inquired into, when it is opposed or hostile to the paper ballot which he has deposited in the ballot-box. We might with the same propriety permit it to be proved that he intended to vote for one man, when his ballot was cast for another; a species of proof not to be tolerated." Per Whittlesay, J. The case of People v. Cicotte, 16 Mich. 283, is also opposed to People v. Saxton. In the Michigan case a slip for the office of sheriff was pasted over the name of the candidate for another county office, so that the ballot contained the names of two candidates for sheriff. It was argued that the slip should be counted as the best evidence of the voter's intention; but the court held that the ballot could be counted for neither candidate, because of its ambiguity.

[1] People v. Mayworm, 5 Mich. 146; Atty.-Genl. v. Ely, 4 Wis. 430.

[2] People v. Furguson, 8 Cow. 102. See also, upon this subject, People v. Cook, 14 Barb. 259, and 8 N. Y. 67; and People v. Tisdale, 1 Doug. (Mich.) 65.

[3] In People v. Furguson, 8 Cow. 102, it was held, that, on the trial of a contested election case before a jury, ballots cast for H. F. Yates should be counted for Henry F. Yates, if, under the circumstances, the jury were of the opinion they were intended for him; and to arrive at that intention, it was competent to prove that he generally signed his name H. F. Yates; that he had before held the same office for which these votes were cast, and was then a candidate again; that the people generally would apply the abbreviation to him, and that no other person was known in the county to whom it would apply. This ruling was followed in People v. Seaman, 5 Denio, 409, and in People v. Cook, 14 Barb. 259, and 8 N. Y. 67. The courts also held, in these cases, that the elector voting the defecting ballot might give evidence to enable the jury to apply it, and

one Christian name, the giving of an initial to a middle name when the party has none, or the giving of a wrong initial, will

might testify that he intended it for the candidate the initials of whose name he had given. In Atty.-Genl. *v.* Ely, 4 Wis. 429, a rule somewhat different was laid down. In that case, Matthew H. Carpenter was candidate for the office of prosecuting attorney; and besides the perfect ballots, there were others, cast for " D. M. Carpenter," " M. D. Carpenter," " M. T. Carpenter," and " Carpenter." The jury found that there was no lawyer in the county by the name of D. M. Carpenter, M. D. Carpenter, M. T. Carpenter, or whose surname was Carpenter, except the relator, Matthew H. Carpenter; that the relator was a practising attorney of the county, and eligible to the office, and that the votes above mentioned were all given and intended by the electors for the relator. The court say: " How was the intention of the voter to be ascertained? By reading the name on the ballot, and ascertaining who was meant and intended by that name? Is no evidence admissible to show who was intended to be voted for under the various appellations, except such evidence as is contained in the ballot itself? Or may you gather the intention of the voter from the ballot, explained by the surrounding circumstances, from facts of a general public nature connected with the election, and the different candidates, which may aid you in coming to the right conclusion? These facts and circumstances might, perhaps, be adduced so clear and strong as to lead irresistibly to the inference that a vote given for Carpenter was intended to be cast for Matthew H. Carpenter. A contract may be read by the light of the surrounding circumstances, not to contradict it, but in order more perfectly to understand the intent and meaning of the parties who made it. By analogous principles, we think that these facts, and others of like nature connected with the election, could be given in evidence, for the purpose of aiding the jury in determining who was intended to be voted for. In New York, courts have gone even farther than this, and held, that not only facts of public notoriety might be given in evidence to show the intention of the elector, but that the elector who cast the abbreviated ballot may be sworn as to who was intended by it. People *v.* Ferguson, 8 Cow. 102. But this is pushing the doctrine to a great extent further, we think, than considerations of public policy and the well-being of society will warrant; and to restrict the rule, and say that a jury must determine from an inspection of the ballot itself, from the letters upon it, aside from all extraneous facts, who was intended to be designated by the ballot, is establishing a principle unnecessarily cautious and limited. In the present case, the jury, from the evidence before them, found that the votes [above described] were, when given and cast, intended, by the electors who gave and cast the same respectively, to be given and cast for Matthew H. Carpenter, the relator. Such being the case, it clearly follows that they should be counted for him." See also State *v.* Elwood, 12 Wis. 551; and People *v.* Pease, 27 N. Y. 84, per Denio, Ch. J.

On the other hand, it was held, in Opinions of Judges, 38 Maine, 559, that votes could not be counted for a person of a different name from that expressed by the ballot, even though the only difference consisted in the initial to the middle name. But see People *v.* Cook, 14 Barb. 259, and 8 N. Y. 67. And in People *v.* Tisdale, 1 Doug. (Mich.) 65, followed, in People *v.* Higgins, 3 Mich. 233, it was

not defeat the ballot;[1] nor will a failure to give the addition to a name — such as "Junior" — render it void, as that is a mere matter of description, not constituting a part of the name, and if given erroneously may be treated as surplusage.[2] But where the

held that no extrinsic evidence was admissible in explanation or support of the ballot; and that, unless it showed upon its face for whom it was designed, it must be rejected. And it was also held, that a vote for "J. A. Dyer" did not show, upon its face, for whom it was intended, and that it could not be counted for James A. Dyer. This rule is convenient of application, but it probably defeats the intention of the electors in every case to which it is applied, where the rejected votes could influence the result, — an intention, too, which we think is so apparent on the ballot itself, that no person would be in real doubt concerning it. In People v. Pease, 27 N. Y. 64, in which Moses M. Smith was a candidate for county treasurer, Selden, J. says: "According to well-settled rules, the board of canvassers erred in refusing to allow to the relator the nineteen votes given for Moses Smith and M. M. Smith"; and although we think this doctrine correct, the cases he cites in support of it (8 Cow. 102, and 5 Denio, 409) would only warrant a jury, not the canvassers, in allowing them; or, at least, those cast for M. M. Smith. The case of People v. Tisdale was again followed in People v. Cicotte, 16 Mich. 283; the majority of the court, however, expressing the opinion that it was erroneous in principle, but that it had now (for twenty-five years) been too long the settled law of the State to be disturbed, unless by the legislature.

  [1] People v. Cook, 14 Barb. 259, 8 N. Y. 67. But see Opinions of Judges, 38 Maine, 597.

  [2] People v. Cook, 14 Barb. 259, and 8 N. Y. 67. In this case, the jury found, as matter of fact, that ballots given for Benjamin Welch were intended for Benjamin Welch, Jr.; and the court held, that, as a matter of law, they should have been counted for him. It was not decided, however, that the canvassers were at liberty to allow the votes to Benjamin Welch, Jr.; and the Judge, delivering the prevailing opinion in the Court of Appeals, says (p. 81), that the State canvassers cannot be charged with error in refusing to add to the votes for Benjamin Welch, Jr., those which were given for Benjamin Welch, without the junior. "They had not the means which the court possessed, on the trial of this issue, of obtaining, by evidence aliunde, the several county returns, the intention of the voters, and the identity of the candidate with the name on the defective ballots. Their judicial power extends no further than to take notice of such facts of public notoriety as that certain well-known abbreviations are generally used to designate particular names, and the like." So far as this case holds, that the canvassers are not chargeable with error in not counting the ballots with the name Benjamin Welch for Benjamin Welch, Jr., it is, doubtless, correct. But suppose the canvassers had seen fit to do so, could the court hold they were guilty of usurpation in thus counting and allowing them? Could not the canvassers take notice of such facts of general public notoriety as everybody else would take notice of? Or must they shut their eyes to facts which all other persons must see? The facts are these: Benjamin Welch, Jr., and James M. Cook, are the

name upon the ballot is altogether different from that of a candidate, and not the same in sound and not a mere abbreviation, the evidence of the voter cannot be received to show for whom it was intended.[1]

Upon the question how far extrinsic evidence is admissible by way of helping out any imperfections in the ballot, no rule can be laid down which can be said to have a preponderating weight of authority in its support. We think evidence of such facts as may be called the circumstances surrounding the election — such as who were the candidates brought forward by the nominating conventions ; whether other persons of the same names resided in the district from which the officer was to be chosen, and if so whether they were eligible or had been named for the office ; if a ballot was printed imperfectly, how it came to be so printed, and the like — is admissible for the purpose of showing that an imperfect ballot was meant for a particular candidate, unless the name is so different that to thus apply it would be to contradict the ballot itself ; or unless the ballot is so defective that it fails to show any intention whatever : in which cases it is not admissible. And we also

candidates, and the only candidates, for State Treasurer. These facts are notorious, and the two political parties make determined efforts to elect one or the other. Certain votes are cast for Benjamin Welch, with the descriptive word " junior " omitted. The name is correct, but, as thus given, it *may* apply to some one else ; but it would be to a person notoriously not a candidate. Under these circumstances, when the facts of which it would be necessary to take notice have occurred under their own supervision, and are universally known, so that the result of a contest in the courts could not be doubtful, is there any reason why the canvassers should not take notice of these facts, count the votes which a jury would subsequently be compelled to count, and thus save the delay, expense, vexation, and confusion of a contest ? If their judicial power extends to a determination of what are common and well-known abbreviations, and what names spelled differently are *idem sonans*, why may it not also extend to the facts, of which there will commonly be quite as little doubt, as to who are the candidates at the election over which they preside ? It seems to us, that, in every case where the name given on the ballot, though in some particulars imperfect, is not different from that of the candidate, and facts of general notoriety leave no doubt in the minds of canvassers that it was intended for him, the canvassers should be at liberty to do what a jury would afterwards be compelled to do, — count it for such candidate.

[1] A vote for " Pence " cannot be shown to have been intended for " Spence." Hart *v.* Evans, 8 Penn. St. 13. Where, however, wrong initials were given to the Christian name, the ballots were allowed to the candidate ; the facts of public notoriety being such as to show that they were intended for him. Atty.-Genl. *v.* Ely, 4 Wis. 420.

think that in any case to allow a voter to testify by way of explanation of a ballot otherwise fatally defective, that he voted the particular ballot, and intended it for a particular candidate, is exceedingly dangerous, invites corruption and fraud, and ought not to
be suffered. Nothing is more easy than for reckless parties thus
to testify to their intentions, without the possibility of disproving
their testimony if untrue ; and if one falsely swears to having deposited a particular ballot, unless the party really depositing it
sees fit to disclose his knowledge, the evidence must pass unchallenged, and the temptation to subornation of perjury, when public offices are at stake, and when it may be committed with impunity, is too great to allow such evidence to be sanctioned. While
the law should seek to give effect to the intention of the voter,
whenever it can be fairly ascertained, yet this intention must be
that which is expressed in due form of law, not that which remains
hidden in the elector's breast ; and where the ballot, in connection
with such facts surrounding the election as would be provable if it
were a case of contract, does not enable the proper officers to apply it to one of the candidates, policy, coinciding in this particular with the general rule of law as applicable to other transactions,
requires that the ballot shall not be counted for such candidate.[1]

The ballot should also sufficiently show on its face for what office the person named upon it is designated ; but here again technical accuracy is not essential, and the office is sufficiently named
if it be so designated that no reasonable doubt can exist as to what
is meant. A great constitutional privilege — the highest under the
government — is not to be taken away on a mere technicality, but
the most liberal intendment should be made in support of the elector's action wherever the application of the common-sense rules
which are applied in other cases will enable us to understand and
render it effectual.[2]

---

[1] This is substantially the New York rule as settled by the later decisions, if we
may accept the opinion of Denio, Ch. J. in People v. Pease, 27 N. Y. 84, as
taking the correct view of those decisions. See People v. Cicotte, 16 Mich. 283,
for a discussion of this point.

[2] In People v. Matteson, 17 Ill. 167, it was held that where " police magistrates " were to be chosen, votes cast for " police justices " should be counted, as
they sufficiently showed upon their face the intention of the voters. So where the
question was submitted to the people, whether a part of one county should be
annexed to another, and the act of submission provided that the electors might
express their choice by voting " for detaching R——," or " against detaching

Where more than one office is to be filled at an election, the law may either require all the persons voted for, for the several offices, to be so voted for by each elector on the same ballot, or it may provide a different receptacle for the ballots for some one office or set of offices from that which is to receive the others. In such a case each elector will place upon the ballot to be deposited in each the names of such persons as he desires to vote for, for the different offices for whose election that box is provided. If, for instance, State and township officers are to be chosen at the same election, and the ballots are to be kept separate, the elector must have different ballots for each ; and if he should designate persons for a township office on the State ballot, such ballot would, to that extent, be void, though the improper addition would not defeat the ballot altogether, but would be treated as surplusage, and the ballot be held good as a vote for the State officers designated upon it.[1] But an accidental error in depositing the ballot should not defeat it. If an elector should deliver the State and township ballots to the inspector of election, who by mistake should deposit them in the wrong boxes respectively, this mistake is capable of being corrected without confusion when the boxes are opened, and should not prevent the ballots being counted as intended. And it would seem that, in any case, the honest mistake, either of the officer or the elector, should not defeat the intention of the latter, where it was not left in doubt by his action.[2]

The elector is not under obligation to vote for every office to be filled at that election ; nor where several persons are to be chosen to the same office is he required to vote for as many as are to be

R——," it was held that votes cast for " R—— attached," and for " R—— detached," and " for division," and " against division," were properly counted by the canvassers, as the intention of the voters was clearly ascertainable from the ballots themselves with the aid of the extrinsic facts of a public nature connected with the election. State v. Elwood, 12 Wis. 551. So where trustees of common schools were to be voted for, it was held that votes for trustees of public schools should be counted; there being no trustees to be voted for at that election except trustees of common schools. People v. McManus, 34 Barb. 620. In Phelps v. Goldthwaite, 16 Wis. 146, where a city and also a county superintendent of schools were to be chosen at the same election, and ballots were cast for " superintendent of schools," without further designation, parol evidence of surrounding circumstances was admitted to enable the proper application to be made of the ballots to the respective candidates.

[1] See People v. Cook, 14 Barb. 259, and 8 N. Y. 67.

[2] People v. Bates, 11 Mich. 362.

elected. He may vote for one or any greater number, not to exceed the whole number to be chosen. In most of the States a plurality of the votes cast determines the election. In others, as to some elections, a majority; but in determining upon a majority or plurality, the blank votes, if any, are not to be counted; and a candidate may therefore be chosen without receiving a plurality or majority of voices of those who actually participated in the election. Where, however, two offices of the same name were to be filled at the same election, but the notice of election specified one only, the political parties each nominated one candidate, and, assuming that but one was to be chosen, no elector voted for more than one, it was held that the one having a majority was alone chosen; the opposing candidate could not claim to be also elected, as having received the second highest number of votes, but as to the other office there had been a failure to hold an election.[1]

The Freedom of Elections.

It is of the utmost importance that every election should be kept free of all the influences and surroundings which bear improperly upon it, or may influence the electors against their judgment or desire. In addition to the constitutional principles to which we have referred, and which protect the secrecy of the ballot, there are express constitutional and statutory provisions designed to accomplish the same general purpose. It is provided by the constitutions of several of the States. that bribery of an elector shall constitute a disqualification of the right to vote or to hold office;[2] the treating of an elector, with a view to influence his vote, is in some States made an indictable offence;[3] the militia are not allowed to be called out on election days, even though the purpose be for enrolling and organizing them, and not for exercise;[4] courts are not allowed to be held, for the two reasons, that the electors ought to be left free to devote their attention to the exercise of this high trust, and that

---

[1] People v. Kent County Canvassers, 11 Mich. 111.

[2] See the constitutions of Maryland, Missouri, New Jersey, West Virginia, Oregon, California, Kansas, Texas, Arkansas, Rhode Island, Alabama, Florida, New York, Massachusetts, New Hampshire, Vermont, Nevada, Tennessee, Connecticut, Louisiana, Mississippi, Ohio, Wisconsin.

[3] State v. Rutledge, 8 Humph. 32. And see the provision in the constitution of Vermont on this subject.

[4] Hyde v. Melvin, 11 Johns. 521.

suits if allowed on that day might be used as a means of intimidation ;[1] legal process in some States, and for the same reasons, is not allowed to be served on that day ; intimidation of voters by threats or otherwise is made punishable ;[2] and generally all such precautions as the people in their organic law, or the legislature afterwards, have thought available for the purpose, have been provided with a view to secure the most completely free and unbiassed expression of opinion that is possible.

Betting upon elections is illegal at the common law, on grounds of public policy ;[3] and all contracts entered into with a view improperly to influence an election would be void for the same reason.[4]

[1] But it was held in New York that the statute of that State forbidding the holding of courts on election days did not apply to the local elections. Matter of Election Law, 7 Hill, 194 ; Redfield v. Florence, 2 E. D. Smith, 339.

[2] As to what shall constitute intimidation, see Respublica v. Gibbs, 3 Yates, 429.

[3] Bunn v. Riker, 4 Johns. 426 ; Lansing v. Lansing, 8 Johns. 454 ; Ball v. Gilbert, 12 Met. 397 ; Laval v. Myers, 1 Bailey, 486 ; Smyth v. McMasters, 2 Browne, 182 ; McAllister v. Hoffman, 16 S. & R. 147 ; Stoddard v. Martin, 1 R. I. 1 ; Wroth v. Johnson, 4 H. & M. 284 ; Tarelton v. Baker, 18 Vt. 9 ; Davis v. Holbrook, 1 La. An. 176 ; Freeman v. Hardwick, 10 Ala. 316 ; Wheeler v. Spencer, 15 Conn. 28 ; Russell v. Pyland, 2 Humph. 131 ; Porter v. Sawyer, 1 Harr. 517 ; Hickerson v. Benson, 8 Mo. 8 ; Machir v. Moore, 2 Grat. 257 ; Rust v. Gott, 9 Cow. 169 ; Brush v. Keeler, 5 Wend. 250.

[4] In Jackson v. Walker, 5 Hill, 27, it was held that an agreement by the defendant to pay the plaintiff $1,000, in consideration that the latter, who had built a log-cabin, would keep it open for political meetings to further the success of certain persons nominated for members of Congress, &c. by one of the political parties, was illegal within the statute of New York, which prohibited contributions of money " for any other purpose intended to promote the election of any particular person or ticket, except for defraying the expenses of printing and the circulation of votes, handbills, and other papers." This case is criticised in Hurley v. Van Wagner, 28 Barb. 109, and it is possible that it went further than either the statute or public policy would require. In Nichols v. Mudgett, 32 Vt. 546, the defendant being indebted to the plaintiff, who was a candidate for town representative, the parties agreed that the former should use his influence for the plaintiff's election, and do what he could for that purpose, and that if the plaintiff was elected, that should be a satisfaction of his claim. Nothing was specifically said about the defendant's voting for the plaintiff, but he did vote for him, and would not have done so, nor favored his election, but for this agreement. The plaintiff was elected. *Held*, that the agreement was void, and constituted no bar to a recovery upon the demand. See also Meachem v. Dow, 32 Vt. 721, where it was held that a note executed in consideration of the payee's agreement to resign public office in favor of the maker, and use influence in favor of the latter's appointment as his successor, was void in the hands of the payee. In Pratt v.

The Elector not to be deprived of his Vote.

It has been held, on constitutional grounds, that a law creating a new county, but so framed as to leave a portion of its territory unorganized, so that the voters within such portion could not participate in the election of county officers, was inoperative and void.[1] So a law submitting to the voters of a county the question of removing the county seat is void if there is no mode under the law by which a city within the county can participate in the election.[2] And although the failure of one election precinct to hold an election, or to make a return of the votes cast, might not render the whole election a nullity, where the electors of that precinct were at liberty to vote had they so chosen, or where, having voted but failed to make return, it is not made to appear that the votes not returned would have changed the result,[3] yet if any action was required of the public authorities preliminary to the election, and that which was taken was not such as to give all the electors the opportunity to participate, and no mode was open to the electors by which the officers might be compelled to act, it would seem that such neglect, constituting as it would the disfranchisement of the excluded electors *pro hac vice*, must on general principles render the whole election nugatory ; for that cannot be called an election or the expression of the popular sentiment where a part only of the electors have been allowed to be heard, and the others, without being guilty of fraud or negligence, have been excluded.[4]

If the inspectors of elections refuse to receive the vote of an elector duly qualified, they may be liable both civilly and criminally for so doing : criminally, if they were actuated by improper and corrupt motives ; and civilly, it is held in some of the States, even though there may have been no malicious design in so do-

People, 29 Ill. 54, it was held that an agreement between two electors that they should " pair off," and both abstain from voting, was illegal, and the inspectors could not refuse to receive a vote of one of the two, on the ground of his agreement.

[1] People *v.* Maynard, 15 Mich. 471. For similar reasons the act for the organization of Schuyler County was held invalid in Lanning *v.* Carpenter, 20 N. Y. 477.

[2] Atty.-Genl. *v.* Supervisors of St. Clair, 11 Mich. 63.

[3] See Ex parte Heath, 3 Hill, 42 ; Louisville & Nashville R. R. Co. *v.* County Court of Davidson, 1 Sneed, 637. See Marshall *v.* Kerns, 2 Swan, 68.

[4] See Fort Dodge *v.* District Township, 17 Iowa, 85.

ing;[1] but the cases generally hold that, where the inspectors are vested by the law with the power to pass upon the qualifications of electors, they exercise judicial functions in so doing, and are entitled to the same protection as other judicial officers in the discharge of their duty, and cannot be made liable except upon proof of express malice.[2] Where, however, by the law under which the election is held, the inspectors are to receive the voter's ballot, if he takes the oath that he possesses the constitutional qualifications, the oath is the conclusive evidence on which the inspectors are to act, and they are not at liberty to refuse to administer the oath, or to refuse the vote after the oath has been taken. They are only ministerial officers in such a case, and have no discretion but to obey the law and receive the vote.[3]

The Conduct of the Election.

The statutes of the different States point out specifically the mode in which elections shall be conducted; but, although there are great diversities of detail, the same general principles govern them all. As the execution of these statutes must very often fall to the hands of men unacquainted with the law and unschooled in business, it is inevitable that mistakes shall sometimes occur, and that very often the law will fail of strict compliance. Where an election is thus rendered irregular, whether the irregularity shall avoid it or not must depend generally upon the effect the irregularity may have had in obstructing the complete expression of the popular will, or the production of satisfactory evidence thereof. Election statutes are to be tested like other statutes, but with a leaning to liberality, in view of the great public purposes which they accomplish; and except where they specifically provide that a thing shall be done in the manner indicated and not other-

[1] Kilham v. Ward, 2 Mass. 236; Gardner v. Ward, 2 Mass. 244, note; Lincoln v. Hapgood, 11 Mass. 350; Capen v. Foster, 12 Pick. 485; Gates v. Neal, 23 Pick. 308; Blanchard v. Stearns, 5 Met. 298; Jeffries v. Ankeny, 11 Ohio, 372; Chrisman v. Bruce, 1 Duvall, 63.

[2] Carter v. Harrison, 5 Blackf. 138; Rail v. Potts, 8 Humph. 225; Peavey v. Robbins, 3 Jones, Law, 339; Gordon v. Farrar, 2 Doug. (Mich.) 411; Caulfield v. Bullock, 18 B. Monr. 494; Morgan v. Dudley, Ibid. 693.

[3] Spragins v. Houghton, 2 Scam. 377; State v. Robb, 17 Ind. 536; People v. Pease, 30 Barb. 588. And see People v. Gordon, 5 Cal. 235; Chrisman v. Bruce, 1 Duvall, 63.

wise, their provisions designed merely for the information and guidance of the officers must be regarded as directory only, and the election will not be defeated by a failure to comply with them, provided the irregularity has not hindered any who were entitled from exercising the right of suffrage, or rendered doubtful the evidences from which the result was to be declared. In a leading case the following irregularities were held not to vitiate the election: the accidental substitution of another book for the holy evangelists in the administration of an oath, both parties being ignorant of the error at the time; the holding of the election by persons who were not officers *de jure,* but who had colorable authority, and acted *de facto* in good faith; the failure of the board of inspectors to appoint clerks of the election; the closing of the outer door of the room where the election was held. at sundown, and then permitting the persons within the room to vote; it not appearing that legal voters were excluded by closing the door, or illegal allowed to vote; and the failure of the inspectors or clerks to take the prescribed oath of office. And it was said, in the same case, that any irregularity in conducting an election which does not deprive a legal voter of his vote, or·admit a disqualified voter to vote or cast uncertainty on the result, and has not been occasioned by the agency of a party seeking to derive a benefit from it, should be overlooked in a proceeding to try the right to an office depending on such election.[1] This rule is an eminently proper one, and it furnishes a very satisfactory test as to what is essential and what not in election laws.[2] And where a party contests

---

[1] People v. Cook, 14 Barb. 259, and 8 N. Y. 67. To the same effect, see Clifton v. Cook, 7 Ala. 114; Truehart v. Addicks, 2 Texas, 217; Dishon v. Smith, 10 Iowa, 212; Atty.-Genl. v. Ely, 4 Wis. 420; State v. Jones, 19 Ind. 356; People v. Higgins, 3 Mich. 233; Gorham v. Campbell, 2 Cal. 135; People v. Bates, 11 Mich. 362; Taylor v. Taylor, 10 Minn. 112; People v. McManus, 34 Barb. 620; Whipley v. McCune, 12 Cal. 352; Bourland v. Hildreth, 26 Cal. 161; Day v. Kent, 1 Oregon, 123; Piatt v. People, 29 Ill. 54; Ewing v. Filley, 43 Penn. St. 384. In Ex parte Heath, 3 Hill, 42, it was held that, where the statute required the inspectors to certify the result of the election on the next day thereafter, or sooner, the certificate made the second day thereafter was sufficient, the statute as to time being directory merely. In People v. McManus, 34 Barb. 620, it was held that an election was not made void by the fact that one of the three inspectors was by the statute disqualified from acting, by being a candidate at the election, the other two being qualified.

[2] This rule has certainly been applied with great liberality in some cases. In People v. Higgins, 3 Mich. 233, it was held that the statute requiring ballots to

an election on the ground of these or any similar irregularities, he ought to aver and be able to show that the result was affected by them.[1] Time and place, however, are of the substance of every election,[2] and a failure to comply with the law in these particulars is not generally to be treated as a mere irregularity.[3]

What is a sufficient Election.

Unless the law under which the election is held expressly requires more, a plurality of the votes cast will be sufficient to elect, notwithstanding these may constitute but a small portion of those

be sealed up in a package, and then locked up in the ballot-box, with the orifice at the top sealed, was directory merely, and that ballots which had been kept in a locked box, but without the orifice closed or the ballots sealed up, were admissible in evidence in a contest for an office depending upon this election. This case was followed in People *v.* Cicotte, 16 Mich. 283, and it was held that whether the ballots were better evidence than the inspector's certificates, where a discrepancy appeared between them, was a question for the jury. In Morril *v.* Haines, 2 N. H. 246, the statute required State officers to be chosen by a check-list, and by delivery of the ballots to the moderator in person ; and it was held that the requirement of a check-list was mandatory, and the election in the town was void if none was kept. The decision was put upon the ground that the check-list was provided as an important guard against indiscriminate and illegal voting, and the votes given by ballot without this protection were therefore as much void as if given *viva voce.* An election adjourned without warrant to another place, as well as an election held without the officers required by law, is void. Commonwealth *v.* County Commissioners, 5 Rawle, 75.

[1] Lanier *v.* Gallatas, 13 La. An. 175 ; People *v.* Cicotte, 16 Mich. 283.

[2] Dickey *v.* Hurlburt, 5 Cal. 343.

[3] The statute of Michigan requires the clerks of election to keep lists of the persons voting, and that at the close of the polls the first duty of the inspectors shall be to compare the lists with the number of votes in the box, and if the count of the latter exceeds the former, then to draw out unopened and destroy a sufficient number to make them correspond. In People *v.* Cicotte, 16 Mich. 283, it appeared that the inspectors in two wards of Detroit, where a surplus of votes had been found, had neglected this duty, and had counted all the votes without drawing out and destroying any. The surplus in the two wards was sixteen. The actual majority of one of the candidates over the other on the count as it stood (if certain other disputed votes were rejected) would be four. It was held that this neglect of the inspectors did not invalidate the election ; that had the votes been drawn out, the probability was that each candidate would lose a number proportioned to the whole number which he had in the box ; and this being a probability which the statute providing for the drawing proceeded upon, the court should apply it afterwards, apportioning the excess of votes between the candidates in that proportion.

who are entitled to vote,[1] and notwithstanding the voters generally may have failed to take notice of the law requiring the election to be held.[2]

If several persons are to be chosen to the same office, the requisite number who shall stand highest on the list will be elected. But without such a plurality no one can be chosen to a public office; and if the person receiving the highest number of votes was ineligible, the votes cast for him will still be effectual so far as to prevent the opposing candidate being chosen, and the election must be considered as having failed.[3]

The admission of illegal votes at an election will not necessarily defeat it, but to warrant its being set aside on that ground it should appear that the result would have been different had they been excluded.[4] And the fact that unqualified persons are allowed to enter the room, and participate in an election, does not justify legal voters in refusing to vote, and treating the election as void, but it will be held valid if the persons declared chosen had a plurality of the legal votes actually cast.[5] So an exclusion of legal votes — not fraudulently, but through error in judgment — will not defeat an election; notwithstanding the error in such a case is one which there was no mode of correcting, even by the aid of the courts; since it cannot be known with certainty afterwards how the excluded electors would have voted, and it would be obviously dangerous to receive and rely upon their subsequent statements as to their intentions, after it is ascertained precisely what effect their

---

[1] Augustin v. Eggleston, 12 La. An. 366.

[2] People v. Hartwell, 12 Mich. 508. Even if the majority expressly dissent, yet if they do not vote, the election by the minority will be valid. Oldknow v. Wainwright, 1 Wm. Bl. 229; Rex v. Foxcroft, 2 Burr. 1017; Rex v. Withers, referred to in same case.

[3] State v. Giles, 1 Chand. 112; Opinions of Judges, 38 Maine, 597; State v. Smith, 14 Wis. 497; Saunders v. Haynes, 13 Cal. 145. But it has been held that if the ineligibility is notorious, so that the electors must be deemed to have voted with full knowledge of it, the votes for the ineligible candidate must be declared void, and the next highest candidate is chosen. Gulick v. New, 14 Ind. 93; Carson v. McPhetridge, 15 Ind. 327. So if the law which creates the disqualification expressly declares all votes cast for the disqualified person void, they must be treated as mere blank votes, and cannot be counted for any purpose.

[4] Ex parte Murphy, 7 Cow. 153; First Parish in Sudbury v. Stearns, 21 Pick. 148; Blandford School District v. Gibbs, 2 Cush. 39; People v. Cicotte, 16 Mich. 283.

[5] First Parish in Sudbury v. Stearns, 21 Pick. 148.

votes would have upon the result.[1] If, however, the inspectors of
election shall exclude legal voters, not because of honest error in
judgment, but wilfully and corruptly, and to an extent that affects
the result, or if by riots or otherwise legal voters are intimidated
and prevented from voting, or for any other reasons the electors
have not had opportunity for the expression of their sentiments
through the ballot-box, the election should be set aside altogether,
as having failed in the purpose for which it was called. Errors of
judgment are inevitable, but fraud, intimidation, and violence the
law can and should protect against. A mere casual affray, however, or accidental disturbance, without any intention of overaw-
ing or intimidating the electors, cannot be considered as affecting
the freedom of the election ;[2] nor in any case would electors be
justified in abandoning the ground for any light causes, or for improper interference by others where the officers continue in the discharge of their functions, and there is opportunity for the electors
to vote.[3] And, as we have already seen, a failure of an election
in one precinct, or disorder or violence which prevent a return
from that precinct, will not defeat the whole election, unless it appears that the votes which could not be returned in consequence
of the violence would have changed the result.[4] It is a little difficult at times to adopt the true mean between those things which
should and those which should not defeat an election ; for while on
the one hand the law should seek to secure the due expression of
his will by every legal voter, and guard against any irregularities or
misconduct that may tend to prevent it, so, on the other hand, it is
to be borne in mind that charges of irregularity and misconduct are
easily made, and that the dangers from throwing elections open
to be set aside, or controlled by oral evidence, are perhaps as great
as any in our system. An election honestly conducted under the
forms of law ought generally to stand, notwithstanding individual
electors may have been deprived of their votes, or unqualified
voters have been allowed to participate. Individuals may suffer
wrong in such cases, and a candidate who was the real choice
of the people may sometimes be deprived of his election ; but
as it is generally impossible to arrive at any greater certainty of

[1] Newcum v. Kirtley, 13 B. Monr. 515.
[2] Cush. Leg. Assemb. § 184.
[3] See First Parish in Sudbury v. Stearns, 21 Pick. 148.
[4] Ex parte Heath, 3 Hill, 42.

result by resort to oral evidence, public policy is best subserved by allowing the election to stand, and trusting to a strict enforcement of the criminal laws for greater security against the like irregularities and wrongs in the future.

The Canvass and the Return.

If the election is purely a local one, the inspectors who have had charge of the election canvass the votes and declare the result. If, on the other hand, their district is one precinct of a larger district, they make return in writing of the election over which they have presided to the proper board of the larger district; and if the election is for State officers, this district board will transmit the result of the district canvass to the proper State board, who will declare the general result. In all this the several boards act for the most part ministerially only, and are not vested with judicial powers to correct the errors and mistakes that may have accrued with any officer who preceded them in the performance of any duty connected with the election, or to pass upon any disputed fact which may affect the result. Each board is to receive the returns transmitted to it, if in due form, as correct, and is to ascertain and declare the result as shown by such returns;[1] and if other matters are introduced into the return than those which the law provides, they are to that extent unofficial, and such statements must be disregarded.[2] If a district or State board of canvassers assumes to reject returns transmitted to it on other grounds than those appearing upon its face, or to declare persons elected who are not shown by the returns to have received the requisite plurality, it is usurping functions, and its conduct will be reprehensible, if not even criminal. The action of such boards is to be carefully confined to an examination of the papers before them, and a determination of the

---

[1] Ex parte Heath, 3 Hill, 42; Brower v. O'Brien, 2 Ind. 423; People v. Hilliard, 29 Ill. 413; People v. Jones, 19 Ind. 357; Ballou v. York County Com'rs, 13 Shep. 491; Mayo v. Freeland, 10 Mo. 629; Thompson v. Circuit Judge, 9 Ala. 338; People v. Kilduff, 15 Ill. 492; O'Farrell v. Colby, 2 Minn. 180; People v. Van Cleve, 1 Mich. 362; People v. Van Slyck, 4 Cow. 297; Morgan v. Quackenbush, 22 Barb. 72; Dishon v. Smith, 10 Iowa, 212; People v. Cook, 14 Barb. 259, and 8 N. Y. 67; Hartt v. Harvey, 32 Barb. 55; Atty.-Genl. v. Barstow, 4 Wis. 567; Atty.-Genl. v. Ely, 4 Wis. 420; State v. Governor, 1 Dutch. 331; State v. Clerk of Passaic, 1 Dutch. 354; Marshall v. Kerns, 2 Swan, 68; People v. Pease, 27 N. Y. 45.

[2] Ex parte Heath, 3 Hill, 42.

result therefrom, in the light of such facts of public notoriety connected with the election as every one takes notice of, and which may enable them to apply such ballots as are in any respect imperfect to the proper candidates or officers for which they were intended, provided the intent is sufficiently indicated by the ballot in connection with such facts, so that extraneous evidence is not necessary for this purpose. If canvassers refuse or neglect to perform their duty, they may be compelled by mandamus; though as these boards are created for a single purpose only, and are dissolved by an adjournment without day, it would seem that, after such adjournment, mandamus would be inapplicable, inasmuch as there is no longer any board which can act;[1] and the board themselves, having once performed and fully completed their duty, have no power afterwards to reconsider their determination and come to a different conclusion.[2]

Contesting Elections.

As the election officers perform for the most part ministerial functions only, their returns, and the certificates of election which are issued upon them, are not conclusive in favor of the officers who would thereby appear to be chosen, but the final decision must rest with the courts.[3] This is the general rule, and the exceptions are of those cases where the law under which the canvass is made declares the decision conclusive, or where a special statutory board is established with powers of final decision.[4] And it matters not how

[1] Clark v. Buchanan, 2 Minn. 346; People v. Supervisors, 12 Barb. 217.

[2] Hadley v. Mayor, &c., 33 N. Y. 603.

[3] State v. Justices of Middlesex, Coxe, 244; Hill v. Hill, 4 McCord, 277; Wammack v. Holloway, 2 Ala. 31; State v. Clerk of Passaic; 1 Dutch. 354; Marshall v. Kerns, 2 Swan, 68; Atty.-Genl. v. Barstow, 4 Wis. 567; Atty.-Genl. v. Ely, 4 Wis. 420; People v. Van Cleve, 1 Mich. 362; People v. Higgins, 3 Mich. 233; Dishon v. Smith, 10 Iowa, 211; State v. Johnson, 17 Ark. 407; State v. Fetter, 12 Wis. 566; State v. Avery, 14 Wis. 122; People v. Jones, 20 Cal. 50; Newcum v. Kirtley, 13 B. Monr. 515; People v. Van Slyck, 4 Cow. 297; People v. Vail, 20 Wend. 12; People v. Seaman, 5 Denio, 409; People v. Cook, 14 Barb. 259, and 8 N. Y. 67; People v. Matteson, 17 Ill. 167.

[4] See Grier v. Shackleford, Const. Rep. 642; Batman v. Megowan, 1 Met. (Ky.) 533. For the proceedings in the State of New York in the canvass of votes for governor in 1792, where the election of John Jay to that office was defeated by the rejection of votes cast for him for certain irregularities, which, under the more recent judicial decisions, ought to have been overlooked, see Hammond's Political History of New York, ch. 3. The law then in force made the decision of the State canvassers final and conclusive.

high and important the office, an election to it is only made by the candidate receiving the requisite plurality of the legal votes cast; and if any one, without having received such plurality, intrudes into an office, whether with or without a certificate of election, the courts have jurisdiction to oust, as well as to punish him for such intrusion.[1]

Where, however, the question arises collaterally, and not in a direct proceeding to try the title to the office, the correctness of the decision of the canvassers cannot be called in question, but must be conclusively presumed to be correct;[2] and where the election was to a legislative office, the final decision, as well by parliamentary law as by constitutional provisions, rests with the legislative body itself, and the courts cannot interfere, as we have heretofore seen.[3]

The most important question which remains to be mentioned, relates to the evidence which the courts are at liberty to receive, and the facts which it is proper to spread before the jury for their

[1] Barstow, being governor of Wisconsin, was candidate for re-election against Bashford. A majority of the votes was cast for Bashford, but certain spurious returns were transmitted to the State canvassers, which, together with the legal returns, showed a plurality for Barstow, and he was accordingly declared chosen. Proceedings being taken against him by *quo warranto* in the Supreme Court, Barstow objected to the jurisdiction, on the ground that the three departments of the State government, the legislative, the executive, and the judicial, were equal, co-ordinate, and independent of each other, and that each department must be and is the ultimate judge of the election and qualification of its own member or members, subject only to impeachment and appeal to the people; that the question who is rightfully entitled to the office of governor could in no case become a judicial question; and that as the constitution provides no means for ousting a successful usurper of either of the three departments of the government, that power rests exclusively with the people, to be exercised by them whenever they think the exigency requires it. A strange doctrine in this country of laws! but which, of course, received no countenance from the able court to which it was addressed. In People v. Cicotte, 16 Mich. 283, the opinion is expressed by two of the judges, that one claiming a public office has a constitutional right to a trial by jury, and that this right cannot be taken away from him by any law which shall undertake to make the decision of the canvassing board conclusive. But see Ewing v. Filley, 43 Penn. St. 384; Commonwealth v. Leech, 44 Penn. St. 332.

[2] Morgan v. Quackenbush, 22 Barb. 72; Hadley v. Mayor, &c., 33 N. Y. 603. And see Hulseman v. Rens, 41 Penn. St. 396, where it was held that the court could not interfere summarily to set aside a certificate of election, where it did not appear that the officers had acted corruptly, notwithstanding it was shown to be based in part upon forged returns.

[3] See ante, p. 133. See also Commonwealth v. Meeser, 44 Penn. St. 341.

consideration when an issue is made upon an election for trial at law.

The questions involved in every case are, first, has there been an election ? and second, was the party who has taken possession of the office the successful candidate at such election, by having received a majority of the legal votes cast ? These are questions which involve mixed considerations of law and fact, and the proper proceeding in which to try them in the courts is by *quo warranto*, where no special statutory tribunal is created for the purpose.[1]

Upon the first question, we shall not add to what we have already said. When the second is to be considered, it is to be constantly borne in mind that the point of inquiry is *the will of the electors as manifested by their ballots ;* and to this should all the evidence be directed, and none that does not bear upon it should be admissible.

We have already seen that the certificates or determinations of the various canvassing boards, though conclusive in collateral inquiries, do not preclude an investigation by the courts into the facts which they certify. They are *prima facie* evidence, however, even in the courts ;[2] and this is so, notwithstanding they appear to have been altered ; the question of their fairness in such a case being for the jury.[3] But back of this *prima facie* case the courts may go, and the determinations of the State board may be corrected by those of the district boards, and the latter by the ballots themselves when the ballots are still in existence and have been kept as required by law.[4] If, however, the ballots have not been kept as required by law, and surrounded by such securities as the law has prescribed with a view to their safe preservation as the best evidence of the election, it would seem that they should not be received in evidence at all,[5] or, if received, that it should be left to the jury to determine, upon all the circumstances of the case, whether they constitute more reliable evidence than the inspectors' certificate,[6] which is usually prepared immediately on the close of

[1] People *v.* Matteson, 17 Ill. 167.
[2] Marshall *v.* Kerns, 2 Swan, 68 ; Morgan *v.* Quackenbush, 22 Barb. 72.
[3] State *v.* Adams, 2 Stew. 231.
[4] People *v.* Van Cleve, 1 Mich. 362 ; People *v.* Higgins, 3 Mich. 233 ; State *v.* Clerk of Passaic, 1 Dutch. 354 ; State *v.* Judge, &c., 13 Ala. 805 ; People *v.* Cook, 14 Barb. 259 ; Same case, 8 N. Y. 67 ; People *v.* Cicotte, 16 Mich. 283.
[5] People *v.* Sackett, 14 Mich. 320. But see People *v.* Higgins, 3 Mich. 233.
[6] People *v.* Cicotte, 16 Mich. 283.

40

the election, and upon actual count of the ballots as then made by the officers whose duty it is to do so.

We have already had something to say as to the evidence which can be received where the elector's ballot is less complete and perfect in its expression of intention than it should have been. There can be no doubt under the authorities that, whenever a question may arise as to the proper application of a ballot, any evidence is admissible with a view to explain and apply it which would be admissible under the general rules of evidence for the purpose of explaining and applying other written instruments. But the rule, as it appears to us, ought not to go further. The evidence ought to be confined to proof of the concomitant circumstances, such circumstances as may be proved in support or explanation of a contract, where the parties themselves would not be allowed to give testimony as to their actual intention, where unfortunately the intention was ineffectually expressed.[1] And we have seen that no evidence is admissible as to how parties intended to vote who were wrongfully prevented or excluded from so doing. Such a case is one of wrong without remedy, so far as candidates are concerned.[2] There is more difficulty, however, when the question arises whether votes which have been cast by incompetent persons, and which have been allowed in the canvass, can afterwards be inquired into and rejected because of the want of qualification.

If votes were taken *viva voce*, so that it could always be determined with absolute certainty how every person had voted, the objections to this species of scrutiny after an election had been held would not be very formidable. But when secret balloting is the policy of the law, and no one is at liberty to inquire how any elector has voted, except as he may voluntarily have waived his privilege, and consequently the avenues to correct information concerning the votes cast are carefully guarded against judicial exploration, it seems exceedingly dangerous to permit any question to be raised upon this subject. For the evidence voluntarily given upon any such question will usually come from those least worthy of credit, who, if they have voted without legal right in order to elect particular candidates, will be equally ready to testify

---

[1] People *v.* Pease, 27 N. Y. 84, per Denio, Ch. J., commenting upon previous New York cases. See also Attorney-General *v.* Ely, 4 Wis. 420.

[2] See ante, 620.

falsely, if their testimony can be made to help the same candidates; especially when, if they give evidence that they voted the opposing ticket, there can usually be no means, as they will well know, of showing the evidence to be untrue. Moreover, to allow such scrutiny is to hold out strong temptation to usurpation of office, without pretence or color of right; since the nature of the case, and the forms and proceedings necessary to a trial are such that, if an issue may be made on the right of every individual voter, it will be easy, in the case of important elections, to prolong a contest for the major part if not the whole of an official term, and to keep perpetually before the courts the same excitements, strifes, and animosities which characterize the hustings, and which ought, for the peace of the community, and the safety and stability of our institutions, to terminate with the close of the polls.

Upon this subject there is very little judicial authority, though legislative bodies, deriving their precedents from England, where the system of open voting prevails, have always been accustomed to receive such evidence, and have indeed allowed a latitude of inquiry which makes more to depend upon the conscience of the witnesses, and of legislative committees, in some cases, than upon the action of the voters. The question of the right to inquire into the qualifications of those who had voted at an election, on a proceeding in the nature of a *quo warranto*, was directly presented in one case to the Supreme Court of New York, and the court was equally divided upon it.[1] On error to the Court of Appeals, a decision in favor of the right was rendered with the concurrence of five judges, against three dissentients.[2] The same question afterwards came before the Supreme Court of Michigan, and was decided the same way, though it appears from the opinions that the court were equally divided in their views.[3] To these cases we must refer for a full discussion of the reasons influencing the several judges, but future decisions alone can give the question authoritative settlement.[4]

[1] People *v.* Pease, 30 Barb. 588.

[2] People *v.* Pease, 27 N. Y. 45.

[3] People *v.* Cicotte, 16 Mich. 283.

[4] Considerable stress was laid by the majority of the New York Court of Appeals on the legislative practice, which, as it seems to us, is quite too loose in these cases to constitute a safe guide. Some other rulings in that case also seem more latitudinarian than is warranted by sound principle and a due regard to the secret ballot system which we justly esteem so important. Thus Selden, J.,

says : " When a voter refuses to disclose or fails to remember for whom he voted, I think it is competent to resort to circumstantial evidence to raise a presumption in regard to that fact. Such is the established rule in election cases before legislative committees, which assume to be governed by legal rules of evidence (Cush. Leg. Assem. §§ 199 and 200) ; and within that rule it was proper, in connection with the other circumstances stated by the witness Loftis, to ask him for whom he intended to vote ; not, however, on the ground that his intention, as an independent fact, could be material, but on the ground that it was a circumstance tending to raise a presumption for whom he did vote." Now as, in the absence of fraud or mistake, you have arrived at a knowledge of how the man voted, when you have ascertained how, at the time, he intended to vote, it is difficult to discover much value in the elector's privilege of secrecy under this ruling. And if " circumstances " may be shown to determine how he probably voted, in cases where he insists upon his constitutional right to secrecy, then, as it appears to us, it would be better to abolish altogether the secret ballot than to continue longer a system which falsely promises secrecy, at the same time that it gives to party spies and informers full license to invade the voter's privilege in secret and surreptitious ways, and which leaves jurors, in the absence of any definite information, to act upon their guesses, surmises, and vague conjectures as to the contents of a ballot.

Upon the right to inquire into the qualifications of those who have voted, in a proceeding by *quo warranto* to test the right to a public office, Justice Christiancy, in People *v.* Cicotte, 16 Mich. 311, expresses his views as follows : —

" I cannot go to the extent of holding that no inquiry is admissible in any case into the qualification of voters or the nature of the votes given. Such a rule, I admit, would be easy of application, and, as a general rule, might not be productive of a great amount of injustice, while the multitude of distinct questions of fact in reference to the great number of voters whose qualification may be contested, is liable to lead to some embarrassment, and sometimes to protracted trials, without a more satisfactory result than would have been attained under a rule which should exclude all such inquiries. Still, I cannot avoid the conclusion that in theory and spirit our constitution and our statutes recognize as valid those votes only which are given by electors who possess the constitutional qualifications ; that they recognize as valid such elections only as are effected by the votes of a majority of such qualified electors ; and though the election boards of inspectors and canvassers, acting only ministerially, are bound in their decisions by the number of votes deposited in accordance with the forms of law regulating their action, it is quite evident that illegal votes may have been admitted by the perjury or other fault of the voters, and that the majority to which the inspectors have been constrained to certify and the canvassers to allow has been thus wrongfully and illegally secured ; and I have not been able to satisfy myself that in such a case, these boards, acting thus ministerially, and often compelled to admit votes which they know to be illegal, were intended to constitute tribunals of last resort for the determination of the rights of parties claiming an election. If this were so, and there were no legal redress, I think there would be much reason to apprehend that elections would degenerate into mere contests of fraud.

" The person having the greatest number of the votes of legally qualified electors, it seems to me, has a constitutional right to the office ; and if no inquiry

can be had into the qualification of any voter, here is a constitutional right depending upon a mode of trial unknown to the constitution, and, as I am strongly
inclined to think, opposed to its provisions. I doubt the competency of the
Legislature, should they attempt it, which I think they have not, to make the
decision of inspectors or canvassers final under our constitution."

The opposite view is expressed by Justice Campbell as follows (Ibid. p. 294) : —

" The first inquiry is whether an election can be defeated as to any candidate
by showing him to have received illegal votes. The authorities upon election
questions are, in this country, neither numerous nor satisfactory. In England,
where votes are given *viva voce*, it is always easy to determine how any voter
has given his voice. And in some States of the Union, a system seems to prevail
of numbering each ballot as given, and also numbering the voter's name on the
poll list, so as to furnish means of verification when necessary. It has always
been held, and is not disputed, that illegal votes do not avoid an election, unless it
can be shown that their reception affects the result. And where the illegality
consists in the casting of votes by persons unqualified, unless it is shown for whom
they voted, it cannot be allowed to change the result.

" The question of the power of courts to inquire into the action of the authorities in receiving or rejecting votes is, therefore, very closely connected with the
power of inquiring what persons were voted for by those whose qualifications are
denied. It is argued for the relator that neither of these inquiries can be made.
No use can fairly be made in such a controversy as the present of decisions or
practice arising out of any system of open voting. The ballot system was designed to prevent such publicity, and not to encourage it. And the course
adopted by legislative bodies cannot be regarded as a safe guide for courts of
justice. There is little uniformity in it, and much of it is based on English precedents belonging to a different practice. The view taken of contested elections
by these popular bodies is not always accurate, or consistent with any settled
principles.

" There is no case, so far as I have been able to discover, under any system of
voting by closed ballot, which has held that any account could be taken of rejected
votes in a suit to try title for office. The statutes here, and probably elsewhere,
require the election to be made out by the votes given. But it is plain enough
that in most cases it would be quite as easy to determine for whom a rejected
voter would have voted as for whom any other actually did vote. In many cases
it would be easier, because the vote is always ready and tendered with better
opportunities of observation than are given where it is received and deposited.
But the element of uncertainty has been regarded as sufficient to cause the rejection of any such inquiry, and, in most cases, probably it would not be admissible under the statutes. But the policy which leads to this result must have
some bearing upon the construction of the whole system.

" So far as I have been able to discover by means of the somewhat imperfect
indexes on this head, there is but one case in which the decision has turned upon
the propriety of allowing inquiry into the qualifications of voters and the identification of their tickets when claimed to be disqualified. That case was the case
of People *v.* Pease, 27 N. Y. 45. In the Supreme Court the judges, although
arriving at a general result, were equally divided on this point. In the Court of
Appeals, the judges elected to that tribunal were also equally divided, and the

majority of the Supreme Court judges, belonging to it by rotation, turned the scale, and decided that the inquiry was proper. The decision was based chiefly upon English authorities; the previous New York decisions having turned principally on other errors which rest upon somewhat different grounds.

" New York, so far as may be inferred from the absence of decisions elsewhere, seems, until recently, to have been the only State preserving the ballot system, in which the right to office by election is open to examination on the merits to any considerable extent. The courts of that State have gone further than any others in opening the door to parol proof. Some of the Western States have, upon the authority of the New York cases, permitted some of these matters to be litigated, but they are not in any majority. And it is quite manifest that the decisions have not in general acted upon any careful consideration of the important questions of public policy underlying the ballot system, which are so forcibly explained by Denio, Ch. J., in his opinion in People v. Pease ; and it is a little remarkable that in New York, while so many doors have been opened by the decisions, the law requires all the ballots, except a single specimen of each kind, to be destroyed; thus leaving the number of votes of each kind, in all cases, to be determined by the inspectors, and rendering any correction impossible. I think the weight of reasoning is in favor of the view of Judge Denio in the New York case, that no inquiry can be made into the legality of votes actually deposited by a voter upon any ground of personal right as an elector.

" The reasons why such an inquiry should be prevented do not necessarily rest on any assumption that the inspectors act throughout judicially, although under our registration system that objection has a force which would not otherwise be so obvious. Neither do they rest in any degree upon the assumption that one rule or another is most likely to induce perjury, as very hastily intimated in People v. Ferguson, 8 Cow. 102. But a very strong ground for them is found in the fact that our whole ballot system is based upon the idea that unless inviolable secrecy is preserved concerning every voter's action, there can be no safety against those personal or political influences which destroy individual freedom of choice.

" It is altogether idle to expect that there can be any such protection where the voter is only allowed to withhold his own oath concerning the ticket he has voted, while any other prying meddler can be permitted in a court of justice to guess under oath at its contents. If the law could permit an inquiry at all, there is no reason whatever for preventing an inquiry from the voter himself, who alone can actually know how he voted, and who can suffer no more by being compelled to answer than by having the fact established otherwise. The reason why the ballot is made obligatory by our Constitution is to secure every one the right of preventing any one else from knowing how he voted, and there is no propriety in any rule which renders such a safeguard valueless.

" It has always been the case that the rules of evidence have, on grounds of public policy, excluded proof tending to explain how individuals have acted in positions where secrecy was designed for their protection or that of the public. No grand juror could be permitted to disclose as a witness the ballots given by himself or others upon investigations of crime. Informers cannot be compelled to disclose to whom they have given their information. And many official facts are denied publicity. In all of these cases, the rule is not confined to one person any more than to another ; for public policy is against publication from any source. And if, as is clear, a man is entitled to keep his own vote secret, it is difficult to see how any testimony whatever can be allowed, from any source, to identify and explain it.

" The statutes contain some provisions bearing upon these topics with considerable force. By sec. 47 of the Compiled Laws, every voter is compelled to deliver his ballot folded ; and, by sec. 52, the inspector is prohibited from either opening or permitting it to be opened.

" The devices adopted for creating different appearances in the ballots of different parties are such palpable evasions of the spirit of the law as to go very far towards destroying the immunity of the voter, and in some States it has been found desirable to attempt by statute the prevention of such tricks ; but the difficulty of doing this effectually is exemplified in People v. Kilduff, 15 Ill. 492, where the evidence seems to have shown that a uniform variation may be entirely accidental. Unless some such difference exists, it would be idle to attempt any proof how a person voted, and it would be better to do away at once with the whole ballot than to have legal tribunals give any aid or countenance to indirect violations of its security ; and the evidence received in the present case exemplifies the impropriety of such investigations. In some instances, at least, the only proof that a voter, complained of as illegal, cast his ballot for one or the other of these candidates, was, that he voted a ticket externally appearing to belong to one of the two political parties, and containing names of both State and county officers. To allow such proof to be received in favor of or against any particular candidate on the ticket, is to allow very remote circumstances indeed to assume the name of evidence. And the necessity of resorting to such out-of-the-way proofs only puts in a clearer light the impropriety and illegality of entering upon any such inquiry, when the law sedulously destroys the only real proofs, and will not tolerate a resort to them. And the whole State is much more interested than any single citizen can be, in emancipating elections from all those sinister influences, which have so great a tendency to coerce or deceive electors into becoming the mere instruments of others.

" But there are further provisions bearing more directly on the propriety and necessity of allowing no inquisition into individual votes.

" County officers are among those included under sec. 31 of the Compiled Laws, which declares that ' the persons having the greatest number of votes shall be deemed to have been duly elected.' The law does not confine this to votes cast by authorized voters, and can only be applied to votes cast and recorded in the manner provided by law. And although this section, standing alone, might be open to construction, yet, when the whole law is taken together, there are provisions not to be reconciled with any rule allowing single voters and their votes to be made the subject of inquiry. It will not be denied, that an inquiry into the legality of a particular voter's qualifications, after his vote has been cast, is of a strictly judicial nature ; and it cannot be proper or legal to allow such an inquiry in one case, and not in another. But it will be found not only that the rejection of votes from the count is required to be in such a way as to preclude any consideration of the person giving or putting them in, but that there are cases where even a legal inquiry into the ballots themselves is prevented.

" In the first place, when two or more ballots are so folded together as to present the appearance of one, and if counted will make the ballots exceed the names on the poll-list, they are to be destroyed. And whenever, for any other reason, the number of ballots found in the box exceeds the number of names on the corrected poll-lists, the inspectors are required to draw out and destroy unopened a number equal to the excess. This is, of course, upon the assumption that the excess has probably been caused by fraud, and assumes that no man's vote ought to be counted, unless the testimony of the poll-lists shows that he actually handed in his ballot. It is, therefore, altogether likely, upon any theory of probabilities, that, in drawing out these extra ballots, they will really be ballots lawfully put in, and this probability is in the ratio furnished by a comparison of numbers between lawful and unlawful votes. In other words, it is more than likely to punish the innocent, instead of the guilty. The true method of arriving at the truth would be to inquire what vote each voter on the list actually cast, and destroy the remainder. The absurdity of this process upon such a large scale is such as to need no pointing out. But unless something very like it is done in such a case as the present, the result obtained by any partial inquiry will be no better than guesswork. Where votes are thrown out, no one can tell whether the illegal voter whose vote is sought to be assailed has not already had his vote cancelled. The adoption of the principle of allotment is the most sensible and practicable measure which could be devised, and I cannot conceive how it can be improved upon by any subsequent search.

But when the inspectors have made their returns to the county canvassers, and *by those returns* a tie vote appears between two or more candidates, who are highest on the list, their right to the office is to be determined by lot, and the person drawing the successful slip is to be ' *deemed legally elected to the office in question.*' Compiled Laws, sec. 76, 132, 133.

"In case the State canvassers (who can only count the votes certified to them) find a tie vote, the legislature has power to choose between the candidates. Constitution, art. 8, § 5. In these cases, there can be no further scrutiny ; and in the case of State officers, if such a scrutiny were had, no end could be reached within any reasonable time, and there would be a practical impossibility in attempting to conduct it in any time within the official term, or to approach accuracy in a count of some thousand or more ballot-boxes before a jury. Yet State officers are not less important to the private elector, and, of course, are not to the community at large, than local. And the nearer a vote approaches a tie, the more likely it is that a rigid scrutiny might change its character. There is no more reason for preventing investigation behind the ballots in the one case than in the other.

" The statute also takes very efficient measures to prevent any needless litigation by shutting out any preliminary resort to the means of information. If the officers do their duty, no one else can ever know whether their count is correct or not, until a suit is brought and issue joined upon it. The ballots are required to be sealed up, and not opened except for the inspection of the proper authorities, in case of a contest. The only ballots open to public inspection are those which are rejected upon the canvass for defects apparent on their face. These ballots are not sealed up with the rest, but are filed ; while, therefore, it can be determined by inspection whether votes which have been thrown out should have been counted, the law does not seem to favor any unnecessary disturbance of the official returns, and any one who assumes to dispute an election is compelled to begin his suit before he can have access to the means of proof. This is not the usual course of litigation, and the rule has a strong bearing upon the policy to be deduced from the law.

" Under our statute, there is no general provision which makes the canvass for local officers conclusive in all cases, and therefore the rule is recognized that the election usually depends upon the ballots, and not upon the returns. These being written and certain, the result of a recount involves no element of difficulty or ambiguity, beyond the risk of mistakes in counting or footing up numbers, which may, in some respects, be more likely in examining the ballots of a whole county than in telling off those of a town or ward, but which involves no great time or serious disadvantage. But the introduction of parol evidence concerning single voters in a considerable district, can rarely reach all cases of ilegality effectually, and must so multiply the issues as to seriously complicate the inquiry. And when we consider, that, for many years, legislation has been modified for the very purpose of suppressing illegal voting, and when we know that hundreds of elections must have been turned by the ballots of unqualified voters, the absence of any body of decisions upon the subject is very strong proof that inquiry into private ballots is felt to be a violation of the constitutional safeguard on which we pride ourselves as distinguishing our elections from those which we are wont to regard as conducted on unsafe principles."

INDEX.

A.

ABBREVIATIONS,
>when ballots rendered ineffectual by, 608, 609.

ACCUSATIONS OF CRIME,
>are actionable, *per se*, 423.
>how made with a view to investigation and trial, 309.
>>(See PERSONAL LIBERTY.)
>varying form of, cannot subject party to second trial, 328.

ACTION,
>against election officers for refusing to receive votes, 616.
>for negligent or improper construction of public works, 571.
>for property taken under right of eminent domain, 559 – 564.
>>(See EMINENT DOMAIN.)
>for exercise of legislative power by municipal bodies, 208.
>for slander and libel, rules for, 422 – 425.
>>modification of, by statute, 430.
>>(See LIBERTY OF SPEECH AND OF THE PRESS.)
>rights in, cannot be created by mere legislative enactment, 369.
>>nor taken away by legislature, 362.
>>nor appropriated under right of eminent domain, 527.
>>nor forfeited, except by judicial proceedings, 362, 363.
>>statutory penalties may be taken away before recovery of judgment, 362 n.; 383 n.
>limitation to suits, 364 – 367.
>>statutes for, are unobjectionable in principle, 365.
>>subsequent repeal of statute cannot revive rights, 293, 365.
>>principle on which statutes are based, 365.
>>cannot apply against a party not in default, 366.
>>must give parties an opportunity for trial, 366.
>for causing death by negligence, &c. 581.

ACTS OF THE LEGISLATURE,
>>(See STATUTES.)

ADJOURNMENT OF SUIT,
>from regard to religious scruples of party, 477 n.

APPORTIONMENT,
>of powers between the States and the nation, 2.
>between the departments of the State government, 33 – 37, 39, 90 – 92.
>of taxes, 495.
>>(See TAXATION.)

APPRAISAL,
>of private property taken by the public, 559 – 570.

APPRAISEMENT LAWS,
>how far invalid, 290.

APPRENTICE,
>control of master over, 340.

APPROPRIATION,
>of private property to public use, 525.
>>(See EMINENT DOMAIN.)

ARBITRARY ARRESTS,
>illegality of, 300, 302.
>>(See PERSONAL LIBERTY.)

ARBITRARY EXACTIONS,
>distinguished from taxation, 490, 491.

ARBITRARY POWER,
>unknown among common-law principles, 22.
>cannot be exercised under pretence of taxation, 490, 508.

ARBITRARY RULES OF CONSTRUCTION,
>danger of, 61, 62.

ARBITRATION,
>submission of controversies to, 399.

ARGUMENTUM AB INCONVENIENTI,
>in constitutional construction, 70, 71 n.

ARKANSAS,
>divorces not to be granted by legislature, 110 n.
>special acts for sale of lands of infants, &c. forbidden, *Preface.*
>protection of person, &c. by law of the land, 352 n.
>liberty of speech and of the press, *Preface.*
>legislature may regulate granting of pardons, 116 n.
>exclusion from office for want of religious belief, 468 n.

ARMS,
>right to bear, 350.
>exemption from bearing of persons conscientiously opposed, 478.

ARMY,
>quartering in private houses, 308.
>jealousy of standing army, 350.

ARREST,
>privilege of legislators from, 134.

ARREST, — *Continued.*

>   on criminal process (see CRIMES).
>
>   of judgment, new trial after, 328 and n.

ART, WORKS OF,

>   criticism of, how far privileged, 457.

ASSESSMENTS,

>   for local improvements, generally made in reference to benefits, 497.
>
>   special taxing districts for, 497.
>
>   not necessarily made on property according to value, 497:
>
>   are made under the power of taxation, 498.
>
>   not covered by the general constitutional provisions respecting taxation, 498.
>
>   not unconstitutional to make benefits the basis for, 499, 505, 511.
>
>   apportionment necessary in cases of, 499.
>
>   may be made in reference to frontage, 507.
>
>   but each lot cannot be compelled to make the improvement in front of it, 508.
>
>   for drains, levees, &c. 510.
>
>   in labor for repair of roads, 512.

ATTAINDER,

>   meaning of the term, 259.
>
>   bills of, not to be passed by State legislatures, 15, 33, 259.
>
>>   cases of such bills, 259 – 264.
>
>   bills of pains and penalties included in, 261.

ATTORNEYS,

>   exclusion of, from practice is a punishment, 263, 264.
>
>   laws requiring service from, without compensation, 393, 394.
>
>   punishment of, for misconduct, 337.
>
> (See COUNSEL.)

AUTHORS,

>   not to be assailed through their works, 457.
>
>   criticism of works of, how far privileged, 457.

B.

BAIL,

>   accused parties entitled to, 309 – 311.
>
>   unreasonable, not to be demanded, 310.
>
>   on *habeas corpus*, 348.
>
>   control of bail over principal, 341.

BAILMENT,

> (See COMMON CARRIERS.)

BALLOT,

>   system of voting by, generally prevails, 604.

41

COMPACTS BETWEEN STATES,
>   must have consent of Congress, 15.
>   are inviolable under United States Constitution, 275 and n.

COMPENSATION,
>   for private property appropriated by the public, 559.
>> (See EMINENT DOMAIN.)
>   what the tax payer receives as an equivalent for taxes, 498.

COMPLAINTS,
>   for purposes of search warrant, 304.
>   of crime how made, 309.

CONCLUSIVENESS OF JUDGMENTS,
>   full faith and credit to be given in each State to those of other
>   States, 16, 17.
>   parties and privies estopped by, 47 – 54, 408.
>>   but not in controversy with new subject-matter, 49.
>   strangers to suit not bound by, 48.
>   irregularities do not defeat, 409.
>> (See JURISDICTION.)

CONDITIONAL LEGISLATION,
>   power of the States to adopt, 117.

CONDITIONS,
>   what may be imposed on right of suffrage, 601, 602.
>> (See ELECTIONS.)
>   precedent to exercise of right of eminent domain, 528, 529.

CONFEDERACY OF 1643,
>   brought about by tendency of Colonies to union, 5.

CONFEDERATION, ARTICLES OF,
>   adoption of, 6, 7.
>   authority to supersede, 8 n.

CONFESSIONS,
>   dangerous character of, as evidence, 314.
>   must appear to have been made voluntarily, 313, 314.
>   excluded if solicitations or threats have been used, 315.
>   will not prove the *corpus delicti*, 315.

CONFIDENCE,
>   between attorney and client, is client's privilege, 334 and n.

CONFIRMING INVALID PROCEEDINGS,
>   of a judicial nature, 107, 108.
>   admissible when defects are mere irregularities, 371.
>> (See RETROSPECTIVE LAWS.)

CONFISCATIONS,
>   require judicial proceedings, 363, 364.
>   during the Revolutionary War, 262.

ELECTIONS, — *Continued.*

preliminary action by the authorities, notice, &c. 602.

mode of exercising the right, 604.

the electors privilege of secrecy, 604 – 606.

a printed ballot is " written," 604.

ballot must be complete in itself, 606.

technical accuracy not essential, 607.

explanations by voter inadmissible, 607.

must not contain too many names, 607.

name should be given in full, 608.

sufficient if *idem sonans*, 608.

what abbreviations sufficient, 608, 609.

erroneous additions not to affect, 610.

extrinsic evidence to explain imperfections, 611.

ballot must contain name of office, 612.

but need not be strictly accurate, 612.

different boxes for different ballots, 613.

elector need not vote for every office, 613.

plurality of votes cast to elect, 614, 620.

effect if highest candidate is ineligible, 620.

freedom of elections, 614.

bribery or treating of voters, 614.

militia not to be called out on election day, 614.

courts not to be open on election day, 614.

bets upon election are illegal, 615.

contracts to influence election are void, 615.

elector not to be deprived of his vote, 616.

statutes which would disfranchise voters, 616.

failure to hold election in one precinct, 616.

liability of inspectors for refusing to receive vote, 616.

elector's oath when conclusive on inspector, 617.

conduct of the election, 617.

effect of irregularities upon, 617, 618.

what constitutes a sufficient election, 619.

not necessary that a majority participate, 620.

admission of illegal votes not to defeat, 620.

unless done fraudulently, 621.

effect of casual affray, 621.

canvass and return, 622.

canvassers are ministerial officers, 622.

canvassers not to question returns made to them, 622.

whether they can be compelled by mandamus to perform duty, 623.

G.

GAMING IMPLEMENTS,
    keeping of, for unlawful games, may be prohibited, 596.
GENERAL INTENT,
    when to control particular intent, 58 n.
GENERAL LAWS,
    required instead of special by some constitutions, 128, 129 n.
    in cases of divorce, 110 n.
    due process of law does not always require, 353 – 355, 389 – 393.
    submission of, to vote of people invalid, 116 – 125.
    suspension of, 391.
    changes in, give citizens no claim to remuneration, 358.
    respecting remedies, power of legislature to change, 267 – 273,
        287 – 294, 361 – 367.
GENERAL WARRANTS,
    illegality of, 299 – 303.
              (See SEARCHES AND SEIZURES.)
GEORGIA,
    divorce cases to be adjudged by the courts, 110 n.
    liberty of speech and of the press in, 417 n.
GOOD MOTIVES AND JUSTIFIABLE ENDS,
    defence of, in libel cases, 464.
    burden of proof on defendant to show, 464.
GOVERNMENT,
    constitutional, what is, 2, 3.
    of the United States, origin of, 5 – 8.
              (See UNITED STATES.)
GOVERNOR,
    approval or veto of laws by, 153, 154.
    messages to legislature, 155.
    power to prorogue or adjourn legislature, 132.
    power to convene legislature, 155.
    legislative encroachment on powers of, 114 – 116.
    power to pardon, 115 n.
    power to reprieve, 116 n.
GRADE OF RAILROADS,
    legislature may establish for crossings, 580.
GRADE OF STREETS,
    change of, gives parties no right to compensation, 207.
    special assessments for grading, 497, 505 – 509.
GRAND JURY,
    criminal accusations by, 309.

INCHOATE RIGHTS,
> power of the legislature in regard to, 359 – 361.

INCOMPETENT PERSONS,
> legislative authority for sale of lands of, 97 – 106.
> exclusion of, from suffrage, 599.

INCONTINENCE,
> accusation of, against female, not actionable, *per se*, 423, 424.
> statutory provisions respecting, 424.

INCORPORATIONS,
> charters of private, are contracts, 279.
> charters of municipal are not, 192, 276.
> control of, by police regulations, 577 – 579.
>> (See CHARTERS; MUNICIPAL CORPORATIONS.)

INDEBTEDNESS BY STATE,
> prohibition of, will not preclude debts by towns, counties, &c. 217, 218.

INDECENT PUBLICATIONS,
> sale of, may be prohibited, 596.
> parties not free to make, 422.

INDEMNIFICATION,
> of officers of municipal corporation where liability is incurred in supposed discharge of duty, 209, 210.
> power of legislature to compel, 211.
> not to be made in case of refusal to perform duty, 212.

INDEMNITY,
> for property taken for public use
>> (See EMINENT DOMAIN.)
> for consequential injuries occasioned by exercise of legal rights, 384.

INDEPENDENCE,
> declaration of, by Continental Congress, 6.
> new national government established by, 6.

INDIANA,
> special statutes licensing sale of lands forbidden, 98 n.
> legislature of, not to grant divorces, 110 n.
> when laws to take effect without governor's signature, 154 n.
> revenue bills to originate in lower house, 132 n.
> prohibition of special laws where general can be made applicable, 129 n.
> title of acts to express the object, 142.
> liberty of the press in, 416 n.
> religious tests for office forbidden, 469 n.
> exemption from bearing arms of persons conscientiously opposed, 478 n.

N.

NATION,
    definition of, 1.
        (See UNITED STATES.)
NATURALIZATION,
    power of Congress over, 10.
NAVIGABLE WATERS,
    made free by ordinance of 1787, 25 n.
    right of States to improve and charge toll, 26 n., 592.
    what are, 589.
    what are private channels, 589.
    are for use of all equally, 590.
    general control of, is in the States, 591.
    Congressional regulations when made control, 591.
    States cannot grant monopolies of, 591.
    States may authorize bridges over, 592.
    when bridges become nuisances, 592.
    States may establish ferries across, 593.
    States may authorize dams of, 593, 594.
    regulation of speed of vessels upon, 594.
    rights of fishery in, 524.
    frontage upon, is property, 544.
        (See WATER-COURSES.)
NAVIGATION,
    right of, pertains to the eminent domain, 524.
        (See NAVIGABLE WATERS.)
NEBRASKA,
    legislature of, not to grant divorces, 110 n.
    privilege of members of legislature from arrest, &c. 134 n.
    title of acts to express the object, 141 n.
    liberty of the press in, 416 n.
    religious tests forbidden in, 469 n.
NECESSITY,
    is the basis of the right of eminent domain, 524, 538.
    extent of property to be taken is limited by, 539.
    destruction of buildings to prevent spread of fire, 594.
NEGLIGENCE,
    carriers of persons may be made responsible for deaths by, 581.
    in the construction of public works may give right of action, 571.
NEGOTIABLE PAPER,
    when municipal corporations liable upon, 212, 215 and n.
NEVADA,
    special statutes licensing sale of lands forbidden, 98.

44

OFFICE,
>   appointments to, do not constitute contracts, 276.

OFFICER,
>   protection of dwelling-house against, 22, 299.
>   general warrants to, are illegal, 300 – 302.
>   may break open house to serve criminal warrant, 303.
>   service of search-warrant by,
>>   (See SEARCHES AND SEIZURES.)
>   privilege of criticism of, 431 – 441, 455, 456.
>   constitutional qualifications cannot be added to, by the legislature,
>   64.
>   duty of, when doubtful of constitutional construction, 73, 74.
>   of the legislature, election of, 133.
>   municipal, may be indemnified by corporation, 209.
>>   but not for refusal to perform duty, 212.

OHIO,
>   legislature not to grant divorces, or exercise judicial power, 111 n.
>   title of acts to express the object, 142 n.
>   general laws to be uniform, 63.
>   appointing power, how exercised, 115.
>   retrospective laws, what not to be passed, 370 n.
>   liberty of the press in, 415 n.
>   religious tests forbidden, 469.
>   impeachment of judges of, 160 n.

OMNIPOTENCE OF PARLIAMENT,
>   meaning of the term, 3, 4, 86.

OPINION,
>   proscription for, is unconstitutional, 390.
>   on religious subjects to be free, 467 – 470.
>   religious tests forbidden in some States, 469 n.
>   of witnesses on religious subjects not to constitute disqualification in
>   some States, 478.
>   judicial, force of, as precedents, 50 – 54.

ORDINANCE OF 1787,
>   how far still in force, 25, 26 n.
>   admission of States to the Union under, 28 n.

ORDINANCES, MUNICIPAL,
>>   (See BY-LAWS.)

OREGON,
>   special statutes licensing sale of lands forbidden, 98.
>   legislature of, not to grant divorces, 110 n.
>   revenue bills to originate in lower house, 132 n.
>   legislative regulation of pardons, 116.

R.

RAILROADS,

authorizing towns, &c. to subscribe to, is not delegating legislative power, 119.

such subscriptions generally sustained, 213 – 219.

appropriations of lands for, 533.

and of materials for constructing, 526.

and of lands for depot buildings, &c. 541.

corporations may take, 537, 538.

(See Eminent Domain.)

appropriation of highways for, 545 – 557.

must be legislative permission, 545.

whether adjoining owner entitled to compensation, 546 – 557.

police regulations in respect to, 573.

requiring corporations to fence track and pay for beasts killed, 579.

regulation of grade and crossings, 580.

provisions regarding alarms, 580.

responsibility for persons injured or killed, 580, 581.

bridges for, over navigable waters, 592.

READING OF BILLS,

constitutional provisions for, 80, 139, 140.

REAL ESTATE,

not to be taxed out of taxing district, 499, 500.

within taxing district to be taxed uniformly, 502.

REASONABLENESS,

of municipal by-laws, 200.

REBELLIONS,

employment of militia to suppress, 11.

RECITALS,

in statutes, not binding upon third parties, 96.

when they may be evidence, 96.

RECORDS,

public, of the States, full faith and credit to be given to, 15, 16.

judicial, not generally to be contradicted, 407.

(See Judicial Proceedings.)

REDEMPTION,

right of, cannot be shortened or extended by legislature, 291.

REFUSAL TO PLEAD,

in criminal cases, consequence of, 311.

REGISTRATION,

of voters, may be required, 601.

REGULATION,
>of commerce by Congress, 10, 581 – 587.
>of navigable waters by Congress, 591.
>police, by the States,
>>(See POLICE POWER.)
>of the right of suffrage, 601, 602.

RELIGIOUS LIBERTY,
>care taken by State constitutions to protect, 467 – 470.
>distinguished from religious toleration, 467 and note.
>does not preclude recognition of superintending Providence by public authorities, 470, 471.
>>nor appointment of chaplains, thanksgiving and fast days, 471.
>>nor recognition that the prevailing religion of the State is Christian, 471.
>the maxim that Christianity is part of the law of the land, 472 – 477.
>punishment of blasphemy does not invade, 472 – 474.
>>or of other forms of profanity, 476.
>Sunday laws, how justified, 476, 477.
>respect for religious scruples, 477, 478.
>religious belief, as affecting the competency or credibility of witnesses, 478.

REMEDIAL STATUTES,
>liberal construction of, 61 n.
>parties obtaining bound by, 96.

REMEDY,
>power of legislature over, in criminal cases, 267 – 273.
>>in civil cases, 287 – 294, 361 – 367.
>legislature cannot take away all remedy, 289.
>>may give new remedies, 361.
>>may limit resort to remedies, 364 – 367.
>for compensation for property taken by public, 560, 561.

REMOVAL,
>of causes from State to national courts, 12, 13.

REPEAL,
>of old English statutes, 25 n., 26 n.
>all laws subject to, 125 – 127.
>of laws conflicting with unconstitutional law, 186.

REPORTS,
>of public meetings, 435.
>of legislative proceedings, publication of, 418 – 420, 457 – 460.
>of judicial proceedings, publication of, 448 – 451.
>>(See LIBERTY OF SPEECH AND OF THE PRESS.)

RETROSPECTIVE LEGISLATION, — *Continued.*
    cannot cure defects of jurisdiction, 382, 383.
    forbidden in some States, 370 and notes.
    statutes generally construed to operate prospectively, 370.
    prospective construction of constitution, 62, 63.

REVENUE,
    in some States bills for, to originate with lower house, 131, 132.
    cannot be raised under right of eminent domain, 527.
                (See TAXATION.)

REVISION,
    of State constitutions, 30 – 37.
    of statutes,
                (See STATUTES.)

REVOLUTION, AMERICAN,
    powers of the Crown and Parliament over Colonies before, 5, 6.
    Congress of the, its powers, 6, 7.
    division of powers of government at time of, 6 n.

RHODE ISLAND,
    ratification of constitution by, 8, 9.
    impeachment of judges of, 26 n.
    charter government, 26 n., 30 n.
    privilege of members of legislature from arrest, 134 n.
    protection by law of the land, 352 n.
    liberty of the press in, 414 n.
    periodical valuation of property, 496.

RIGHT,
    distinguished from the remedy, 285 – 287.
    vested,
                (See VESTED RIGHTS.)
    in action,
                (See ACTION.)

ROADS,
    appropriation of private property for, 533.
    appropriation of materials for constructing, 526.
    appropriation of, for railroads, &c. 545 – 557.
                (See EMINENT DOMAIN.)
    regulation of use of, by States, 588.
    action for exclusion from, 543 n.

RULES OF CONSTRUCTION,
                (See CONSTRUCTION OF STATE CONSTITUTIONS.)

RULES OF EVIDENCE,
    power of the legislature to change, 288, 367 – 369.
                (See EVIDENCE.)

45

T.

TAKING OF PROPERTY,
> of individuals for public use, 524.
> > (See Eminent Domain.)

TAX LAWS,
> directory and mandatory provisions in, 75, 76.
> > (See Taxation.)

TAX SALES,
> curing defective proceedings in, by retrospective legislation, 382, 383.
>
> what defects should avoid, 521.
> > (See Taxation.)

TAXATION,
> and representation to go together, 24 and note.
>
> right of, compared with eminent domain, 559.
>
> exemptions from, by the States, when not repealable, 127, 280.
>
> can only be for public purposes, 129, 487 – 495.
>
> must be by consent of the people, 117 n.
>
> license fees distinguished from, 201, 586, 587.
>
> by municipalities, power of legislature over, 230 – 235.
>
> reassessment of irregular, may be authorized, 209.
>
> necessary to the existence of government, 479.
>
> unlimited nature of power of, 479 – 485.
>
> of agencies of national government by the States impliedly forbidden, 480 – 483.
>
> of agencies of the States by the national government also forbidden, 483.
>
> of the subjects of commerce by the States, 485, 486, 586.
>
> discriminations in, as between citizens of different States, 487.
>
> legislature the proper authority to determine upon, 488 – 495.
>
> apportionment essential to, 495.
>
> taxing districts, necessity of, 495, 499.
>
> apportionment not always by values, 496, 501.
>
> license fees and other special taxes, 496.
>
> assessments for local improvements, 497.
>
> > benefits from the improvement may be taken into the account, 497, 505, 511.
> >
> > general provisions requiring taxation by value do not apply to these assessments, 498.
>
> taxation of persons or property out of the district is void, 499, 500 – 504, 516.
>
> must be uniform throughout the district, 502.

TRUSTEES,
>
> special statutes authorizing sales by, constitutional, 97 – 106.
>
> rights of *cestuis que trust* not to be determined by legislature, 105.

TRUTH,
>
> as a defence in libel cases, 424, 438, 464.
>
> necessity of showing good motives, 464.

TURNPIKES,
>
> exercise of eminent domain for, 533.
>
> appropriation of highways for, 545.
>
> change of, to common highways, 546 n.

TWICE IN JEOPARDY,
>
> punishment of same act under State and national law, 18.
>
> > under State law and municipal by-law, 198, 199.
>
> > (See JEOPARDY.)

TWO THIRDS OF HOUSE,
>
> what constitutes, 141.

U.

UNCONSTITUTIONAL LAW,
>
> definition of the term, 3, 4.
>
> first declaration of, 26 n.
>
> power of the courts to annul, 159.
>
> > (See COURTS; STATUTES.)

UNEQUAL AND PARTIAL LEGISLATION,
>
> special laws of a remedial nature, 389.
>
> local laws, or laws applying to particular classes, 390 – 393.
>
> proscription of parties for opinions, 390.
>
> suspensions of the laws must be general, 391, 392.
>
> distinctions must be based upon reason, 393.
>
> equality the aim of the law, 393.
>
> strict construction of special burdens and privileges, 393 – 396.
>
> discrimination against citizens of other States, 397.

UNIFORMITY,
>
> in construction of constitutions, 54.
>
> in taxation, 495, 499.
>
> > (See TAXATION.)

UNITED STATES,
>
> division of powers between the States and Union, 2.
>
> origin of its government, 5.
>
> Revolutionary Congress, and its powers, 6, 7.
>
> Articles of Confederation and their failure, 6 – 8.
>
> formation of Constitution of, 8.

WORKS OF ART,
> liberty of criticism of, 457.

WRITS OF ASSISTANCE,
> unconstitutional character of, 301, 302 n.

WRITS OF HABEAS CORPUS,
> (See HABEAS CORPUS.)

Y.

YEAS AND NAYS,
> in some States, on passage of laws to be entered on journals, 140.

Cambridge: Printed by Welch, Bigelow, and Company.